The Routledge International Companion to Gifted Education

The Routledge International Companion to Gifted Education is a ground-breaking collection of fully-referenced chapters written by many of the most highly-respected authorities on the subject from around the world. These 50 contributors include distinguished scholars who have produced many of the most significant advances to the field over the past few decades, like Joseph Renzulli and Robert Sternberg, alongside authorities who ask questions about the very concepts and terminology embodied in the field – scholars such as Carol Dweck and Guy Claxton.

This multi-faceted volume:

- highlights strategies to support giftedness in children, providing ideas that work and weeding out those that don't.
- is written in jargon-free language in an easy-to-use themed format.
- is the most authoritative collection of future-focused views, ideas and reflections, practices and evaluations yet produced.
- includes chapters dealing with the major controversies and concerns in the field today, from the problems of identification to changing understandings of giftedness and creativity.

The international aspect of the Companion, and its juxtaposition of points of view – whereby chapters are deliberately positioned and accompanied by editorial commentary to highlight the contrasts with each other – ensures that different views are addressed and allows the reader to absorb and reflect upon the many perspectives of each issue.

The Companion is a guide to the new ideas and controversies that are informing gifted education discussion and policy-making around the world. It is a first-class resource for students and researchers alike.

Tom Balchin is a Research Fellow and Lecturer in gifted education, based in the Brunel Able Children's Education Centre at Brunel University, UK. He is also a Visiting Lecturer at the Institute of Education, Reading University, UK.

Barry Hymer is a Visiting Lecturer at Newcastle University's Centre for Teaching and Learning in the UK. He is a freelance educator, chartered psychologist, trainer and writer, specialising in the fields of thinking skills, creativity and gifted education.

Dona J. Matthews is a Visiting Professor at the Ontario Institute for Studies in Education of the University of Toronto and, until recently, the Director of the Center for Gifted Studies and Education at the Hunter College, City University of New York, working with the New York City Department of Education on gifted education policies and practices.

The Routledge International Companion to Gifted Education

Edited by
Tom Balchin
Barry Hymer
Dona J. Matthews

Routledge
Taylor & Francis Group

LONDON AND NEW YORK

First published 2009
by Routledge
2 Park Square, Milton Park, Abingdon, Oxon, OX14 4RN

Simultaneously published in the USA and Canada
by Routledge
270 Madison Avenue, New York NY 10016

Routledge is an imprint of the Taylor & Francis Group, an informa business

Typeset in Bembo by Swales & Willis Ltd, Exeter, Devon
Printed and bound in Great Britain by
TJ International, Padstow, Cornwall

British Library Cataloguing in Publication Data
A catalogue record for this book is available from the British Library

Library of Congress Cataloging in Publication Data
The Routledge international companion to gifted education / edited by Tom Balchin, Barry Hymer
& Dona J. Matthews.
    p. cm.
   Includes bibliographical references and index.
   1. Gifted children—Education. 2. Gifted children—Education—Cross-cultural studies. 3. Gifted
children—Education—Research. I. Balchin, Tom. II. Hymer, Barry. III. Matthews, Dona J.
   LC3993.R69 2008
   371.95—dc22   2008009721

ISBN10: 0–415–46136–7 (hbk)
ISBN10: 0–415–46137–5 (pbk)

ISBN13: 978–0–415–46136–8 (hbk)
ISBN13: 978–0–415–46137–5 (pbk)

Contents

v

Part 5: Expanding horizons: supporting gifted development more broadly

Notes on contributors

Susan Assouline, Ph.D., is the associate director of the Belin-Blank Center and an adjunct clinical associate professor in school psychology. She is co-author (with Ann Lupkowski-Shoplik) of *Developing Math Talent: A Guide for Educating Gifted and Advanced Learners in Math*, co-author (with Nicholas Colangelo and Miraca U. M. Gross) of *Nation Deceived: How Schools Hold Back America's Brightest Students*; and co-developer of the *Iowa Acceleration Scale*. She is lead investigator on the Belin-Blank Center's national study on twice-exceptional children.

Thomas Balchin, Ph.D., is a lecturer in gifted education at Brunel University and runs the Masters programme in gifted studies at Reading University, UK. A former schoolteacher, he has written many papers in national and international journals. His main research interest is the recognition and evaluation of creative achievement. He has developed the *Creativity Feedback Package* (CFP) for British teachers to use for the identification of able learners.

Maud Besançon, Ph.D., received her doctorate from Paris Descartes University. She is currently a temporary junior lecturer at the University of Bourgogne. Her research focuses on the development of creativity in childhood and the influence of pedagogical environments on children's competencies (creative or logical reasoning).

Denis Bonora, Ph.D., has devoted his research life mainly to school learning and conditions, encompassing the clarification of educational objectives, as well as an improvement of educational system efficiency. He took an active part in the second international survey of The International Association for the Evaluation of Educational Achievement (IEA) Six Subjects Survey in 19 countries, and in various national secondary school surveys. More recently, he has contributed to several publications concerning the educational treatment of high potential children in France and around the world.

Cristina Cardona, Ph.D., is Professor of Special Education at the University of Alicante, Spain. She has taught children with special educational needs in a variety of settings and has worked in teacher education in Spain and abroad. Her research interests include instructional and curricular adaptations for differentiation, inclusive education and quantitative research on knowledge and attitudes toward difference, particularly in ability. She is also the convener of the Inclusive Education Network of the EERA (European Educational Research Association).

Graham Chaffey, Ph.D., is an Honorary Fellow with The University of New England, Australia. Graham is currently occupied facilitating the ongoing development of the Coolabah Dynamic Assessment method and a provision model appropriate for gifted children from indigenous and other under-represented communities.

David Chan, Ph.D., is Professor in the Department of Educational Psychology and Director of the Programme for the Gifted and Talented of the Faculty of Education at the Chinese University of Hong Kong. His research interests in gifted education include assessment of giftedness and talents, stress, coping, and social and emotional needs of gifted children and youth.

Guy Claxton, D.Phil., is Professor of the Learning Sciences at the University of Bristol Graduate School of Education. His recent books include *Hare Brain, Tortoise Mind*, *Learning for Life in the 21st Century*, *Building Learning Power* and *The Wayward Mind*. His main interest is in narrowing the gap between formal and informal models and practices of learning.

Nicholas Colangelo, Ph.D., is the Myron & Jacqueline Blank Professor of Gifted Education at The University of Iowa and the Director of The Belin-Blank International Center for Gifted Education and Talent Development. He co-edited (with Gary Davis) the *Handbook of Gifted Education, Editions I, II, and III*, and he co-authored *A Nation Deceived: How Schools Hold Back America's Brightest Students* (with Susan Assouline and Miraca Gross). In 2002, he received the President's Award from the National Association for Gifted Children.

Carmen Crețu, Ph.D., is Professor of Psychology and Educational Sciences at University Alexandru Ioan Cuza, Iasi, Romania. She is Director of the Master's Programme on Policy and Management in Education; and president of RO-Talent (Romanian Association for Talented People). Her fields of expertise are giftedness, curriculum theory and development and educational policy.

Boris Davidovich is the head of the mathematics department in Moscow state school 57. He has been teaching children gifted in mathematics and physics for over 40 years. He helped create a system for teaching mathematics to gifted children in Russia and has developed a unique method of teaching gifted children. His students have received five gold medals in IMO and over 60 of his students have gone on to earn a Ph.D. in mathematics.

Eva Dougali is a Ph.D. candidate at Brunel University, UK, advised by Valsa Koshy and Thomas Balchin. Her research focus is curriculum provision for the Gifted and Talented in Greece. She is also working in collaboration with Elias Matsagouras at Marasleion Didaskaleion of the University of Athens, in a training programme for the education of high ability children.

Annie Dreux is a vocational advisor and training officer at INETOP (Institut National d'Etudes du Travail et d'Orientation Professionnelle – Institute for Vocational Guidance and Work Studies). She is involved in counselling programmes for young sporting talents at INSEP (Institut National du Sport et de l'Education Physique – The French National Institute of Sport and Physical Education).

Carol Dweck, Ph.D., is the Lewis and Virginia Eaton Professor of Psychology at Stanford University. She is a leading researcher in the area of motivation, having pioneered the study of how self-beliefs and goals influence learning and academic achievement. Her recent books include *Self-Theories: Their Role in Motivation, Personality, and Development* and *Mindset*, which has been translated into twelve languages. In recognition of her contributions, she was elected to the American Academy of Arts and Sciences.

Åke W. Edfeldt, Ph.D., is a Professor of Education, retired (Emeritus) and has been a researcher in the fields of reading and communication ever since the time of his doctoral dissertation, *Silent Speech and Silent Reading* (University of Chicago Press, 1960). Beside gifted education, his main interest has been the work against parental use of corporal punishment, which has resulted in contributions to national bans in Sweden 1979, Germany 2002 and New Zealand 2006.

Mercedes Ferrando, Ph.D., did her doctorate in gifted and emotional intelligence at Murcia University. She is now doing postdoctoral research sponsored by Fundación Séneca with Robert Sternberg at the PACE Center. She works with the High Ability Research Group directed by Dr. Lola Prieto. She was a visiting research fellow at Warwick University (UK) and at Canterbury Christ Church Universities (2005–2006). Her research is focused on creativity, intelligence, gifted and talented children, thinking skills and emotional intelligence.

Robert Fisher, Ph.D., is a speaker, writer and researcher on teaching thinking, learning and creativity. His books include *Teaching Children to Think, Teaching Children to Learn, Teaching Thinking*, and the *Stories for Thinking* series. He taught for 20 years in schools in the UK and abroad before becoming Professor of Education at Brunel University. His Ph.D. was for research on philosophy with children. He is a consultant to many professional development projects and keynote presenter at national and international conferences.

Christy Folsom, Ph.D., teaches at Lehman College, City University of New York. She developed the Teaching for Intellectual and Emotional Learning (TIEL) Design model and uses it in teacher education courses and professional development to teach curriculum design. Her research focuses on teaching the self-regulation skills of decision making, planning and self-evaluation.

Joan Freeman, Ph.D., has worked in the area of gifts and talents for more than 30 years. For this, she has been honoured with the Lifetime Achievement Award by the British Psychological Society. She is the author of 16 books, translated into many languages, and several hundred scientific and popular publications. She is founding president of the European Council for High Ability (ECHA) and Visiting Professor at Middlesex University, London.

Lisa French, Ph.D., has recently completed her doctorate in School/Applied Child Psychology at McGill University in Montreal, Quebec, Canada, advised by Bruce Shore. She is beginning her career as a professional psychologist in Montreal. She will be continuing her research affiliation with the High Ability and Inquiry Research Group at McGill University.

Françoys Gagné, Ph.D., is a French Canadian from Montreal, Quebec. A professor (now retired) in the Department of Psychology at l'Université du Québec à Montréal, he has been active in gifted education since the early 1980s. He is best known internationally for his Differentiated Model of Giftedness and Talent (DMGT). He has won major awards, among them from the American MENSA Association (1993, 1998). In 1996, he received from the National Association for Gifted Children (USA) the Distinguished Scholar Award 'for significant contributions to the field of knowledge regarding the education of gifted individuals'.

John Geake, Ph.D., is Professor of Educational Neuroscience, Westminster Institute of Education, Oxford Brookes University, where he leads the Institute's research into giftedness and gifted education. He is also a Visiting Academic at the Centre for Functional Imaging of the Brain, University of Oxford, where he conducts fMRI research into creative intelligence. He is the founding convenor of the Oxford Cognitive Neuroscience Education Forum, and was keynote speaker on The Neurobiology of Giftedness at the World Conference of Gifted Education, Warwick, UK, in 2007.

Asta Georgsdottir, Ph.D., completed her undergraduate studies of psychology at the University of Iceland, Reykjavik and her graduate degrees at the University Paris Descartes. Her main research interests include the study of cognitive flexibility, its measurement and its development, as well as its role in creative problem solving. She collaborated in the founding of the first French centre for gifted and talented children in difficulty. She has also been a co-author of several articles and book chapters on creative giftedness.

Elena Grigorenko, Ph.D., received a doctorate in general psychology from Moscow State University and a doctorate in developmental psychology and genetics from Yale University in 1996. She is Associate Professor of Child Studies and Psychology at Yale and Adjunct Professor of Psychology at Moscow State University. She has published more than 200 peer-reviewed articles, book chapters and books. Dr. Grigorenko has worked with children and their families in the US as well as in Africa (Kenya, Tanzania and Zanzibar, the Gambia and Zambia), India and Russia.

Annie Haight, Ph.D., is a Senior Lecturer in Education at Oxford Brookes University and works with in-service teachers in gifted and talented education. She is also the editor of cpdgifted, Oxford Brookes University's website for educational professionals interested in gifted education. Her research interests include the identification of gifted and talented students, teacher attitudes and ethical issues and vocational giftedness.

Kurt Heller, Ph.D., is Professor Emeritus of Psychology and Director of the Center for the Study of Giftedness at the University of Munich (LMU). He is founding director of the International MA Study Program 'Psychology of Excellence' at LMU and has published over 400 books, psychological tests, book chapters and peer-reviewed journal articles. He has won several awards, most recently the Choice (USA) Award for the second edition of the *International Handbook of Giftedness and Talent* (2000, rev. reprint 2002) and the 2003 National (Bavarian) Prize in Educational Sciences.

Jan Hughes is a gifted and talented co-ordinator for a local education authority in the north of England. She is a teacher of physical education and a leader of learning. A living theory practitioner, she has led school action research into educational processes that promote and support exceptional performance and produce autonomous learners.

Marie Huxtable is a senior educational psychologist, working within an English local authority where she coordinates the APEX (Able Pupils Extending Opportunities Project) and related work. She holds to the belief that all learners have the capacity for extraordinary achievement, and is working to develop her inclusive and inclusional practice through living theory research to reflect her growing understanding of what she means by extraordinary achievement and the educational environment in which it can flourish.

Barry Hymer, Ph.D., is a freelance educator, chartered psychologist and visiting fellow at Newcastle University's Centre for Teaching and Learning. He is the author of numerous books, papers and articles in the field of giftedness, learning and teaching and he serves as Consultant Editor for the journal *Gifted Education International*. He received the ICPIC (International Council for Philosophical Inquiry with Children) Award for Excellence in 2003.

Ida Jeltova, Ph.D., is an Assistant Professor of the School of Psychology, Graduate Center, City University of New York, USA. Her research focuses on a process-oriented approach to cognitive and behavioural modifiability in children and adolescents. Her special areas of interest are approaches to identification, diagnosis and interventions for gifted and learning disabled students with exceptional profiles of abilities. Her clinical research has focused on addressing behavioural and academic problems encountered by schoolchildren in special education.

Valsa Koshy, Ph.D., is Director of the Research Centre for Gifted and Talented Education at Brunel University, UK, and founded the Brunel Able Children's Education Centre in 1996. She was previously a teacher and a member of the mathematics advisory team in London. She is the author of several books and journal articles on gifted education and mathematics education. Her research interests include search and fulfilment of inner-city talent, provision for gifted children aged 4–7, and aspects of giftedness in mathematics.

Wiesława Limont, Ph.D., is the Head of the Department of Art Education at the Faculty of Fine Arts of the Nicolaus Copernicus University in Toruń, Poland. She is the chairperson of the programme council in Toruń, which offers gifted education, and the chairperson of the Centre for Gifted Education and Study of Giftedness at Nicolaus Copernicus University. She is the author and editor of many books, as well as scientific and popular-science papers. She investigates specific abilities, creative talents and creative imagination.

Todd Lubart, Ph.D., is Professor of Psychology at the Université Paris Descartes and Member of the Institut Universiatire de France. He received his Ph.D. from Yale University. His research focuses on creativity and creative giftedness, its identification and development in children and adults, the role of emotions, the creative process and intercultural issues. He is author or co-author of numerous scientific reports on creativity, including most recently *Enfants exceptionnels* [Exceptional Children] (Bréal, 2006).

Konstantin Lukin, Ph.D. candidate, is a clinical psychologist at Fairleigh Dickinson University, USA. Lukin's research focuses on the identification and diagnosis of psychiatric disorders using psychometric data. His special interest is the application of taxometric analysis to research data to ascertain their latent structure (i.e. categorical versus dimensional).

Elias Matsagouras, Ph.D., is Professor of Didactics in the faculty of Primary Education at the University of Athens and vice-president of the Institute of Education of Greece. Areas of interest include personal theory of teaching, reflective teaching, teaching thinking through the curriculum, cooperative learning, interdisciplinary curriculum teacher education and gifted education. His books include *Educating the High Ability Children: Differentiated Syneducation* (2008), *School Literacy* (2007), *Interdisciplinarity in School Knowledge* (2004), *Genre Approach to Written language* (2003) and *Strategies of Teaching* (2002).

Dona Matthews, Ph.D., is a Visiting Professor at the Ontario Institute for Studies in Education. From 2003–2007 she was at Hunter College, City University of New York, as the first director of the Center for Gifted Studies and Education, where she taught graduate courses and worked with the New York City Department of Education on gifted education policies and practices. She has written dozens of articles and book chapters on gifted education and co-authored (with Joanne Foster) *Being Smart about Gifted Children*.

Sara Meadows, Ph.D., is a Senior Lecturer in education at the University of Bristol Graduate School of Education. She has been teaching developmental psychology and writing about children's cognitive development since the 1970s. Her latest book is *The Child as Thinker*. Her research interest throughout her career has centred on the ways in which interactions between parents and children do (or do not) set children up as 'self-running problem-solvers'.

Diane Montgomery Ph.D., is Emeritus Professor in education at Middlesex University, London. She is a qualified teacher, teacher educator and chartered psychologist. Her doctorate is in improving teaching and learning, and she researches giftedness and learning difficulties. She writes and runs Distance Education MAs in SEN, SpLD (Dyslexia) and Gifted Education and the Learning Difficulties Research Project. She has written 20 books and many articles on gifted education, underachievement, dyslexia, behaviour problems, appraisal, learning difficulties and classroom observation. She lectures widely internationally.

Carole Nassab, Ph.D., is an associate of the Center for Creative Learning in Sarasota, Florida and earned graduate degrees at Harvard University and Lesley College. She has been a middle school teacher, guidance counsellor, principal, pupil personnel director, adjunct professor and school board member. Carole has authored or co-authored several publications for school and community use, including *Expanding and Enhancing Gifted Programs: the Levels of Service Approach* and the *Talent Development Planning Handbook*.

Maria Dolores Prieto, Ph.D., is Professor of Educational Psychology in Murcia University (Spain). As the director of the research group titled high abilities, she is currently working with local educational authorities to identify and develop programmes for G&T. She has many international publications on these topics: history of creativity in Spain; creative abilities in early childhood; Sternberg triarchic abilities theory; and multiple intelligences theory.

Sally Reis, Ph.D., is Professor of Educational Psychology at the University of Connecticut, where she also serves as a principal investigator for the National Research Center on the Gifted and Talented. She was a teacher for 15 years, and has authored or co-authored hundreds of articles, books, book chapters, monographs and technical reports. She is past president of the National Association for Gifted Children (NAGC), was recently awarded the NAGC Distinguished Scholar award and named a Board of Trustees Distinguished Professor at The University of Connecticut.

Joseph Renzulli, Ph.D., is a Board of Trustees Distinguished Professor at the University of Connecticut where he also serves as director of the National Research Center on the Gifted and Talented. In June 2003 of he was awarded an Honorary Doctor of Laws degree from McGill University, Montreal, Canada. His work has focused on the development of theories and research related to broadened conceptions of human potential, the identification and development of creativity and giftedness in young people, organisational models and curricular strategies for differentiated learning environments and total school improvement, and using technology to promote high-end learning.

Edwin Selby, Ph.D., is an associate with the Center for Creative Learning and also an Adjunct Professor with Fordham University's Graduate School of Education (USA). He is the principal author of *VIEW: An assessment of problem solving style*, as well as a co-author of the *Talent Development Planning Handbook* and numerous journal articles on creativity, talent development and individual style. He served for many years as a public school music and drama teacher. He founded, and directed for 25 years, the Sussex Student Theatre, in which students wrote and produced their own musical plays.

Bruce Shore, Ph.D., is Professor of Educational Psychology in the Department of Educational and Counselling Psychology in the Faculty of Education, McGill University, Montreal, Canada. He is one of the principal academic staff in the High Ability and Inquiry Research Group (HAIR) at McGill University and the inter-university Centre for the Study of Learning and Performance.

Dean Simonton, Ph.D., is Distinguished Professor of Psychology at the University of California, Davis. His more than 330 publications treat various aspects of genius, creativity, leadership, talent and aesthetics. His honours include the William James Book Award, the Sir Francis Galton Award for Outstanding Contributions to the Study of Creativity, the Rudolf Arnheim Award for Outstanding Contributions to Psychology and the Arts, the Theoretical Innovation Prize in Personality and Social Psychology, the Mensa Award for Excellence in Research and the President's Award from the National Association for Gifted Children.

Robert Sternberg, Ph.D., is Dean of the School of Arts and Sciences and Professor of Psychology at Tufts University and an Honorary Professor at the University of Heidelberg. He received his PhD from Stanford and his Bachelor's degree from Yale, and holds eight honorary doctorates. He has published roughly 1200 referenced books, chapters and peer-reviewed journal papers and is a past president of the American Psychological Association. He is currently president of the Eastern Psychological Association and president-elect of the International Association for Cognitive Education and Psychology.

Kirsi Tirri, Ph.D., is Professor of Religious Education at the University of Helsinki, Finland and a visiting professor at King's College, London. She is also president elect of ECHA (European Council for High Ability). Her research interests include gifted education, moral and religious education, teacher education and cross-cultural studies. She has published several books and journal articles related to these fields.

Donald Treffinger Ph.D., is President of the Center for Creative Learning, Inc. and has worked for more than three decades in the areas of creativity, and gifted and talented education. He has authored or co-authored more than 360 books, monographs and articles, and has received many honours, including the National Association for Gifted Children's Distinguished Service Award, the E. Paul Torrance Creativity Award, the *Risorgimento Award* and the

International Creativity Award from the World Council for Gifted and Talented Children. Dr. Treffinger has served as editor of the *Gifted Child Quarterly* and *Parenting for High Potential*.

Joyce VanTassel-Baska, Ph.D., is the Jody and Layton Smith Professor of Education at the College of William and Mary, where she runs graduate programs at masters and doctoral levels in gifted education and directs a research and development centre. She has published widely, including 22 books and over 500 journal articles, book chapters and reports. She is the past president of the National Association for Gifted Children.

Pierre Vrignaud, Ph.D., is Professor of Vocational Psychology at University of Paris 10. His main topics of interest are differential psychology and psychometrics. He is author of several papers on these topics as well as questionnaires and software. He provides expertise in assessment survey of adults' skills for French Ministries (Work and Education) and for international organizations (OECD, UNESCO). He is senior research fellow at International Global Leadership Center at INSEAD. He has conducted several research studies on gifted and talented schooling in France.

Belle Wallace is Director of TASC International. She was co-director of the Curriculum Development Unit, University of Natal, SA and was senior author of a series of language and thinking skills texts to redress cognitive underdevelopment in pupils from 6 to 17 years. Belle has served on the executive committee of the World Council for Gifted and Talented Children, and has been editor of *Gifted Education International* since 1981. Her main interest is the development of problem-solving and thinking skills across the curriculum.

Ian Warwick is Senior Director of London Gifted & Talented, part of the London Challenge. He taught at inner city comprehensives for 20 years and in 2000 became G&T Strand Coordinator for the Royal Borough of Kensington and Chelsea, and Westminster. In 2003, he wrote the vision document and assembled the consortium of higher education and local authorities, which formed London Gifted & Talented. His chief areas of interest are urban education and disadvantaged and underachieving students. He has written many articles and chapters for educational journals and spoken at national and international conferences.

Helen Wilson is a Senior Lecturer in primary science education at Oxford Brookes University, Oxford, England. She is particularly interested in the potential of science for providing challenge and is the co-author of *Challenges in Primary Science: Meeting the Needs of Able Young Scientists at Key Stage 2*. She was the course leader of England's training programme for primary gifted and talented co-ordinators within the Excellence in Cities programme and has been involved in projects that have shown a clear link between challenging, exciting science and raised pupil engagement and achievement.

Inger Wistedt, Ph.D., is Professor in the Department of Education, Stockholm University and visiting professor at Växjö University, Sweden. Her main research focus lies within the field of mathematics learning, ranging from studies of very young children to university students. She has also taken an interest in gender studies and is presently engaged in studies of gifted education in mathematics, another aspect of her general interest in equity issues.

Victoria Yurkevich, Ph.D., is the head of a gifted children's psychology laboratory at Moscow Town Psychological Pedagogical University. Born in Orenburg, South Urals, Russia, she graduated from the General and Pedagogical Psychology College of Moscow (at present Psychological College of Russian Academy for Education). She defended her thesis on 'Problems of self-regulation development in gifted children' in 1973. Since then she has continued to study gifted children, and is the author of a concept of 'naïve and cultural creativity' and a theory of 'developing discomfort'.

Foreword

James H. Borland
Teachers College, Columbia University

Initially, upon reading the introduction to this volume, I had some misgivings. After all, the editors aspire to a great deal – perhaps, I thought, more than can be achieved between two book covers.

Consider the scope of the work. Not only have the editors attempted to collect chapters that, in the aggregate, address issues in gifted education in a comprehensive fashion, a difficult feat of editorship in itself, but they have attempted to do so from an international perspective. This is crucial because, whereas other works have drawn on the perspectives of authors of diverse nationalities (one thinks of Heller, Mönks, Sternberg and Subotnik's estimable *International Handbook of Research and Development of Giftedness and Talent*), the goal in this volume is to have the authors address issues specific to the development of gifted education in their own countries. This has made the collection international in more than a nominal fashion, which is very refreshing for those of us who tire of seeing everything in the field viewed through American-centric lenses. In addition, asking the contributors to comment (in 150 words or fewer!) on how they would like to see the field develop in their countries was a masterstroke of editorial genius that has resulted in some pithy and provocative aperçus.

Also consider that the intended audience, as described in the book's introduction, would seem to subsume most of literate humanity: policy makers, parents, educators, psychologists, researchers, undergraduate students, graduate students, academics, general readers. The book cannot possibly appeal and be accessible to all of these groups, one would logically think, but the results contradict that logic. Without compromising the quality of their scholarship, the authors whose work is collected herein have delineated, analyzed, synthesized and critiqued the critical issues in the field in a manner that is lucid, unusually jargon-free (or at least -reduced), and, *mirabile visu*, readable.

As the editors assert, the field of gifted education is in flux. Virtually everything is up for grabs, and I think that is a good thing. We have been stuck in conceptions and practices based on received wisdom for far too long, and that received wisdom, consisting of ideas that were fresh and served us well in the revivified field of the 1970s and 1980s, now seems tired, rote and reflexive. This collection of papers is bracing in the freshness of so many of the ideas, perspectives and recommendations it contains. All of this suggests reasons for optimism, even among orthodox pessimists such as me.

And to top things off, the editors and contributors have agreed to donate all royalties to two very deserving charitable causes (and to think of the good the $10 from my last book could have done!). Publishing this collection was nigh on to a charitable act; this makes it literal.

Playing on the title of this volume, one can define *companionable* as 'Having the qualities of a good companion; friendly' (http://www.answers.com). Companionable this volume is, and by that I do not mean to suggest a lack of appropriate gravitas. I expect to spend a good amount of time with it, and I do not think I will soon tire of its company.

References

Heller, K. A., Mönks, F. J., Sternberg, R. J., & Subotnik, R. F. (Eds.). *International handbook of research and development of giftedness and talent.* London: Pergamon Press. (pp. 587–594)

Introduction: reflections on the road ahead

Welcome to *The Routledge International Companion to Gifted Education*.

Gifted education is a worldwide concern. Although there is as yet no internationally accepted definition of giftedness, and in fact, no two experts in the field will agree entirely on what giftedness means or what one ought to do about it, there is almost certainly a wide range of students with gifted learning needs in any given school or country, as well as many others who might be helped to develop gifted-level abilities with the right kinds of support and opportunities to learn.

Your specific needs with respect to this book are likely to reflect your professional or parental stance: you may be an educational leader or policy maker with a remit to provide for gifted education in your community or country. You may be an education or psychology practitioner, university lecturer or academic researcher seeking advice about how giftedness is viewed and provided for worldwide. You may be an undergraduate or postgraduate student in education, youth studies, psychology, sociology or social policy, with a wish to have a robust and future-focused guide to a certain dimension of your chosen field. You may be a parent of a gifted child and want to know more about how you can help your child, school, or community. You may be a reader who is simply interested in finding out more, and wanting a clear, comprehensive and 'mystery-free' explanation that has, until now, been hard to find.

Whoever you are, welcome. Your ultimate goal is the same as ours: like us, you are a learner who wishes to understand and enhance opportunities for gifted-level development. We hope that you derive as much benefit and enjoyment from the journey through this volume as we did in constructing and shaping it, and we trust that it will be of use in myriad ways. We have carefully prepared the volume to be read sequentially, but also recognise that, like the best journeys, some of the most fruitful encounters occur when you dip into an area without planning a route and explore as you will. Whichever way you travel through it, we designed this volume in the hope that it becomes a fixture in your library and a favourite first port of call. We intend that this series of challenging, comprehensive and intellectually provocative chapters will help you understand the common themes that underpin the way gifted education is viewed, presented and conducted internationally, and gauge its parameters now and for many years into the future.

The 54 contributors to this *Companion* are drivers of major initiatives of the past, present and future. Some of the most established and well-respected international leaders in the field are here, along with other notable academics and practitioners whose voices are just beginning to be heard. The 39 chapters in this book have been chosen as representative of major themes and issues in gifted education worldwide, and whilst there is a Euro-American emphasis, contributors are drawn from around the world.

This volume distinguishes itself from comparable handbooks by its focus on contributors' perspectives on the ways in which the field is developing and ought to develop. It started life in our desire as editors to present to readers futures-led perspectives in gifted education. In approaching contributors, we looked for experts with dynamic conceptions both of human development and of the field of gifted education, people around the world who might share their experiences with innovative practice in the field, and provide suggestions for implementing better practice over time.

At present, gifted education initiatives around the world are in a state of flux, reflecting a dissatisfaction with twentieth-century conceptualisations, and the need to respond to the particular challenges of the new century. This volume presents both what is occurring in existing practice, and the evolving directions, concomitant challenges and solutions that new practices and technological innovations bring to gifted education. In addition to their chapters, we asked authors to provide a personal comment of 150 words on the way they thought things should go in their countries over the next ten years in order to provide the best prospects for gifted education. Many of our authors tell us that this was the hardest task they faced. We will know soon enough whether the actions advised by these authorities have been acted upon by their country's leaders, psychologists, educators and parents.

So, who and what are we talking about here? Regardless of the volume's title, should we even be talking about 'gifted children' – or 'gifted education'? Our authors take contrasting positions on these questions. Some focus on identifying certain percentages of gifted children as a subset of the broader population of children and young people, and meeting their educational and psychosocial needs, whereas others dismiss 'actuarial' approaches to giftedness as representing a twentieth-century mindset – one which they argue we need to move on from and concentrate instead on optimal conditions for human growth and development, and the creation (rather than discovery) of gifts and talents. We hope that you will find yourself interrogating these contrasting conceptual positions and other related ideas as you're reading these chapters. We also hope that you find yourself thinking about how you can help your children, your classroom, your school, your community or your country to provide appropriate learning opportunities for students, including those whose learning needs are so advanced compared to others their own age that they require additional or different training or coaching. We hope that you will also be wondering if there are ways you might work to support gifted-level learning much more broadly than is typically done.

The volume is split into five themed sections, each with seven or eight chapters. In the introduction to each of the overarching thematic sections, we highlight the key concepts addressed by the authors and illustrate some of the ways the constituent chapters play with and through each other. The first theme, 'Models, definitions and conceptual challenges', sets the scene by examining ways in which the experts are currently constructing and deconstructing the field of giftedness, providing descriptions, discussions and critiques of existing international conceptions of giftedness models, definitions and approaches to identification. Our authors address some traditional and controversial responses to the foundational questions in the field, such as, What is intelligence? What is giftedness? What is creativity? How should we assess these attributes?

The authors included in the second themed section, 'International perspectives', are experts on gifted education from Germany, France, Sweden, Greece, Russia, Australia and China. Although we wish that space had allowed an even wider sampling of expertise from around the world, we think there are useful understandings to be gained for all of us from these discussions of diverse cultural, historical and educational experiences and perspectives, particularly when considered in the context of the volume as a whole. We invite readers to deepen their conceptions of the field and broaden their awareness of possibilities, as they think about implications of distant perspectives to local issues, policies and practices.

The chapters included in the third thematic section, 'Psychosocial development', focus on the extra-cognitive dimension, considerations of ethical, moral, social and emotional development, which we ignore or downplay at our peril. This is an area – psychosocial development as it intersects with giftedness – which is attracting attention in the field. Historically it is this same area that has perhaps generated more controversies, conflicting research findings and widely held misconceptions than any other. We hope that you enjoy seeing how our authors fearlessly wade into the controversies, thoughtfully weigh conflicting research findings and valiantly attack the misconceptions. We also hope that their musings and conclusions on these topics are useful in informing your own evolving understandings and practice.

Our fourth theme is entitled 'Theory into practice: differentiation strategies, tools, and approaches'. The chapters in this section explore the dynamic interplay between theory and practice, the ways in which each engenders, informs and changes the other, leading to richer and more engaging learning experiences for children and adolescents. From the beginning, we have attempted with this book to avoid simplistic dualisms, including the traditional theory-versus-practice distinction. You will see that the chapters in this section situate practice at the heart of theory-generation, and constitute examples of practice and theory working complementarily to refresh and inform each other.

In our fifth and final theme, 'Expanding horizons: supporting gifted development more broadly', our authors push the craft out further, exploring proximal and more distant horizons for gifted education. Each one of these authors has invested enormous efforts over many decades in the trenches of teaching and learning, and has concluded that gifted education, to remain viable in the twenty-first century, needs to reach out more broadly, become dramatically more inclusive and inclusional, and focus more on supporting and creating diverse kinds of giftedness, than identifying and classifying an ossified notion of general intelligence. Collectively, they make the point that just as global survival depends on respect for ecological diversity, the future of gifted education (and education more generally) depends on opening our minds and hearts and practices, and finding ways to respect and incorporate human diversity of every kind – racial, cultural, socioeconomic, cognitive, spiritual, gender, religious and linguistic.

We hope that you enjoy your journey through this volume as you are escorted, counselled, entertained, guided, challenged, updated, instructed, encouraged, forewarned, nudged and perhaps even inspired in your consideration of the field of gifted education in its variety. Although the authors vary greatly in their focus as in their experience, there are some underlying recurrent themes. As we see it, the overall message from this volume concerns the importance of the way we conceive of giftedness and our attitudes toward its development, our evolving understanding that 'giftedness' is not a static attribute of certain individuals, but rather a dynamic aspect of our humanity that requires considerable encouragement and effort to bring into realisation. This was nicely observed many years ago by English philosophical writer, James Allan (1864–1912), who was best known for the 1902 verse 'As a Man Thinketh'. He wrote also:

In all human affairs there are *efforts*, and there are *results*, and the strength of the effort is the measure of the result. Chance is not. Gifts, powers, material, intellectual and spiritual possessions are the fruits of effort; they are thoughts completed, objects accomplished, visions realised.

We have serendipitously come upon a 'spiritual navigator' in this volume in the form of one of our contributors, Carol Dweck. Although we had not planned this, we have found that her extensive research on motivation and the 'mindset' we bring to challenges has been referenced by many contributors, both implicitly and explicitly. Her work is seminal, challenging and timely, and as we see it, likely to have far-reaching consequences for the way that giftedness is understood, and for the ways that gifted education will be constructed worldwide over the next few decades.

In weaving the book together, we have also noticed a source of inspiration more closely aligned to the field itself in the person of Jim Borland and his seminal work, starting in the 1980s, urging a move away from labelling children and toward providing appropriate intellectual challenge for all learners. He has been at the vanguard of the paradigm shift toward giftedness as 'doing' (rather than 'being') that many of our authors discuss, and with his colleagues at Columbia University, has led the battle against the elitism and exclusive practices that characterised so much of the earlier work in the field.

He has kindly agreed to write the foreword to the volume.

There are many, many others whom we wish we had had the space and time to include. We say a collective thank you to them all here, all of the giant thinkers in the field on whose shoulders we are standing today.

Interestingly, the process of shaping and editing the volume has reflected its underlying principles and focus on future trends and possibilities. It has been a dynamic, respectful, collaborative, interactive process from the beginning. We three editors have shared perspectives, prodded each other to think again, to grow, to bend, to learn. In the relentlessly ongoing transatlantic discourse in which we have participated over the past year, we have joked and lamented in equal measure. We have had heated online discussions about substantive issues, and always found a congenial way through to focusing on what was right, rather than who was right. Our interactions have not all been about the book; we have also chatted about our pasts and futures, and shared what was happening in our present lives with families and home and work, as each one of us has experienced major moves and life changes. The chapter authors have participated in this discourse in their thoughtful responses to our careful editing and re-editing of each chapter. Our work has been technologically mediated in so many ways – email, Internet information-gathering and sharing, innovative editing software – that the warmth, speed, intensity and extent of this collaboration would have been impossible even a decade ago. And in one of the many delightfully serendipitous coincidences that have marked this process, several of our chapter authors focus on the possibilities for teaching and learning that are provided by emerging technologies.

We are delighted to report that all the authors in this volume have agreed unhesitatingly to join in donating their time and expertise to two charitable causes that build upon the kind of work we advocate throughout the book. All authorial fees and future royalties for the *International Companion to Gifted Education* are being shared equally between two causes close to the editors' hearts. The ARNI Trust is a UK-based charity, which concentrates on rehabilitating people from the effects of paralysis – usually caused by stroke – after out-patient assistance is discontinued. ARNI (Action for Rehabilitation from Neurological Injury) was founded in 2001 by Thomas Balchin, who suffered a brain haemorrhage ten years ago. The techniques he teaches – a unique system composed of techniques derived from many styles of martial arts and strength training – were acquired from his own near total recovery from the effects of partial paralysis. The charity now has over 100 qualified instructors around the UK who concentrate on rehabilitating those who have suffered brain injuries progressively to recover movement, balance, physical strength and confidence. Please visit http://www.arni.uk.com for more information.

The other charity to which editors and authors are donating their proceeds from the book is the Kinamba Nursery Project in Kigali. This is a remarkable and superbly managed grassroots educational initiative, established 'on a shoestring' in 2005 by a group of Rwandan volunteers who set about trying to meet the educational, social and material needs of the poorest and most marginalised people in their local area. It is ably supported by Meg Gleave, a retired headteacher and former VSO volunteer from Cumbria, England. For further information about the project and its funding, and regular newsletter updates, contact Meg Fletcher at megfletch@hotmail.co.uk. We appreciate the donation of our authors' time and talents, and see these reflected back in the faces of the beneficiaries – these remarkable Rwandan children and volunteers.

Notes on contributors appear in the front of the book and email contact addresses can be found at the end of each chapter.

Now, an eye-opening volume of future-focused academic strategies, procedures, opinions, projects, plans, and systems from numerous countries around the globe awaits your attention . . .

Your editors, Thomas Balchin, Barry Hymer and Dona Matthews

Part 1

Approaching giftedness: models, definitions and conceptual challenges

One of the most striking aspects of gifted education today is the extent to which the underlying constructs are being questioned, investigated and puzzled over. In this section, we raise explicitly many of the thorny questions that authors throughout the volume address more implicitly. For example, what is intelligence? What is giftedness? What are talents? What is creativity? Who is intelligent/gifted/talented/creative? How should we assess these attributes?

We open the book with a provocative chapter by Guy Claxton and Sara Meadows, who make a compelling case for moving beyond traditional notions of giftedness as innate and unchangeable, and for rethinking the lifetime pigeon-holing that too often results from gifted identification and labelling practices. This is followed by John Geake's intriguing chapter on the ways that emerging findings on the nature of neural interconnectivity not only explain the creative intelligence associated with giftedness, but also provide important information for educators. Specifically, Geake illustrates that 'brain-based' learning styles assessments have little or no educational value, that curriculum should emphasise interdisciplinarity and content connectedness, and that we should expect to find, and celebrate, individual differences.

Although you will find many different perspectives and controversial points of view here, most of the authors in this section would agree with Dona Matthews and Christy Folsom that categorical notions of gifted versus non-gifted are more harmful than useful in practice, and that all educators are involved with gifted education whether they know it or not. Many would also agree with their suggestions that include integrating cognitive and emotional processes in educational practices, and providing a wide range of programming options that are available for educators to select for every student for the purpose of addressing individual and developmental diversity.

You will see as you read through the chapters in this thematic grouping that the nature/ nurture question is being turned upside down and inside out. Dean Keith Simonton addresses this fundamental question as it unfolds over the lifespan, and concludes that giftedness is more like a 'matching grant' than an outright gift; it requires the recipient to do the work that converts a genetic gift into reality. Similarly, Françoys Gagné argues that outstanding natural abilities, or gifts, must go through a complex and systematic domain-specific talent development process before they can be useful to the individual or society.

Todd Lubart, Asta Georgsdottir and Maud Besançon grapple with the fundamental questions surrounding creative giftedness and talent, addressing issues of definition, development, identification and education. They recommend infusing creativity into teacher development, as well as taking it into consideration in gifted identification and curriculum design and delivery, and also affirming the importance of supporting the development of creative giftedness in all students. In our final chapter in this section, Thomas Balchin writes about findings from his survey and interviews with over 800 gifted and talented education coordinators throughout England, and about the problems that are caused in practice by their confusion over foundational principles, including definitions of terms. He argues for the importance of a developmental, practical definition that embodies an understanding of the dynamic nature of giftedness, and leads directly to effective implications for educators.

Although we raise a lot more questions than we are able to answer definitively and conclusively, we hope that our authors' various considered responses to the burning questions of the field today inform your own dynamic conceptions of what giftedness is, and how it develops.

Brightening up: how children learn to be gifted

Guy Claxton and Sara Meadows
Bristol University, UK

> I have always maintained that, excepting fools, men did not differ much in (talent), only in zeal and hard work; I still think this is an eminently important difference.
> Charles Darwin (1808–1882), English evolutionary biologist

This chapter addresses the issue of whether the dominant conception of 'gifted and talented' is justified by psychological research, and what effects holding this conception have for learners. It argues that both the research base and practical and moral considerations should lead us to exclude ideas of innate and unchangeable degrees of 'giftedness' from our educational practice as incorrect, inhuman and counter-productive.

It is easy to forget that 'brightness' or 'giftedness' are inferences and attributions, not statements of self-evident fact. In this chapter we want to go back to the behaviours and dispositions on which these inferences and attributions are based and explore the ways in which they might have been learned, and thus could be subject to further systematic modification. We ask: To what extent do young people learn to act in ways that will lead parents and teachers to attribute 'brightness' to them? To what extent are such behaviours capable of further modification?

When children first arrive at school it is likely that within weeks, if not hours, judgements will be made about how 'bright' they are. Let us say for the sake of argument that Neneh is quickly seen as 'bright', while Jacob is soon thought of as 'un-bright'. How are these judgements made and justified? On the basis of a brief sampling of teachers' views, we offer the following as behaviours that could be taken as symptomatic of the difference in apparent brightness between Neneh and Jacob:

- Neneh is usually physically alert and energetic – 'bright-eyed and bushy-tailed'. Jacob is often listless and slouches.
- Neneh is strongly oriented to adults and alert to their presence. She orients to their voices, makes eye contact and reads their faces for clues as to what they want her to do. Jacob is less sensitive to adults and their non-verbal messages. He sometimes looks like he does not know what he is (supposed to be) doing.
- Neneh's facial expressions clearly signal to adults that she is oriented to them and

3

picking up their messages; her face is mobile and expressive and changes quickly when she is confused. Jacob's face is harder to read.

- Neneh is sensible: her choices and reactions are mostly appropriate to what is possible or legitimate in the classroom, and she is alert and responsive to cues as to 'what goes around here'. Jacob is more impervious to such subtle indicators, and so is more often 'silly' or inappropriate.

- Neneh is already able to maintain focus on a chosen or prescribed activity and ignore some distractions. She knows how to stick at things. When distracted she soon remembers to come back to the task. Jacob does not have such a strong 'anchor' to his prime activity. If things don't go smoothly he quickly loses interest or focus, or gets upset.

- Neneh is more articulate. Her questions and responses are more appropriate to the context of the moment, and more precise than Jacob's. Jacob is less fluent at expressing his interests and thoughts.

- Neneh seems to latch on to the core of ideas and the purpose of activities more quickly than Jacob. She is 'quicker on the uptake'.

- Neneh is more used to sitting still and listening to, or watching, grown-ups. Jacob has not developed this habit. He is used to being more physically active around adults, except when he is watching a screen.

- Neneh has greater ease and fluency with her peers. She is already able to discuss and argue with other children in a calm and rational way. Jacob is rougher and more 'gauche' in his dealing with other children.

- Neneh often remembers and makes links to things that happened a while ago. Her questions suggest she is trying to link things up inside her head. Jacob seems more 'captured' by the immediate present.

- Neneh is proactive and inquisitive; she is keen to explore new things. Jacob is more hesitant or timid.

- Neneh will often see and remark on sensory details and patterns that Jacob does not notice. She seems more perceptive.

We could argue about the detail of this picture, but it is abundantly clear that 'bright' is a portmanteau word that contains a number of ingredients. Neneh's 'brightness' reflects the fact that she is more socially sensitive, more adult-oriented, more inquisitive, more resilient, more focused and more interested in connecting ideas and experiences. She also remembers things better, asks better questions, makes more appropriate comments and interacts better with her peers than Jacob. Once we unpack some of the implicit dimensions and observations on which the judgement of brightness depends, we can see that being 'bright' is not a single thing; it is woven together from a number of separable developmental achievements, some social, some perceptual, some cognitive and some linguistic.

We are seeing Neneh and Jacob at the start of school, at age five. If we had seen them as babies, we might have seen some differences between them in some of these components of 'brightness'. But there is obviously a lot of learning that has gone on in the first years of these children's lives that will have contributed to the differences in their behaviours at school entry. We do not yet have to reach for the genetic explanation of brightness.

How could children's family life teach them to be oriented to learning in different ways – one that appears 'bright' and one that (viewed through the filter of the dominant conceptions of school culture) looks dimmer? There are a host of experiences that could have nudged Neneh and Jacob into different behaviours (Hart and Risley 1995; Meadows 2006). We know that 'middle-class' and 'working-class' children are immersed in surroundings which differ on average in the quantity, content and style of adult–child use of language. We know that mothers talk more, and in different ways, to their daughters than to their sons. Some carers are more adept at coaching young children in the art of 'joint attention' than others. Some get down to the child's level in shared play more often, or find it easier to engage sympathetically with the child's own interests.

The habitual ways in which carers scaffold, guide, interpret, comment on and evaluate children's activities set up corresponding habits and expectations in the child, some of which may be education-positive and others not. (When you tell an outrageously exaggerated story, do grown-ups regularly laugh and clap, or tell you off for bragging or lying? How often do you have a story read to you and discussed with you? Are you allowed to play with things around the house or are you continually told 'don't touch'?). Recurrent rituals sow and water the seeds of certain ways of thinking and talking. Family mealtimes, for example, are an important arena in which habits of debate and discussion are displayed, and a child's 'legitimate peripheral participation' as fledgling debaters may be invited and shaped – or not (Pontecorvo and Sterponi 2002). All the time, adults model ways of solving problems such as trying to remember where possessions have been left (Tharp and Gallimore 1988) or how to understand other people's feelings (Meadows 2006). They are continually teaching through their actions how to react when things go wrong, what to do with leisure time, what is worthy of note and what things (that may be perfectly obvious and interesting to the child) get regularly and strategically ignored (Billig 1999).

Thus the habits of thinking, remembering, noticing and talking that go to make up 'brightness' are, as sociocultural researchers have long known (Vygotsky 1978), highly socially contagious. If we push our attention back to individual differences at birth, or focus on heritability studies in twins or adoptees, or look at the problems associated with genetic disorders (Meadows 2006), we see that there probably is some inherited ingredient to 'brightness'. People do seem to differ somewhat in their genetically underwritten 'mean position' on such dimensions (Plomin and Daniels 1987). But there is such a wide indeterminate zone around that mean position, that effectively it is your environment and your learning that most influence where you actually end up. Genes do programme development but they operate in continual interaction with environment and experience, and their programmes are generally flexible.

Most researchers (e.g. Resnick 1999) now believe that young minds are better thought of as 'developing muscles' than 'fixed-capacity engines'. The mind is made up of many interwoven strands which get stronger with exercise. Like musculature, minds have a genetic element to them. Different people are born with different physical 'potential', different ranges and aptitudes. But the training which these muscles receive determines whether they get stronger, much more so than differences in 'potential'. In practice the hypothetical 'ceilings' set by genetic differences are so far away from where a child currently is that there is no excuse for anyone to impute 'lack of innate ability' when a child finds something hard to master. There is plenty of room for virtually everyone's physical fitness to improve, and likewise there is plenty of room for everyone to get brighter, whatever portfolio of capacities and dispositions their genes and their early years has provided them with. Of course those early years have a big influence on the kind of learner you might become. But a child's learning style and capacity is not fixed: far from it. We conclude that it is strategically practical and morally preferable to focus our attention as educators on how children's minds might be capable of development, rather than on what is immutable.

Despite the broad consensus about the learnability of 'brightness' amongst scholars, the contrary idea, that children's minds, like light bulbs, come in a range of pre-determined wattages that we can do nothing about, is still surprisingly popular. The language of 'fixed ability' and the injunction to determine students' 'ability' and teach them accordingly, suffuse educational policy and practice in the UK today. Yet such ideas affect the lives of many children for the worse. Once ability attributions are made, they create long-lasting expectations in the minds both of youngsters and of their teachers, expectations that may be misleading or even damaging. For example, the general-purpose 'capacity' assumption can lead teachers to ignore how variable students are from day to day, subject to subject, and from in school to out of school. A bland simplistic summary of a student's performance can be mistaken for 'the truth', and without meaning to, teachers can thereby box students in and cramp their style, reducing their ability to *be* different.

Students who have come to see themselves as 'dim' often stop attempting difficult things, asking themselves what the point is of trying, if they haven't got what it takes? And students who have been led to think of themselves as 'bright' or 'gifted' can also become very conservative learners, afraid to accept new challenges where their chances of success are uncertain, in case their status as 'bright' or 'successful' is put in jeopardy (Dweck 1999, this volume). Such students may also come to expect to be treated as 'special', and get upset if they are not.

The fixed-pot view of ability is often associated with a restricted and rather academic view of intelligence in general. Yet recent research tells us that intelligence is as much about thinking slowly as it is about quick answering, and that true intelligence should not be confused with verbal fluency or mere cleverness (Claxton 1997). Yet there are still schools where 'slow' is used as a euphemism for stupid. Students with more practical or creative forms of intelligence can, as Sternberg (1997a, p. 1036) puts it, be 'essentially "iced out" of the system, because at no point are they much allowed to let their abilities shine through'.

Like adults, any group of children will vary widely on their current levels of achievement and performance (CLAPs) on any kind of skills or subject matter. To deny the fixed-pot theory of ability is not to deny these differences; it is merely to deny a particularly common but pernicious way of talking about them, how they came to be, and what can be done about them. How might we understand the differences between young people's CLAPs differently?

Neneh came to school with high CLAPs on a set of skills and dispositions that matched those that her teachers valued, and on which the smooth and successful running of a school has been assumed to depend. Whatever her 'genetic envelope of possibility', her early apprenticeship has developed her dispositions to be attentive and responsive to adults' non-verbal cues, to search her own memory for links, to sit still and listen, to make appropriate contributions to debate and so on. Through repeated interactions and observations, over hundreds of bathtimes, mealtimes and storytimes, she has developed the proto-educational mindset that her teachers think of as 'bright'. Not only is she already more disposed than Jacob to the kinds of learning that will go on in her reception (kindergarten) class; she is also more disposed to 'learn the ropes' that she has not already mastered. Jacob's epistemic apprenticeship has cultivated a different set of habits and sensitivities that do not mesh so well with the cultural demands of school. His ride through school may well be rockier as a result.

When you start looking seriously at why Neneh is 'bright' and Jacob is 'dim', or why Zeinab is such a 'talented' violinist, you find that it is mostly down to masses of experience and practice and an amalgam of conditions, social and material, that enabled and encouraged that amount of learning. People with high CLAPs, whether it be in quiet listening or physical clowning, have got there because they have done a great deal of learning and have learned how to learn in effective ways. Across a wide range of activities — sports, musicianship, writing, chess, oratory, electronic games — if you want to be outstanding, you need to invest around 10,000 hours of good practice (Ericsson and Charness 1994).

If you track their histories carefully, you find that the 'gifted and talented' have generally been lucky enough – and obsessive enough – to have the support and opportunities required. Mozart's father immersed his children in music from their infancies, carefully marketed their ability to perform and to compose, opened up every opportunity to be a musician and persuaded his own employers to employ his son. Some small seed of their particular 'talent' may be there initially in the form of a mild interest or even a small aptitude, but that seed could equally well have been sown by a chance event, or even by the unjustified attribution of talent by a proud parent. Your elder siblings might have 'bagged' being good at sports and socialising, so you are looking around for something to be good at in your own right, when along comes a second-hand violin. The reason that virtuosi are so rare is because most of us don't put in the hours. We lack the desire, the emotional support, the material resources, and we have too many other interesting things to do.

So it is more accurate to see Neneh not as 'innately gifted' but as 'skilled-up' in particular ways. As a result of her intense apprenticeship, she arrived at school already 'gifted and talented' in all the pro-educational behaviours previously identified. These learned skills will enable her to grasp ideas more easily; to retain what she hears and sees and refer back to it; to be more confident in communication with unfamiliar adults and so on. In other words, she looks all-round 'brighter'. But these skills are not in her genes. Her 'giftedness' lies in the ways she has already learned to learn in more sophisticated ways than her peers. And it is more helpful to see Jacob not as 'at the back of the queue when the brains were doled out', but rather as playing catch-up in certain social, cognitive and linguistic capabilities. What he needs, if he is to do well at school, is a lot of experience and practice in school-type learning, and the supportive coaching and explanation to engage in it. He would also benefit from people around him adopting a less blinkered view of 'intelligence', so that his existing learning talents and methods can be appreciated. Neneh could benefit from watching how Jacob goes about learning, as well as vice versa.

As Charles Darwin astutely observed, almost everyone is born with the ability to be bright, and to be G&T in something. Some children do not get that ability fed. And some get the joy of learning knocked out of them by too much chaos or too tight a prescription of what it means to be 'good', or by an education system apparently driven by assessment and labelling. And for some of those it will be hard or even impossible for them ever to catch up completely. Nevertheless our job is surely to help them develop the 'zeal and hard work' that will enable them to emerge as gifted and talented in their own unique ways.

We can coach everyone in the generic skills of learning. We can help Neneh get over her performance anxiety and the fear of failure that hobble her curiosity and creativity, just as we can help Jacob learn how to listen more attentively and ask sharper questions. Everyone can be coached in how to persist more in the face of difficulty; how to make more use of their imaginations to get ideas; how to learn more productively alongside others; how to capitalise more on the resources around them; how to be their own critical friend; how to look at a situation through other people's eyes; how to choose and create the right kind of challenge for themselves and move on positively from it (Claxton 1999a, 2002).

Summing up the research in this area, Lauren Resnick (1999, p. 39) put it like this:

Students who, over an extended period of time are treated as if they are intelligent, actually become more so. If they are taught demanding content, and are expected to explain and find connections . . . they learn more and learn more quickly. They (come to) think of themselves as learners. They are (better) able to bounce back in the face of short-term failures.

According to recent research on 'student voice', what adolescents want from school is respect, challenge and responsibility (Flutter and Rudduck 2004). Give them the opportunity, and many of them will find and engage with learning challenges that are well beyond what the prescribed curriculum demands – just as many of them are already doing on their bedroom computers in the evenings. They say they like challenge. They like stretching their learning muscles, provided they see demanding exercise as a way of getting stronger, not as exposing their 'weakness'. And they know when things are getting too easy and it is time to make it more difficult for themselves. Working with the giftedness in young people should not be about the busy teacher finding an endless succession of new mind games to entertain the fast-finishers. It should be about giving young people the support they need to take on challenges that interest them, and to build their own learning power in the process. Those with both high and low CLAPs can be encouraged to stretch themselves, without having to be labelled and stigmatised. And this applies, we are sure, to learners of all ages, in school and out of school, and from birth until death.

Yet the pressure on teachers to use students' CLAPs to infer ability, to use these bogus judgements as a basis for predicting future performance, and for schools then to be judged on whether these targets have been reached, remains strong. There is even a current suggestion on the Department for Children, Schools and Families website that we should identify gifted and talented students when they are eleven, hive them off into a 'distinctive in-school teaching and learning programme' and put them on a special national register, and censure secondary schools that do not ensure they all end up with distinguished first degrees from Oxford (or equivalent) – without any recognition of the avoidable damage that would result (see http://www.standards.dfes.gov.uk/giftedandtalented/).

Why is the idea of fixed ability so tenacious? Perhaps it is because the education system has always been concerned with sorting, grading and labelling young people and their educational outcomes, and with finding justifications for so doing. Or maybe ability attributions are attempts by harassed teachers to reduce the overwhelming complexity of a room of 30 young people to something graspable. Bright, average and weak; motivated and unmotivated; well- or badly-behaved; high- or low-achieving: however inadequate these filters are in capturing any-thing very interesting about students and their lives, perhaps they are necessary filters and defences. If this is so, they come at a high price. And it may be time to find alternative ways of supporting teachers, ways that do not damage students or distort their psychology so much. As Hart et al. (2004) point out, it is perfectly fine to arrange your students, for practical purposes, into those whose CLAPs are above average, average or below average. But to transmute these pragmatic and provisional groupings of how people are behaving right now into labels that can stick, and harm, for life . . . that has to stop.

Contact address: guy.claxton@bristol.ac.uk

Future Perspectives

Suggested priorities for gifted education over the next decade

In ten years' time, the antiquated and dysfunctional idea that 'giftedness' is an innate, abiding and situation-independent quality of a fortunate minority of young people must have been removed from the discourse of educational practice and policy. It must instead be widely recognised that this idea exists primarily as a stress-reduction device for teachers, one that comes with unacceptable side-effects for the majority of young people – both those who are designated 'gifted' and those who are not. In its place must come a more humble and pragmatic commitment to helping all youngsters (a) stretch their mental capacities (whatever level those capacities may currently be) i.e. become more 'gifted' and (b) discover the domains of human achievement they would most like to become good at i.e. become more 'talented'. We must accept that transitory levels of achievement in any sphere, including sociolinguistic fluency, reflect composites of learned habits, and provide only poor guides to future learning and performance.   Guy Claxton and Sara Meadows

2

Neural interconnectivity and intellectual creativity: giftedness, savants and learning styles

John Geake
Oxford Brookes University, UK

There is considerable evidence that intelligence as a brain function occurs through the synchronised integration of information processing, involving a myriad of interconnected functional modules. Consistently, the brains of gifted children show relatively higher levels of cerebral interconnectivity when engaged in cognitive tasks. An important part of the evidence for integrated brain function as the seat of intelligence comes from studies into cross-modal processing, where sensory information in one modality e.g. vision, is processed in multiple sensory areas e.g. auditory, sensory. Thus, so-called learning styles such as VAK (Visual-Auditory-Kinaesthetic) based on processing information in a single modality, fail to acknowledge how the brain actually works. This could explain why no independent evidence has been found for the learning efficacy of VAK and similar learning style inventories. Moreover, as an anti-integration pedagogy, VAK is implicitly anti-intellectual and anti-giftedness. Savants are an intriguing example of high-functioning individuals. Despite their extremes of performance, this chapter argues that in terms of their neural interconnectivity, the brains of savants are qualitatively different from those of children we usually classify as gifted.

Our integrated brains

One important generalisation that has emerged from the past decades of neuroscience research is that there are common brain functions for all acts of intelligence. This very much includes learning at school and engaging in classroom activities. These fundamental brain functions, and the brain areas which seem to be critically involved, include

- sequencing of symbolic representations in the (left) fusiform gyrus and temporal lobe;
- quasi-spatial conceptual inter-relationships in the (inferior) parietal lobes;
- long term memory via the hippocampus (and connected cortical areas);
- decision making via the orbitofrontal cortex;
- emotional mediation from various components of the limbic subcortex;
- integration of information within working memory (WM) with the (bi-) lateral frontal cortex;
- integration and possible rehearsal of output in the cerebellum.

All but the very simplest of cognitive tasks demand all of these contributions. This is not to say that the brain is not modular, it is; but such modularity can only be expressed through interconnectivity, i.e. through combination of the contribution of various modules to the cognitive task at hand. It is a common misunderstanding of neuroimaging data that those appealingly coloured areas of brain that represent areas which are significantly active during an experiment (and are said to 'light up') are solely responsible for the behavioural response elicited by the experimental stimuli. Such a misunderstanding ignores the statistical ontology of the coloured blobs. Whereas they certainly represent important if not critical areas of relevant brain function, these are not the only areas that are necessary to perform the cognitive task in question. In fact, to get such contained focal maps, activations from a carefully designed control task are usually subtracted from those associated with the criterion task. To coin an analogy, imagine making a map of the ocean's mountains but only showing those that protrude above sea level (the level of the sea being the statistical threshold set by the experimenter who, in order to see more or less activation, simply raises or lowers the threshold).

Moreover, the various functional modules evolved eons ago when our primate ancestors were adapting to very different conditions from those we face in modern society, including schooling. There are modules which enable us to speak in our mother tongue, but none as such which singly enable us to be literate or numerate. To achieve these cognitive abilities we have to learn to integrate and synchronise a number of modules originally evolved for other purposes.

A good illustration of this is seen with a neuroimaging (functional magnetic resonance imaging, fMRI) study of Staneslas Dehaene (1997) doing repeated subtraction (100 minus 7, minus 7, minus 7 . . .). This ostensibly simple task activates at least ten functional modules throughout the brain, left side and right, front and back. The various contributions of these modules to the task of arithmetic subtraction include the recognition of number words and digits, visually or aurally; the representation of quantity; the updating of a short-term memory buffer; strategic decision-making and planning; and the articulation of the answer. What is remarkable is how well, usually, we can seamlessly coordinate the inputs and outputs of these modules to come up with the correct answer in a fraction of a second. This suggests, in turn, that children with learning difficulties might suffer from some deficiencies in neural connectivity rather than in modular function, if for no other reason that there are many more connection pathways than modules (Geake 2006).

It has to be said that this view of the interconnected brain, while concordant with contemporary neuroscience, is somewhat at odds with the location-equals-function view popular in the media (Geake 2004). This has come about, it seems, by the misunderstanding of neuroimaging data as indicative of self-contained function rather than contributions to a web of interaction: the exclusive consideration of cerebral locations has produced a new phrenology, this time beneath the skull. But, as Nobel Laureate Charles Sherrington (1938) warned in Oxford some 70 years ago, 'To suppose the roof-brain consists of point-to-point centres identified each with a particular item of intelligent, concrete behaviour is a scheme over simplified and to be abandoned' (p. 181).

For example, a voxel-based morphometric (VBM) study which mapped the grey matter density of the brain, found some six areas throughout the brain (about 6 per cent of the total) where density correlated positively with IQ (Haier et al 2004). These included regions in the frontal, parietal, temporal and occipital cortices, as well as the cerebellum. A sensible interpretation is not that these multiple sites somehow represent multiple, independent intelligences, but rather, that these areas, among many others, contribute to the intellectual enterprise.

11

The other reason that interconnectivity has not featured so prominently in popular accounts of brain function is that neuroimaging technology that specifically records neural connectivity, such as diffusion-weighted MRI (diffusion tensor imaging, DTI), has only recently become available in most neuroimaging laboratories. Previously, the technology has only permitted the interrogation of brain functions in time and space. Of course, data about the spatial distribution of functional modules are necessary precursors to understanding what gets connected to what, and now neuroscience studies typically report circuits of activity rather than just lists of the most active sites.

An interconnected model of brain function begs the question of integration. Many neuroscientific studies into the neural correlates of intelligence have found that the frontal cortices play a critical, if not exclusive, role in the integration of information from around the brain for intelligent application to cognitive tasks (Rypma et al. 1999). This has been explained by Duncan (2001) as the selective adaptability of frontal neurons which enables focused attention or emphasis on relevant inputs while filtering out irrelevant inputs. Moreover, such focused frontal information processing supports information processing in other relevant areas of the brain by maintaining persistent activation of relevant inputs from other brain areas. The combined effect of this is to create a temporary dominant active state of concern toward a particular problem under consideration. This regional involvement increasingly recruits overlapping regions of the frontal cortex as problem engagement continues. In this way, sustained and focused thinking requires a high working memory demand.

Consistently, several neuroimaging studies report neuroanatomical correlates with intelligence test scores (IQ), which involve the frontal cortices. In a longitudinal MRI study of intellectual ability and cortical development in 300 children and adolescents (Shaw et al. 2006), data sampled over six years indicated that the trajectory of change in the thickness of the cerebral cortex, rather than cortical thickness itself, was most closely related to levels of intelligence. The cortex was thinner in the high-IQ group when these children were young, but rapidly grew so that by the time the gifted children had reached their teens, their cerebral cortices were significantly thicker than average, especially in the prefrontal cortex. This is not to say that the prefrontal cortex is the only region in which neural correlates with intelligence can be found. The Haier et al. (2004) VBM study found IQ-correlated grey matter density distributed in several places throughout the brain, and in a similarly designed VBM study, Frangou, Chitins and Williams (2004) found IQ correlates in regions of the non-cortical hind-brain, the cerebellum.

Giftedness as enhanced cerebral interconnectivity

To summarise the preceding section, the brain is a processor of information via structural cerebral interconnectivity, mediated through executive cognitive control in the form of attentional focus and selective inhibition (albeit mostly unconscious) as central functions of the frontal lobes. Behavioural measures of intelligence correlate with structural and functional characteristics of these frontal areas, not in isolation, but within a fronto-parietal network (Gray et al. 2003). It should be predicted, then, that gifted children should display relatively enhanced frontal (and other correlated) activity, enabling high-level performance in the various facets of working memory. There is psychophysical and neuroscientific evidence for such a prediction. For example, in an ERP study of highly mathematically gifted pre-adolescents, O'Boyle et al. (1995) concluded that:

a finely tuned capacity for activating (or inhibiting) the very brain regions known to play (not play) specialized roles in the performance of a given task. . . . That is, precocious individuals are especially facile at knowing [sic] what steps to take in solving a given intellectual problem.

(p 478)

Moreover, it would be predicted that gifted children should have greater or more efficacious neural interconnectivity (Singh and O'Boyle 2004). There is neuroimaging evidence for such a prediction. An fMRI study of mathematically gifted primary school children undergoing a spatial rotation task showed significant bilateral activations in the brains of the gifted subjects (O'Boyle et al. 2005). The researchers suggested that enhanced bilateral activation of the parietal, frontal and anterior cingulate cortices is indicative of

an all-purpose information processing network . . . that is relied upon by individuals who are intellectually gifted [and which] may provide finely-tuned general information processing capacities for handling and integrating various types of task demands across a variety of domains.

(p. 586)

Further direct evidence for enhanced interconnectivity of gifted subjects comes from an fMRI study of Lee et al. (2006) with two groups of participants: adolescents from the Korean national academy for the gifted (Ravens Advanced Progressive Matrices > 99%) and an aged-match control group from local high schools. High g [general intelligence]-loaded tasks increased activity in bilateral, prefrontal regions. But for the gifted subjects, there was a stronger activation in the anterior cingulate, a region involved in emotionally weighted decision making, and in the posterior parietal cortices, regions involved in forming conceptual inter-relationships. Lee et al. concluded that 'These results suggest that superior g may not be due to the recruitment of additional brain regions but to the functional facilitation of the fronto-parietal network particularly driven by the posterior parietal activation' (p. 578).

The extent to which such neural support is more extensive and focused for gifted individuals can be interpreted as a manifestation of greater working memory efficacy, particularly in cognitive tasks with high demands for creative outcomes (Geake and Dodson 2005). High creative intelligence has been conceptualised at a cognitive level as an enhanced ability for fluid analogising (Geake 2007a; 2007b). Two fMRI studies of the neural correlates of fluid analogy making found that the level of neural activation in certain areas of the frontal lobes was positively correlated with static measures of IQ (Geake and Hansen 2005; in progress). That is, what the gifted brain 'buys' with its relatively enhanced neural interconnectivity is a greater ability to create conceptual connectivity by way of fluid analogy making. As Wright (2007) describes, hearing or seeing a word causes stimulation, first of the associated primary cortex, but then progressively of the other interconnected parts of the brain:

In some persons at all times, and in some other persons at some times and in some states, the 'ripples' may be limited; but in other persons, or at other times, the ripples may be more widespread. . . . Therein lies the difference between the dullard, the person of inflexible mind who interprets everything literally, and the person of fertile imagination, the 'lateral thinker' who has . . . 'the power to connect the unconnected'. . . . When such a connection is perceived . . . another metaphor has been born.

(p. 283)

13

Consistent evidence for this claim comes from an electroencephalographic study by Carlsson et al. (2000), who found significant differences in frontal activity between high and low creative subjects, the high creative group utilising bilateral prefrontal regions, while the low creative group used frontal functions, predominantly on the left. Not only is cerebral interconnectivity necessary for creativity, individual differences in the quality of creative intelligence can be explained by qualitative differences in the distribution of that interconnectivity.

The neuromythology of Visual-Auditory-Kinaesthetic learning styles

The notion that individual differences in academic abilities can be partly attributed to individual learning styles has considerable intuitive appeal if we are to judge by the number of learning style models or inventories that have been devised – 170 at last count, and rising. The myriad ways that approaches to learning can seem to be partitioned, labelled and measured seem to know no bounds. Just click on to a website and send money. The disappointing outcome of all of this endeavour is that, overall, the evidence consistently shows that modifying a teaching approach to cater for differences in learning styles does not result in any improvement in learning outcomes (Coffield et al. 2004).

Despite the lack of evidence, the education community has been swamped by claims for a learning style model based on the sensory modalities: visual, auditory and kinaesthetic (VAK). The idea is that children can be tested to ascertain which is their dominant learning style, V, A or K, and then taught accordingly. Some schools have even gone so far as to label children with V, A and K shirts, presumably because these purported differences are no longer obvious in the classroom. There is plenty of evidence as to why such recommendations are nonsense. What is more insidious is that focusing on one sensory modality flies in the face of the brain's natural interconnectivity. VAK might, if it has any effect at all, be actually harming the academic prospects of the children so inflicted. Certainly such a divisive pedagogy runs counter to the interconnectedness that characterises intellectual giftedness.

A simple demonstration of the ineffectiveness of VAK as a model of cognition comes from asking five-year-olds to distinguish different-sized groups of dots where the groups are too large for counting (Gilmore et al. 2007). So long as the group sizes are not almost equal, young children can do this quite reliably. Now, what happens when one group is replaced by as many sounds played too rapidly for counting? There is no change in accuracy! Going from a V versus V version of the task to a V versus A version makes no difference to task performance. The reason is that input modalities in the brain are interlinked: visual with auditory; visual with motor; motor with auditory; visual with taste, and so on.

Evidence for this comes from fMRI studies of cross-modal binding, especially visual-auditory cross-modal binding, where visual information is directed to and processed by parts of the auditory cortex, and vice versa. This is not just a simple interconnection of sensory information processing where there is congruent visual-auditory information, such as a speaker's lips coinciding with the sounds heard. Both cortical areas activate in a supra-additive effect (Calvert et al. 2000). Similarly, where the visual auditory information is incongruent, as in when the video is out of synch with the audio on a television broadcast, the two sensory areas display supra-subtractive activations. There are well-adapted evolutionary reasons for this. Out on the savannah as a pre-hominid hunter-gatherer, coordinating sight and sound makes all the difference between detecting dinner and being dinner. The brain sees with its ears and touch, and hears with its eyes (Kaiser 2007). Moreover, as primates, we are predominantly processors of visual information. This is true even for congenitally blind children who instantiate Braille, not in the kinaesthetic areas of their brains, but in those parts of their visual cortices that sighted children dedicate to learning written language. Moreover, unsighted people create the same mental spatial maps of their physical reality as sighted people do (Kriegseis et al. 2006).

Obviously, the information to create spatial maps by blind people comes from auditory and tactile inputs, but it gets used as though it were visual. Wright (2007) points out just how interconnected our daily neural processes must be. Eating does not engage just taste, but smell, tactile (inside the mouth), auditory and visual sensations. Learning a language, and the practice of it, requires the coordinated use of visual, auditory and kinaesthetic modalities, in addition to memory, emotion, will, thinking and imagination. Input information is abstracted to be processed and learnt, mostly unconsciously, through the brain's interconnectivity (Dehaene et al. 1998).

VAK is not about differences in learning but pre-learning biases in perceptual acuities. Following a VAK regime in real classrooms would lead to all sorts of ridiculous paradoxes: What does a teacher do with the V and K learners in a music lesson? the A and K learners at an art lesson? or the V and A learners in a craft practical lesson? The images of blindfolds and corks in mouths are all too reminiscent of *Tommy*, the rock opera by The Who. As Sharp et al. (2007) elaborate, VAK trivialises the complexity of learning, and in doing so, threatens the professionalism of educators. Fortunately, many teachers are not taken in; instead, ironically, VAK has become, in the hands of practitioners, a recipe for a mixed-modality pedagogy where lessons have explicit presentations of material in V, A and K modes. Teachers quickly observed that their pupils' so-called learning styles were not stable, that the expressions of V-, A- and K-ness varied with the demands of the lessons, as they should. As with other learning style inventories, research has shown that there is no improvement of learning outcomes with VAK above teacher enthusiasm, where 'attempts to focus on learning styles were wasted effort' (Kratzig and Arbuthnott 2006).

We might speculate in passing why VAK and other 'learning-styles' approaches seem so attractive? I wonder if two aspects of folk psychology – where we seem to learn differently from each other, and that we have five senses – have created a folk neuroscience where the working of our brains directly reflects our folk psychology. Of course if our brains were that simple we would not be here today!

How are savants differently gifted?

Savants are those rare people whose prodigious talent in one well-defined area is quite inconsistent with their general intellectual abilities, measures of which are typically below the normal range. Autistic computational savants such as Kim Peek, portrayed as Raymond Babbitt by Dustin Hoffman in the film *Rain Man*, seem to be able to bring a much greater than normal focus of neural resource to a computational problem that would defeat most of us. Artistic savants are remarkable in their precocity and seemingly effortless talent, usually either in visual art or music performance. For example, Nadia could draw life-like sketches of animals, especially horses, at age three. Savant pianists such as Tom, aged four years, could accurately reproduce an entire piece having heard it only once (Hermelin 2001). Nevertheless, just like their normally talented peers, savants demonstrate persistence, practice and self-motivation, and respond positively to encouragement and praise. However, the asynchrony in their level of talent compared with their general cognitive functioning suggests that there is something quite different about the brains of savants.

There is diverse evidence for the neural characteristic of savants (Snyder et al. 2003). Savant talents sometimes disappear; e.g. Nadia's extreme drawing skill in early age was lost once she started to talk later on in childhood. Savant talents sometimes appear. Asperger savant Daniel Tammet attributes his extraordinary calculating and language-learning abilities to his epilepsy, which first occurred at the age of four (Tammet 2006). Some elderly stroke patients suddenly demonstrate artistic prowess. Transcranial magnetic stimulation (TMS), a neuroscientific investigative technology which creates a temporary lesion to a focal area of the brain when applied to the temporal lobes, seems to enhance visual artistic abilities in some subjects. Alan Snyder interprets these data as suggesting that the savant brain is characterised by deficits in its interconnectivity, at least with those parts of the brain responsible for our social cognition (Snyder et al. 2003, 2006; Snyder and Bossomaier 2004). Snyder proposes, therefore, that artistic genius can be unlocked in all of us by closing down our brain connections with our social world (Snyder 2001).

Such a conjecture raises the question: are savants really creative? Certainly, much savant artistic output is remarkable in its accuracy, e.g. Tom, and Nadia. But the want of originality or interpretation counts against savant output as being highly creative. In fact, artistic talent at a professional level in savants is extremely rare. Although comparisons of artistic savants and high ability artists demonstrate little difference in artistic execution (Pring and Hermelin 1993) there are important differences in the intellectual understanding of meaning, symbol and context. To demonstrate this point, an American college student was trained to perform calendrical calculations, computing the day of the week for any date in the past or future, at savant level (Young 2000). For this student, the training was perceived as extremely boring, the task lacking intrinsic merit.

This highlights the differences between savant abilities and those of the creatively gifted. For an artistic product to be regarded as creative requires a high degree of original intellectual or emotional connectivity to areas of human experience which are external to the art form itself (Geake and Dodson 2005; Sternberg 1999a). Such connectivity is often unconscious or implicit, all the more so in what comes to be regarded as creatively great works. Self-referential art, often the province of student artists, is not usually destined for providence. Non-referential art, such as savants typically produce, counts even less. To be creative we don't need to switch to a savant-like view of the world. Rather, we need to exploit the very rules and mindsets that we have acquired over the years. It is the mental exploration of putative links between concepts at this higher cognitive level that constitutes creative thinking. For example, in music, creative epitomes are found in orchestral conducting and composition, fields devoid of savants. In sum, a high level of creative intelligence requires dense, high-functioning cerebral interconnectivity; an induced reduction of higher brain functioning is unlikely to lead to creativity or genius. It might be noted in passing that Professor Snyder is proof of this himself in that his theory and experiments require his higher brain functions to create them in the first place.

But this critique does not explain the prodigious gifts of savants like Tammet (2006), who in a record-breaking public performance in Oxford in 2005, accurately recalled the decimal expansion of pi to over 20,000 digits! Tammet speaks ten languages, including Icelandic (which he learnt in a week), Lithuanian and Welsh. He attributes his extraordinary abilities to his synaesthesia, a condition where several sensory modalities strongly coincide. Typical synaesthetes 'see' numbers or words in colour. Some composers 'see' musical notes in colours; some chefs 'see' tastes in shapes. These multi-modal associations have been tested, and are quite stable across the lifespan (Steven et al. 2006). For Tammet, every number (and many words) has a consistent and stable colour and shape. The advantage of synaesthesia for memory is that the act of recall is re-journeying through a mental spatial map of coloured shapes in virtual locations.

For Tammet, his description of recalling pi to over 20,000 places was remembering going on a long (mental) journey. His description of his memory processes is consistent with that of Luria's (1968) account of his patient S, the man who could not forget, whom Luria diagnosed as a synaesthete. Synaesthesia presumably occurs from excessive neural interconnectivity between the primary sensory cortices. Wright (2007) notes that if the information flow between the sensory cortical areas is disrupted by some insult to the association cortex, such as a temporal lobe epilepsy as happened to Daniel Tammet, then some abnormal functioning of multi-modal sensory processing, such as synaesthesia, might be the result.

Concluding remarks

The aim of this chapter is to demonstrate the utility of applying a fundamental structural and functional feature of the brain – neural interconnectivity – to three issues pertinent to the education of gifted children. First, neural interconnectivity throughout the brain provides an in-principle explanation of the conceptual interconnectivity or fluid analogising which characterises the creative intelligence of gifted people. Second, an analysis of sensory interconnectivity shows the futility of basing classroom pedagogies on so-called brain-based learning styles such as VAK. Third, possible irregularities in neural interconnectivity provide a means of beginning to understand the enigma of extreme functioning posed by autistic savants. Together, these accounts suggest not only that the learning needs of gifted children will be best met through curricula and pedagogies which emphasise interdisciplinarity and content connectedness, but that we should expect to find, and celebrate, individual differences within the population of children we call 'gifted'.

Contact address: jgeake@brookes.ac.uk

Future Perspectives

Suggested priorities for gifted education over the next decade

Academic giftedness, when it presents itself in schools, should receive a similar empathic and professional response to other, more accepted, individual differences such as physical disability (in most countries, affirmative school policy towards children with physical disabilities is mandated by law), Language Other Than English Background (LOTEB), or even athletic or artistic precocity. For each of these latter cases, schools have long-standing policies of individual provision, with designated, trained teachers in charge of the various special programmes. So it should be with the gifted. Giftedness should be treated as another 'ordinary' difference requiring appropriate differentiation of educational provision to meet the individual child's specific learning needs. Consequently, universal pre-service and in-service teacher professional development in gifted education is essential.   John Geake

---

3

Making connections: cognition, emotion and a shifting paradigm

Dona J. Matthews
Ontario Institute for Studies in Education of the University of Toronto, Canada

Christy Folsom
Lehman College, The City University of New York, US

A paradigm shift in progress: from mystery to mastery

Over the past few decades, there has been a change in prevailing definitions and understandings of intelligence, in the ways that giftedness is identified and in the programming that is recommended for exceptionally capable learners. After a brief description of the historical and conceptual underpinnings of this paradigm shift, we discuss here its practical consequences, including connections to current psychological research on mindsets, and to teaching that promotes both intellectual and emotional learning. Throughout, our focus is on what this means for understanding and supporting high-level development in diverse kinds of learners.

The observed shift is grounded in current findings about human development, neural plasticity, psychometrics and the complex interacting processes that underlie exceptional intellectual ability and achievement (Dai and Renzulli in press; Geake this volume; Horowitz 1987; Lohman 2005; Worrell in press). Increasingly, accepted practice in education and psychology is moving away from a categorisation of some children as *gifted* (with all others implicitly assigned to the *not gifted* category), and toward a focus on individual differences in developmental trajectories, recognising that pathways to high-level achievement are diverse, domain-specific, and incremental (Bransford et al. 2000; Dweck 2006; Keating in press).

For purposes of discussion, we have called the traditional categorical perspective a *mystery* model of giftedness, and the emerging developmental perspective a *mastery* model (Matthews and Foster 2006). While we acknowledge the mysterious complexity of human development, we use the term mystery model to describe the now-outdated idea that gifted children are special, superior to others in an innate, categorical, and global way. We have observed how confusingly mysterious (or problematically elevating) this is to children who are identified as gifted, and to their parents and teachers. We also recognise the dynamic nature of the development of expertise, and use the term mastery to describe the ongoing process that leads to gifted-level learning, rather than the static end-state that the term sometimes signifies.

Gifted education is frequently criticised for exacerbating social, economic and racial disparities. When it is conceptualised as providing a dynamically responsive curriculum match for educationally advanced students, however, not only are the results better targeted at students' actual learning needs, but there are also fewer problems with concerns of equity and social justice (Matthews and Kitchen in press). That is, when educators employ a special education approach, and provide a wide range of learning options to address individual students' diverse gifted learning needs, the resulting programmes are more consistent with emerging knowledge of child and adolescent development, and they are better able simultaneously to foster both excellence and equity in a diverse society (Lohman 2005; Worrell in press).

The mastery model is aligned in many ways with the talent development literature (Subotnik and Jarvin 2005; Tannenbaum 2003), and is leading to a simple, practical, education-based definition of giftedness: 'Giftedness is exceptionally advanced subject-specific ability at a particular point in time such that a student's learning needs cannot be well met without significant adaptations to the curriculum' (Matthews and Foster 2005, p. 26).

One of the important points of difference between the categorical/mystery model of giftedness and the emergent developmental/mastery model is the relative emphasis on either innate genetic causality or environmental dimensions interacting over time. Most psychology and education professionals today concede the interactive contributions of both nature and nurture, but are increasingly interested in the developmental nature of intelligence, its dependence on a child's opportunities to learn and the importance of the goodness of fit with the environment. This can be contrasted with the historic emphasis on giftedness as genetic superiority that might be measured at birth if only we had the right psychometric instrument.

Another point of difference concerns duration. From a mystery model perspective, giftedness denotes an intellectual superiority across the lifespan, sometimes expressed, 'Once gifted, always gifted'. Increasingly, however, educators are recognising the tremendous variability in individual developmental trajectories, and are conceptualising giftedness as a current need for educational modifications, subject to change over time.

Domain-specificity is a key component of a developmental or mastery approach. Intelligence used to be considered a global attribute of a person, so that one might say about a given child, 'He is gifted', and mean that he is exceptionally capable in every intellectual endeavour. As we learn more about human development, however, we realise that it makes better sense to identify cognitive exceptionality in particular domains, saying for example, 'She is mathematically gifted'. Or musically gifted, or linguistically, etc.

With the mystery model, the sooner giftedness is identified the better, and intelligence tests are the gold standard for measuring its presence and extent. From a mastery perspective, however – where giftedness is defined less categorically and more developmentally – looking to provide an appropriate educational fit is an ongoing process, flexibly responsive to changing circumstances and developmental needs, and a natural part of a child's education. Intelligence tests can certainly be useful, particularly where a child has had problems with access to academic learning, but are used sparingly, as a supplement to a combination of dynamic classroom assessments and high-ceiling tests of academic reasoning.

The models differ also in the educational placement implications once a child has been identified as gifted. With the mystery model, the first choice is usually a full-time, segregated classroom where a gifted child is educated with categorically similar children. Mastery model theorists, on the other hand, advocate a broad range of learning options, including many kinds of acceleration, extracurricular and enrichment opportunities, online learning, and full-time, gifted classes, as appropriate to the child's learning needs at a given point in time.

Because of the mastery model's flexible responsivity to individual differences, and fluid connections with general education, it takes into account racial, economic, gender and cultural diversity, and is more equitable than the mystery model, while being equally conducive to excellence. When gifted learning options are (and are seen to be) flexibly targeted to special learning needs, giftedness can be found in every school in every district, regardless of socio-economic status, race, language, or culture. For obvious reasons, this goes a long way toward addressing the longstanding political and funding problems of the field.

A final point of contrast between the two models is that of programme evaluation. When we use intelligence or creativity tests to identify giftedness, we do not have any increased understanding of the specific learning needs that distinguish identified-gifted students from others. This makes it difficult to make sound programming decisions, and even more difficult to evaluate success. Are we perhaps looking for gains in IQ or creativity test scores? Mastery model programming, on the other hand, because it is based on identifying students' current needs for special gifted education, can be evaluated by discerning whether a given child is actually learning, and at what rate. This can be assessed using domain-specific measures of academic achievement, including portfolio assessment, standardised tests, grade-normed tests and other measures, depending on a number of factors, including the student's developmental stage, interests and domain of learning (Lohman 2005).

By conceptualising gifted education as an educational match for students who otherwise experience a mismatch with the curriculum normally provided, the mastery model represents a changing mindset which not only better addresses the learning needs of students who demonstrate exceptionally advanced ability under traditional approaches, but also encourages high-level learning in those whose exceptionality might not otherwise be identified.

The role of mindsets in understanding giftedness

Carol Dweck (2006, this volume) distinguishes between two different perspectives on one's own ability that she calls a *fixed mindset* and a *growth mindset*. Interestingly for those engaged in gifted development, these overlap closely with the mystery and mastery models of giftedness (see Table 1). From the vantage point of a fixed mindset, as with a mystery model, ability is seen as innate and permanent: some people are intelligent and some are less so. From a growth mindset, as with the mastery model, ability is seen as growing incrementally over time with appropriate opportunities to learn: intelligence develops. The outcome differences between these two mindsets are strikingly large and persistent across age, sex, culture, ability level and socioeconomic status. Results in repeated studies in a number of lines of research show that those who hold the growth mindset in a particular area of their lives are happier, healthier, more fulfilled and more successful in those areas, whether it is school, work, sports, business, love, friendships or family relationships.

Dweck's concept of growth versus fixed mindsets may come to represent the tipping point in the shift from mystery to mastery. Our conceptualisations of intelligence and giftedness are foundational to gifted education. These shift dramatically when we move from a fixed mindset, where some students are categorised as inherently smart and some are not, to a growth mindset, where intelligence is seen as dynamic, as developing over time with appropriately scaffolded opportunities to learn. Looked at from this perspective, teachers who encourage their students' continued engagement in the learning process are fostering gifted development, quite independently of where their students may score on ability or intelligence tests: 'The great teachers believe in the growth of the intellect and talent, and they are fascinated with the process of learning' (Dweck 2006, p. 188).

From a fixed mindset, as with a mystery model of giftedness, some people are inherently smart, and some are not, and there are ways accurately and reliably to measure this. From a

Table 1 A comparison: giftedness models and mindsets

Belief or Attitude	Mystery Model/Fixed Mindset	Mastery Model/Growth Mindset
Theories of giftedness creativity, and talent	Innate and categorical; some people are born gifted, creative or talented, and some are not	Dynamic; giftedness, creativity and talent develop over time with appropriate opportunities to learn
Measurement reliability and predictive validity	Static; IQ or creativity tests accurately measure ability and predict future achievement	Fluid; intelligence and creativity ebb and flow; a current score does not predict the future very well
Speed of learning	Gifted people learn quickly	All learning and achievement require time; are often slow
Effort	Gifted people don't need to work hard; things come easily without much effort	All worthwhile achievements require persistence, an investment of hard work over time
Failure	A failure or challenging obstacle signifies lack of ability in an area, leads to avoidance	A failure is welcomed as a learning opportunity, and signifies the need to work harder
Praising intelligence	Beneficial; supports positive self-concept	Detrimental; reduces learning motivation by fostering fixed mindset
Labelling giftedness and creativity	Beneficial; supports positive self-concept	Better to label programmes than children

growth mindset (or mastery model), on the other hand, intelligence develops over time with appropriately scaffolded opportunities to learn. There are many fewer limits on who might or might not be gifted, and many opportunities along a given developmental trajectory to become gifted; intelligence is a moving target that cannot be measured with much expectation of reliability over time. This is consistent with current findings on neural plasticity (Nelson 1999) and gifted development (Gottfried et al. in press). It is also an important perspective for whose who are concerned about minority under-representation and giftedness (Graham, in press; Warwick and Matthews this volume; Worrell in press).

Referring to Ellen Winner's work with child prodigies (Winner 1996), Dweck addresses the topic of extreme giftedness. She concludes that there is a prevalent misconception that such exceptionality is innate, and that the emphasis ought to shift from what might be genetically endowed to the essential temperamental and motivation dimensions that are connected to mindsets: 'Most often people believe that the "gift" is the ability itself. Yet what feeds it is that constant, endless curiosity and challenge seeking' (Dweck 2006, p. 63).

Another recommendation emerging from *Mindset* for our work in supporting high-level development is that rather than praising children for innate and permanent attributes, we should instead praise them for their growth-oriented processes, for what they accomplish through practice, study, persistence and good strategies. Even better than praise is to ask them about their work in ways that appreciate their effort and choices. Many parents and educators are surprised to learn that, 'Praising children's intelligence harms their motivation and it harms their performance' (Dweck 2006, p. 170).

When asked if there any recognisable signs of giftedness, many people identify speed of thinking or learning: 'Gifted kids are fast thinkers' or 'They learn really quickly'. According to Dweck's research, this is fixed mindset thinking: from a fixed mindset, if you learn very quickly, you are gifted, but if you have to work hard at something, or learn it slowly, you are not. By contrast, from a growth mindset, as with a mastery model of giftedness, skills and achievement come through persistence and intense effort, expended over time. Instead of being markers of giftedness, speed and perfection are enemies of high-level learning. Real achievement comes from a lot of hard work; thoughtfulness (which can be slow) is a good thing.

People operating from a fixed mindset have much to lose by failing. When given a choice, they take easier academic courses they know they can do well on, and avoid competitions they are not sure they can win. The best way to address and prevent underachievement may be to help students learn how to approach things from a growth perspective, where failures are perceived as learning opportunities, chances to see what we don't know yet or need to work on. Indeed, the growth mindset is associated with higher academic and career achievement levels over time: 'People in a growth mindset don't just seek challenge, they thrive on it' (Dweck 2006, p. 21).

From a fixed mindset, we measure a person's potential every time we give them a test. From the growth perspective, as with the mastery model of giftedness, the concept of potential is avoided because there is too much open to development over time and to variables like motivation and effort: 'An assessment at one point in time has little value for understanding someone's ability, let alone their potential to succeed in future' (Dweck 2006, p. 29). Every child has tremendous potential, and it is dangerous to think we can accurately determine which one has more than others, and which one has less. Mindsets are learned, and can be unlearned. Parents, educators and others can have a long-lasting beneficial impact on children and adolescents when they model and foster the growth mindset. Dweck (2006, this volume) provides strong evidence for mindsets' susceptibility to change, as well as practical suggestions for changing mindsets.

A final recommendation that emerges from the work on mindsets concerns labelling: 'Telling children they're smart, in the end, made them feel dumber and act dumber, but claim they were smarter. I don't think this is what we're aiming for when we put positive labels – "gifted", "talented", "brilliant" – on people' (Dweck 2006, p. 75). These labels communicate innate and permanent exceptional qualities, over time corroding confidence, self-esteem, and achievement. When we label a child 'gifted', then we foster the fixed mindset in that child, as well as in the adults in her life. Rather than labelling children as gifted (or not gifted), we might consider labelling educational programming descriptively by level of challenge.

Making connections: the role of teaching for intellectual and emotional learning

As Dweck's work illustrates, understanding giftedness and gifted education involves issues of motivation and self-theory, as well as advanced cognitive abilities. And as we move beyond the traditional categorical model of giftedness, and toward a more fluid domain-specific understanding of gifted development, it is becoming increasingly apparent that all teachers – not just those working with identified-gifted students – need the training and support required for a skilful integration of high-level cognitive and emotional processes with advanced content. In order to implement a mastery model of giftedness and encourage the growth mindset, thus fostering giftedness more broadly, we must find ways to connect gifted with regular education, and to help all educators connect thinking and feeling processes for themselves and their students.

The Teaching for Intellectual and Emotional Learning (TIEL) model is a scaffolding tool for teachers interested in developing the complex curriculum required by advanced learners, and in fostering high-level development in others, in ways that are consistent both with the mastery approach and with the growth mindset. It provides a framework for thinking about the cognitive and emotional components of teaching and learning, helping educators and students consider the connections between the intellectual and emotional dimensions of their learning, and thereby addressing and motivating gifted development in diverse kinds of learners. It has been used effectively in a wide range of classroom settings, from full-time gifted programmes to regular classrooms that include students with diverse learning challenges and special needs (Folsom 2004, 2006).

Graphically represented by a colour-coded wheel (see Figure 1), the TIEL model includes five thinking operations identified by Guilford in his investigation of the structure of intellect (1977), and five qualities of character described by John Dewey as seminal to effective learning (Archambault 1964). The thinking operations (cognition, memory, evaluation, convergent production and divergent production) and the qualities of character (reflection, empathy, ethical reasoning, mastery and appreciation) were selected because of their connections to contemporary theoretical and empirical work on optimal learning and gifted development. Although they are paired on the TIEL wheel through an analysis of connections in the empirical and theoretical literature, the specific operations and qualities, as well as the pairing, should be considered flexibly and heuristically, not as rigid or exclusive, but rather as ideas that help educators and students think systematically about interconnected dimensions of thinking, feeling, and learning.

Cognition and reflection

As used here, the thinking operation *cognition* includes observing, discovering, knowing, being attentive and recognising relevant information. Dewey described observation as being allied with *reflection* in identifying connections and organising facts, and advocated that teachers strike a balance between 'routine and reflection' (Zeichner and Liston 1996). Instead of following a traditional one-size-fits-all routine, a teacher who effectively uses the cognition/reflection axis

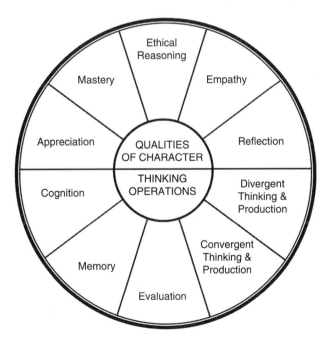

Figure 1 Teaching for Intellectual and Emotional Learning (TIEL) Curriculum Design Wheel

is better able to differentiate learning activities and assignments for advanced students, whether in a gifted or regular classroom.

Memory and empathy

Memory plays an essential role in forging connections from new to old information, among concepts and between experiences. In order to identify and address the misconceptions that interfere with learning, and to motivate interest in new knowledge, teachers need to activate students' prior relevant experience; that is, their memories. One of the best ways to do this is to engage their empathic attention, which is one of the reasons that stories work so well as motivators for learning (Bruner 1996).

Evaluation and ethical reasoning

The thinking operation *evaluation* includes analysing, criteria-setting, decision-making and self-monitoring. The explicit teaching of self-organisation skills – setting criteria, making decisions, planning, and evaluating one's own achievements – helps students become more responsible learners (Folsom 2004); works to reverse underachievement (McCoach and Siegle 2003); and plays a central role in addressing learning disabilities (Konrad and Trela 2007). *Ethical reasoning* is connected to evaluation through the processes of setting criteria and making decisions. The evaluation/ethical reasoning axis can be particularly helpful with those learners who have intense feelings about ethical issues (sometimes associated with giftedness; see for example von Karolyi 2006).

Convergent production and mastery

Guilford (1977) describes *convergent thinking and production* as the search for the one right answer, and as including logical and sequential thinking. It is linked to *content mastery* through a shared focus on domain-specific foundational knowledge. Underachievement is a predictable result for students whose urge to mastery is frustrated by instruction that does not challenge them, a frequent problem for exceptionally capable learners (Neihart et al. 2002).

Divergent production and appreciation

According to Guilford (1977), *divergent production* refers to creative thinking that produces 'alternative ideas . . . which satisfy a somewhat general requirement' (p. 92). Inventing, designing and composing (and other processes involving divergent production) depend on an appreciation of the beauty, diversity, and possibilities inherent in human nature and the world around us.

Conclusions

The mastery model, the theory of mindsets and the TIEL model work to build bridges between gifted education and regular education, and make connections between cognition and emotion.

Taken together, the three perspectives advocated here have many implications for those interested in the policy and practice of gifted education. These include the suggestion that educators:

1 integrate cognitive and emotional processes in their teaching, in fluid, dynamic, and interactive ways, both explicitly and implicitly;
2 minimise categorical distinctions, for example, by labelling programming challenges rather than children;
3 provide all students with optimal levels of challenge, by subject area, as this changes over time;
4 celebrate successful learning processes and resilient responses to setbacks, rather than inherent 'gifts' or 'talents'; and provide a wide range of programming options to address individual and developmental diversity.

Many of our colleagues writing in this volume are advocating similar or allied perspectives, based on their work in this field around the world. As we move forward into the twenty-first century, these policies and practices can help us do a better job of addressing gifted learning needs and fostering high-level development in diversely gifted students everywhere.

Contact address: donamatthews@gmail.com

Future Perspectives

Suggested priorities for gifted education over the next decade

How should gifted education develop over the next ten years in Canada and the United States? The first thing to do is to improve the quality of teaching and learning in general education classrooms. Too often, parents see gifted education as a remedy for inadequate teaching, classroom discipline problems and low expectations. Teachers who understand how to challenge all of their students intellectually and encourage their social/emotional learning – and who are given the time, support, and resources they need to do that – are much better prepared to recognise individual developmental differences, plan appropriately differentiated learning experiences and recommend other settings or options on an as-needed basis. The needs of all students – including the intellectually advanced – will be much better met if all teachers have the training and support that they need to provide high-quality learning experiences, and when a range of learning options is available to address individual developmental differences, by subject area.

Dona J. Matthews and Christy Folsom

4

Giftedness: the gift that keeps on giving

Dean Keith Simonton
University of California, Davis, US

Human beings usually live a long time. During their lifetime, certain attributes will follow them from birth to death. For almost everyone, gender is one of these persistent characteristics. Most of us who are born a male will die a male. Other traits may come and go. An obvious example is the developmental categories that we all put on and take off as we pass through life. Our days of infancy, childhood and adolescence are now long past, and some of us may even find ourselves walking about the earth as so-called senior citizens.

The question that has preoccupied me for more than 30 years is where giftedness falls along this dimension. Is giftedness confined to childhood and perhaps adolescence? Or can it be like gender – something that we possess from the moment of conception and which remains with us until the day we die? Needless to say, we have a strong tendency to see giftedness as something that is associated with children. Other developmental periods, in contrast, have a more tenuous connection with the ascription.

This differential emphasis is apparent if you do a web search. When I Googled 'gifted children' in the mid-summer of 2007, I obtained 1,440,000 hits. No other period got close to this figure. On the later end, 'gifted adolescents' produced 39,600 ('gifted teenagers', 1,670), 'gifted adults', 24,700, and 'gifted elderly', 56 ('gifted senior citizens', 8). On the earlier end, 'gifted babies' yielded 6,660, 'gifted infants', 540, and (just out of curiosity) 'gifted zygotes', 1. The attribution of giftedness appears to be a curvilinear inverted-U function of the person's age since conception, with the peak in childhood.

Yet I would argue that the actual distribution should be more egalitarian. A gifted child was probably a gifted infant, even zygote, and may later become a gifted adolescent and adult, and may even die being gifted. The only difference across the life span is changes may take place in the nature of the gift or in the degree of its manifestation. To make this case I will offer a brief review of what we know about giftedness from a lifespan developmental perspective. The review starts with conception to birth, turns to childhood through adolescence, and ends with adulthood and maturity.

But before I begin, a warning is in order. The overview will stress giftedness of the highest order, giftedness that leads to exceptional achievement. In order words, the gift that the individual received eventually creates gifts that are given to others. My reason for this focus is to increase the signal to noise ratio (i.e. ratio of relevant to irrelevant data). Take intellectual giftedness as a case in point. Children with IQs of 120 or higher represent about 10 per cent of the population, whereas those with IQs of 140 or higher represent the top 1 per cent of the population. Where the former are sometimes called 'potentially gifted', the latter are more often called 'geniuses' (e.g. *American Heritage Dictionary* 1992; Storfer 1990). As a consequence, the latter's intellectual gifts will stand out more from the crowd, like mountain peaks above the foothills. Moreover, as Terman (1925–1959) showed in his classic longitudinal study, gifts of so high an order are more likely to prove prominent throughout the life span. Despite this restriction, I believe that what I say about genius-level giftedness still applies to less selective levels of giftedness. The applications will just have more exceptions and qualifications.

Conception to birth

The sole hit for 'gifted zygote' was a comment on some quip of the comedian Jon Stewart, not a serious site devoted to the topic. Even so, that's exactly where giftedness begins – with the fertilised egg. The future child at that moment acquires the unique combination of genes that will partially decide the degree and type of giftedness that will later emerge. The idea that genius is born goes back very far, but it was first investigated scientifically by Francis Galton (1869) in his *Hereditary Genius*. Using the family pedigree method, Galton showed that eminent achievers in a wide assortment of domains tended to come from highly distinguished lineages. Moreover, the probability of a family connection closely followed the degree of relationship. Parent-child pairings of the eminent are much more common than grandparent-grandchild pairings. For example, Charles Darwin had one distinguished grandfather (Erasmus Darwin) and three distinguished sons (George, Horace, and Francis Darwin) – plus his cousin Francis Galton.

Of course, Galton's extreme genetic determinism very quickly provoked criticism (e.g. Candolle 1873), so that later he was forced to admit that high achievers are influenced by nurture as well as nature (Galton 1874). Nevertheless, modern research in behaviour genetics has shown that Galton was at least partly correct (Simonton 1999b, 2005). It is not that there is a single 'gene' for giftedness but rather that each gift or talent depends on a large number of intellectual and personality traits that are inheritable to some reasonable degree. For instance, I have estimated that the general heritability of talent in the sciences could be no less than 10–20 per cent and probably may range even higher (Simonton 2007b, 2008). For artistic talent the impact of genetic endowment is in all likelihood even larger still, perhaps twice as large as seen in science.

Nonetheless, contemporary research also imposes some complications in the genetic contribution to giftedness. Two complications stand out:

First, the endowment doesn't happen all at once, but rather it unfolds over the course of personal development. That is, giftedness is 'epigenetic' (Simonton 1999b, 2005). The full force of a gift may not fully materialise until adolescence and even early adulthood. In a sense, the growth of giftedness is a positive monotonic function that doesn't max out until after childhood. Moreover, because genetic endowment is epigenetic, the actual nature of the gift is dynamic rather than static. Given that different component traits have distinct growth trajectories, the precise mix of those traits changes over time. A gift for music performance might evolve into a gift for music composition.

Second, genetic endowment may operate according to a multiplicative rather than additive model (Simonton 1999b, 2005). In other words, giftedness can be 'emergenic' (Lykken 1982, 1998). This means that a particular gift may require a unique configuration of intellectual and personality traits. If one or more traits is absent from the set of inherited traits, the individual may be said to have no gift whatsoever. Emergenic inheritance has already been demonstrated for certain forms of giftedness, such as creativity and leadership (Lykken et al. 1992; Waller et al. 1993). Such inheritance has some fascinating implications. For one thing, it predicts that giftedness will not be normally distributed. The distribution will be highly skewed instead, with a long upper tail. This indicates that a very small percentage of the population will have the bulk of the talent. In addition, emergenesis implies that a given gift will not necessarily exhibit familial inheritance. This latter prediction helps explain why some high achievers e.g. Newton, Beethoven and Michelangelo, did not necessarily enjoy distinguished family pedigrees (e.g. Simonton 1994).

Before moving on to the next phase in the development of giftedness, I must acknowledge that the natural endowment that contributes to giftedness may also include non-genetic contributions (Simonton 2008). A patent candidate is the prenatal environment. There's no doubt whatsoever that embryonic development is strongly shaped by the chemical world in which the fetus prepares itself for birth. For instance, it has been suggested that elevated *in utero* testosterone sometime after the 20th week of gestation may be responsible for some kinds of exceptional mathematical, spatial or musical giftedness (Geschwind and Galaburda 1987; McManus and Bryden 1991). If so, the nine-month interval between conception and birth may constitute a critical phase in which a gift is given to the talent to be.

Childhood through adolescence

From the moment of birth to the beginning of childhood, giftedness enters a period about which we are almost entirely ignorant. The very idea of a gifted infant has relatively little meaning from the standpoint of extraordinary giftedness. That is because the criteria by which we might judge a baby's development are so far removed from anything associated with later achievement. Babbling, crawling, etc. are just not relevant to our comprehension of giftedness. And sometimes, precocious development can even be counter-predictive. For instance, some kinds of extreme giftedness may involve delayed linguistic development (Winner 1996). The first few years of post-natal development can thus be called the dark ages in our portrayal of giftedness.

Somewhere in early childhood the genetic and prenatal gifts become reconnected with observable talent development. The exact age is difficult to pin down with any precision, but some clues are provided by child prodigies. According to Cox's (1926) study of 301 geniuses: Mozart began composing around age five, and had published his first work by seven; J. S. Mill was only five when he discussed the comparative merits of the British generals Marlborough and Wellington with Lady Spencer and at six-and-a-half wrote a history of Rome; and Galton could read a book at two-and-a-half, sign his name before three years, and compose simple letters in his fourth year without assistance. The six contemporary prodigies studied by Feldman and Goldsmith (1986) were comparable. They consisted of:

> a child who read music before he was four, two children who played winning chess before they entered school, another who studied abstract algebra in grade school, a youngster who produced typed scripts of original stories and plays before his fifth birthday, and a child who read, wrote, began learning foreign languages, and composed short musical pieces before he was out of diapers.

(p. 3)

Even savants do not do any better than the prodigies. Blind Tom could improvise on any tune by age six and Nadia was an autistic savant who was making phenomenal drawings by five-and-a-half years (Winner 1996). So I think the earliest that the dark ages end is somewhere between four and six years of age.

From this time forward we have a good understanding of the many familial and educational experiences that appear to nurture the development of various forms of giftedness (Simonton 1987, 1999a). For example, a child's birth order appears to influence several intellectual and dispositional factors that underlie many gifts (Galton 1974; Kristensen and Bjerkedal 2007; Sulloway 1996; Zajonc 1976). This is actually a relatively straightforward example because ordinal position in the family is not confounded with genetic endowment. Other apparently environmental variables are not so clear-cut. For instance, geniuses are more prone to appear in highly educated families in which the parents place a strong emphasis on learning (e.g. Roe 1953). But this positive correlation may only reflect the fact that very intelligent parents are more inclined to have very intelligent children. Sometimes, too, certain genetic proclivities start to exert themselves in a manner that's conflated with experiential factors.

As a result of epigenetic growth, the child may begin to develop interests and values that show an early preference for specific domains of achievement. These preferences will assume the guise of particular hobbies and activities that reshape the environment in which the child develops. Thus, future physicists may exhibit an attraction to mechanical contraptions and future biologists may display a fascination with collecting biological specimens (Roe 1953). Genetic and environmental effects begin to become inextricably intertwined the moment that youths can decide what they want for their birthday, what they do with their spare time and what kinds of objects they want to decorate their bedroom.

Although the environmental inputs are quite diverse, there is one environmental factor that is universal across almost every domain of achievement: namely, the need for expertise acquisition (Ericsson et al. 2006). Giftedness is not an outright gift. It's more like a matching grant. Natural endowment will contribute so much, but you have to do the rest. This necessity is epitomised by the so-called 'ten-year rule' (Ericsson 1996; Hayes 1989). This rule says that you cannot expect to make a name for yourself in any domain without first devoting a full decade to mastering the knowledge and skills essential to achievement in the domain. One of the unfortunate realities of gift development is that sometimes this requirement is not met. For various reasons, a talented youth may be distracted from the arduous need for study, practice and sheer hard work. The teenage years may be especially critical. Too often peer-group pressures operate to nudge young talents off the optimal developmental path (Csikszentmihalyi et al. 1993). Some may later recover and merely become late bloomers. Others may not be so lucky, and join the ranks of the underachievers – those who failed to live up to their potential.

Still, I must point out that giftedness can ameliorate this requirement a bit (Simonton 2000). Because giftedness is associated with accelerated expertise acquisition, highly gifted individuals take less than a complete decade, whereas less gifted individuals may take more than a decade (e.g. Simonton 1991b). In general, genius-grade achievers in a given domain will be able to launch their careers earlier than their less illustrious colleagues. Just as importantly, the magnitude of genius is positively correlated with total output and the length of the productive career (Albert 1975). The gifts that permit the acceleration of domain-specific expertise also enhance the manifestation of that expertise. But now we must turn to the next developmental phase.

Adulthood and maturity

It's now time for the potential gifts to become actual gifts. Potential genius must become actual genius. Naturally, the particular manner in which this promise is actualised depends greatly on the domain of achievement. A creative contribution is not the same as a contribution in leadership, and neither is comparable to accomplishments in sports or the performing arts. So let me narrow the discussion to just one type of giftedness, namely, creativity. Certainly of all human gifts, this is among the most important.

With respect to creativity, the most crucial indication of giftedness is provided by each creator's career trajectory (Simonton 1997; see also Simonton 1988). This trajectory is characterised by several distinct parameters: at what age did creative output begin? What was the average rate of output across the entire career? At what age did output peak? And at what age did creative productivity cease? Moreover, associated with this trajectory are three career landmarks: the age at first notable contribution, the age at best single contribution, and the age at last notable contribution (Raskin 1936; Simonton 1991a, 1991b, 1992). These parameters and landmarks help us identify the level and type of creative genius. The higher the level of creative genius, the higher the overall rate of creative productivity, the earlier that productivity begins, the later it ends, and the longer the number of years separating the first and last major contribution. Furthermore, because highly creative geniuses are so prolific, their first landmark arrives closer to the outset of output and their last landmark arrives closer to the termination of output.

What about the location of the middle career landmark – the single best work? First of all, the age at best contribution is strongly correlated with the age at maximal output (Simonton 1991b, 1997). The peak of the career trajectory is thus a double peak: the most creative products and the best creative product. What is more, the age at which this double peak turns up is indicative of the type of genius. To illustrate, poets tend to peak at an earlier age than novelists (Simonton 1975, 2007a) and mathematicians tend to peak earlier than geologists (Dennis 1966; Simonton 1991a). There are also telling contrasts among creative domains in the slope of the post-peak decline (Dennis 1966; Lehman 1953; Simonton 1997). In some fields the age-decrement is rapid and in other fields it is almost nonexistent. This holds for the poetry-versus-novel comparison, for example.

This domain variation in peak and decrement has a curious consequence: there are substantial discrepancies in expected life span across domains of creative achievement. Poets and mathematicians not only peak earlier, but they also die younger (Kaufman 2003; Simonton 1975, 1991a). Part of this effect may simply reflect the fact that because poets and mathematicians can produce their best work at a younger age they can die prematurely and still be famous (Simonton 1994). But there are also complexities that go beyond this simple explanation (McCann 2001). As an example, the versatility of the genius has repercussions concerning their life expectancy as well (Cassandro 1998). To add more niceties, the effect of versatility depends on the main domain of achievement.

While I am speaking of death, I might as well mention another aspect of adult giftedness. I noted a little earlier that the greatest geniuses have very long, prolific careers. Most often, they are still active right up to the day they die. What is intriguing is that their creativity tends to change in the final years before their death. This shift has been called the 'old-age style' or the 'swan-song phenomenon' (Lindauer 2003; Simonton 1989). Thus, classical composers who see the end approaching soon have a higher probability of writing shorter, simpler, but more profound and influential music (Simonton 1989). It's as if they feel the necessity of ending their careers with one last artistic testament that encapsulates their creative life. They seem to take advantage of their last opportunities to demonstrate the magnitude of their giftedness. The gift keeps on giving right to the very end.

Conclusion

I have tried to depict giftedness not as a childhood attribute, but rather as a characteristic that the gifted emanate throughout their lives. I began with the instant that the egg's fertilisation fixed the genetic basis of the gift, and from there progressed, however briefly, through the intra-uterine environment. After skipping the dark ages of infancy, I then picked up with the factors that contribute to giftedness in childhood and adolescence, and ended the survey with the achievements of adulthood and maturity. To be sure, this demonstration was predicated on those individuals whose gifts reach the highest levels. Surely a variety of reservations would have to be imposed if we extended these findings to the less stellar exemplars of giftedness. For instance, although the most outstanding creators make major contributions right to the very end – the late-life and swan-song works – the less celebrated creators will usually end their productive lives sooner. Despite that limitation, one fact remains true for all eminent achievers at any magnitude of genius. All have managed to convert the natural endowment that delineates their gift into some contribution that left a big impression on their chosen domain of achieve-ment. And some of those contributions will ensure their reputation for generations to come. So: that is another sense in which giftedness can be the gift that keeps on giving.

Contact address: dksimonton@ucdavis.edu

Future Perspectives

Suggested priorities for gifted education over the next decade

Gifted education in the United States has a long way to go before it can even be considered barely adequate. If anything, the situation has grown worse in recent years. Because of enhanced stress on meeting minimum progress standards, particularly as gauged by stand-ardised assessments, scarce resources have become channeled toward 'teaching to the test' and 'one size fits all' instruction. Hence, before anything else, there must appear a rededica-tion to the special needs of gifted children. Without this reversal of the 'dumbing down' trend, the plight of the gifted can only become more precarious. To be fully effective, this revival should be reinforced by improved methods for identifying the potentially gifted. Too often identification is based on psychometric assessments or teacher nominations that fail to capture the full range of giftedness, especially in under-represented minorities. Unfortunately, at present it is difficult to conceive effective tactics for accomplishing these goals.

Dean Keith Simonton

5

Talent development as seen through the differentiated model of giftedness and talent

Françoys Gagné
Université du Québec à Montréal

This chapter surveys the Differentiated Model of Giftedness and Talent (DMGT), a talent development theory whereby outstanding natural abilities, or gifts, are progressively transformed into outstanding systematically developed skills and knowledge, which define expertise or talent in a specific occupational field. The text briefly describes complex interactions among the six components that help or hinder that process, and succinctly answers a fundamental question: 'What factor(s) differentiate(s), on average, between those who emerge among the talented and those who remain average?'

The field of gifted education defines its special population around two key concepts: giftedness and talent. For the vast majority of scholars, these two terms are considered synonyms (e.g. the gifted and talented are . . .). Yet, these same scholars keep mentioning one particular idea in almost every discussion of the giftedness construct, namely a distinction – implicit or explicit – between early emerging forms of giftedness, to some extent innate and usually manifested in childhood, and fully developed, adult forms of 'giftedness'. The distinction will be expressed with terms like potential versus achievement, aptitude versus realisation, promise versus fulfilment. But it will rarely, if ever, systematically be operationalised. I believe it can be done. Aptitudes can be described as natural abilities in a particular domain, and achievement as systematically developed skills in a particular occupational field. Since its first presentation (Gagné 1985), the Differentiated Model of Giftedness and Talent (DMGT) has used that distinction to anchor its definitions of the field's two key concepts.

Giftedness as used in this model designates the possession and use of untrained and spontaneously expressed outstanding natural abilities or aptitudes (called gifts), in at least one ability domain, to a degree that places an individual at least among the top 10 per cent of age peers. Talent in the DMGT designates the outstanding mastery of systematically developed competencies (knowledge and skills) in at least one field of human activity to a degree that places an individual at least among the top 10 per cent of 'learning peers' (all those who have accumulated a similar amount of learning time from either current or past training).

These definitions reveal that the two concepts share three characteristics: (a) both refer to human abilities; (b) both are normative, in the sense that they target individuals who differ from the norm or average; (c) both refer to individuals who show outstanding behaviours. These commonalities help us understand why professionals, as well as people in the street, so often confound them.

The DMGT introduces four other components (see Figure 2) that help represent more accurately the complexity of the talent development process: intrapersonal catalysts (I), environmental catalysts (E), learning/practice (D) and chance (C). Moreover, as stated in the formal definitions above, precise thresholds quantify the meaning of 'outstanding'. Finally, the DMGT addresses the long-term process of talent development, proposing various dynamic interactions among the six components.

A componential overview

The six components of the DMGT can be subdivided into two trios. The first describes the core of the talent development process, namely the progressive transformation, through a long learning and training process, of outstanding natural abilities into the high level competencies (knowledge and skills) typical of a particular occupational field. The members of the second trio have in common the concept of 'catalyst' since they facilitate or inhibit the talent development process.

The talent development trio

The DMGT's differentiation of gifts from talents is a particular case of the general distinction between aptitude (or potential) and achievement. Angoff (1988) built a strong defence for such a distinction, using the following differentiating characteristics: (a) slow growth for aptitudes versus rapid growth for achievement; (b) informal learning versus formal; (c) resistance to stimulation versus susceptibility to it; (d) major genetic substratum versus major practice component; (e) more general content versus more circumscribed; (f) 'old formal' learning versus recent acquisitions; (g) more generalisable skills and knowledge versus narrower transfer; (h) prospective use (predicting future learning) versus retrospective use (assessing amount learned); and (i) applicable to general population evaluation versus limited to systematically exposed individuals. These characteristics apply perfectly to the DMGT's differentiation of gifts from talents.

Gifts

The DMGT identifies four areas of gifts (G), or aptitude domains (see Figure 2): intellectual, creative, social and physical. Each can be divided into any number of sub-categories. Figure 2 shows exemplars borrowed from various sources. Natural abilities can be observed through the various tasks confronting children in the course of their development. They include the intellectual abilities needed when learning to read, speak a foreign language, or understand new mathematical concepts, and the creative abilities applied to solving various technical problems or producing original work in science, literature and art. Physical abilities are involved in sports, music or carpentry, while social abilities manifest themselves in the children's daily interactions with peers and adults. These natural abilities are present in all children to a variable degree; the gifted label will be used only when the level of expression becomes outstanding. High aptitudes or gifts can be observed more easily and directly in young children because environmental influences and systematic learning have exerted their moderating influences in a limited way. However, gifts still manifest themselves in older children, even in adults, through the facility and

33

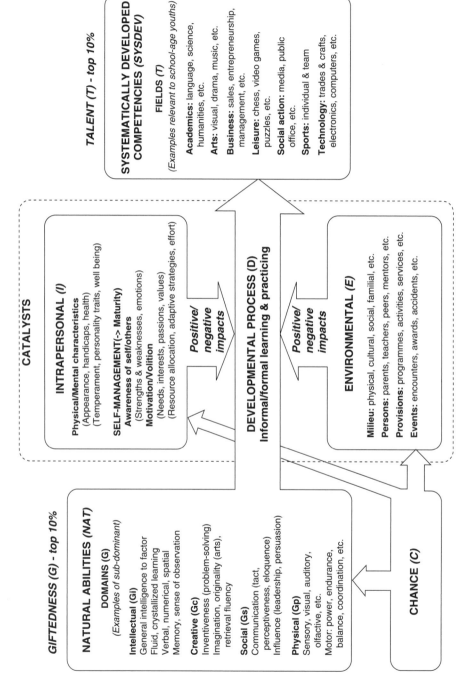

Figure 2 Gagné's Differentiated Model of Giftedness and Talent (DMGT 2006)

GIFTEDNESS (G) - top 10%

NATURAL ABILITIES (NAT)

DOMAINS (G)
(Examples of sub-dominant)

Intellectual (Gi)
General intelligence to factor
Fluid, crystallized learning
Verbal, numerical, spatial
Memory, sense of observation

Creative (Gc)
Inventiveness (problem-solving)
Imagination, originality (arts),
retrieval fluency

Social (Gs)
Communication (tact,
perceptiveness, eloquence)
Influence (leadership, persuasion)

Physical (Gp)
Sensory: visual, auditory,
olfactive, etc.
Motor: power, endurance,
balance, coordination, etc.

CHANCE (C)

CATALYSTS

INTRAPERSONAL (I)

Physical/Mental characteristics
(Appearance, handicaps, health)
(Temperament, personality traits, well being)

SELF-MANAGEMENT(-> Maturity)
Awareness of self/others
(Strengths & weaknesses, emotions)
Motivation/Volition
(Needs, interests, passions, values)
(Resource allocation, adaptive strategies, effort)

*Positive/
negative
impacts*

DEVELOPMENTAL PROCESS (D)
Informal/formal learning & practicing

*Positive/
negative
impacts*

ENVIRONMENTAL (E)

Milieu: physical, cultural, social, familial, etc.
Persons: parents, teachers, peers, mentors, etc.
Provisions: programmes, activities, services, etc.
Events: encounters, awards, accidents, etc.

TALENT (T) - top 10%

**SYSTEMATICALLY DEVELOPED
COMPETENCIES (SYSDEV)**

FIELDS (T)
(Examples relevant to school-age youths)

Academics: language, science,
humanities, etc.

Arts: visual, drama, music, etc.

Business: sales, entrepreneurship,
management, etc.

Leisure: chess, video games,
puzzles, etc.

Social action: media, public
office, etc.

Sports: individual & team

Technology: trades & crafts,
electronics, computers, etc.

speed with which some individuals acquire new skills in any given occupational field. Within the DMGT, ease and speed in learning are the trademark of giftedness.

Nowadays, few researchers in the social sciences deny the significant contribution of genetic factors to human characteristics, including physical and mental abilities, interests, or temperament. The two domains with the best measures of natural abilities are also those with the most extensive analyses of the nature-nurture question. Especially during the last two decades, dozens of studies have examined the contribution of genes to individual differences in general cognitive functioning: comparing identical twins reared together or apart (Bouchard 1997), identical twins with fraternal ones, or adopted siblings (Rowe 1994). If any degree of contention remains, it concerns essentially the precise relative contributions of nature and nurture to individual differences. Similar proof has been accumulating with regard to psychomotor abilities (Entine 2000; MacArthur and North 2005).

Talents

Talents (T) progressively emerge from the transformation of high aptitudes into the well-trained skills characteristic of a particular field of human activity. These fields cover a wide spectrum; indeed, any occupational field in which a set of knowledge and skills needs to be mastered generates large individual differences in performance, from minimum competence to high-level expertise. The DMGT labels as talented all individuals whose outstanding skills place them among the top 10 per cent within their occupational field, when compared to peers having done a similar amount of learning and practicing. Measuring talent is a straightforward enterprise: it simply corresponds to outstanding mastery of the specific skills of any occupational field. During the developmental phase of most talents, many occasions for normative assessment present themselves: teacher exams, achievement tests, competitions and so forth.

Talent is a developmental construct, which means that soon after youngsters have begun learning a new set of competencies, it becomes possible to assess their performances normatively, comparing them with others who have been learning for an approximately equal amount of time. In schools, such assessments begin as early as kindergarten. Assessments also exist for beginners in music, dance, visual arts or sports. Note that the level of achievement can change as learning progresses. During their first years in school, students can obtain grades within the top 10 per cent of their class and, consequently, be labelled academically talented. Then, for whatever reason, their progress may slow, justifying a decision to remove them from the talented group. The reverse is equally possible. However, high correlations between yearly achievements indicate that most academically talented students maintain their label throughout their formal schooling.

Developmental process

The talent development process (D) consists in transforming specific natural abilities into the skills that define competence or expertise in a given occupational field. Competence corresponds to levels of mastery ranging from minimally acceptable to well above average, yet below the defined threshold for talented or expert behaviour. Thus, academic talent is to gifted education what competence is to general education, that is, the goal of the enterprise. As usually defined (see Ericsson 1996b), the concept of expertise largely overlaps the DMGT's concept of talent.

Developmental processes can take three different forms: (a) maturation, (b) informal learning and (c) formal (non-institutional or institutional) learning. Maturation is a process almost totally controlled by the genotype; it ensures the growth and transformation of all biological structures: bones, internal organs, brain, etc. That developmental process in turn impacts other functions at the phenotypic level. Informal learning corresponds to knowledge and skills acquired during daily activities. Much of what is called 'practical intelligence' (see Wagner and Sternberg 1986) results from such informal or unstructured learning activities. The general knowledge, language skills, social skills or manual skills mastered by young children before they enter the school system also emerge in large part through such unstructured activities.

The third developmental process is formal learning. Here, there is a conscious intention to attain specific learning goals, and a systematically planned sequence of learning steps to reach these goals. The first sub-type, non-institutionalised, corresponds to autodidactic or self-taught learning. Many individuals, young and old, decide to develop competencies in a particular field, most of the time as a leisure activity. Few achieve performances that would compare with the best in these fields. But, sometimes, a self-taught pianist may outperform a majority of music students who have trained for five or six years. In the DMGT framework, these outstanding autodidacts would be labelled talented (Gagné 1993). Still, most learning activities are institutionally based, and lead to some form of official recognition: attending school, joining a sports team, a music school or conservatory, a cooking academy, and so forth. Because of the definition given to the concepts of giftedness and talent, it follows logically that the three processes contribute to the development of gifts in inverse proportion to their degree of formality. In other words, the major developmental agent for gifts is maturation, closely followed by informal learning. In the case of talents, it is the opposite, with institutional (or autodidactic) systematic learning accounting for most of the developmental impact.

The supporting trio

In chemistry, the term 'catalyst' designates substances introduced into a chemical reaction, usually to accelerate it. The DMGT comprises two types of catalysts: intrapersonal and environmental. Also included here are chance factors. Each of them may be examined with regard to two dimensions: direction (facilitating versus hindering) and strength of causal impact on the developmental process.

Intrapersonal catalysts

Based on a conception of self-management proposed by De Waele et al. (1993), the intrapersonal catalysts were recently redefined and given a much broader and more central role. This redefinition produced a new dichotomy among intrapersonal catalysts: physical and mental characteristics on one side, and processes on the other. The physical characteristics placed here differ from those that serve as underpinnings to physical abilities (e.g. morphology, height, weight); they concern phenomena like physical appearance or general health that can impact the talent development process. Mental characteristics cluster around two major constructs: temperament and personality, which represent the nature and nurture poles respectively, or basic propensities as opposed to behavioural styles (McCrae et al. 2000). Most personality researchers recognise the existence of five basic bipolar personality dimensions, commonly called The Big Five (Digman 1990). They are usually labelled: Extraversion (E), Agreeableness (A), Conscientiousness (C), Neuroticism (N), and Intellect/Openness (O). There is growing evidence for a close relationship between temperament dimensions and adult personality traits; that relationship probably explains why all five dimensions have significant genetic underpinnings (Rowe 1997).

Self-management, as redefined in this model along the lines of De Waele et al.'s (1993) work, becomes the overarching governing process of a person's self-development. Its goal is to foster personal maturity and self-actualisation. As shown in Figure 2, it comprises two major dimensions. The first one, labelled awareness, includes both of Gardner's (1983) personal intelligences (intra and inter), as well as any process having an influence on the development of the self-concept and self-esteem. The second dimension, labelled motivation/volition, proposes a clear distinction between goal-setting behaviours and goal-attainment behaviours. This distinction is borrowed from Kuhl and Heckhausen's Action Control theory (see Corno 1993). The term 'motivation' is reserved for goal-setting processes (e.g. identifying and selecting interests, needs, motives, passions, values), whereas the term 'volition' covers all goal-attainment activities (e.g. delay of gratification, effort, perseverance, self-regulation). Both constructs play a significant role in initiating the process of talent development, guiding it, and sustaining it through obstacles, boredom, and occasional failure.

Environmental catalysts

In the DMGT, four environmental inputs are distinguished (see Figure 2). The milieu can be examined both at macroscopic (e.g. geographic, demographic, sociological) and microscopic levels (e.g. size of family, socioeconomic status, neighbourhood services). For example, young gifted persons who live far from large urban centres do not have easy access to appropriate learning resources (e.g. sports training centres, music conservatories, magnet schools). Within the child's home environment, the parents' financial comfort, the absence of one of the caregivers, or the number and age distribution of siblings can impact upon the child's access to talent development opportunities. Psychological factors (for instance, the parents' value of educational pursuits or their personal psychological health) belong to the 'persons' category, below.

The concept of environmental input usually brings to mind significant persons: parents, siblings, the extended family, friends, educators, mentors, idols, etc. The significant impact of interpersonal relations is probably easier to imagine than that of any other environmental source of influence. Moreover, the traditional environmentalist beliefs of most professionals in the social sciences stress the primary importance of humans as significant agents in the lives of fellow humans. Thus, it is not surprising that a good percentage of the professional literature on talent development focuses on the potential influence of significant individuals in the immediate environment of gifted or talented youngsters (Bloom 1985; Hemery 1986; Simonton 1994).

The provisions sub-component includes a large diversity of individual or group interventions specifically targeted at talent development. Provisions have been traditionally subdivided into three groups: enrichment of the curriculum (often labelled 'differentiation'), grouping (either within a classroom, within a school, or in special schools), and acceleration (e.g. early entrance to school; grade skipping; Advanced Placement Programme (College Board 2001). Finally, significant events (e.g. the death of a parent, winning a scholarship, suffering a major accident or illness) can markedly influence the course of talent development.

Chance

Tannenbaum (1983) first introduced chance as a contributing factor to talent development. It could be added as a fifth causal factor associated with the environment (e.g. the chance of being born in a particular family; the chance of the school in which the child is enrolled developing a programme for talented students). But, strictly speaking, it is not a causal factor. Just like the type of influence (positive versus negative), chance characterises the predictability (controllable versus uncontrollable) of elements belonging to three other components, namely gifts, intrapersonal and environmental catalysts. Although no longer considered a catalyst chance still plays a major role in talent development. Tannenbaum cites Atkinson's belief that all human accomplishments can be ascribed to 'two crucial rolls of the dice over which no individual exerts any personal control. These are the accidents of birth and background' (Tannenbaum 1983: 221). Atkinson's 'accidents of birth' stress the role of chance outside environmental catalysts, especially through the action of the genetic endowment in gifts and intrapersonal catalysts. In brief, as shown in Figure 2, some degree of chance affects all the causal components of the model, except the developmental process itself.

The prevalence issue

This section briefly explains why a complete definition of giftedness or talent should include a prevalence estimate, and how the DMGT deals concretely with that fundamental issue (see Gagné 1998, for a detailed discussion). The term 'prevalence' refers to the percentage of a subgroup within a larger population. Concepts used to demark subgroups (e.g. poverty, obesity, mental deficiency, genius, deafness) are based on normative judgements. Galton (1892/1962) was among the first to argue that a complete definition of a normative concept requires a quantitative operationalisation. He applied that principle in his study of eminent Englishmen, defining eminence as 'high enough renown to be among the top 1:4000 within the general population'. Knowledge about the size of a special population further clarifies the meaning of a normative concept: if we define the gifted as the top 1 per cent of the population it conveys a totally different image about their exceptionality than if we define them as the top 20 per cent of the population.

Identifying appropriate thresholds is a difficult task, because no objective markers on a measurement scale indicate the passage from one category (e.g. average ability, normal weight) to the next (e.g. gifted, overweight). Any proposed threshold is localised somewhere within a grey zone, with some experts showing more openness and others defending stricter positions. Because there is no 'correct' answer, specialists within a field will have to eventually agree on a best choice, one that they will generally adopt in their research. In gifted education, the authors of major handbooks very rarely discuss the subject of prevalence, and only one (Marland 1972) of the more popular definitions of the last three or four decades includes a prevalence estimate. The fact that the prevalence question is not discussed does not mean that estimates have not been regularly proposed. In fact, they abound; and the result of that 'creativity' is huge variability. Scholars' proposals can easily range from the 1 per cent adopted by Terman (1925) with his threshold of a 135 IQ, or the 3 to 5 per cent in the above-mentioned Marland definition, to the 20 per cent advanced by Renzulli (1986) to create the talent pools in his Revolving Door model. Note the huge 20:1 ratio between the two extreme estimates.

The DMGT proposes a five-level metric-based (MB) system of cut-offs, hence the choice of 10 per cent as the initial threshold. Although that minimum leans slightly toward the generous pole of the range observed in the literature, it is counterbalanced by the introduction of five degrees of giftedness or talent, labelled mildly (top 10 per cent), moderately (top 1 per cent), highly (top 1:1000), exceptionally (1:10,000), and extremely (1:100,000) respectively. Following the metric system rule, each group represents the top 10 per cent of the previous group. The 10 per cent estimate applies to each natural ability domain and each talent field.

Since there is only partial overlap between domains and fields, it follows that the total percentage of gifted and talented individuals far exceeds 10 per cent.

Toward a talent development theory

The third part of this chapter briefly covers two major questions (see Gagné 2003, 2004, for a more extended discussion). First, what relationships do the six components of the DMGT entertain among themselves? Second, is it possible to create a hierarchy of the five factors in terms of their relative causal power? In other words, where lies the difference between those who become talented and those who do not?

Basic overview

The relationships among the six components are expressed through a complex pattern of interactions. The most fundamental is the causal relationship between natural abilities (gifts) and competencies (talents), illustrated by the large central arrow in Figure 2. Because gifts are the constituent elements (or raw materials) of talents, it follows that the presence of talents implies underlying gifts. But that statement needs to be qualified. Of course, intrapersonal and environmental catalysts, as well as the developmental process, play a significant facilitating (or hindering) role in the emergence of talents. As causal agents they take away from gifts part of their predictive power for talent emergence, thus reducing the causal power of gifts to a moderate level. Consequently, at low levels of talent, we could observe individuals with natural abilities below the gifted level reaching talent-level performances through strong inputs from intrapersonal and/or environmental catalysts, as well as from the developmental process itself (amount and intensity of learning and practising). This moderate relationship between gifts and talents also means that gifts can remain undeveloped, as witnessed by the well-known phenomenon of academic underachievement among intellectually gifted children. The causal components usually act through the developmental process, facilitating or hindering the learning activities and thus the performance. But any pair of components can interact, and in both directions (e.g. gifts influencing intrapersonal catalysts, and vice-versa). High achievements (talents) or their absence can even have a feedback effect on the other components.

What makes a difference?

Are some components generally recognised as exercising more powerful influences on talent emergence? It is possible to find in the scientific literature strong defenders for each of the DMGT's components. It is clear, for instance, that strong environmentalists (e.g. Bloom 1985) will choose the E catalysts; for his part, Ericsson (Ericsson et al. 1993) has been insisting for almost two decades that his 'deliberate practice' construct (a part of the developmental process component) is the crucial element in talent development. My own review of the existing literature has brought me to propose the following hierarchy among the four components: (a) gifts, (b) intrapersonal catalysts, (c) developmental process and (d) environmental catalysts (see Gagné 2003, 2004, 2005, for a detailed discussion of that ranking). Because of its pervasive role through most components, I have put aside the chance factor. Still, that pervasive role achieved through non-controllable genetic and environmental influences would give it a top ranking.

Creating a hierarchy should not make us forget that (a) all components play a crucial role in the talent developments process, and (b) that each individual story of talent emergence reveals a unique mixture of the four causal components (see Gagné 2000 for an illustration). In a nutshell, the emergence of talents results from a complex choreography among the four causal components, a choreography unique to each individual situation.

Comparing the DMGT with other conceptions

Space does not allow a detailed comparison of the DMGT with other leading conceptions. To do that process justice would require examining each of them individually. As a shortcut approach, I have summarised four characteristics of the DMGT that appear to me very specific, and, in conjunction, make it a distinct and unique conception of giftedness and talent.

First, the DMGT stands alone in its clearly differentiated definitions of the field's two key concepts. The separation of potentialities/aptitudes from realisations/achievements is well operationalised through a distinction between natural abilities and systematically developed skills, concepts associated with the labels *giftedness* and *talent* respectively. This distinction leads to another clear definition, that of talent development, which becomes the transformation of natural abilities into the systematically developed skills typical of an occupational field. Only in the DMGT does the concept of talent become as important as that of giftedness in understanding the development of outstanding skills and knowledge. Finally, this differentiation between potentialities and realisations permits a much clearer definition of underachievement among gifted individuals. It becomes simply the non-transformation of high natural abilities into systematically developed high-level skills in any occupational field.

Second, the introduction within the giftedness and talent definitions of prevalence estimates (top 10 per cent) also constitutes a unique facet of the DMGT among existing conceptions of giftedness. Because it confronts the prevalence issue and proposes a metric-based system of five levels that applies to any giftedness domain or talent field, the DMGT helps maintain a constant awareness of levels of giftedness and talent. The availability of clear thresholds and labels could facilitate not only the selection and description of study samples, but also the comparison of results from different studies. Moreover, the metric-based system of levels should remind educators in the field that the vast majority of gifted or talented individuals (90 per cent) belong to the lowest (mild) category, and that only a tiny fraction of those identified as gifted or talented in their youth will ever achieve eminence in their chosen field. The concept of 'eminence' is usually defined as a very high level of achievement. For instance, Galton defined it as the top 1/4000 among British adults. The rarity of eminent people means that most youth identified as gifted or talented (top 10 per cent) will never achieve such an exceptional status

Third, the DMGT's complex structure clearly identifies every significant etiological factor of talent emergence, especially those located within the intrapersonal and environmental catalysts. But, that comprehensive outlook maintains the individuality of each component, clearly specifying their precise nature and role within this talent development theory. The giftedness construct remains well circumscribed, thus more easily operationalised. The catalysts are clearly situated outside the giftedness and talent concepts themselves. This sets the DMGT apart from many rival conceptions where disparate elements are lumped together in the giftedness definition itself. For instance, Feldhusen (1986) defines giftedness as follows: 'Our composite conception of giftedness then includes (a) general intellectual ability, (b) positive self-concept, (c) achievement motivation, and (d) talent' (p. 112).

Finally, most published conceptions focus almost exclusively on intellectual giftedness and academic talent, as well as academically based professions (e.g. scientists, lawyers, doctors, and so forth). The DMGT follows an orientation adopted explicitly by only a few past scholars (e.g. De Haan and Havighurst 1961; Gardner 1983; Marland 1972), namely to broaden the concept of giftedness and acknowledge its various manifestations. In that respect, the DMGT stands almost alone in bringing physical giftedness within the fold of the giftedness construct, defining that domain much more broadly than Gardner's (1983) bodily-kinesthetic intelligence. This openness should foster closer ties between professionals focusing on academic talent development and those who devote their energies to athletic talent development.

Contact address: gagne.francoys@uqam.ca

Future Perspectives

Suggested priorities for gifted education over the next decade

Currently, gifted education in Quebec does not officially exist. No law puts pressure on school boards. Not a single professional supervises that area, neither in the Education Ministry nor in school boards. No provisions wearing the 'giftedness' label are available for students from elementary through high school, except for a twenty-year-old hard-won Early Entrance programme for precocious Kindergarten (age 5) or Grade 1 (age 6) students. And, to top it all, the teachers' union ferociously attacks anything they perceive as elitism. Still, some parents and educators have found a way to bypass union resistance. Close to one hundred high schools (mostly public) offer an International Baccalaureate 'track' that parallels the five-year regular curriculum. That system flourishes. The outlook for the next ten years? More of the same, namely unpublicised efforts to enrich the school life of talented students. Why? Because educational reforms, not just in Québec, but almost everywhere, spread very slowly indeed.

Françoys Gagné

6

The nature of creative giftedness and talent

Todd Lubart, Asta Georgsdottir and Maud Besançon
Université Paris Descartes, France

Creativity: definition and measures

The first studies of giftedness, such as Terman's (1925) investigation, focused on intelligence test scores (IQ) as the main criterion. However, a number of recent theories have suggested that giftedness should not be limited to traditional conceptions of intelligence and have highlighted creativity as an important dimension. In this chapter, the notion of creative giftedness is examined. First, creativity is defined and some current measures are described. Second, the main components of creativity and their development are outlined. Third, the role of creativity in the education of the gifted is discussed. Fourth, we suggest some studies that should be done during the next ten years in order to assist in identification of the creatively gifted.

Creativity can be defined as the capacity to produce novel, original work that fits within task constraints (Lubart 1994). Work refers to all types of ideas and productions. This work must be novel in the sense that it goes beyond a replication or copy of that which exists. The extent to which the work produced is novel can vary from being original only for the person who completed the work (this is the notion of re-inventing ideas known already in the larger social context) to being original for a limited social group, to being original for all of humanity. The second component in the definition concerns the 'fit within task constraints'. We distinguish creative ideas from bizarre ideas, which are also novel, because creative ideas take into account the parameters of a situation, the constraints. Depending on the field of endeavour, such as art, science, literature, or engineering and design, the weight given to the two components, novelty and constraint satisfaction varies.

Operationally, creativity in children is often measured through divergent thinking tests, evaluations of specific productions such as drawings or stories, or parent/teacher nominations (Lubart 1994; Sternberg and Lubart 1992; Wallach 1985). Divergent thinking tests of creativity, such as the Torrance Tests of Creative Thinking or the tests proposed by Wallach and Kogan, require children to produce as many original ideas (uses of an object, questions, consequences, or titles for a picture) as possible concerning a stimulus (Torrance 1974; Wallach and Kogan 1965). This stimulus may be a hypothetical situation (e.g. strings attached to clouds), a drawing (e.g. picture of a boy who looks in the water), an object (e.g. a box, a paperclip), or other things. These tests are usually time limited (five to ten minutes for a task). Divergent thinking tasks provide three indices of performance: fluency, which is the number of ideas produced; flexibility, which is the number of different categories from which the ideas are drawn; and originality of the ideas.

Some divergent thinking tasks take into account the elaboration of ideas, or the number of details included in the productions. An alternative to divergent thinking tests is the use of integrated production tasks in which the child must produce an elaborated idea, such as a short story, a drawing, a collage, or a musical composition. This production is then evaluated by adult judges for its creativity. Finally, creativity may be measured by asking parents or teachers to nominate children who show creative thinking in their actions at school or at home. Of course, each of these three types of creativity measures has its strengths and weaknesses (Lubart 1994).

However, other measures exist such as questionnaires of personality and motivation, questionnaire of self-assessment of the creative activities, and finally, parents' or teachers' judgements. The scholastic and extra-scholastic activity questionnaire can concern diverse domains such as the arts, science, literature, leadership and music. The publication of a poem, a prize for an invention or leading a school club, are examples of accomplishments which can be reported. Milgram and Hong (1999) developed and used a questionnaire (Tel-Aviv Activities Inventory) in several countries, allowing for detection of children's involvement in diverse self-selected activities.

These various measures of creativity can be categorised in two groups. Some are measures of creative potential, whereas others are measures of creative talent, i.e., the realisation of potential. Tests of divergent thinking and questionnaires of creative personality measure potential. Evaluations of specific productions, such as drawings or invented stories, and questionnaires of self-assessment of creative activities and fulfilment, are mainly measures of creative talent. The global evaluations of children's creativity by teachers or the social environment (family, friends) can concern an estimation of creative potential, creative talent, or both. Knowing that the diverse measures of creativity capture various facets of the phenomenon, it is recommended to use various creative measures in order to identify and follow the development of creative potential and talent.

Factors involved in creativity and their development

In the last twenty years, several authors have sought an integrated approach to the factors involved in creativity. Accordingly, in the multivariate approach to creativity, creativity depends on cognitive, conative, and environmental factors that combine interactively (Amabile 1996; Lubart 1999; Sternberg and Lubart 1995). Results of recent empirical studies have begun to provide support for this multivariate approach (Conti et al. 1996; Lubart and Sternberg 1995). A continuum of creative ability from very low levels (non-creative individuals) to very high levels (eminent cases of creativity) is postulated. Case studies suggest that a combination of person-centred and environment-centred variables is involved for each eminently creative person (Gardner 1993a). Consider now the nature of the cognitive, conative, and environmental factors involved in creativity.

Cognitive factors

Several intellectual abilities are considered important for creativity. These include selective encoding (the ability to notice relevant stimuli in the environment), selective comparison ability (allowing for analogical and metaphorical thought), selective combination ability (to facilitate the generation of complex ideas from disparate elements), and divergent thinking (to generate numerous alternatives when facing an impasse), and cognitive flexibility (Georgsdottir and Lubart 2003).

These abilities develop with age. In our recent work, we have devised specific measures of some of these capacities and examined their development. For example, we constructed a test of sensitivity to cognitive change using visual stimuli, which relates to selective encoding capacity. In this test, a child sees a series of images that change gradually (e.g. the face of a lion that becomes a face of a monkey). The child indicates what is portrayed on each image and we score when the child notes that the initial object or animal displayed has become something different. This test correlates with children's creativity in diverse tasks, such as the Urban-Jellan drawing test (Georgsdottir et al. 2000; Lubart et al. 2000).

It is important to note that the development of cognitive abilities particularly involved in creative thinking, such as divergent thinking, is not isolated from the development of other cognitive abilities such as logical reasoning. In fact, some of our research suggests that there may be temporary slumps in creative development when other aspects of cognition that require contrasting types of thinking are put into place (Georgsdottir et al. 2002; Lubart and Lautrey 1995).

In addition to basic information processing skills, the acquisition of knowledge is also important. Knowledge is the raw material on which creative thinking draws. It provides a platform from which creative ideas can be generated. In this vein, Isaac Newton noted that his achievements were due, to a great extent, because he had 'stood on the shoulders of giants'; the predecessors in his field. When we speak of knowledge, we include the accumulated facts, theories, and personalised experiences that concern various content domains, but also an understanding of task-relevant constraints and other implicit parameters that play a role in problem solving. It seems especially important to be aware of constraints in order to distinguish creative ideas from simply eccentric ones. The capacity for evaluative thinking, which has been shown to relate to children's and adult's creative performance (Runco 1992), depends on the development of one's knowledge base in a domain. Of course, as with most things, too much of a good thing can become detrimental; the negative side of acquiring substantial knowledge on a topic is that it can lead to rigid, fossilised thinking.

Conative factors

Creativity is more than purely cognitive. Certain personality traits are particularly relevant for the development of original, adaptive thinking during childhood. In particular the traits of risk taking, openness, individuality, perseverance, and tolerance of ambiguity seem to play roles in creativity (Sternberg and Lubart 1995; Zenasni et al. in press). For example, creative thinking involves taking risks, going against standard ideas, and exposing oneself to failure and negative comments from peers, teachers, or parents. We have found that people who respond to hypothetical domain-specific situation scenarios in a way that shows willingness to take risks tend to produce more creative work in tasks in the domain examined (Lubart and Sternberg 1995).

These considerations among others led to the development of what we call the investment approach to creativity (Sternberg and Lubart 1995). In this view, many people are not creative because they are unwilling to pursue unknown or little valued ideas: they don't 'buy low'. 'Buying low' involves investing one's energy and resources in new, risky, or currently low-valued ideas. Some of these ideas may turn out to be worth the investment. Being creative is, in part, a philosophy of life, which is acquired through childhood experiences. In addition to personality traits, motivational variables have also been shown to be important for creativity. Motivation refers to the force that drives an individual to engage in a task. There are both intrinsic motivators, such as curiosity and the enjoyment gained from expressing one's self through visual or verbal modes, as well as extrinsic motivators, such as social recognition from peers or teachers. Intrinsic motivation is considered more conducive for creativity, although extrinsic motivation can also contribute in certain circumstances (Amabile 1996).

Environmental factors

Several authors have proposed that the physical and social environment of the child is a key influence on creative development. In this section, we consider the family, school, and societal spheres of the environment. The family environment may provide cognitive (e.g. intellectual stimulation) and affective (e.g. emotional security) support for creativity as well as providing the physical setting in which a child grows (Harrington et al. 1987). For example, families that provide stimulating settings with many books, magazines, and cultural activities tend to foster creative thinking (Simonton 1984). Rogers (1954) suggested that a warm, secure family will serve as a base from which creative work can be attempted. Other authors (Lubart and Lautrey 1998; Mumford and Gustafson 1988) have explored a social-cognitive dimension of the family environment, the 'structure of family rules' for daily life, finding positive relations between flexibility of parental rules and children's creative performance (Lubart and Lautrey 1998).

In addition to the family setting, the school environment plays a crucial role in the development of creativity, or its lack of development in many cases. First, children acquire cognitive abilities and knowledge in school. Often schools emphasise convergent thinking, finding the 'correct' answer to problems and emphasising memorisation and recall. However, as we will discuss in a later section, some curricula emphasise the dynamic, context-specific nature of knowledge, using knowledge in diverse ways, and building links across different content areas.

Second, teachers serve as role models for children. Teachers may value or de-value the expression of creative ideas in the classroom. Studies of teachers' conceptions of the ideal student show that teachers often value characteristics that are socially important (obedience, courtesy) but are not especially propitious for creativity. Working with teachers on their attitudes towards creative behaviours in the classroom is important as they are in a privileged position to stimulate or stifle creativity. Cropley (1997) identified some common characteristics of teachers who foster creativity in the classroom: they encourage independent learning, have a cooperative teaching style, motivate students to learn the facts in order to have a solid base for divergent thinking, encourage flexible thinking, delay judging students' ideas until they have been fully considered and promote self-evaluation of ideas. They also take students' questions and suggestions seriously, offer opportunities to work with a variety of materials in varied conditions, and help students to cope with frustration and failure in order to build the courage to pursue new ideas.

Beyond the local school setting, the macroscopic social environment conditions creative development in numerous ways. For example, cultural activities such as concerts, artistic expositions, museums, and television shows on diverse topics can all contribute to children's creative development. Historiometric studies have shown that the presence of eminent role models (such as great scientists or writers) in one generation tends to predict the creative accomplishments of future generations in the same domain (Simonton 1984, 1996). The proximity of a city, state, or country with respect to other different cultural centres also seems to have an influence, through the potential for stimulation and cross-fertilisation of ideas (Simonton 1975b, 1984).

Creativity in the education of the gifted

For more than 40 years, creativity has generally been considered an important component of high potential and talent (Gardner 2000; Getzels and Csikszentmihalyi 1976; Hong and Milgram 1996; Maker 1993; Naglieri and Kaufman 2001; Renzulli 1986; Runco and Albert 1986; Treffinger 1980). In a recent study, Guignard and Lubart (2007) examined performance on convergent and divergent thinking tasks in gifted (IQ > 130) and control children. Participants were 5th and 7th grade students (age 10 to 12) in a semi-private French school which provided a traditional pedagogy with enrichment programmes for the gifted.[1] As expected, the gifted children compared to the control subjects tended to show superior performance on convergent thinking tasks.

Somewhat less expectedly, however, the gifted and control groups showed differences in their divergent thinking performance that changed over the period covered in this study. In 5th grade (age 10), gifted children obtained significantly higher scores than non-gifted children, but no advantage for the gifted was observed in 7th grade children (age 12). The design was cross-sectional, but if these results were replicated in a longitudinal study they might be interpreted to suggest that the special activities for the gifted serves to reinforce their academic convergent thinking abilities to the detriment of other kinds of thinking, notably creative thinking. These data also fit with the finding from long-term longitudinal studies that gifted children tend, more often than not, to go on to become competent professionals rather than creative geniuses.

It is therefore interesting to note that some programmes for the education of gifted learners seek to foster creative thinking as an enriching educational activity that differs from traditional academics. Some educators and psychologists have proposed, more generally, that traditional pedagogy should be replaced by 'modern' or alternative pedagogies. According to Piaget (1969/2004), it would be stimulating for children to make discoveries by themselves and thereby construct their knowledge through actions. The teacher's role is, in this view, to provide the pupil with a rich environment including situations favouring the emergence of cognitive and socio-cognitive conflicts, viewed by Piaget as the engines of development. For Montessori (1958/2004), teachers should let children evolve freely (giving them the freedom to choose an activity, to handle objects placed at their disposal) but within a well-established framework. In a similar vein, Freinet (1994), a French expert on teaching and learning, proposed that each child has a natural dynamism which should not be opposed; that error is a means to acquire knowledge; and that creativity should be allowed and fostered in various activities in which children themselves create their own productions from their knowledge or personal experience.

In more recent work, Maker (1996; Maker and Nielson 1995) has advocated a DIscovering Strengths and Capabilities while Observing Varied Ethnic Responses (DISCOVER) curriculum for gifted and talented children that fosters creative problem solving, although it is still in the development stage for all age groups and grades. The DISCOVER curriculum model is based on the concepts of multiple intelligences, and provides a continuum of problem types from well-defined to open, creative ones, as well as research indicating that children learn best if they construct their own learning. The teacher's role is more a guide for information and

---

[1] In France, the first grade for 6-year-olds corresponds to 'Cours Préparatoire'; we have 5 years in the elementary school, 4 years in the middle school and then 3 years in high school (before university).

learning than a source of knowledge, and teachers should detect children's strengths and interests and use these to foster learning in a wide range of domains with a wide range of problem types.

The effect of alternative pedagogies on children's creative development has been examined in a few studies (see Horwitz 1979 for a review). There have been mixed findings, but, in general, children who were exposed to alternative pedagogy (a) showed more initiative, better capacity to face problems, knowledge acquisition, and social participation, (b) described themselves as less rigid, more imaginative, more open, and less conventional, and had fewer stereotypes concerning social roles, (c) were more cooperative, less competitive, and more accessible than children exposed to traditional pedagogies; and (d) showed more creative performance. Thomas and Berk (1981) examined creative performance in first and second graders in six different schools and found a complex interaction effect on the development of creativity, suggesting that it is influenced by the type of school, the pupil's gender, and the type of creativity (verbal or figural). Notably, they found that the environment that fosters best creative development is an intermediate one with some structure and some openness to experimentation, play, and problem finding. Teachers using alternative pedagogies may grant greater freedom to pupils than in traditional classrooms, allowing them to express themselves, and fostering students' initiatives, qualities that contribute to the development of creativity.

To investigate further the influence of alternative and traditional pedagogies on the development of creativity, we conducted a study of elementary school children (Besançon et al. 2006). Three hundred and seventy-one children in 1st grade to the 5th grade (age 6 to 10) were studied. They were enrolled either in alternative schools (Montessori or Freinet), or in traditional schools in Paris or its suburbs. In order to examine distinct facets of creativity, we used various measures of creativity, which differed on domains of expression (verbal versus figural) and on type of task (divergent versus integrative thinking). In the literature (Runco 1999; Torrance 1968), a slump in the development of divergent thinking had been observed in the 4th grade (age 9). Our results showed a slump in divergent thinking tasks in 4th grade for children in traditional schools, consistently with findings in the literature, but the same slump appeared in 3rd grade (age 8) for children in alternative schools. For the integrative task, the developmental timing was the same across the two types of pedagogies, with a stagnation occurring across conditions for children between the 3rd and the 4th grade. These observations must be interpreted carefully because this portion of the study used a cross-sectional design.

Afterward, 210 children participated in a longitudinal part of the study. They were enrolled in 1st grade to the 4th grade (age 6 to 9) the first year and from 2nd grade to 5th grade (age 7 to 10) in the second year. As previously, they were schooled in alternative schools, or else in traditional schools in Paris or its suburbs, and the same creative tasks were administered. Our results indicated that children schooled in alternative pedagogies obtained higher creative performance than children schooled in traditional pedagogy regardless of the task used (verbal or figural, and divergent or integrative thinking). Moreover, we find, from one year to another an effect of the school: the alternative school students becoming more creative relative to their traditional school peers (Besançon and Lubart in press). So these results suggest an overall effect of pedagogy, with differentiated development according to pedagogy in favour of creative thinking in alternative pedagogical settings. However, some family environments could also support more creative development than others and it is also possible that teacher's personality play a role on children's creative development.

Pointers for the future

We conclude by expressing our views concerning the studies that will be most useful to carry out during the next ten years. A gap is often observed when we compare the potential of a child and the expression of talent later as an adult. Most frequently, the identification of gifted children is based on the IQ, which measures perhaps some but not many of the capacities linked to creativity. Indeed, in a survey of 418 school districts in the United States, Hunsaker and Callahan (1995) examined the definitions and criteria used to identify gifted and talented children. They found that 69.6 per cent of the districts included creativity in their definition, but only 35.2 per cent of the districts actually measured it, mainly with divergent thinking tests which, as we noted, are only partial measures of creative potential. In addition, the multivariate nature of the constituents of creativity which intervene during children's development makes it difficult to predict adults' talents from children's potential.

Studies on gifted children's personality traits and on gifted children's motivation could help explain the difference between early potential and eventual adult talent. Moreover, these differences depend also on the domain of activity. Given these issues, studies could be devised concerning the influence of different factors on the development of creative potential. For the cognitive factors, it would be particularly interesting to study how transitions between logical reasoning, IQ, and creativity can be introduced into the school curriculum (Rieben 1978). Such studies could lead to new possibilities to identify gifted children based on how they use their intelligence, rather than on their level of measured intelligence.

Research on creativity has practical implications to help children and adults realise their potential. First, the identification of gifted children could benefit from finding ways to distinguish 'academic giftedness' from 'creative giftedness'. Second, a better understanding of creativity could enhance teacher training. Specific training concerning high potential could help teachers to integrate creative problem solving activities in each content area, and thus foster interest in high-level learning in a wide range of students in heterogeneous classes, including high potential pupils.

Finally, a better identification of giftedness, taking into account not only IQ but also creativity, could develop curricula better adapted to children's potential and thereby better equipped to develop this potential. By finding methods to evaluate creativity that allow us to track creative development, and providing more attention to creativity in curriculum design and delivery, we could greatly improve the development of creative giftedness in all students.

Contact address: todd.lubart@univ-paris5.fr

Future Perspectives

Suggested priorities for gifted education over the next decade

It will be important for France to develop valid, easy-to-use assessments of creative potential that classroom teachers can administer and score in order to identify creative potential. These measures will serve, as well, to assess progress after intervention programmes that seek to develop it. A key to gifted education, in terms of creativity enhancement, will be the ability to accurately track children's development. A second key to gifted education in terms of creative potential will be teacher training on this topic. Few teacher-training programmes cover creativity in any detail. Creativity is a capacity that involves cognitive, personality-motivational and environmental factors that differ from those solicited in the regular classroom learning activities. Thus, learning goals, learning methods and grading procedures need to be redesigned in order to value creativity.

Todd Lubart, Asta Georgsdottir and Maud Besançon

7

The future of the English definition of giftedness

Thomas Balchin
Brunel University, UK

The English definition

In this chapter I examine the practical value of the English definition of giftedness, and propose an alternative developmental conception that I argue is more suitable for future practice. The chapter is illustrated with quotes from some of the 800 primary and secondary school Gifted and Talented education (G&T) coordinators responsible for about 400,000 of the nation's students between the ages of four and 18, who responded to an enquiry sent to 23,000 schools around England in November 2005 concerning the problems they face on a daily basis (Balchin 2007a). The sample represents about 12.5 per cent of English schools that had produced a G&T register in 2005.

Most people outside the gifted education field are unaware of the decades-long search for consensus over any single definition of giftedness. They naturally assume that 'gifted' and 'talented' mean roughly the same thing when applied to students at school. However, the English government's Department for Children, Schools and Families currently defines 'gifted' pupils as those who have exceptional abilities or potential in one or more subjects in the statutory school curriculum other than art and design, music and physical education. 'Talented' pupils are defined as those who have exceptional abilities in art and design, music, physical education, sports or performing arts such as dance and drama (OfSTED 2001). The term 'very able', which referred to academically gifted learners who demonstrated exceptionally high-level performance either across a range of endeavours or in a limited field (Freeman 1998) was changed to the term 'gifted and talented' in 1999 by the English government's Department for Education and Skills with reference to the 'Excellence in Cities' programme, for which 'Gifted & Talented' constituted one strand. Although the government statutory document or research base explaining the reasons for the change in terms has not been made easily available, it would be very useful to find out why the new terminology was put in place. In the study under discussion here, the G&T co-ordinators reported very clearly that these distinctions are not helpful for their practice.

Results of the 2005 national study strongly indicated that the English definitions of gifted and talented education (and corresponding legal requirements) are puzzling for many teachers who are trying to understand high ability in order to provide support for the students in question. The Department for Children, Schools and Families acknowledges that gifted children are those who have one or more abilities developed to a level significantly ahead of their year group, or with the potential to develop such abilities (Department for Education and Skills 2006). However, the application of different meanings to 'gifted' and 'talented' emerged as a serious problem for teachers; it ranked fourth of 14 self-identified issues which most hindered them from making successful nominations of gifted children (Balchin 2007a). The teachers reported that the 'gifted and talented' term does not adequately explain the phenomena for them, or focus on what is meant by high performance.

G&T co-ordinators are requesting a useful definition of terms. Currently, to combat problems with the existing lack of definition, many G&T education providers at local level in England have been looking to the United States and Canada for help, often referencing Gagné's Differentiated Model of Giftedness and Talent (Gagné 1991) that is included in their information packs for school G&T co-ordinators (see Gagné this volume). Although many English teachers sampled in the 2005 study reported that Gagné's model of giftedness and talent aids their understanding of G&T, we must still exercise caution, for there are some suggestions that it is perhaps not as definitive and unifying an approach as some had hoped it might be. Some critics suggest a need to take into account the incremental nature of learning and move beyond the relatively 'fixed' view of potential that this model posits. For example, Morelock (1996) recommends that 'giftedness' should be thought of as precocious or advanced development, rather than outstanding human ability, and that 'talent' is a trait present in each and every child.

Matthews and Foster (2006) argue that it is impossible to ascertain the limits of possible achievement for any given child, and conclude that we are on very shaky ground when we presume to rank order children on their relative potentials. This is because the science of cognitive measurement is too imprecise for us to ascertain with any degree of certainty which child has more potential than others, or in which areas. The more we learn about brain development, especially neural plasticity – the changes that occur in the organisation of the brain as a result of experience (Drubach 2000; Tortora and Grabowski 1996) – the clearer it is that developmental pathways are highly variable, and we have to be very careful when setting limits on students' potential for learning. This does not mean that there should not be gifted education, but rather that we should be concentrating on identifying which learners are so advanced relative to their age peers as to require adaptations to the curriculum in order to continue learning.

Over the past few years, many experts in gifted education have written about the need for major changes in the way giftedness is perceived (Borland 2003a; Feldhusen 2003a; Rogers 2002b; Subotnik et al. 2003). Proposals to imbue the terms 'gifted' and 'talented' with different meanings have been presented in the US, including the talent development approach (Subotnik et al. 2003), the integrated curriculum model (VanTassel-Baska and Little 2003) and an intrinsic motivation addition (Gottfried et al. 2005). These approaches tend to be grounded in understandings of individual developmental differences along complex continua, rather than categorical dichotomies such as gifted/not gifted (Matthews and Foster 2006).

My problem with the English definition as it stands, therefore, is that it aligns itself with a 'mystery' view of giftedness, which experts in the field, including both practitioners and theoreticians, are moving away from (Matthews and Foster 2006). This position states that gifted children are born with high potential and their ability stays relatively constant over time. The mystery model (see Matthews and Folsom this volume) is implicit when children are labelled as gifted or not gifted without any explicit links to specific educational programming based on their particular strengths or abilities. Put simply, this approach is mysterious because it is difficult to figure out what giftedness means using this definition, and what to do about it once it is identified.

This is exactly the problem our G&T co-ordinators are currently facing in England. I believe that for our teachers to have imposed on them an approach that they have doubts about, is to impede or discontinue their search for truth. We want our G&T co-ordinators to keep thinking, and maintain a real interest in learning more about G&T education in order that they can transmit their enthusiasm about gifted learners to colleagues, rather than come to feel that they have become ciphers of centralised control, with their views not taken into account. For their sake as professionals, and for the sake of their students who require thoughtfully critical role models, teachers should, ideally, be trained to question and analyse, not silently accept that which is handed to them. There are important long-term consequences for a civilisation that does not foster critical thinking in its teachers.

It must be remembered that for many teachers in England, giftedness is still regarded as a 'bonus' which does not require from them such urgent attention as more obvious special needs such as dyslexia. A large-scale survey in 2006 showed that less than half of all teachers in the UK think that gifted students ought to be given special attention (Hewston 2006). Many teachers lack empathy for these students, and resist any calls for adaptive education for them.

I am not saying that the English definition is untenable, but rather that we need to countenance a change. English teachers acknowledge that the current distinction between the 'gifted' and the 'talented' is difficult to translate into practice (Balchin in press). For example, Design and Technology in England is traditionally conceived as a practical (non-academic) subject, but Design and Technology teachers defend its academic content, arguing that the learning of the design process is not simply a 'non-academic exercise' (Balchin 2008b). The gifted/talented distinction is meant to aid identification practices, but English G&T co-ordinators claim that it has the effect of making their colleagues who are tasked with nominating individuals for further programmes uncomfortable with their duty.

Many teachers in England are confused about what giftedness and talent really are, and work out somewhat idiosyncratic approaches to identification. For example, in 2005, a primary school head teacher was interviewed: '. . . "G&T" implies to us a much more able group than most pupils nationally, so we don't like this term when defining a top percentage of a cohort, regardless of ability'. She stated that: '. . . we just identify the most able children in a class and also those who in our collective experience at this and other schools, stand out as being significantly more able than children of their age usually are'. Another primary school teacher stated: '. . . we have a number of children who are more able than their classmates, but are not necessarily G&T. Drawing the distinction between the two can cause problems, especially if the majority of a class are poor at a given area'.

A secondary school biology teacher stated: '. . . in fact when you ask staff to identify G&T students and even give them descriptions, they actually just give you a list of most able'. Here we see the 'mystery' model delineated by Matthews and Foster (2006), at work, where teachers are thinking about giftedness and talent as some kind of global superiority. However, as they are being tasked to identify the top 5–10 per cent of the most able, then regard them as 'gifted', it is not surprising that they are unsure about what this means for their practice.

There is another limiting angle to the English definition that I wish to explore briefly. Any definition that does not consider those who are gifted or talented at communication, making things, buying and selling, creating new ideas, caring for others, cooking, building, gardening, and so on, is narrowly restrictive. We do not currently consider these critically important skills and abilities in anything other than a marginal way when identifying giftedness and talent in children. For the future, we will need to make sure we are not simply giving the students who score well in scholastic achievement tests, and some others who play the piano outstandingly well or run unusually fast, the opportunity to receive further provision to develop their burgeoning skills. Although it is important, this is another topic to be addressed separately, however, as it applies to all educational practices, not just giftedness and talent.

An alternative definition

I argue that for G&T education to thrive in English schools in the future, a viable alternative definition must be found which does not differentiate between 'gifted' and 'talented' as terms. I take as my start-point the notion that a student's attitude towards personal progression is a strong sign of his or her ability to benefit from advanced level work. Not surprisingly, high motivation and engagement in learning have consistently been linked to reduced dropout rates and increased levels of student success (Kushman et al. 2000). Intelligence and extra-cognitive factors such as self-esteem, support and opportunity are not the only determinants of high performance (Freeman 2005; Shavinina and Ferrari 2004). Freeman (2006) shows that the best predictive factors for adult success are hard work, emotional support and a positive, open personal outlook. Flack (2000) tells us that 'willingness to work' must play a role in any definition or understanding of giftedness.

I have interviewed many children labelled as 'gifted and talented' by English schools, who have expressed to me the view that they do not need to work hard, experiment or look further '. . . because I'm gifted and talented!' Hearing a child say that to you once is surprising, but it is depressing to hear it so frequently, like a broken record, by so many students at a formative time in their lives when one would hope that their minds are at their most open and receptive to new challenges. This attitude is the antithesis of what we want to create, and suggests that the current definitions of giftedness and talent are contributing towards a generation of youngsters who will be disappointed, frustrated and low-achieving when they reach the world of work and its concomitant challenges.

The very word 'gifted' reinforces the notion that cleverness is something that you cannot do much about: either you have been given the 'gift' or you have not. There is an abundance of evidence (Dweck 2006 this volume) that attaching this label can be destructive, fostering arrogance and closing off young minds to the awareness that hard work is an essential pre-requisite to all success. By using this word, we are implicitly telling children that they have been given a fixed ability that sets them apart and makes them more intelligent than others. These may be exactly the circumstances under which talent fails to grow.

G&T co-ordinators in the 2005 sample reported finding that many of the students identified as gifted would adjust their responses to tasks (both set by teachers and self-set) in response to the application of the label. They tended to stick to what they knew would return them good marks. They rejected the possibility of failure (in the eyes of peers, teachers and parents) by 'going out on a limb'. Teachers who teach the more practical subjects also reported that students nominated as gifted may initially take risks with open-ended tasks, but if their work has not been finished in time or is badly done, there is often little that they can do to help out – the students will fail assessment criteria. These rigid assessment profiles (currently prolific in English state schools), which do not acknowledge risk-taking, creative effort and persistence, encourage what Dweck (this volume) calls 'fixed mindsets' in the short term . . . and waste time, money and talent in the long term.

The US has had a Federal definition (and three subsequent iterations) of gifted and talented since the Marland Report (1972). Cramond (2004) writes that if everyone truly believed the last part of the definition ('they require services or activities not ordinarily provided by the schools') then special services for gifted students would be clearly understood as necessary.

Cramond, whilst questioning why we require one single definition, is right, ethically, to high-light this particular part of the federal definition. Might it be best for a new definition simply to emphasise a mismatch between a child's current developmental level in a given subject area and the educational programming that is usually offered at that student's age and grade level, as suggested by Matthews and Foster (2006)?

Such a view is consistent with evidence in psychology and education about individual differences in developmental trajectories, and the highly diverse and incremental ways that learning actually happens (Bransford et al. 2000; Howe 1990; Shonkoff and Phillips 2000). From this perspective, a child is considered gifted only when their learning needs in any given subject area are so advanced relative to their age-peers' that special adaptive programming is required for continued challenge and academic development.

This 'mastery' model means that there is no mystery about what giftedness is: it is essentially about matching exceptional learning needs with appropriate educational provisions. The study of giftedness should not be about sorting people into categories but rather it should be con-cerned with exploring how to address the needs of students who are advanced in relation to their peers and monitoring closely the current intensity and drive they bring to their schooling. Addressing this need should involve a reaction to action rather than a reaction to a 'condition'.

Distinguishing among motivation, achievement, and ability is important when assessing school difficulties and developing specific interventions, but the relationship between motiv-ation and academic success has been better established with older children and adults than with younger children (Broussard and Garrison 2004). The few studies that have examined motiv-ation in young children have found that (as measured) it is a weak predictor of achievement (Stipek and Ryan 1997), so it is perhaps better to concentrate on research using adolescents when attempting to link motivation with giftedness.

Of particular interest in the pursuit of forming alternatives for a new English definition of giftedness is a longitudinal research study by Gottfried et al. (2005). This research took adoles-cents with extremely high academic intrinsic motivation (i.e. gifted-level motivation) and compared them to a cohort of their peers on a variety of educationally relevant measures from elementary school through the early adulthood years. The assessment of academic intrinsic motivation was based on the Children's Academic Intrinsic Motivation Inventory. Academic intrinsic motivation is defined by Gottfried (1990) as the enjoyment of school learning charac-terised by an orientation toward mastery, curiosity, persistence and the learning of challenging, difficult and novel tasks. In the study, cross-time, pervasive differences resulted, favouring the gifted motivation group, as compared to the cohort comparison group, on motivation, achievement, classroom functioning, intellectual performance, self-concept and post-secondary educational progress.

Critically, the Gottfried study seems to offer excellent evidence that there is a need to consider the construct of gifted motivation in its own right. Could it be that gifted-level outcomes result simply from fostering a mindset that includes hard work, drive, motivation and persistence over time in diverse subjects? When we are sure that a student has reached an advanced relative to peers, it reflects applied intrinsic motivation. The Gottfried study, by documenting an important distinction between gifted motivation and gifted intelligence, has opened the door for researchers in England to recommend identifying students with gifted motivation for entry into programmes for the gifted.

Eminent investigators contributing to the literature concerning motivation and expertise theory (e.g. Ericsson et al. 1993; Howe 1999; Sloboda et al. 1996) have produced persuasive studies to show that the 'magic' ingredient in success (particularly socially recognised success) is usually practice. Persistent endeavour has been shown to require a degree of positive feedback to maintain motivation. This was well considered a decade ago with social cognitive construct additions (described in Dai et al. 1998) to Gagné's Differentiated Model of Giftedness and Talent (Gagné 1991), and current supporting neurological evidence (Geake and Hansen 2005).

By attending to the special learning needs of exceptionally able learners, and emphasising the recognition that they are currently working hard and have thereby earned the right to further provision, we will be giving them this positive feedback. I agree with Cramond's view in that it is possible that there is no need to define something completely in order to understand it (Cramond 2005), but I also recognise that it would be useful for England to listen to North American scholars such as Carol Dweck, Allen and Adele Gottfried, and Dona Matthews (this volume), and English scholars like Guy Claxton (this volume) and Belle Wallace (this volume) who are promoting the view that engagement in learning and motivation are essential to the development of giftedness and talent. The English definition would do well to reflect these evolving understandings. Doing so would help us move away from a categorical, rigid and confusing conceptualisation of giftedness as an endowment of skill in one or more areas of learning, and towards a more developmental, practical definition that embodies an understanding of the dynamic nature of giftedness, and leads directly to reasonable implications for educators.

Contact address: tom@arni.uk.com

Future Perspectives

Suggested priorities for gifted education over the next decade

The English definition of giftedness will surely be recast. Its current mechanism does not assist schools to understand what to do with able learners, who must not be labelled and congratulated for being 'gifted'. Funding currently directed toward compiling school registers and maintaining a national register (a goal which is focused mainly upon who is gifted – not how to foster talent), must be redirected towards a goal of placing a gifted education specialist in every school. These people will be trained to identify high ability with empirically sound techniques that integrate neurocognitive findings, and supported to develop and deepen their own understandings of giftedness. They must guide teachers (via school-based and online training) to ramp-up the effectiveness of nominations for extra provision. More time must be allocated to teachers; attitudes toward parental input must change from wariness and non-consultation towards welcoming collaboration and co-advocacy. In return, parents must work with schools to set appropriate targets against which students' academic successes can be measured.   Tom Balchin

Part 2

Widening the focus: international perspectives and cultural issues

Although all of the chapters in this volume might be well-placed in the 'International Perspectives' thematic section, we have collected here the chapters of authors who have focused specifically on practices in their own country that might have useful application elsewhere. To get an even broader cross-section of national perspectives, you might want also to read Thomas Balchin's chapter on the English definition of giftedness, Ian Warwick's description of work he has been doing to expand gifted education provisions in England, Joyce VanTassel-Baska's chapter on the role of gifted education in promoting cultural diversity in the United States, Nick Colangelo and Susan Assouline's chapter on the use of acceleration in the US, Maria Dolores Prieto's chapter based on her work in Spain with emotional intelligence, Todd Lubart, Asta Georgsdottir and Maud Besançon's discussion of creativity as it is assessed and educated in France, or Wiesława Limont's discussion of working with Asperger Syndrome in Poland.

One of the reasons to create a book like this is to challenge the assumptions and misconceptions that so easily develop in closed systems: when something is always done in a certain way, it comes to be seen as the only way it can be done. By learning how things are done elsewhere, as with travelling, our eyes can be opened to fresh perspectives and possibilities that lead to better and more robust practices. Although specific observations may or may not apply to practices in your own jurisdiction, there are almost certainly elements of commonality or difference that you will find instructive in each of the chapters in this section.

Kurt Heller has been a strong advocate of evidence-based approaches to gifted education and counselling for many years now, and describes in his chapter in this volume the state of affairs in Germany. He makes a compelling case for systematic programme evaluation, as well as serious attention to teacher and counsellor training in gifted development that every jurisdiction would do well to heed. Similarly, many elements of the analysis of Pierre Vrignaud, Denis Bonora and Annie Dreux of the French educational approaches to giftedness would apply to many jurisdictions; their conclusions include the need for teacher education concerning giftedness, and for providing the same kind of support to intellectual and academic development as is provided for athletic and artistic development.

Some countries have longer histories than others of focusing on gifted education, and Åke Edfeldt and Inger Wistedt describe Sweden as a 'late starter' in this area. Their review of the pathway to gifted education in Sweden highlights opportunities and challenges that may be instructive to educators elsewhere who want to strengthen provisions in their own communities. Elias Matsagouras and Evangelia Dougali describe a situation in Greece where gifted education is in an even earlier stage of implementation, and propose a plan of development that promises to address this. Although education is context-specific, and must be responsive to local circumstances and values, many elements of their plan would apply elsewhere.

You will find two chapters on gifted education in Russia in this section. Ida Jeltova, Konstantin Lukin, and Elena Grigorenko discuss Russia's illustrious history of national support for high-level mathematical and scientific education, and wonder whether this will continue with the changing financial, political, and social circumstances facing Russia today. Victoria Yurkevich and Boris Davidovich describe alternative strategies that are being used to support gifted development in Russia, perhaps providing some answers to the questions raised by Jeltova, Lukin and Grigorenko.

Graham Chaffey raises the issue of under-representation of children from cultural minorities in programmes for the gifted, and discusses research he and his colleagues have conducted with underachieving indigenous populations in Australia and Canada. He describes a new cognitive intervention in the form of the *Coolabah Dynamic Assessment Instrument* which seeks to optimise cognitive performance and reverse the trend towards academic underachievement by addressing socio-emotional issues and questions of academic self-efficacy and engagement. To illustrate the way these children's gifts can be identified and facilitated, he offers 'snap-shot' reports of two children, one of Aboriginal descent and one from a low socio-economic status environment, who have been helped to become gifted achievers.

David Chan also illustrates the importance of honouring cultural differences as they lead to different conceptions and experiences of what giftedness is, how it develops and how it is best fostered. His chapter on lay conceptions of gifted education in China provides an intriguing window on the kinds of fresh conceptions that can be useful to educators and psychologists everywhere. He concludes his chapter and this thematic section by discussing the Chinese practice of *ren* (benevolence), suggesting the integration of a socio-emotional component into gifted education by fostering the self-cultivation that transforms and changes one's beliefs, attitudes, and values, and leads to a deep concern for the well-being of others.

8

Gifted education from the German perspective

Kurt A. Heller

Center for the Study of Giftedness at the University of Munich, Germany

Social psychologists understand 'ability' as an individual potential for achievement, with the conditions in the social and cultural learning environments playing important roles in its development and transformation into manifest achievements. In contrast, learning or educational psychologists focus on the individual utilisation of learning opportunities, and see the pivotal point for individual success as being learning and achievement motivation, as well as personal inclinations and interests in high-level achievement or expertise.

From the point of view of developmental psychology, ability, in the sense of intellectual and creative abilities, is initially manifested as relatively unspecific individual achievement potential that interacts with the social learning environment. This interactive process is understood as the reciprocal influence of childlike behaviour and parental goals and practices. Inherited genetic conditions become effective primarily through individual selection and the utilisation of learning opportunities in the social environment (Scarr and McCartney 1983; Sternberg and Grigorenko 1997; Thompson and Plomin 1993).

The early indicators of high ability, such as cognitive curiosity, indicate that before their first birthday, these children actively attempt to institute a supportive learning environment by attempting to satisfy basic cognitive and socio-emotional needs. The nature versus nurture debate acquires a new dimension in which individuals develop by participating in the active formulation of their social environments, resulting in the construction of dynamic systems. The direction in which this development moves is, naturally, dependent on the socio-cultural conditions placed on the learning environment; in other words on the academic opportunities offered by – or neglected by – the school in the promotion of talent and giftedness. What roles do creativity and intelligence play here?

The term giftedness refers primarily to cognitive abilities that contribute to problem solving both in general, as well as in specific domains (e.g. mathematics, the natural sciences, social abilities). Although intellectual talents are commonly associated with convergent thinking, the term 'creativity' is mainly associated with so-called divergent (multi-track) thinking. Because of this distinction, which reaches back to a suggestion made by Guilford (1950), it is not unusual to encounter contradictory postulations, although Guilford's intention was to establish complementary intellectual mental competencies. Characteristic of convergent thought production are classic intelligence tasks which require single track (inductive, conclusive) thinking, while relatively unstructured, open problems – such as those found in creativity tests – provoke divergent thought production. The problem is structured in a more or less restrictive manner, in other words it is characterised by 'closed' (e.g. intelligence tests) versus 'open' (e.g. creativity tasks) problems.

This system of dealing with different types of problems implies inherent qualitative differences in the respective thought processes. In the initial phases of seeking a solution for a complicated problem one relies primarily on divergent (creative) abilities in order to formulate questions or generate hypotheses, after which convergent thought competencies are increasingly needed. In order to model complex, demanding problem solutions, multi-dimensional concepts are needed. Single dimensional ability constructs cannot deal with all the facets of difficult problems and do not play a major role in modern theories of intelligence and creativity (contrary to what is still often encountered in practice). Prime examples are Gardner's theory of multiple intelligences (1983), Sternberg's three-component theory of information processing (1983; Sternberg et al. 2001) or his recent WICS model (this volume), as well as the Munich Model of Giftedness (Heller 2001, 2005b; Heller and Hany 1986; Heller and Perleth 2004; Heller et al. 2005). For meta-theoretical perspectives, see Ziegler and Heller (2000).

Gifted education: individual needs and instructional conditions

Individually differentiated talent prerequisites and learning needs demand differentiated scholastic curricula and instructional strategies (Heller 1999). This postulate is based on the theoretical assumption that between the cognitive learning prerequisites (aptitudes), and the social learning environment or instructional method (treatment), specific interactions are generated (Aptitude–Treatment–Interaction, ATI). According to the ATI model, not all instructional methods are equally suitable for all pupils. For example, a more rigidly structured instructional format is more effective among younger, anxiety-prone or less intelligent students, while an open instructional format which offers the opportunity for discovery learning has been proven to be, by and large, more advantageous for older and generally more intelligent students (Corno and Snow 1986; Cronbach and Snow 1977; Snow and Swanson 1992).

Consequently, the learning needs and interests of intellectually gifted students should be accorded as much consideration as that offered to individuals from handicapped groups. With respect to potential college preparatory (Gymnasiasten) students, long periods of understimulation in more or less undifferentiated, heterogeneous talent groups can lead to adverse developmental effects or even behavioural problems. This danger is particularly potent for the 10–20 per cent most talented Gymnasium students. These pupils are often characterised by cognitive curiosity, originality, an unquenchable thirst for knowledge and a broad (not necessarily scholastic/academic) interest profile. Their quick learning tempo and particularly effective information processing capabilities and memory skills, in conjunction with highly pronounced task motivation in the face of challenging performance situations, require open and comprehensive learning environments. How are such learning environments identified?

In order to answer this question empirically, one might compare particularly successful teachers with less successful teachers. Compared with less successful colleagues, the 'effective' teachers show higher levels of flexibility and greater acceptance of their pupils. They demonstrate a positive approach to particularly talented students, resulting in an altered role perception: 'The positions of student-teacher are, in comparison to traditional instruction, often exchanged. The teachers find themselves in the role of fellow-student in a course, which is partially organised by the students themselves' (Grotz 1990, p. 17; free translation). The goals of promoting independent thinking, learning and problem solving are optimally combined with discovery learning.

According to Neber (2006), discovery learning in an instructional environment means that the student does not receive learning material as a finished product, but rather that learning environments are designed to enable the student to engage in knowledge acquisition processes. The goal of discovery learning is to promote the learner's independence. The student should acquire flexible, practical knowledge. As Neber explained, discovery learning has so far been realised in three basic forms:

- discovery learning through example, such as the acquisition of terminology and rules;
- discovery learning through experimentation, such as the acquisition of the knowledge of rules in natural science instruction;
- discovery learning through the resolution of conflict.

Identification and programming

When the purpose of identification is clear, one can decide on a specific concept of giftedness, or at least decide between single- and multi-dimensional models. With respect to practical pedagogic and/or psychological measures, multi-dimensional models of giftedness are highly recommended.

In general, a graduated process (or sequential selection strategy) is preferable (Hany 1993, 2001; Heller 2000, 2004, 2005a). The Munich High Ability Test Battery (Münchner Hochbegabungs-Testbatterie; MHBT) developed by Heller and Perleth (2007) contains more

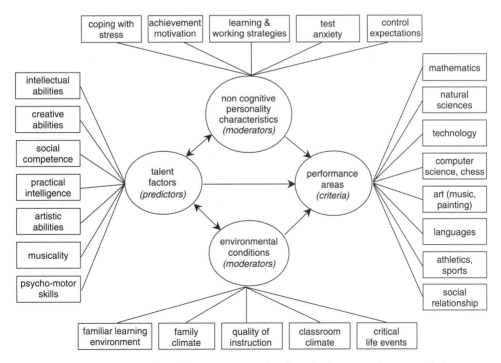

Figure 3 The Munich Model of Giftedness as an example of a multi-dimensional concept of talent

than two dozen tests and standardised questionnaires for the differential assessment of the predictor and moderator variables illustrated in Figure 3. The MHBT scales, which assess differentiated forms of talent on a high level, consider ability predictors as well as moderator variables, assessing cognitive and non–cognitive (primarily motivational) personality characteristics and socio-environmental variables which are relevant for the development and promotion of giftedness. The individual tests and questionnaires have been developed within the framework of the Munich Giftedness Study for use with talented children and adolescents, and great efforts have been taken to adapt them to these target groups (Heller and Perleth 2007). Furthermore, checklists can be used to establish a rough estimate of individual talent levels for children and adolescents in the following areas: intelligence, creativity, musical ability, social skills and psycho-motor skills (Heller 2004, 2005a/b).

In gifted education, the following questions must be considered: (1) *Why* should the highly gifted be promoted? (2) *What* should be promoted – special knowledge and domain specific competencies, or the development of general thinking skills? (3) *How* and *where* are the promotional measures to be conducted?

In order to answer the first question – *why* gifted education?, a pro and con analysis can be conducted. Critics of gifted education are concerned about loss of opportunities for children who are not highly gifted. However, financial and remedial learning efforts for handicapped children in Germany are many times greater than for highly gifted children and adolescents. Clearly, the promotion of gifted children does not occur at the expense of less advantaged children. This misconception, often voiced in public discussions, is upheld with assumptions of elitist attitudes and socially inept 'nerds' being produced by gifted programmes, although scientific investigations have actually suggested the opposite (e.g. Heller 2001; Rost 1993, 2000). In fact, the disappointments when highly gifted children and adolescents are not offered appropriate learning opportunities are far more serious and can lead to developmental and/or parenting problems (Freeman 2000). A basic right guaranteed to all citizens – including handicapped and non-handicapped children and adolescents – is optimal developmental opportunities.

The second question – *what* should be promoted? – is best answered with respect to individual learning needs. Gifted education can be adjusted to individual strengths and weaknesses, using academic acceleration and remedial learning. The enrichment model can be considered a specific and creative variant of remedial learning for the highly gifted, whereby the ability potential of talented individuals is augmented by stimulating and challenging learning environments. Appropriate enrichment measures focus on broad support for the development of gifted children. Academic acceleration for domain-specific expertise is for the most part superior to the enrichment approach, although a combination of enrichment and acceleration is the quickest way to promote general thinking skills and learning abilities as well as domain specific knowledge. For curricular planning, Gallagher (1985) suggests taking the following aspects into consideration: formulating relationships between thoughts and ideas, developing well-founded theories and opinions, and operating within a large knowledge system. For knowledge to progress, a large array of disjointed facts is not enough. What is needed instead is 'intelligent' knowledge (Weinert 1995), for which basic cognitive and metacognitive competencies are required (Heller and Hany 1996).

The third question – *how* and *where* are the promotional measures to be conducted? – is tightly bound to the differentiation problem, and to the formation of learning groups. Many terms are used to describe grouping; ranging from 'tracking' to 'within-class-grouping'. The separation of secondary school pupils into three different types of learning institutions (Gymnasium, Realschule, Hauptschule; roughly understood as high schools which prepare students for college, trade schools, or apprenticeships), common in German-language societies, is an example of tracking. Further sub-tracking variations can be instituted within these main tracks, for example with respect to language, mathematics, or athletic abilities. Grouping allows for a better fit between an individual's cognitive level, and the learning environment: 'Although tracking is an attempt to group students of like ability in order to make instruction more effective, . . . grouping without curriculum differentiation serves only to stratify, not to educate, students' (Borland et al. 2002, p. 101). For this reason, many educational experts advocate flexible grouping, accompanied by appropriately differentiated curriculum. In contrast to the 'classic' tracking concept, pupils should be instructed according to individual progress in different domains or school subjects, thereby maintaining a better fit between individual profiles and instructional/learning environments.

Flexible groups are consistent with the ATI model, but presuppose that a school system can offer sufficiently individualised learning and curricular conditions. In reality most German comprehensive schools are managed quite differently, as recently documented by two major international studies, the Third International Mathematics and Science Study (TIMSS), conducted by the International Association for the Evaluation of Educational Achievement, and the Programme for International Student Assessment (PISA), conducted by the Organisation for Economic Cooperation and Development (OECD) (Baumert et al. 1997; Deutsches PISA-Konsortium 2001, 2002). These findings led Borland et al. (2002) to the conclusion that, 'flexible grouping is easier to advocate than it is to put into practice'. It is hardly surprising then that the German comprehensive schools are not as strong as three-track secondary schools in promoting gifted pupils (cf. Deutsches PISA-Konsortium [German Pisa Consortium] 2002; Heller 2003b).

This is not an attempt to use a single case as a universal explanation. On the contrary, the degree of differentiation in a school system is merely one element of a complex structure affecting academic success (Heller 2002a/b, 2003b; Heller et al. 2000/2002; Heller and Hany 1996). A validation of differentiated measures for gifted education can be found in the plethora of empirical studies confirming cumulative learning and knowledge expansion in the context of challenging, complex problems and tasks. These cumulative effects can be seen in the increase in achievement differences over time between better and poorer pupils in heterogeneous learning groups. This variance can only be absorbed by instruction in more or less performance-homogeneous learning groups. The optimal promotion of giftedness is best guaranteed through scholastic and instructional differentiation (Reimann 2002a/b).

German gifted programme activities and their evaluation

The increase in gifted programming activities has been rapid, and the current figure is too high to estimate accurately. But are theoretical advances and practical applications keeping pace? Reservations must be voiced due to the fact that no more than one dozen scientific programme evaluations have been conducted within the last decade in German-language countries. Hany (2000) has also been sceptical of the value of many of the activities conducted in the name of gifted education and counselling. Why is it that programme evaluation studies are conducted so infrequently? In addition to financial reasons, proper methodology is often unavailable or insufficient, and psychological barriers are also responsible here.

Programme evaluations must take into consideration not only the usual measurement standards (objectivity, reliability, validity, etc.), but also many other important criteria. The Joint Committee on Standards of Educational Evaluations came up with no fewer than 30 criteria that can be subsumed in four categories: utility, feasibility, propriety, and accuracy (Sanders 1994).

Callahan (1993, 2000) developed a nine-point approach to evaluating gifted programmes: the threat, the definition and programme description, finding 'the programme' and isolating its effects, formulating appropriate questions and setting priorities, comparison or standards and the control group problem, the teacher as programme, aptitude treatment interactions, success and instrumentation, and evaluation utilisation (Heller 2002b). The first factor (threat) highlights a special psychological problem of programme evaluations:

> Educational programme evaluation has never been an easy task, for the evaluator or those who are being evaluated. Nor has it been perceived by most as a welcome part of programme activities. Evaluation within any educational programme is, in fact, most often regarded at best as a nuisance, and at worst, as a threat.
>
> (Callahan 1993, p. 607)

Some major gifted programmes in Germany have been scientifically evaluated. For the evaluation of enrichment programmes inside and outside of school, see Hany and Heller (1992), Heller (1995), Neber and Heller (2002). For academic acceleration programmes and related evaluation studies see Heller and Reimann (2002). Methodological problems of using talent searches as gifted programmes are treated by Hany (1993, 1997, 2001, 2004) and Neber (2004).

Academic competitions and programmes designed to challenge the exceptionally talented at school, university, and work have been evaluated in a few large-scale studies (Heller and Lengfelder 2000, 2006; Heller and Viek 2000; Lengfelder and Heller 2002; Trost 2000). For an international overview, see Campbell, Wagner and Walberg (2000).

There are two main functional goals of programme evaluation studies: formative evaluation and summative evaluation (Scriven 1967). Formative evaluations aim to optimise gifted programme activities as well as to identify and eliminate unwanted side effects. Summative evaluations serve primarily to assess the effects of programme activities, based on an input-treatment-output design. In this manner the evaluation functions supplement each other. It would be beneficial to certify gifted programmes that have been confirmed through scientific evaluations. However, in Germany we do not seem to have arrived at this point (Hany 2000), and have quite a way to go before we reach it. Possibly this article will help German educators focus their efforts more actively on quality and less on quantity (Heller 2002b). Programme evaluations conducted according to scientific standards provide not only important insights into the pedagogic value of such programmes, but also important financial information for planning and realising gifted programme activities (Heller and Neber 2004).

Conclusion

The belief that highly gifted children and adolescents should be given an opportunity for optimal development through special educational measures and counselling opportunities, much in the same way other exceptional children and adolescents are dealt with, has slowly, over the past two decades, established itself in German public opinion. After parental initiatives led to the foundation of the German Society for the Gifted Child in 1978, the first school-based gifted programmes were implemented in Lower Saxony (at a private school in Braunschweig), and in Baden-Wuerttemberg, with enrichment and academic acceleration programmes at the secondary school level that were scientifically evaluated. At this time the first professional gifted counselling centres opened their doors at public universities in Hamburg and Munich. These were followed in the 1990s by similar centres in Tübingen and Cologne, and recently in

Marburg, Rostock, Ulm and Würzburg. In the meantime a very large number of promotional programmes and counselling activities for the gifted, both within and outside of school, have been established across Germany (Holling and Kanning 1999; Persson et al. 2000; Stapf 2003).

It appears that no more than 10–20 per cent of these programmes have been subjected to scientific evaluation, in that no valid or reliable information is available regarding the utilisation or side effects of most of these activities (Hany 2000). The exceptions to this have been documented in this article. Of course, non-evaluated gifted programmes can be effective. However, one should exercise a healthy scepticism when considering participation in such programmes, and not place blind faith in the promises printed in glossy brochures, especially when the programmes are expensive.

The fact that the necessity for gifted programmes and counselling centres has found a broader resonance in Germany can be interpreted as an encouraging sign. Now it is vital that this realisation be implemented in teacher development and counsellor training. Only then will we be able to rely on a sufficient base of qualified personnel for the development and evaluation of gifted education and counselling programmes, including methodological competencies for talent searches and the identification of giftedness. Here one should make use of the longer experience with special gifted programmes in the Eastern part of Germany, as well as internationally (Heller et al. 2000/2002b).

Contact address: heller@mail.paed.uni-muenchen.de

Future Perspectives

Suggested priorities for gifted education over the next decade

Reflections on where we must go in gifted education in Germany over the next ten years should be focused on at least three tasks. Firstly, the heterogeneous nature of giftedness and talent requires comprehensive theories like the Munich Model of Giftedness. Synthetic research approaches, e.g. a combination of prospective psychometric and (retrospective) expertise paradigms, are also needed for epistemological purposes in the explanation of giftedness and talent. Individual learning potentials must be transformed into corresponding scholastic or academic achievements. Secondly, these learning potentials must be maximised by enabling independent learning – a function of lifelong learning. Hence I expect a strong increase in gifted classes and special schools for gifted students in Germany over the next years. Thirdly, German gifted education policy should focus on underrepresented populations, especially gifted females in mathematics and the sciences. This should affect not only gifted individuals' educational opportunities but also national prosperity in the future – in Germany as well as worldwide.   Kurt A. Heller

9

Education practices for gifted learners in France: an overview

Pierre Vrignaud
Université de Nanterre, Paris

Denis Bonora and Annie Dreux
INETOP/CNAM Laboratoire de Psychologie de l'Orientation

In France, educational practices concerning gifted and talented young people have long been the object of discussion. These discussions can be traced back to work carried out by Binet (1911), whose name is usually associated with studying pupils with learning difficulties, but whose research also led to pedagogy for young people with high results in his intelligence test. There is a real contrast when we compare the attitude of the educational authorities in France toward the gifted on one hand, and the talented on the other.

Attitudes toward giftedness

Debates in France surrounding practices for the gifted have always been dominated by arguments expressing 'giftedness's' total opposition to the values of French society in general, and 'republican egalitarianism' in particular. A consideration of the debate concerning specific practices for the gifted, shows France to be a country averse to addressing these questions (see for example Urban and Sekowski 1993). This situation however is not so radical as first perceived, as demonstrated in our report on the schooling of gifted children in France (Vrignaud et al. 2000). Indeed, our findings indicated that amongst the key measures recommended to improve adaptation of the school system to the gifted – acceleration, enrichment and special classes – as referred to in international literature (Callahan 1993; Clark and Shore 1998), the first two appear to be well established in French National Education texts and programmes. However, explicit reference to the fact that these practices can be a response to the situation of gifted children is never made in these documents.

In addition, the absence of institutional debate concerning giftedness is changing. Following the report referred to above, the Ministry of Education (Ministére de l'Education Nationale)-(MEN) set up a deliberative committee for the schooling of gifted children[1] and published a report on their findings (Delaubier 2002). A new awareness arose from this action, which broke down the taboo that had long surrounded the question. Consequently, the 2005 Law of Orientation and Program concerning the Future of School (Law 2005–380) grants explicit

---

[1] One of the authors of this paper, Pierre Vrignaud, took part in the deliberations of this commission.

permission to offer specific adjustments for the gifted: 'Adapted measures will be taken in order to allow students who are advanced or with special aptitudes, to fully develop their potential. Schooling will possibly be speeded up in accord with student learning rate' (Art. L. 321–4).

Before being able to realise the reach of this new legislation, we must wait for the application decrees, which are expected to clarify these curriculum adjustments, as well as the gifted identification procedures to apply in order to select those who will benefit from them.

With regard to research, the Institut de France (Académie des Sciences, Academy of Sciences) instructed the Cognition and Development Laboratory in the University of Paris 5 to produce a report relating to 'the Current State of Research Concerning Children Known as Gifted' (Lautrey 2002). This report was later published as a special issue of Psychologie Française, one of the main French scientific psychological journals edited by the French Psychological Society. Various publications run by research scientists who belong to this laboratory are worth recommending (e.g. Lubart 2006; Pereira 2006).

Practices for the gifted

The three principal practices: acceleration, enrichment and special classes – referred to in international literature for the education of the gifted – all exist in France.

Acceleration

There are two types of accelerated courses of study: grade-skipping and intensive programmes (schooling in special classes where the mainstream curriculum is covered in a shorter time). The educational texts overseeing preschool and primary schooling make provision for grade-skipping. Intensive programmes have been subjected to various trials, which are mentioned below in the paragraph devoted to special classes. Preschool and primary education is divided into three stages, known in France as cycles: the early learning stage (first two years of nursery school), fundamental learning (last year of nursery school and the first two years of primary education) and improvement (last three years of primary school). Moving up to each stage is decided by a board of teachers. Progressing more quickly through these stages is just one of the decisions that is examined by this board.

It is usually the board of teachers of each cycle that applies for acceleration, and frequently examines applications put forward by parents. Specialist opinion (educational psychologist, school doctor) is not obligatory. However, it remains a standard practice that the child is examined by an educational psychologist who does not systematically check the intellectual development of children, but rather comes to a conclusion about their maturity in general, and capacity to adapt to the teaching and social and emotional context of a class in which the general age is higher than theirs.

Grade-skipping is the most popular practice with precocious children in France, although statistically the figures for it are low, and have been constantly decreasing over the last fifty years. In 2006, 1.3 per cent of children were enrolled in their first year of primary school at the age of five instead of six, and 2.5 per cent of children were enrolled in the 'collège' (the sixth year) at the age of ten instead of eleven (MEN 2006).

Enrichment

Primary and secondary education

Enrichment or rather individualisation of course programmes is the practice regarded by the MEN as best adapted to the needs of gifted children. This position is developed at length in Delaubier's report (2002). In primary school, enrichment is built into the organisation of the different learning stages (mentioned above) and the methods of class supervision in place. In the collège (ages 11–15) the principle of diversification is specified within the 96–465 decree. This ruling specifies that it is not a question of drawing up the syllabus, rather the text envisages grouping pupils together so that they can 'go further, to further their knowledge of certain topics or subjects, but also to express and to develop their talents, to enjoy seeking and creating'. It should also be noted that these regulations were drawn up more to enable better integration of children with learning difficulties, than to accommodate precocious development.

In the lycée and institutes of higher education

In the French 'lycée' (college), the programme content of various sectors and the possibility of taking more or fewer options make it possible for gifted children to be provided with a stimulating environment. Pupil selection and streaming has led in certain cases to the emergence of some pools of excellence where pupils can be found with exceptionally high academic ability and who are one to two years advanced. Being advanced by more than one year is theoretically impossible, according to laws and regulations; however some hundreds of children (400 in 1999) reach the sixth form two years in advance (and sometimes even three years: 30 in 1999). The regular age for undergoing the 'baccalauréat' examination is 18 years; in 2006, 3.3 per cent of the candidates who took this examination were aged 17 or less (MEN 2006).

Special classes and programmes

When referring to special education, we can mention some special classes set up in the public sector in various pilot programmes (for more detailed information see Vrignaud et al. 2005). There are, in addition, some institutions recruiting pupils with high potential who are having difficulty in state schools. These initiatives seem more frequent and better encouraged by the heads of the Education Department since the publication of the 2005 Law of Orientation and Program concerning the Future of School (Law 2005–380). An interesting example is the opening in 2005 in the lycée Janson de Sailly, one of the great Parisian lycées, of a special curriculum for intellectually precocious children who had encountered difficulties during their primary school years.

In the private sector, there are institutes that work in conjunction with the State, receiving a government grant, which obliges them to teach the national curriculum and make provisions for pupils to progress from one class to another. There are also institutes without contracts. These have more leeway but, as they do not receive government aid, they are more expensive for parents. In the case of government-funded, contractually-bound schools there exist, on one hand, institutes which set themselves up as 'educating precocious children' but do not systematically draw up individualised programmes, and, on the other hand, institutes drawing up pedagogical programmes adapted to gifted children.

An official list of such institutes does not exist. Compiling information from websites, documents of parent associations of gifted children, and directories listing private institutes, has allowed the identification of up to 70 institutes to date showing an interest in the schooling of precocious children. However, according to the results of a questionnaire sent to these organisations (Vrignaud 2006), it appears that the vast majority of them do not admit gifted children, or simply integrate them into mainstream classes. Few institutes practise an explicit policy of identification; even fewer have also established a specific pedagogy aimed at gifted children.

Examination of the alternative education sector indicates a broad diversity. There are schools linked to parent associations of gifted children, which put options for gifted children into practice. Others, it would appear, are profit-focused. In 1988, the Lycée Michelet in Nice created the first class to combine 6th year and 5th year pupils in the same year level; it practises systematic acceleration of the school syllabus, sometimes to the detriment of certain subjects. Its pupils sitting the baccalauréat exam are regularly classified as being among the youngest in France.

Associations for giftedness

Parent associations of gifted children play a significant role in the schooling of gifted children, on one hand by lobbying the media and governing bodies, on the other hand by information campaigns and counselling provided to families. These associations also play an important role in disseminating knowledge by organising conferences and by publishing books, reviews and setting up websites. In general, associations hold rather extreme viewpoints regarding the special needs and/or adaptation difficulties of gifted children in the school system. They exaggerate the dangers of underachievement and the advantages of special classes. Indeed the INETOP (Institut National d'Etude du Travail et d'Orientation Professionnelle [French National Institute of Work and Vocational Guidance])report (Vrignaud and Bonora, 2000) was the reaction of Jack Lang (who was Education Minister at the time) to a request from a parent's association, demanding what he was intending to do about schooling gifted children. To underline the importance of the role of French associations, we can refer to one of the French associations, which founded a European one: Eurotalent. This European association has taken the initiative for having the 'Recommendation 1248' law (1994) voted in at the Council of Europe's Parliamentary Assembly on Educating the Gifted.

Identification of gifted children

In France a systematic policy of identifying gifted children has never really existed. In general, identification of giftedness is carried out using tests during an individual consultation. These tests could be requested for an expert evaluation following an application for acceleration, or due to learning or behavioural difficulties in school. It is important to distinguish between situations where the test is administered by a psychologist belonging to an educational institution (educational psychologist, career counsellor), a health institution (Centre Médico-Psycho-Pédagogique (CMPP): Children's Mental Health Centre; a psychiatrist or a paediatrician) or a liberal body member.

There is little or no information available concerning school psychologists' attitudes toward requests for tests of precocity. The hypothesis seems plausible that given their workload, this type of request is not given priority over those concerning pupils with learning difficulties. Nonetheless, certain professionals are now aware of these questions, but there is a lack of systematic training for administering such tests. The counselling responses to young people and their families will vary according to the psychologists' expertise with regard to these problems. Writing or psychomotor difficulties can be dealt with within the structure of rehabilitation laid out in the national education system (Réseau d'Aide Spécialisée aux Elèves en Difficulté [Help Resources Network for Pupils Encountering Learning Problems]). Any relational difficulties can be handled by consultation with a psychotherapist in specialised centres such as the CMPP.

It is possible to generalise to psychologists in private practice some of these views related to test administration. The number of requests for such psychological assessment has considerably increased in the last twenty years. More and more families wish to get a psychological assessment of their child's intellectual potential with a view to obtaining a diagnosis of giftedness. Psychologists are usually self-taught in this area, with the attendant limits and risks, as there are no special courses on gifted development and education in most French universities.

Nearly all psychologists use the Wechsler Intelligence scales for assessing giftedness. For practical reasons – that is, a lack of valid tests and questionnaires in French – they do not assess other facets of giftedness, including creativity. Some books on giftedness well known by French psychologists (Terrassier 1991/1999) contain questionnaires used to identify giftedness, which have not been subjected to scientific validation. For example, the majority of items in one questionnaire used to detect and identify gifted children based on memory and behaviours do not discriminate when comparisons are carried out using a control group, with matching age and social background criteria (Vrignaud 2006).

Parents receive verbal and written information on the test results, but the report often lacks recommendations. In summary, we wish to emphasise the urgent need for continuing education for psychologists engaged in identifying and counselling gifted children and adolescents.

The talented

Attitudes toward the talented

In contrast with attitudes toward academically gifted learners, the governing body's attitude toward specific practices for the talented, whether in the artistic or sporting fields, has consistently been favourable. The majority of special classes and institutes were set up in the 1960s, with special programmes and timetables, allowing the practice of artistic and sporting activities at a high level. Identification of pupils likely to enrol in these programmes is clearly defined and managed by the various relevant institutions.

The question that arises, as soon as devotion to an artistic or sporting activity becomes a full-time activity or a life vocation, is how schooling can be reconciled with it. For teachers and career counsellors this question is formulated in the following way: how is it possible to help young people prepare for their futures while taking into account their investments outside school, while at the same time facing the risks involved with artistic recognition or athletic achievements? For the last thirty years, identifying and encouraging artistic and sporting talent in France has led to specially organised academic programmes, specialised training programmes, and the possibility for pupils following the mainstream syllabus to select artistic or sporting options. These three options are differentiated by the time dedicated to training in the artistic or sporting disciplines, as well as the prominence of the professional project. The institutional partners involved, the training sessions and the programmes differ rather markedly between the artistic field and the sporting field, and so we approach them separately.

Artistic talent

Setting up classes with specially adapted schedules is possible from the end of the early learning stage onwards (fourth year). These classes are rare in primary education. The best known example is a class for young choir singers recruited by Radio France. It is obligatory for these young people to pursue their schooling until the legal age of 16, regardless of their specialised programme.

Classes with specially adapted programmes are more frequent in secondary schools for musicians and dancers in partnership with music and dance academies. Music and dance classes with specially adapted schedules were introduced in France in 1974 by an interdepartmental decree. They aim to maintain a high level of teaching and to allow the trainee musicians and dancers to continue their tuition under satisfactory conditions.

In general, admission into classes with specially adapted schedules at the 'collège' level is subject to a dual selection procedure: passing the entrance exam of the artist academy, and having an application dossier accepted by the collège board. In addition, extra qualities are required: organisation, rigour, discipline and motivation, all prerequisites for coping with a demanding regime.

There is a professional syllabus leading to a technological baccalauréat with a music or dance option. A second option leads to a general literary baccalauréat with a substantial artistic content, of which there are currently seven options: music, theatre, dance, visual arts, cinema-audio-visual, circus, history of arts. Parents and educational staff consider it regrettable that the curricula are primarily literary, whereas the scientific syllabus leads to more professional openings. Even high-achieving pupils in scientific disciplines are obliged to abandon their scientific studies if they want to give priority to their artistic development.

In the field of dance, the schools concerned have signed agreements with schools responsible for organising specially adapted schedules in their sector. These schools are the Opera National de Paris, the dance department of the Conservatoire de Paris and the Marseille dance school. In the field of music, the famous Conservatoire Supérieur de Paris works in association with four high schools proposing part time tuition.

Athletic talent

The case of young sportsmen/women is more specialised because the duration of their sporting career is usually short (about ten years) compared to their professional lives. It is thus important to provide them with vocational training that will facilitate productive employment at a later date. For talented young athletes, there are two possibilities for reconciling their sporting ambition with schooling: the élite syllabus reserved for young French national or at least regional hopes, and which admits fewer than 2000 young people each year, and the 'school sports option', which is more open and provides education for more than 50,000 pupils.

The school sports options in lycées propose setting up schedules, which allow intensive training of four to eight hours a week and means that the highest achievers are recognised as 'high-level sportspeople'. This enables them to gain entry onto the most prestigious teams: the Pôles Espoirs (young hopefuls) and the Pôles France (French national team) set up in 1995 by a circular issued by the Ministry for Youth and Sports stipulating in particular the conditions of specially organised schooling.

The élite syllabus assembles talented young athletes with the potential to gain access to the Pôles France, thereby bringing together pupils committed to competition on a national or international level. More than a simple reorganisation of their timetable, the sports pupils signed on by these two associations receive individualised help in organising training sessions and schoolwork . . . and they also benefit from social, medical or psychological support, if necessary. The special programmes, a result of close collaboration between the ministries concerned, the Ministry of Education, and the Ministry of Youth and Sports, greatly facilitate the schooling of these adolescents who must get up early, go to bed late and take part in competitions during their week-ends.

INSEP (Institut National du Sport et de l'Education Physique [French National Institute of Sport and Physical Education]) is an institution available to high-level athletes. This institute, governed by the Ministry of Youth and Sports, offers the French sporting elite optimal conditions for reconciling their athletic training with university or vocational tuition. The INSEP demonstrates strong attachment to the policy of ensuring that each new recruit establishes a dual plan, alerting the young person to the need to elaborate his career plan at the same time as his sporting project. The question that arises for guidance experts is how the young person can be helped to see the dual project as a total life plan integrating sport with life after sport, rather than a restriction.

Within the framework of practices in place to support guidance and life-long learning, assistance for high-level athletes goes beyond schooling, and also offers specially adapted qualification contracts for the under-30s keen to enrol on paid vocational training courses or to enter employment. A 'Convention d'Insertion Professionelle' (professional contract) can be signed between the government and the employer; the contract allows sports students to have 50 per cent of working time free so that they can take part in training sessions and sporting competitions. Other procedures also exist such as employment relocation, timetable adjustment for civil servants, help in setting up a business, encouragement grants, local authority support, all of which means that the young athlete is assured of permanent employment while pursuing a high-level sports career.

We have observed during our research for the Ministry of Education (Vrignaud and Bonora 2000) that attitudes and practices for the gifted and the talented vary widely from country to country. One approach to evaluating the effectiveness of educational measures and counselling activities is to consider international competition results. In the field of sport, the Olympic Games provides one such evaluation. In the intellectual domain, the Fields medal, sometimes considered equivalent to a Nobel Prize in Mathematics, provides a short and interesting example of this comparative approach. Since 1998, 41 Fields medals have been awarded to mathematicians from 12 countries. Five countries have been distinguished more than once and these countries share more than 80 per cent of the awarded medals: USA (11), France (9), Great Britain (6), USSR (5) and Japan (3). It would be heuristically useful to compare these figures with the measures designed to encourage mathematical talent; certainly they suggest that France has been doing an excellent job of fostering mathematical giftedness.

Conclusion

In this brief overview of the situation in France, we have seen how the French system encourages talent in the artistic and sporting fields but has not sought until recently systematically to address academic giftedness. For the talented there are many practices, from primary education onwards, which allow schooling to be reconciled with sports studies or artistic tuition. For the academically gifted, practices are restricted to different courses of study, and especially to the development of elitist courses for the 'best' pupils. From the point of view of multiple intelligence theory (Gardner 1983), high achievement in certain school subjects like mathematics can be deemed a talent. In that respect, the French school system addresses intellectual talent. However, there is much work still to be done in developing assessment practices that effectively differentiate between high achievers and the gifted As we mentioned above, educational consideration of gifted development is in the early stages in France, and without formal training of concerned professionals, these considerations will not go beyond being merely good intentions.

Contact address: vrignaud.pierre@wanadoo.fr

Future Perspectives

Suggested priorities for gifted education over the next decade

Concerning the gifted, we provided in our chapter several examples of the improving acceptability and visibility of issues pertaining to gifted identification and schooling. In the field of research, several laboratories are involved in programmes dealing with gifted children's psychology, and more and more students are working on the gifted in the framework of their PhD theses. A national hospital (at Rennes, Bretagne) has opened a specialised consultation for maladjusted gifted children. Numerous secondary schools are about to offer special courses for the gifted. The stream described in the first report to the Minister of Education (Vrignaud and Bonora 2000) is constantly widening, and gives birth to more and more actions in favour of the gifted. Concerning the talented, the special courses devoted to them will quite probably become more and more effective in the future, and will progressively encompass many more aspects of their lives, both at the present time and in the future.   Pierre Vrignaud, Denis Bonora and Annie Dreux

---

10

High ability education in Sweden: the Swedish model

Åke W. Edfeldt

Stockholm University

Inger Wistedt

Stockholm University and Växjö University

Sweden – late starter in the field of gifted education

In the 1980s, L.M. Cohan commented on the state of gifted education in Sweden in the *International Encyclopedia of Education* (Husén and Postlethwaithe 1985). Cohan summed up his observations by noting that in Scandinavia there were few provisions for gifted children, '. . . since the egalitarian ethic is dominant, and special provisions for the gifted are viewed as a means of maintaining the privileged positions of certain groups' (p. 48). However, at the end of the twentieth century this state of affairs eventually lost its legal support. A new national curriculum was passed in 1994, leaving a door open for specific support programmes in favour of high-ability students fully in line with European Council Recommendation 1248 (1994). Yet, until the turn of the century, no Swedish Minister of Education was willing to jeopardise his or her political existence for the benefit of gifted children.

In 1999 Åke Edfeldt received money from the then conservative majority leadership of Stockholm city council to invite leading European researchers in the field of gifted education to the first Swedish seminar on high ability students. At short notice he managed to assemble about a dozen of the best known European experts in this area. Obviously many other European countries were interested in a possible Swedish turnaround on this issue. A direct request two years later to the Social Democratic Minister of Education enabled government-funded training of specially selected teachers and student teachers as part of Sweden's first experimental gifted education initiative. These trained assistants were intended to guide the studies of high-ability students at various levels within our schooling system, in accordance with a curriculum individually adapted to learners in selected subjects. High-ability students were also expected to pass an examination geared to these tailored curricula.

To whom?

Let us now address to whom we intended to give gifted education support in Sweden. Such support was not to be given to schools or to special study levels (Edfeldt 1990a). Only individual pupils within our ordinary school system would qualify for this kind of assistance.

Requests for gifted education support might come from students or their parents. The applicant's teacher or some other relevant school representative would be expected to testify to the desirability of the requested support.

As a first step, candidates would be given the opportunity to discuss their subject of interest with an ECHA (European Council for High Ability)-certified teacher, who would then draft a skeletal plan for the requested curriculum and locate relevant learning environments within the Swedish school system where the desired tuition could be realised. The ECHA-certified teacher would also help the candidates apply for the right to carry out external studies at the institution in question. During the resulting study period the ECHA-certified teacher would aid the candidates in negotiating school matters in the external environment.

Pupils who obtained such guidance from an ECHA-certified teacher would not be transferred from their original school setting, but would continue to be regarded as belonging to their native educational environment. It would also be expected that these pupils would report back on any interesting developments resulting from their advanced studies.

In what way?

Since we do not expect to find pupils with specific qualifications for all types of advanced studies, we have not proposed early general-ability testing or tuition aimed at facilitating studies in general. Unlike the old regulation-ruled school with a detailed curriculum for the teachers to follow in their daily tuition, today's Swedish 'aim-and-result-steered school' enjoins schools to help pupils gain certain competencies at successive school levels. After general-ability assessments using a series of benchmarks, the teachers and the school administrators will know if and how well these competences are being achieved by individuals as well as by classes or other groups of pupils. How individual children succeed in their studies is also the most useful basic data for local school administrators who have to distribute available funds to those most in need, those whom they may regard as both the high-achieving and low-achieving students.

Gifted education in reading

Experiences in human engineering, which strongly affected most behavioural sciences in the post-Second World War era, led to a concern with the mere instruction and training of students within the field of education. In its most extreme form, this kind of education brought about both 'teaching machines' and 'scrambled books', mechanical devices used to support programmed individualised instruction Not until the 1970s was this crisis in education finally resolved.

In the mid-1970s a group of psychologists from the University of Gothenburg led by Ference Marton (Marton and Säljö 1976) started to study learning in a new way. They used qualitative data to characterise the outcome of their experiments and introduced a new and elegant way of depicting the well-known difference between surface readers and depth readers. The number of individuals within these two groups in their studies, however, did not match the proportions usually found in research on reading. The high-achieving students, distinguished by their deep-reading habits, were fewer in number than was typical in other studies on reading. When asked about the content of the text used in Marton's experiment, the deep-reading subgroup showed a good ability to report on the text content when both summary responses and itemised details were sought.

The main subgroup, on the other hand, had the usual surface-reader problem of summing up the text's content. This subgroup, in Marton's elegant terms, was said to read and 'learn the signs'. The small elite subgroup, on the other hand, was said to read and to have 'what is signified' as their object of focal attention. The difference between 'learning the sign' and 'learning what it signifies' does not sound that immense, but it makes all the difference.

Good readers are characterised by their ability to interpret new texts directly at sight, and unconsciously to test their interpretations against what they already know. As a result they might come up with new or at least modified ideas concerning phenomena generally significant to their own lives. Marton wrote that the small top group from his Gothenburg study was characterised by this ability. Reports from Marton's experiments also show that the small deep-reading group had excellent qualifications for advanced studies.

However, in 1985, two representatives of Marton's research group tried to show positive results from a carefully controlled experiment in the teaching of reading (Dahlgren and Olsson 1985). All their good intentions were effectively undermined by the fact that they were not free to choose the method by which the students were taught how to read. They had to accept the conventional synthetic method (with phonics) preferred in their hometown, about which Edmund B. Huey (1908) had issued a stern warning for its notoriously bad effects. During the year in which the teaching of reading began in earnest, the children lost much of their spontaneous linguistic ability. Thus the most important aspect of the children's linguistic development, viz. their meta-linguistic understanding/competence, actually decreased during the learning-to-read period. Normally children's meta-linguistic ability increases as a result of even moderately successful reading instruction. The researchers concluded that the method used to teach reading had been a source of the unexpected outcome of this study.

At that time we began our own study, entitled 'Teaching reading with newspapers as the sole reading material' (Edfeldt 1990b). The results from the Gothenburg study were then the most recent among many indications that we should use an analytic method for our experimental teaching of reading. The experimental teaching was carried out during the consecutive school years of 1985–1986 and 1986–1987, and in 1987–1988 the project was evaluated and reported on. Three classes from each of the three levels of the comprehensive school took part in the experiment. Thus some 300 children from grades 1–3, 4–6, and 7–9 (i.e. children aged 7–9, 10–12, and 13–15 respectively), learned how to read and/or further developed their reading skills by making daily use of three major newspapers as their only reading texts.

The results from the experimental classes were compared with the results from a matched control group. Considering the limitation of the sample sizes, we also chose to compare our experimental results with the outcome of a corresponding field study concerning the teaching of reading. This study included 7515 students from grades 1–9 who had also received reading instructions according to the analytic method, though using conventional readers or textbooks. Let us emphasise that in both our studies the basic issue was the differences in outcome between analytic and synthetic methodologies. Those results have been reported elsewhere (Allard and Sundblad 1991).

> In the synthetic method, however, 'breaking the code' is the key ability. The written text is treated as if it were a brand new language to be learned and thus the decoding procedure has to be drilled into over-learning before any questions about the meaningful content of the decoded words and/or phrases may be raised at all.
>
> (p. 6)

Huey (1908) and later Bloom (1985) had already talked about this uneconomical use of the elementary school children's time and suggested ways to reduce such mismanagement. In his report Edfeldt (1990a) also reports on results that indicate that the same kinds of school problems still exist.

In the analytic method, on the other hand, one makes optimal use of the linguistic auto-maticity established by structural learning within the process of acquiring one's mother tongue. Reading is thus a communicative process, which means that there is always a message prior to any decoding. This in turn means that the pupil's urge to use all possibly pertinent, earlier knowledge and experiences should always proceed and thus control the decoding efforts. Our results from the research period 1985–1988 indicated that the beginners needed between one and a half and two years' less time to reach the point of reading fluently than did the control children. During the same period of time the older children managed to achieve qualitatively better reading competency than had previously been possible for most students throughout their entire nine years at school. Their results equalled those of the elite group from Marton's studies, i.e. those who were reading/learning what is signified (Marton and Säljö 1984). That is the reason why we have decided to add the same reading instruction to our gifted education programme in reading, starting with test activities at Öjaby School close to Växjö University in the south of Sweden where the developmental centre of the Swedish gifted education movement is now located.

Conclusions to be drawn from the reading projects

We have tried, of course, to understand why this teaching approach was so successful. Even with a scrupulously effected analytic methodology it had not been previously demonstrated that such first rate results could be achieved. We ourselves had conscientiously used the analytic formula before, but without such success. In our 1989–1990 evaluations, however, we found that newspaper texts intended primarily for communication and the analytic method of teach-ing reading each reinforced the other's positive effects. Ordinary school reading texts do not seem to have similar communicative qualities or effects.

We also noted additional positive results. In our 1985–1988 study with newspapers as sole reading texts we found that the parents of the study's subjects were highly interested in the experiment. We also found that both the children and their parents talked about the reading texts being used, on an almost daily basis, not because of the exceptionality of such texts, but more often because of their interesting contents. The parents seemed as happy as their children that the usual question, 'How was school today?' was replaced by their mutual interest in topics about which the children were then reading. These parents behaved therefore in the same supportive way as the parents did in Bloom's (1985) famous interview study of 120 US geniuses.

In his text, *Conversations in Comparative Education with Torsten Husén*, Tjeldvoll (Tjeldvoll and Lingens 2000) quotes Husén's view on '. . . parental commitment, which has been diminishing. This is what we have found in all highly industrialised countries. To an increasing extent the family does not involve itself in the school. In many instances it does not care at all.' (p. 35). Deprived of parental help, students have to rely on school teaching to develop their reading skills. In a follow-up study from 1958 to 1988 (Edfeldt 1962) we found that only those individuals who had learned to read before entering elementary school were able to reach the highest achievement levels. We concluded that these students were the only ones who stood a chance of escaping the notoriously bad effects of the traditional synthetic methods used in Swedish elementary schools.

Gifted education in mathematics

A short background

The general educational situation for the gifted students in Sweden, as described above, also applies to students with high mathematical abilities. Few schools offer able children any special assistance, which means that even students who have developed an interest in mathematics at a young age may soon get bored of the subject as it is presented at school. International evaluations, such as TIMSS (Trends in International Mathematics and Science Study) (Mullis et al. 2004) and PISA (Programme for International Student Assessment) (Swedish National Agency for Education 2004), show that many Swedish students have negative attitudes towards mathematics pared with poor results. Clearly something needs to be done.

During the 2002 ECHA summer conference in Nijmegen the Swedish representative, Åke Edfeldt, who had struggled for years to establish gifted education as a research field in Sweden, prepared an introductory activity plan for the period 2003–2005. This plan was sent to the Swedish Ministry of Education together with a proposal that national funds should be used for development projects in gifted education, located at two relatively new universities, one in the north and one in the south of Sweden. In the Swedish government's budget bill of 2002/03 two million Swedish crowns were allocated for the advancement of gifted education in Sweden, one million to each of the two universities.

Due to unfortunate circumstances, the project in the north of Sweden, specialising in musically able students, was never properly implemented. However, the project in the south of Sweden, located at Växjö University and specialising in gifted education in mathematics, was soon underway. The government funds were used to plan for and implement a teacher-training course on gifted education in mathematics which ran for the first time in 2005 and which is still offered as a distance course to Swedish teachers and teacher candidates. The government funds were also used to prepare for a research project on gifted education in mathematics, the first of its kind in our country. In 2004 the application was approved by the Swedish Research Foundation for the period 2005–2007. The project is carried out by a group of three senior researchers and two research students with Inger Wistedt functioning as project leader (Wistedt 2005). We have now received funding from the Swedish Research Foundation for a continuation of that project for the period 2008–2010.

Ongoing research efforts

Concern for the education of students with keen interests and high abilities in mathematics has a long international research history. However, these advancements have had a minimal impact on research and practice in Sweden. The public debate on mathematics learning has mostly focused on students' deficiencies in mathematics, a trend even more pronounced in the backwash of recent international comparative studies (PISA, TIMSS) which show that Swedish students are lagging behind in the international ranking of learning outcomes and attitudes towards the subject. However, focusing on pupils' learning difficulties tends to colour teachers' perspectives on their pupils as well as their views of the subject to be learnt. We firmly believe that it would serve all students better if teachers were to look for talent and ability in their students instead of failure and deficits.

When our project started, we discovered that it is hard to change the perspectives on mathematics teaching and learning which have dominated the Swedish school debate for decades. Thus, we have spent much time over the last three years countering the many myths about mathematically able students, which are rooted and nurtured in Swedish society. Many associate such students with elite schools for the already privileged. But students with a mathematical aptitude are not a homogeneous group, nor are they privileged (Winner 1996). They have different social backgrounds, different interests, and some of them do not attain the levels of achievement matching their potential (Mönks et al. 2000). Preliminary results from our ongoing project show that high-ability students exist in many Swedish classrooms, but that they often lack the opportunity to develop their abilities, finding little challenge in textbooks, the use of which dominate pedagogical practice. In case studies we have observed mathematically able students over a period of three years, and we have found that much could be done to help these students grow intellectually and socially, if good practices in identification of high-ability students were to be accompanied by good teaching practices adapted to these students' needs.

Let us provide an example from a case study of a highly talented boy whom we met at the beginning of our project and have followed through his three school years in junior high school (grades 7–9, 13–15 years of age). This boy was certainly privileged in the sense that he was born into a family where the parents took an interest in the development of their child and were sensitive towards his developing talents and interests; not in the sense that they trained him in any particular area, but they were keen observers of his developing abilities, praised him for even small efforts in his chosen fields of interest, and encouraged his mathematical curiosity. His father and grandfather were powerful role models, both of them interested in mathematics. His mother took an interest in his creative play with building blocks where he often constructed complex patterns. When travelling, the family passed their time by engaging in logical quizzes and multiplication games, and when the child started school he was familiar with all four fundamental rules of arithmetic and a lot more.

This playful way of familiarising him with mathematics was followed when he arrived at school by a textbook-based instructional method dominated by pen-and-pencil calculations in books of sums. Since he already knew how to do these calculations in his head, he swiftly worked his way through the books. When he was done with one book he was given another, and another, until he had covered all books from grade one to grade six. This happened in grade four, and by that time he was bored with school mathematics. Since he was a long way ahead of all the other pupils in his class, he was allowed to spend his time on other matters. And he did. His mathematics was put on hold.

We met him when he was in grade seven. When we tested him we found that he had an astonishing logical ability, he was independent in his reasoning, he had a well-developed mathematical imagination, but he had problems tracing his routes of thought and he was unfamiliar with the terminology used to communicate mathematics to other people. No wonder! Covering mathematics textbooks had for years been a lone occupation, which had eventually bored him rigid. Being ahead of all the others had also isolated him from his peers, which he reacted to by hiding behind bulky clothes, and at our first meeting he entered the classroom wearing a headset, demonstrating that he was not interested in communicating with us. Today he has changed his dress habits, and he is now taking part in the social life of his class.

How did this transformation happen? During the last two years he has had a tutor who has observed him and given him challenging tasks to work on. He has been encouraged to work with two other talented students in the class, which has led to a vast improvement in his communicative skills. When we were invited to a regional television show to present our ongoing project on gifted education in mathematics, we asked him and a highly talented girl in the same class to accompany us and to demonstrate how they worked on challenging mathematical problems. Not only did he solve a rather complex mathematical task in real time, but he also succeeded in presenting two rather different solutions to it in a concise and simple way.

Moreover, he adapted to an audience who could not be expected to be familiar with high-level mathematics.

Could this be a solution to be used to inspire and support other highly able students? Probably not. First of all, there is no one solution that could suit all mathematically able students. As mentioned, they are not an homogeneous group. Second, we will not, in the foreseeable future, be able to recruit fully educated tutors to meet the needs of all these students. Survey studies conducted within our current project show that lack of resources paired with the myth that these students will develop their talents regardless of educational support, results in a situation where very little is done to help able students develop their abilities – even if this is their right according to Swedish law.

Future plans

The Swedish educational system is, like most other publicly funded school systems around the world, based on the administrative logic that school children should be grouped by age. When compulsory school attendance was introduced in the 1900s, this was a convenient system for grouping pupils, and was seen as necessary for making sure that all students entered school at a certain age. It may still be a convenient model, since children in the same age group tend to have much in common. As mentioned before, we do not believe in separating young children from their peers and playmates by taking them out of their original school forms (Reed 2004). But since children's needs do not always follow their biological age, we need to expand the borders of the classroom in order to give highly able students a proper chance to develop their talents. What we wish to do is to find ways to enrich the intellectual and social environment of these students within and outside of their ordinary classrooms.

As mentioned above, we have recently received funding for a continuation of the current project for the period 2008 to 2010. In this new project we wish to further our understanding of how mathematical abilities can be developed innovatively within ordinary classrooms by bringing mathematics into the modern world of human communication. Mathematics is primarily based on textbook presentations of the subject. This does not apply only to Swedish schools but is a common way of presenting mathematics in most countries. If we obtain funding we plan to develop ICT (Information and Communication Technology)-settings where modern technology is used to create collaborative math-learning communities amongst high-ability students. This will make it possible for students with a keen interest in mathematics to meet with other students who share their interest and with whom they can collaborate on equal terms.

In this new project, we will adopt a dialogical approach to learning, focusing on students' communicative projects when learning mathematics – an approach that also permeates our views of other mathematical activities and abilities. The technological tools to be used in the project are developed by the CeLekt group at Växjö University within two international projects sponsored by the European Union. These tools are made available to us through our collaboration with a national project, 'Young Communication' (http://www.ungkommunikation.se), sponsored by the Swedish Knowledge Foundation. The interactive tools will be developed and adapted to mathematics learning by a multidisciplinary research team representing the fields of mathematics, computer science and education; they will also be implemented and evaluated by the team in co-operation with teachers, teacher candidates and, not least, with the students taking part in the study.

Concluding statement

It is obvious even from our short discussion of the first public endeavour to introduce gifted education into the Swedish national school system that persistence pays off and that there is always hope for change – even for late starters. Today Sweden has a gifted education movement that is fully functioning and capable of funding itself as far as continual research is concerned. Our priorities are now to link these research efforts to the training of ECHA-certified teachers. Sweden already has an ECHA-approved curriculum and two full professors with the ECHA ordinance to examine Swedish ECHA student teachers. And, of course, all of this will benefit the many gifted students in Sweden, who within a ten-year period we hope will have a chance to develop in accordance with their qualifications and their civic rights.

Contact address: ingerw@ped.su.se

Future Perspectives

Suggested priorities for gifted education over the next decade

It is obvious even from our short description of the first public endeavour to introduce gifted education into the Swedish National School System that persistence pays off and that there is always hope for change – even for late starters. Today Sweden has a gifted education movement, which is fully functioning and capable of funding itself as far as continual research is concerned. Our priorities are now to link these research efforts to the training of ECHA-certified teachers. Sweden already has an ECHA-approved curriculum and two full professors with the ECHA ordinance to examine Swedish ECHA-student teachers. And, of course, all of this is for the benefit of the many gifted students in Sweden, who within the mentioned ten-year period eventually will have their chance to develop in accordance with their qualifications and their civic rights.

Åke W. Edfeldt and Inger Wistedt

11

A proposal for gifted education in reluctant schools: the case of the Greek school system

Elias G. Matsagouras and
Evangelia Dougali
University of Athens, Greece

In Europe, the idea of fostering intellectual excellence can be traced back to the ancient Greeks. Plato's *Republic* grouped society into classes based on intelligence. Only those who performed well in advanced studies could undergo further training to become philosopher-kings. As far as choosing the rulers of the future, Plato asserted that a higher education – namely, the studies of geometry, astronomy and other disciplines of the highest order – be assigned to the surest and the bravest and those with natural gifts which would surely facilitate their education (Tannenbaum 2000). Plato was convinced that the survival of Greek democracy was dependent on the education of those excellent citizens who were going to work in leading positions.

Unfortunately, a commitment to the full development and understanding of one's special abilities and special talents is not a feature of the modern Greek school system, where educational objectives have focused primarily on the needs of average students. The Greek Ministry of Education and Religious Affairs is responsible for the administration of the educational system, which has been shown over a long period to be catering poorly for the educational needs of gifted and talented students, and which in fact has been characterised by the absence of any strategic policy (Matsagouras 2000). During the last 15 years, some secondary public schools have started to accept and support students with musical talent, and only in the big cities are there classes to support athletes. There are no schools to support and educate any other category of gifted and talented students. Moreover, special classes, schools, enrichment programmes, and acceleration procedures are not available, at any level, either in the Greek public school system or in the majority of private schools.

As far as education for highly able students is concerned, Greek primary and secondary education teachers are inadequately trained, and in-service training does not exist (Pigiaki 1995; Starida 1995). Although an interest in supporting gifted and talented students is slowly emerging, it is accompanied by a suspicion of elitism and the fear that it might lead to an undemocratic education. The purpose of this chapter, therefore, is to present a plan for educating gifted and talented learners in the Greek centralised school system, a plan that is feasible with currently available human, material and technical resources, and that will benefit the Greek education system as a whole.

The needs and rights of the gifted and talented

Education is acknowledged worldwide as a fundamental right for everyone. This does not mean, however, that all students benefit from the same education. Clark (1997) stated that '. . . in a democracy, equal opportunity cannot and must not mean the same opportunity' (p. 7). She further argued that unchallenged individuals frequently become bored, discouraged, and angry, and suffer physical and psychological pain, creating a critical need for improving services for the gifted. On this basis, Greece must develop the most appropriate education policy in relation to the needs of all pupils, with a view to promoting educational opportunity and enabling all young people to develop their potential to the full.

Providing equal opportunities for learning is a basic principle of every democratic society, and a country's educational system plays a significant role in the fight against social inequality. Equal opportunities should be provided to all pupils, including those who belong to minority groups, as well as those with disabilities and other special educational needs, so that they can be helped to conquer issues like societal exclusion or unemployment. Providing equal opportunities for learning should not be interpreted, however, as providing uniform educational benefits that lead to uniform abilities and behaviours. Providing for the gifted and talented pupils in our schools is a question of equity. As with all other pupils, they have a right to an education that is suited to their particular needs and abilities.

Social and educational context

It is evident, then, that an emphasis should be placed on the implementation of gifted and talented education services in the Greek public education system. As elsewhere, gifted education has had to wait until other priorities were attended to, with the result that it has all too often been ignored. In order to be accepted by the educational community and Greek society in general, an educational plan for provision for gifted and talented students, should fulfil two basic requirements. First, it should be feasible with currently available human, material, and technical resources. Second, it should be of educational benefit for the whole education system.

Taking into account relevant international research, experience, and developments in gifted education, as well as current trends in the Greek educational system, in this chapter we present a plan for provision for the gifted and talented children in Greece. In developing this plan, we took into consideration the following components: (a) the inadequacy of the regular classroom as it functions today to address the cognitive, emotional, and social needs of gifted and talented students; (b) the fundamental rights of all students to develop their potentials to the full, through an education that is suited to their particular needs and abilities; and (c) the philosophy that a child should be considered gifted only when their learning needs exceed those of their peers, so that special adaptive programming is required.

Gifted educational policy and practice ought to focus on about 20,000 primary school pupils, or 2 to 3 per cent of the student population. The same percentage may be considered talented in the visual and performing arts. We suggest that provision for the gifted and talented population should: (a) meet the learning and developmental needs of students who demonstrate high intellectual and performance abilities or potential abilities; (b) constitute a comprehensive programme of intervention, and be accessible and acceptable to all parties concerned (families, teachers, administrators, pupils); and (c) incorporate support for the education of gifted and talented children into special education funding, under Law 3194/2003, which refers to gifted/talented students as students with special educational needs (this law seeks further to develop special programmes and teaching methods, as well as requiring improvements in the availability of specialist materials, aids, and services [European Agency 2003]).

As for our view concerning the nature of giftedness itself, the Greek model rests on a multidimensional conceptualisation that includes multiple abilities and factors, focusing on the needs of the whole child (intellectual, academic, social/emotional, physical). By including these abilities and recognising that different profiles/types of intelligence might exist, we seek to base our identification procedures and provision model on a synthesis of Gardner's multiple intelligences theory (1983), Renzulli's triad model of giftedness (1977), and Sternberg's triarchic theory of intelligence (1997c) and his recent wisdom, intelligence, and creativity synthesized (WICS) model (2003c).

We recommend school-based enrichment programmes, acceleration practices and cluster groupings of gifted students in 600 to 650 'reception schools' all over the country. To create this number of schools, the heads of the directorate and education offices, and education officers at the prefecture level of government, will decide which schools in their region should accommodate the needs of the gifted and talented students. For the needs of the programme, the Peiramatika (experimental) schools that operate in every region, and the primary schools which accommodate 'integration classes' and 'reception classes' (classes which have been established to provide for the needs of immigrant groups), can be used. If we estimate that six trained schoolteachers are required for each reception school, the total number of teachers that should be trained will be roughly 4,000. Furthermore, it will require the appointment of 1,800 gifted education teachers to undertake the role of gifted and talented education co-ordinators at school and district levels.

In addition we suggest the need to develop curriculum resources. The Department of Primary Education of the University of Athens and the Pedagogical Institute (PI) can take on this task. The latter is a consultative body to the Ministry of Education, and its field of responsibility is curriculum development, overseeing the writing of textbooks and the study of matters related to primary and secondary education.

Identification of giftedness

Correct identification of giftedness and talent is essential to providing highly able learners with an appropriate education. This can be a difficult task. We know that bright students are often confused for gifted students, and gifted underachievers are often overlooked. Based on recommended best practice in the field of gifted education, we have included three basic components in our proposal that pertain to identification: nomination, assessment and notification of parents.

The identification process begins with nomination. Identification of gifted and talented pupils should start as early as kindergarten, so that high ability can be given the maximum opportunity to develop to its full potential. The reason for considering such early years identification is that we know early childhood to be a crucial stage of life in terms of children's physical, intellectual, emotional, and social development. In the first few years of their lives, children are receptive to new ideas and cognitive restructuring at a greater speed (Koshy 2002). Important considerations include that nominations should be made annually, every student must be considered, nominations must be accepted from any source, and parents must be given information about the identification process. Identification of gifted children should be transparent, non-discriminatory, flexible and effective. That means that a variety of objective and subjective measures are needed.

Suggested objective measures include standardised tests of achievement and aptitude that are valid, reliable, and free from bias. Nominating students with high standardised test scores helps to guarantee that underachievers who have strong domain-specific reasoning skills, but who do not show their abilities through their performance in classrooms, will be included. Such measures are economical and relatively uninfluenced by teacher bias.

Suggested subjective measures include teacher nominations based on subject-specific checklists, and parent nomination, peer nomination, and self-nomination (Balchin 2007a). Teachers often notice talents in students that are not necessarily reflected by school grades. Students who are very creative or have unusual or special areas of interest are frequently overlooked when nominations are based on standardised testing alone. There are also many situations where test scores are not available. Therefore, teachers have much to offer when assessing students' abilities; in fact, teacher nomination is one of the most widely used and recommended means for identifying the gifted and talented (Balchin 2007a). Along with teacher nominations, we suggest the use of student portfolios, performance-based assessments and projects that involve collaboration with peers as supplements to standardised testing.

Notification of parents is the next step. The Department of Primary Education of each region will send a letter of notification to the parents of all students who have been nominated. The letter should include a comprehensive description of the identification process. It should also explain the nature of the school that their child may become eligible to attend, if identified as gifted, and invite parents for an orientation meeting. Once students are nominated, their names will be placed in a talent pool and all individuals in the talent pool will be screened. Multiple instruments must be used, so that a student cannot be denied admission to the gifted and talented education programme based on one single assessment. All screening instruments will be based on current research and theory, and their reliability and validity must have been thoroughly proven. The Centre(s) for Diagnosis Evaluation and Support (CDES) of each region will be responsible for offering models of screening instruments to help determine students' strengths. These centres are new institutions established by the Ministry of National Education and Religious Affairs, with the aim of locating, diagnosing, and supporting pupils with special educational needs or disabilities.

After all assessment data have been recorded for every student, a special committee based at each CDES (a committee comprised of educational psychologists and special education teachers) will decide whether or not each student is eligible either for admission into a reception school that provides a gifted and talented education programme, or for acceleration.

Acceleration

We recommend early entrance to primary school and grade skipping as two possible forms of acceleration for gifted students. Many gifted children are ready academically for school before the required age of admission, and they develop more rapidly than their classmates in the school environment. Early entrance allows students to graduate from school earlier and enter sooner into the practice of their careers and professional development (Gross 2004; Schiever and Maker 1997). It also cuts down on the cost of education because students are simply moved into existing programmes, requiring no additional resources for developing and instructing the curriculum. In order for early entrance to be successful, the identification process must be thorough, the teacher must be aware of the student's needs, and have a positive attitude towards acceleration (Mares and Byles 1994). We consider the latter strategy, grade skipping, to be effective also, but believe a child should not be accelerated in this way more than two grades or years ahead. Clearly, careful consideration should be given when deciding to use acceleration. A psycho-educational evaluation to determine a child's levels of ability in various academic and social areas is an essential tool when contemplating advanced grade placement.

Admission to reception schools

We believe that the best role of reception schools is to provide a wide range of challenging learning opportunities which enables each individual, including those with exceptional abilities, to realise their potential. Our commitment is to identify and meet the needs of gifted pupils stemming from our principles of

- ensuring equality and inclusion;
- facilitating the achievement of excellence;
- facilitating every pupil's achievement of her/his potential;
- raising achievement for all through a curriculum that is balanced, broad and appropriately differentiated;
- developing talents by providing opportunities that match the expectations and needs of our children.

The reception schools will develop specific programming plans for the students who have been admitted into them. School policies will be operated with flexibility to take into account individual needs and circumstances. Pupils' needs will be served by having a school with the highest possible emphasis on academic achievement, a rich and varied experience for all, and effective partnership with parents, pupils, teachers and members of the CDES. We estimate that each year group will have five to six gifted pupils who will be clustered in a mixed-ability classroom. The number of gifted/talented pupils in each reception school will be roughly 30 per year.

Differentiated teaching and learning in special cluster classrooms

We aim to differentiate curriculum and instruction. Following the advice of Pierce and Adams (2004), instruction may be differentiated in content (through the use of probing and open-ended questions), process (through the use of simulations, higher level thinking questions, and guided and unguided independent study) and/or product (by guiding students to gather exciting resources and demonstrate ways to put them to good use) according to the learning style, readiness or interest of the student. Content is differentiated with the use of more advanced and complex texts and resource materials, interdisciplinary learning, curriculum compacting and learning contracts. Curriculum compacting will be used to modify the regular curriculum so that previously mastered content is eliminated, seeking to avoid highly able students becoming bored with repetition, and also freeing up time for more challenging academic pursuits (Renzulli and Reis 2003).

The implementation of the new cross-thematic curriculum is working towards this, because by eliminating overlaps and minimising duplication, we aim to save time. The point of accumulating 'spare' time is to allocate it back to the students in order that they may use it to concentrate on developing the necessary core knowledge and skills in diverse subjects (Matsagouras 2004). In Greece's compulsory education, the timetable provides for the establishment of a 'flexible zone' programme. This programme comprises at least two teaching hours per week, and involves cross-thematic activities and projects. These aim at the qualitative upgrading of educational results. They also promote collective effort, the development of critical thinking, active participation of pupils, including those of high abilities, while at the same time allowing the teacher to take the initiative and act with flexibility in the context of upgrading and differentiating the teaching and learning.

Another way to teach gifted and talented students is through enrichment practices. When teachers learn how to differentiate the curriculum and provide for clusters of gifted pupils, they also learn to provide modified versions of the same opportunities to the entire class, thereby enhancing learning of all students (Winebrenner and Delvin 2001). In order to support self-directed learning and talent development, enrichment requires the design of interest-based curriculum extension activities. An enrichment programme should be a systematic plan for extended student learning (Schiever and Maker 1997). Thus, our enrichment programme goal will be to deepen and broaden the curriculum. It will include activities such as Saturday classes, summer classes and resources rooms, in addition to regular classroom curriculum and afternoon clubs based on pupils' interests. Summer and weekend programmes sponsored by universities will also be made available.

Reception schools will be in position to offer a variety of locally and nationally sponsored extracurricular opportunities, such as business studies, athletics, art, music and drama. Gifted students can heighten their strengths by becoming involved in extracurricular activities in areas that interest them. These activities also afford them the opportunity to develop positive social skills, such as co-operation and sportsmanship. This may give them a sense of belonging to a community of learners. Each school can provide access to the Internet, distance learning labs, universities, government agencies, and independent organisations, through which students can participate in courses that are not offered by their schools. These opportunities will enable gifted students to pursue their areas of interest to a degree of depth that is not possible within the regular curriculum.

Reception schools may also offer special classes through 'pull-out programmes', where pupils are pulled out of the regular classroom for specialised instruction in one or more specific academic areas. Burton-Szabo (1996) believes that these types of classes allow gifted students to '. . . use their creativity in unique ways, and have a teacher who understands their particular needs' (p. 12), giving them an important opportunity to interact with similarly gifted students. However, pull-out classes should not exceed 20–25 per cent of a student's total in-school time, because this would diminish opportunities for them to develop social skills in heterogeneous groups.

The gifted and talented education coordinators' duties will be similar to that which such co-ordinators carry out internationally. They will be responsible for developing a scope and sequence based on students' needs and interests. They should work with classroom teachers to help them carry out individual programming plans within and outside of the classroom, and with their district's gifted and talented education advisor. The district gifted and talented education advisor must also provide diverse resources and materials, technological support, and adequate funding. A variety of resources and tools, including updated technology, and sufficient funding are necessary in order to develop differentiated learning opportunities. The resources should be based on current research and theory and must be made easily accessible within the district. The funding should ideally be roughly equal to that of other comparable programmes within the district.

Administrative support and programme evaluation

The administration of this type of gifted and talented education service will require careful planning and organisation. Firstly, teachers must be appropriately trained in the education of gifted and talented students. We estimate that approximately 6,000 teachers should be trained in university departments of primary education or in long-duration training programmes, so that they will be capable of using the appropriate instructional approaches and personalising available educational materials.

Secondly, there will be a connection between the gifted and talented education services provided in reception schools and general education countrywide. The programme cannot operate independently from the regular classroom programmes. Gifted and talented education coordinators should work with classroom teachers to help them carry out individual programming plans within and outside of classrooms, and the gifted and talented education advisors of each district should also work with administrators to develop provisions for gifted and talented services.

Thirdly, positive collaboration among parents, teachers, students and the CDES specialists is critical. The goal will be to achieve ongoing collaboration among all parties concerned. This will involve putting the whole plan for the education of the child in writing so that parents may be kept 'in the loop', and ensure the system is working for them and their child. As Silverman (1991) points out, many parents feel inadequately prepared to raise a gifted child. A school district can help parents to understand their gifted child's emotional development by hosting meetings on various gifted and talented issues and by maintaining consistent communication regarding the child through regular conferences. When parents understand reasons for their child's behaviour, they have a better idea of how to respond to it.

Finally, the Ministry of Education and Religious Affairs must evaluate the effectiveness of the programme to ensure that it upholds the philosophy and standards that are defined by the administrators. Evidence of the effectiveness might include written evaluations from head teachers and from gifted and talented education co-ordinators, as well as short reports from classroom teachers and parents.

To conclude, we believe that society must fulfil two important promises to its children. The first is to prepare a world that accepts them, and provides them with opportunities to live, grow and create in safety. The other is to help them develop their whole being to the fullest in as many ways as possible. Education is our best vehicle for working to keep these promises, and our proposal for gifted education policies and practices can help us in that work.

Contact address: ematsag@primedu.uoa.gr

Future Perspectives

Suggested priorities for gifted education over the next decade

We believe that the best way to foresee the future of gifted education in Greece is to create it. Those of us who understand gifted children and their needs must advocate for them, and make the Greek ministry of education and other official institutes see the need for special provision and the value of devoting recourses in gifted education. The situation in Greece seems to have improved since the Greek Parliament introduced special educational provision to cater for those who have special mental abilities and talents. Nevertheless, progress in the field of gifted education can only be made if policy makers, practitioners, administrators, teachers and parents move beyond perceptions of the field as elitist. This can only be achieved by offering gifted programmes that serve students from all social backgrounds and ethnic groups, whether achievers, underachievers or handicapped, and by considering these programmes as an integral part of the general education system. Moreover, we need to help people see Reception Schools as schools that work to improve learning, intellectual stimulation and challenge for all pupils.   Elias G. Matsagouras and Evangelia Dougali

12

We can still do this, or can we? The Russian system of educating and promoting talent in mathematics and science

Ida Jeltova

City University of New York, US

Konstantin Lukin

Fairleigh Dickinson University, US

Elena L. Grigorenko

Yale University, US

In August 2006, a Russian mathematician from St. Petersburg named Grigori Yakovlevich Perelman was awarded the Fields Medal for his contributions to the fields of geometry and topology (specifically for his proof of the geometrisation conjecture, which includes the famous Poincaré conjecture as a particular case). In December 2006, *Science* acknowledged Perelman's discoveries as the 'Breakthrough of the Year'. Perelman declined the award, did not appear at the award ceremony at the International Congress of Mathematicians in Madrid, and has been avoiding media attention. Nonetheless, his achievement drew attention to his biography and, subsequently, to the Russian tradition of educating gifted youth. Perelman was educated and trained during the Soviet era, with its government-sponsored specialised schools, university programmes and research institutions emphasising mathematics and science over other disciplines and guaranteeing conditions for talent development. The contemporary Russian educational system is struggling with the many economic and social issues that resulted from the global instability following the collapse of the Soviet Union, when much of the financial, political, and social support for education in general and gifted education in particular eroded.

This chapter addresses the current state of affairs in mathematics and science education for the gifted in post-Soviet Russia and describes (a) the infrastructure of gifted education; (b) the identification of giftedness; (c) the nature and scope of gifted and specialised programmes (and schools), with a separate discussion of programmes in mathematics and science; and (d) the trajectory of talent development and realisation (i.e. performance in mathematics and science olympiads for youth compared with adult employment). The chapter expands and supplements the discussion offered in Yurkevich and Davidovich (this volume) on general trends in the education of gifted children in Russia and focuses specifically on such trends in the teaching of mathematics and science, the domains in which gifted education in Russia has previously been recognised as one of the world-leaders (Grigorenko 2000). Today, there are many interesting innovations in teaching the social sciences and humanities to gifted children, but this field is still in development and needs further crystallisation.

The infrastructure of contemporary Russian education for gifted children

Overall, contemporary Russian gifted education is centralised but only in part sponsored by specialised federal funds and initiatives (Donoghue et al. 2000; Dorfman 2000; Grigorenko 2000; Jeltova and Grigorenko 2005; Post 2005). Regions of the Russian Federation establish and run their own programmes for gifted youth. Talent development is now more commonly supported through extra-curricular activities delivered in specialised centres rather than through school-based programming. Moscow and St. Petersburg stand alone in that their school and after-school programmes for gifted children remain the most intact.

Financial support for gifted education comes from both governmental and private sources. In the late 1980s, many schools for the gifted were started by the government with government funds. At the same time, legal regulations for education were modified and the country witnessed a proliferation of 'alternative' schools. Alternative schools were often run by enthusiastic, highly educated teachers, scientists, psychologists and parents, who made schooling child-centred as opposed to the achievement-centred, product-oriented schooling of traditional schools. Alternative schools attracted most gifted students away from public (federal) schools. Soon after this brief period of autonomy, legal mandates were introduced that effectively eradicated most of the alternative gifted schools by withdrawing federal support and making it very difficult for schools to accept private help from sponsors. The combination of limited financial support, strict regulation of the schools' financial activities, great pressure to focus on 'profitable' activities and overall social instability began to re-shape gifted education in mathematics and science, spurring modifications in traditional programmes and innovations in new ones.

For example, the highly respected Lavrentiev Physics–Mathematics Boarding School (Evered and Nayer 2000), which developed leading mathematics and science professionals by selecting talented students and then providing them with a rigorous curriculum, began to offer programmes in humanities, language, business and economics. As the Russian government shifted its focus from producing the finest scientists to succeeding in a market-driven economy, funds for schools became limited. Now, teachers earn minimal salaries and are often forced out of the field. Many schools need to charge tuition and therefore fill some of their seats with students who can afford to pay as opposed to the brightest and most gifted children. These changes in curriculum and student population are likely to have an impact on gifted education and on Russian performance in mathematics and science in the decades to come.

In 1996, by a decree from the Ministry of Education, regulations for specialised classes in mathematics and science were modified as well (for comparison, see Grigorenko and Clinkenbeard 1994). The selection criteria for these classes were loosened and allowed typically developing children with a higher than average interest and ability in mathematics and a sound knowledge of eighth grade mathematics to be accepted. Prior to 1996, specialised classes accepted only highly able students with evidence of significantly above average ability in mathematics or science. The curriculum for specialised classes, however, did not change. In these, the regular curriculum is enhanced and stresses a thorough development of the pupils' abilities and potential by amplifying educational opportunities (e.g. for entry into scholastic competitions or higher-education institutions).

To reflect the diverse needs of Russian youths, in 2002 a number of new programmes were created under a programme called 'Children of Russia' [*Deti Rossii*]. In particular, a programme called 'Gifted Child' [*Odarenyi Rebenok*] was established to identify, support and secure the growth of gifted learners in the Russian Federation. The government appropriated 200,950,000 rubles (US$783,705, or £388,637) for this programme; some financial support also came from non-governmental agencies (10,400,000 rubles; US$405,600, or £197,600).

Gifted Child is an ambitious programme. It aspires to increase the number of gifted children for whom government support is warranted; create a systematic approach to working with gifted children; improve pedagogy for gifted children; and provide the necessary technology for the gifted programme, among other goals. In addition, the programme aims to inform the public of issues and concerns regarding the education of the gifted in Russia and to deliver training to professionals working with the gifted. Gifted Child is delivered via the National Center for Gifted Children across seven regions headed up by regional offices.

In general, throughout Russia, the Gifted Child initiative has already been shown to increase the number of olympiad participants, both regionally and nationally. Specifically, an analysis of participation has shown annual growth in the number of participants in national (all-Russia) scholastic olympiads in mathematics, physics, chemistry and biology. The number of Russian prizewinners in international competitions has also increased: in 2004, 23 participants were awarded diplomas for first, second and third place. In 2005, that number climbed to 28 and leapt to 37 in 2006.

In terms of funding, the majority of support comes from the Russian government; it is appropriated through the national Gifted Child programme and distributed through its regional and local offices. There is also help from a variety of private donations and local sources, but this funding constitutes a minor portion of the overall support for gifted education. In addition, a number of schools charge tuition. In terms of structure, the system preserved many of its old features, capitalising on the Soviet tradition of boarding and specialised schools and after-school programmes. In terms of content, gifted programmes are extremely diverse and reflect national and local economical, political, and cultural influences. Here we describe some regional and local realisations of the programme. Snapshots of the various programmes indicate their diversity.

Ingushetiya region

The Ingushetiya region, adjacent to Chechnya, has been riddled with political and social conflicts. Financial support for the gifted programme in Ingushetiya comes from the regional budget and is meant to stimulate and promote gifted education. More specifically, students are awarded grants for winning all-Russian and international scholastic olympiads. The system of science and mathematics olympiads was developed in the former Soviet Union and is now sustained in the Russian Federation primarily for two reasons: (a) to identify the most precocious and talented youth throughout the vast and many regions of the country; and (b) to prepare Russian teams for international competitions. The olympiad system typically penetrates all levels of the educational system (school, district, city/town, region, republic, country) to identify successive winners who then participate at the higher level competitions. Winners of these olympiads are held in high regard and are invited to participate in television programmes that celebrate academic achievement. As a result of the federal initiative, children from the Ingushetiya region have been increasingly represented in international and national scholastic olympiads over the past three years.

Krasnodar region

The Krasnodar region has expanded the Gifted Child initiative to include sporting and cultural events. Hence, dozens of different cultural and sporting events, musical festivals and exhibitions of technical and artistic creativity have been sponsored by the programme since its inception. Local youth has participated and even excelled in these regional and international art and music festivals.

Far East Region

The development and realisation of the Gifted Child initiative in the Far East Region has led to creative competitions, educational projects, and regional sports competitions for nearly 2,000 children and adolescents. Regional winners in the research competitions (similar to US science fairs) have taken part in national research competitions and been awarded diplomas and medals for national achievement. To foster success in these gifted programmes, the Far East Region has created specific gifted boarding schools or 'scientific centres', which rely heavily on training seminars that emphasise organisational skills, development of students' theoretical and practical ability, decision making, and formulation of scientific inquiry.

Identification of giftedness

Traditional practice dictated the use of criterion-referenced assessments, prior performance, and interviews in the process of identifying giftedness. Today, in general, there is currently no single uniform practice for identifying giftedness in the Russian system, which has led to a great variety of selection procedures that schools can use. Some schools require a general background check for a child's 'giftedness' Some merely let the teachers determine whether they consider any individual teachable (Zhilin 2007). Other schools have a more formal process. For example, applicants to Lavrentiev Physics–Mathematics Boarding School must first participate in mathematics and physics competitions. The most successful students (winners and near-winners) get invited to the summer programme as a trial run to determine whether they are qualified to be admitted to the school's full-time programme. No more than half of the students who take the entrance exam at the end of the summer will be admitted to the programme, and it is only after two and a half months, during which they must prove their commitment and adjustment to the school, that they may be inducted formally into the school. More than half the students who graduate from Lavrentiev Physics–Mathematics Boarding School work as professionals in the fields of mathematics and science.

Some schools, such as the All-Russian Specialised Boarding Schools (serving children in various regions of the country), involve three years of study. Pupils in these schools study mathematics and physics extensively, having more classes in these subjects than they would in an ordinary school. Very often, university professors teach in these schools. After completion, these students are more likely to attend competitive universities such as Moscow State University and compete successfully in olympiads. For example, from 1963 to 1980, students attending one such programme in Moscow won 14 first, 29 second, and 27 third prizes in the All-Soviet-Union Olympiad. This school uses performance indicators (e.g. results from mathematics and science fairs and olympiads) as admission criteria. Currently, in collaboration with colleagues from St. Petersburg University in Russia, we are translating and adapting a new test for giftedness, the Aurora Battery, based on Sternberg's triarchic theory of intelligence (Chart et al. 2007). Hopefully, the availability of the Aurora Battery in Russian will diversify the portfolio of tests available there for the identification of gifted students.

The nature and scope of gifted education

In response to the 1996 decree from the Russian Ministry of Education, mentioned earlier, some regular schools began to label themselves as special mathematics and physics schools. Not all of these schools are truly special in any way; however, some of the new schools do indeed have programmes that can rightfully be called specialised or gifted, and it remains to be seen whether these newly labelled schools will be able to survive amidst the creation of so many truly specialised schools.

Programmes do exist to support the intellectual growth of students who do not attend special schools but are still interested in mathematics and physics, but they are limited and poorly funded. In some ordinary schools, 'math weeks' are held to spur pupils' interests. Some schools are affiliated with universities and have specific scientific centres. Other schools have special mathematics classes that are taught by professors instead of regular teachers. Evening mathematics classes and summer programmes are sometimes offered at youth centres to prepare for mathematics olympiads. Here we briefly describe some of the enrichment regimens at a handful of specialised schools.

For example, Lavrentiev Physics–Mathematics Boarding School emphasises discipline and diligence. Students wake up at 7.15 a.m. and classes run from 8.30 a.m. to 9.25 p.m. Students go to bed at 11.00 p.m. The school requires a core set of classes in mathematics, science, Russian language, literature and physical education. In addition, students must spend four class hours per week in elective courses on priority subjects like mathematics, physics and biology and two hours in humanities courses. Students receiving a mark or grade of 2 (out of 5) can be expelled from the school.

The Novgorod Lyceum and Boarding School for gifted children

The Novgorod Lyceum and Boarding School for gifted children offers unique opportunities for gifted education at the secondary and tertiary levels. The curricula of its 15 classes were developed with consideration of concentration areas: linguistics, physics and mathematics, technology, chemistry and biology, history and philology, social studies, and economics. The school offers quality facilities to its students, including a psychological centre, a medical and health centre, a counseling centre, and a sports complex, and is a venue for a number of all-Russian competitions. The Lyceum describes itself on its website as promoting education not only for knowledge, but also for social maturity, character, leadership and citizenship.

Some schools have initiated experimental programmes in their academic curriculum to reflect the Ministry of Education's revisions to the national standards. Public School 92 in the Rostov-na-Donu Region focuses on developing the mathematical skills of its students. To that end, the school is designed to accommodate scholastic olympiads, competitions and conferences. Teachers are encouraged to conduct research in their fields of interest. Parents are provided with resources and consultation to help their children achieve the highest standard. The school evaluates its 'high standard' by improvement in progress and quality of work, frequency of olympiad winnings, and the rate of acceptance of its students to colleges and universities.

In some regions, after-school programmes have been developed to reflect the growing needs of children identified as gifted. Specialised coordination centres were established across the Stavropol' area in response to the call for school reform. With the support of the regional committee on the affairs of youth, after-school centres were created to promote and deliver 'education for the future' in a variety of domains, from foreign languages and thinking strategies to astronomy. Youths come to these centres to gain more advanced knowledge in a variety of domains; classes and group activities are typically led by professionals (e.g. university/college teachers, engineers, researchers). In Stavropol', 'A Small Academy of Sciences' [*Malaya Akademiya Nauk*] is a voluntary association of pupils of the senior high school classes (grades 7–11) studying at comprehensive public schools. This extracurricular establishment was created as a place for youth to conduct research and create inventions after school under the direction of experts (scientists and upper-level students, employees of research establishments, teachers).

The Lyceum of Chelyabinsk carries out the Gifted Child initiative in the Ural'skii region through a programme called 'The Ecology of Creativity' [*Ecologiya Tvorchestva*]. The Lyceum is a creative association of teachers, psychologists, scientists and parents whose purpose is to reveal, educate, and promote conditions for realising the potential of gifted children. The education process in the Lyceum emphasises creativity. Various forums allow for an exchange of ideas and dialogues that help gifted children realise their potential. The Ecology of Creativity is geared toward identifying uniqueness, creativity, cognitive ability, logical thinking, 'outside the box' thinking and the preservation of spiritual and moral values. Numerous training sessions are held every year to promote the social development of gifted children (training in dialogue, assertiveness, sensitivity and empathy, development of emotional stability and personal growth, and personal self-determination and goal setting).

The nature and scope of gifted education varies across regions, depending on traditions as well as financial and intellectual resources. The underlying assumption, however, is that the education for gifted children, in any form, is aimed at providing these children with a general education and much more, including both mastery of knowledge and academic competencies, as well as the acquisition of thinking skills and the ability to engage in research.

Olympiads as the ultimate criterion: past and current performance

Olympiads are the rigorous competitions – existing at the district, town, regional, national and international level – by which Russia has traditionally winnowed the field of academic excellence to identify its best and brightest minds.

The Russian Mathematics Olympiad for youth began in 1934 when a group of famous mathematicians initiated the first Leningrad City Mathematics Olympiad. By the 1940s and 1950s, many Soviet Republics had established regional mathematics olympiads, and the first All-Soviet-Union Olympiad took place in 1961. Already well-attended, the success of the USSR in space exploration generated interest in physics and astronomy as well, and a massive increase in participation caused the USSR Olympiad Committee to introduce the 'Republican' exam to reduce the number of participants in the final stages of competition.

First conducted in 1934 as the Leningrad Olympiad, the St. Petersburg Olympiad has been held annually ever since, except during the Second World War. The Olympiad is conducted by official city referees, who follow the general guidelines of all Russian Olympiads – at least since such guidelines were first introduced – but remain largely independent in their decisions and the development of competition problems. The St. Petersburg Olympiad has three rounds: a district-wide round, which is frequently attended by anyone who wants to take part, as well as by those who were advised to do so by a teacher; a written round for each city district; and an oral round, which is citywide. Each of the rounds is conducted separately for each grade; thus, those participating in the district-wide round – say, seventh graders from all the schools in the district (30–40 schools) – gather together in one of the schools for identical assignments.

This emphasis on mathematics education for the gifted is obvious in the performance of the Russian team in the international mathematics Olympiads, where it has placed in the top six every year, and been one of the top three teams in 15 of the past 22 years (http://www.imo-official.org). Similarly, physics olympiads remain a central element in gifted education in Russia, although international comparisons are not available.

The St. Petersburg Olympiad is one of the most prestigious mathematics olympiads in all of the former Soviet Union. To examine Olympiad performance as an indicator of future success and gather informed opinions on mathematics education Russia, Karp (2003) studied former St. Petersburg Olympiad participants and tried to evaluate how their lives turned out and to what degree they could be considered successful, as well as how they now viewed and rated their education. The search yielded 354 names; however, some of the participants were unreachable, mostly because of emigration in the 1980s and 1990s. A survey was sent to the remaining 148, once in 1991 and again to the same individuals in 2001.

The results of the survey were not terribly surprising. All of the respondents had received a higher education, an overwhelming majority of them at prestigious schools. And because an intensive mathematical education constitutes a highly valued aspect of Russian educational culture, the graduates of such prestigious specialised mathematics schools – including these Olympiad participants – form a notable proportion of the Russian *intelligentsia*. It is easy to name graduates from such schools who went on to become delegates in the Russian parliament or editors of the largest Russian newspapers; these graduates also constitute about 90% of the faculty of the mathematics department of St. Petersburg University.

In a case of those supporting a system that has led to their success, the respondents' views on education, and especially on mathematical education, proved to be conservative. The ideal was generally seen as the preservation and expansion of the type of education that had existed during the respondents' school years, without accounting for the changes that have taken place since that time. In 1991, in keeping with the dominant mood in intellectual circles, their views acquired a reformist tinge, while ten years later, again in keeping with the spirit of the times, they became noticeably more conservative.

It is difficult to make any judgements concerning the mechanisms responsible for success in gifted individuals. There are grounds for assuming that the most important step in the development of an academic or other career on the part of former Olympiad winners was entering a prestigious school. The statistics about Olympiad winners who did not attend the top three schools are unfortunately too sparse, but the fact that the financial situation of graduates of these schools has noticeably improved in recent years, when opportunities for further advancement have opened up, deserves consideration. However, responses to Karp's questionnaires also revealed the important role of individual teachers. Some statistics even reflect this importance, such as an increase in the number of Olympiad winners from one of the schools outside of the top three during the tenure there of one or another teacher (Karp 2003).

Conclusions

In this essay, we briefly outline the state of gifted education in mathematics and sciences in New Russia. In general, the federal educational system has preserved a tradition of early identification and specialised education of young talents, but forms and types of such education are much more 'localised' than ever before. It is reassuring that in these years of economic difficulty and the redefinition of the Russian Federation, its government is still concerned enough with gifted education to commit a substantial amount of money to it. Yet, although the Russian Federation still produces mature (as in the case of Perelman) and developing (in the case of Russian winners of international science and mathematics olympiads) talent, the impact of these changes can only be fully appreciated with time.

Completing this brief overview/illustration, we would like to comment on some general issues that pertain to the question of gifted education specifically in Russia. Any system of gifted education has to be of financial (although it might be potential!) value and practical importance to the country developing or maintaining such a system. The system of education for gifted children in mathematics and physics as that existed in 'Old' (Soviet) Russia was extremely valuable, both financially and reputationally, because it contributed to the system by developing a highly qualified cadre of scientists, for academia, industries and social practices and by enhancing the reputation of Soviet science and education around the world. The first, the financial, aspect was very important for establishing the continuity between identifying gifts and talents, providing proper education for them, and then realising both the abilities and knowledge in those most valued arenas of hard sciences and technology by guaranteeing jobs, salaries and possibilities for professional growth. Thus, the system was easily justifiable, both administratively and financially, since the early investment in the best schools for gifted children 'paid back' with innovations, discoveries, and hard, enthusiastic work at their jobs, delivered by gifted children educated through the system. Of course, this is in part an idealisation because many examples of dissidence and resistance to the regime came from this same population of highly educated individuals. However, in general, the system of gifted education in the Old Soviet Russia worked extremely well primarily due to this continuity between early identification of gifts, their proper upbringing, and their utilisation in the context of a technocratic society of which Soviet Russia was an example. The second, reputational, aspect was also important, but only in the context of the existing society with its clear priorities on the development of technology and industry. When that society dissolved, the first, financial, connection disintegrated very quickly – there were no or very few jobs in the early 1990s that still required highly talented and well-educated youth. As a result, the continuity broke and, financially, the New Russia experienced, for the first time, a huge loss rather than a gain from its system of gifted education; instead of employing the graduates of this system itself, it was 'letting them go' to find employment opportunities abroad. This development, from the country's cost-benefit analysis, called for a significant reorganisation of the system of gifted education. As a result, this system nearly disintegrated and is now rebuilding itself, based primarily on the remains of the old system and in the context of the programme 'Gifted Child'. This programme is also interested in building a positive reputation; so developing its 'presentational' aspect through the preparation and representation of participants from the Russian Federation in international competition is a relatively low-cost solution which is accomplishable primarily on the remains of the old system of gifted education. It is the restructuring and redesigning of the first, financial aspect that is difficult and requires collaboration between secondary and tertiary educational institution, the federal and local governments, and the advocates for gifted education. How, and if, this component is to be formed, are questions for the future. The structure of the economy of the New Russia is very different from that of the Soviet Union; guaranteed job placements are simply impossible and there are no direct connections any longer between tertiary educational institutions and the job market. And, unless such a financial connection is established, in one way or another, gifted education in Russia will remain what is it now – immersed in old traditions, but helpless in terms of protecting the future of the gifted and talented, innovative in aspects and places, but mostly fragmented and asystematic.

Acknowledgment

Preparation of this essay was supported, in part, by a generous gift from Karen Jensen Neff and Charles Neff. The authors also wish to thank Ms. Robyn Rissman and Ms. Mei Tan for their valuable editorial assistance.

Contact address: elena.grigorenko@yale.edu

Future Perspectives

Suggested priorities for gifted education over the next decade

As the Russian Federation undergoes changes, and stabilises and defines its political system, its educational system will keep reshaping as well. Currently, the system of gifted education in the Russian Federation is supported through two main federal programmes, Children of Russia and Gifted Children. Both programmes are not institutionalised and need regular reauthorisation and, thus, are both open to change and financially vulnerable. Right now, similar to what is going on in the educational system in general, the system of gifted education is extremely localised and fragmented. Based on the general trend toward centralisation common to many aspects of Russian life today, it is likely that gifted education will also become centralised and institutionalised, which, from one point of view, will add security to the system, but, from another point of view, will reduce the diversity of implementations that characterise Russian gifted education today.

Ida Jeltova, Konstantin Lukin and Elena L. Grigorenko

13

Russian strategies for talent development: stimulating comfort and discomfort

Victoria S. Yurkevich

Russian Academy of Education, Moscow, Russia

Boris M. Davidovich

Moscow City Psychological and Pedagogical University, Moscow, Russia.

A very brief history of Russian gifted education sets the scene for this chapter's exploration of two successfully implemented techniques for developing talent. In Russia, the year 1958 is generally acknowledged to be the year that we started knowingly to attempt the successful identification and provision for gifted children. It was the beginning of Russian liberalism, and the successes of our space programme propelled Russia visibly to the forefront of international public recognition in the field of scientific progress.

In this year, the first physics and mathematics school was opened in Moscow (the Moscow school No. 2), which attracted world famous mathematicians Israel Gelfand and Eugene Dynkin to teach there. The quality of the school was clear from the beginning; teachers treated pupils with respect and created a special atmosphere of learning. In 1964 new physics and mathematics boarding schools were established in the Universities of Moscow, Leningrad, Kiev and Novosibirsk. For the first time, our huge country (then the USSR) could be scoured for highly able children to receive tuition. The era of 'special schools' oriented precisely towards working with gifted children had started. Moscow School No. 57, started in 1968, is a good example. Forty years on, it is the top school in Russia for gifted education.

At present, although these 'special schools' for gifted children are notable for their higher quality of education (and consequent competitiveness for places), the differences between these and regular schools are relative. We know that, in a similar fashion to that which may occur around the world, there may be gifted children present in every non-'special' school and that a majority of each 'special' school probably consists of children who simply have shown a higher than average (rather than exceptional) ability.

One result of the restructuring of Perestroika (a term which has come to denote the economic reforms introduced in 1985 by the then Soviet leader Mikhail Gorbachev) was to create a definite countrywide system of working with gifted children. Sometimes in schools, it was little more than a formality, with a focus on assimilating gifted children with the rest of the class. However, more often than not, there were attempts in both regular and provincial schools to make this work rich in content and worthwhile for gifted learners. Now, for example, common and special courses, so-called masterclasses and practical training, have been put in place. Graduates from these institutions come back to work with gifted children who have specialist requirements that they may be able to support. Similarly, professional scientists are brought in to demonstrate their ideas and innovations. New methods that allow schools to work individually with each gifted child have been explored, despite the relatively large class sizes (25–30 children per class) common to Russian schools.

As far as extracurricular training is concerned, provision has been introduced via evening schools, summer and winter camps for gifted children. 'Olympiads' (or competitions) in many different subjects, especially the sciences, were introduced. The results of these are now one of the main criteria used by outsiders to judge the school's effectiveness. For example, the International Olympiad 'Tuymaada' is an annual competition for secondary school students held in Republic of Saka, Russia. The contestants compete individually, in four independent sections: computer science, mathematics, physics and chemistry. There are clearly many potentially negative issues that have been raised concerning this type of competition, but we have shown over the years that competition intensifies the rate of gifted child identification and raises the quality of their learning.

Another significant factor we face is that not all of our schools for the gifted have the same outlook as each other towards the children's education. For example, some are extremely demanding academically and demand high discipline levels whilst working, while others consider freedom whilst working to be paramount in the pursuit of excellence. Some schools consider that specialisation in the ability that the child is identified as possessing is necessary until 11–12 years old, while others try to do the opposite and develop a wider knowledge in the child for as long as possible, usually until 16 years of age. Some schools put forward the view that their main purpose is to give high-quality knowledge, and hold the development of creative thinking in lesser regard. Others regard their main purpose to be to teach children how to think creatively, considering that they themselves can obtain the knowledge they require.

Is there any optimal strategy for developing and educating a gifted pupil? This simple question can result in many diverse answers from distinguished educators around the world, and many of these are to be found in this book (see for example, Colangelo and Assouline; Treffinger; Nassab and Selby this volume). According both to the literature and our own long-term experience a basic problem faced by the highly gifted can be the difficulty in self-actualisation (achieving their potential) that they encounter after schooling. Though the majority of these children finish undergraduate programmes after leaving school and around 35–40 per cent of them write dissertations, only a very small proportion of gifted children, from 2 to 5 per cent, really achieve significant successes when growing. This percentage range was produced by counting the group of remarkable art workers, scientists, and social activists about whom enthusiastic epithets are often used.

We believe that the major reason for this is that the 'distance' between expectation levels from schools (where teachers and parents are often ambitious for the children and the children work very hard to realise their ambitions) and where the support network is removed (i.e. where children are on their own to 'sink or swim' in the real world) is great. A significant percentage of our gifted people who cannot realise their abilities during adolescence have been shown to display symptoms of depression. In the worst cases, this has culminated in 'existential neurosis' (Frankl 1967) and has contributed to the reasons for contemplating or committing suicide.

The problem seems to be worse for the exceptionally talented. It sounds like a paradox, but the prognosis for this small minority with obvious prodigious ability is more pessimistic than for children who display the levels of giftedness that would allow them access to the gifted education programmes. We have noticed that not only are the distances between hopes and realistic achievements greater in exceptionally talented children (this is clear from a mathematical point of view), but the achievements of those with 'normal' giftedness who have attended our programmes are usually higher than those of the exceptionally talented children. To combat this, the most crucial production to implement is an effective educational method for training gifted children, which effectively prepares them to accept and actualise their abilities as they mature. This goal, to create and implement an efficient educational experience to facilitate self-actualisation sounds obvious, but has barely been tackled yet in Russia. We believe that this emphasis is a priority for change over the next few years.

The idea of stimulating comfort or discomfort

For four decades we have examined the development of gifted children, including their development outside of school in their professional activities. We have found that those gifted pupils who achieve and become successful in creative activities usually have an intrinsic, constant requirement for difficult problem solving, and thrive on hard work. We do not think it is a surprise that the gifted people whom we know have achieved success in creative activity later in life usually have formed an explicit need for complex, hard work at an early age. However, this 'sweet, hard labour' that often requires maximal effort (or 'strained working') often never forms spontaneously in highly talented children, because they are used to improving in an intellectual way very easily. We believe that if the habit of working hard is developed at school age then it becomes a significant part of that person's mental outlook. To optimise this effect in highly talented children, it is necessary for them to have feedback concerning their creative activities, and for someone to judge task outcomes in relation to task requirements. This feedback need not be criticism *per se*, rather a helpful indicator for progression. However, the level of feedback should be defined individually for children according to their productions, opportunities and real levels of development (see Balchin this volume).

If the feedback and suggestions for improvement are too relaxed, they will not have the intended developing effect. If the criticism is too great, success will seem to be improbable and the child will lose interest in work. Optimal feedback, bordering on negative criticism, is especially important for highly talented children who are used to the ease of knowledge-acquisition, to its fascination and visible imperceptibleness. We want to see them work hard; strong-willed efforts should be obvious and constant for each child, especially a gifted child.

Stimulating a need for sustained mental work is therefore critical in order to teach the highly talented that they must also work hard for their successes. This will allow them mental strategies to diversify if necessary in later life, rather than remain in the comfort-zone of their exceptionalities. They will need to make a make a living once free of the academic arena. With this principle in mind, we define below the strategies of stimulating discomfort and comfort.

The general principle of stimulating comfort and discomfort embraces harmony. It is about teachers matching their high expectations of the gifted child with consideration and respect for their abilities. It is the harmony of a high academic load and the gifted child's opportunity to choose the content and level of difficulty of the work. It is the harmony of the child's responsibility and his or her freedom. It is also the harmony of the teacher's attitude to successes and failures of pupils matched with the level of difficulty of work and freedom they allow.

This concept of harmony is clearly an ideal; total harmony is unattainable as there are difficulties, problems and crises in every school. It is more like a question of strategy upon which the school is oriented. So what does this look like in reality? Firstly, let us consider the level of complexity in teaching. This is raised to a very high level; as a rule, this means very serious work with science (for example) instead of treating it as a school subject. In the senior classes pupils study mathematics at a professional level, thus avoiding duplication of a university course. We have found that very high loading of work does not destroy pupils, but becomes stimulating. The highly complex nature of the material is meant to challenge the children intellectually, rather than challenging them to cope with a large volume of set work. The number of class periods does not exceed the set physiological norms and the academic load is planned so that all pupils have the free time necessary for social development.

The discomfort strategy is implemented in particular by allocating one teacher to each child, or as near to that ratio as is possible. As a rule, these teachers are selected from the excellent young scientists, post-graduate students, or even current students of the Moscow State University. These teachers are told to demand excellent output from the gifted learners, but to regard themselves as close and benevolent colleagues to the students; to share ideas and material almost as equals or co-learners. Under their guidance, students quickly take charge of their own learning and as part of this, the content and depth of their own investigative work. Even the methods by which tasks will be achieved are discussed and targets agreed. Such a system helps us to ensure that each student is 'working on the edge', working hard and successfully at the level of difficulty suitable for him or her.

The teachers are in charge of giving appropriate feedback to the students concerning failures in their work. We ask the teachers not to shirk from their duty in admonishing students if their work is not up to the standard that they believe the student is capable of achieving. This criticism must be constructive, but should leave the student in no doubt that they have 'collided' with failure. It is important for the gifted child that risk of failure and failure itself (a large part of the preparation, and need, for creative action) become part of the child's mental outlook upon the world.

Due to the one-to-one ratio between teachers and students desirable for schools that are running this 'discomfort' strategy, we try to facilitate children to work in teams from the moment they join the schools. The children in these small teams, with five to six teachers accompanying them simultaneously in lessons, are gradually allowed to bond together by a general sense of the importance of hard work. Extra activities like museum visits and foreign trips are aimed at providing opportunities for teams to cement relationships between themselves to make a 'small learning unit'. This recipe for stimulating the need for complex work and for the intellectual and social development of the students has resulted in very impressive work emerging from schools using this strategy. For example, the majority of the Moscow School No. 57 graduates are professionally and socially successful, and every year at least a fifth of them go on to become high-level scientists in Russia and around the world.

The second strategy, that of stimulating comfort, has much in common with the strategy described above. For instance, the academic workload of pupils is again kept high, with an emphasis on complexity and intellectual difficulty rather than volume. Attention is given to encouraging the seeking of knowledge via research, rather than learning-presented information by rote. Children are taught in an individual way by teachers and are grouped together as collectives.

However, the 'comfort' strategy, as its name may suggest, advises a more liberal approach to study. Teachers will tend to present only the best marks of a student as indicators of performance, and students are encouraged to conduct much wider research work than the subject(s) they are required to study (unlike the focused study advised with the first strategy). No one forces the children to study hard and no punishments follow during the educational process, even if the pupil is judged to have prepared for the lessons badly and cannot cope with the difficulty of the programme. However, many schools, especially boarding schools, have a psychologist on hand to help with any problems, particularly because this strategy can creates a real pressure to deepen subject knowledge very quickly. There have been cases where interventions have been necessary in order to persuade some students to reduce the amount of subject knowledge they are absorbing, as the effort has made them physically ill.

Only those students inclined towards very serious mental work are therefore selected. A complex system of selection methods has been developed for this purpose, which includes 'trial lessons' so that the children can prove they possess the ability to work intensively. Certainly, gifted children who have not been accustomed to regular patterns of scholarly work are sometimes selected for these schools, but we have found that these individuals gradually start to work in a serious fashion like their peers because most of their classmates (in their very small groups) have the desire to work hard. Each group contains some students who are 'profoundly gifted' (advanced) and some who are 'base gifted' (which corresponds to the educational standard required for entry to the school). Such a strategy of working with gifted children is rather demanding and expensive to operate, but is undoubtedly successful in Russia.

Both strategies – stimulating comfort and stimulating discomfort work – have been proven to work in Russia to further the education of the highly able. We firmly believe that our schools for gifted education are not in existence to entertain and delight the children. They are there to facilitate students, as individuals, to work hard in order practically to deepen their knowledge and skills, in order that they can make the transfer smoothly to a successful future professional career.

Contact address: vinni-vi@mail.ru

Future Perspectives

Suggested priorities for gifted education over the next decade

On one hand, in our opinion, the outlook for work with gifted children in the next ten years in Russia will generally remain positive. This is closely connected with increasing interest from the government and society to these children's development. On the other hand, some difficulties will remain and new ones may be added. The Gifted Children Development Center will be functioning in Moscow in 2008. We believe that in ten years the majority of large cities will have such centres. Of course, these innovations may lead to excessive formal work for gifted schoolchildren. The gap between regional and metropolitan schools will be reduced. Furthermore, we predict that in spite of the obvious increase in quality of training for teachers and psychologists working with gifted children, there will continue to be a problem of finding the right personnel.

Victoria S. Yurkevitch and Boris M. Davidovich

14

Gifted but underachieving: Australian indigenous children

Graham W. Chaffey

University of New England, Australia

The under-representation of children from cultural minority and/or low socio-economic status (SES) backgrounds in programmes for the gifted in Australia is emerging as an issue of national concern (Braggett 1985; Chaffey 2002; Taylor 1998). Indigenous Australians constitute the most under-represented group of all. Conflicting definitions and terms used in gifted education as well as the absence of effective identification methods are key factors implicated in this under-representation. Coolabah Dynamic Assessment (CDA) (Chaffey 2002) is a promising identification tool for children from cultural minority and/or low SES backgrounds which has created the need for an appropriate provision model to cater for those identified.

Underachievement

If gifted underachievers are not meaningfully accounted for in conceptions of giftedness and talent, it is highly unlikely that underachievers will be effectively sought. This is especially so for gifted underachievers from cultural and social minority groups where giftedness is often heavily masked (Ford 1996). Most conceptions of giftedness and talent do not give sufficient emphasis to the gifted underachiever, one exception being Gagné's (1995) differentiated model of giftedness and talent.

Accepted definitions of underachievement depend on performance on some measure or indicator of potential (Reis and McCoach 2000), but the most commonly used methods to assess this potential are static standardised tests and teacher nomination, the very assessment forms where minority students have been shown to under-perform (Braggett 1985; Davis and Rimm 1998). It has long been recognised that high-ability children may under-perform both in the classroom and on commonly used measures of aptitude or potential (Butler-Por 1993; Reis and McCoach 2000; Whitmore 1987). However, a review of the literature reveals the absence of a consistent term for this type of underachievement.

The establishment of a consistent definition for this type of underachievement is a simple and necessary step if gifted children from cultural minority and/or low SES groups are to be included in enrichment programmes in similar proportions to their membership within the wider community. For our purposes here, then, the term 'invisible underachiever' is used to refer to individuals who under-perform in the classroom and on commonly used measures of aptitude or potential (Chaffey 2002).

Identifying invisible underachievers using dynamic assessment

Dynamic testing may constitute part of the solution to the problem of providing suitable assessment for underachieving children (Grigorenko and Sternberg 1998; Lidz 1997). Essentially, dynamic assessment seeks to optimise, rather than simply sample, cognitive functioning and it is here that a paradigm shift in intellectual assessment is apparent (Grigorenko and Sternberg 1998, p. 77; Lidz 1997, p. 291). Explaining the significance of the paradigm shift, Tzuriel and Feuerstein (1992) state:

> The assessment of cognitive modifiability requires an investment in attacking the cognitive impairments, deficient learning habits, and motivational patterns that are responsible for the poor performance. This assessment has special significance for disadvantaged and special needs children, who are jeopardised by conventional psychometric methods.
>
> (pp. 187–188)

Dynamic testing can be considered a subset of dynamic assessment, which has been defined as 'approaches to the development of decision-specific information that most characteristically involve interaction between the examiner and examinee, focus on learner metacognitive processes and responsiveness to intervention, and follow a pre-test intervention post-test administrative format' (Lidz 1997, p. 281).

Dynamic testing is different from dynamic assessment, however, in that it only seeks to determine the learning potential of an individual, rather than to establish long-term cognitive change (Grigorenko and Sternberg 1998). It follows the test–intervention–retest format of classic dynamic assessment, but involves a comparatively short intervention which is designed to establish learning potential by determining the extent to which the individual has the ability to benefit from the intervention experience. The intervention is designed to address issues that are thought to contribute to the under-performance of an individual in the initial pre-test which provides a baseline indication of cognitive aptitude. A post-test given some time after the intervention determines the extent of improvement from the pre-test and thus establishes what is assumed to be a better indication of learning potential. Consequently, dynamic testing has the potential to identify giftedness in individuals who under-perform on one-off tests of cognitive ability.

Coolabah Dynamic Assessment

Coolabah Dynamic Assessment (CDA) was developed through a doctoral study (Chaffey 2002) working with Australian Indigenous children in regional New South Wales. The CDA utilises a classic *test-intervention-retest* dynamic assessment approach. It has been specifically designed as an identification instrument that seeks to reveal learning potential rather than facilitate long-term cognitive change (Chaffey 2002; Chaffey et al. 2003). In common with other dynamic assessment approaches, CDA uses the Raven's Standard Progressive Matrices (RSPM) instrument at pre-test and post-test to examine children's potential to learn.

Details of research outcomes and data analysis methods from two studies, one of Australian

Indigenous children and the other involving Canadian Indigenous children are reported in Chaffey et al. 2003; Chaffey et al. 2005 and Chaffey and Bailey 2006.

The CDA intervention: the Gate, the Mountain and the Goldmine

The CDA intervention seeks to optimise cognitive performance by addressing the key issues implicated in underachievement in test-taking situations of children from cultural minority and/or low SES backgrounds. Indigenous children will be considered as a separate cultural group in this discussion as they are also impacted by a variety of issues associated with involuntary minority status (Ogbu 1994). In order to create a coherent model for the intervention, the terms 'the Gate', 'the Mountain' and 'the Goldmine' will be used. The CDA cognitive intervention takes three hours to complete (this includes a one-hour break) with four children assessed at once. The cognitive intervention is preceded by an 'ice-breaker' session that is designed to defuse possible socio-emotional issues, which can impact on initial engagement.

The Gate

The Gate refers to a group of socio-emotional factors that can act as inhibitors to test taking. If a child's test performance is inhibited by fear, self-doubt or the impact of low expectation or alienation from education, then a true estimation of academic potential is highly unlikely.

Factors perceived as possible inhibitors for these children are the forced-choice dilemma (Gross 1989), expectation issues (Lovaglia et al. 2000; Rosenthal and Jacobson 1968; Steele and Aronson 1995), fear of failure and cultural differences (Ford 1996). For Indigenous children the issue of involuntary minority status is crucial. Involuntary minorities have been placed in long-term subordinate positions as a result of colonisation, conquest or slavery (Ogbu 1994). Involuntary minority status peoples often experience a powerful forced-choice dilemma (Ford 1996; Gross 1989) and oppositional behaviours to education. For academically able Indigenous students the dilemma is clear: should the students 'act white' and risk alienation from their cultural peers or retain peer acceptance and shun academic excellence (Colangelo 2002; Ogbu 1994)? The CDA provider has the task of addressing these issues employing a range of carefully structured strategies. In essence, a successful CDA intervention will depend entirely on 'having the Gate opened wide'.

The Mountain

The Mountain refers to the issue of academic self-efficacy. Self-efficacy is considered as a separate issue due to the perceived importance of this construct in the CDA process. Lack of academic self-efficacy can act to block any substantial progress in the intervention. Self-efficacy has emerged as the pivotal factor in engaging the children in the cognitive processes necessary in the final stage of the intervention.

Invisible underachievers have been revealed as consistently displaying low academic self-efficacy (Chaffey 2002), which is a common feature of underachieving children generally (Bandura 2003). Numerous strategies to enhance self-efficacy on cognitive tasks are imbedded in the cognitive intervention. Self-efficacy is defined by Bandura (2003) as 'beliefs in one's capabilities to organise and execute the courses of action required to produce given attainments'.

An individual's self-efficacy is of primary importance as it determines how much effort will be expended and how long that effort will be sustained in the face of difficulties (Bandura 2003). In plain terms it will determine if an individual engages at all, how quickly and intensely they engage, how persistent they are, and how resilient they are. Self-efficacy has been identified as an important component in developing expertise (Sternberg 2001) and in the test performance of involuntary minority students (Chaffey 2002; Lovaglia et al. 1998). Bandura (2003) identified individual mastery, vicarious experience and verbal persuasion as the most powerful of the factors that influence self-efficacy.

The long-term consequences of low academic self-efficacy are, too often, disastrous for the academic development of the child. Further, the behaviours associated with low academic self-efficacy provide a potentially powerful talent mask. For underachieving children, especially gifted invisible underachievers, low academic self-efficacy may be the key talent mask that must be removed before underachievement is reversed.

A teacher who encounters an unmotivated child, one who engages poorly in the learning process, or who gives up quickly, could be forgiven for having low expectations of his/her academic potential. The teacher may be correct. However, the teacher may be looking at a bright, even gifted, child with low self-efficacy toward academic learning. This is especially so if the child comes from a background that provides few academic role models and where education has not been an important part of family life.

The Goldmine

The term 'Goldmine' refers to the cognitive intervention that is at the heart of the CDA method. The cognitive intervention has been designed to access, and work in, each child's zone of proximal development (Vygotsky 1978). If a child has undeveloped or immature cognitive abilities, substantial advances can occur if the CDA provider can successfully engage the child in the 'flow' zone (Csikszentmihalyi 1982; Kanevsky 1992). For a chronically disengaged child, as many gifted underachievers are, this is no simple task. It is here that the socio-emotional and academic self-efficacy strategies are essential. What impact can be expected working with an intellectually gifted, but totally disengaged child?

The cognitive intervention involves a CDA provider delivering a range of simple meta-cognitive control and knowledge skills (Schraw and Graham 1997) that will allow the child to engage independently in the cognitive processing of 23 intervention items. The intervention items developed for the CDA are cognitive analogues of the RSPM and contain similar cognitive processes to the RSPM, but use dissimilar presentations. It is important to note that the reasoning required to solve any of the intervention puzzles is never directly taught. The children discover the cognitive pathways through their own efforts. Of course, the higher the learning potential of the child the more she/he can discover.

Although the Gate, the Mountain and the Goldmine are presented separately for ease of understanding, it is important to note that there is constant interaction between the three intervention components of CDA.

Revealing the gifted cohort using CDA

The impact of poor test performance, even using a relatively culture fair instrument such as the RSPM, on the participation of Indigenous children in programmes for the gifted is highlighted in two studies with Australian and Canadian Aboriginal children. In the Australian study

(Chaffey et al. 2003) not one child of the 79 participants reached the gifted benchmark (90th percentile) on the one-off delivery (pre-test) of the RSPM. At post-test, five achieved the benchmark (see Table 2). In the Canadian study (Chaffey et al. 2005) one child out of 19 reached the gifted benchmark at pre-test, but four did so at post-test (see Table 3).

The 'gifted' Australian children made mean raw score gains of 12.20, compared to 8.39 for the whole group. The 'gifted' Canadian children achieved a 8.75 mean raw score gain from pre-test to post-test, as compared to 4.90 for the Canadian group as a whole. The mean raw score gains for both gifted groups are substantially above those of their respective whole groups, suggesting that both the Canadian and Australian gifted children are amongst the greatest underachievers at pre-test.

The Gate, the Mountain, and the Goldmine – the Chaffey model

A profile of Angus, an invisible underachiever, is presented to give an insight into some of the problems that arise in establishing suitable provision for these children. Angus was eight years old when assessed using the CDA. He is a proud Indigenous Australian whose parents both left school at the minimum age. He rarely hands in homework and often spends time helping the two other Indigenous children in his class. Mrs Jones, his teacher, estimated that Angus was achieving academically at about the middle of the class although she felt that he was capable of 'a little more'. She described Angus as prone to give up quickly in the more difficult aspects of academic programmes, although she said she felt his classroom outcomes were consistent with his literacy and numeracy skill levels. At pre-test Angus scored at the 48th percentile band (raw score 32). Following the CDA intervention Angus achieved 47 raw score, an outcome equivalent to the 98th percentile band.

Most existing gifted education provision caters for achieving gifted children. Programmes

Table 2   Raw Scores of the Australian Indigenous 'Gifted' Group at Pre-test and Post-test

| | Pre-test | | Post-test | | |
	Raw Score	Percentile Band	Raw Score	Percentile Band	Gain
Terry	23	26%	45	96%	22
Adam	21	18%	44	91%	23
Kate	35	58%	43	91%	8
Ian	45	86%	50	97%	5
Leisha	41	81%	45	93%	4

Table 3   Raw Scores of the Canadian Aboriginal 'Gifted' Group at Pre-test and Post-test

| | Pre-test | | Post-test | | |
	Raw Score	Percentile Band	Raw Score	Percentile Band	Gain
Angela	46	91%	48	95%	2
Catherine	39	75%	46	98%	7
Diane	30	38%	43	91%	13
Susan	33	46%	46	95%	13

(Chaffey, McCluskey and Halliwell 2005)

110

assume high-level academic skill development and aptitudes to cope with the greater demands of the programmes. Angus, with his relatively poor literacy and numeracy skills, low academic self-efficacy, and the probable burden of a forced-choice dilemma, is a likely candidate for failure if admitted into any of these programmes. Existing mainstream programmes for the gifted are generally not suitable for the invisible gifted. Failure is highly likely.

A solution to this predicament may well reside in the theoretical model underpinning the CDA method. A provision model incorporating the Gate, the Mountain and the Goldmine was created in 2002 and applied in the highly successful Wii Gaay programme for gifted Indigenous children (Armidale, NSW, Catholic Diocese). A number of other major Australian projects utilising the Chaffey Model with Indigenous children and children from low SES schools are currently in progress. The initial outcomes are very positive with research currently in progress or in press.

The Chaffey Provision Model has a number of basic steps:

Effective identification

While CDA outcomes are the primary source of identification, any reliable indication of high learning potential is sought.

Reversing underachievement

As many of the children identified have been substantial underachievers, reversing under-achievement is the necessary starting point. To accomplish this, the Chaffey Model requires investments in overcoming socio-emotional barriers (the Gate), building/enhancing academic self-efficacy (the Mountain), and deeply engaging the child in cognitive efficiency growth (the Goldmine). Operationally, the broad goals are

- creating an un-pressured environment where the children feel safe;
- enhancing/building academic self-efficacy;
- creating a love of academic learning;
- identifying and closing academic skills gaps;
- improving cognitive efficiency;
- empowering teachers, parents and the school to understand and support the children;
- working closely with the community to establish trust and an exchange of ideas;
- providing appropriate programmes for the achieving gifted children;
- accounting for cultural differences with special consideration for involuntary minority status issues.

On-going personal and academic growth over 3 years

The reversal of academic underachievement is expected to be a long-term task. The children are expected to take part in the project for three years.

While every component of this model is important, the necessary starting point is the building of academic self-efficacy. To bring the Chaffey Provision Model to life an overview of two Australian CDA programmes are presented, the *Klebawan Programme* for Indigenous children and the *Lighthouse Project* for children from low SES communities.

The Klebawan Programme

This project, based in the Sunshine Coast Region, Education Queensland, began in 2006 with the training of a team of CDA providers. The providers must be excellent teachers, as they have to break through the talent masks that have long hidden most of these invisible underachievers. In early 2007 the CDA providers assessed 202 Indigenous children in grades four and five (eight and nine years old) from 23 schools. The top 10 per cent of this cohort (along with two extras) were then offered places in the project. By way of descriptive comparison, the lowest raw score at post-test equated to the 91st percentile band while five students had reached the 99th percentile band (RSPM ceiling). Approximately five of these children were achieving close to their assessed potential while the rest were mildly to highly underachieving. The achievers were selected to provide vicarious experience for the others. Twenty-one of the 22 families accepted the invitation to participate. The academic/cognitive provision has two major focuses:

Learning Clubs

The Learning Clubs are two-day academic camps, with an intense focus on literacy, numeracy and computer technology. In the first camp, the Gate is the major focus with the Mountain as the secondary focus. This is the beginning of the engagement phase. If the children return home feeling happy and carrying a quality product of their efforts, the goal has been achieved. In subsequent Learning Clubs the children are scaffolded to gradually improve their outcomes by building academic and meta-cognitive skills while systematically enhancing academic self-efficacy. This automatically moves the children to the Goldmine. The Learning Clubs provide non-academic activities as well that are designed to be challenging and fun.

Learning Clubs are held twice a year away from school. It is necessary to work with the children in a different environment for two main reasons. Firstly, an opportunity is created to provide intense application of the Chaffey Model components. Secondly, surrounding the children with similar bright minds creates an environment where the forced-choice dilemma can be eliminated. The Learning Clubs provide the environment for the breakthrough in reversing underachievement that the Chaffey Model demands. The response to the two Learning Clubs in 2007 has been outstanding with very high attendance rates, excellent engagement and an absence of behavioural problems. After two Learning Clubs, all children are engaged most deeply in the academic tasks, with significant improvements being reported in school performance and attitude.

In-school support

A Field Officer supports the children throughout the year and facilitates most aspects of the programme. The Field Officer works closely with the class teachers, the children, the parents and communities. Teachers of the project children participate in a comprehensive professional development programme designed to develop understanding and effective pedagogy. The teachers are assisted in identifying and remediating academic skills gaps the children may have and in developing curriculum extensions as the children begin to achieve to their potential.

The Lighthouse Project

In 2006 the Lighthouse Project, catering for gifted underachievers from low SES schools, was initiated. Based at Broken Bay Diocese Catholic Schools Office, New South Wales, this project has the same fundamental design as the Education Queensland project, with slight modifications to cater to local conditions. The outcomes have been most encouraging with outstanding participation and significant improvement in classroom performance and growth on state literacy and numeracy assessments. To conclude, I offer two profiles (one from each project) that seem to indicate worthwhile interventions with the CDA.

A snapshot of Suzi

Suzi was eight years old when assessed using CDA. She is of Aboriginal descent and until this year her educational needs had been met by distance education. Suzi's teacher reported that she was academically achieving in the bottom third of the class and that her fundamentals in literacy and numeracy were extremely weak. In the CDA pre-test Suzi scored at the 5th percentile band, while at post-test she achieved at the 97th percentile band, demonstrating that Suzi is an invisible underachiever. Two key factors have been implicated as the likely origin of this extraordinary post-test gain. Firstly, Suzi had almost no meta-cognitive understanding of the processes involved in the pre-test. Secondly, her academic self-efficacy had been very low. In the intervention when meta-cognitive pathways were revealed she began engaging and simply 'took off' much to the delight (and surprise) of the assessor. During the first Learning Club, Suzi, in the absence of fundamental skills, created her own conceptual framework in a mathematics task. She astounded the experienced mathematics provider. Although Suzi represents an extreme case, she clearly demonstrates the potential of CDA and the need for the Chaffey Provision Model.

A snapshot of Ryan

Ryan was nine years old when assessed using CDA. Ryan is from a low SES school where he was achieving at about the middle of the class, although his teacher thought he had more potential. In class Ryan was academically disengaged, disorganised, constantly complaining of being sick, and easily distracted. In the CDA pre-test, Ryan scored in the 88th percentile band, revealing him as an underachiever. At post-test he achieved at the 96th percentile band. Two years after entering the Lighthouse Project, Ryan is rapidly reversing his academic underachievement. He is deeply engaged in academic tasks with commensurate improvement in literacy and numeracy skills as revealed by large gains in statewide testing and a prestigious 'school excellence in studies' award. Ryan now rarely complains of sickness, is displaying leadership qualities and is very positive in class.

Contact address: gchaffe4@une.edu.au

Future Perspectives

Suggested priorities for gifted education over the next decade

The inconsistent usage of terms and definitions in gifted education in Australia has created bewilderment at the grass roots level and divisions amongst those in the field. A start was made to address this problem when the Federal Australian Government (2005) delivered a nationwide professional development package for teachers in gifted education. Over the next ten years I hope that uniform application of terms and meanings in gifted education will be achieved in Australia. This outcome will not only strengthen gifted education overall but will also remove one of the major barriers to the equal inclusion of gifted children from cultural minority and/or low SES backgrounds in programmes for the gifted. Within the next ten years I see a stream of gifted Indigenous children moving through provision programmes that truly cater for their needs. Much of this stream will, in time, be ready for mainstream gifted programmes. A national desire for genuine reconciliation will hopefully give life to this hope.   Graham W. Chaffey

15

Lay conceptions of giftedness among the Chinese people

David W. Chan
The Chinese University of Hong Kong

It is generally acknowledged that educators and researchers in gifted education have different views on how best to conceptualise and define giftedness, and a seemingly simple question of 'What is giftedness?' will evoke different answers, depending on where you are and to whom you talk (Pfeiffer 2003; Sternberg and Davidson 1986, 2005; Winner 2000a). Indeed, even if one endorses the Western conception that giftedness is associated with high ability or intelligence above a certain cut-off score (Callahan 1996; Feldhusen 2003b), one readily realises that this once popular notion has been seriously challenged, as theorists have now broadened the notion of intelligence (Guilford 1967), and distinguished different and distinct human cognitive abilities (Cattell 1971; Gardner 1983, 1999; Sternberg 1985, 2003b). Further, giftedness could involve more than just a high intelligence quotient (IQ), and has non-cognitive components such as socio-emotional competence, creativity, and motivation (Renzulli 1978, 2003; Runco 1993; Sternberg 2000a, 2000b, 2003c). Finally, considering giftedness across cultures, educators are reminded to take into account the cultural contexts in which giftedness is conceptualised, socialised and nurtured, and honour different cultural conceptions to make giftedness relevant for children in different cultural settings (Sternberg 2007; Stevenson 1998).

Chinese implicit theories and Confucian thinking

In Chinese societies, the valuing and nurturing of *shen-tong* (godly children) has a long history dating back to the times of imperial China. The various names given to gifted children such as *tian-cai-er-tong* (children with heavenly abilities) or *zi-you-er-tong* (children with superior genetic endowment) reflect the lay conceptions of giftedness among the Chinese people. In avoiding the use of these and similar terms with connotations that seem to favour nature over nurture, Chinese psychologists in Mainland China started in 1978 to adopt the use of a more neutral and perhaps statistical term, *chao-chang-er-tong* (supernormal children), to describe gifted children in Mainland China (Shi and Zha 2000). But psychologists and educators in Hong Kong and Taiwan continue to use *zi-you-er-tong* to describe gifted children in Chinese societies outside Mainland China.

Despite the long history of identification and nurturing of gifted children, systematic gifted education in contemporary Chinese societies is generally regarded as a relatively recent development, based largely on Western conceptions of giftedness (Chan 1998). However, it is of interest to explore Chinese people's lay conceptions of giftedness; the common cultural views that dominate Chinese thinking on this topic. Arguably, these views or implicit theories are likely to have the most influence on actual life and practices, and hence on identification and programming in gifted education (Sternberg and Zhang 1995). One approach to uncovering these implicit theories is to examine giftedness and related constructs in Chinese thinking as embodied in Chinese folk stories, idioms and proverbs. In this process, one has to examine more closely the thinking and teaching of Confucius (551–479 BC) who has deeply influenced Chinese thought and civilisation for over 2,500 years. Although Confucius left few (if any) writings, his disciples have recorded many of his ideas and dialogues in the twenty chapters of *Lun-yu*, or the *Analects* (Wu 2003), which provide insight into Confucian philosophy and teaching.

Nature and nurture

Perhaps the Chinese construct that comes closest to the Western construct of giftedness is *tian-cai* (heavenly ability), which is at the top of the hierarchy of *cai* (abilities), and is regarded as an inborn ability or a natural endowment from heaven. Second to *tian-cai* is *ren-cai* (human ability), which can be acquired or developed through effort and effortful learning. At the low end of the hierarchy is *yong-cai* (mediocre ability), which can be interpreted as a lack of ability. The recognition of a spectrum of abilities gives rise to the notion of *yin-cai-shi-jiao* (all individuals should be educated according to the levels of their abilities) in Confucian teaching, which is in complete agreement with the contemporary notion of a commitment to individual differences in teaching and learning. However, *tian-cai* does not appear originally in the chapters of the *Analects*. Its popularity could probably be attributed to the often cited verse of the poet Li Bai in Tang Dynasty, *tian-sheng-wo-cai-bi-you-yong* (heaven gives me abilities that must be put to use). Thus, contrary to the assertions by many educators and researchers who contrast Eastern with Western thoughts, that Confucius emphasised only effortful learning and nurture against nature (Tweed and Lehman 2002; Wu 2005, 2006), Confucius did recognise the role of nature in conceptualising giftedness. Indeed, in associating giftedness with intelligence (*zhi* or *zhi-li*), Confucius highlighted that there are the *shang-zhi* (the most highly or exceptionally intelligent) and the *xia-yu* (the most lowly or extremely foolish or mentally retarded), and the abilities of these individuals occupying the extreme ends of the continuum of abilities cannot be changed (Analects, 17:3). Since the *zhi* as in *zhi-li* (intelligence) is the same word as *zhi* as in *zhi-shi* (knowledge) and *zhi-dao* (to know or understand), it is understandable that Chinese people perceive connections among intelligence, knowledge and learning. Thus, Confucius also maintained that those who are born to know (*sheng-er-zhi*) are the best, and those who learn to know (*xue-er-zhi*) or acquire the knowledge through learning are second best (Analects, 16:9). Taken together, Chinese thinking, in line with Confucian teaching, does recognise the importance of nature in the conceptualisation of giftedness. Further, nature and nurture do interact to lead to the unfolding of talents, and to gifted or talented performance and achievement.

The story of 'Grieving for Zhong-yong' or *Shang Zhong-yong*

The complementary roles of nature and nurture can be best illustrated by the story of Fang Zhong-yong as told by Wang An-shi, a Song Dynasty Confucian scholar, in his collected works,

Lin-Chuan-Ji. The story has been adopted as a reading for secondary school students in Hong Kong (Bu et al. 1999b). The following is my translation from the Chinese text. The story first emphasises the role of nature in the development of a prodigy or *shen-tong*:

> In the town of Golden River lived Fang Zhong-yong whose fathers and forefathers were farmers. The five-year-old Zhong-yong, who has never set eyes on books and stationery, suddenly cried and demanded them to be given to him. His father was surprised but managed to borrow them from a neighbour. Zhong-yong wrote a poem with four verses, and wrote down his own name. The theme was on filial piety and the cohesiveness of clans-people. The incident attracted the attention of a learned person from the town, and he came to read the poem. Thereafter, Zhong-yong was given various objects as topics, and he could immediately write good poems on them.
>
> (Bu et al. 1999b, p. 218)

The story then continues to point out the importance of nurture and education in Zhong-yong's development:

> The townspeople marvelled at Zhong-yong's literary ability, invited him and his father to their homes, and gave money in exchange for his works. Zhong-yong's father, tempted by the financial benefits, brought him to meet different people in town, and did not send him to school.
>
> I have heard about Zhong-yong for some time. In the year of Ming-dao, I went back to my hometown with my father, and met Zhong-yong at my uncle's house. Zhong-yong was 12 or 13 at the time. When he was asked to compose a poem, his work did not measure up to what was once claimed. Seven years later, I went back to Yangzhou and visited my uncle. I asked about Zhong-yong. My uncle replied that he has become an ordinary person.
>
> (Bu et al. 1999b, p. 218)

Finally, Wang An-shi ended the story with his commentary on the tragic end of Zhong-yong, and how nurture could interact with nature in a child's development:

> Zhong-yong's talent or giftedness is from heaven (*shou-zhi-tian*), and he was even far better than other children with high abilities. He eventually became an ordinary person, because human support and nurturance (*shou-zhi-ren*) did not come to him. A gifted person without human nurturance will become an ordinary person. Those who are not gifted will start as ordinary people, and if they are not supported or nurtured, could they still stay as ordinary people?
>
> (Bu et al. 1999b, p. 221)

Thus, Wang An-shi's grieving for Zhong-yong was also his call for providing nurturance and education for all children.

Effortful learning for achievement and talented performance

While the story of Fang Zhong-yong is a broken-twig story that has often been cited to make the point that nurture is important for all children, including gifted children, Wang's commentary illustrates the Chinese view of the complementary and compensatory roles of nature and nurture. Specifically, Chinese people recognise that a small number of children may have higher innate abilities, or a stronger *shou-zhi-tian* component than most children. However, all children, including gifted children, require as much human support and education as possible, and an adequate *shou-zhi-ren* component is necessary to allow the unfolding of potentials or talents, leading to talented performance and achievement. Assuming that the *shou-zhi-tian* component is not changeable, it is appropriate to stress the importance of *shou-zhi-ren* component and promote effortful learning in attaining success in life. Viewed from this perspective, Confucian teaching aims to address the ordinary people, and to urge them to devote efforts in learning to attain success in life, even though they might not be gifted. Thus, in another classic Confucian text, *Zhongyong* or *The Mean* (Lao 2000), it is said that the passion for learning (*hao-xue*) will make one approach (*jin-hu*) being intelligent (*zhi*), that is, *hao-xue-jin-hu-zhi*. The emphasis on effortful learning is sometimes interpreted as supporting the position that Chinese people endorse an incremental model of intelligence, believing that ability increases as a result of effort (Dweck et al. 1995; Shi 2004). However, a more accurate conceptualisation is that Chinese people view effort as influential, not by improving ability, but by overpowering the effects of deficits. According to the Chinese proverb, *qin-neng-bu-zhuo*, diligence (*qin*) can (*neng*) compensate (*bu*) for foolishness (*zhuo*). Alternatively, if ability is assumed to be largely similar across persons (that is, when one is not dealing with individuals with extremely high or low abilities, the *shang-zhi* or the *xia-yu*), what determines success in life is effort. Thus, Confucius pointed out that people are similar by nature (*xing-xiang-jin*) but effort or practice set them apart (*xi-xiang-yuan*) (Analects, 17:2).

The importance of effort and effortful learning leading to success in life can also be observed in numerous Chinese sayings, idioms and proverbs, and stories about how people could achieve success through determination, hard work, diligence, and perseverance (Wu 2006). For example, popular Chinese proverbs embedded in everyday conversation to encourage effortful learning include: 'Jade will not become an article if it is not polished (*Yu-bu-zhuo, bu-cheng-qi*)', and 'those who are determined will achieve what they desire (*You-zhi-zhe, shi-jing-cheng*)'. In extreme cases, determination, perseverance, and effort can even help one tackle formidable tasks beyond human limits, as in the story of Yu-gong described below.

The story of 'Yu-gong Who Moved Mountains' or *Yu-gong-yi-shan*

The important role of effort in achievement is also firmly and deeply implanted in Chinese thinking beyond Confucian teaching. The well-known story about Yu-gong, a fable recorded in *Lie-Zi*, a Taoist classic, epitomises the supremacy of effort in Chinese thinking. The story has also been adopted as a reading for secondary school students in Hong Kong (Bu et al. 1999a). The story starts with a straightforward description of Yu-gong's initiation of a project that was subsequently pursued with thoughtful plans. It is interesting to note that it seems natural for Yu-gong (literally the Foolish Old Man) to act 'foolishly' and take on perhaps an unnecessarily formidable task. The following is my translation from the Chinese text:

> Taixing and Wangwu Mountains stretch some seven hundred square miles and rise to several thousand feet high. They were originally located south of Jizhou and north of Heyang.
>
> North of the mountains lived Yu-gong (The Foolish Old Man) who was nearly 90 years old. With his house facing the mountains, he found it inconvenient that he had

to take a roundabout route whenever he went out and came back. He gathered his family members to hold a discussion, 'Let us work to level the mountains so that we have a direct route to South Yuzhou and the bank of Han River.'

Everyone agreed to his suggestion. Only his wife voiced her doubts, 'You don't even have the strength to level Kuifu the small hill. How can you tackle Taixing and Wangwu? And where will you dump the earth and rocks?'

'We can dump it at the Bo Sea and north of Yintu,' said everyone.

Yu-gong then set out with his sons and grandsons. Three of them could carry loads on their shoulders. They dug up rocks and earth, and carried them to the edge of the Bo Sea in baskets. A seven-year-old boy, the son of his neighbour, a widow by the name of Jingcheng, also came happily to help them.

It took them nearly a year to make one trip.

(Bu et al. 1999a, pp. 64–66)

The story takes a turn here in bringing in the contrasting view of Zhi-sou (literally the Wise Old Man). One is left with wondering whether Yu-gong is *yu* (foolish) and Zhi-sou is *zhi* (wise or intelligent). The flavour of Chinese paradoxical thinking or Taoist dialectical thinking is apparent (see Nisbett et al. 2001; Wong 2006):

Zhi-sou (The Wise Old Man) who lived in Hequ (the river bend), laughed at their efforts and dissuaded Yu-gong from continuing: 'Enough of this folly. You are old and weak. You cannot even destroy a blade of grass, not to speak of digging up earth and stones.'

Yu-gong sighed, 'You are so stubborn that you do not even have the sense of the widow's little boy. I shall die, but my son lives on. He will have sons, and they will have sons. My sons and grandsons will multiply, but the mountains will not grow in size. Why worry about not being able to level them?'

Zhi-sou was left speechless.

(Bu et al. 1999a, pp. 66–68)

The story then takes another turn in introducing forces beyond human activities:

The mountain god who held a snake in his hand heard about this. Fearing that Yu-gong would not stop digging, he reported it to the King of Gods. The King of Gods was moved by Yu-gong's sincerity, and commanded the two sons of Kua-e-shi, a god with great strength, to carry away the two mountains on their backs to put one east of Shuozhou and one south of Yongzhou. From that time onwards, no mountain stood between the south of Jizhou and the Han River.

(Bu et al. 1999a, p. 68)

The ending of the story is intriguing in that what is humanly impossible remains humanly impossible (at least at the time of ancient China), but paradoxically possible through the intervention of the power of a higher being who was moved by the determination, motivation, and effort of Yu-gong.

Beyond achievement and talented performance

Given that Chinese thinking stresses effort and perseverance as most important in learning and achievement, Chinese learners are often regarded as focusing more on the practical outcomes of learning than on learning per se (Salili 1996; Sue and Okazaki 1990). Indeed, learning and education have been recognised as a pathway to secure government positions throughout Chinese history (Lee 1996). However, research findings also indicate that among Chinese learners, performance goals and social goals are often positively correlated with mastery or learning goals (Salili et al. 2001), suggesting that Chinese learners' concerns for pragmatic outcomes such as getting high marks, securing jobs, and acquiring high status, generally co-occur with the striving for learning-related goals. Confucius also emphasised the importance of practical applications of learning, as he questioned the use of a person knowing three hundred odes if he failed when given administrative responsibilities and sent to foreign states (Analects, 13:5). Thus, a learned person should apply his knowledge to become a government official to serve other people, and an official should engage in continuing education to better himself. In the words of Confucius' student Zi-xia, '*Shi-er-you-ze-xue* (A government official should devote his time to learning after discharging his duties); and *xue-er-you-ze-shi* (a student should serve as a government official after completing his learning)' (Analects, 19:13).

According to Confucian teaching, a person who has completed his learning and can apply his knowledge and skills to serve as a public official might be regarded as having achieved talented performance or *cheng-cai* (becoming *ren-cai*). This social-interest orientation is also part of the expanded Western conceptions of giftedness, such as Renzulli's Operation Houndstooth (Renzulli 2003) and Sternberg's WICS model (Sternberg 2003c). However, in addition to talented performance and achievement, the ultimate goal of learning should be self-cultivation and self-transformation to attain *ren* (benevolence).

Ren as the supreme ideal encompassing different virtues is mentioned 109 times in the Analects, more than any other terms in Confucian teaching. *Ren* has many behavioural and interpersonal manifestations, such as loyalty (*zhong*) and forgiveness (*shu*) (Analects, 4:15; 15:24). Confucius, in response to a student's question, explained in simple terms that *ren* is *ai-ren* (love and care for others) or a deep concern for others (Analects, 12:22). Confucius recognised that *ren* is an ideal, and talked about approaching and practising *ren*. A learned person practising *ren* is a *jun-zi* who will even sacrifice his life for achieving *ren* (*sha-shen-cheng-ren*) (Analects, 15:9). But the practice of *ren* is completely accessible to all people, hence the notion of human perfectibility as advocated by some educators (Lee 1996).

In explaining to students how one might know that one is on the right path to practising *ren*, Confucius said, 'When in establishing oneself, one thinks of helping others to establish them-selves (*ji-yu-li-er-li-ren*); when in achieving something for oneself, one thinks of helping others to make their dreams come true (*ji-yu-da-er-da-ren*)' (Analects, 6:30). From this dialogue come two well-known proverbs on the relationships on self (*ji*) and others (*ren*). They are: *Tui-ji-ji-ren* (Starting from self and reaching out to others), and *li-ji-li-ren* (from establishing for oneself to establishing for others). Thus, *ren* always starts from self to others, and one does not have to be in a high position to practise *ren*. The famous and gifted Tang Dynasty poet Du Fu is said to have brought his talented performance to a higher level of giftedness with his deep concern for other people. Living in poverty and with his hut battered by thunderstorm, he wrote, 'How could we build houses by the thousands (*An-de-guang-sha-qian-wan-jian*), so that poor learners in the country could be sheltered and could stay smiling (*da-bi-tian-xia-han-shi-ju-huan-yan*)?' In summary, Confucian teaching emphasises effortful learning that leads to talented performance, and more importantly, to self-cultivation and the practice of *ren*.

Conclusion

As there are many different conceptions of giftedness across cultures and within cultures, there must be many different lay conceptions of giftedness among the Chinese people. One approach to uncover these implicit theories is to ask people what they mean by giftedness (Zhang and Hui 2001; Zhang and Sternberg 1998). A second approach is to examine Chinese thinking on giftedness as embedded in folk stories, idioms and proverbs of the Chinese people (Shi 2004; Wu 2006). In taking this second approach, I have also focused more on Confucian thinking that dominates, permeates, and has been part of Chinese thoughts for centuries. While Chinese people recognise that only a few individuals might be endowed with exceptional innate cognitive abilities, this innate superiority is not absolute, and what is generally understood to make the greatest contribution to talented performance, achievement, and success in life, are non-cognitive personality factors, including motivation, perseverance, and effort. Even more importantly, effortful learning does not have to end in talented performance, but can be brought to a higher level of accomplishment through self-cultivation that transforms and changes one's beliefs, attitudes, and values to a deep and ultimate concern for the well-being of others. The practice of *ren* with enhanced socio-emotional competence is perhaps the new dimension that could be added to traditional Western conceptions of giftedness.

Contact address: davidchan@cuhk.edu.hk

Future Perspectives

Suggested priorities for gifted education over the next decade

With the many different conceptions of giftedness in Chinese societies, including those associated with IQ and with multiple intelligences imported from Western countries, China has been struggling with many of the issues confronted by other countries, including how best to define giftedness, to develop gifted programming, to evaluate its effectiveness, and to train teachers of gifted students. While the focus on academic giftedness and the emphasis on talent search and accelerative options have dominated gifted education in Mainland China for the last three decades, enrichment options based on valuing giftedness in multiple specific academic and non-academic domains initiated outside the Mainland have gradually gained wider acceptance among educators. An integrated articulation of talent search and accelerative options with school-based enrichment programmes – while honouring and incorporating the traditional Chinese concept of *ren* – is a major task in the development of gifted education in China in the next decade. David W. Chan

---

Part 3

Whole child considerations: psychosocial development and extra-cognitive issues

There are many controversies, conflicting research findings and widely-held misconceptions about psychosocial development as it intersects with giftedness. Coming at the field from a thoughtfully unconventional angle, Annie Haight considers whether gifted education has anything to learn from the field of medical ethics. She addresses the applicability of the Hippocratic oath, as well as other important principles, and provides practical suggestions for educators and psychologists wishing to implement ethically sound practice, including 'doing no harm'. Kirsi Tirri also considers ethical issues and giftedness, this time from the standpoint of educational practices that can be implemented to support gifted learners' ethical sensitivity and moral development. Joan Freeman addresses another of the controversies in the field, and argues that although advanced academic ability may be correlated with higher scores on tests of moral reasoning, it does not necessarily lead to more moral behaviour.

Emotional intelligence has been less well-investigated than many other kinds of intelligence. Lola Prieto and Mercedes Ferrando review literature that touches on this area, and report on a series of studies that lead them to conclude that generally speaking, high ability does not lead to a greater likelihood of emotional problems, but that individual outcomes depend on the individual and the situation. Valsa Koshy considers another dimension of giftedness with important psychosocial implications, that of early childhood development. She makes a strong case for providing appropriately differentiated learning experiences in the early years.

Grounded in her experience as a student and as an experienced educator, Jan Hughes advocates that educators attend to motivational and other psychosocial factors in all students, observing that giftedness develops when students experience their educational challenges as interesting, relevant, and achievable. Most of the volume's authors would agree with Hughes' recommendations, as they would with Carmen Cretu in her emphasis on the dynamic and multi-dimensional nature of gifted-level development.

One of the controversies in the field with a history of conflicting findings concerns whether or not giftedness leads to a preference for independent study. Lisa French and Bruce Shore provide a comprehensive review of the literature on this topic, describing a study they have recently completed, and reporting on their nuanced findings. They conclude that it is really a question of 'match': when exceptionally capable learners do not feel supported, they prefer to learn alone, but when they are in situations that facilitate their learning goals, they can thrive in mixed groups.

16

The ethics of gifted education: what can we learn from medical ethics?

Annie Haight
Oxford Brookes University, UK.

An earlier version of this chapter appears in K. Tirri and M. Ubani (eds.) (2007), *Holistic Education and Giftedness*, Helsinki: University of Helsinki.

In developed countries, education, like medical provision, is a key focus of social welfare. Recent years have seen a tendency to compare education to medicine in the call for evidence-based policy and practice (Hargreaves 1996; Slavin 2002). The problematical aspects of this are significant and have been explored elsewhere (Parlett and Hamilton 1987; Thomas 2004). In this chapter, I suggest an area for more fruitful comparison between the two domains: a consideration of how the ethical principles informing the medical profession might shed light on the ethics of gifted education.

Since the time of Hippocrates, medical practitioners have been concerned to ground their activities in a set of ethical principles that govern the doctor–patient relationship and reflect wider conceptions of a good society. These principles may be grouped into four key areas: respect for autonomy, beneficence, non-maleficence (doing no harm) and justice. I consider here the extent to which these principles overlap with and might inform the ethics of gifted education. In particular, I seek to identify and explore key ethical issues and tensions in gifted education related to them, including respect for autonomy – consent and the right to underachieve; beneficence – what good is done by gifted education, and to whom; non-maleficence – the character and competing claims of potential harms to gifted students and others; and justice – equal rights for giftedness as a special educational need, distributive justice, and parity of esteem.

In recent years, the search for 'evidence-based' models of educational practice in the UK has fostered a tendency among governmental advisory bodies to look to medical paradigms (Hargreaves 1996). While this has prompted discussion around the issues of comparing 'hard' medical science and 'softer' educational research, there has been no effort to shift the focus to the ethical commonalities of the two domains. I would like to suggest that, for a number of reasons, a consideration of medical ethics is helpful in understanding issues in educational ethics. Gifted education by its very nature exemplifies key issues in educational ethics, raising questions such as: 'What is education for?' 'Who is it for?' 'How is it to be provided equitably?' and 'How are conflicts between the interests of different groups to be settled?'

Why look at medical ethics?

Medical ethics is a well-established field of applied ethics in a parallel social welfare domain. As with education, in medicine the stakes are high, public expenditure (at least in developed countries), is considerable, and provision is regarded as a key indicator of a civilised society. Both medical and educational issues represent crucial areas of public concern and political debate. Medical ethics is a well-established field, with resonance for education. In both fields, commitment to public service is an important motivator for practitioners.

Both fields share features with regard to the practitioner–client relationship, which is characterised by professional expertise and authority on the part of the practitioner, and a degree of vulnerability on the part of the recipient. In both cases, the power dynamic is unequal: both patients and pupils must take what is on offer. To guard against potential abuses of this situation, doctors traditionally take the Hippocratic oath; nurses and other healthcare practitioners have equivalent codes of conduct. Similarly, the teaching profession requires demonstration of rigorous standards of conduct before individuals are admitted.

Neither medicine nor education is a purely personal endeavour. The experiences of recipients and practitioners alike are influenced by cultural, structural, and policy issues. Both medicine and education reflect their times, key issues are often contested, and abundant historical examples illustrate that the approved practices of one age are often seen in hindsight to be erroneous or even inhumane.

Of course gifted education, like education as a whole, has its own set of burning ethical issues, including those of definition, excellence versus equity, inclusiveness, and social justice. These issues are all hotly debated, as they should be. But too frequently discussion becomes channelled into established adversarial discourses and entrenched positions. Medical ethics has generated a thoughtful and provocative literature, and its example provides educators with the opportunity to look beyond the parameters of our own field to see what relevant lessons might be learned.

Principle-based and virtue-based ethics

There are two main approaches in medical ethics: principle-based and virtue-based. The principle-based approach relies on the consideration and application of general ethical values. The authors of a leading textbook on medical ethics note that, 'A set of principles in a moral account should function as an analytical framework that expresses the general values underlying rules in the common morality. These principles can then function as guidelines for professional ethics' (Beauchamp and Childress 2001, p. 12).

The 'virtue-based approach' grounds its arguments in the characters of the individuals involved in particular ethical situations. Its proponents claim that considering 'what the moral person should do' allows important emotional and interpersonal issues to be considered, and addresses the complexity and specificity of ethical issues better than a principle-based position.

In this chapter, I consider the 'principle-based approach'. Principle-based ethics emphasises action, while virtue ethics focuses on the person performing the action. Some commentators emphasise the complementarity of principle- and virtue-based ethics (Campbell 2003). I accept this refinement and would not wish to discount the importance of the virtue-based approach. Nevertheless, in this brief discussion, I feel there is much to be learned from the principles informing medical ethics. Ethics is about moral decision-making, and many of the key issues in gifted education, explicitly or implicitly, are about weighing the competing moral claims of one course of action against another.

My discussion is based on the four fundamental principles identified by Beauchamp and Childress (2001), and discussed in Ranaan Gillon's clear and helpful short book (1985). These four principles are respect for autonomy, non-maleficence, beneficence and justice. These values may be justified by 'deontological' and/or 'consequentialist' arguments. Deontological arguments appeal to duties (for example the moral duties arising from religious adherence). The most well-known secular statement of a deontological position is Kant's categorical imperative, briefly summarised here: we should treat other human beings as ends in themselves, rather than as means to ends, and we should behave in a way that we would be willing to have universally applied. (A simplified version of this is the golden rule: 'Do as you would be done by'.) Consequentialist arguments are based on the outcomes of actions. The most important formulation of this stance is utilitarianism, expressed in notions such as maximising pleasure and minimising pain, and promoting 'the greatest happiness for the greatest number'.

Several other important moral formulations relevant to medical and educational ethics will be considered in the section on justice. In the next section, I briefly consider the principles of respect for autonomy and beneficence, and suggest issues in gifted education to which they might relate. I focus at greater length on the principles of non-maleficence and justice, before concluding with a consideration of ways of deciding among the claims of competing principles, and a description of the features of ethically defensible programmes of gifted education.

Respect for autonomy

Respect for autonomy – sometimes termed respect for the person – is the principle which, in Gillon's view, takes precedence over the other principles, all things being equal. The preferences of patients regarding their own medical treatment, while not necessarily definitive, are a crucial factor guiding doctors' actions and decisions. This principle of respect can be justified both on deontological and consequentialist grounds, and balances the unequal power relationship between doctor and patient.

In medicine, the principle of respect does not of course justify complete patient autonomy in dictating medical treatment. Circumstances that curtail this include: the superior professional knowledge and experience of practitioners, the need for patients' preferences to be restricted to medically effective and defensible options, and the need for patients to be legally and mentally adults.

Respect for the person entails respect for the range and variety of crucial differences among people. Applied to education, it calls in my view for respect for individual differences in ability at higher as well as lower levels than the norm – and by extension it also demands provision appropriate to these differences. It calls for respect for unrealised potential as well as demonstrated achievement, and for educational responses that address the full range of a child's or young person's needs, including social and emotional ones.

Key medical issues related to the principle of respect for autonomy include informed consent and the right to make independent choices and to refuse interventions. Clearly children and young people are not fully autonomous individuals either in a developmental or legal sense, and may not have the ability to make fully autonomous choices. They are, however, on a continuum of autonomy, and have preferences, desires, and an ability to make choices that are autonomous to some degree. This is exemplified by the 1985 British House of Lords decision in Gillick v West Norfolk and Wisbech AHA [1985] 3 All ER 118, in which the Law Lords ruled that a thoughtful and morally mature fifteen-year-old girl (still technically a legal minor) had the right to give consent to medical intervention without parental involvement (Montgomery 1997). Even given the crucial differences between schooling and medical care, and between the right to consent between children and adults, issues of consent also pertain to gifted education.

Research evidence on the preferences of gifted students to control their own learning is compelling (Gallagher et al. 1997; Hallam and Ireson 2006; Kanevsky and Keighley 2003; Plucker and McIntire 1996). Respect for autonomy requires educators to consult the preferences of young people, including gifted students, about schooling. The current personalisation agenda and interest in 'pupil voice' are examples of efforts to apply this principle to educational policy (see for example Claxton, Fisher, Huxtable and Hymer this volume).

A critical aspect of autonomy is the right to refuse interventions. For gifted education, this might mean a young person's decision not to participate in a programme or perhaps to underachieve. One team of researchers has studied the motivations of a group of 'underperformers' in mainstream schooling in British Columbia and described their decisions as 'honourable', primarily because the classroom provision they received failed to allow them sufficient discretion over the pace and content of their learning (Kanevsky and Keighley 2003).

Beneficence

According to Gillon (1985), beneficence – proactively doing good – is the principle entailing the weakest moral obligation on doctors. This is not to say that practitioners should not aim for beneficial outcomes of their treatments. But even a brief consideration of doctors 'doing good' against their patients' wishes (forcing a blood transfusion on a Jehovah's Witness, for example) raises issues as to whose conception of 'good' should prevail. It also illustrates the fact that one ethical principle can conflict with another in such a way that one of them must be contravened. In the example of the Jehovah's Witness, medical benefit is at odds with respect for the patient's autonomy. Even if everyone agreed that a doctor's actions were nothing but good, however, there would still be the need for a kind of triage of beneficence, informed by other, superordinate principles, to prioritise which 'good' the doctor should perform first. Issues such as these demonstrate that beneficence often needs to be bounded or directed by other principles.

Nevertheless, we should still consider gifted education programmes, like doctor's interventions, in terms of the good they produce. We may ask first, whether they do any good at all, and second, how we are to judge this question. I am using the term 'good' here to mean positive benefit to relevant individuals or groups of people. This raises a third question: who has the right to be considered a relevant person in this determination of benefits? In other words, who should benefit?

Few educators would disagree that the main purpose of gifted education programmes should be to benefit their recipients, children and young people of high ability. It is notable, however, how often this deontological grounding is subordinated in public discussion to instrumental arguments that emphasise the benefits to society as a whole, to a country's global competitiveness, and so on. This is certainly the case where gifted education programmes are publicly funded. As Carl Rogers put it, 'Wasting the potential of a gifted mind is reckless for a society in desperate need of creativity and inventiveness' (quoted in Steineger 1997).

It is outside the scope of this discussion to propose tests for ascertaining the benefits of gifted education programmes. Fair and accurate evaluations are difficult, and must certainly be context-specific. The question of evaluation raises ethically connected issues such as (a) Who evaluates and who sets the terms of reference? (b) What is the balance of interests between individual recipients and society? (c) How long should programmes be allowed to run before they are judged? and (d) Who sets the standards against which they are assessed?

In practice, standards for publicly funded programmes are most often confined to 'key performance indicators' such as percentages of students with high marks on tests, high grade point averages, and so on. If there are other, social, benefits included among the aims of a programme, such as social justice for gifted disadvantaged students, the indicators often include factors like the numbers of students progressing to higher education. Programme evaluations are necessarily short-term in scope (for example, five rather than twenty years) and tend to focus on whether taxpayers are receiving value for money. They are typically determined by a neo-liberal mindset whose assumptions include the belief that market dynamics can and should govern social welfare activities, and that the results of programmes can be identified and quantified in the relatively short term.

It is not my intention here to condemn efforts to evaluate the benefits of publicly funded gifted education programmes. While the need for accountability and the responsible use of funding is evident, we must be aware that this type of evaluation gives us only a partial, macro-level, and short-term picture of a much more complex reality having to do with individual lives in the present and future. Moreover, in this type of exercise it is much easier to identify failures and shortcomings than benefits and successes. This is especially true if the programme is linked to ambitious political targets or aspirations. In any more finely granulated assessment, the voices of the students and other stakeholders such as parents and teachers must be sought and given evidential weight.

If asking about the benefits of gifted education programmes is a hard question, it is much easier to identify their disadvantages. The two major criticisms levelled at gifted education programmes, whether explicitly or implicitly, are that they are harmful and that they are unfair.

Non-maleficence

Non-maleficence is the principle that holds that, in providing medical care, doctors must not make matters worse. This is often formulated as the Latin dictum '*primum non nocere*' – 'first (or above all) do no harm'. As Gillon (1985) points out, absolute compliance with this shibboleth of medical ethics is both overly simplistic and impossible in practice, as many types of treatment involve certain disadvantages (for example, the side effects of a drug whose overall effect is curative).

For gifted education, the principle of non-maleficence may be considered in light of these questions: (a) Do gifted education programmes cause harm? (b) If so, to whom? and (c) Does the harm outweigh any good that can be presumed or demonstrated?

There are four main ways in which programmes might be harmful: (a) Programmes could harm gifted children in some way, either educationally or by neglecting or abusing their wider emotional, social, or physical needs; (b) Programmes could be unjust by excluding unrecognised gifted students; (c) Programmes could be harmful to children not regarded as gifted, for example by making them feel inferior; and (d) Programmes could be harmful to society as a whole, for example by reinforcing socio-economic deprivation.

In fact, all of these harms have been imputed to gifted education, either generally or with regard to specific programmes. There are those, such as the British educationalist John White, who believe that gifted programmes are by definition pernicious because they perpetuate false constructs of ability, create invidious distinctions between children and demand an undue share of resources (White 2006; see also Hart et al. 2004). In the United States, Mara Sapon-Shevin claims that gifted education programmes foster a type of 'educational triage' that siphons off resources from the majority of children, and fosters schools' self-deception regarding their own effectiveness (Sapon-Shevin 1994).

A number of critics argue that, because notions of ability are culturally constructed, programmes reinforce and exacerbate social inequities. David Gillborn, a colleague of White's and a leading researcher on race and education in the UK, cites the UK government's own statistics showing that black children are under-represented in gifted programmes in England (DfES 2005, p. 36). His research indicates that in mainstream schooling black children are disproportionately placed in programmes 'for which the highest possible grade is commonly accepted as a "failure" ', and he contends that gifted education programmes perpetuate the assumptions that lead to such outcomes (Gillborn 2005, p. 4).

These arguments are typical of criticisms in a number of countries that gifted education programmes foster social harm. In terms of harm to individual children, critics within and outside the field are concerned that programmes might cause harm through inaccurate and unjust identification procedures, inappropriate educational strategies, lack of suitable pastoral care, labelling, stereotyping and so on.

The gifted education field has accepted and responded to criticisms of harm, with a number of scholars and practitioners (a number of them represented in this volume) striving to create more defensible approaches that ameliorate real or potential harms to gifted children, those not regarded as gifted, and society as a whole.

Some educationalists outside the field, such as White (2006), argue that this is insufficient, and that only a paradigm shift that dispenses with the dominant models of intelligence and ability will eradicate these harms. The two camps could perhaps be summarised as those who believe the baby should not be thrown out with the bathwater (reformists within the field), and those who believe there *is* no baby in the bathwater (the abolitionists).

It is of course worth noting that a number of commentators, as well as parents, teachers and gifted individuals themselves, point out the potential harms to individuals and society of *not* having gifted education programmes. As in medicine, the complete eradication of harm in educational programmes is a practical impossibility. The best we can do is to weigh the balance of possible harms against possible benefits and construct programmes that minimise the former and maximise the latter. Certainly, in seeking to promote the greatest good for the greatest number, this approach has an element of utilitarianism. It also raises issues about whose interests are to have priority in the balancing of good against harm, and leads to a consideration of the fourth principle, justice.

Justice

Justice is the principle appealed to most frequently in public debates over the ethics of gifted education programmes. As we have seen, critics argue that programmes are unjust by treating gifted and non-gifted children differently, and by denying non-gifted children the esteem and resources bestowed on gifted students. Defenders of programmes argue that it is unjust to treat gifted children as though they were not gifted, and that they have a right to the type of education they need.

Many of these disputes arise out of competing philosophical interpretations of justice. One of these is Aristotle's 'formal principle' that defines justice as equality: 'Equals should be treated equally and unequals unequally in proportion to the relevant inequalities' (Gillon 1985, pp. 87–88). This stance can be seen to defend gifted education programmes, as it provides a justification for differences in treatment, as long as the 'inequalities' are 'relevant' (a point that critics such as White (2006) particularly contest).

In terms of distributive justice, the Marxist maxim 'from each according to his abilities, to each according to his needs', might be seen to justify a levelling of educational provision, with the 'neediest' being seen as the most deserving. This is sometimes interpreted in education to mean that 'deficits' always trump 'over-endowment', for example that children with learning difficulties should be accorded more resources than children who find learning easy.

Another relevant interpretation is that of John Rawls, who conceives of justice as fairness. Rawls hypothesises that a truly fair society would allow deliberate inequalities (in the sense of preferential treatment, perquisites, and the like) only if they work to the advantage of the least advantaged in society (Rawls 1976). Proponents of gifted education could argue that different treatment for gifted students is likely to work to the advantage of society. Critics might counter that research evidence points to a weak correlation between childhood giftedness and outstanding achievement in adulthood (Arnold 1995; Holahan and Sears 1995; Trost 1993), so the link between gifted programmes and social benefit is tenuous (Gottfried et al. 2005). In any case, a justification based on Rawls's theory regards gifted students in an instrumental sense, as potential deliverers of future social good, rather than as ends in themselves. It is worth noting that both the Marxist and Rawlsian positions entail moral duties on gifted individuals, who are enjoined to benefit society 'according to their abilities'.

A theory more in keeping with a deontological approach is offered by the legal philosopher Ronald Dworkin, who argues in defence of the rights of minorities against the 'tyranny of the majority' (Dworkin 1977). Dworkin's position counters the utilitarian view by asserting that minorities retain certain inalienable rights even when this works against the interests of the majority. This leads us to the question: do gifted students have special (minority) rights by virtue of their giftedness?

Carrie Winstanley addresses this rather neatly by emphasising that gifted students have the same rights as all students, but that the right involved is the right to 'equality of challenge'. This is defined as provision appropriate to develop their particular talents as they are, without being linked to an overriding age norm (Winstanley 2004). To relate this to both Aristotle's formal principle and the Marxist dictum, the 'relevant inequality' becomes a difference in the character, not the degree, of need. Consequently the emphasis on 'to each according to his needs' can justify specific provision for the character of gifted students' needs. This stands as a counter-argument to the notion, often found among both educators and the general public, that gifted students' supposed superfluity of ability represents an unfair advantage deserving no further enhancement. It also invokes Kant's categorical imperative by treating gifted children as ends in themselves, that is, as children with specific needs demanding educational responses.

Resolving ethical conflicts

Ethical values often conflict with one another and educators and policy makers must steer a course through competing moral claims. Can medical ethics help us devise defensible approaches to gifted education that go some way to reconciling such conflicts? One possible route is represented by the intuitionist approach of the British philosopher W. D. Ross, which holds that, because moral issues are complicated, conflicts between moral imperatives should be settled on a case by case basis, guided by moral intuitions (Gillon 1985). This seems to me a persuasive, if commonsensical, answer, but perhaps one that does not leave us much the wiser, or hold much promise for policy-makers.

Beauchamp and Childress (2001) have elaborated on this notion, however, advancing a helpful and rigorous systematisation of the intuitionist approach. They offer a set of tests to guide in the selection of one prima facie ethical principle or norm over another, in cases where they conflict (see Table 4). These tests are general enough to apply to ethical conflicts in many spheres, and are relevant to the ethical questions arising over gifted education programmes.

Beauchamp and Childress emphasise that moral disagreements can occur even when these tests are applied to a situation by people of equal moral seriousness and probity. Such tests are unlikely to prevent disagreements, but might help both proponents and critics reflect on their own moral intuitions and allow them to understand better those of people holding opposing views.

Features of ethical gifted education programmes

This overview of the principles of medical ethics and their possible relevance to gifted education leads me to suggest the following characteristics of ethically defensible gifted education programmes.

Ethically defensible programmes

- treat gifted children and young people as ends in themselves;
- prioritise the needs of gifted students over societal agendas seeking to make use of them;
- respect the 'relevant inequalities' of gifted students while according them equal rights to appropriate educational provision;
- are designed to be flexible and permeable, with multiple entry and exit opportunities;
- are self-challenging, aware of the fallibility of systems and the fact that conceptions of high ability (and pedagogical approaches) are contested and change over time;
- respect the autonomy of gifted students by allowing them optimal levels of discretion over learning processes and content, and even over their right to opt out of a programme;
- are sensitive to individual variances among the gifted population, and provide for these;
- seek to prevent harm to gifted children in their emotional, social, and physical well-being;
- seek to prevent harm to the self-esteem and educational opportunities of other children not identified as gifted;

Table 4 Tests for selecting between competing ethical principles

---

1. 'Better reasons can be offered to act on the overriding norm than on the infringed norm'. People who have rights under a particular principle deserve special consideration over people with no comparable rights. Here the question is whether gifted children's rights of 'equality of challenge' override the rights of other children not to suffer the potential disadvantages of not being considered gifted.
2. 'The moral objective justifying the infringement must have a realistic prospect of achievement'.
3. 'The infringement is necessary in that no morally preferable alternative actions can be substituted'.
4. 'The infringement selected must be the least possible infringement, commensurate with achieving the primary goal of the action'.
5. 'The agent must seek to minimize any negative effects of the infringement'.
6. 'The agent must act impartially in regard to all affected parties; that is, the agent's decision must not be influenced by morally irrelevant information about any party'.

(from Beauchamp and Childress 2001, pp. 19–22)

- are outward-looking and sensitive to the larger social context and strive – in terms of definitions of ability, identification approaches, entry procedures, pedagogy, assessment and pastoral support – to reduce rather than perpetuate inequity and disadvantage; and
- seek to promote maximum and balanced benefit to gifted children and young people in terms of their intellectual development, emotional well-being, physical health and social fluency.

It is likely that some of these features conflict with one another, and virtually certain that the list is not exhaustive. Perhaps indeed there are other desiderata for gifted education programmes outside this ethical framework, for example, intellectual rigour and faithfulness to the evidence emerging from scientific research on aspects of giftedness.

In any case, an exploration of the principles underlying the parallel professional and social-welfare domain of medicine can help educators forge a better understanding of the ethical issues and values surrounding gifted education. We may hope that this will contribute to the process of improving the design, organisation, and delivery of ethically defensible programmes.

Contact address: ahaight@brookes.ac.uk

Future Perspectives

Suggested priorities for gifted education over the next decade

Among OECD countries, the UK registers high in both educational excellence (a good thing) and educational inequality (a bad thing). In the past decade there have been import-ant attempts to redress inequality of access to gifted education, but certain entrenched systemic features of the prevailing 'factory' model of education limit their effectiveness. Introducing flexibility for the age of entry to primary school (later as well as earlier), abolishing 'age lock-step' in progression through school and exams, removing the aca-demic–vocational divide, and providing multiple opportunities for success would all be helpful developments. A few of these are in train already under the 'personalisation agenda'. Finally, the current inconsequential definitions of 'giftedness' as academic ability/ potential and 'talent' as artistic or kinaesthetic ability should be replaced with Gagne's definitions of 'giftedness' as potential, and 'talent' as realised performance. This would disarm accusations of essentialism among critics and affirm the transformative role of education in nurturing gifts into talents.

Annie Haight

17

Ethical sensitivity and giftedness

Kirsi Tirri

University of Helsinki, Finland

In this chapter the current empirical research on morality and giftedness is reviewed with an emphasis on ethical sensitivity. The component of moral judgement has been the most studied aspect in morality. Although high ability students have been shown to be superior in moral judgement when compared to average ability students, morality includes other components as well, such as sensitivity, motivation, and character. In this chapter the component of ethical sensitivity is introduced with both quantitative and qualitative empirical results regarding gifted students. Recommendations for the moral education of gifted students are made based on the research findings.

Research on morality and giftedness

According to Bebeau et al. (1999), morality is built upon four basic component processes: moral sensitivity, judgement, motivation, and character, of which moral judgement has been the most widely studied.

Most of the studies in the area of moral development have been based on the cognitive-developmental theory of Lawrence Kohlberg (e.g. 1969). The Defining Issues Test (DIT) is a well-documented measure of moral judgement that has been used all over the world (Rest 1986). The index most frequently used is the 'P score', which reflects an individual's principled reasoning ability (Kohlberg's stages five and six). Kohlberg's procedures have been criticised for lack of diversity in the moral dilemmas that have been in the interviews (Yussen 1977). In addition, the hypothetical dilemmas have been criticised as being too abstract and removed from the daily experiences of most people (Straughan 1975). Recognition of these aspects of hypothetical dilemmas has led educational researchers to study real-life moral problems (Walker et al.1987). The research shows that the actual dilemmas formulated by adolescents are very different from the hypothetical dilemmas used by Kohlberg and his colleagues to assess moral reasoning (Binfet 1995; Yussen 1977). Most of the dilemmas formulated by Kohlberg focus on issues of ownership, public welfare, and life-and-death. In Yussen's (1977) study, the moral dilemma themes formulated by adolescents focused most frequently on interpersonal relations. Colangelo (1982) and Tirri (1996) found the same tendency with gifted adolescents.

Andreani and Pagnin provided a comprehensive review of the literature (1993). According to these authors, gifted students are presumed to have a privileged position in the maturation of moral thinking because of their precocious intellectual growth. Terman's (1925) sample of gifted children showed superior maturity in moral development in choosing socially constructive activities and in rating misbehaviour.

In the 1980s, Karnes and Brown (1981) conducted an initial investigation of moral development and the gifted using Rest's DIT. Their sample included 233 gifted students (9–15 years in age) who had been selected for a gifted program. The results of the DIT were compared to the students' results in a test that measured their intellectual ability (WISC-R). The empirical results of the study showed positive correlation between the two tests. According to researchers, intellectually gifted children appear to reach a relatively high stage of moral reasoning earlier than their chronological peers (Karnes and Brown 1981).

Other studies of moral judgement using DIT scores have shown that gifted adolescents scored higher than their peers as a group (Janos and Robinson 1985; Narvaez 1993; Tan-Willman and Gutteridge 1981). However, the data with high-achieving adolescents have indicated that the relationship between apparent academic talent and moral judgement scores is more complex. According to Narvaez's study, high academic competence is necessary for an unusually high P score, but does not necessarily predict it. High achievers generally have average to high moral judgement scores, whereas low achievers seldom achieve high scores in moral judgement (Narvaez 1993).

Ikonen-Varila (2000) reported DIT principled scores of Finnish 9th graders ($n = 1631$), and according to her, the proportion of post-conventional moral reasoning or principled reasoning was 22.6 per cent. When P scores in this study were classified according to academic competence (using a measure of average success in school which varied from 4 to 10), she observed that when average school success was under 7, the DIT mean score was 15.4, and when average school success varied between 7 and 9, the DIT score was substantially higher, at 24.2. Finally, Ikonen-Varila found that those who succeeded best in school (average success over 9) attained an average P score of 29.7. Ikonen-Varila (2000) concludes that because cognitive factors regulate moral reasoning in childhood and adolescence, it is not surprising that success in school is the main factor that predicts moral reasoning. Her results support the connection between giftedness and moral reasoning: the more academically gifted, the more capable an individual is of principled moral reasoning.

Tirri and Pehkonen (2002) explored the moral reasoning and scientific argumentation of a group of Finnish adolescents who are gifted in science. Sixteen girls and 15 boys (14–15 years of age) participated in a gifted programme at the University of Helsinki. There were three research instruments. Raven's Standard Progressive Matrices (SPM) was used to compare students' capacities for observation and clear thinking. Their moral reasoning was measured by DIT. The students were also asked to write essays on scientific moral dilemmas, and finally the researchers interviewed the students. The average DIT P-score for these 14- and 15-year-olds was 41, the average score for 18-year-olds. The variance was very high, with scores ranging from 7 to 78 ($SD = 15.8$); some students demonstrated well-developed post-conventional moral reasoning, and some did not. Another interesting finding was that the correlation between DIT and SPM was near zero (Tirri and Pehkonen 2002). This finding might be due to the small sample size in the study and more research with bigger samples are needed to confirm this result.

In a recent Finnish study with 51 academically gifted 9th grade students, their DIT tests were compared with those of average-ability students of the same age ($n = 77$) (Räsänen, Tirri and Nokelainen 2006). As with the Tirri and Pehkonen (2002) study, the researchers reported very large standard deviations. When studying the moral reasoning of gifted students with DIT,

Narvaez (1993) got parallel results. The more gifted the students in question, the larger the standard deviation. Narvaez also concluded that academic competence is necessary but not sufficient for principled thinking. The Finnish researchers draw the same conclusions.

The DIT score distribution was investigated separately for the male and female sub-samples. The average score for gifted males ($n = 21$) was 35.0 per cent with a standard deviation of 15.5. The principled scores ranged from 16 per cent to 79 per cent in the male sub-sample. The average score for gifted females ($n = 25$) was not much different than that of the males: 35.9 per cent with a standard deviation of 15.4, with P scores ranging from 15 per cent to 75 per cent (Räsänen et al. 2006).

Antti Räsänen and his colleagues (2006) further classified the DIT scores into four classes on the basis of quartiles: 1st quartile (DIT score values below 25.0), 2nd quartile (DIT score values from 25.0 to 33.9), 3rd quartile (DIT score values from 34.0 to 44.4) and 4th quartile (DIT score values above 44.4). No statistically significant difference between the DIT scores of male and female respondents was found, $\chi^2(3, 41) = 4.733$, $p = 0.192$. In Narvaez's research (1993), girls had an average score of 28.2, while boys had an average score of 25.6. The difference was not significant.

Rest (1986), reporting on a meta-analysis of 56 DIT studies, concluded that contrary to some statements (see for example Gilligan 1982), females actually score higher on the DIT than males but that gender accounts for no more than 0.9 per cent of the variance in DIT scores, and that age and education are 250 times more powerful than gender in explaining DIT score variance.

Of course, morality includes other components besides moral judgement as measured by DIT scores. Real-life moral dilemmas also require moral sensitivity and moral motivation (Narvaez 1993). Before an individual can make responsible moral judgements, he or she needs to identify real-life moral dilemmas in different contexts. A broad conception of morality requires more than just skill in abstract reasoning. Affective and social factors play a vital role in moral conduct. The few empirical studies available provide contradictory results on the relationships among general intelligence, social competence and altruism (Abroms 1985). Earlier studies on deviant behaviour and crime among the gifted have also shown that there is no necessary relationship between morality and intelligence (Brooks 1985; Gath et al. 1970). Furthermore, earlier studies show that there are qualitative differences in the moral reasoning of gifted adolescents (Tirri and Pehkonen 2002).

Research on ethical sensitivity and giftedness

According to Muriel Bebeau and her colleagues, moral sensitivity

> . . . is the awareness of how our actions affect other people. It involves being aware of the different possible lines of action and how each line of action could affect the parties involved (including oneself). Moral sensitivity involves imaginatively constructing possible scenarios (often from limited cues and partial information), knowing cause-consequent chains of events in the real world, and having empathy and role-taking skills. Moral sensitivity is necessary to become aware that a moral issue is involved in a situation.
>
> (Bebeau et al. 1999, p. 22)

To respond to a situation in a moral way, a person must be able to perceive and interpret events in ways that leads to ethical action. The person must be sensitive to situational cues and must be able to visualise various alternative actions in response to that situation. A morally sensitive person draws on many skills, techniques, and components of interpersonal sensitivity. These include taking the perspective of others (role taking), cultivating empathy for a sense of connection to others and interpreting a situation based on imagining what might happen and who might be affected. Ethical sensitivity is closely related to a relatively new suggested intelligence type, social intelligence, which can be broadly defined as the ability to get along well with others and get them to cooperate with you (Albrecht 2006; Goleman 2006).

Numerous tests of ethical sensitivity have been developed over the years, but most of them are very context-specific, for example, relating to medicine and dental education (Bebeau et al. 1985) or to racial and gender intolerance (Brabeck et al. 2000). Our most recent study (Tirri and Nokelainen 2007) used the Ethical Sensitivity Scale Questionnaire (ESSQ) to examine ethical sensitivity self-evaluations of 7th–9th grade students ($n = 249$) in two urban Finnish schools.

The questionnaire is based on Narvaez' (2001) operationalisation of ethical sensitivity: (1) reading and expressing emotions, (2) taking the perspectives of others, (3) caring by connecting to others, (4) working with interpersonal and group differences, (5) preventing social bias, (6) generating interpretations and options, and (7) identifying the consequences of actions and options. Three research questions were formulated: Firstly, are the psychometric properties of ESSQ adequate for scientific work? Secondly, are there sex differences in ethical sensitivity?, and thirdly, are there any differences in ethical sensitivity between academically average and above average students? Results showed that psychometric properties of the ESSQ were satisfactory for scientific work. However, further development of the ESSQ would benefit from larger, especially cross-cultural, samples. According to the results of this study, female students estimated their ethical skills higher than those of their male peers. This tendency was explained by the nature of items, which mostly measure caring ethics with emotional and social intelligence. In earlier Finnish studies, both sixth- and ninth-grade girls were shown to be more care-oriented in their moral orientation than their same age male peers, who demonstrated a stronger justice-orientation in their responses (Tirri 2003).

Academically gifted students estimated their ethical skills higher than did average ability students (Tirri and Nokelainen 2007). This finding is consistent with other researchers' suggestions that gifted students hold a privileged position in the maturation of moral thinking because of their precocious intellectual growth (Andreani and Pagnin 1993; Karnes and Brown 1981; Terman 1925).

An empirical study emphasising ethical sensitivity investigated moral concerns and orientations of Finnish students (Tirri 2003). The data included sixth-grade students ($n = 100$) and ninth-grade students ($n = 94$). The students came from four different schools. The method used in the study was an essay in which the students were asked to write about a moral conflict in their school involving themselves or their friends. In addition to the interpersonal relationships presented in the stories, special emphasis was given to the moral orientations of justice (Kohlberg 1969) and care (Gilligan 1982), as reflected in the stories. Both sixth- and ninth-grade boys were strongly justice-oriented in their solutions to moral conflicts in schools. Justice-oriented moral reasoning was reflected in the emphasis on rules and equal treatment of everybody. The following quote is a typical story written by sixth-grade gifted boy:

> The coach treated me and my friend very unjustly. He didn't let us play more than a half game out of three. He argued it was a critical situation all the time. We felt very bad. It was so wrong to use the same players all the time. After the game, we asked the coach why he had asked us to play if he only let us play for a half a game. I think he should have been more just, and let everybody play equally.
>
> (Sixth-grade gifted boy)

137

On the other hand, the girls were shown to be care oriented in their solutions to moral conflicts in both grades six and nine. Furthermore, the girls expressed a greater ability to empathise and take the role of a third person than did the boys (Tirri 2003). The following quote illustrates the capacity of girls to empathise with a person who is very different from themselves:

> We had a Gypsy boy in our class whose name was Hate. He was quite fat but very nice. The boys always harassed him but he was still very happy all the time. He gave free stickers to the other boys and hoped to make friends with them. He couldn't help it that he was a Gypsy and a little bit fat. The girls were friendly to him and much nicer than the boys were. I think the girls were able to take his role and understood it is not nice to be harassed.
>
> (Sixth-grade gifted girl)

In our previous study on moral reasoning and scientific argumentation of Finnish adolescents who are gifted in science (Tirri and Pehkonen 2002), we also paid attention to their ethical sensitivity. In the qualitative essays and interviews the pupils were asked to identify moral dilemmas in science and to provide solutions to them. The findings showed that the students paid attention to different aspects in discussing the same moral dilemma. Furthermore, the principles and values used in solving the dilemma revealed qualitative differences in students' moral sensitivity. We analysed students' arguments and justifications for doing archaeological research in graves with the help of technical terminology developed by Toulmin (1958). All the students reached the conclusion that research in graves is morally justified. However, those students who gained the highest scores in the DIT reflected on the dilemma with different justifications and values than the students who attained only average scores. Furthermore, girls and boys differed qualitatively from each other in their argumentation processes (Tirri and Pehkonen 2002).

We present two cases that illustrate some general trends in the argumentation pattern of the whole group studied (Tirri and Pehkonen 2002). Tina is a good example of a gifted girl whose argumentation is logical and elegant and who provides theoretical and ethical backing for her arguments. Furthermore, she demonstrates emotional and spiritual sensitivity in her reflection on moral dilemmas in science. Tina's argumentation for the disadvantages of archaeological research in graves is based on her moral sensitivity in respecting other people's feelings and values. She does not limit her arguments to rational and scientific evidence only. Tina considers the sacred nature of the grave and understands the religious concept of holiness. The reasons she uses for her position are based on ethical values of respecting things that are considered holy by some people. Tina demonstrates very good judgement in her reflection on the advantages of archaeological studies as well. She admits that sometimes graves have to be studied. However, the reasons need to be valid and the grave must be old enough. For the final conclusion, Tina states that we should negotiate contracts and laws on how to conduct archaeological studies in graves. Compared to the whole group of gifted students, Tina's argument is outstanding, including critical thinking, logic and moral sensitivity. Her final conclusion provides some concrete, but not naïve, ways to approach this dilemma. It is no surprise that Tina ranked at the highest level of post-conventional moral reasoning in the DIT.

Alex's argument for the advantages of archaeological research in graves was typical of the whole group of gifted students. The majority of the arguments students used to justify conduct in science were based on utilitarian ethics. The new knowledge in science was identified as the leading value that brings the greatest benefit to people. However in most cases the students acknowledged the need to provide some exceptions to this rule. Even in science the researchers should pay attention to the feelings of those people who are affected by the research. In our study, archaeological research in graves was advocated, with the exception of those graves that are so new that the relatives of the dead could still be alive. Alex's argument for the disadvantages of archaeological research in graves was not typical of the whole group of gifted students. His strong identification with the scientists led him to consider scientific moral dilemmas only from the scientists' point of view. This emphasis made him neglect the relatives and other people who may have different values concerning studies in graves.

Alex's score in the DIT was below average compared to the whole group of gifted students. Compared to his almost perfect score on the Raven test, it appears that his general intellectual ability may be more highly developed than his moral reasoning. A qualitative analysis of his argument reveals in part the reasons for his only average score in the DIT: Alex's reflection on the disadvantages of doing research in graves lacks attention to universal concerns. He considers the dilemma only from his own standpoint. However, the ability to take into account universal moral judgements by an impartial moral agent is considered the most mature moral reasoning, according to Kohlberg's procedures (Strike 1999).

The results of our study revealed qualitative differences in the moral reasoning of gifted adolescents, as compared with their less academically advanced age peers. Contrary to previous reports of superior moral reasoning in gifted students, we found that high intellectual ability does not predict mature moral judgement, and that responsible judgements of moral dilemmas in science require moral motivation and moral sensitivity. Implications of our findings include the suggestion that educators nurture the moral growth of future scientists by exploring and discussing the ethical aspects of scientific studies. The model presented in our article can serve as a pedagogical tool for teachers in reflection on moral dilemmas in science with their students (Tirri and Pehkonen 2002).

Implications for moral education of the gifted

According to ethical competence theory (Narvaez et al. 2002), morality can be taught. Moral character is viewed as a set of skills that can be honed to expert levels of performance. The Greek philosopher Plato believed that the just person is like an artisan who has particular, highly cultivated skills that have been developed through training and practice.

Persons of good character, then, have better developed skills in four areas: moral sensitivity, moral judgement, moral motivation, and moral action (Bebeau et al. 1999). For example, the skills of moral sensitivity enable one more quickly and accurately to 'read' a moral situation to determine what role one might play. The skills of moral judgement include many tools for solving complex moral problems in different contexts. The skills of moral motivation include the cultivation of an ethical identity that leads one to prioritise ethical goals. The skills of moral action include the ability to keep the goal orientation, to stay on task and take the necessary steps to get the ethical job done. Persons of character have specific moral skills that can be divided into these four categories (sensitivity, judgement, motivation, action). The moral person is guided by a personal moral commitment that calibrates moral perception and awareness.

The moral education of high ability students should include a deliberative process to determine a just and caring solution to a moral issue in hand. This process should include (a) better and worse interpretations of the moral issues discussed (moral sensitivity); (b) better and worse justifications for actions (moral judgement); (c) expectations for behaviour in particular contexts, for example; 'the good citizen', the 'just student' (moral identity) and indicators of commitment to moral ideals; as well as (d) indicators to judge courage, persistence, and follow through (moral character) and prototypes for effective responses to problematic contexts (e.g. 'just say no') (Bebeau et al. 1999). According to empirical findings, real-life moral conflicts and interpersonal relationships should be among the topics used in these discussions.

Empirical studies also point to the need for teachers to discuss moral, spiritual, and religious questions influencing adolescents' futures. Furthermore, spiritual and religious questions are among the issues with which pre-adolescents and adolescents are concerned (Tirri and Nokelainen 2006). These questions should be addressed in every culture to help the youngsters find answers to questions such as: 'Who am I?', 'Where do I belong?', 'What is my purpose?' and 'To whom or what am I connected or responsible?' All the leading religious and spiritual traditions in the world have studied these questions. Our adolescents need the knowledge and wisdom of these traditions in order to grow not only cognitively but also morally and spiritually. Moral, spiritual, and religious questions are part of gifted students' concerns and the pedagogical task of education. They are also part of moral and citizenship education. To be as meaningful as possible, the education of gifted students should address questions like these.

Contact address: ktirri@mappi.helsinki.fi

Future Perspectives

Suggested priorities for gifted education over the next decade

International comparative studies have shown that Finnish students score well in tests measuring mathematical abilities. In 2003 the PISA follow up study focusing on mathematics literacy and involving 276,165 15-year-old students was conducted in 41 countries (OECD 2004). The results of overall student performance in different countries on the mathematics scale showed that Hong Kong students had the highest and Finnish students had the second highest mean student score (OECD 2004, p. 89). In the future the challenge in Finland is to address more the holistic education of gifted students. Future scientists need ethical expertise that includes skills in ethical sensitivity, ethical judgment, ethical motivation and ethical action. Holistic education supports the development of the whole person, rather than merely the cognitive domain. This kind of education acknowledges the importance of social and affective domains in students' development including their spiritual and moral concerns.

Kirsi Tirri

18

Morality and giftedness

Joan Freeman
Middlesex University, UK

Morality does not exist in a theoretical limbo; it is an entirely practical concept, the warp and weft of the way people live together. Like giftedness, the concept of morality can only be understood within its historical and cultural contexts. And also like giftedness, morality is always relative, in that what is gifted or moral to me is not necessarily gifted or moral to you. It also shares the ephemerality of giftedness – being infuriatingly difficult to define precisely, although a checklist of characteristics that morally gifted people may possess can be useful (see Spreacker 2001).

Based on my reading in the field, I would argue that a moral person characteristically:

1 chooses the ethical rather than the expedient alternative when faced with an inter-personal dilemma;
2 stands against public sentiment when such sentiment threatens to compromise personal values;
3 feels allegiance and responsibility for principles and causes;
4 identifies with humanity beyond the immediate confines of their own group;
5 feels compassion for wrongdoers without condoning their specific acts;
6 perceives and admits to personal shortcomings; and
7 holds to personal ideals transcending such qualities as appearance and social acceptability.

In brief, 'Moral motivation means prioritising moral values over other personal values' (Bebeau et al. 1999).

Morality is inextricably bound up with 'wisdom', a currently fashionable concern in education. Wisdom too demands action, such as giving advice and getting people to take it – all of course for their own good. And wisdom also depends on the individual in context. Sternberg's (2003e) examples of wise people – Nelson Mandela, Mother Teresa, Martin Luther King and Mahatma Ghandi – all fall into the Western Judeo-Christian mould. Yet other ideas of morality are held just as strongly, such as those promoted by the Ayatollah Khomeini and Osama Bin Laden who are/were also revered for their wisdom, as indeed were Comrades Lenin and Stalin. For Germans, Hitler was (and still is to some) the ultimate voice of morality and wisdom, as is Kim Jong-il of North Korea today. There appears to be no shortage of people ready to lead others in their vision of morality, which may be diametrically opposed to other people's morality.

Here is an excerpt from an audio-recorded example of a gifted boy and his moral thinking in England in 1986 (longitudinal study, Freeman 2001). Melvin, the speaker, was undeniably gifted in terms of IQ and school achievement. He was a round, beaming 14-year-old with the manner of a bank manager who knew what was best for you. He explained to me carefully:

> I often feel that I have a more mature outlook from most people my age. It sounds a terribly high-minded attitude to take, and some people pretend not to understand me, because if they did, then I'd explode all their myths about their petty little values. Sometimes it seems that the only way that everybody agrees is when they all disagree with me.

His mother told me with concern what would happen:

> He was always morally two years ahead of any of his peers. Where they were still hitting each other for fun, Melvin had worked out that this was silly. He used to try and reason with them, but they didn't know what he was talking about. So while they were hitting him, he was busily pointing out the reasons why they shouldn't.

Melvin was one of the 210 gifted and non-gifted youngsters I have interviewed in their homes across Britain, comparing their developing attitudes and achievements regularly since 1974 (Freeman 2001). One part of the investigation was to look at a possible relationship between giftedness and morality. It seemed to me that in Melvin's case, it was neither his extraordinary intellect nor his advanced morality that had denied him friends, as is so often claimed for the gifted. Rather, it was his lack of genuine acceptance of others and of simple friendliness towards his fellows.

Whose morality?

Morality has a two-way relationship with gifts and talents. The first is cultural morality, the everyday conduct and expectations of a society. The second is the personal morality of the gifted and talented themselves.

Cultural morality

Prevailing societal morality affects the values placed on all gifts and talents within it. What is seen as moral behaviour to the majority is bound to influence the emphasis placed on provision for different kinds of learning and what is consequently respected as excellence (Freeman 2005). Cultural morality determines which children are eligible for special opportunities for learning. This is influenced by groupings such as gender and social-status, so that while some youngsters are effectively selected to succeed, others are permitted to fail. Educational scholarships are not available, for example, to enhance the fine skills and creative talents required to crack open other people's safes.

Personal morality

Because the adjectives 'gifted' and 'talented' are usually understood to refer to a statistically small percentage of individuals, myths and stereotypes about them circulate, so that the outlook and behaviour of this 'abnormal' cluster is expected to be different from that of 'normal' people at all ages. Such assumptions may be totally wrong, but they can affect the individuals who may try to live up to them. The personal morality of the gifted and talented is like two sides of a coin, and people who see one side cannot always see the other. The gifted are often seen as having a higher morality, a view overwhelmingly more popular than the alternative – that they are morally more fragile.

Investigation into the development of morality in children is usually done using Kohlberg's moral development theory. The form of the test is a base of cognitive organisational stages onto which stages of moral developmental are superimposed (Kohlberg 1984; Leroux 1986). In this approach, moral stages become increasingly comprehensive, idealistic, and of a higher order than the preceding stage. Individuals move through the levels at different rates, though they cannot skip a level and may never reach the top one. There are three levels, with two stages in each. The first is the pre-conventional, notably with concern for physical consequences. The second is conventional, showing support for the established order. The third is the post-conventional, autonomous, or principled level. Kohlberg believed that the majority of adults in America were at the conventional level.

Youngsters who score well on paper-and-pencil intelligence tests score equally well on paper and pencil tests of moral development (see Tirri this volume). Terman's Californian study has shown the greater law-abidingness of his gifted sample over two generations (Holahan and Sears 1995). Although this work is highly contentious (see below), Herrnstein and Murray (1994) provide considerable evidence to demonstrate that the lower the intelligence quotient (IQ), the more likely a life of crime and depravity, whereas the 'cognitive elite' with an IQ of above 125 are less likely to commit crimes, become pregnant out of wedlock, abuse illicit drugs and alcohol, or remain unemployed or underemployed, while having success in school, career and income.

The assumption that the gifted are morally superior is particularly evident in the selection of children for leadership courses by IQ (almost all in America). The selected children are tutored in the appropriate skills to direct the lives of others. From earliest childhood, the potential leader is supposed to show enthusiasm, easy communication, problem-solving skills, humour, self-control and conscientiousness, as well as very high intelligence (Sisk 2001). Sisk also sees the gifted as in greater need of moral education than non-gifted, saying, 'Moral education is particularly essential for gifted students in order for them to further develop and utilise their capacities to reason' (Sisk 1982, p. 221).

The less popular opposite side of the coin claims that the intellectually gifted are morally more susceptible to temptation and delinquency than other children. Hence, if they are frustrated when they do not get the education they need to stretch their powerful minds, they are more likely than lower-IQ children to turn to crime. Instead of spending years in higher education, they will spend these in prison. This was the premise on which Margaret Branch founded the National Association for Gifted Children (NAGC UK) in the 1960s. A recent British textbook for teachers states without hesitation, 'There is evidence that some of these (gifted) children who are not recognised and supported become involved in crime and turn to delinquency' (George 1992, p. viii). What evidence? In my detailed overview for the Office for Standards in Education (UK) of world-wide scientific research on the development of the gifted, I could not find the slightest evidence of any greater moral weakness of the gifted (Freeman 1998).

In the longitudinal research project that Melvin participated in (above), with a total pool of 210 subjects, 170 children scored at the 99th percentile of the Raven's Matrices (Freeman 2001). Stanford-Binet IQs ranged from below 120 (46 children) to the test ceiling of 170 IQ

(13 children). Family finances ranged from very poor to very rich. Attrition over the decades has meant that from 1974 to 2007, the sample declined from 210 to 97 subjects, although fortunately the proportions of students in the groups has remained relatively constant. For most participants in this study, their individual styles of thinking and reasoning were already well formed even in their teenage years. Now in their forties, their attitudes to morality have hardly changed and are very much in line with those of their parents, as they usually had been since childhood. It is not possible to say that the gifted in this sample are morally any different than the non-gifted, though what has happened to the sample drop-outs is of course unknown.

So many of the gifted high-achievers seemed to have spent such a high proportion of their young lives in ardent study, that they had difficulty with the questions which asked for a touch of imagination. This was particularly noticeable with one question concerning how they would deal with vast sums of money. Responses were mostly conventional, such as 'banking it for a rainy day', buying small luxuries like tape recorders, a car, or even 'a new house for Mum and Dad'. One or two, though, decided to give it all away. On the whole, this sample had little interest in politics, and in fact not one has taken up politics as a career. They felt deeply about the environment and inequality, long before it was fashionable, but very few have sought to do anything about it in adulthood.

Gender comparisons

Historically, it is only relatively recently that females were seen as deserving of the same opportunities in learning as males, at least in Western society (though the situation has still not changed in other parts of the world, such as most of the Middle East). Across European history, educating women like men was immoral in the eyes of the church and society. As a woman, Marie Curie encountered this more than a hundred years ago. I summarise Quinn (1995): When Marie Curie won her first French science prize the judges did not send the informing letter to her. It went instead to her husband, Pierre, who was congratulated on his wife's success. Later, her Nobel Prize hung in the balance for the same reason; it seemed more appropriate to give it only to her husband. But fortunately the excellence of her work was known to her associates who pleaded her case, and the Swedes finally awarded it to her. The world was fascinated with this female first, though she was still cast in a feminine supporting role. The *New York Herald* (among many similar put-downs from the world's papers) reported that Madame Curie 'is a devoted fellow labourer in her husband's researches and has associated her name with his discoveries'. A French journalist who camped outside her home to watch the Curie's daughter, Irene, being served her supper, described Marie's poor morality, describing how the child was neglected so that her mother could win the Nobel Prize.

In fact, we might find a clue to the relationship between morality and intelligence by using males and females as experimental control groups. Looking at moral behaviour over the millennia, for example, we might observe that women rarely start wars, torture people or behave in other highly destructive ways; and in fact we might also observe that they are traditionally the carers in their families and societies. In the absence of controlled experimental studies, we cannot conclude anything firm about this, but it may well be that if actual moral behaviour (rather than high IQ) was the entry ticket to leadership courses for the gifted, they would be filled almost entirely by girls – which they are not. And then, if we also demonstrated that females were significantly more or less intelligent than males – we might think further about the association between morality and intellectual gifts.

As it happens, a natural and statistically analysed comparison has emerged between boys and girls, in the gender outcomes of a cross-national school study of the sciences and mathematics. In the UK, gifted girls have completely reversed the situation of many centuries by gaining higher grades than boys in all the 'hard' subjects, but not so in America, where boys continue to have the higher grades (Freeman 2003). If high-level achievement (and by association, the intelligence needed to reach that level) and morality are indeed correlated, one might reason that girls are morally superior in the UK, and boys are morally superior in the USA. It is more likely, though, that morality is independent of high-level school achievement, and thus probably of IQ too. The most likely reasons for these educational gender differences are both cultural and educational. There have been changes in education in the UK, notably improved provision and expectations for girls, which has probably altered the balance between girls' and boys' school achievements – in all subjects – in favour of the girls.

The confusion of giftedness and morals

The confusion of giftedness and morality seems to have begun in 1869, when Sir Francis Galton published his *Hereditary Studies of Genius*, in which he first spelled out a positive association of high-level intelligence with high-level morality – the kind he approved of. In his eyes, this morality was shown only by people from the 'right' social level in the 'right' society; an early pronouncement on the 'right stuff' that Thomas Wolfe wrote about two centuries later in the USA. Galton's interest in the 'mental peculiarities of different races' was stimulated by his trip to Africa. On his return, he wrote that high intelligence can only be associated with 'high culture', meaning European culture, promoting what he called the best of the 'English race'. He considered men of other races, particularly black ones, to be the bottom of the human pile, although (European) women and Jews were only marginally better. There could be no change in this moral order: he believed totally in the unalterable inheritance of abilities, and accordingly of morality.

Many years after Galton had died, the effects of the widespread acceptance of his views – then and still today – were pointed out by Kamin (1974). He quoted documents showing how in the early part of the twentieth century, immigration to the USA had been controlled by the manipulation of IQ tests to detect immorality. The new science of mental testing was used by psychologists in New York to vet the non-English speaking immigrants as they staggered sick and exhausted off the boats. The efficient white-coated psychologists considered IQ to be a cleanly objective measure, unsullied by culture (as some still do). Their results 'showed' that 83 per cent of Jews, 87 per cent of Russians, 80 per cent of Hungarians and 79 per cent of Italians were 'feeble minded'. It was, they claimed, for the secure future of decent American society that those morally deficient 'races' must be kept out, whereas the higher scoring 'races' from Britain, Canada and Scandinavia should be allowed in.

This tangled thread of moral expectations associated with IQ ran through Terman's *Genetic Studies of Genius* (1925–29), with its heavy weighting of white middle-class subjects as exemplars of the high-IQ child. More recently, it emerged again in the survey of research by Herrnstein and Murray in *The Bell Curve* (1994). These authors were in no doubt as to the relationship between intelligence and virtue, reiterating Galton's claims that 'high intelligence also provides some protection against lapsing into criminality' (p. 235). Arthur Jensen, notably in his famous 100-page paper in the *Harvard Educational Review* (1969), has always been sure that IQ and crime are associated. He has stated that 60 per cent of black Americans have an IQ below 90 and that a peak crime rate occurs in the IQ range 75–90.

Eysenck too, in his posthumous book, *Genius* (1995), surveying more than a century of research, was in general agreement with Galton, although he was less concerned with race. But to Eysenck, all geniuses are men, and gender achievement differences, he wrote, 'are of course genetic'. He demonstrated this by showing how genius was tied to high scores on his psychoticism scale, on which males score twice as highly as females. Real genius, he concluded, demands psychopathology, which men have in far greater abundance than women. He recognised though that high-level psychopathy implies a fine line between a life of universal acclaim and one of big-time criminality. Thus, on Eysenck's psychopathy scale women are more moral than men, a decided handicap in achieving the status of 'genius'.

Measuring people

When one person sets out to measure another, there is always some value judgement implied in the comparison. Galton was one of the founders of the Eugenics Society, an organisation devoted to a policy of improving the human gene-pool by selective breeding – ideas enthusiastically taken up by the Nazis. However, a paler version of this happened in other countries too, including the USA and Sweden. Fearing the effects on society of the assumed poor morality of children of low-intelligence, the authorities set about sterilising them – almost always girls – often without either the parent's or the victim's knowledge. Thousands of girls, many of them with normal intelligence, were denied motherhood. Boys, however, were not sterilised. Not only was the male operation easier, but boys, whether of low or high IQ, whether moral or immoral, had by far the greater ability to procreate. In 1975, William Shockley, the Nobel Prize-winner who invented the transistor, took a gentler approach by suggesting that extra welfare payments might be awarded to low-IQ women who volunteered to be sterilised. Again, low-IQ (immoral) males were exempt and free to have as many children as they wanted. If the sterilisation plan was about preserving social morality, one might expect to see boys sterilised even more rigorously than girls. We can only conclude that there were other kinds of agendas operating for the policy-makers in question.

Morality and intelligence test questions

Looking carefully at some frequently asked IQ questions, it is possible to see the moral values of the test makers which were (and still are) taken for granted and assumed to be culturally universal. In the beginning, the test-makers were all white Anglo-Saxon Protestant (WASP) men – men of a decidedly Protestant ethic (Weber 1930). For nearly a century, new tests and revisions continued to be modelled on the older ones in order to be designated as having psychometric validity, and so the thread of testing for WASP morality continued. Here are some examples from older versions of widely used tests of intelligence:

> Q. 'What is the thing to do if another boy/girl hits you without meaning to?'
> The correct response, for which the highest score is given, must involve the Christian ideal of forgiveness. An eye-for-an-eye or tooth-for-a-tooth response gets a lower score, thereby penalising the honour-vengeance morality practised in many parts of the world, and in many communities in predominantly Judeo-Christian countries.
> Q. 'What is the thing to do when another child takes your toy?'
> Instead of suggesting grabbing it back or fighting over it, which is a healthy normal reaction, the response that gains the most points is one of cool problem-solving, reining in any anger, and inhibiting any desire to lash out. We might observe that this is not always a good lesson for real life: What higher authority would you run to in the

cut-throat market place when someone snitches a deal from under your nose? In some communities, the right-answer behaviour would lead to serious trouble, and be considered very unintelligent indeed.

Q. 'What should you do if a smaller child starts to fight you?'

To score well, a child of any age should say that he or she would place a protective arm around the weaker child and explain gently that, 'Hey, that's not a good idea'. But in the rough and tumble of everyday life a youngster often replies quite honestly – 'I would hit him back, because that way the smaller child will learn not to fight bigger people', the message being – 'Don't take on City Hall, kid!' Which is really the more caring response?

These questions and 'right answers' illustrate that the world of the psychologist and the child may reflect quite different cultures and moral value systems. Perhaps it is the still-prevalent Protestant work ethic which has brought about the assumption in testing that children will do their sincere best, so that comparative norm-referenced scores (like IQ) continue to be seen as valid reflections of differences in intellectual ability, rather than of degree of socialisation into a particular cultural mindset.

Mistaken relationships

What, then, about the unarguably positive correlation between scores on intelligence tests and morality tests, such as Kohlberg's popular test of moral development (1984)? The assumed morality of some of the questions on that test is questionable. Look at this moral dilemma and consider your answer before you read the following paragraph: A married couple are extremely poor. The wife is dying and the husband cannot afford the drugs needed to save her. Should the man break into a pharmacy and steal what his wife needs?

The underlying assumption is that because the man does not have enough money, he cannot get the drugs, and his beloved will die if he does not steal the drugs. I ask – how moral is the society that obliges someone to consider such drastic, immoral and dangerous action to save his beloved? Most developed countries have adequate social benefits, providing essential medicines and medical treatment. What intellectual convolutions do children in some western societies have to perform to score a point on this test when they live in a society that provides medicines as of need? In fact, they must play the test-maker's game. A clever test-taker knows how to do this. But if a child were to think more deeply and question the question in terms of the social morality the question assumes, he or she would quite simply lose the mark or point, and be given a lower test score for morality.

There is often a difference between what children reply in a test situation and what they do out of the sight of adults. In a wide survey of research into intelligence and morality, no recognisable relationship between measured giftedness and actual behaviour could be found (Pagnin and Adreani 2000). A study of young gifted children showed that although their scores were higher than average in tested moral reasoning, their playground behaviour did not reflect that (Abroms 1985). Rothman (1992) pointed out that 'IQ explains but little in the development of moral reasoning' (p. 330). He suggested that the higher morality scores of high-IQ children are due to their special social relationships with adults. So, it seems that although the intellectually gifted know what they should answer on the morality tests – they know how to play the game – they may or may not choose to abide by the rules in real life.

In fact, there is no reason to think that there is any relationship at all between high IQ and decency. Many top ranking Nazis were extremely intelligent and beautifully cultured (Zilmer et al. 1995). Hitler's propaganda minister, Joseph Goebbels, could easily have risen to the dizzy heights of Mensa, though the Führer himself might not have made it. The IQs of other cruel despots are not known, but it can be guessed that if they were running a country and countering clever plots to topple them, they were probably highly intelligent. Whatever you may feel about his morality, Fidel Castro is likely to be extremely intelligent, as is Osama bin Laden.

Conclusion

In spite of the beliefs and anecdotes about a relationship between morality and giftedness – positive or negative – the only evidence for a relationship lies in paper and pencil tests which share a grounding in western morality. In real life, there is no measured evidence of a relationship between morality and intellectual gifts, whether in children or adults.

We have begun to realise that what we call the 'civilised' values of reason and morality are in fact only a veneer of current social sanction, a veneer which cracks and breaks only too easily, a veneer which too often masks ethically questionable motives. There is no reason to think that suicide bombers and their leaders are less intelligent than those who band together to advocate peace, and certainly both groups believe wholeheartedly in the morality of what they are doing.

In accord with ethical competence theory, morality can be taught in schools, e.g. via class discussions and working through real-life problems (see Tirri and Pehkonen 2002; Tirri this volume). Moral character can be seen as a set of skills that can be honed towards expert levels of performance through training and practice. The skills of moral sensitivity enable quick reading and decision-making for moral dilemmas in a variety of contexts. These skills include keeping a goal in mind, staying on task, and making sure the ethical task is done, and that the task is done ethically.

Yet in the end, the only morality each of us can promote is what we believe – flexibly – to be the best way. The intellectually gifted, I suggest, have no greater claims to morality than anyone else, but what they do have is the capacity to understand moral conundrums in life, and to perceive arguments for what they are, set in their social contexts. Whether they actually chose to use their gifts to understand and see different points of view is another matter.

Contact address: joan@joanfreeman.com

Future Perspectives

Suggested priorities for gifted education over the next decade

Children's gifted and talented potential is too often lost in the UK by restricting selection to small percentages of pupils for extra education. This misses children who do not fit teachers' ideas of giftedness, because their gifts may lie elsewhere or are not immediately obvious. Freeman's Sports Approach (Freeman 1998) suggests that – as in sport – children should be encouraged to opt for study at a more advanced and broader level in any available area and engage with other keen learners. This identification by provision means that such facilities must be available to all, as sport is, rather than only to those selected by teachers, tests, family support or money to pay for extras. Such open access makes use of research-based understanding of the gifted and talented, notably the benefit of early focus on children's interests, as well as providing the motivated with facilities to learn and high standards to rise to.

Joan Freeman

19

Emotional intelligence: re-examining some preconceptions

Maria Dolores Prieto and Mercedes Ferrando

Murcia University, Spain

This chapter focuses on the emotional difficulties encountered by gifted children as they attempt to respond appropriately to the situations and people they encounter on a daily basis. The emotional needs of gifted children have been the topic of much research (Clark 1992; Hollingworth 1942; Janos and Robinson 1985; Silverman 1994), but as yet there are no definitive conclusions that gifted children cope any differently with environmental demands than their less able peers. The overall evidence suggests that individual outcomes depend on the individual and the specific situation.

This chapter reviews the central arguments concerning gifted children's potential social and emotional coping problems, and then discusses a number of recent studies. Finally, a study carried out in Spain, using an emotional quotient inventory to assess variations in emotional intelligence, is presented, concluding that gifted children have far fewer emotional problems than non-gifted children (Ferrando 2006).

Social and emotional predispositions of gifted children

There are three predominant perspectives concerning this issue in the literature. Gifted and talented (G&T) students can show (a) more emotional problems, or (b) more social problems than their less able peers, or (c) be better adjusted to social and emotional change than their age-peers. Clark (1992) and Silverman (1994) argue that a gifted child can be characterised as possessing an advanced sense of moral judgement, heightened self-awareness, and sensitivity to the expectations and feelings of others. Silverman (1994) points out that while these, and concomitant factors like introversion, idealism, perfectionism, and higher levels of emotional depth and intensity, are all perceived to be general indicators of the emotional complexity of gifted children, it is equally possible that many of these traits are not generalisable for all gifted children.

The descriptors above are all related to what Dabrowski (1964) called 'overexcitabilities' (OEs). Dabrowski argued that creatively gifted individuals have more pronounced responses to various stimuli. OEs may be thought as an abundance of physical energy, heightened acuity of the senses, vivid imagination, intellectual curiosity and drive, and a deep capacity to care

(Silverman 1994). There is evidence to indicate that gifted children have stronger OEs than their less gifted peers (Nelson 1989; Silverman 1993) making them more vulnerable to psychological problems than their peers. Sensitivity (concern for others and emotional ties), perfectionism (feelings of inadequacy and inferiority), intensity (extremes of emotion) and introversion (inhibition such as timidity and shyness), are all aspects of emotional OE (Silverman 1994).

Contrarily, there exists evidence that shows that gifted children do not necessarily show the social problems mentioned, but instead are more sensitive to interpersonal conflicts (Lubinski and Benbow 2000; Terman 1925). They experience greater degrees of alienation and stress than their less able peers, due to their higher cognitive capacities (Grossberg and Cornell 1988; Hollingworth 1942; Janos and Robinson 1985; Neihart 1999; Roedell 1986; Tannenbaum, 1983). In particular, Hollingworth (1942) suggested that highly intelligent children are prone to social and emotional adjustment problems. She originally proposed the concept of 'optimum intelligence', arguing that a certain range of intelligence is optimal for a child's personal happiness and adjustment to society. She proposed that children with Stanford–Binet intelligence test scores (IQ) levels between 125 and 155 are likely to have enough interests in common with their peers to enable cooperation and mutually fulfilling relationships, but beyond this range, were likely to incur a risk of psychosocial isolation.

Dauber and Benbow (1990) emphasise that the verbally gifted, in particular, are at risk. Roedell (1986) maintains that the more profound the giftedness, the more likely the student is to experience adjustment problems. In contrast, Grossberg and Cornell (1988) hypothesise that it is not the ability itself that is to blame, and that gifted children experience adjustment problems for the same reasons as other children; e.g. family or school issues. However, the idea that all individuals across the 'gifted' range possess an increased risk of psychosocial problems continues to exist among some practitioners and researchers.

According to Garland and Zigler (1999), the connection between giftedness and psychosocial problems becomes more apparent when heightened intellect combines with heightened sensitivities to diverse phenomena, or to a collection of characteristics with the potential for promoting adjustment problems, including perfectionism, non-conformity, idealism, developmental asynchrony, excitability, and unrealistic goals or expectations. In general, gifted children who report feeling different from their peers also report more negative perceptions of their social adjustment (Cross et al. 1995). They report that they have few friends, that they feel 'different', that they are often teased about being smart, and that they feel helpless to do anything about world problems.

A third group of researchers (e.g. Baer 1991; Freeman 1983) put forward evidence to support the idea that gifted children do not have more social and emotional problems than their non-gifted peers. In general, supporters of this view believe that the gifted are capable of greater understanding of themselves and others, due to their heightened cognitive capacities, and therefore cope better with stress, conflicts and developmental asynchrony (Garland and Zigler 1999). Freeman (1983) found no differences in rates of emotional deviance when she compared 70 high-ability children with two matched control groups. Baer (1991) found that gifted children are generally better adjusted than peers of average and below average intelligence. Baer believes that gifted students overall are characterised by mental flexibility, emotional resilience, and the ability to think positively. Such traits may account for better emotional adjustment. McCallister et al. (1996) contend that research studies show a mostly positive picture of gifted children, but that reports based on experience are more negative. They suggested that the discrepancy between experience and research may be due to small samples, or errors that may occurred when data was being analysed.

Freeman (1979) has observed that intellectual giftedness, whether measured by IQ or a non-verbal reasoning test, is not generally related to adjustment success. She has found that the life events that can bring about poor adjustments in gifted children are the same ones that affect other children adversely. However, there are aspects related to giftedness, such as hypersensitivity, perfectionism, and inflexible schooling, which can cause problems for a minority of gifted children, and bring about conflict, anxiety, and unwelcome behaviour. One problem she found was that gifted children do not necessarily benefit by the imposition of the label 'gifted', which brings myths and stereotypes with it. Freeman concluded that the gifted child has the same emotional needs as other children, and the same educational needs for expression and exploration, but that the difference lies in their intensity (Freeman 1979 this volume).

New perspectives on emotional intelligence

Several major research studies have been carried out using models of emotional intelligence (EI). These models conceptualise the abilities and skills which define emotional intelligence, and researchers have used various instruments to assess it. Four studies are presented here, as they inform conclusions from our own research.

The first study (Mayer et al. 2001), was an ethnographic attempt to check the relationship between the concepts of EI and emotional giftedness, as proposed by Dabrowski (1964). The sample consisted of 11 gifted children (aged 13 to 17) who were given the Multi-factorial Emotional Intelligence Scale (MEIS) and the Peabody Picture Vocabulary Test (PPVT) (Dunn and Dunn 1981). The children were also interviewed in order to find out how they coped with emotionally difficult situations, and to assess their social behaviours.

The results indicated that emotionally gifted children showed greater intelligence, involvement in tasks, and creativity than non-gifted children. The children who scored highest in EI (independent of their verbal IQ measure) appeared to cope better with varieties of peer relationships, as compared to those with lower EI. Those higher in EI discussed emotional situations in richer ways, including identifying many more of the subtle and sometimes conflicting feelings of those around them, compared even to other participants who roughly matched them in verbal IQ. Mayer et al. (2001) established that the individuals who had obtained the highest scores in the EI tests fitted the profile of emotional giftedness in children proposed by Dabrowski and Piechowski (1977). This profile presented emotionally gifted children as highly conscious of feelings and able to establish deeper relationships, as well as better able to clarify differences between themselves and others.

The objective of a second research study was to examine differences in EI between gifted and non-gifted students, and to explore the role of measurement procedures on the direction and magnitude of any observed group differences (Zeidner et al. 2005). This study took 83 academically gifted and 125 non-gifted high school students from Israeli secondary schools and compared EI scores, using the Mayer-Salovey-Caruso Emotional Intelligence Test (MSCEIT) (Mayer et al. 2002) and the Schutte Self-Report Inventory (SSRI) (Schutte et al. 1998). The results pointed to higher MSCEIT scores but lower SSRI scores for the gifted children, demonstrating that individual differences depend on the means used for evaluation. According to the study authors, the SSRI is not a very clear measure of EI because it overlaps with some personality factors, while the MSCEIT reproduces concepts of the theory on which it is based. In other words, whether or not gifted students differ significantly from their non-gifted peers depends entirely on the way EI is measured.

The third relevant study (Chan 2003) attempted to evaluate the EI and management of social conflict situations of 259 gifted children aged 13 years old. For this, the SSRI (Schutte et al.

1998) and the Social Coping Questionnaire (SCQ) (Swiatek 1995) were used. In this study the mean item responses and mean scale scores indicated that students obtained higher scores on Social Skills and Self-Management of Emotions, followed by Empathy and Utilization of Emotions.

The G&T pupils' highest scores from the SSRI were related to their social skills and ability to cope with emotions. The results of the study showed a correlation between emotional intelligence and gifted students' social coping strategies. Thus students with high IE scores used positive coping strategies such as 'valuing peer acceptance' and 'involvement in activities' which demanded higher 'social skills' and in addition, good 'utilisation of emotions'. On the other hand, poor self-management of emotions led to the use of the strategy of 'attempting avoidance'.

The fourth study relevant to our own (Schewean et al. 2006) focused on examining the social-emotional competences of gifted children, and the relationship between their school environments and their psychological well-being. Of interest in this study is the congruence across ratings of EI by the children and their parents and teachers. One hundred and sixty-nine gifted children were sampled first (84 male and 85 females, with a combined mean age of 11.45). Of these, 123 were enrolled in an academic programme specifically designed for gifted children and adolescents, and the other 46 were being taught in regular classroom settings.

A second sample of 1200 non-gifted children comprised a subset of cases from a large community-based sample of children and adolescents. Emotional intelligence was measured with the Bar-On Emotional Quotient Inventory: Youth Version (BarOn EQ-i: YV) (Bar-On and Parker 2000) in its two forms: self-report and 360°. The EI dimensions measured were intrapersonal, interpersonal, stress management, adaptability and total EI. Students had two scores on each EI dimension, one self-estimated, and the other estimated by their parents.

Schewean et al. (2006) found that the non-gifted students rated their inter-personal abilities significantly higher than did the gifted students. However, gifted students rated their intrapersonal and adaptability abilities significantly higher than did their peers. Furthermore, they found that the parents of the gifted students rated their children's abilities significantly higher in the areas of adaptability, stress management and in the total EI, than did the parents of the less able children.

The findings showed that within the gifted sample, those who remained in regular class settings scored slightly but significantly higher only on self-reported adaptability, as compared with those in special programmes. Parent and teacher ratings also supported the higher adaptability scores for gifted children in regular classes. In summary, the data showed that intellectually gifted children were seen by themselves, their parents, and their teachers to be as emotionally healthy overall as their non-gifted peers, at least as measured by the BarOn EQ-i: YV (Bar-On and Parker 2000)

With the conclusions of these four studies as a reference point, we decided to study the EIs of Spanish children who had been identified variously as gifted and non-gifted. The sample of gifted learners included 98 boys and girls ranging from 6 to 12 years old, from different schools in Murcia, Spain. They were identified as gifted using teacher nominations, ability tests scores, and creativity test scores (Torrance Thinking Creative Test; Torrance 1974b). We also gathered a sample of 945 non-gifted learners. All of the participants took the BarOn EQ-i: YV (Bar-On and Parker 2000).

The differences were statistically significant only for Adaptability (t = 4.466; df = 977; p < .001), in this case meaning a higher self-perception of the capacity to be flexible and to adjust emotions, way of thinking, and behaviours in accordance to environmental demands.

Table 5 Descriptive statistics for the EQ-i:YV dimensions

	Means & SD		Adjusted* Means & SD	
	G&T (n = 98)	Non-G&T (N=949)	G&T (n = 98)	Non-G&T (N=949)
Mood	57.4615	57.1371	3.3801	3.3610
	(6.3740)	(6.8219)	(.3749)	(.4012)
Adaptability	33.2553	30.7412	3.0232	2.7947
	(5.2954)	(5.1773)	(.4814)	(.4706)
Stress Management	38.8587	37.8146	2.9891	2.9088
	(6.4306)	(6.2461)	(.4946)	(.4804)
Interpersonal	28.1889	27.8681	3.1321	3.0965
	(3.7383)	(4.4254)	(.4153)	(.4917)
Intrapersonal	14.6947	14.7976	2.4491	2.4663
	(3.5791)	(3.7434)	(.5965)	(.6239)
EQ-i:YV total	11.6014	11.3150	3.0533	2.9993
	(1.3171)	(1.3459)	(.3142)	(.3020)

*Adjusted means: min = 1 to max = 4

Additionally, the gifted children showed more well-developed abilities to identify, define, and implement effective problem-solving solutions (Ferrando and Bailey 2006). However, no statistically significant differences were found for the total EQ score, neither for the other dimensions measured byt the EQ-i:YV

Conclusion

According to the data discussed here from five studies using different models and measurements of emotional intelligence, none of the earlier ideas about the personal and social maladjustment of high ability students was corroborated. It appears that emotional and social problems are not characteristic of gifted children.

These findings emphasise the importance of evaluating emotional intelligence in addition to cognitive skills when studying gifted children, supporting Weschler's (1950) suggestion that non-cognitive aspects are needed in order to provide a full understanding of the complex thinking of gifted children.

Further to our findings, we recommend the study of psychosocial variables related to giftedness, such as how some gifted and talented learners develop unusual degrees of compassion, or why gifted children sometimes decide to work below their capacities, hiding their talents, and how they cope with the high expectations placed on them by parents and teachers. A better understanding of social and emotional variables can provide useful information for those who are interested in supporting and fostering gifted development.

Contact address: lola@um.es

Future Perspectives

Suggested priorities for gifted education over the next decade

In Spain, optimal provision of gifted education can be considered through the following aspects. Efforts should be made to achieve more challenging opportunities for all children. For example, we must develop relevant educational strategies to identify our gifted and talented students and provide suitable, more inclusive curricula in our schools. Opportunities in terms of out-of-school provision need to be created and money invested from central government for researching and studying gifted education. To embrace this progression, we will need to collaborate with colleagues in other countries, such as the US and England, in order to take on board the new directions and knowledge that is currently available. Working effectively with policy makers, educators, communities, and families will also be emphasised. If we do all of this, the needs of our gifted students can be more effectively met.

Maria Dolores Prieto and Mercedes Ferrando

20

Too long neglected: giftedness in younger children

Valsa Koshy

Brunel University, UK

This chapter reports on the outcomes of a three-year project, commissioned by the British government, involving fourteen local education districts drawn from a range of socio-economic settings. The project was carried out as a set of action research projects, with practitioners working collaboratively with university academics, exploring practical strategies for enhancing educational provision for gifted children aged 4 to 7. Each project was designed to address the local schools' and education districts' needs within the context of a rapidly developing national agenda for gifted and talented education in the UK. Analysis of the fourteen case studies generated a number of issues with implications for classroom practice and policy. The findings from the projects enrich and extend the knowledge base and understanding of gifted and talented education in foundation and key stage one settings (4 to 7 years) in England and Wales.

Gifted education provision for young children in Britain

Two radical new initiatives gathered momentum in England and Wales between 1998 and 2003. A national strategy was launched for the enhancement of provision for children in the early years. Twenty-five early excellence centres were set up across the country, which were to serve as models for high quality practice in both education and child care (Sylva and Pugh 2005). Curricular guidance for teaching children in the foundation stage (3 to 5 years old) was provided by the government (Department for Education and Skills/Qualifications and Curriculum Authority 2000). Around the same time, the British government launched a gifted and talented initiative, initially aimed at driving standards in inner-city areas (DfES 1999). Secondary schools (with students aged 12–16 years) were required to identify the top 10 per cent of their intake as gifted and talented and provide a distinctive teaching and learning programme for them. In the following four years the gifted and talented initiative was extended to more local districts across the country and after a further two years, primary schools (whose intake includes children aged 9–11) were also included in the initiative.

It is interesting to note that neither the early years' programmes nor the gifted and talented initiatives made any provision for identifying or developing giftedness in younger children. As a consequence of canvassing support for this neglected group, in 2003 the author was commissioned by the British government to support groups of practitioners (themselves responsible for the education of children aged four to seven from local education districts across England and Wales) to carry out action research projects. These projects explored aspects of both identification and provision for younger gifted and talented children.

A cohort ignored?

A review of research literature undertaken by Koshy and Robinson (2006) suggests that of all the children with special needs, younger gifted children are the group most frequently ignored throughout the world. There are many educators who maintain that this age group of children has no special gifted learning needs whatsoever, and that it is far too early to think about their gifts and talents. Internationally, there are very few studies exploring aspects of giftedness in younger children, and we ask 'what may be lost by retaining the *status quo*?' We believe that there are losses for the children, for science, and for society at large. In societies that care about their children, it is difficult to justify the continued neglect of children for whom the ordinary preschool or school programme may be a poor fit. Like all children, gifted children deserve a happy childhood full of vigour, joy, optimism and growth, whether or not early intervention produces long-range differences in their attainment.

Gifted individuals of all ages thrive best in environments that match the level and pace of their development, with the joys and strengths that come from mastering challenges, as well as companions who share their interests, curiosity, depth of understanding, and sense of humour (Neihart et al. 2002). So, we must stop neglecting this group of students. In this chapter I have described some attempts by practitioners to make a start in meeting the needs of these children.

Who are these younger gifted and talented children? Defining giftedness in early childhood is a challenging task and no accepted definition exists (Coleman 2004; Cramond 2004; Gagné 2004; Sternberg and Davidson 2005). So, we must make do with a theoretically informed starting point toward a definition. For the study reported in this chapter we considered children who showed significantly advanced abilities and skills in any domain. In most of the research studies or initiatives in the research literature, it is the most advanced who are considered sufficiently different from their age peers as to need special attention outside their ordinary settings.

Although there is a paucity of research about young gifted and talented children, what we do know provides some guidance to build on. A landmark study of adults who were world-class achievers in sports (swimming, tennis), the arts (pianists, sculptors), and academics (mathematics, research neurology) by Bloom and his colleagues (1985), showed that precocious talents could often be observed in early childhood. The importance of the early years in areas such as classical music and dance has been affirmed many times (Winner 1996). There are significant implications of this for parents and others who work with younger children.

Early intervention programmes

There is evidence of the important role of parents in the early identification of giftedness and talent. Robinson found that at the University of Washington, when parents were asked to 'volunteer' precocious young children, they did so successfully (Koshy and Robinson 2006). Four such studies have been carried out by investigators associated with the Robinson Centre.

In each one, parents not only accurately identified very young children with advanced development; they could also claim that the advancement remained, or even steadily increased, during the next two to five years.

The most extensive literature on early school options for gifted children relates to early entrance to kindergarten or first grade (Robinson 2004). Almost all countries have dates by which children are supposed to enter kindergarten or regular school. Robinson (2006) points out that early entry has many advantages for gifted children since it is the least disruptive in terms of friendships and curriculum, is inexpensive, and at least in the beginning can provide appropriate challenges for the academically precocious child. Based on her research in the USA, Robinson maintains that very precocious readers will need additional curriculum adaptations, and that a one-grade acceleration is likely to prove insufficient by itself later on. This alternative does require decision-making when the child is quite young, however, and is difficult to reverse.

There are conflicting views on early school entry ranging from studies showing that younger accelerated children are less mature in terms of achievement and adjustment and are more often referred, because of suspicion of learning disabilities (Maddux 1983) and other studies which assert that children usually thrive academically after early entrance. Studies on acceleration have shown that social-emotional indicators in such situations tend to be slightly (but not dramatically) positive and that accelerated children do as well as other children (Colangelo, Assouline and Gross 2004). The few long-term studies (Hobson 1963; Worcester 1956) have tended to show early entrants in positions of leadership later on in school.

There are only a few reports in the literature of programmes specifically designed for younger gifted children, and even fewer that have used reliable research designs to evaluate the effectiveness of the interventions. Some of the programmes have targeted children whose development is distinctly advanced, while others have tried to encourage children 'of promise' who were growing up in unpropitious circumstances. Morelock and Morrison (1999) argue that a 'developmentally appropriate' curriculum for young, gifted children must take their advancement into account. They describe a framework for a multidimensional, five-level curriculum that proceeds from children's concrete, direct experiences through increasingly contextual and abstract dimensions crossing disciplines.

The Early Years project

The Early Years project drew on several important and respected models and perspectives concerning the emergence of giftedness. We drew on Gardner's (1993b) theory of multiple intelligences, Renzulli's (1976) three-ring model and Sternberg's (2000d) view of intelligence as developing expertise, to guide teachers through the complex processes of identification and provision. Several of VanTassel-Baska's (1998) guidelines for managing gifted programmes – e.g. accelerated groupings, differentiated curriculum resources, and appropriate teaching styles, were also taken into account.

There were three main objectives of the project. Firstly, we wanted to guide groups of practitioners, in collaboration with university tutors, in exploring aspects of educational provision for younger gifted children. Secondly, we wanted to identify issues which are of particular significance in the education of younger gifted and talented children. Thirdly, we hoped to contribute to a database of evaluated practices for wider dissemination so as to inform both policy and practice.

Action research was the selected methodology, and in-depth case studies were produced by each of the project teams. Practitioners undertaking research in collaboration with academic researchers has been growing in popularity in the UK for the past six years, enabling as it does both knowledge transfer and accessibility (Furlong 2004). Our aim was to encourage groups of teachers in the 'production of new knowledge' (Gibbons et al. 1994), in the context of their application to practice. All 150 local districts in England and Wales were invited to apply to be included in the action research projects. Of these, 91 districts applied; and 14 socio-economically representative groups were selected. Each group consisted of advisers and three practising teachers. Topics for exploration included a range of issues relating to gifted education.

Our intention was to provide in-depth case studies, which would serve as documentaries and the basis of replicable models in other similar contexts. The action researchers were in full-time posts when they began their journey of exploration of the complex terrain of gifted and talented education, with very little knowledge and experience of the topic. They were involved in constructing a framework of understanding for themselves and for fellow practitioners within their institutions, as well as others, through sharing experiences. They received support in research methodology and literature analysis. As government initiatives in gifted education are fairly new in the UK, they also needed considerable input relating to all aspects of giftedness, and giftedness in younger children in particular. Data were gathered from the following sources:

- demographics of participating institutions and their intake of students
- questionnaires
- interviews of students and colleagues
- participant observation notes
- notes of visits by university tutors
- group discussions of participants at the university
- video recordings
- practitioners' logs
- interim and final reports and case studies
- recorded evidence of ongoing samples of children's work and responses during lessons.

Although project participants were aware of the limitations of action research in terms of generalisability, it was possible to identify common themes and issues across cases. The richness of the gathered data helped the project teams to make useful interpretations for early years practitioners. Each project was designed to address the local schools' and education districts' needs within the context of a rapidly developing national agenda for gifted and talented education in the UK. Hence, some projects focused more on approaches to identifying young gifted and talented learners, while others took curriculum provision as their main focus.

Some projects were subject specific (music, mathematics, and writing), while others explored cross-curricular and thematic approaches to provision. For some of the research projects, the individual needs of specific subgroups of gifted learners predominated; for example, gifted children with hearing impairments, those with English as an additional language (EAL), and those with behaviour issues. And yet again, for some projects, the broader themes of transition, or relationships with parents or the wider community provided the key focus. Despite the diversity of the projects, it was possible to discern a range of common themes and shared experiences across the cases (Koshy et al. 2006). The following analysis of a representative sample of the case studies shows the developing expertise of a group of practitioners concerned with creating opportunities for the education of very young gifted children.

The challenge of meeting the needs of the exceptionally gifted was one of the major issues highlighted in several of the projects. Not surprisingly, practitioners found that the needs of the truly exceptional young child were difficult to meet within a whole class situation. An enrichment cluster set up in a central venue, following the principles of Renzulli's (1976) enrichment triad, was found highly effective in one district where twenty schools sent their most able pupils to the cluster. They carried out in-depth explorations, created mathematical games, planned and built model bridges – all scaffolded by adults including experts from the local university. Three projects highlighted the conflicts and dilemmas faced by teachers who were expected to follow a nationally imposed curriculum employing whole class teaching methods, knowing that there were students in their class whose understanding of both mathematical content and the use of sophisticated processes were years ahead of their peers.

Strategies for nurturing the talents of the exceptionally able included adopting principles of the Reggio Emilia programme, which offers students personalised learning opportunities arising from their interests. Another strategy, which resulted in positive outcomes, was the use of older mentors (17-year-olds) to work with groups of gifted 6-year-olds. Young students who worked with mentors described their pleasure in communicating with them about complex mathematical topics. Two pioneering projects involved designing curriculum materials for special groups of younger children whose identification and inclusion in gifted programmes posed particular difficulties. One of the projects targeted deaf children, and the other was situated in an inner-city school in an area of high social deprivation. In both cases the 5- to 6-year-olds had difficulties with spoken language and with reading. Activities which provided opportunities to demonstrate their talents thorough doing or making things were used successfully. This led to the identification of giftedness in children whose talents were otherwise masked by disadvantage.

Video recordings showed situations that teacher researchers described as 'magic moments': one showed a deaf child of 5 demonstrating initiative in transferring water: she showed a firm understanding of hydraulic pressure by siphoning water from a higher to a lower level. Another gifted young child reproduced from memory a map of her neighbourhood, showing a remarkable talent for spatial awareness. Teachers' documentation of conversations as the project developed and displays of work were other major features of this project. They heard that 5-year-old Matthew had claimed during an interview that he called himself a 'waiter'. By this he meant that he was always 'waiting for others to catch up'. Another 5-year-old, Sam, had declared at the start of the project, 'I am on the hardest shelf, but it is still all too easy'. He used to be on the 'disruptive register' and had been being taken off that list after joining the gifted cluster.

In demonstrating the effectiveness of many different approaches to adapting learning opportunities for exceptionally advanced young children, the results of this study challenge the assumption that whole-class teaching and adherence to a prescribed curriculum are the best ways to meet the needs of gifted younger children. Happily, I can report that the importance of investing in the curiosity of the very young and the pursuit of exceptional personal intellect has been affirmed in the new UK national quality standards for gifted and talented education (DfES 2006b): education in the early years (4 to 7 years old) has now been included.

Contact address: valsa.koshy@brunel.ac.uk

Future Perspectives

Suggested priorities for gifted education over the next decade

I would like to see the development of three aspects of gifted education, within the next ten years in the UK. First, that gifted and talented children are to be nurtured from the early years. As we have evidence of the significant impact of early years education on children's future development, realising and developing their potential is important for both the children themselves and for the country. Second, the waste of talent in areas of social deprivation should be addressed through the search for and fulfilment of submerged talent through well-researched interventions. Third, I think we as a developed country should provide leadership in talent development of children in developing countries, thereby accelerating the radical change of purpose of globalisation for the benefits of all children and adults of the future. Then, there is also a general need for more research, academics and practitioners working together, to generate new knowledge and perspectives in gifted education.
Valsa Koshy

21

Teaching the able child . . . or teaching the child to be able?

Jan Hughes

Doncaster Education Service, UK

The philosophy of education posited in this chapter is my own. It stems from my natural way of being, my intrinsic knowledge and beliefs, and has been honed by a lifetime in the teaching profession. My experiences have led me to a deeper understanding of myself, my values and my motivations. At times my practitioner research matches the validated research of others, and this will be referenced where appropriate. Overall, though, this work documents the conclusions of a reflective practitioner, and reflects the tacit knowledge described by Whitehead and McNiff (2006): 'Practitioner researchers already know what they are doing in their everyday lives in the sense that knowledge is embedded in what they do' (p. 13). It is a lived experience.

The beginning

At first I skipped to school, then I walked, more slowly. I can trace my disillusionment: the infant class where, bursting with good things inside my head, I began to write; until stilled by a voice. I did not have permission to write, nor would I know what to write since I had not been told. This was a new concept: knowledge was not within me; I had to wait to have it placed there. My intrinsic understanding was irrelevant. So I discovered that school was not about my thoughts or feelings, and I learned to be guarded.

Then, in the first junior class, I battled alone with my sums, misunderstood the concept, and received pages of red crosses; not such a problem until I and fellow unfortunates were forced to hold up our ignorance to the rest of the group for them to view our lack of intelligence. I learned three more things in school that day: a deep-rooted fear of maths, a realisation that 'cleverness' is not seen to be a process and never to trust. As a middle junior, aged nine, I risked bringing to school the writings I had done for pleasure, at home. These were rejected as not being my own work. I was placed alone to write a poem, as proof that I could do it. So I learned to have less faith in my ability, and to be defensive. In the older junior class, aged eleven, I came across the concept of ranking. All 48 of us were given a number. Mine was three. I wondered what it felt like to be number one, and I wondered about the other 45 with numbers below mine. What might be the differences between us all? Which were important, and why?

I had ceased to be an eager learner. We had all ceased to be the divergent individuals we once were, full of unknown promise. We had been moulded into an amorphous mass ready to be sorted and divided by our convergent responses. If they had noticed the beauty of my different wings, maybe they would not have clipped them. My learning experiences diminished my self-efficacy. Claxton (1999b) draws attention to the fact that believing in your ability to control events affecting your life has a powerful influence in learning. Resilience, and therefore mastery, is reduced in those who believe their self-efficacy is weak.

Learning

I carried all my learning with me to the high school. I had been streamed. How was it possible to judge me when no-one knew me? I had never been asked questions about myself, or had the opportunity to ask questions of others. How could anyone know how my brain worked, or where my thoughts led? I discovered that the trick was to guess what was inside the teacher's head and to say The Right Thing. The trouble was that my head was full of questions and curiosities and I had lots of possible Right Things that I wanted to air. According to Bob Samples, quoted in George (1992), 'Children never give a wrong answer . . . they correctly answer a different question. It is our job to find out which one they answered correctly and honour what they know' (p. 18). It is easy to assume that a different or unusual response is wrong. Before teachers intervene and correct they must create opportunities to explore children's minds. Misconceptions need guidance, but to realign another's thinking without exploration is presumptuous and obstructs the reasoning processes from which new knowledge is created and new insights gained. Being listened to is empowering. It boosts understanding and creates confidence in the learner.

But I knew from previous experience that knowledge was not to be found within me, so thinking wouldn't be helpful. I had learned that there were no strategies for improving: I either knew The Right Thing, or I didn't; I was able, or I wasn't. I did not accept this easily. I lost confidence and gained lots of detention slips. I decided that school was an emotionally risky business. I had acquired the fixed or 'entity' view of intelligence that Dweck (1999 this volume) describes from her research studies: those who believe in a fixed state of intelligence are threatened by intellectual challenge and failure; they do less well than growth-oriented ('incremental') learners who believe a focus on effort and strategy will bring success.

What I did well, I was prepared to repeat. I wouldn't risk trying something new: the consequences of failure were humiliation and loss of self-esteem. Effort highlighted my lack of ability. Perseverance was pointless: I had been shown that there was no process to intelligence. Where I was unsure or held other opinions, I withdrew or became aggressive – a result of the fear, anxiety and panic engendered in me by my educational environment. I held fast to my different beliefs in the complex, imaginative, and creative world of my mind. For some, I became a difficult pupil. I found freedom in physical education. My body soared, and so, mutely, did my mind. This was the 'optimal experience' ('flow') described by Csikszentmihalyi (1990): 'The autotelic experience, or flow, lifts the course of life to a different level. Alienation gives way to involvement, enjoyment replaces boredom, helplessness turns into a feeling of control, and psychic energy works to reinforce the sense of self . . .' (p. 69).

I knew I had become worthy when I was awarded the Physical Education (PE) prize, but not so worthy as others, since the PE prize was always presented last.

Status quo

I believe the UK education system violates basic tenets of social justice in its preoccupation with narrow bodies of knowledge, hierarchically arranged. Those who have fared well in the system, including many teachers, perpetuate it; they may indeed have a vested interest in maintaining the status quo. Privileged classes fare better in education, where opportunities, support, resources, self-belief and values are essential to success in a narrow academic agenda. Our top schools and universities are testament to the promotion of those with an advantaged family background. We have created an educational underclass. Gardner (1993b) suggests that this uniform view of the assessment of minds, based on IQ measurement and the pencil-and-paper testing of facts, is elitist, benefiting certain already-advantaged people and schools. Based on neurological, educational, clinical and cognitive evidence, he proposes a different view; that of recognising multiple intelligences.

Being able

The term 'able' needs qualifying: able to do what, and in what circumstances? If acquiring a body of knowledge is important, who decides which body of knowledge, and by what criteria? How should this be measured? What is the point of knowledge unless applied in a meaningful way? Knowledge acquisition alone does not define a superior brain. Able people demonstrate intelligent behaviours resulting in products; they make connections, identify possibilities, and create solutions; they question the known and travel further to create the new. Renzulli (2006, this volume) argues for moving beyond 'schoolhouse giftedness'. History tells us that it has been the creative and productive people of the world, the producers rather than the consumers of knowledge, the reconstructionists of thought in all areas of human endeavour, that have become recognised as truly gifted individuals. History does not remember persons who merely scored high on IQ tests and/or learned to do their lessons well.

In contrast to the English definition that divides giftedness and talent by domain of concentration, I subscribe instead to Gagné's view that giftedness refers to a student's outstanding potential and ability in one or more domains, (intellectual, creative, socio-affective, and sensorimotor), and that talent refers to outstanding performance in one or more fields of human activity, and emerges from ability as a consequence of the student's learning experience (1997 this volume). However, since potential is limitless, and not always readily recognisable, it is an unknown, and therefore developmental for all. The learning process is complex and changeable; chance is a crucial factor. It is time to re-examine our understanding of intelligence and education, to reassess the usefulness of our definitions and measurement procedures. The Reggio Emilia project in Italy supports the concept of the 'competent child'. Rinaldi (2006) writes: 'The answer . . . for Reggio has been the "rich child" . . . based on the understanding that all children are intelligent, meaning that all children are embarked on a course of making meaning of the world, a constant process of constructing knowledge, identity and value' (p. 13).

The necessity for change

'Don't go, you make me feel good'. Jane and I were going places, but I was leaving. She sat beside me at the end of the last lesson of my teaching career, and her words echoed my feelings for her, feelings of trust, belief, respect and expectation. Jane had long ago acquired a perception of herself as an average pupil, with limitations. I had aimed to help her break through that limiting label by concentrating on the process of learning. My experience echoes the work of Hart et al. (2004). Their case studies support a rejection of ability labelling, limited grade expectations, and subsequent glass ceilings, in favour of inclusive practices that allow all pupils to grow. We all need to feel good about ourselves, or the idea of 'believe to succeed' is beyond us. In my teaching career I have learned a lot. I am not prepared to be the omnipotent voice, giving students the benefit of my judgements of them, exercising limiting decisions that are not mine to make. I do not know how far my students can go, or in which fields they can excel in the future. I believe we all have the capacity go beyond our current positions, and all we can be sure about is that no-one knows our limits: a view endorsed by Wallace (2000a): 'Can any of us say that we have reached our full potential?' (p. 7).

Wallace proposes that, while we challenge and excite the obvious high performers, we should also be mindful that there are others whom we have yet to intrigue, who might surprise us if we can engage them. Identification of abilities through wide provision is essential. Sternberg's triarchic theory of intelligence (this volume) posits that successful intelligence is an interplay between conventional (analytic), practical, and creative intelligences. Hymer with Michel (2002), invoking Sternberg, explain:

> Conventional conceptions of intelligence are incomplete and inadequate . . . They've configured schooling and society in unfortunate ways, but applications of the broader concept of Successful Intelligence can actually improve people's cognitive abilities in the classroom and at work. The concept will result in substantial benefits to individuals, institutions and society.
>
> (p. 15)

Knowledge bases, and global accessibility, are changing more rapidly than at any other time. Young people need to think flexibly and adapt to unknown situations to be able to function in a changing society where yesterday's certainties are now shifting sands. There is a desperate need for them to think, as individuals and interdependently, and visualise themselves as part of a global community. Freeman (2001) found in her longitudinal study of giftedness that:

> The most successful examinees of all, normally from the selective schools, showed a lack of broad concern . . . their natural curiosity had been sated because of heavy spoon-feeding . . . One father spoke sadly of his highly successful daughter, 'The disappointing thing to me is her lack of desire to find out for herself. She lacks the questing mind of a good scientist.'
>
> (p. 131)

A major reason for disillusionment with teaching is the advance of the 'I' culture. Students are more self-centred, expect more, are perceived to be blameless, and are more detached from society. Our education system has some responsibility here. We have removed from their experience the idea that they should connect their thinking to society and realistic situations, take reasoned actions and accept responsibility for the consequences. They are told what and how to think, and what it is important to know. Depth of thought and breadth of creative responses to problematical situations are less important. This convergence and closing down of original thought has created individuals who lack awareness and feel no responsibility to themselves or their role in society. Freeman's studies support this argument:

'I feel disadvantaged . . . I crammed a lot of science and didn't develop myself culturally, I've never read novels . . . I've never bought a book in my life . . . I was quite happy to be railroaded, and I didn't think a lot or question things. That's how I came to try LSD . . .' (2001, p. 208).

My childhood experiences of education and my experience and reflection as a teacher have led me to believe that ranking students is simplistic and unhelpful to their development. It reflects a fixed view of intelligence, which leads to limiting expectations, both for the teacher and the pupil. I have felt and observed the frustration and misery of learned helplessness and the damaging belief that value and worth are gained only through examinations. Gardner argues that in assessment of individuals our society suffers from three biases: cultural values, a focus on readily testable abilities, and the belief that certain approaches, such as logical mathematical thinking are superior. He believes we need to embrace wider views of intellect: 'If it can't be tested, it sometimes seems it is not worth paying much attention to . . . assessment can be much broader, much more humane . . . (we) should spend less time ranking people and more time trying to help them' (1993, p. 12).

Our exam systems isolate students and do not for the most part relate to realistic situations – thereby increasing stress and anomie. Those who cope well, however, have mastered or accepted this environment. Since educators rarely give credence to intelligence in practical situations, it should not be a surprise that high academic achievement does not predict career or life success. To achieve highly in life we must have passionate, obsessive commitment to our own goals; we must make decisions, create a plan, try our ideas and reform our thinking as a result of experience. Csikszentmihalyi observed that, 'One must develop skills that stretch capacities, that make one become more than what one is' (1990, p. 213).

The numbers game

Education is obsessed with the (easily) measurable; we have reduced the complexities of abilities and intelligence to numbers. We have created artificial intelligence. Students must answer set questions of isolated knowledge in a limited amount of time, and at given times in the calendar. The frequency of right answers can be converted into comparative numbers; these will then decide who is able (and who is not). Thus has been devised an absolute measure, with no room for deviation, making it easy to classify, box, and label students. Those who refuse to enter the box become the designated deviants, to be differently labelled (behaviour problem? low achiever? able underachiever?), and/or brought back into line.

The educational system has somehow taken on an omniscient voice on what is important, with a fatal flaw that the importance ranking has little reference to the real world. The numbers are used to predict other numbers, to be similarly gathered at a later date, the resulting totals deciding which students are ultimately successful (and unsuccessful) in their education. This makes no sense. It is impossible to abstract the interwoven facets of intelligent behaviours across the spectrum of human activity and stack them in a neat numerical order of importance. Chen and Gardner (1994, quoted in Torff 1997, pp. 37–38) state that '. . . human beings have unique combinations of abilities that are qualitatively different and cannot be quantitively ranked and sorted'.

Changing the goalposts

'I thought I understood. I thought I could do this subject. What else can't I do, that I thought I could?' This profound and reflective question came from a pupil who had discovered that, following a disappointing test result, she was to move down in the group rankings.

She internalised the self-doubt, the effects becoming noticeable in judgements of herself as a capable human being. The destruction of a child's belief has devastating consequences; actions that cause this are indefensible. Did we ask the right questions of the child, or of all the children we have 'grouped according to abilities'? How can we be sure that our system of sorting and classifying children is the right one? Is it accurate, or merely an administrative convenience? If it is possible to be accurate, what are the consequences of inaccurate assignments? What self-perceptions are we engendering, and how is this limiting, for both top set and lower set children? What are we measuring when we decide for children what they are capable of achieving? Would a child moving up or down a set have become more able, or less able? Or should we question the system of assigning children to ability levels?

I am reminded of the Hippocratic oath of the medical profession: 'First, do no harm' (Haight this volume). Yapp (2005) envisages a transformed education system supporting lifelong learning, where students are equipped with skills, competencies, attitudes and self esteem to enable them to make best use of their talents. He believes education should focus on the journey, not the destination; that the need to apply learning in changing circumstances and maintain confidence in unknown contexts is an essential factor.

The keys to learning

Teachers hold the keys to learning for future generations; we also have enormous power to curtail and prevent learning. Too often, we have exercised the latter (consciously or unconsciously) to the detriment of countless numbers who have exited our schools. If you ask many adults, they are immediately able to say what they cannot do. Many will trace awareness of their inability back to schooldays. Some believe that, given different circumstances, they could learn to overcome their difficulties. Others are antagonistic towards the origin of their failure; they do not believe in their potential to improve, and lack the interest or desire to do so. Their learning capacity and motivation have been disastrously impaired. Many others, despite doing poorly in their education, have made successes of their lives. There are famous examples, and also many unsung heroes and heroines, who have capitalised on qualities which go unrecognised and unrewarded in our schools.

Conversely, there is evidence that too often we have failed to equip children labelled 'gifted' and 'able' at school with the necessary resources for living and thriving in the real world. Torff (1997) observed that standardised tests are a poor predictor of adult success; real world application of skills bears little resemblance to a decontextualised exam situation. Goleman (1998a) argues that emotional intelligence is a better indicator and predictor of success in life than IQ, citing (for one example) studies which compared successful and failing executives and demonstrated that the crucial differential was the failure to perform well in the emotional intelligence domains.

We should be looking for the skills and qualities that are found in successful adults, and integrating these into the processes of education, recognising and affirming in our actions that we can grow ability. This will enable more young people to become autonomous, highly functioning adults. I have seen, repeatedly, the passionate, resilient, persistent child eventually outstrip the achievements of the child who appears to be 'naturally talented', and who often falls at the first hurdle. I have also seen the child with innate ability become the brightest star, when desire, commitment, belief and ability to learn combine.

Process

In our most enabling nursery classes the children are more likely to be curious, ask endless questions, expound theories and take risks. They shape their own learning, often with others, with the teacher as a guide. They understand by talking and applying, and they create their own knowledge. They may be true learners in their preparedness to try something out and structure actions from failures without the 'self' being diminished. It is possible to observe in them the learning process, and the growth of intelligence, and to appreciate the beauty of their different wings.

Fifteen years later I have observed passive, dependent 6th formers (aged 18), with predicted high grades in Advanced Level exams who are completely divorced from the process of learning. They are unable to create meaning from their knowledge, so it becomes meaningless. They are unaware that they have become disabled. Lipman describes similar observations, stating, 'We must capitalise on the natural gifts that children bring to school – their curiosity and hunger for meaning' (cited in Fisher 2003, p. 27). He asserts that children in co-operative and collaborative situations function at an intellectually higher level. They construct meaning together and think more deeply than those in more isolated, factual learning environments.

Claxton (1998) defines an effective learner as a discerning individual who can successfully combine 'the different ways of knowing'. He argues that active discovery creates confidence, and a sense of competence as an explorer on the learning journey. Children must be enabled and encouraged to think freely, and to question. Knowledge, concepts, and skills must be purposeful, and learners need to play an active part in defining, acquiring, shaping, and using them. Strategies and effort are worth rewarding: outcomes, less so. If we reward the obvious we are teaching children to protect the self when the going gets tough: we are preventing learning. Those who are rewarded for 'natural ability' become performance oriented, and stay within their comfort zones, as I learned to do as a child; those who seek mastery value effort and are motivated to persevere, a position supported by Dweck's studies (1999, this volume). We need to uncover the motivations of individuals and light the passions, so that they become self-sustaining. Claxton (1999a) states:

> Contrary to common belief, virtuosi are characterised much more by their dedication than by their innate ability. They do not have some God-given talent that makes learning easy. What they do have . . . is usually a fortuitous set of circumstances that gives them the confidence that mastery can be obtained, and therefore the commitment to go for it.
>
> (p. 81)

Independence

The ultimate objective of education should be independent, interdependent lifelong learning for all. This agenda will flourish where the individual is at the centre; where education providers believe that success is individual and incremental, and challenges are personalised and developmental; where expectations are high and glass ceilings eliminated. Students will risk stretching themselves where a fluid view of intelligence allows them to believe that they can become cleverer, and the varied nature of learning is communicated and facilitated. Since desire is the key, our young people need to find challenges interesting, relevant, and achievable. There must be collaborative learning opportunities in a non-threatening environment where abilities in divergent fields are celebrated and equally valued; where thinking processes are made visible and creativity is facilitated; where challenge through the creating and solving of problems is the basis for the development of intellect and autonomy.

Giftedness is not a fixed state and I view the term 'gifted education' with caution. I believe in the fluidity of intelligence and I value achievement in all domains. Children who exhibit advanced performance or aptitude, relative to their peers, in any given arena need to experience the conditions for learning and the opportunities for both intellectual and applied challenge which will enable them to move beyond the comfort of their current status and towards mastery. At times differentiated provision may be required.

However, as educators we are working with the unknown. We must temper control with humility and provide the conditions for all children to have confidence in themselves as learners. Teachers must stand alongside their pupils and equip them to go beyond accepted wisdom. We must teach all children to become able. This is my vision of inclusive gifted and talented education.

Contact address: Jan.Hughes@doncaster.gov.uk

Future Perspectivess

Suggested priorities for gifted education over the next decade

Giftedness is complex. In the UK, we must review systems for measuring intelligence and success and recognise crucial factors like personal qualities and learning processes. We must remove unsubstantiated divisions between gifts and talents; adopting a definition rooted in research evidence. The validity of the National Register must be questioned, and labelling discontinued. Giftedness evolves and factors are developmental: it cannot be definitively fixed and measured. It is grown, not diagnosed. We must enable effective recognition of gifted behaviours in all aspects of human endeavour, while deconstructing the myth of a hierarchy of gifts and talents. Conformist testing and limiting age-related expectations in schools must be reduced. School curricula for creativity, emphasising creativity and risk-taking must be promoted. Giftedness is not a ready-made package. Exceptionality is developed through the interplay of many factors, and is earned through passionate and dogged pursuit of personal goals with effort over time.   Jan Hughes

22

Global success and giftedness

Carmen Creţu
Alexandru Ioan Cuza University, Romania

Understanding Global Success

Global Success (GS) is a complex reflection of personal excellence, achieved as a result of tackling challenges. The GS concept has been built from a holistic perspective, and considers the multitude of forms that an individual's personal successes might take (e.g. learning, profession, social life, relationship, family life, etc.). GS addresses the complex linkage of each form to all other forms of personal success at a certain moment of an individual's life. The global interaction among all these forms of success affects each of the various aspects of every human being: vitality/health; financial welfare; intrinsic occupational satisfaction; aesthetic satisfaction; civic participation; and moral/spiritual/religious fulfilment. GS, as a developing theory, suggests that the identification and multi-dimensional analysis of one's personal values, or axiological system, from a lifespan perspective, is important for understanding the interrelationship between success and giftedness.

Usually, the concept of success is perceived as a sociological construct and is understood more as an outcome than as a dynamic developmental process. I think that global success involves many more dimensions than is captured in the usual social, external connotations of success. I propose that it be understood as incorporating a person's entire life construction. Also, we consider the impact of GS on what giftedness means from a gifted individual's point of view.

In order to achieve a better understanding of the significance of personal global success to real-life contexts, such as the learning experience for gifted students in schools, we refer to current psychological theories of learning, and to curriculum models. We also recommend the development of life-long educational strategies to improve global success.

Global Success' main characteristics

GS may be viewed as multi-determined, multi-dimensional, multi-levelled, individualised, and multi-functional. By taking these characteristics into account, we build a theoretical base for the holistic appraisal of high ability characteristics. GS is multi-determined insofar as the complex human personality is biologically, psychologically, culturally and socially multi-determined (Figure 4).

Note that from a non-positivistic knowledge perspective we could include in the 'other variables' a new line of causality: chance, hazard, or even a cosmic/universal or religious dimension. We should dare to consider such novel perspectives even if our available research methodology is far from scientifically adequate. We have to be aware of the evolution of

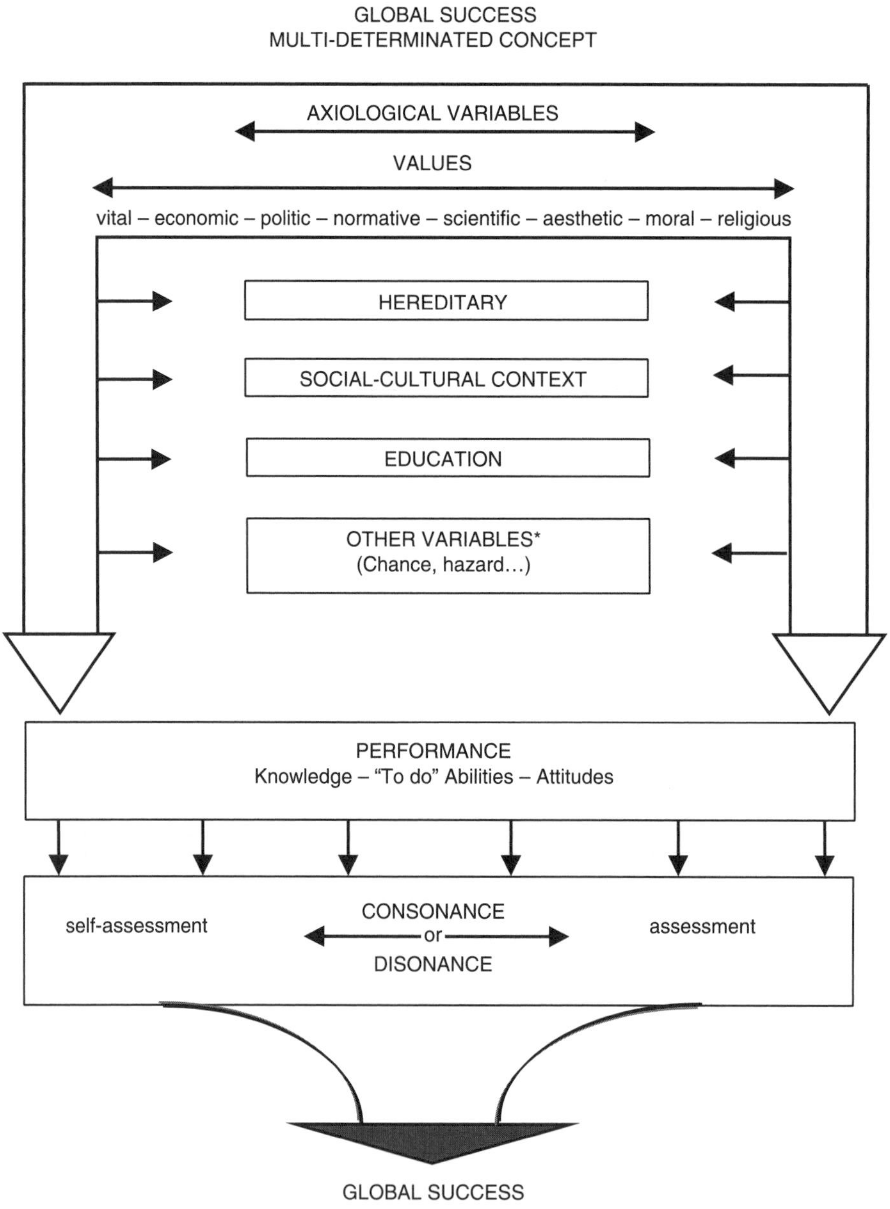

GLOBAL SUCCESS
MULTI-DETERMINATED CONCEPT

AXIOLOGICAL VARIABLES

VALUES

vital – economic – politic – normative – scientific – aesthetic – moral – religious

HEREDITARY

SOCIAL-CULTURAL CONTEXT

EDUCATION

OTHER VARIABLES*
(Chance, hazard...)

PERFORMANCE
Knowledge – "To do" Abilities – Attitudes

self-assessment   CONSONANCE   assessment
              —or—
             DISONANCE

GLOBAL SUCCESS

Figure 4 Global success as a multi-determined concept

170

non-conventional fields of knowledge. Actually, many of these non-scientific determinants like chance or hazard are referred to by scientists as 'black box concepts'.

The issues of multi-determination and multi-affiliation of human excellence are the focal point of the investigation of the relationship of GS to giftedness. The development of this world-view of giftedness simultaneously involves several fields of knowledge: sciences, philosophy, mythology, religion and other spiritual traditions of different cultures on the earth. Their merging leads mainly to the co-evolution of the specific knowledge fields and to the gradual break-up of knowledge boundaries. The investigation of GS implies not only a cross-field approach, but also an intercultural one. Although discovering and recognising a multitude of forms of expression of human excellence, the traditional psychological and sociological approaches of education fail to satisfy our curiosity about talents that are hidden or manifested unconventionally.

GS is multi-dimensional, incorporating diversity in dimensions of talent expression (see Figure 5 for a visual depiction of the six dimensions):

- the nature of abilities (general, special, systematic and non-systematic developed abilities (Gagné 1991, 1993, this volume)); multiple intelligences (Gardner 1983, 1994); wisdom, intelligence, and creativity synthesised (Sternberg 2003c, this volume); emotional intelligence (Goleman 1995);
- areas of social expression (school, family, friends, groups of people coming together to participate in shared hobbies, etc.), where GS can be examined through the individuals' projects, actions, and results (Figure 5);
- psychological processes (cognitive, sensory, perceptual, representational, intellectual, imaginative, memory-related, linguistic, intuitive; emotional; motivational; volitional;
- developmental factors (heredity, social environment, education, chance, spiritual or religious);
- fields of aspiration (professional, familial, social);
- personality style (competitive, co-operative, demonstrative, aggressive, restrained).

GS is multi-levelled when interpreted from a systemic perspective. GS, as a system that incorporates the whole range of individual potential abilities and manifest performances, is the result of the co-development of all its dimensions. The development of particular dimensions is typically unequal and sometimes compensatory. The complex continuum is perceived and expressed at an individual level as personal GS.

Feelings of self-achievement, self-esteem and happiness are derived from a positive correlation between a person's value and successes. Opposite feelings occur when individuals place at the top of their hierarchy values different from those emphasised in their fields of professional expertise. For instance, a man may be financially successful, but if his current priority is success in different arenas – e.g. scientific or political – he may have few chances of achieving something he will experience as real success. We have observed that such cases are less frequent in real life, because there is generally a convergence and a balance between the nature and the level of abilities and motivation. Conforming to the theory of 'personal talent' (Moon 2003), people seem happier when their awareness of personal talent facilitates a values/success balance through the development of goal selection and self-regulation skills.

The individualised character of GS reflects the uniqueness of each individual, and leads to a recommendation for the individualisation of curriculum for gifted learners. Differentiation for highly able children should include the recognition of and respect for children's feelings of GS.

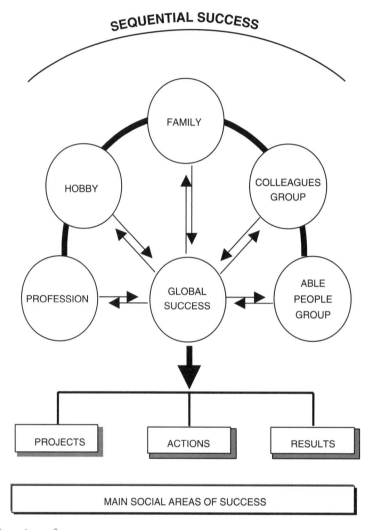

GLOBAL SUCCESS

MULTI-DIMENSIONAL CONCEPT

Figure 5 Dimensions of success

Design and development of differentiated curriculum should be adopted as professional stand-ards in teacher training and teacher assessment processes.

Historically, success has been an object of reflection for philosophers and novelists more than for psychologists or educators. Of course the concept of success has enjoyed a great deal of attention from both theoretical and empirical sociological research, but has not typically been connected with giftedness. Recently there has been an explosion of 'how-to' literature on success, pragmatic and commercial books purporting to teach people how to obtain maximum success in their lives. Many of these how-to books are all too happy to tell readers exactly what 'real' success is and how to achieve it.

What makes success?

The literature on excellence has provided several different theoretical models. The GS model emerged from the outcomes of several theories (Gagné 1991; Gardner 1983, 1999; Goleman 1995; Renzulli 1978; Sternberg 1999d) and more recently, Moon (2003). The common components of giftedness/high ability/talent across these theories include general intelligence, successful intelligence, multiple intelligence, emotional intelligence, personal talents, motivation, and creativity.

Global success factors

Many empirical studies stress the importance of nurturing giftedness. Mönks and his collaborators (Mönks et al. 1983, 1985) have provided a dynamic description of the development of giftedness in a lifespan view, with three main external factors responsible for gifted development in adolescence – family, school and peers – and the same factors can be applied to adulthood. Another interesting factor, the courage to present oneself as gifted has been identified by Landau (1991). Alongside this kind of 'inner world factor', we have found two others to be vital for giftedness development and affirmation (Creţu 1993, 1997, 1998): (a) the attitudes responsible for an individual's movement toward universal values; and (b) the emotional/affective development responsible, along with motivation, for the individual's involvement in activity. In the framework of the GS model, we can view both factor categories as working together as a global system of nurturing excellence (see Figure 6).

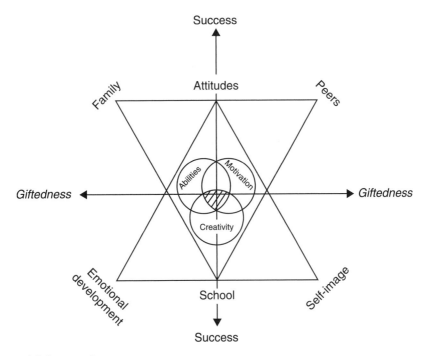

Figure 6 Global success factors

How do giftedness and success correlate?

Figure 7 illustrates the dynamics of GS in real contexts. Understanding how to improve GS strategy and implement it in education, as well as in other life contexts leads to a consonance between success and the promotion of giftedness/talent.

The gifted and the successful population is like a fuzzy system

In trying to describe the concept of global success, we have examined the concept of 'fuzzy systems'. By this we mean a class of vague relationships. If some traits include behaviours that allow for their exact measurement and psychometric description, many other processes either lack psychometric properties or have not yet been investigated sufficiently well to allow reliable measurement. Thus arises the need for a theoretical approach able to operate with a degree of imprecision.

The incompatibility principle was discovered by an outstanding specialist in systems theory, the American professor Zadeh (1973; Zadeh et al. 1975). He observed that as the complexity of system increases, our ability to make precise statements and at the same time significant ones, decreases, until it gets to a point beyond which precision and significance are almost excluded (Zadeh 1973; Zadeh et al. 1975). The price of an increase of complexity, then, is a decrease of

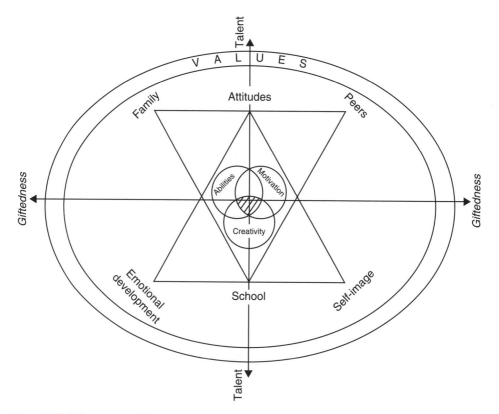

Figure 7 Global success model

precision of measurement. And as a system develops in time, that is, as the planning horizon increases, so does ambiguity. The anticipation process, lacking all the data of the system whose trajectory is to be predicted, leads to a multitude of trajectories arranged in a fan-like shape, or a fuzzy and imprecise system.

How does this relate to giftedness? High ability should be evaluated on an ongoing basis, for each individual through all stages of development, in a dynamic, multi-determined, way, taking into account the instability of the gifted construct. In addition, teachers should be given the training and support that they need to plan, design, and deliver context-sensitive educational projects and assessments, taking into account the multi-dimensional and unique nature of human development.

Contact address: carmencretu@rdslink.ro

Future Perspectives

Suggested priorities for gifted education over the next decade

Gifted education in Romania should embrace the following interventions over the next ten years. We need to develop and implement better legislative frameworks, differentiated curriculum strategies for the formal curriculum, and more programmes for able learners within the non-formal curriculum; and introduce compulsory initial and in-service teacher training on gifted education. The development of national talent-development programmes by specialised non-governmental organisations is advised.

We must carry out further research into gifted education in our universities, extend international partnerships in terms of visiting professors, student exchanges, doctoral co-supervisions and international master's programmes in an effort to gather and disseminate research and practice. Further to this end, the organising and hosting of important national and international events for the field of giftedness is seen as an important goal for the future as we seek to enhance the reputation of Romania on a global scale.   Carmen Crețu

23

A reconsideration of the widely held conviction that gifted students prefer to work alone

Lisa R. French and Bruce M. Shore
McGill University, Quebec, Canada

Although gifted children are not a homogeneous group, they are reported to share many characteristics (Clark 1997), including a preference for working alone (Alexander and Muia 1982; Davis and Rimm 2004; Gowan and Bruch 1971). Whitmore (1980) stated that 'The gifted child enjoys independent investigation outside the classroom, and often finds it difficult to conform to a group activity in school' (p. 154). Griggs and Price (1980a) found that gifted students 'prefer a quiet learning environment, and prefer to learn alone rather than with peers' (p. 361). Seagoe (1974) cited 'independence in work and study; preference for individualised work; self-reliance; and need for freedom of movement and action' (p. 44) as characteristics of the gifted student.

This purported preference has been attributed to the 'gifted personality' – a constellation of social and intellectual characteristics including a tendency toward introversion (Ruf 2002). Myers (1980) asserted that a tendency toward intuition-introversion increases with academic giftedness (also see Delbridge-Parker and Robinson 1988; S. A. Gallagher 1990; Hoehn and Bireley 1988). In the popular media, Sanjay Gupta, CNN's medical correspondent, in a 2006 broadcast stated that, 'In the popular imagination, the genius is a loner'. Even recent literature regarding standardised intelligence tests includes the claim that teachers of those individuals achieving IQ scores of 120 and above need to 'create opportunities for [these] student[s] to seek and find information independently, [as these] individual[s] . . . enjoy reasoning things through alone' (Roid 2003, as quoted in Ruf 2003, p. 8). However, empirical evidence addressing this persistent view is mixed.

Challenges from the cooperative learning literature

In a 2001 study, gifted learners' parents valued group-learning activities within an inquiry-based classroom less than they valued individualised instruction (Syer and Shore 2001), and ranked group-learning tasks lower than did teachers. Parents may have been expressing a desire for their children's fair share of individual attention, or to perform at full potential and receive suitable recognition, but their response is consistent with the assumption that gifted children prefer to work alone. Teachers also may be divided into similar camps: depending on whether

176

the teacher is working in a gifted education or cooperative learning setting, group learning activities for gifted students are accorded varying importance or desirability (J. J. Gallagher et al. 1993).

In cooperative learning, students in small groups help each other complete projects or master content. The strategy is widely used across North America 'to promote peer interaction and cooperation for studying academic subjects' (Sharan 1980, p. 242). It is 'often cited as a means of emphasising thinking skills and increasing higher-order learning . . . as a means of improving race relations . . . and as a way to prepare students for an increasingly collaborative work force' (Slavin 1991, p. 71). Proponents have pushed to return students to mainstream classrooms (Utay and Utay 1997) for numerous reasons, for example, presumed costs of pull-out enrichment, 'inter-ability' relations among students, and to improve academic achievement of all students.

Although children with learning disabilities benefit socially and academically (Jenkins et al. 1994; Wood et al. 1993), evidence concerning gifted education is more conditional. Important contextual factors influence gifted students' receptiveness to and benefits from cooperative learning, as described below.

Nelson et al. (1993) questioned 20 cooperative learning advocates and 20 gifted education advocates about using cooperative learning with gifted students, and surveyed 400 further experts from both groups (314 responded: 173 identified themselves as primarily cooperative learning experts, and 141 identified primarily themselves as experts in gifted education, although some may have had expertise across these fields). Cooperative-learning educators responded more positively on a four-point scale that the curriculum in cooperative learning is sufficiently challenging for gifted students, and that all students can be educated in hetero-geneous settings. The two groups agreed that there was a need for more teacher preparation in the appropriate uses of cooperative learning with gifted students. In open-ended comments, cooperative learning educators responded favourably to heterogeneous grouping, but the gifted and talented group had reservations, and favoured homogeneous (ability peer) groups.

Stevens and Slavin (1995) longitudinally compared mainstream classrooms using cooperative learning versus traditional lecturing. Students were matched on achievement pre-test mean scores (the *California Achievement Test*) for reading, language and mathematics. Cooperative learning teachers and administrators were previously trained on goals and components. Those using traditional methods were not provided with any additional training; they continued using their regular methods and curriculum, complemented by a part-time pull-out gifted pro-gramme. Attitude and social relations were also assessed. Two years later, there were significant overall effects favouring the cooperative learning group on reading vocabulary, reading com-prehension, language expression, mathematics computation, self-perceived ability in reading and language arts, and social relations. Gifted students in the cooperative learning schools demonstrated significantly higher academic achievement in several areas compared to their counterparts in the traditional programme, as well as higher attitude and social relations outcomes.

Coleman and Gallagher (1995) compared heterogeneous versus homogeneous groups in cooperative learning in research addressing achievement and social behaviour of gifted students in mainstream classrooms. Two year-long studies analysed five cooperative learning sites. In the heterogeneous grouping condition, gifted students were paired within the mainstream classroom with non-identified peers to solve problems. In the homogeneous grouping condition, gifted students were paired within the mainstream classroom with other gifted students. Researchers observed classrooms, noting variables such as teacher enthusiasm, task complexity, and student enthusiasm. They probed students' opinions about their learning environments with question-naires and interviews. Gifted students expressed 'clear and overwhelming enthusiasm' (p. 380) for cooperative learning in homogeneous groups. There were no differences between social behaviours of gifted children in either grouping. Students in heterogeneous cooperative learning groups highlighted having to act as the teacher (of the less able), doing all of the work, being slowed down, and feeling uncomfortable when they appeared 'too smart'. Gross (1993) strongly advocated that ability grouping is 'absolutely essential for exceptionally and profoundly gifted children if they are to have any chance of finding intellectual and social companionship' (p. 272; also see Colangelo, Assouline and Gross 2004).

Diezmann and Watters's (2001) exploratory case study video-recorded, observed and surveyed six mathematically gifted students aged 11 and 12 years engaged in collaborative activities, selected from mixed-ability classrooms within a single elementary school. During a problem-solving sequence, students worked in a quiet zone (independently), work zone (beside each other), chat zone (group task discussion), and teacher zone (for teacher assistance). 'Gifted students preferred minimal interaction with others when they worked on at- or near-grade-level tasks, and they were independently successful on these tasks' (p. 24), but preferred collaborating with similarly able peers on challenging tasks, and reported enjoying such collaboration. This study suggests that gifted students value collaboration when engaged in new learning, and prefer working independently when practising past learning.

We found no studies indicating that cooperative learning had a deleterious effect on gifted children's academic or social outcomes. Especially in homogenous groups, cooperative learning can serve some needs of gifted children in mainstream classrooms. Nonetheless, it remains a last resort for many educators of gifted and talented learners. In a meta-analysis of learning-styles research (Rogers 2002a), cooperative grouping ranked as the least preferred of eight common educational strategies by gifted learners. We theorise that these students possibly identify cooperative learning with negative experiences they may have had in heterogeneous ability groups.

The contributions of age or grade

Positive outcomes for group learning with gifted children vary when we look beyond the elementary years. Boultinghouse's (1984) gifted early elementary students (ages 5 to 8) preferred to work alone and rejected peer teaching on a locally developed learning-style scale. Dunn and Price (1980) challenged this outcome. Using Dunn, Dunn and Price's *Learning Style Inventory* (LSI) (1975), they surveyed 109 gifted students (IQ 130+ on the *Otis Lennon Test of Mental Abilities*, or between 120 and 129 plus 95th percentile scores in standardised mathematics or reading achievement) and 160 non-gifted students. They showed that gifted learners neither preferred to work alone nor with others. Dunn and Price speculated, 'It may be that the gifted are so goal-oriented that with whom they learn is of less importance to them than where (formal design) and how (persistently and creatively)' (p. 34). However, at the junior high school level (grades 7 through 9 – ages 12 to 15), Griggs and Price (1980b) found that 170 gifted students (using the *Lorge-Thorndike Test of Mental Ability and Stanford Achievement Tests*) preferred to learn alone significantly more than did non-gifted learners.

Price and colleagues found somewhat different grade outcomes. In one study (Price et al. 1981), when 70 gifted 7th through 9th grade students (ages 12 to 15) who achieved *Lorge-Thorndike Intelligence Test* scores of 130+ (or IQ scores of 125 to 129 and two or more years above grade levels in reading or mathematics on the *Stanford Achievement Tests*), were compared with 100 randomly selected average performing students on the LSI, gifted students preferred to work alone more than their non-gifted grade peers or other elementary-aged groups. One year previous, 109 4th- through 8th-grade (ages 9 to 13) students with *Otis-Lennon* IQs of 130+ (or between 120 and 129 plus scores in the 95th percentile on standardised mathematics or reading achievement tests) were compared to 160 randomly selected other students. These young gifted students demonstrated a preference for learning with others (Dunn and Price 1980).

Sex differences in learning preference

A synthesis of psychological types of gifted adolescents (Sak 2004) involving the *Myers-Briggs Type Indicator* revealed that, although gifted adolescents overall were found to be more introverted than the normative group, gifted females were significantly higher in extraversion than gifted males. However, Haier and Denham (1976) studied 71 7th, 8th and academically accelerated 9th-grade boys (ages 12 to 14), and 25 academically accelerated girls. On the *California Personality Inventory* (CPI), a self-report personality inventory consisting of several hundred 'yes-no' questions and yielding scores on a number of scales including dominance, self acceptance, self control, socialisation, and achievement, mathematically gifted girls rated themselves as being more successful on 'Achievement via Independence' compared to mathematically gifted boys. Moreover, Lessinger and Martinson (1961) had found the tendency toward gifted female extraversion to be inconsistent across grades. Their study used the CPI with 929 gifted students in grades 1 through 12 (ages to 18), including 436 in junior and senior high school (ages 11 to 18). Gifted 11th-grade girls (ages 16 and 17) rated themselves significantly higher on 'Achievement via Independence' than did gifted 8th-grade girls (ages 13 and 14). In in-depth observations of informal and organised peer activities in a middle school setting (approximately 250 students per grade in 6th, 7th, and 8th grades – ages 11 to 14), Eder (1985) revealed early adolescent girls (not boys) as more focused on interpersonal relations than on school achievement. These findings are in keeping with a large body of related research on girls and popularity, the development of relational aggression, and so on but description of those studies goes beyond the scope of this review.

Other challenging findings

Burns et al. (1998) further countered previous findings concerning the tendency of gifted learners to prefer to work alone. In their own survey of 500 students, they found that students not identified as gifted preferred to learn alone, whereas the gifted in their sample did not. Similarly, Li and Adamson (1995) reported that a significant preference for working alone did not appear in their sample of 30 gifted secondary students (when compared with 32 of these students' siblings who were within four years of the gifted students' age) on the abridged *Learning Preference Scale-Students* (Owens and Straton 1980) (which identifies participants' learning style preferences as cooperative, competitive, or individualised), and the *Self-Perception Profile for Adolescents* (Harter 1986) (which measures eight domains of adolescents' judgements of their own competencies – scholastic, social, athletic, physical appearance, job, romantic appeal, behavioural conduct, close friendship, as well as global self-worth). Ewing and Yong (1992) surveyed 155 African-American, Mexican-American and American-born Chinese junior high school gifted students (90th percentiles on the *Raven Standard Progressive Matrices* or *WISC-R*) using the LSI. Unlike Price et al. (1981), they found no evidence of a preference for working alone overall or in individual cultures.

179

Csikszentmihalyi et al. (1993) commented that ordinary children come home after school to play; gifted children come home eager to paint, play music, do mathematics problems, read or write. They commented that 'Although gifted children gain more than others from solitude, they still seek peer contact'. It is difficult to find like-minded peers (Winner 2000b), especially in age-assigned classrooms. Enersen (1993) wrote that gifted children tend to '[go] off alone, but never [give] up the hope of finding peers who will accept and like them just as they are' (p. 173).

A promising theoretical framework

One explanation for prior mixed results may be the lack of a consistent theoretical framework. A powerful theory that drives much contemporary curricular thinking is Vygotsky's (1978) social constructivism. Vygotsky emphasised the criticality of culture and social context (cultural mediation) in cognitive development. He believed that learning is never purely an internal process but that, through interactions with more knowledgeable others (including but not limited to classmates, playmates, teachers and parents), learners understand new cognitive concepts and strategies. Properly supported individuals eventually are capable of applying and extending these to other contexts (Hiebert and Raphael 1996).

Another tenet of social constructivism is that the extent to which children develop within a classroom depends on the learning context. Peers, teachers, instructional strategies, curriculum, and activity format all contribute.

> Social constructivists see motivation as both extrinsic and intrinsic. Because knowledge is actively constructed by the learner, learning depends to a significant extent on the learner's internal drive to understand and promote the learning process. Because learning is essentially a social phenomenon, learners are partially motivated by rewards provided by the knowledge community.
>
> (*Theories of Learning*, n.d.)

Perhaps mixed findings on learning conditions mirror the varying quality of the environmental support provided in the childhoods and adolescences of able students. This support may, at times, lack productive and positive social interaction. Classroom activities and content adaptation may inadequately support development in a balanced way. This idea is supported by homogeneous ability grouping being preferred over heterogeneous: 'collaboration provided students with a supportive learning environment in which there was practical and affective support to assist them in overcoming obstacles within a task' (Diezmann and Watters 2001, p. 25).

In a mixed-ability or 'inclusive' classroom, gifted children may not feel consistently supported, or that their work is appreciated. Typically, curricular needs of gifted children are addressed in a token manner, if at all (Archambault et al. 1993), leading some to prefer independent activities or working alone. Within a larger group, gifted individuals fall into the category of those who are 'non-normative' or 'non-standard', and may suffer for it (Csikszentmihalyi et al. 1993; Enersen 1993). Whitmore (1980, 1986) noted a tendency for gifted children to perceive negative social feedback as rejection and to feel socially isolated: '[B]ecause the gifted child is different by virtue of superiority, the social penalties will include indifference in the forms of ignoring accomplishments and encouraging independent activity alone' (1980, p. 150). Feeling compelled by others to work alone, gifted individual therefore runs the risk of this becoming habitual and comfortable and coming to be regarded as the preferred or normal way of learning. Buescher et al. (1987) drew on clinical case studies to delineate eight specific coping strategies used by gifted adolescents. Of these eight, one emerged as 'isolating oneself' and another as 'hiding academic ability from other students (especially among adolescent girls)'.

Working alone therefore may not represent a natural preference; it may be a default option. Given adequate and appropriate support in the learning process, perhaps these same students might report a preference for working with others. When describing social constructivism, it is necessary to include cognitive support (e.g. scaffolding), but support as encouragement and appreciation are equally important for gifted learners.

Methodological issues behind mixed results

Several studies did not include control groups or random selection, and some classes studied had very few gifted students identified in the cohort. For example, an earlier study by Griggs and Dunn (1984) had no comparisons and only two gifted students. Such issues limit generalisability of results to the broad gifted population (Burns et al. 1998). Stahl (1988) highlighted questionable reliability and validity in some learning-style instruments, for example, none of Boultinghouse's (1984) items in the Learning Styles Inventory had demonstrated internal validity or reliability.

Some limitations seem unavoidable. Random assignment cannot be achieved when identifying giftedness. Most gifted students in the studies quoted are identified by IQ testing, making high IQ individuals over-represented in populations of 'gifted' individuals, especially in elementary schools. The research question driving the majority of the studies listed this far was typically 'Do gifted children prefer to work alone?' This is perhaps a leading question; in no study we have found did participants choose learning activities from a series of options, or compare and contrast activities. Neither were participants asked open-ended questions about most or least preferred learning activities or situations. Participants more typically responded to situations they actually experienced, a necessarily narrower range (e.g. Diezmann and Watters 2001).

Pedagogical issues

Advocates of acceleration and academic enrichment for the gifted are more likely to emphasise individual accomplishment and support competition than their cooperative-learning counterparts who focus on teamwork and group accomplishment (Oakes 1985; Slavin 1991; Thorkildsen 1994). These 'world-views' of the competitive versus cooperative have powerful implications for social development of gifted students and their classmates, and future career success (Thorkildsen 1994). Spence and Helmreich (1983) reported that entrepreneurs who are low in competitiveness and high in work-rate and desire for mastery (communal orientation) earned the highest annual incomes. Similarly, academic scientists with a communal orientation had the greatest impact (Thorkildsen 1994). Teachers with collaborative working styles have more opportunities to learn varied strategies, and may have access to a greater variety of materials.

Finally, gifted students' social and emotional well-being are also important (Garland and Ziegler 1999; Neihart 1999). Although Terman (1925) had suggested that bright children were better adjusted than their less gifted counterparts, Hollingworth (1942) proposed otherwise:

Gifted individuals can experience difficulties making educational and social adjustments; they have multiple issues to face in life, including 'to suffer fools gladly, to keep from becoming negativistic toward authority, and to keep from becoming hermits' (p. 299).

Conclusion

The original question, 'Do gifted students prefer to work alone?' obscures the underlying mechanisms behind this preference. The theory of motivation in social constructivism predicts that gifted children who do not feel socially and cognitively supported by their environments, regardless of grade, sex, or formal identification, will claim a stronger preference for learning alone. A comprehensive re-analysis of the learning-preference question is needed with a larger sample across grade (age), sex and giftedness assessed in different ways, utilising well-documented, valid and reliable instruments.

Under some conditions – perhaps those that characterised classrooms when the question was first asked – gifted children have been found to prefer to work alone. However, we believe that now, under conditions such as an inquiry-driven constructivist pedagogy that necessarily includes purposeful student-student interaction, and mutual respect and appropriate support for all students (without implicitly assuming that gifted pupils are deficient in social attitudes), a different response to this question might be found. Gifted students might express a preference to work with others when the learning situation is appropriate to their learning goals, and if the nature of interaction supports their needs as well as those of others.

Contact address: bruce.m.shore@mcgill.ca

Future Perspectives

Suggested priorities for gifted education over the next decade

Whether or not gifted learners prefer to work alone is not a uniquely Canadian question. A connection may emerge in the growing policy commitment to treat learning as a social constructivist phenomenon. Only three of Canada's 13 provinces and territories currently mandate gifted programmes, and services are not universal. Provisions typically follow familiar models such as programme compression, career exploration, subject-specialised or magnet schools, social development, acceleration and university transition. Provinces and territories are totally autonomous in general education, and most have recently moved toward social-constructivist curricular models and policies that encourage or even require students and teachers to be inquirers and co-constructers of the curriculum. Overall levels of Canadian student achievement are high in most international comparisons. Nonetheless, perhaps in ten years we can hope for increased buy-in to inquiry-based instruction and learning. This would, in turn, benefit gifted students, given their willingness to work collaboratively with intellectual and creative peers rather than alone in such learning environments.

Lisa R. French and Bruce M. Shore

Part 4

Theory into practice: differentiation strategies, tools and approaches

For many educators, this section will be the heart of the volume, providing as it does an emphasis on differentiation strategies, tools, and approaches for practice. As with the other sections, however, many chapters in other sections might just as well have been included here.

In addition to arguing for a certain perspective on understanding giftedness, many of the chapters in the sections on models, definitions, and conceptual challenges provide suggestions for practitioners, as do the chapters in the international perspectives and psychosocial development sections. And each of the chapters in the final section on expanding horizons is also directed squarely at improving practice.

You will find that there are several themes that recur across the chapters within this section, themes that also run throughout many of the other chapters in the volume. These include a focus on individual developmental differences, the need for increased and improved teacher development and support regarding gifted development and learning needs, a need to attend to cultural differences and context-sensitivity, and of course, the provision of practical differentiation tools for educators.

In their chapter, Joe Renzulli and Sally Reis describe the *Renzulli Learning System*, a way that teachers can use technology to differentiate effectively for a broad range of individual differences and diverse student needs, and increased pressures to improve student achievement. Nick Colangelo and Susan Assouline report on many kinds of acceleration practices in the US, and provide compelling evidence for the effectiveness of acceleration in differentiating learning for gifted students.

Thomas Balchin, in his chapter on recognising and fostering creative production, reviews some of the myths and confusions about the nature, identification and development of creativity, and provides information about the *Creative Feedback Package*, a tool that he has developed to help teachers support creative development in their students. Donald Treffinger, Carole Nassab, and Edwin Selby are also very concerned with creative development, and describe the Levels of Service (LoS) approach that has been in use in schools internationally for over twenty years, and has proven itself to be a contemporary, flexible, and inclusive model for nurturing the strengths and talents of students through the collaborative efforts of the school, the home, and the community.

We have two chapters that address giftedness as it intersects with other special educational needs. Diane Montgomery considers many kinds of dual exceptionality and concludes that the educational provisions that exceptional learners need are essentially the same as those that all students need: she states that a positive and supportive classroom climate, in combination with an appropriate level of challenge and discipline, gives the best chances of educating all our students, including those who are doubly exceptional. After reviewing literature on Asperger Syndrome, Wiesława Limont describes in some detail a case study of a child who has been diagnosed with Asperger's and shows evidence of giftedness. In a consideration of educational implications of this kind of dual exceptionality, she emphasises the importance of attending to strengths and interests, as vehicles for learning to cope with challenges.

This section ends with two chapters that emphasise the need for all children to learn to think, and for teachers to ensure their students have the time and support they need for that learning to happen. Helen Wilson raises a provocative question: 'Are pupils too busy working to have time to think?' She makes a strong argument for the importance of encouraging the development of all children's higher-order thinking skills, not just those who are identified as gifted and/or talented. Similarly, Robert Fisher argues for putting the learner at the heart of the educative process, and discusses the ways that philosophical dialogue can be used effectively to do just that. He provides delightful quotations from work that he and colleagues have done in classrooms, describing and illustrating effective practices for stimulating philosophical intelligence, and emphasising, as with Wilson, the critical importance of providing structured time and opportunity for real thinking.

24

A computerised strength assessment and internet-based enrichment programme for developing giftedness and talents

*Joseph S. Renzulli and
Sally M. Reis*
The University of Connecticut, US

A new system developed at the University of Connecticut is designed to use our long-standing research on strength-based assessment and high-end learning as a theory-based model for providing differentiated learning experiences for gifted and talented students. The Renzulli Learning System (RLS) is based on the enrichment triad model. The diversity of talents and interests that we serve in gifted programmes requires a wide range of resources and inordinate amounts of time on the parts of teachers working with gifted students.

The RLS is a research-based approach that is built around four components. The first component consists of a computer-based diagnostic assessment that creates an individual profile of each student's academic strengths, interests, learning styles and preferred modes of expression. The online assessment, which takes about 30 minutes, results in a profile that highlights individual student strengths and allows teachers to form groups based on common interests, learning styles and other strength areas.

In the second step, a differentiation search engine examines thousands of resources that relate specifically to each student's profile. In this component the search engine matches student strengths and interests to an enrichment database of 16,000 enrichment activities, materials, resources, and opportunities for further study.

The third component of Renzulli Learning is a project organisation and management plan for students and teachers called *The Wizard Project Maker*. This guide allows teachers to help students use their web-based explorations for original research, investigative projects, and the development of a wide variety of creative undertakings. This management device is designed to fulfil the requirements of a Type III Enrichment experience, which is the highest level in the Enrichment Triad Model.

The final component in the RLS is an automatic compilation and storage of all student activity from steps one, two and three into an ongoing electronic student record called the Total Talent Portfolio. Teachers and parents can review the portfolio online at any time, enabling them to give feedback and guidance to individual students and creating opportunities for parental involvement. The Total Talent Portfolio 'travels' with students throughout their educational career. In this chapter, research about the use of this approach will be discussed, as will practical applications of the use of this exciting new tool.

Every teacher has had the satisfaction of seeing a child 'turn on' to a topic or school experience that demonstrates the true joy and excitement of both learning and teaching. We sometimes wonder how and why these high points in teaching occur, why they do not occur more frequently, and why more students are not engaged in positive learning experiences. Teachers are also painfully aware of the boredom and lack of interest that so many of our young people express about much of the work they do in school. Highly prescriptive curriculum guides and relentless pressure to increase achievement test scores, often prevent educators from the kind of teaching that results in those joyous times when we see truly remarkable engagement in learning.

One teacher interviewed as part of a research project dealing with high engagement in learning said, 'I could easily improve student enthusiasm, enjoyment, and engagement if I had about a dozen teaching assistants in my classroom!' It was comments like this, and the seemingly limitless resources that are now available through the Internet, that inspired the development of the RLS at the University of Connecticut's Neag School of Education.

The use of instructional technology, and especially the Internet, has evolved rapidly over the past decade. First generation use of technology consisted mainly of what might be called 'worksheets-on-line', with the added advantage of providing students with immediate feedback about correct responses and remediation for incorrect answers. The next generation included courses-on-line, and although this innovation enabled students to have access to teachers and professors with expertise beyond what might be available locally, it usually followed the same pedagogy of traditional courses (i.e. read the chapter, answer questions, take a test). The third generation was a leap forward because of the advent of 'hypertext'. Students could now click on highlighted items in online text to pursue additional, more advanced information, making the process of locating and reading information more individualised.

The RLS is the next generation of applying instructional technology to the learning process. This programme is *not* a variation of earlier generations of popular e-learning programmes or web surfing. It is a unique use of the Internet that combines computer based strength assessment with search engine technology, thus enabling true differentiation, as thousands of carefully selected resources are matched to individual students' strengths. The RLS is based on a learning theory called the enrichment triad model (Renzulli 1977b), which is supported by research studies dealing with the model implementation (Reis and Renzulli 1994). The triad model focuses on the kinds of creative productivity that develop higher-level thinking and investigative skills, and it places a premium on the application of knowledge to learning situations that approximate the practices of a professional in that field. The RLS is a four-step procedure that is based on more than 30 years of research and development dealing with the diagnosis and promotion of advanced level thinking skills, motivation, creativity and engagement in learning.

Step 1: Strength assessment using the electronic learning profile

The first step consists of a computer-based diagnostic assessment that creates a profile of each student's academic strengths, interests, learning styles and preferred modes of expression. The online assessment generates a personalised profile that highlights individual student strengths, and sets the stage for step two of the RLS. The profile acts like a compass for the second step, which is a differentiation-type search engine that examines thousands of resources and selects them for each student based on his or her profile. Teachers can use information from the student profiles to form groups of students who share common interests or learning styles, design instruction based on identified interests or learning preferences, or assign curricular activities or projects to be completed independently or in groups. Parents may also access their child's profile and web activities, promoting at-home interest in learning and parent involvement.

Step 2: Enrichment differentiation database

In step two, the differentiation search engine matches student strengths and interests to an enrichment database of 16,000 enrichment activities, materials, resources, and opportunities for further study that are grouped into the 14 categories listed on Table 6.

These resources are not merely intended to do more than enable students to occupy time surfing the web. Rather, they are used to help students find and focus a problem or creative exploration of personal interest that they might like to pursue in greater depth. Many of the resources provide the methods of inquiry, advanced level thinking and creative problem solving skills, and investigative approaches that approximate the modus operandi of the practising professional. Students are guided toward the application of knowledge through the development of original research studies, creative projects and action-oriented undertakings that put knowledge to work in personally meaningful areas of interest. The resources also provide students with suggestions for outlets and audiences for their creative products. All resources in the database are classified and cross-referenced by subject area, thinking skill, subject and grade level. The database includes resources reserved for teachers' use, including learning maps for each of the fourteen enrichment resource categories and lesson plans organised by subject area.

Research on the role of student engagement clearly shows that high engagement results in higher achievement, improved self-concept and self-efficacy, and more favourable attitudes toward school and learning. A strong body of research points to the crucial difference between time-spent and time-engaged in school achievement. In a recent Organisation for Economic Cooperation and Development (OECD) Programme for International Student Assessment (PISA) study, the single criterion that distinguished between nations with the highest and lowest levels of student achievement was the degree to which students were engaged in their studies. In a longitudinal study comparing time-spent versus time-engaged on the achievement

Table 6 RLS categories of enrichment activities, materials, resources and opportunities for further study

Virtual Field Trips
Real Field Trips
Creativity Training
Critical Thinking
Projects/ Independent Study
Contests and Competitions
Websites
Fiction Books
Non-Fiction Books
How-To Books
Summer Programmes
On-Line Classes and Activities
Research Skills
Videos and DVDs

of at-risk students, Greenwood (1991) found that conventional instructional practices were responsible for students' increased risk of academic delay, and a study by Ainley (1993) reported that there were important differences in achievement outcomes favoring engaged over disengaged students of similar ability.

The resources available in step two also provide students with places where they can pursue advanced level training in their strength areas and areas of personal interest. Online courses and summer programmes that focus on specific academic strengths and creative talents are ways that any school or parent can direct highly able and motivated students to resources that may not be available in the regular school programme.

Step 3: The Wizard Project Maker

The third feature of RLS is a project organisation and management plan for students and teachers called *The Wizard Project Maker*. This guide allows teachers to help students use their web-based explorations for original research, investigative projects and the development of a wide variety of creative undertakings. This management device is designed to fulfil the requirements of a Type III Enrichment experience, which is the highest level of enrichment described below in the discussion of the Enrichment Triad Model. Specifically, the Wizard Project Maker supports students in developing the metacognitive skills required to define a project and set a goal and identify and evaluate both the resources to which they have access and the resources they need to commit (e.g. time, Internet sites, teacher or mentor assistance). The Wizard Project Maker establishes a creative and viable responsibility for teachers in their role as 'the guide on the side' (King 1993). By helping students pursue advanced levels of challenge and engagement through the use of the Wizard Project Maker, students see teachers as mentors, rather than disseminators of knowledge. As one teacher recently said, 'The Wizard Project Maker helps my students understand the "why" of using the Internet'.

Step 4: The Total Talent Portfolio

The final step in the RLS is an automatic compilation and storage of all student activity from steps one, two and three into a cumulative electronic student record called the Total Talent Portfolio, which can be viewed by teachers, parents, and students at any time. Work saved within students' individual Portfolios include a list of their favourite sites, a record of all sites visited, student self-assessments and evaluations of sites visited, notes from their online research and any projects they have undertaken. Teachers can give feedback and guidance to individual students and provides parents with information about students' progress. The portfolio can also be used to inform future teachers, select subsequent enrichment preferences, design future projects and creative activities, explore online courses and competitions, participate in extracurricular activities and guide college progression and career. The Total Talent Portfolio can travel with students throughout school and serve as a reminder of previous activities and creative accomplishments that they might want to include in college applications. It is an ongoing record that can help students, teachers, guidance counsellors, and parents make decisions about future educational and vocational plans.

The theory and research underlying the Renzulli Learning System

The RLS is based on a learning theory called the enrichment triad model, which was developed in 1977 and implemented in thousands of schools in the United States and several overseas nations (see Figure 8). The enrichment triad model was designed to encourage advanced level learning and creative productivity by: (1) exposing students to various topics, areas of interest, and fields of study in which they have an interest or might develop an interest, (2) providing students with the skills and resources necessary to acquire advanced level content and thinking skills, and (3) creating opportunities for students to apply their skills to self-selected areas of interest and problems that they want to pursue.

Type I Enrichment is designed to expose students to a wide variety of disciplines, topics, occupations, hobbies, persons, places and events that would not ordinarily be covered in the regular curriculum or that are extensions of regular curriculum topics. In the RLS, Type I Enrichment includes virtual field trips, online activities that challenge student thinking, exciting websites, books, videos and DVDs related to areas of special interest. Type I experiences might be viewed as the motivational 'hook' that causes individual students to become turned-on to a particular topic or area of study that they will subsequently pursue in greater depth.

Type II enrichment consists of materials and activities designed to develop a broad range of higher level thinking processes and advanced enquiry skills. Some Type II training is general,

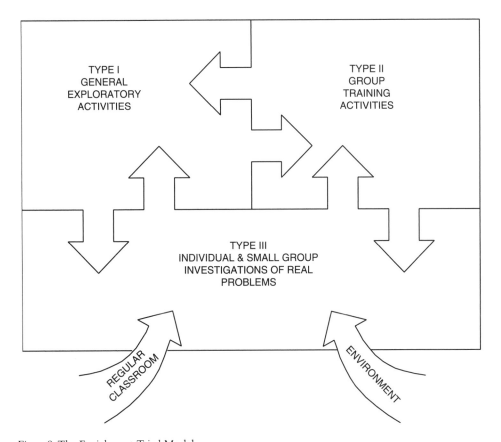

Figure 8 The Enrichment Triad Model

189

including the development of (1) creative thinking and problem solving, critical thinking and affective processes; (2) specific learning how-to-learn skills; (3) skills in the appropriate use of advanced-level research methods and reference materials; and (4) written, oral, and visual communication skills. Teachers can use general Type II Enrichment activities (e.g. a lesson in creative thinking) that are available online for whole group or small group instruction, or an online activity can be recommended for individuals or small groups to pursue on their own.

Other forms of Type II Enrichment are specific to a particular project that a student might be pursuing. For example, a small group of students became interested in mechanical engineering after a Virtual Field Trip that dealt with some of the world's most imaginative bridges. Using Renzulli Learning, they located resources on the Internet that provided instruction for designing, planning and building a model of a bridge. They also found a number of model bridge competitions to which they subsequently submitted their designs.

Our experience with the enrichment triad model has shown that Types I and II enrichment and/or interests gained in the regular curriculum or out-of-school activities will motivate many students to pursue self-selected topics in greater depth. We call these advanced types of involvement Type III Enrichment, which is defined as individual or small group investigations of real problems. When students choose to become involved in Type III Enrichment, they usually are interested enough in a topic to pursue a self-selected area of study in great depth. They are also willing to commit the time necessary for advanced content acquisition and process training in which they assume the role of a first-hand enquirer. The goals of Type III Enrichment are:

- to provide opportunities for applying interests, knowledge, creative ideas and task commitment to a self-selected problem or area of study;
- to acquire advanced level understanding of the knowledge (content) and methodology (process) that are used within particular disciplines, artistic areas of expression and interdisciplinary studies;
- to develop authentic products directed toward bringing about a desired impact upon a specified audience;
- to learn self-directed learning skills in the areas of planning, organisation, resource utilisation, time management, decision making and self-evaluation; and
- to further develop task commitment, self-confidence and feelings of creative accomplishment.

In the RLS, the Type III component can emerge from almost any of the options that students choose to pursue. They might get an idea after taking a virtual field trip or a real field trip, or a creativity training exercise or critical thinking activity might spark an interest. There are numerous options in Renzulli Learning for students to pursue Type III studies in specialised areas (e.g. Math League, Invention Convention or National History Day Competition).

Type III Enrichment is different from the types of projects and reports that students typically do in connection with their regular schoolwork. The best way to describe this difference is to list the three things that make a problem 'real' to a student. First, real problems are based on a sincere interest of the student rather than one assigned by the teacher. It is something the student wants to do, rather than something he or she is assigned to do. You may discuss and provide guidance in helping a student find and focus a problem, and the problem might be within the general curriculum area you are covering, but the subject or theme on which a student chooses to work must represent a personalisation of the topic for him or for her.

The second distinguishing feature of working on a real problem is that the students will use the methods of investigation of the practising professional. They're going to do what the real geologist, scenery designer or community activist does, but at a more junior level than an adult professional working in one of these fields. This focus will help to distinguish a bona fide Type III project from the reports that students typically complete by gathering and summarising information from reference books or Internet sites. The most powerful tools for giving students the know-how of authentic methodology, such as the 'How-To Book for Conducting Research and Creative Projects', can be found in the Enrichment Database under the category How-To Books. Material in these books can be used for whole-class and small group lessons on teaching research and investigative skills, such as questionnaire design, for example.

The third characteristic of a real problem is that it is always geared toward an audience other than, or in addition to, the teacher. In the adult world, practising professionals carry out their work because they want to have an impact on one or more relevant audiences – people who voluntarily attend a performance, read a newsletter or go to a science fair. Presenting to classmates occasionally may qualify as a real audience, but such presentations should be viewed more as practice sessions for more real-world settings such as a presentation to the local historical society, submission of one's writing to a magazine that publishes poetry or short stories or entering an invention contest. The enrichment category entitled Contests and Competitions will give students ideas about opportunities for audiences in all areas of student interest. And the Websites category includes many organisations and professional societies that produce journals and newsletters where high quality student products might be included.

The goal of Type III Enrichment is to transform the role of the student from a person who merely acquires information to a role in which she or he is thinking, feeling, and doing – i.e. acting as a practising professional – by actually engaging in authentic activities, addressed by enabling students to use the Wizard Project Maker. This form also highlights the specific ways in which teachers can provide guidance in helping students find and focus a problem, examine potential outlets and audiences and obtain the necessary resources to carry out their investigative activities.

One of the questions that teachers frequently ask is, 'Where will students find the time to do Type III projects?' All students can use the RLS, but we have found that gifted and above average ability students – those who can master the regular curriculum at a faster pace than others – can 'buy' some time for enrichment activities through a sub-component of the Enrichment Triad Model called Curriculum Compacting. Compacting is a process through which the teacher uses formal and informal assessment at the beginning of a unit of study, to determine which students have already mastered basic skills, and therefore do not need the same amount of practice material as others.

The value added benefits of learning *with* technology

The conditions of learning have changed dramatically for young people going to school today. Don Leu and his team of New Literacies researchers at The University of Connecticut (2004, 2005) have pointed out that the Internet is this generation's defining technology for literacy and learning. There was a time when teachers and textbooks were the gatekeepers of knowledge, but today virtually all of the world's knowledge is accessible to any student who can turn on a computer and access the Internet. One of the dangers of a content-abundant resource such as the Internet, however, is that we might be tempted to use it simply to cram more information into students' heads! But by applying a learner-centred pedagogy rather than a traditional drill-and-practice approach, we can harness the power of the Internet in a way that respects principles of high-level learning developed by the Task Force on Psychology of the American Psychological Association (APA 1997). These technologies make it possible to apply to all students the pedagogy typically used with high achieving students, a point we summarise in several other studies (Renzulli 1988; Renzulli and Reis 1994).

With almost unlimited access to the world's knowledge, a critical issue for educators is selecting the software and providing the training that will help young people use this access safely, efficiently, effectively, and wisely. Leu and his colleagues (2004, 2005) define the five major skill sets of the new literacies as follows: identifying important questions; locating relevant information; critically evaluating information; synthesising information; and communicating effectively.

The major goals of the RLS are a series of metacognitive tools that result from computer based learning environments. Metacognition is generally defined as the monitoring and control of one's own thinking processes. Metacognitive tools are skills that help students organise and self-regulate their learning so that they can make the most efficient use of time, resources, and the cognitive skills that contribute to higher levels of thinking.

Several researchers studying constructivist models of learning and metacognition have developed or modified traditional theories of learning to explain the role of computer environments in mediating the interactions between and among the cognitive, metacognitive, affective, and social processes that are involved in learning complex material (Bandura 1986; Corno and Mandinach 1983; Pintrich 2000; Schunk 2001). Promising results have emerged from these new developments in theory and research, concerning the ways in which computer learning environments facilitate metacognitive skill development. Promising research on RLS has also been completed. Field (2007) found that after 16 weeks, students who participated in Renzulli Learning for two to three hours each week demonstrated significantly higher growth in reading comprehension ($p < 0.001$), in oral reading fluency ($p = 0.016$) and in social studies achievement ($p = 0.013$), than those students who did not participate in RLS.

An even more promising trend is emerging as computer use evolves from traditional e-learning to RLS, which is an enquiry-based software that focuses on the application of knowledge to creative productivity, and investigative research projects which promote high levels of student engagement. Students learn via problem-based learning, acquiring and using skills such as problem finding and focusing; stating research questions; task understanding and planning; identifying appropriate investigative methodologies; searching, skimming, selecting, and interpreting appropriate resource material; identifying appropriate outlets, products, and audiences; and preparing effective communication vehicles. All of these skills underlie the Enrichment Triad Model and provide powerful learning opportunities when combined with the vastness of resources available through the Internet.

The Renzulli Learning System – summing it all up

The RLS is designed to be an aid to busy teachers who seek the tools for effective differentiation as they go about the process of dealing with a broad range of individual differences, diverse student needs and increased pressures to improve student achievement. Through the use of technology and an approach to learning that is the opposite of highly prescriptive instruction, the RLS provides teachers with the tools to provide engaging differentiated learning opportunities for all students in the classroom. The main goal of the RLS is simultaneously to increase achievement and the enjoyment of learning by making available an easy-to-use, research-based system that promotes student engagement. Although student engagement has been defined in many ways, we view it as the infectious enthusiasm that students display when working on something that is of personal interest, and that challenges them to 'stretch' for the use of materials and resources that are above their current comfort level of learning. Research on the role of student engagement is clear and unequivocal: high engagement results in higher achievement, improved self-concept and self-efficacy, and more favourable attitudes toward school and learning. Numerous students involved in our field tests of the RLS summed it up with one word – 'Awesome!'

Contract address: joseph.renzulli@uconn.edu

Future Perspectives

Suggested priorities for gifted education over the next decade

The increasing diversity of the US population, coupled with new theories and research that have given us a much broader conception of human potential, has already begun to influence more flexible approaches to identifying and serving gifted students. The application of instructional communication technology has begun to allow educators to develop more personalised approaches to assessing multiple strengths, interests, learning styles, preferred modes of expression and matching resources to individual student profiles. The development of creativity is starting to be emphasised rather than traditional advanced course approaches to serving gifted and talented students. Our focus on preparing students for the information age will be replaced with an emphasis on conceptual growth, expanded artistic development, and co-cognitive factors such as empathy, optimism, courage, and a sense of power to change things. Gifted programmes have begun to identify and develop the so-called 'soft intelligences' such as organisational, collaborative, and leadership skills, interpersonal and affective skills, and concerns related to social and environmental issues.   Joseph S. Renzulli and Sally M. Reis

25

Acceleration: meeting the academic and social needs of students

Nicholas Colangelo and Susan Assouline
The University of Iowa, US

In this chapter, we report on acceleration in American schools. There may be cultural and educational nuances elsewhere that require modifications to the way acceleration is implemented in the United States. However, the essential elegance and simplicity of both the rationale behind acceleration (academic readiness) and intervention (providing more advanced curriculum to a student) remains true across settings. We encourage our colleagues elsewhere to analyse their own acceleration practices, so that we may learn more about how acceleration can work worldwide. We believe that in the not-too-distant future, acceleration will no longer carry the burden of ambiguity and misunderstanding. Instead, it simply will be seen as a more effective curricular intervention for gifted students that has a robust research base. This will be true, not just for US schools, but for schools around the world.

Acceleration is a simple and elegant academic intervention. Its purpose is to move students through the traditional curriculum at rates faster than typical or at ages younger than usual (Pressey 1949, in Colangelo, Assouline and Gross 2004). This definition has not changed over the decades and the various iterations mirror what Gold (1965) so neatly captured as the goal of acceleration: 'Reduce the time spent by superior students in formal education' (p. 238). In order to do this, acceleration requires first and foremost appropriate educational planning, which means matching the level and complexity of the curriculum with the readiness and motivation of the student. The elegant simplicity of this concept – matching student readiness with complexity of curriculum – is the true core of gifted education.

Regardless of the elegance of academic acceleration for matching the curriculum to the learner's readiness, and despite the fact that acceleration has a long and consistent history of research supporting its effectiveness, school officials routinely avoid it. Throughout the history of education there are multiple examples of disparities between research evidence and popular belief; however, when the issue is academic acceleration, the degree of disparity between the research-based evidence and the application of the intervention is unparalleled. This disparity exists because of two major issues, one academic and the other social. The academic concern revolves around a belief that accelerated students may 'learn' the material but not adequately comprehend the content, and that their superficial understanding will become a negative at a later time. The second issue, which seems to cause even greater resistance, is a concern about students' social development. This is based on the belief that removing students from the traditional trajectory of a specific grade for a specific age can jeopardise their social development.

The negative energy from inaccurate beliefs about acceleration has neutralised the positive energy from research evidence accumulated over the last 50 years, which highlights the academic and social benefits of acceleration. Despite those benefits, schools routinely avoid academic acceleration or set up unnecessary barriers to its implementation. Acceleration has become the classic casualty of belief trumping evidence.

In 2004, after more than a decade of working with academically accelerated students and helping educators make appropriate decisions about academic acceleration, we authored a national report, *A Nation Deceived: How Schools Hold Back America's Brightest Students*, synthesising more than half a century of research on acceleration and gifted students. The goal of the report was to eliminate the victimisation of acceleration as an educational practice. Boldly and deliberately, it presents what we know about acceleration rather than what we fear about it, in order to start a new dialogue about the role of acceleration in the education of gifted students. *Nation Deceived* is a two-volume publication that synthesises the information from eminent experts in the field and makes this information understandable and accessible to educators.

Since the 2004 publication of *Nation Deceived*, significant changes have occurred in the dialogue about acceleration. The report exposed the disparity between the beliefs that were driving educational practice and the research. Upon its publication, *TIME* Magazine (September 27, 2004) featured academic acceleration in general, and *Nation Deceived* in particular. In one fell swoop, the issue of the appropriateness of acceleration was brought to the attention of millions of households as well as educators. The media has continued to play a vital role in informing the nation; a variety of newspapers, radio and TV stations across the United States have carried the message.

In addition to the more than 42,000 print copies of the publication in circulation, a website was established at the Belin-Blank Center for Gifted Education (B-BC), to make the report available at no charge. In the three years since the website (http://www.nationdeceived.org) was established, more than 2 million visits have been logged, and 70,000 copies have been downloaded. That *Nation Deceived* has been and continues to be available in its multiple formats at no charge, is due to the generosity of the John Templeton Foundation. The purpose of this chapter is to present some of the most critical findings, by highlighting the academic and social effects of acceleration as well as by presenting some special issues.

Academic effects of acceleration

Types of acceleration

Although acceleration is typically associated with whole-grade skipping, there are at least 18 types of acceleration (Southern and Jones 2004). These are either subject-based or grade-based, and the type varies with respect to the impact on the student as well as on the system (see Table 7).

Before presenting the evidence supporting the academic effects of acceleration, we discuss some concerns about acceleration. Contrary to popular opinion, it is more than a 'grade-skip'; in addition, there is more to acceleration as an academic intervention than placement into another class. Southern and Jones (2004) identified five dimensions of acceleration that are useful in distinguishing among their 18 types: pacing, salience, peers, access and timing. All but one of the dimensions, salience, are fairly self-explanatory. Salience refers to the degree to which the accelerative option is noticeable by others. Consequently, grade-skipping, a very

Table 7   Continuum of accelerative options

Individual Students	Small Group	Large Group
Grade-skipping	Single-subject mentoring	Advanced Placement classes
Early entrance	Combined classes	Post-secondary
Curriculum compacting		

visible decision for many, including peers, educators and other parents, is very high in salience. Enrolment in correspondence courses is less perceptible to others, and so is considered low in salience.

Also helpful in distinguishing among the forms of acceleration is Rogers' (2004) categorisation into subject-based acceleration and grade-based acceleration. According to Rogers, grade-based acceleration shortens the number of years that a student is in the elementary and high school system, and subject-based acceleration permits exposure to advanced content at an earlier age than usual.

Summaries of research from Kulik (2004), Lubinski (2004) and Rogers (2004), illustrate the impact of acceleration as an intervention. The evidence from their collective work is strong and unambiguous: acceleration results in growth in academic achievement (Kulik 2004; Rogers 2004). In fact, no other arrangement for gifted children works as well (Kulik 2004). Contrary to popular belief that accelerated students regret the decision to skip a grade, Lubinski discovered that intellectually precocious students, who experienced educational acceleration in middle school and high school, did not regret their decision to accelerate. A small percentage even indicated that they regretted not accelerating more.

Growth in academic achievement

Educational research is often descriptive in nature or, at best, quasi-experimental. However, the meta-analyses conducted by Kulik (2004) and Rogers (2004) depend upon results obtained through an experimental design using a control group and a treatment group. According to Kulik,

> Meta-analysts thus added precision and weight to reviews of research on academic acceleration. They not only identified relevant studies, but they showed exactly how strong the statistical effects were in each study and precisely how strong the evidence was on the major questions about acceleration.
>
> (2004, p. 13)

Since the early 1980s, Kulik (1997) has emphasised the 'value added' nature of meta-analyses when interpreting results. The value added is comprised of robust and consistent findings, as well as the use of combined effect size calculations, to illustrate the degree of impact of aggregated study findings.

The effect-size statistic represents 'the standardised difference between treatment and control means on an outcome measure' (Kulik 2004, p. 14). Calculated across studies, it allows the meta-analyst to address questions about the effectiveness of acceleration as an intervention, both descriptively and statistically. The short descriptive answer on Kulik's meta-analyses is that accelerated students perform better than their non-accelerated, same-age, same-ability, peers. The short statistical answer is that the

> median effect size in the studies was 0.80 . . . An effect size of 0.80 implies that the scores of the accelerated students were approximately one grade-equivalent above the scores of the bright, non-accelerated students. The overall message from these studies is therefore unequivocal: acceleration contributes greatly to the academic achievement of bright students.
>
> (Kulik 2004, p. 15)

Long-term academic effects

Lubinski (2004) offers a different perspective based on results from longitudinal studies of the Study of Mathematically Precocious Youth. He has investigated what happens if the intervention is *not* to accelerate students who are academically ready for acceleration. The students themselves tell us that a slow-paced curriculum leads to boredom and discontent. The opportunity for accelerative experiences is therefore critical to the development of world-class leaders, especially in the areas of mathematics and science, areas that are specifically a part of Lubinski's work.

The decision-making process

For certain forms of acceleration, e.g. enrolment in Advanced Placement classes (similar to British 'A levels') in the final two years of high school, there is little dispute. For other forms, especially whole-grade acceleration – commonly known as grade skips – the intervention is so salient that many districts have developed anti-acceleration policies. At least that was the case prior to *Nation Deceived*. The *Iowa Acceleration Scale* (Assouline et al. 2003) is providing additional support for changing practices, and has proven effective for educators and parents who want to make an objective evidence-based decision about whole-grade acceleration.

When it comes to acceleration, our experience has been that concerns about social effects are the primary reasons for a negative view. Social effects include interpersonal relationships, emotional well-being, self-esteem and attitudes about school, as well as hopes and aspirations for the future. Understandably, teachers, administrators and parents want to be assured that acceleration will not have negative social consequences. The overall research findings are that acceleration leads to either positive social adjustment (social adjustment actually improves), or there is no noticeable change. The research evidence has not supported negative consequences. However, people tend to recall hearing about highly publicised students who did not adjust well (e.g. the case of William Sidis, as reported by Montour 1977). When someone is opposed to an idea, a representative sample is not necessary – one case suffices.

There are two issues here. One is that the concern about social adjustment assumes that acceleration is restricted to early entrance to school, whole-grade acceleration, and early entrance to college. In response to this misconception, it is important to note that many other forms of acceleration have minimal, if any, social consequences; this would include, for example, dual enrolment or Advanced Placement courses. The other issue is that measuring social adjustment is more subjective than measuring academic progress. For all their limitations, standardised tests and classroom grades provide acceptable markers of academic progress. Social variables are more subjective and the markers of social development are not as clearly agreed upon as those for academic progress. Although understanding the effects on social development are important, the measurement of these effects is not very reliable. This makes the decision-making process more difficult.

General social effects

In Kulik's (2004) meta-analysis of acceleration, he reported that only a small number of the studies reviewed also investigated social effects. Investigations of social effects are complicated for many reasons, which can make it necessary to glean results from investigations of other variables such as scholarly achievement. For example, enrolment in college is easily measured, and at one time was also an indicator of two important affective characteristics: ambition and aspiration. However, college enrolment no longer distinguishes American gifted students from their same-aged peers, because college attendance is much more widespread than it once was. Nevertheless, there are ways to assess these important attributes. Kulik reports that when compared to non-accelerated students, accelerated students have *elevated* educational ambitions (e.g. desire to attain an advanced degree) as well as higher career aspirations. Accelerated students are willing to commit to longer periods of preparation, which is often needed to complete advanced degrees. In other words, acceleration is positively related to educational ambition. Kulik also observed that some differences between accelerated students and non-accelerated students were minimal in terms of educational aspirations and goals, but even in those cases, the differences favoured accelerated students. Kulik concluded that when it comes to educational ambition, acceleration has a positive effect.

When comparing accelerated students with bright not-accelerated students, Kulik's (2004) comprehensive review indicated that the few studies that investigated students' attitudes about school and subject matter were mixed. On the one hand, some studies indicated that accelerated students liked both school in general and their accelerated subject (e.g. mathematics, if mathematics was the area of acceleration). On the other hand, in some cases, the findings indicated a slight downturn in accelerated students' attitudes about school and their accelerated subject. Kulik's interpretation was that students needed to work harder in accelerated situations; in some cases, they realised that they might not be the 'best', as had often been the case in less challenging situations.

Regarding self-acceptance, there are trends suggesting that accelerated students might drop slightly in self-acceptance when compared to their older peer groups. Kulik (2004) contends that this is consistent with findings about bright students who go from academically hetero-geneous situations to more homogenous (select) situations, the 'Big-Fish-Little-Pond' effect (Gross 1998; Marsh and Parker 1984; Marsh et al. 1995). Time is required for an accelerated student to reorient to the possibility that he or she is no longer at the top of the class.

Kulik summarises that while the academic effects of acceleration are strong and positive, the social effects are fragmentary. Acceleration appears to stimulate educational ambition for college and beyond. Also, accelerants participate in extra-curricular activities as much as non-accelerants; acceleration does not diminish school involvement. The one area that appears to need attention is self-esteem. Quite predictably, a more challenging academic environment can cause students to reassess their ability relative to others. This may be more useful in the long run because bright students who recognise that there are others who are equally or more advanced in certain areas will be better suited for future challenges than bright students who have never encountered their intellectual peers.

Nancy Robinson (2004) provides a comprehensive review of the effects of acceleration on the social status of gifted students. Like Kulik (2004), she acknowledges that accelerated students can have a slight (and usually temporary) dip in self-esteem when placed in settings with older children. There does not appear to be evidence of serious, long-term negative effects on self-esteem.

Social effects of early entrance to school

Assessing the effects of early school entry is another difficult-to-measure area because the children are young and the consequences are difficult to predict. In reporting on several reviews of the literature on early entrants to school, Robinson (2004) indicated that such students are well served academically and there are slight positive effects (although not significant) for socialisation and psychological affect. As reported by Colangelo, Assouline and Lupkowski-Shoplik (2004), Gagné and Gagnier (2004) found few adjustment differences between early entrants and regular-age students, but when these differences appeared they were in a positive direction for early entrants. Robinson's recommendation is that early entrants be no more than three months away from the required birthday (except in very exceptional cases), and that a psychological evaluation should include academic readiness *and* emotional regulation, social skills, and social maturity. In their review of literature on early entrance to school, Colangelo, Assouline and Lupkowski-Shoplik (2004) concluded that, in general, early entrants adjust well, both academically and socially.

Social effects of grade-skipping

There is considerable research evidence that grade-skipped students have good perceptions of their social relationships and their emotional development, and that they tend to have fewer serious school behaviour problems than others. For example, Richardson and Benbow (1990) reported that high-ability students (both accelerants and non-accelerants) reported high self-esteem and an internal locus of control. Also, they found that acceleration did not relate to social and emotional difficulties. Robinson (2004) states, 'We can, then, conclude that grade-skipping is a highly viable option for gifted students, although one that is not currently in vogue. There is no evidence that being younger than one's classmates is associated with social or psychological difficulties' (p. 63). As previously discussed, the *Iowa Acceleration Scale* (IAS) (Assouline et al. 2003) has proven to provide useful guidelines for whole-grade acceleration. The IAS recognises the non-academic (as well as academic) factors that need to be considered in whole-grade acceleration, and pays particular attention to social-emotional issues when considering whole-grade acceleration. These issues include the interpersonal skills of the child, emotional maturity, motivation to accelerate, as well as attitude of the receiving teacher and attitude of the school. Part of the rationale for developing the IAS is the fact that whole-grade acceleration is a public event and puts the accelerant into a new environment of peers and teachers. Effective social skills and social maturity are needed to complement exceptional academic skills.

Social effects and early entrance to college

Early entrance to college is typically viewed as a decision that is easier to make than a decision about early entrance to kindergarten or first grade. Not only does the student have a strong say in the matter, but also considerable academic and social evidence can support the decision to accelerate. However, as Muratori (2007) and Brody et al. (2004) acknowledge, because adjusting to college is a challenge for most first-year students, there is considerable concern about a decision to enter college earlier than usual. As Brody et al. aptly state, 'Obviously, society expects more from early entrants than from regular-age college students. Early entrance programs have sought to minimise adjustment problems, and our recommendation is that early entrants attend universities as part of a structured program rather than as a single entrant' (2004, p. 104). Whereas the studies on early entrance have been positive, a few rare, yet public, cases of negative or mixed outcomes have received considerable attention. Brody et al. indicate that although the social-emotional adjustment of early entrants to college has overall been positive, the 'literature has not painted the clear and compelling picture of success that educators and parents arguably need in order to feel comfortable with this curricular option' (p. 104).

Robinson (2004) highlights studies that report the reactions of early entrants regarding their decision to leave high school at a much younger age than the typical graduate (i.e. ages 17, 18, or 19). A review of these surveys and interviews indicates that early entrants generally are satisfied that they left high school early, and few regret their decision. This should not be surprising because these students made the choice, and may well have been very ready (and eager) to leave high school. Of course, it cannot be known how their adjustment to college would have been any different (either easier or more difficult) if they had waited. The evidence we do have in the social-emotional adjustment area is not uniform, but is positive.

Muratori (2007) provides an in-depth look at early entrants, their parents, and their college experiences. What this excellent and comprehensive text indicates is that early entrants are not only successful in college, but are also very satisfied with their decisions. There are numerous quotes from early entrants regarding both their academic and social experiences in college. Also, attending college early through a structured early-entrance programme, with reliable support and a peer group, has significant advantages over entering college early but not through a specialised programme.

Muratori (2007) argues that adjustment to college is a challenge for most, and students who enter college earlier than their peers are not absolved from the typical stresses of such adjustment. However, the evidence indicates that, typically, these are just the normal stresses of a new and demanding environment, and that early entrants adjust well to both the academic and social demands. This information is consistent with other information on early-entrance programmes (Brody et al. 2004; Muratori et al. 2003).

Long-term social effects

Educators require answers not only to the short-term effects but also to the long-term effects of acceleration. Whenever there is an intervention, and acceleration is clearly a curriculum intervention, we need to know its likely consequences well down the educational road. The most impressive work we currently have on long-term effects for highly capable students stems from the Study of Mathematically Precocious Youth, investigated over the years by Julian Stanley, Camilla Benbow, David Lubinski and others. Lubinski (2004) summarises the long-term effects of acceleration on large groups of students, and concludes that even in adulthood, students who were accelerated in middle and high school recall their pre-college experience 'much more positively than their intellectual peers who were deprived of such experiences' (p. 36).

Summary

Acceleration is certainly not a new educational intervention. However, it maintains its place as the intervention that generates more controversy than others. The major problem has *not* been the lack of evidence on its effectiveness, but the disparity between this evidence and educational practice and beliefs.

We advocate strongly for a consideration of acceleration for gifted students. The evidence is compelling when it comes to academic effects. The evidence for beneficial social effects is also positive, but not as clear and compelling as the evidence regarding academic effects. Acceleration can be a powerful and easily implemented intervention for gifted students, but a number of issues need to be researched, and many studies need to be replicated. We believe the more carefully educators look at the evidence, the clearer the need to use acceleration as an intervention will become.

The future: the Institute for Research and Policy on Acceleration

We end this chapter on a vibrant note. Acceleration is a dynamic topic, and in continuation of the work initiated by *A Nation Deceived*, the John Templeton Foundation awarded the Belin-Blank Center a grant to establish the Institute for Research and Policy on Acceleration (IRPA) (http://www.accelerationinstitute.org). The purposes of IRPA, established in 2006, are:

1 to generate new research on acceleration;
2 to act as a clearinghouse for research and information on acceleration;
3 to develop instruments that will guide educators and parents to make effective decisions;
4 to provide consultation on acceleration policy and practices based on research evidence; and
5 to provide research grants to stimulate worldwide research on acceleration.

The Research Director for IRPA is the highly respected educational psychologist Dr. David Lohman, a faculty member at The University of Iowa, as well as the senior author on the Cognitive Abilities Test (CogAT), Form 6.

Contact address: nick-colangelo@uiowa.edu

Future Perspectives

Suggested priorities for gifted education over the next decade

We predict that acceleration for highly gifted students is going to become a mainstream intervention and that more countries will develop policies that are supportive of acceleration. This elegant and research-supported means of offering a challenging curriculum intervention is going to become part of the fabric of our education of gifted students. We also predict that there will be greater understanding among professionals about the necessary role of assessment with respect to the decision-making process regarding acceleration. On the surface, this may sound rather ordinary, i.e. that acceleration will become an integral part of gifted education. It doesn't resonate with new or big ideas. Education is complex and often we don't know what works. We do know acceleration works with gifted students and the transformation will take place by acting on this knowledge. Acceleration practices are elegant in their simplicity and effectiveness.

Nicholas Colangelo and Susan Assouline

26

Recognising and fostering creative production

Thomas Balchin
Brunel University, UK

The demand to place value upon creative effort

Global interest in the phenomenon of creativity has grown incrementally since J. P. Guilford's (1950) presidential address to the American Psychological Association. For nearly six decades now it has been subject to many types of enquiry and analysis, experimental manipulation and control. The 'mystery' conception of creation has been largely removed (Simonton 2000b). Creativity is generally seen as the ability to produce work that is both novel (i.e., original, unexpected), and appropriate (i.e., useful, adaptive to task constraints) – see Sternberg and Lubart 1999. Several researchers in the cognitive science field, e.g. Mandler (1995); Schank and Cleary (1995); Smith et al. (1995); Weisberg (1993), suggest that creative thinking is simply the result of ordinary mental processes (i.e. the same as those we use to solve everyday problems). Similarly, the psychology field is in general agreement that the ability to express novel, orderly relationships is not a rare form of genius, and that any area of human endeavour can be fertile soil for fresh ideas to flourish. However, creative work is not easy, and serious task commitment and motivation are also required (Eysenck 1993; Dweck 2006; Gardner 1993a). Creativity should undeniably be encouraged in schools, but can (and should) creative effort be identified, judged and graded in schools in order to identify and support gifted learners? Some scholars in this book, e.g. Donald Treffinger, have tackled this question for decades.

English teachers are currently assured, through their school gifted education co-ordinator, local authority (LA) gifted education co-ordinators, or own reading, that creativity (along with other intellectual processes) is strongly related to giftedness (Balchin 2008). They are usually shown Renzulli's enrichment triad model (Renzulli 1986; Renzulli and Reis this volume) which includes creativity as one of three components required for giftedness (along with above-average ability and task commitment). The implicit message is that they need somehow to recognise, acknowledge, corroborate, and authenticate creativity if it occurs, when nominating students for gifted programmes. However, a tool for doing all this simply does not exist, at least in the English educational market, and its absence is one of the biggest problems facing teachers tasked with identifying gifted learners.

The most comprehensive English study to date of the views of gifted education co-ordinators concerning the efficacy of subject teacher nominations of gifted learners, took place in 2005 (Balchin 2008). Results showed that creativity was a major psychological construct within 800 coordinators' conceptions of 'giftedness'. When asked what signs they typically looked for (having been given no suggestions or choices that may have influenced their answers), the majority of the gifted education co-ordinators (71 per cent) reported that indications of creative achievement were the best indications of giftedness, although they acknowledged that they possessed no suitably standardised tool to allow them to assess this. They were, in effect, waiting for appropriate creativity tests to become available for their schools, and did not feel able to adapt any other kinds of creativity assessments for their own purposes with authority. They observed that because creativity is seen to be such a subjective matter, they could not justify their opinions concerning students' creative efforts (or indeed failure to bring original ideas to fruition), without some kind of appropriately validated test or tool.

The problem is exacerbated in England, because teachers are mandated to foster creative habits of mind and outcomes in their students. For instance, the government's curriculum for design and technology (arguably a school subject which should aim to provide a good degree of creative expression for able learners) highlights this obligation, requiring students to 'be creative', 'intervene creatively to improve quality of life' and 'become autonomous and creative problem solvers' (DfEE/QCA 1999, p. 4). The dilemma is that a word search of the relevant 60-page examination boards' teachers' guides and corresponding 60-page coursework guides reveals not one mention of 'creativity', 'creative', or 'innovation', let alone suggestions for how to recognise it or attach value to these constructs. There is a vacuum of support concerning this issue which teachers have tried to fill either by factoring creativity into mark schemes under the guise of something else, or by ignoring it completely (Balchin 2006). From the English study it emerged that co-ordinators fell more or less into three groups. Eleven per cent believed that is not possible or desirable to evaluate creative effort; 13 per cent believed that insufficient attention is given to recognising students' creativity, but evaluation is implicit in marking schemes; a significant majority, 76 per cent, believed that it would be useful for students' creativity to be evaluated through explicit assessment criteria, but did not know how to assess it (Balchin 2008).

Using the example of the same school subject as mentioned above, investigations which tackle the question of assessments of creative outcomes in design and technology (Balchin 2005b; Kimbell et al. 2004) have revealed that the current predilection of UK examination boards is to reward staged design work, usually featuring beautifully rendered pictures, complete with pretty borders. Given the deficit of both formative and summative assessment support for creative effort in English schools, how can use of paradoxes, analogies and risk-taking by young minds be rewarded? What about the frivolous thoughts, the practical ideas, the re-definitions of the question, the experimentation, the happy accidents, the stickability, the attitude, the consulting, the vision of another artefact and its application, the combining of ideas (often completely unrelated), the wackiness, the what-ifs, the copying, the alteration, the adaptation, the trying of options, the debate, consideration and acceptance of diverse ideas and perspectives? All these attributes are associated with the phenomenon of creativity, but they may all be missed unless teachers possess some kind of tool that allows them to disseminate work in terms of creativity during marking processes, for subsequent reference to when nominating a certain percentage of students for enhanced provision.

The indications from my own research are that creativity evaluations, to be of real use to schools and students, should be focused on both process and product, and look more like helpful 'feedback' than a standardised assessment measure. Marton (1981) considered that conceptual understanding of learning is based upon the relation between the students' experience of learning and their reflections upon the experience. Research (e.g. Lubart this volume) suggests that valuation – the effort towards appreciation – may be more important than critical evaluations, both for gifted children and their parents and teachers. This point seems to validate the effort to help teachers produce feedback on students' creative efforts, rather than seek to add it to the lists of measures and evaluations they already have to perform. Introducing ways to add to the assessment burden of teachers would therefore not be a good idea (Balchin 2002; Hall and Shultz 2003). Finding ways in which creativity can be promoted and nurtured without adding to teachers' workload would be better. Thus, the focus of this chapter concerns the introduction of a set of assessment tools for both teachers and students to use in conjunction with their workload, which reflects and raises awareness of real creative effort taking place.

It is my contention also that decisions about the value of creative effort should initially be made more to inform the creator than for the purposes of identifying the gifted. This primary focus may stimulate further excellence and identify areas of future learning over which the creator or facilitator has some control. Bringing students explicitly into assessment priorities can be highly productive in this process. The secondary aspect of such feedback is to facilitate the identification of giftedness, providing information that helps identify those students who are so advanced relative to their age peers such that they require adaptations to instruction.

Creative products

It seems now to be possible, via neuroimaging, to 'view' types of creative activity in the brain (for reviews, see Cabeza and Nyberg 2000; Damasio 2001). However, as the notion of discreet monitoring of a student's brain activity in the regular classroom to display whether creative responses are occurring whilst on-task is still some way into the future, and would probably be regarded as unethical, we need to devise a way of gaining evidence of creative productivity in order to identify a student as creatively gifted.

Cropley (2006) explains that the kind of free production of variability in the brain through unfettered divergent thinking holds out the seductive promise of effortless creativity. However, it is likely that if thinking about innovative ideas is all students do, they actually run the risk of generating quasi-creativity or pseudo-creativity, as ideas have not been grounded in reality. How do we see this reality? It can be a physical manifestation – a tangible piece of evidence, something that can be touched, criticised, praised, and judged – but it may also be a tune, a fractal algorithm, or a recipe. It is essentially a window through which a glimpse of the creativity of the product's makers can be seen – 'Products are the artefacts of thought' (Rhodes 1961, p. 305).

Teaching to maximise students' intellectual abilities, therefore, should include fostering their creative ability through defining high-quality creative output, and providing the necessary challenges to produce it. Products in schools may be essays and many other forms of writing including reports, diaries and reflective logs, poems, the products of electronic discussions, posters, and the results of problem working, design, and synthesis – like independent projects, and laboratory or field notebooks. They may include visual and graphical representations – designs, sketches, drawings, paintings, photographs, videos, computer animations, physical and virtual models and constructions, performance – theatre, role play, simulation, dance, songs and live or recorded presentations.

> Although the topic of criteria for evaluating creative products has a long history, it is not the case that there has been 'closure'. There is yet no conclusive 'set of criteria' for evaluating creative products. Thus there may be many benefits from continued inquiry in this area.
>
> (Besemer and Treffinger 1981, p. 161)

To date, this is still true. While we may never attain global agreement concerning criteria, we can certainly seek to examine the past research in this area, which has been proven to be reliable, and adapt that which we find efficacious to our national contexts and requirements. New neurological understandings must also be highlighted inside new tools. The *Creative Feedback Package* (CFP) has been developed in England to help with the creativity component of gifted learner identification (Balchin 2007b). It includes a tool to help teachers and gifted education co-ordinators to understand and produce information about elements of creative processes (Creative Moments Space), a tool for evaluating the effectiveness of the environment for creativity (Creative Climate Indicator), and a tool to evaluate outcomes (Creative Product Grid). Of Rhodes' '4 P's' contextual organiser (process, product, person and press, Rhodes 1961), Murdock and Puccio warn that 'it might neither be possible, necessary or practical to examine all interactions' (Murdock and Puccio 1993, p. 250). The decision was therefore taken early on during the CFP's construction to acknowledge the existence of the 'person' during creativity evaluation, but to avoid going into the realms of psychometric testing or having to validate subjective observations. Personality measures are viewed by many educators to be a minefield of potentially contradictory measures.

The Creative Product Grid (CPG) provides seven criteria against which teachers score students' products. These criteria were generated in 2004 by acknowledging the descriptors of products from the works of several researchers who have examined this area and produced reliable tools (Amabile 1982; Besemer 1998; Reis and Renzulli 1991), then removing some descriptors and combining or adding others. The Grid was then refined by continually discussing different permutations with panels of teachers until only the most critical essentials were left.

Seeking to define creative products can easily produce a tautological nightmare of interconnected nuances, which are difficult to separate out and find clear space between criteria. The CPG therefore aimed to utilise significantly fewer criteria than the 23 product dimensions included in Amabile's 1982 consensual assessment technique (CAT). The CAT has been successfully applied to evaluate the innovativeness of a product or response in situations where functional measures like technical performance are not available (Conti et al. 1995). The collaborative/discursive process in consensual assessment has been shown to effectively offset individual bias and frames of reference (Amabile 1996; Amabile et al. 1997). Amabile asks judges to use their own subjective definition of creativity and rate the degree to which an idea is creative relative to the others presented. Hickey (2001) urges caution, commenting that in order to rate the creativity of products, there is the need to rate the expertise of an appropriate judge. Inter-judge reliabilities reported in this area of research nevertheless have been found to be high – in excess of $r = .90$. For example, Dollinger and Shafran (2005) achieved a mean correlation rating of $r = .91$ with a sample of 200 students' drawings, drawn in response to stimuli provided by the TTCT, and assessed with Amabile's CAT.

It can be seen that the CPG derives some elements of its format from the *Creative Product Analysis Matrix* (CPAM) theory produced by Besemer and Treffinger in 1981. The CPAM is a three-dimensional model of creativity in products, which hypothesises novelty, resolution, and elaboration/synthesis as the three factors that most help judges to focus their attention on relevant attributes of products. Bearing the simplicity of CPAM in mind, the CPG was designed to be as straightforward as possible to use, yet retain as much as possible of the complexity of the phenomenon of creativity. Four criteria assess the creative concept or ideas, and three criteria assess the quality of outcome (which evaluates how well the creative thoughts are demonstrated in the final product). It is proposed that creativity be seen in both the concept and the standard of production. It is the creative concept stage where the unique ideas can be seen, and the quality of outcome stage where their manifestations show up. The latter cannot occur without the former; in this model, the quality of outcome is seen as a vehicle for the creative thought (Balchin 2005b). The criteria for this latter stage can be altered according to the subject area. The format for assessing products is shown below:

1 Uniqueness – what is the degree of deviation from the normal incidence?
2 Association of ideas – is there a link or attempt at synthesis of two or more broad ideas?
3 Risk-taking – is it a bold attempt? How ambitious is it? Is there a clear challenge taken on?
4 Potential – does it have the capacity to succeed/solve the problem? What is its likely promise?
5 Effectiveness – is it functional? Does it really work?
6 Well-craftedness – is it carefully/neatly/robustly done/made?
7 Pleasure – is it enjoyable/surprising/attractive to the senses?

These criteria attempt to capture the multifarious ways we sense the creative effort that has gone into the composition of any artefact. For example, risk-taking – being able to make decisions when the outcome is uncertain, imagining and analysing future scenarios, and learning from the situation if failure occurs – is an important personality trait that contributes to creativity in the classroom (Craft 2000; Davies 2000; DeSouza-Fleith 2000; Meador 1999; Wickes and Ward 2006; Wilson this volume). It was added in an effort to see whether judges could diagnose signs of risky behaviour from the product. To test this, 25 panels (of three to five UK teachers) were given design and technology products (e.g. a chair, a necklace, a dress, an electronic board game) made by KS 3 (age 11–14) students (Balchin 2005b). During the year-long trialling of the tool, strong evidence emerged to show that the judges could diagnose how the student had pushed the barriers of possibilities and experimented, by the different ideas, techniques and resources that they could see had been used to make the product, and what kind of learning they felt had taken place. Furthermore, they appreciated that feedback resulting from examining products in relation to this criterion could facilitate the acknowledgement of those who make genuine efforts but are defeated by pressures outside their control, the counsel of students who do not heed their teacher's advice and proceed with unworkable solutions, and of the consequences of starting to put creative ideas into fruition without the corresponding motivation and drive to finish.

The 'association of ideas' is the criterion on the CPG that needs the most justification for its place – and therefore needed the most careful trialling in schools to see if, using the descriptors, the phrase would be useful for teachers. However, it is at the heart of many of the accepted definitions of creativity. We accept the absence of a universally accepted definition of creativity, however the notion that creativity is the combination of ideas from different and largely separated fields is at the heart of many proposed definitions since Rogers (1949) wrote: creativity is the ability to make unusual relationships or unexpected connection between elements. The reason for highlighting it is that it has only been within the last few years (Dietrich 2004) that we have been producing the direct neurological evidence that creative relational processing requires the ability to see unusual connections and links in order to think around the nature of a problem. For example, one of the first neuroimaging studies which specifically looked at brain function whilst creative thought is taking place (Geake and Hansen 2005) found that intelligent individuals tend to consider more analogical combinations. Cognitive neuroscientists Heilman, Nadeau and Beversdorf (2003, p. 370) found that '. . . the more mental relationships that are evoked by an element (via general intelligence, domain-specific knowledge, and special skills), the more likely it is that another element will be combined with it in a meaningful way'.

The CPG challenges teachers to see whether they can diagnose the products for signs of the associative insights that had occurred in order to make the product the way it was. During the year-long trialling of the tool, strong evidence emerged to show that a surprising amount of information could be deduced concerning evidence of novel combinations of information inherent in the artefacts, simply by the judges using specialised knowledge of the particular task and previous outcomes done by others, and their general knowledge of the world around them (e.g. current trends that the student might have incorporated into the designs of their products). The products nearly always yielded strong enough clues to the combinations of ideas involved to allow the teachers to feel confident about reaching conclusions. However, upon asking students to explain the creative associations they may have gone through, many features had eluded the panel, simply because complexity of thought may be hidden or undetectable on the product itself (e.g. the novel use of a manufacturing process to construct an artefact may be highly creative, but the outcome may not show clear evidence of this). Moreover, if the condition of the production, whether it is an essay or a toy car, is poor, creativity is harder to see and score.

The CPG incorporates an adapted 12-point Likert scale for each criterion. It is intended to mirror traditional letter-grade marking schemes, with the corresponding pluses and minuses. We found that using this scale had the same effect of forcing opinions as a four point scale, as the marker cannot 'sit in the middle' (Balchin 2005a). Importantly, measures taken from the scale can be looked upon as enabling educators:

1   to force judgements by facilitating scorers to focus their attention on the criteria;
2   to show students which aspects of their work they might need to improve in order to be successful in terms of creativity;
3   to produce a concrete 'score of creativity', assisting gifted education co-ordinators in identifying creative individuals for provision programmes;
4   to facilitate students in articulating and harnessing their own creative processes, becoming progressively more aware of their own work patterns; and
5   to facilitate teachers to understand students' emerging products, and grow their awareness of the creative possibilities inherent in the tasks they set.

This tool has begun to be distributed by English school gifted education co-ordinators variously to teachers of art, design, performing arts, information technology, creative writing and music in many primary and secondary schools (Balchin, 2008). Co-ordinators are free to adapt it for their own purposes in order to discuss the creative responses of their students. School gifted education co-ordinators report informally that it can be used three or four times a year, without too much hardship to teachers or wasted time. We have found that when using the CPG in conjunction with marking products made as part of curriculum coursework, teachers (the people who may best act as 'judges' who understand the contexts in which the outcomes have been produced) can produce high correlations of agreement concerning the criteria for creative products shown in the CPF. It seems that even two teachers, who understand the nature and fit of the product can achieve a very high level of agreement (ranging from $r = 0.89$ to $r = 0.95$) concerning the creative effort exerted by the student (Balchin 2007a).

Clearly, knowledge of the task, the processes required, and the skills level of the creator assists assessments. To this end, students can usefully be included in the evaluative process of their own products (Fryer 1996), and enjoy the experience of critical and constructive analysis of their own creativity. Understanding students' creativity may depend therefore to some extent on the students' own ability to understand and explain it. There is convincing evidence that metacognitive training, such as getting students to verbalise their thinking, can be effective in enhancing children's perceptions of their own strengths and weaknesses, especially as far as creative abilities are concerned (Shore et al. 2003). This raises the issue of students' involvements in negotiating the criteria against which they will make claims and by which they will be judged. The coordinators report informally that the CPG can assist students to harness their creative powers once they begin to understand that time spent thinking about ideas and taking imaginative risks during design phases can be directly rewarded, and that incomplete work resulting from brave experimentation and working outside comfort zones will not be penalised (Balchin 2008a). As top marks, inevitably, are a concern, they view these assessments as providing a way to show students that they need to improve some aspect of their work in order to gain higher marks, whether this be to concentrate more on creative thinking, or on the presentation of their ideas:

> . . . if my pupils knew that creativity was being scored and rewarded in equal terms as their outcomes, they might be encouraged to problem solve in a more novel way in order to get those marks for creativity!
>
> (Mr. E, School AS)

A way for educators to use this tool may be to provide a start-point for students by showing them the feedback from each criterion (marked with these consensual assessments), in order to allow them to reflect on their own creative efforts, and perhaps then construct new understandings of what their personal creativity means in the particular contexts in which it was utilised.

It is often hard to distinguish creative and useful novelty from unintended and unimportant differentness, especially where products produced in classes are generally similar because a set task has been carried out with a defined outcome (i.e. to learn specified content or skills) rather than a more fluid or open-ended one. Information concerning unique creative processes, used to complement decisions about the creativity of student products, can be generated by students themselves using the CFP's CMS or other records of process. We are currently experimenting with giving pupils handheld personal digital assistants (PDAs) to record and download ideas and photos at half-hour intervals while fulfilling tasks (Balchin 2008a).

While helping school gifted education co-ordinators ramp up the efficiency of their identification process is encouraged, extra assessments inevitably generate concern. For co-ordinators to ask teachers to spend their time completing a product page to gauge creativity (if appropriate), the process of generating feedback therefore needs to be justified further. A possible rationalisation is that in addition to producing important identification data, the process of consensual evaluation also facilitates rich discussion about creativity and giftedness – which can provide important baseline knowledge for negotiations with students in the interest of promoting desirable 'growth mindsets' (Dweck this volume).

The use of neuroimaging tools (Geake and Cooper 2003) in combination with psychometric measures might help test the efficacy of this strategy for encouraging and/or testing creativity. Unfortunately, however, not even the most established psychometric measures of creativity, such as Guilford's (1967) test of divergent thinking, Torrance's (1974a) *Test of Creative Thinking* (TTCT), or Mednick's (1962) *Remote Associates Test* (RAT), have yet been used in combination with functional neuroimaging tools, optical imaging tools, trans-cranial magnetic stimulation, or electroencephalograph (EEG) equipment (Dietrich 2004). Until neuroanatomical correlates of mental processes can combine with the knowledge base of the field of creativity to produce new and more precise psychometric measures of creativity, there is little doubt that the identification and support of creatively gifted students in English schools will continue to be an inefficient and inadequate operation. Adopting reliable and positive approaches of recognising creativity in products like the CPG may help to facilitate the fostering of student's creativity in the meantime.

Contact address: tom@arni.uk.com

27

Programming for talent development: expanding horizons for gifted education

Donald Treffinger, Carole A. Nassab and Edwin C. Selby
Center for Creative Learning, Florida, U.S.

> *The only man I know who*
> *Behaves sensibly is my tailor; he takes*
> *My measurements anew each time he sees me.*
> *The rest go on with their old measurements*
> *And expect me to fit them.*
> George Bernard Shaw (1856–1950), Irish playwright and critic

Those of us in the field of Gifted Education need to be more like George Bernard Shaw's tailor. We must develop forward-looking programming options for all students, and especially for those with high potential whose needs must be met in appropriate and flexible ways. The twenty-first century presents unique challenges and will require answers to questions that have not yet been formulated. We know that political, business and religious leaders worldwide are clamouring for individuals who can work collaboratively with others, think critically and creatively, and solve complex problems. If our challenge is, as often expressed, to 'prepare the leaders of tomorrow', the task has never been more formidable.

Students – their characteristics, their strengths and talents, and their needs for instructional services that are stimulating and satisfying – must be the central focus of the next generation of programming that will carry us, in the words of this book's editors, 'beyond gifted education'. After nearly four decades of involvement in the field, the heart of our vision for the future rests in recognising and nurturing students' unique strengths, talents, sustained interests, and needs rather than in labels and categories which anoint a few students as 'gifted' and exclude all others. Too often our vision seems so shallow or myopic that the effects or impact on students are all but forgotten in the process. We must not neglect the critical question, 'In what ways will this benefit students?' (Treffinger and Selby in press).

There are many ways to expand, extend, or enhance learning opportunities for students. We use six broad themes or areas of educational programming as starting points for planning programming for talent development. In each of these six areas, many provisions can be made quite effectively in the mainstream classroom (e.g. Treffinger et al. 2004; Treffinger et al. in press), although effective programming can also extend beyond the regular classroom and outside the walls of the school. The six themes follow:

Differentiating basics. Concern for differentiating basic instruction recognising and responding to students' learning styles and interests, adjusting the content and the rate and pace of instruction according to the student's needs, and providing opportunities for students to use a variety of higher level thinking skills.

Effective acceleration. Students who display strengths in any area need access to teachers, mentors and materials for advanced learning opportunities. Through advanced curricula and deliberately planned accelerative strategies, content instruction can become more stimulating and challenging for learners.

Appropriate enrichment. Enrichment is another essential attribute of programming for talent development. Rather than 'more of the same', enrichment involves the need to explore new and varied topics, to develop thinking and research skills, and as Renzulli (1977b) proposed, to pursue individual or small group investigations of real problems.

Independent, self-directed learning. Fostering of effective, independent, self-directed learning, is another important component of talent development programming (e.g. Treffinger and Barton 1979; Treffinger 2003). Students need to learn how to define goals, locate and use appropriate resources, plan appropriate learning activities, create and evaluate products and present or share their work.

Personal growth and social development. The affective and social-emotional needs of students should also not be overlooked in the talent development commitment. Students must be able to develop a healthy perspective about their own talents and limitations and those of others; a positive self-image, a positive regard for the processes of learning and inquiry and a commitment to a guiding set of moral and ethical values.

Career exploration with a futuristic perspective. As learners discover and develop their talents, they will also need support in exploring career opportunities and information, and in learning how to deal effectively with rapid change and the uncertainty of the future.

Three foundations of programming for talent development

Our work on meeting the challenge of expanding, extending or enhancing learning opportunities for students, spanning more than four decades of theory, research, and practice, draws upon three important foundations. These are: a contemporary, inclusive programming model; attention to differentiation of instruction that is responsive to personal creativity characteristics, learning style, and problem solving style; and deliberate instruction in productive thinking and change management. Taken together, these foundations will guide us in our efforts to enhance, enrich, and strengthen the fabric of twenty-first-century practice in both gifted and general education. In this chapter, we offer a brief overview of each of these foundations and a discussion of their importance in understanding gifted education as a complex, evolving and dynamic educational concept.

A contemporary, inclusive programming model

The Levels of Service (LoS) approach (Treffinger 1981, 1998; Treffinger and Selby 2007; Treffinger et al. 2004; Treffinger et al. in press) is a contemporary, flexible and inclusive model for nurturing the strengths and talents of students through the collaborative efforts of the school, the home, and the community. Based on more than two decades of research, development, and practical application, the LoS approach serves as a framework for ensuring appropriate, challenging, and developmental learning experiences for high-ability students and for differentiating instruction, recognising strengths, talents, and interests, and nurturing the potential among all students. From its origins as the IPPM approach (Individualised Programming Planning Model) (Treffinger 1981) to its contemporary expression today, our approach calls upon educators to consider the most appropriate decisions for the student (Colon and Treffinger 1980; Treffinger 1998; Treffinger et al. 2004) and seeks to guide them in designing, organising, and carrying out effective educational responses.

The LoS approach involves four levels of educational programming or services that serve varying numbers of students, based on the individual student's strengths, talents, and sustained interests (rather than on inclusion or exclusion of students from a single 'gifted program' based on a fixed test score or criterion). LoS involves a variety of programming activities or services, building on student interests, problem solving, and learning style preferences to differentiate instruction and curriculum. Let us consider each of the four levels of service; the model is depicted graphically in Figure 9.

Level I services reach all students, providing many and varied ways to engage the interest and attention of learners. Level I involves the exposure of all students to appropriate and challenging experiences that create a foundation for talent development, such as higher-level thinking, problem solving, decision making, research and inquiry, and high-interest content. Level I also involves assessing and clarifying students' personal characteristics, interests, problem solving and

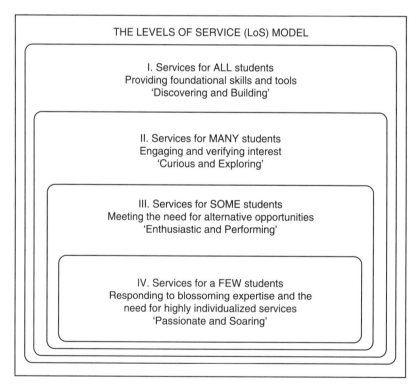

Figure 9 The Four Levels of Service (Treffinger et al. 2004)

© 2004, Center for Creative Learning. Reproduced by Permission.

212

learning style preferences . . . helping parents, teachers, and the students themselves to understand their strengths and to clarify the ways in which they can be at their best. Level I activities, which are generally brief in duration, can readily be accomplished in the classroom or through specific events (such as assemblies with guest speakers or field trips). They expose students to many different topics and experiences in order to clarify strengths, talents, and interests for subsequent development.

Level II services invite students to participate in activities through which they can verify and extend their strengths, talents, and interest areas. We might say that '. . . anyone might, but not everyone will' participate in any given Level II activity. They involve opportunities for students to explore themes, topics, or talent areas about which they have an initial curiosity, or for which they demonstrate interest or aptitude as observed by parents, teachers, or others. Level II activities provide students with experiences that may be deeper, more challenging, or sustained over a longer period of time than Level I. Students can now put their skills and interests to the test, confirm or disconfirm their interest in future work in a specific area, or identify other new (or spin-off) directions to pursue. At the same time, Level II activities can be sufficiently finite in duration that a student is not required to make a long-term commitment to an area that might not sustain their interest or enthusiasm.

Both Levels I and II serve as a 'staging platform' for the emergence and development of specific talent areas for any student. They are essential to the overall talent recognition and development process, because they can help, create or clarify promising opportunities and directions for students to pursue.

In Levels III and IV the focus shifts to linking an increasingly smaller number of students with programming opportunities that provide highly personalised responses to their unique strengths, accomplishments, and growing expertise. The services students need at Level III or IV often build directly on, and extend significantly, previous Level I and Level II experiences. The focus also shifts from foundational group opportunities to small group and individual opportunities that respond to the unmet needs of specific students.

Educators considering Level III or Level IV services for students, examine specific criteria that relate directly to (or identify) the students' unmet, high-level needs in any talent area or domain, seeking demonstrated student interest, motivation, preparation, and readiness to engage in the activity. Evaluation may be based evidence of the student's ability and/or achievement in the specific content or talent area of the proposed programming, rather than on generic ability measures and labels or arbitrary 'cut-off' scores. Level III offers services within the school or through other agencies to help students reach a higher level of accomplishment and build a commitment in a particular talent area or domain, and may involve collaborative efforts among schools to make advanced offerings practical from a scheduling or cost perspective.

Finally, Level IV recognises and responds to an individual's 'blossoming expertise', providing individually tailored services that help the student rise to an outstanding level of talent development, expression, and productivity. The challenges of responding to the programmatic needs of a student who demonstrates the need for Level IV services are unique, and require the collaboration of student, parent, school, and community resources. Often it involves the development of a deliberate Talent Development Action Plan. In some cases this includes making exceptions to standard rules and procedures, crossing traditional age or grade-level (or school) boundaries and doing whatever may be necessary to ensure that the student's needs are being met.

The benefits of providing an appropriate, challenging, and developmental educational opportunities across the four levels of service far outweigh any inconveniences that educators incur. We believe that implementation of the LoS approach does not imply more work for educators, but enables them to discover (or, re-discover) the motivation, commitment, and rewards that initially led them into teaching.

To learn more about LoS, visit http://www.creativelearning.com

Differentiation responsive to creativity characteristics and styles

When we look at talent development from the perspective of the LoS approach, it is essential to recognise that, over several decades of educational and psychological theory and research, our conception of talent, intelligence, and giftedness has expanded significantly (e.g. Reis and Renzulli 1982; Treffinger, Young, and Nassab 2005), so that it is essential today to hold a multi-dimensional perspective of those constructs.

Major theorists and researchers in intelligence and human behaviour have stimulated today's practitioners to expand significantly their understanding or definition of giftedness. Since the 1950's, research by many pioneers, including J. P. Guilford (1959, 1967) and C. W. Taylor (1968, 1985) expanded our thinking about the nature and assessment of cognitive abilities and skills. More recently, the theories of R. J. Sternberg (1985) and Howard Gardner (1983) have reinforced our understanding that traditional conceptions of ability or intelligence have been far too narrow in scope and definition. Renzulli (1978) defined giftedness as the interaction among ability, creativity, and task commitment, while both Amabile (1983) and Torrance (1979) also emphasised that creative productivity arises from a synthesis of abilities, skills, and motivation. Dunn et al. (1992) proposed that giftedness involves achievement and creative productivity, over a sustained period of time (perhaps years or even decades), in a domain that matters to the person.

Through the work of developmental scholars, such as Piaget and Bruner, for example, we have also learned that human cognitive abilities grow and change over time, and that different abilities mature, change, and decline quite differently, which suggests that it is more fruitful to think of giftedness as a qualitative, dynamic construct, rather than as strictly quantitative and static. One's score on a test (such as an IQ test) is a snapshot of a person's responses to a particular set of questions, in a certain context, at a given time; that is much less than the more complex, richer, more varied collage of a person's strengths and talents that yields insights into the person's giftedness over time and experience.

Through the work of many scholars from a variety of perspectives and disciplines, then, we have come to the unambiguous and unavoidable conclusion that giftedness can no longer be defined in relation to a single score or simple quantitative index or cut-off point. The LoS approach builds on the need to recognise that talents are complex and multifaceted. Our emphasis on bringing out the best in all students also takes into account our understanding that, within any student, personal creativity characteristics and style add uniqueness, breadth, and power to the construct of gifts and talents (Selby et al. 2005). We ask: 'How do we help individuals to grow in the knowledge of themselves as learners?' 'How might we help individuals and groups to work together more efficiently and harmoniously?' 'How might educators tailor their instruc-tion to accommodate the emerging needs of a greater number of students?' Thus, our work also involves studies of personal creativity characteristics, learning styles, and problem solving styles.

Treffinger et al. (2002) reviewed research on personal creativity characteristics as part of a larger research project on creativity assessment. In so doing our efforts shifted from asking how creative one is, towards asking how an individual might be as creative as possible. We identified four categories into which we clustered creativity characteristics: Generating Ideas, Digging Deeper into Ideas, Openness and Courage to Explore Ideas and Listening to One's 'Inner

Voice'. We affirmed the importance of assessing such characteristics in many ways (e.g. through formal and informal assessment, self-report and rating tools, and authentic performance data). This was carried out less for the purposes of labelling and selection, and more for the important tasks of designing effective, appropriate instruction and building meta-cognition and self-understanding of the students' strengths and talents.

Theory and research on learning style (e.g. Dunn 1993, 1998), while not universally embraced, yields valuable and useful insights into the varied ways in which learners prefer to function when learning new and challenging material. Research on the Dunns' model indicates, for example, that a number of style factors (such as low structure, learning alone [unless with others who are high achievers], and learning in a variety of ways) often differentiate high-ability students from other age peers (Dunn et al. 1992; Dunn 1998; Selby and Treffinger 2003). Although there was considerable variation within and across talent domains, cultures, and tasks, Dunn (1998) reported that students with strengths in a specific talent domain demonstrated similar learning preferences across cultures. Awareness of learning style offers individuals a deeper understanding of themselves as learners, and provides educators with opportunities to develop their students' creative productivity in personal and effective ways (see http://www.learningstyles.net).

Problem solving styles are consistent individual differences in the ways people prefer to generate ideas and focus them in order to gain clarity, produce ideas and prepare for action when managing change or solving problems (Selby et al. 2004). Problem-solving style involves three dimensions and six specific styles (Treffinger et al. 2007). 'Orientation to Change' deals with an individual's preferences for responding to and managing structure, authority, and novelty when solving complex problems or managing change. It includes the 'Explorer' and 'Developer' styles. Explorers tend to prefer highly original approaches and solutions, often find external structure limiting, and seek distance from authority. Developers tend to prefer new solutions that are clearly workable and add value to the current reality, and are comfortable working with the guidance of structure and authority.

The second dimension, 'Manner of Processing', addresses preferences for turning first to one's own inner resources (an 'Internal' style) or to draw early and often on interaction and the resources of others (an 'External' style) in solving problems and dealing with change. The 'Ways of Deciding' dimension deals with preferences for a 'Person'-oriented style (emphasising relationships or harmony) or a 'Task' style (emphasising the quality and demands of the task) in problem solving and change management. By understanding and using knowledge about problem-solving style, individuals choose issues and challenges and apply strategies and tools in ways that draw upon and nurture their strengths and talents. Team members find ways to collaborate successfully across differing styles and to appreciate the strengths each person brings to the process. Educators can use problem-solving style data to differentiate instruction and to enable learners to discover and apply their problem-solving skills in powerful ways.

Earlier in this section we posed three questions, each of which assumes that our goal is to bring out the best in all students. Because talents evolve over a period of time, in different circumstances, and within a variety of talent domains, our responses as educators must take into account personal creativity characteristics, learning styles, and problem-solving styles.

Deliberate instruction in productive thinking and change management

The third component of the foundation for our work on responsive, contemporary programming involves deliberate instruction in productive thinking (including both creative thinking, critical thinking, and Creative Problem Solving (CPS)) and the application of those skills to complex, open-ended tasks and challenges, and to change management. The LoS approach builds on recognition that students must be able to think creatively and critically. As they develop and apply their strengths and talents in any domain, students are also called upon to manage change and to deal with complex, open-ended opportunities and challenges (Isaksen et al. 2000; Treffinger and Isaksen 2005; Treffinger, Isaksen and Stead-Dorval 2006). Students must also learn and be able to use the research and inquiry tools required in investigations of real problems, and in making real-life plans and decisions. These skills include: using library resources; conducting reviews of literature, using the Internet effectively and wisely, learning basic procedures of data collection and conducting data analysis and data presentation. They also include higher-level knowledge of the specific methods, instruments and techniques related to inquiry in a certain discipline (e.g. an astronomer must be able to use a telescope, or an engineer must be able to conduct a particular kind of stress or strength of materials analysis).

Teachers do not hesitate to teach their students how to take notes, how to study for a test, how to use mnemonic devices or memory aids to review knowledge or other 'process technology' for the knowledge and comprehension levels of learning. By the same token, learning and applying the appropriate technology for processes is also important. If we expect students to learn to solve complex problems and to develop and carry out effective plans of action, we must accept the responsibility to help them acquire and apply the necessary tools. There is also a second set of tools – focusing tools – to help individuals or groups to produce many, varied, or unusual possibilities, to develop new and interesting combinations of possibilities, or to add richness and detail to new possibilities. Brainstorming is an example of a generating tool, although there are also several other generating tools (see, for example, Treffinger and Nassab 2000, 2005). It also includes a second set of tools to help individuals or groups analyse, organise, refine, develop, prioritise, evaluate, or select options from the set of possibilities they have at hand, or 'focusing' tools. Students can apply these basic tools for generating and focusing options independently, or teachers can easily incorporate them into a variety of content or curriculum areas. For other tasks – opportunities and challenges that are complex, ambiguous, important, and open-ended – individuals and groups often need to employ a systematic approach to attain clarity about the problem, to generate possible solutions, or to prepare for action and successful implementation.

These challenges call for applications of the Creative Problem Solving (CPS Version 6.1™) framework (Treffinger, Isaksen and Stead-Dorval 2006; Treffinger et al. 2006). The CPS framework emphasises the importance of a natural, descriptive, and flexible approach to problem solving (in contrast with the prescriptive, sequential approach of traditional 'step/stage' models). CPS includes three process components: 'Understanding the Challenge' (examining opportunities in constructive ways, exploring data to clarify the central themes and issues and framing a specific problem statement), 'Generating Ideas' (producing many, varied, unusual and detailed options for responding to one's challenge) and 'Preparing for Action' (developing or strengthening promising solutions and building acceptance by others with specific action commitments). The CPS framework also includes a metacognitive or management component, 'Planning Your Approach', to guide individuals and groups in determining the appropriateness of CPS for a specific task or challenge and to enable them to analyse and select relevant and appropriate process components to apply.

Productive thinking and CPS can be helpful to educators who work with students of all ages and across many content areas with students in regular education, special education, and gifted education (Isaksen and Treffinger 2004; Treffinger and Isaksen 2005). Helping students to learn and apply practical tools for generating ideas and for focusing their thinking, in addition to applying the components and stages of CPS, will enhance student learning in powerful ways that extend beyond memorisation and recall. Even in times in which there is great emphasis on basic learning and doing well on standardised tests – indeed, particularly in such times – it remains important to balance the emphasis between process and content in teaching and learning. Students who are competent in the basics of productive thinking and CPS, as well as the basics of content areas, will be lifelong learners, creators and problem solvers who can live and work effectively in a world of constant change. (You can download a PDF summary of our contemporary CPS model and find additional resources at the CPS area of our website http://www.creativelearning.com)

Summary

Shaw benefited each time his tailor took his measurements anew. For us to meet the challenges and opportunities of the decades ahead, we, too, must learn from that metaphor. Gifted education is – and always has been – a dynamic, constantly evolving discipline, in which both new knowledge and new questions continue to proliferate. By adopting natural, flexible, inclusive programming models, understanding our own styles and creativity characteristics (as well as those of our students), and arming ourselves with powerful, but practical tools for solving problems and managing change, we will be confident and competent to meet the future and give it shape and direction. A recent quote, of un-cited origin, posed both the opportunity and the challenge quite well:

> *Innovation is not found in the middle of the status quo . . .*
> *Innovation always starts at the edge. . . .*
> *On the edge, the landscape is uncertain and unstable . . .*
> *But the edge is also home to the beginning of the future.*

Contact address: don@creativelearning.com

Future Perspectives

Suggested priorities for gifted education over the next decade

Historically, the inaccuracy of experts' forecasts of the future makes this an exercise for the brave or the foolhardy. The diversity of American education compounds the challenge. Clearly, we have little reason to forecast greater consensus than now exists. Two paths open before us: a contemporary, inclusive path focusing on our ability to bring out the best in varied ways among many students, and a traditional path seeking to serve a narrow, very precisely defined set of individuals designated as the gifted. We chose to walk along the first path, and hope others will journey with us. Both paths will continue to exist, neither will be empty, and all will seek to serve children and youth to the best of their ability. Ultimately, the question is not which path is 'better', but whether those on each walk with respect and appreciation for those they serve.

Donald Treffinger, Carole A. Nassab and Edwin C. Selby

28

Special educational needs and dual exceptionality

Diane Montgomery
Middlesex University, UK

Dual exceptionality (2E) is well known in the special educational needs (SEN) field, where it is termed 'comorbidity'. Comorbidity often occurs in dyslexia when the dyslexic child also shows symptoms of attention deficit hyperactivity disorder (ADHD) or Asperger Syndrome (AS). The incidence of comorbidity is in the region of 30 per cent – meaning that 30 per cent diagnosed with one condition have at least one of the others (Clements 1966; Tanguay 2002). In all three conditions, dyslexia, ADHD and AS, there is also a high frequency of co-occurrence of hand-writing coordination difficulties, creating multiple exceptionality. In the gifted education field, 2E is a term used to describe those who are intellectually very able (gifted) or who have a talent (a special gift in a performance or skill area), and in addition to this have a special educational need. This is made more complex because children may not demonstrate their 'gifts' and the SEN may be hidden.

SEN is defined in the UK as a need for educational or other support to access the mainstream curriculum. Additional resources may be given for learning support, assistive technology, adapting access to school buildings, or providing special education in a special-ist environment. Only recently has funding for special provision been made available for the gifted and talented (Department for Education and Employment [DfEE] 1999). Most state funded grammar school provision was replaced by comprehensive education in the 1970s.

Some problems arising from dual exceptionality

Giftedness in combination with other special educational needs brings about special problems. Handled badly, students given remedial teaching and supportive strategies for their dyslexia, for instance, may be placed in the lowest classes or sets because of their low educational attainments. This is extremely frustrating for them, for then they do not have the stimulation needed for their high ability. The result is that they can develop behavioural and emotional problems as well. At each point the SEN other than giftedness is the focus for intervention, and the high ability is overlooked. Even when high ability is identified and special provision is made for that, there may be a lack of teaching skill in relation to the SEN, or there may be a problem because of the need for dual funding, which the system is not set up to do. Funding for one need cannot be allocated to another.

Underachievement and dual exceptionality

A significant number of highly able 2E pupils are never identified as either gifted or learning disabled, and are at serious risk of underachievement. Estimates of underachievement vary from 25 to 70 per cent depending on the criteria used. My observations in 1250 ordinary classrooms suggested that 80 per cent of pupils in these classrooms were underachieving much of the time (Montgomery 2002). Having a special need, whilst also being highly able, frequently conceals or masks high ability (Baldwin 2002). This can result in a progressive deterioration in school performance (underachievement) and low self-esteem. The frustration and boredom engendered by this situation can lead to social, emotional, and behavioural difficulties.

Profile of typical underachievers

There have been several attempts to describe the 'typical' underachiever (Kellmer-Pringle 1970; Montgomery 2000; Silverman 1989; Wallace 2000a; Whitmore 1980):

- large gap between oral and written work
- failure to complete schoolwork
- poor execution of work
- persistent dissatisfaction with achievements
- avoidance of trying new activities
- does not function well in groups
- lacks concentration
- poor attitudes to school
- dislikes drill and memorisation
- difficulties with peers
- low self image
- sets unrealistic goals
- satisfactory performance at level of peers.

The underlying theme of some of the abovementioned characteristics is an inability or an unwillingness to produce written work of a suitable quality to match the perceived potential. I have argued (Montgomery 2000, 2003) that hidden beneath this profile are two problems – a handwriting coordination difficulty and a spelling problem. Both lead to difficulties in coding and writing speed that underpin the ability to construct good composition (Berninger 2004; Connelly and Hurst 2001). If such difficulties go uncorrected, they lead to low attainments, with boys achieving 10 per cent poorer than girls. However the same research (Kellmer-Pringle et al. 1970) suggests that the positive side of this picture is that pupils with 2E can be identified because they are:

- inventive and original when motivated
- quick to learn new concepts
- very good at posing and solving problems ingeniously

219

- good at asking awkward and penetrating questions about everything
- able to persevere when motivated
- streetwise and full of commonsense wisdom
- perceptive about people and motives
- able to find novel answers to difficult questions or problems.

Patterns of giftedness and special educational needs

A summary review of the research in the field suggests that there are five main types of difficulty that children with SEN might have (with some children having complex learning difficulties involving several conditions):

- general or global learning difficulties
- specific learning difficulties (learning disabilities)
- physical, sensory, and medical difficulties
- social, emotional, and behavioural difficulties
- learning disorders – Autistic spectrum disorders; Down Syndrome; central communicative disorders, or specific language disorders.

Normal functioning can be expected once a specific difficulty has been overcome or circumvented and a catch up programme implemented. With disorders, on the other hand, the system is considered to be dysfunctional and requiring specific training from an early age, and is expected to remain problematic and not normal in function. In each of the five areas, the associated difficulties and disorders are on a continuum from mild through moderate and severe to profound.

General learning difficulties and 2E

In norm-referenced terms the condition known as 'general learning difficulties' (GLD) is common and occurs on a continuum from mild through moderate to severe and profound. Children falling into this group are often referred to as 'slow learners'. The core difficulties are problems with memory, language, and thinking, and these affect development and intellectual functioning across all areas of the curriculum. Thus while students may have specific talents, they generally do not appear in the gifted end of the 2E spectrum.

Specific learning difficulties and 2E

Specific learning difficulties (SpLD) can occur in either or both verbal and nonverbal areas:

Verbal learning difficulties

Developmental dyslexia. A diagnosis of dyslexia is often based upon lack of progress in reading, and intervention is thus targeted there. The core disability would appear to be a lack of progress in spelling, particularly initial sound-symbol correspondence and phoneme segmentation. The bright dyslexic child (IQ 120 and above) constitutes 10 per cent of the dyslexic group and will eventually learn to read and write but with considerable effort and an Alphabetic-Phonic-Syllabic-Linguistic (APSL) multisensory programme. If started at the end of the reception year (the year in which the child turns five), the consequences of first level dyslexia may be avoided. Most bright dyslexics are discovered late and are able to read slowly but write and spell very poorly. They need second level intervention with a strategic approach to spelling for subsequent transfer to reading (see below).

Developmental Dysorthographia. This is a specific spelling problem, accompanied by adequate or even very good reading skills, and is common in gifted students. They may have learned to read in the pre-school period or have begun school with a reading difficulty, which subsequently cleared up. The same cannot be said of their spelling, which is often regarded as 'atrocious'. Such children typically hate the rote learning strategies they are frequently exposed to, such as *Look-Cover-Write-Check,* and these strategies generally do not work with them. However, approaches that engage their reasoning and problem-solving abilities, such as *Cognitive Process Strategies for Spelling* have been found effective for addressing these second level dyslexic problems (Montgomery 2007).

Mild developmental dysphasia/specific language disorder. Children with dysphasia are slow to speak, or have limited vocabularies and powers of self-expression. They find it difficult to achieve well in schools; both conceptually and perceptually they may be very bright, but unable to demonstrate their intellectual abilities except in nonverbal areas. If they can draw, design, sing, or perform well in another non-academic area such as sport, they can gain fulfilment; otherwise they are often bullied or become despairing (Edwards 1994).

Nonverbal learning difficulties

In most *Nonverbal learning difficulties* (NLD) there is an associated motor coordination problem (Tanguay 2002).

Developmental coordination difficulties (DCD). Dyspraxia is a difficulty with motor skills, or with putting a motor plan into fluent operation after a reasonable period of skill acquisition. There is a range of dyspraxic difficulties, from gross motor coordination (a general clumsiness in running and walking), to specific problems of fine motor coordination (e.g. handwriting, bead threading, shoe lace tying and buttoning). Characteristic situations include exercise books being filled with scruffy, scrappy work and loaded with crossings out and holes (Soloff 1973). Typically, children with DCD are not picked in team games, and are frequently bullied even by teachers, becoming the butt of jokes and blame (Gubbay 1976; Chesson et al. 1991). Despite ungainly behaviour and sometimes a lack of control of emotional responses, the individual may be highly intelligent, trapped in a body that will not do as instructed unless specific training is given. Generally speaking, if the child's writing is legible, the DCD is ignored (Montgomery 2008), despite characteristic difficulties with spelling and maths – and the pupil might be condemned to underachieve in school (Chesson et al. 1991).

Dysgraphia. There is a significant number of pupils who will have handwriting coordination difficulties. Estimates vary. Sassoon (1990) reported that 40 per cent of boys and 25 per cent of girls at age 15 stated that they found writing painful and avoided it whenever possible. My studies show that the incidence is in the region of 30 per cent, on a continuum from mild to severe (Montgomery 2008) with boys more prone to difficulties than girls by a 3:1 ratio.

The ability to write neatly secures higher marks regardless of content mastery (Soloff 1973), although untidy writing from boys is more tolerated. Young gifted children's thoughts may run much faster than their writing skills, leading to criticism for presentation rather than content. Problems writing at speed with reasonable legibility are given little attention, but they can have a serious effect on school achievement. Such problems result in lower SAT (School Attainment Test) scores at 7, 11, and 14 scores and degree classification – such as gaining a lower second rather than an upper second class degree. It is a hidden SEN, and a significant cause of under-achievement (Connelly et al. 2005).

Attention deficit hyperactivity disorder. Estimates of the population incidence of attention deficit hyperactivity disorder (ADHD) vary from 3 to 5 per cent in the USA, to 1 to 2 per cent in the UK, with a sex ratio of two to three boys to every girl. It has been speculated that the narrower UK definition leads to the lower incidence (Cooper and Ideus 1995).

It is not uncommon for very bright children on entry to school to be absorbed by the newness of it all for a week or so, and then to become bored by the routine and the sameness and slowness of everything. Such children can begin to leak a nervous energy that has no intel-lectual outlet, and that teachers try to overcorrect and suppress. Students like this are sometimes mislabelled as hyperactive, and recommended for medication. For a genuine diagnosis of ADHD, there are three main symptoms: distractibility or inattention, hyperactivity (extreme and incessant mobility and restlessness) and impulsivity (e.g. shouting and calling out, inability to take turns, poor judgement). Over-activity does not always continue into adolescence, and may be replaced in some cases by under-activity, inertia and lack of motivation.

When the symptoms are present without the hyperactivity, the diagnosis is sometimes known as attention deficit disorder (ADD); in other situations, ADD and ADHD are used interchangeably. The non-hyperactive condition is frequently overlooked, as it can appear to be dreaminess, disorganisation, or quiet withdrawal. Such a child might be easily managed in a busy classroom, but little learning takes place. In pre-school, ADD and ADHD can manifest as a pattern of uninhibited curiosity and meddlesomeness. There tends to be continual trial and error learning, with very little retention; wandering away from the guarding adult; rash accept-ance of strange adults; and proneness to accidents. Studies show that those with hyperactivity are more likely to show aggressive behaviours whilst those without hyperactivity show a slug-gish, cognitive tempo. For planning purposes for parents and teachers, it is important to dis-tinguish between the high energy levels of gifted students who are not being sufficiently challenged and ADHD as a disorder.

What we tend not to see is the positive side of ADHD. Jaksa (1999) reported cases of people who learn to manage and use it to advantage, such as Phil, who insisted that it made him a more exciting speaker, comedian and motivator. He claimed it was a gift, although he joked that at school, teachers took early retirement when they found he was going to be in their class. Until children learn to manage and cope with their distractibility, impulsivity and hyperactivity, however, ADHD is not a joke, and can interfere with effective learning. This can be seriously troubling to all children and may be even more frustrating for children who are capable of high-level learning and reasoning.

Physical, sensory and medical difficulties

Students with physical, sensory and medical difficulties are relatively few in number compared to those with specific learning disabilities, or with social, emotional, and behavioural difficulties, and the difficulties they have similarly range from mild through moderate, to severe and profound. It is those with severe and profound difficulties whose giftedness most easily goes unobserved.

Students with physical difficulties such as cerebral palsy and medical difficulties such as spina bifida, multiple sclerosis and epilepsies need access not only to buildings but also to an intel-lectually challenging curriculum suited to their individual levels of ability. Measures used to aid identification of sensory difficulties (visual and hearing impairments) tend to recognise current levels of attainment, rather than potential (Starr 2003). Further barriers for 2E children who have exceptional learning needs both for giftedness and physical and sensory problems, are that teachers who work in gifted programmes may be reluctant to include children with such difficulties because they lack experience of working with these concerns.

Visually impaired gifted students have observed that they have to be better than gifted students without disabilities in order to be recognised (Corn 1986). They share this in common with gifted girls, and disadvantaged and minority ethnic groups. For those with hearing impairments, visual scales on cognitive tests and nonverbal tests of reasoning, such as *Raven's Progressive Matrices* (Raven 2008) can be useful in assisting the identification of giftedness. In brief, when gifted students with physical, sensory, and medical problems have their physiological needs attended to, their educational needs are much the same as other gifted children.

Social, emotional and behavioural difficulties

Social, emotional, and behavioural difficulties (SEBD) are common hidden causes in under-achievement for gifted learners. Schlicte-Hiersemenzel (2000) recorded the plight of many gifted German pupils who had become behaviourally and emotionally disturbed by their unchallenging mainstream education, and Sisk (2000, 2003) described similar results of 'ill fitting environments' for American students. McCluskey et al. (2003) recorded the same for Canadian students, and in the UK, similar findings have been reported by Kerry (1983) and Montgomery (1992).

Small misdemeanours designed to provoke the teacher and to 'amuse' the learners can, in hostile or coercive school environments, cause the student to be labelled as a problem and a career in disruption is set in progress. Others are dismissed as the 'class clown'. In gifted students the schooling frequently is one of the root causes of SEBD (Slichte-Hiersemenzel 2000), although some will come from disadvantaged and dysfunctional backgrounds (McCluskey et al. 2000). In the latter cases their problem behaviours might mask their abilities and so prevent their adequately accessing the curriculum.

Special populations with disorders

Asperger Syndrome

Asperger Syndrome (AS) was originally thought to be high functioning autism, but more recently this has become somewhat contentious, and there are some who claim a distinction. In AS there is serious impairment in social skills, there are repetitive behaviours and rituals, problems in fantasy and imaginative activities and play, concrete and literal comprehension of speech and a monotonous speech pattern (Wing, 1996), and motor impairment in 90 per cent of cases (Henderson et al. 2001). This latter is in contrast to autism in which there is usually good coordination, even gracefulness but severe impairment in language, perception and social skills (Wing 1996).

In those diagnosed with AS, isolated 'gifts' (such as musical or artistic ability, or a facility with number calculations) may emerge in some 10 per cent of cases. Gifted adults with AS can be highly successful, holding important jobs especially if they have good self-care skills and a placid nature, but they usually remain socially isolated and idiosyncratic. They appear to lack insight into their own thinking processes, as well as understanding of the perspective of others and the ability to attribute mental states – beliefs, intents, desires, and knowledge – to oneself and others. According to Neiehart (2000), the child with AS is differentiated from the ordinary gifted by the following:

- pedantic, seamless speech-usage, with a mixing of fact and personal detail;
- low tolerance for change, and a tendency to ignore class and school routines completely;
- failure to appreciate nuanced humour, literal understanding;
- clumsiness in 50–90 per cent of cases;
- inappropriate affect and lack of insight – e.g. may laugh at a funeral;
- tendency towards stereotypic behaviours and rituals.

Early identification of the giftedness of a child with AS may be vocabulary-based, as they are generally hyper-lingual, although with comprehension deficits (Cash 1999a; Neihart 2000). In later school years they may be very successful in subjects requiring recall of large amounts of factual material (Wing 1996). However, problems ensue if they are not interested in a subject, and they can make naive and overt criticisms of others' methods and personal attributes (Cash 1999a; Attwood 2000).

The behaviours of students with AS can be rigid and resistant to change, which brings them into conflict with other children and school staff; so that having been told to sit still and be quiet they might continue questioning loudly, or get up and walk around, oblivious to the instruction. Some engage in compulsive rituals such as shelf tidying or hand flapping; others are prone to sudden, aggressive outbursts, temper tantrums, hyperactivity, anxiety, or phobic attacks (Jordan and Jones 2001). They are very sensitive to teasing, but continually engage in precisely those asocial behaviours that provoke it. A structured approach for AS students is needed in the rules of interaction in conversation, such as to look at the person when they are speaking and only get ready to speak when they signal they are coming to a close by looking away and then looking back (National Autistic Society 1997). How to 'chat up' a potential girlfriend was high on the 'wants lists' of youths with AS (Rogers 1996).

The more gifted a student with AS, the more likely it is that by adolescence he has learned to cope with most regular demands of school, but he will still need specific instructions for tasks – whilst the rest of us learn by experience. For example, specific teaching in how to take a bus and a train and go shopping were all necessary for a university applicant with AS who was on his way to a place in a prestigious university (Teasdale 2000).

Conclusions

The problems of the education of doubly exceptional children bring into focus two key issues in gifted education – identification and provision. We might ask why we need to identify giftedness at all. The answer usually offered is that we wish to select the most able for some sort of special provision that the ordinary curriculum is not providing. This leads to an observation that instead of treating students' exceptionalities as though they were a problem we might better address the ordinary curriculum and the way it is taught, to make sure it meets most of their needs. Differentiation and inclusive teaching are powerful strategies for teachers to use in these situations.

We might begin by recognising that gifted individuals in mass schooling systems are ill-served. They need much more freedom and autonomy built into programmes of study, with room for creativity and real world problem solving. In the UK, schools are being encouraged to do this by personalising learning. This involves five strategies: assessment for learning; a focus on effective learning and teaching; bringing flexibility to the curriculum; making the required organisational changes to the school in order to facilitate personalised learning; and building partnerships beyond the classroom.

Schools are also encouraged to free up curriculum time so that 20 per cent of it may be devoted to offering out-of-school options, master classes, independent projects and so on. This needs, however, to go hand in hand with reframing ordinary provision for gifted learners.

There seem to me to be four crucial aspects forming good basic provision which can be offered by every teacher to support the education of gifted and talented students who are doubly exceptional, and we should seek to offer the same to children of all abilities in the mainstream classroom. The first is to enhance the skills of mainstream teachers so that the everyday provision they offer is more cognitively challenging within the normal classroom. We need to allow students to be more participative and able to choose from a range of response modes to cater to their different talents. We need to recognise that writing is still widely used as the main assessment response mode in schools; we should help teachers therefore to develop kinder attitudes to writing difficulties, and show them how to intervene to support and develop writing skills, without inadvertently creating a problem or other special need.

All learners – exceptional, doubly exceptional and apparently average – need to experience intellectual challenge in their learning that can be provided at least partly by embedding a cognitively challenging curriculum (i.e. emphasising thinking and reasoning, problem solving and investigative learning, creative learning, games, and simulations) in all subjects. They also require a curriculum that values and embeds talking and reflection about learning before writing and recording in a variety of response modes – the 'talking curriculum' – with less teacher talk and more legitimised pupil talk and leadership. A whole school approach to developing handwriting and spelling skills in both primary and secondary schools – the 'developmental writing curriculum' – can scaffold the acquisition of organisational skills in all learners, whether identified as exceptional or not. A school ethos that encourages a positive classroom climate, matched with an appropriate level of challenge and discipline, will give the best chances of educating all our students, including those who are doubly exceptional.

Contact address: dmont507@aol.com

Future Perspectives

Suggested priorities for gifted education over the next decade

The model of separate provision for the gifted in special schools, pull out programmes and special classes that operates in many countries will change. The latest research on curriculum and learning needs has shown that the gifted need to be helped to develop study and research skills, reasoning capabilities and creative problem solving. This change in focus will move provision towards the mainstream setting and the gifted will be identified on the basis of their performance on the extending and enriching tasks. Increasing differentiated in-class provision is the goal so that the more able are offered more challenging work to extend their skills and abilities across school subjects alongside peers. As they extend their range of intellectual skills and cognitive abilities they will require more opportunities for extended and autonomous learning. Teacher education will need to be extended and enhanced to cope with this.   Diane Montgomery

29

Visual thinking: a gifted boy with Asperger Syndrome

Wiesława Limont
Nicolaus Copernicus University in Toruń

Over recent years, there has been a growing research interest in the educational needs of gifted individuals with learning problems (Baum 1984, 1988; Baum et al. 1998; Reis this volume). This research concentrates on the nature of learning problems experienced by gifted individuals, as well as the need for appropriate curriculum differentiation for them (Attwood 1998; Baum et al. 1991; Cash 1999b; Montgomery this volume; Neihart 2000).

The term 'Asperger Syndrome' (AS) was popularised in a paper by British researcher Lorna Wing (1981), where she introduced the research of Hans Asperger, an Austrian psychiatrist and paediatrician. Asperger, who published the first definition of AS in 1944, called children with AS 'little professors' because of their ability to talk about their favorite subject in great detail. In four boys (initially), he identified a pattern of behaviour and abilities that he called 'autistic psychopathy', meaning autism (self) and 'psychopathy' (personality disease). Asperger considered social isolation to be a feature which differentiated this group of children from others, quite frequently accompanied by relatively outstanding talents.

The term has now come to describe children of normal or higher intelligence than their age-group peers, who nevertheless have trouble with social communication, demonstrate no empathy for their peers, and sometimes possess low levels of physical fitness (Attwood 1998; Grandin 1992). There are some interests and abilities frequently seen in people with AS, including in the natural sciences, complex calculations, and computer programming (Silberman 2001). Typically, individuals with AS show prodigious memory, and are keen on collecting objects they feel attached to. Some demonstrate outstanding savant (exceptional genius-level) skills, including special abilities with numbers, mathematics, mechanical or spatial skills, which tend to manifest themselves in activities connected with science, inventions, complex machines, and, currently, computers (Asperger 1944/1991; Silberman 2001).

The group of behaviours referred to as AS was also observed independently by another researcher at the same time as Asperger, but in a different part of the world. Whilst Asperger described cases of children with characteristic psychiatric and social impairments who, at the same time, revealed outstanding skills and abilities (and defined the symptoms as 'autistic psychopathy'), Leo Kanner (1943) in the United States observed children who showed unique but nearly uniform symptoms which he referred to as 'early infantile autism'.

An attribute of children with AS which differentiates them from those with other autistic disorders is that by the fifth year of life they usually speak fluently, even if their language development started late. As adults, it is sometimes possible for them to adapt reasonably well to social life, and some AS people are successful in their professional lives, thanks to their intellectual abilities and special talents, even though they have the tendency to extreme self-centredness and social isolation (Asperger 1944/1991; Frith 1991). The behaviour of people with AS usually strikes others as 'strange', even when they are intellectually talented and manage their disability well (Attwood 1998; Grandin 1992; Tantam 1988). Some researchers claim that today, the diagnostic label of 'AS' is used much too often, both with reference to people of limited potential and difficulties coexisting with others, to people of outstanding intelligence who have a special interest in numbers, computers, and systems (Wing 1991; Silberman 2001). Steve Silberman describes AS people as characterised by the 'geek syndrome'; the term, on the one hand, describes an alienated person, socially maladjusted, but, on the other hand, points to the person's profound interest in science, computers, or other technologies.

As previously stated, some people with AS have highly specialised skills that lead them to prominence, and the ambiguity of the definition of AS can cause some confusion. There can be mistakes in distinguishing people with outstanding abilities from people who have outstanding abilities but who also demonstrate AS characteristics. Similarities between these groups include the intensity of their experiences, their passions, strong motivation, profound involvement in the work undertaken, and social inadequacies. At a younger age it can be difficult to differentiate between the genius and the individual with autism, and in fact, some highly gifted learners are described as working with 'autistic singularity' (Rimland 1978). Sensory sensitivity is also characteristic of people in both groups. The high sensory sensitivity of those with autism corresponds in the gifted literature to descriptions of overexcitability: Dąbrowski (1979) claimed that people with outstanding abilities show intellectual, imaginative, and emotional overexcitability.

Visual thinking

There are many cases of people with autism demonstrating highly-developed visual thinking, and they are often referred to as visual thinkers (Grandin 2006). Temple Grandin is arguably the most accomplished and well-known adult with autism in the world at the moment, renowned for her work on the design of livestock handling facilities. She has become a prominent author and speaker on the subject of autism, and she has conducted many interviews with verbally fluent autistic adults. Grandin has demonstrated that in their thinking, these verbally fluent autistics mostly use visual images. She claims that outstanding savant skills, evidenced by such feats as solving difficult jigsaw puzzles, quickly navigating around cities, and memorising large amounts of data, are indicative of these individuals' visual acuity. She herself has an autistic tendency of seeing a picture of nouns in great detail (Attwood 1998; Grandin 2006).

People with AS think best by producing concrete, literal pictures, often in the form of drawings or designs. Correspondingly, some with autism have been shown to possess well-developed visual thinking skills. Evidence of the importance of the development of visual thinking for the creative process at a young age can be found in biographies of outstanding socially creative adults (Csikszentmihalyi 1996; Ghiselin 1952; Hadamard 1945; Kosslyn 1983; Limont 1996; Shepard 1978). I now attempt to ground this brief introduction to Asperger Syndrome and giftedness by presenting readers with a case study of a gifted child with autism, whose gift for expressing ideas visually indicates to us that he is 'seeing' the process of thinking, which is normally described by others with words.

Matej

Matej (born May 1997, in Bratislava) is a gifted autistic child. He has a brother, two and a half years younger, and a sister, five years younger. According to his mother the children in the family are emotionally close to each other. Matej was born to 26-year-old parents, each of whom had a degree in higher education; his father is an information and communications technology manager and his mother is a microbiologist. His mother reports that he was a very anxious child; he cried often and it was difficult to soothe him. Over time, however, he became progressively calmer. At seven months, he started crawling and getting to know his immediate surroundings. At that time his favourite toy was clothes pegs; he used to take close looks at each of the pegs in his collection, and then put them one by one in orderly rows, carefully putting the damaged ones aside (Martinková 1995, 2006).

Matej spoke his first words according to normal child development milestones, at around the age of one. However, he used them to name objects, and not for communication with other people. Between the ages of two and four, symptoms of autism appeared more prominently. He could repeat a single activity for a long time, even two hours. During daily walks, he followed the same route and would not tolerate small changes, even as small as circumnavigating a parked car. Any changes annoyed him, and he expressed this in the form of loud yelling. In everyday life, he did not notice others, although some people terrified him; he hated being looked at, and neither did he like looking at others. He liked neither family meetings nor group family photographs being taken. The first gift he really appeared to enjoy was a set of magnetic letters, which he got as a birthday present at age three. At first, as usual, he did not want to accept the new gift, but once he understood how the letters worked, he was very happy with them (Martinková 1995, 2006).

Matej demonstrated his intellectual skills at an early age. Before he turned three he knew the entire alphabet well; he had learned it himself. Between ages four and five he could also write and demonstrate understanding of numbers up to 100. He used to change letters into character-istic geometrical shapes, and this is how he started writing words. He also learned Roman numerals and learned hand-writing by imitating his mother's activities. He got to know zodiac signs from horoscopes available in papers; he noticed that there are 12 signs of the zodiac, which correspond to the number of hours on the clock; and so he combined the two facts by marking clock face hours with signs of the zodiac. Observing houses in the street marked with even and odd numbers, he started creating sequences of odd and even numbers. Then he produced drawings, which included numbers with dividing lines between them.

Between ages five and six Matej was also developing Slovakian map drawing skills, repro-ducing parts of Bratislava, the city and the surroundings as well as the Carpathian mountain region. He began to produce maps of the European continent with countries, cities and rivers. He knew how power is generated in power stations, he learned the Greek alphabet himself, and he also used to invent other alphabets. He was interested in physics, especially changes of different states of matter, their properties, electromagnetic radiation as well as nuclear reactors, and nuclear disintegration at the atomic level. A children's encyclopedia provided him with a lot of knowledge on the lives of stars and the nuclear syntheses and reactions in stars.

Between ages six and seven he was studying the prehistory of the Earth as well as changes in the continents' patterns over centuries. He got to know high-level embryology within two months. He was studying organogenesis and immunology. He knew the human anatomy in detail as well as the DNA structure. At the age of eight his interest in chemistry started. Having revised what he learned a few months before, he focused on organic chemistry which he studied by applying characteristically visual ways of thinking and representation. Interested in organic chemistry, he then focused on learning the structures of enzymes and vitamins. (Martinková 1995, 2006).

As a two-year-old child, Matej neither wanted to draw nor to paint on paper, even though he liked to observe his mother drawing. However he used to play with coloured pencils for long periods, taking them out of the case one by one, and placing each in turn on his arm. Having done this, he looked at them carefully and, finally, put the coloured pencils on the floor and started from the beginning. He could play that way all day, from dusk till dawn. One day, by accident, he drew a line with the crayon, which he held in his hand. From then on, he started drawing; within a month he had covered the entire wall in his room with his drawings. Since the age of about two years and five months, drawing has been a source of pleasure to him. He stopped using the wall and began producing drawings on paper.

Matej's first drawings were a repetition of schemes he had observed in adults. Whenever he wanted others to draw something for him, he placed a crayon into their hands; very rarely did he ask for something using words. He often expected a specific object found in his surroundings to be drawn; if something else was drawn, he reacted by yelling. As early as three years of age he learned to draw objects in three-dimensional space with the use of perspective and object size inconstancy, yet maintaining appropriate proportions and spatial arrangements. At age three years and four months, spatial, three-dimensional drawings appeared; he used to draw chess figures as well as letters and digits (Figure 10).

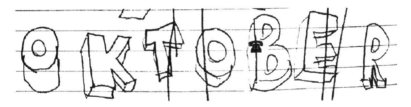

Figure 10 Spatial letters – three years and nine months old

At the age of three years and five months Matej started drawing with a pen, so he could create a thin blue line and create precisely drawn details. At the age of four he was making unusual spatial drawings of rooms, e.g. his bathroom (Figure 11) and electric kitchen devices, e.g. the washing machine (Figure 12).

Words written on paper were treated by Matej as living creatures he could talk to and which could talk to each other. Drawings became a method of obtaining information on his interests, thoughts, feelings, or problems faced. His works show a wide interest in all kinds of installations

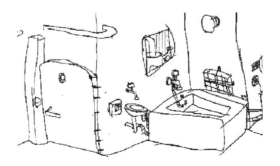

Figure 11 Bathroom – five years and four months old

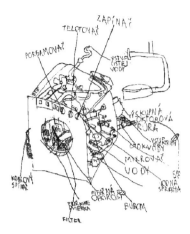

Figure 12 Washing machine – five years and five months old

and systems: he was interested in the rules of water and nuclear power plant operations. He was also fascinated with the operation of the sewage and water distribution systems; from the source through the structure of the underground pipes to the actual sewage discharge. The first drawings provided the main structural components of the static structure, and show that very early on, he had started drawing the structure of entire systems.

Matej was also producing drawings of the internal structures of cars and other devices, e.g. turbines, gears and cables which, whilst not externally visible, are important for the operation of entire devices or systems. At the same time he made a drawing of a tower, clearly showing his associative thinking (Figure 13):

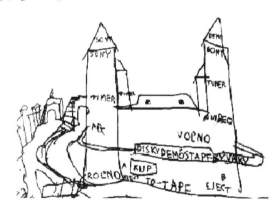

Figure 13 Associating the castle towers with 'Sony' tower – five years and one month old

Another interesting example of Matej's thinking is provided in Figure 14. This is based on the creation of new meanings – which in turn are based on associating similarities of shape and transformations of abstract marks into specific objects. The boy made these drawings whilst performing exercises of lower-case and capital letters writing practice. The capital letter 'E' gets transformed into organic structures and into an animal with four paws.

At the same age Matej was drawing 3-D devices to open the doors in the house, room and kitchen cabinets, with the use of finely drawn perspective (Martinková 1995, 2006). At a slightly later age he designed equipment and its electronic parts – for example, a microprocessor

Figure 14 Transformations of letters 'E' and 'e'

design to be used in 'fantastic' equipment (Figure 15), showing both his cognitive skills as well as his creative thinking skills.

At the age of five Matej joined an art group, which he liked a lot. During classes, he was producing drawings on self-chosen subjects. He neither considered nor accepted the tutor's comments on his work, yet, at the same time, carefully observed the work of others. A characteristic feature of his drawings is the great detail. His drawings show his potential connected with outstanding spatial, visual thinking and with an apparently photographic memory. Before he turned six, he created his own unique letters and made drawings of the underwater world he perceived. In the summer he was drawing the views of landscapes he remembered from walks. At the age of seven he was making embryology drawings (Figure 16), drawings of organogenesis with its pathological variations, and of immunology.

Matej's drawings revealed scenes of social situations he did not understand, which made him anxious, annoyed and which made him yell in protest. At the age of eight, he began to show an

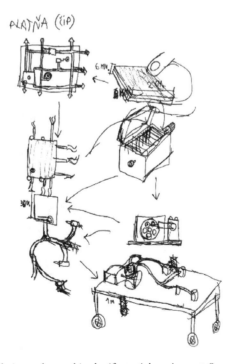

Figure 15 Microprocessor design to be used in the 'fantastic' equipment: 8 years and six months old

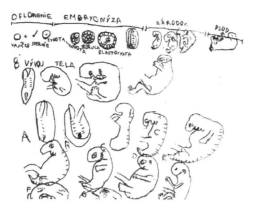

Figure 16 Embryogenesis – six years and eleven months old

intense interest in chemistry and astronomy. Thanks to the maternity leave of his mother, who could afford a longer stay at home, the boy calmed down, which can also be seen in his drawings. He also resumed 'comic-book' drawings, geometrical figures communicating and talking to each other. The drawings reveal what is important to him, what he is thinking of, and what he feels. (Martinková 1995, 2006).

The figure referred to as '*Metabolism – joke*' by the boy (Figure 17) depicts streets with a large number of details, with lamps on the sides. The characteristic quality of this work is a careful and detailed presentation of roads, which make it possible for the vehicles to move freely in different directions. The picture is a metaphor of metabolism and biochemical cycles connected with the biochemical transformation and the energy transformations that accompany these cycles in living cells. The picture includes some use of cognitive visual metaphors with which the boy tries to understand a complex phenomenon with the use of earlier experience of the reality around him (Lakoff and Johnson 1980, 1999; Miller 1996). In the picture the roads going in different directions stand for biochemical cycles and the dynamics of energy transformations (highways and lamps shedding light on the road).

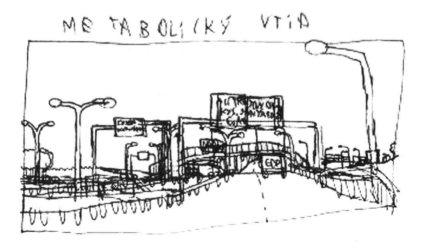

Figure 17 Drawing showing '*metabolism*' – eight years and four months old

Reasoning through visual metaphor is seen in many people with creative talents who use it when learning and problem solving as well as explaining and interpreting new, complex phenomena (Limont 2004). In metaphorical expressions, one field of knowledge is referred to using the terms of the other. In the case of this picture, Matej is describing metabolism using a situation he knows well from his everyday life.

Discussion and conclusion

Matej is an example of a person with a developmental deficit who has learned to cope by using drawings to communicate his ideas, and to facilitate his intellectual development. He thinks with images and drawings, which help him solve problems and develop his thinking. In addition to his intellectual abilities, he is also artistically gifted, albeit differently than many others with savant syndrome: his drawing talents are accompanied by strong intellectual abilities and the drawing is used as a means to solve cognitive and creative problems. In the pictures discussed above, at a very early age the boy's outstanding skills were revealed to be connected with spatial thinking – which is also a good predictor of mathematical skills (Webb et al. 2007).

People whose visual thinking is well developed are better learners and better at problem-solving if they use specific objects or images or mental visual images (Miller 1996). Such thinking could be seen in Matej whose drawing activity is clearly connected with the process of visual thinking. Grandin, with outstanding cognitive giftedness allied to her AS, describes her thinking as specific and occurring in visual pictures in her mind. Visual images found in her imagination are her thoughts, which move on the 'computer screen in her head'. Grandin can also 'see' the process of thinking, which is described by others with words (Grandin 2006). Similar properties of their thinking were described by Albert Einstein (1946; Holton 1972) and other outstanding creators, including James Watt (Shepard 1978), and Michael Faraday (Koestler 1964). Each of these stories, including Matej's, illustrates the importance of attending to children's strengths, and helping them use their strengths and interests to learn to cope with their challenges and weaknesses. When we listen, the twice-exceptional child can teach us something important about human development and possibility.

Acknowledgement

The author is grateful to Michaela Martinková for her permission to use Matej's drawings.

Contact address: wlimont@poczta.onet.pl

Future Perspectives

Suggested priorities for gifted education over the next decade

At present, the Academic Secondary School of Nicolaus Copernicus University in Toruń is one of the more important educational projects concerned with the education of the gifted in Poland. We plan to create more of these kinds of schools at other Polish Universities. At present, the Centre for Gifted Education and the Study of Giftedness is being created at the university in Toruń whose task will be to conduct scientific research, provide teacher education and disseminate expertise in giftedness and creativity. The other important project is the Polish Children's Fund, a non-governmental organisation which helps gifted students to develop their academic and artistic talents within the framework of the out of school educational enrichment and support programmes. The students participating in these two projects mentioned are from all social backgrounds including small towns and villages.   Wiesława Limont

30

Challenge and creativity: making the links

Helen Wilson
Oxford Brookes University

Over the past seven years, I have had the privilege of being the course leader for the national primary gifted and talented (G&T) co-ordinators' training programme within Excellence in Cities, a government funded British programme with the aim of driving up standards in schools in major cities to match the standards of excellence found in our best schools. Over two thousand primary teachers have participated in this training, and through this work, I have met a remarkable group of teachers from schools in the most deprived parts of England, working in challenging circumstances. Most had 'been volunteered' to be the G&T co-ordinator and many did not at first realise that this involved taking part in a five-day assessed course. All had been subjected to the intense barrage of strategies and initiatives that have been the lot of English primary teachers in recent years. However, once convinced that providing challenge for gifted and talented learners will raise standards for all, and will really benefit the children in their schools, they were prepared to go to all lengths to develop appropriate provision. I take my hat off to them – these are very special people, and I have learnt so much from them. This chapter contains my reflections upon what I have gained from working with these professionals.

There is a significant tension in the English education system (as elsewhere) that requires urgent attention. On the one hand, we have an increasingly data-driven system in which pupils' external test results are published; the position of the school in the league tables is considered crucial and there is great pressure to raise achievement scores. On the other hand, there is a simultaneous drive for creativity, and criticism is levelled at teachers if schools are not flexible in their provision. A government document entitled 'Excellence and Enjoyment' (The Department for Education and Skills, DfES 2003) gave schools the freedom to be more creative with the curriculum to meet pupils' needs. However, in the Annual Report of Her Majesty's Chief Inspector for Schools 2004/5 (The Office for Standards in Education, OfSTED 2005), it was noted that many schools continue to take a cautious approach to this freedom.

This caution is hardly surprising – teachers are being encouraged to be creative and to take risks in their teaching and yet schools are judged by outcome measures such as scores on tests taken at the end of a pupil's time in primary school (the Standard Assessment Tests or SATs). Quite predictably, teachers feel that they cannot afford to take risks because they need to deliver the factual content of the curriculum as preparation for the all-important external tests (see

Balchin, this volume). Black and Wiliam (1998) noted that, 'Such tests can dominate teachers' work, and insofar as they encourage drilling to produce right answers to short out-of-context questions, this dominance can draw teachers away from paths to effective formative work'. (p. 17). Teachers generally want the best for the pupils they are teaching. Black and William went on to make the crucial point that the effect of these external tests is for teachers to 'act against their own better judgement about the best ways to develop the learning of their pupils'. (p. 17). Most teachers enjoy creative, exciting teaching, but they often feel bound to adopt a more standard delivery style of teaching, so that their pupils will be well-equipped for the all important tests. This has repercussions throughout the education system. Wilde et al. (2006) in their report, which investigated the outcomes that higher education lecturers seek from the age 14–19 education system, stated:

> There was widespread concern that the current system, with its associated accountability mechanisms, was forcing teachers into a position of 'teaching to the test': Schools are too interested in performance and league tables. They are conscious that what students study has an effect on the performance of the school.
>
> (p. 10)

I well remember a teacher-training day I delivered some years ago about challenge and creativity in primary science. At the end of the day, one of the teachers sat back in his chair, folded his arms and said, 'Good ideas but I can't do any of them'. When asked why not, his response was simply, 'There is too much work to be got through in Year 6'. It is not uncommon to hear of schools where the Year 6 (final year of primary school) pupils prepare throughout most of the year for the SATs, where the main focus is literacy and numeracy, so that there is little space for other subjects (Mansell 2007). One wonders what effect this has on the pupils, and in fact, Montgomery (2002) commented that, 'What we do know is that boredom and lack of cognitive challenge in the daily curriculum is playing a more significant role in causing pupils across the ability range to become disaffected than was originally suspected' (p. 130).

This is in no way a criticism of teachers but more an indictment of our assessment-driven system. Certainly this ongoing revision is an issue for the more able and one of the points highlighted by Rogers (2002c), in her synthesis of research findings regarding provision for gifted and talented learners, was that gifted students are significantly more likely to forget or mislearn content when they must drill and review it more than two or three times. In other words, they become bored and switch off.

There is a wealth of evidence that the primary curriculum, particularly in the latter years, is generally perceived as content laden and assessment driven. Newly released statistics (Mansell 2007), show how non-tested subjects (typically the very subjects which allow the most scope for creative experimentation and expression) have been cut back drastically over the last five years due to the pressures of high-stakes testing in English, maths and science. PE, art, design and technology and music are typically affected, and this cannot help teachers tasked with nominating gifted students.

This has an inevitable impact on teaching styles, and Galton and MacBeath (2002) in their study for the National Union of Teachers on the impact of changes on primary teachers' working lives, pointed out that 'more whole class teaching, more pressure to move on, less time for discussion, left less time to explore, to make meaning, to use illustration and anecdote to develop understanding' (pp. 51–52). Certainly the teachers I have worked with on the primary gifted and talented co-ordinators training programme have echoed these concerns. Galton and MacBeath (2002) went on to state that:

Spontaneity is seen as a thing of the past although this is something that teachers have always valued and been good at exploiting. Teachers feel they cannot be sidetracked by children's questions, they can not veer off what has been planned.

(p. 40)

In my opinion, one of the key challenges facing the English education system today is to encourage and enable our teachers to take risks, to be creative in their teaching, and to be prepared to be sidetracked and to follow the children's interests. I could go so far as to say that what is needed is a restoring of the professional confidence of our teachers.

I was originally a secondary physics teacher and then became a primary teacher. My intro-duction to primary teaching coincided with the introduction of the National Curriculum, which filled a whole shelf in the staff room. I was amazed and impressed by the way the teachers adapted willingly to this innovation and came to terms with the need to plan schemes of work from scratch in all subject areas. Since then, I have never ceased to be amazed at teachers' willingness to cope with the scattergun of initiatives that have bombarded them and to work all hours to assimilate these for their pupils' benefit. Possibly it is a measure of the perceived importance of education that so many initiatives have emerged in recent years. However, there is a desperate need to make links so that the best of these innovations is extracted and there is an holistic approach to the education of our children.

The lessons we have learned in recent years from the gifted and talented field can go some way to making these links. Because provision that is suitable for the gifted requires creative teaching, lessons we have learnt about teaching for challenge can help resolve the widespread tension between creativity and raised standards. Research on teachers rated as particularly successful with gifted children (Cropley 1997) has made a direct link between giftedness and creativity: These teachers, among other things, emphasised 'creative production', showed 'flexibility', accepted 'alternative suggestions', encouraged 'expression of ideas', and tolerated 'humour'. They were themselves creative and had stronger personal contacts with their students. The role of the teacher in fostering creativity is widely recognised (Alexander et al. 1996; Shagoury-Hubbard 1996). According to Cropley (1997) creativity-fostering teachers are those who:

- encourage students to learn independently;
- have a co-operative, socially integrative style of teaching;
- motivate their students to master factual knowledge, so that they have a solid base for divergent thinking.

One of the things that teachers have valued most about the primary gifted and talented co-ordinators training programme is that it has been acknowledged that they cannot be expected or asked to do any more work. Our teachers already work very long hours, and they can do no more than they are already doing. But they can learn to work differently, more creatively. I remember a young teacher who on the third day of the course admitted that he was very confused and uncomfortable. He went on to describe this visually: he put his arms straight out in front of him and explained that he felt that he had been trained to teach like that – narrowly; he widened his arms and said that now he was being challenged to teach like this – expansively and creatively. Here surely is a lesson for our education system: teachers need to be released to teach expansively. It is encouraging that this has obvious resonance with *Excellence and Enjoyment*, a current government policy document for primary schools, which opened with the words, 'Children learn better when they are excited and engaged . . . When there is joy in what they are doing, they learn to love learning' (DfES 2003).

This is not easy though, and Howe (2004) suggested that, 'Teachers need "permission" to follow their instincts to make learning more meaningful and enjoyable' (p. 16). Perhaps, though, this is merely idealistic and rote revision is a bitter pill that just has to be swallowed by teachers and pupils alike so that standards are met? After all, pupils need to pass examinations so that they can reach their full potential. In the gifted and talented world, Renzulli's contention that a rising tide raises all ships is often quoted (1998); in other words, teaching for challenge on an inclusive basis to the whole class will raise standards for all. However, more hard evidence is needed in England to back this assertion so that teachers can have confidence to teach in this way.

One of our aims in the AstraZeneca project: Conceptual Challenge in Primary Science (Mant et al. 2007) was to explore the link between inclusive challenge for the whole class and attainment in the national tests, the SATs. The project in 2002/3 involved 16 schools and two key teachers from within each school. The project teachers created a classroom environment characterised by a high degree of conceptual challenge, rather than by an emphasis on rote preparation for the SATs. Changes in their lessons included encouraging focused recording by their pupils, which meant less but better writing and which released more time for the discussion of scientific ideas and for practical investigation. The teachers also overtly encouraged the pupils' use of higher order thinking. There were 412 Year 6 pupils involved in the project, and the number attaining the highest level in the SATs at the end of that year was 12 per cent above the national average, whereas the figures for the same schools in the previous year were much in line with those nationally. This substantial and statistically significant outcome goes some way to show that inclusive challenge can result in raised standards for all. These findings (among others) suggest that teaching creatively is beneficial for both teachers and pupils. In addition to the raised levels of student achievement, the project teachers enjoyed their teaching more; for example, one commented, 'I have enjoyed science more and think this has rubbed off on the class'. The pupils were very enthusiastic and the words of one were particularly memorable: 'That was good, you had to think a lot more . . . it makes science much more fun'.

One of the activities on the primary gifted and talented co-ordinators training programme was for small groups of teachers to note all the current initiatives within their schools. To our amazement, the list always filled a piece of clip chart paper – evidence of the plethora of innovations that are raining into our schools. The teachers then mapped the possible links between these initiatives and provision for the gifted and talented. One initiative in particular is the Assessment for Learning agenda. Its seminal booklet, *Inside the Black Box* (Black and Wiliam 1998) has had a profound influence upon English education. Elements within this, such as allowing pupils time to think before answering a question, the development of effective classroom dialogue, and the giving of formative feedback, are also key ingredients of provision for the gifted. In the subsequent booklet, *Science Inside the Black Box*, Black and Harrison (2004, p. 5), argued that to create an environment where effective feedback occurs, the essential ingredients are

- challenging activities that promote thinking and discussion;
- rich questions;
- strategies to support all learners in revealing their ideas;
- opportunity for peer discussion about ideas; and
- group or whole-class discussions which encourage open dialogue.

This perfectly and succinctly describes the environment required for a classroom where inclusive challenge is paramount; an environment where standards will be raised for all, and the needs of gifted and talented learners will also be met.

However, as with most educational innovations, the Assessment for Learning agenda has been subject to a degree of mechanistic corruption. Whilst working with a group of teachers recently, I mentioned, as one strategy for challenge, the use of 'must, should and could' learning objectives. This is a simple but effective way of differentiating, and three lesson objectives are shared with the whole class by the teacher. The teacher explains that they all 'must' fulfil the first objective, they all 'should' reach the second and they 'could' reach the third, most challenging objective. The intention is that use of the 'could' objective provides an exciting incentive and a challenge to all. I often say to the teachers that they will be surprised who rises to the challenge of the 'could'. This strategy is usually received with interest but to my surprise, this particular group of teachers groaned audibly. It transpired that many of these teachers' schools were in difficulties and were involved in an intensifying support programme run by their local education authority. Within this system they were required to differentiate every lesson on a 'must, should and could' basis but the pupils were divided according to perceived ability and were actually labelled as 'musts', 'shoulds' and 'coulds'. Hence the 'musts' were given one learning objective, the 'shoulds' another, and only the 'coulds' were allowed to try to meet the most challenging lesson objective. This can only be described as a travesty and an anathema – the pupils had been labelled and expectations fixed. No wonder the teachers groaned.

This brings us on to an issue at the heart of the gifted and talented field: is it right to label children as gifted and/or talented? Every school in England is expected to keep a register of its gifted and talented learners and a national register is being established which comprises an amalgamation of the school registers. Is it fair to label a child in this way? And what will be the effect on their future development? The issue of labelling is discussed during the primary gifted and talented co-ordinators training programme, and the position that is encouraged is not to describe individuals as gifted and talented pupils, but rather to think about pupils with particular gifts or talents. One potential difficulty with labelling was highlighted by Dweck (2000, this volume): if individuals have a view that intelligence is fixed, and their self esteem is built upon the gifted label, they will be reluctant to take risks in their learning. Over time the situation can change, and a child who shows early promise does not always continue to develop at the same pace; it is vital that a child's self-esteem is not reliant on being 'gifted'.

Put bluntly, every child needs to learn to fail, and to learn from failure. I often ask teachers to perform a quick mental audit of the gifted and talented provision in their schools. This involves answering a very simple question: 'Are there pupils in your school who always get everything right?' If this is the case, it is an extremely unhealthy situation. Failure is an important step in the learning process, and a person's awareness that they do not understand something is often the springboard from which deep learning can take place. The concept of failure leading to the production of creative ideas is a natural progression from this idea. Unfortunately it is impractical for schools who all have too many time limits, budgets and curricula to get through to allow the luxury for students to work like inventors for instance. However it is worth noting that Nobel Laureate physicists such as William Shockley who invented the transistor (Rudberg 1956) and Richard Feynman, who explored quantum electro-dynamics (Feynman et al. 1997), both used what is called the 'creative failure methodology'. Feynman states that, 'to develop working ideas efficiently, I try to fail as fast as I can'.

Even without intentional effort to fail (in order to narrow options and point the way toward novelty) everyone will fail at some time or other in their efforts. If an individual's self-esteem has been built upon being a high achiever, who does not fail, this kind of failure, without the proper perspective put on it, can be a devastating blow if it first happens at university or even later in life. Dweck (1999) has noted that this can be a particular issue for bright girls, and suggests that '. . . what must be addressed is the whole framework in which these girls are operating, a framework in which challenge is a threat and errors a condemnation' (p. 55). Some countries, like Russia, have whole educational systems to deal with this important issue (see Yurkevitch this volume).

Wilde et al. (2006) highlighted the importance of intellectual risk-taking at university and noted that, 'What higher education tutors are looking for is . . . students who are committed to studying a subject, engaging critically with ideas, prepared to take some intellectual risks' (p. 4). Unless educators are supporting the development of critical thinking and risk-taking habits of mind in the early years, students are unlikely to show up at university with them fully formed. And unless teachers are fully supported in fostering such attitudes and habits, it will not happen. The final answer may well be that if you are going to reward risk, we must reward failure (to an extent) too. For example, attempted risk-taking should be recognised, but failure to take on board basic recommendations from the teacher, which also results in failure, should not. This would help those students who do not have the self-confidence to experiment with their ideas without believing that they will adversely affect their own chances of success – but should not mean simply giving students more leeway to do whatever they wish, secure in the knowledge that they will achieve good marks even if their work is not of good quality (Balchin 2005a).

One of the most frequently quoted references in the written assignments at the end of the primary gifted and talented co-ordinators' course has been that of Professor Philip Adey:

> What the research shows consistently is that if you face children with intellectual challenges and then help them talk through the problems towards a solution, then you almost literally stretch their minds. They become cleverer, not only in the particular topic, but across the curriculum.
>
> (Adey and Shayer 1994, p. 13)

It is not surprising that teachers find this quotation memorable, because a true grasp of its meaning underscores the immense importance of the role of a teacher. It is a privilege to facilitate the process by which our pupils can become cleverer and to encourage them to reach their full potential.

How do we best 'face children with intellectual challenges'? Monitoring pupils' performance when they are faced with cognitive challenge is a powerful tool for identifying the extent of their ability. This is identification through provision, which Freeman (1998 this volume) calls the Sports Model. The sports analogy is apposite because, in order to identify the best high jumper, for example, the bar is raised in increments for all, and we watch to see who can keep on making the leap. Providing the whole class with increasingly challenging tasks and questions will result in opportunities for pupils to demonstrate the depth and breadth of their thinking and understanding. We can watch to see who makes the highest leaps, and the results are often surprising.

Elitism is a major concern of many about the whole idea of gifted and talented education. Within the primary classroom though, often the most effective way of providing for the gifted and talented is through inclusive challenge for all, which is anything but elitist, because it provides opportunities for all students to rise to a variety of challenges every day. It is often easier to pay lip service to the needs of the more able by providing bolt-on activities, but what really matters for them surely is what takes place in the classroom on a daily and hourly basis. The depth of pupils' thinking will not necessarily be uncovered unless this type of contextually embedded challenge is offered.

I found it humbling to discover the potential reach of an eleven year old's thinking when I asked a class how they know that the Earth is a sphere – pictures from space excluded. One pupil replied, 'Because gravity comes from the centre of the earth, because a sphere is the smallest shape you can make from the centre, it would most likely be pulled up into a sphere'. This was stunning: he had realised that a sphere is the only shape where all points on the circumference are the same distance from the centre, and so it would probably be the resulting shape, because gravity pulls equally in all directions towards that point. I was expecting a mundane answer, but this boy had worked from first principles and had synthesised his understanding from science and mathematics. Having taught both primary and secondary science, I became uncomfortably aware that I had no idea that an eleven year old could show such grasp of scientific thinking. Presenting the whole class with challenging problems can indeed result in surprises.

Another key message of the primary gifted and talented co-ordinators' course has been that there is no prescribed 'one size fits all' approach for learners with gifted and talented educational needs in the participants' schools. The course contains many ideas and strategies, but it has been left to the individual teachers to analyse their particular circumstances and to judge what is best within that context. As the work with gifted and talented education is taken beyond the original Excellence in Cities areas to the whole of England through the national strategies, it will be vital to retain a respect for the need for flexibility within different schools.

Recently in England, gifted and talented institutional quality standards and classroom quality standards have been developed to assist in schools' self evaluation. Used correctly, these can be valuable tools for schools to reflect on current provision, and to plan future developments. However, quality standards are also being developed for a variety of other areas and there is an inherent danger that they will be viewed by school staff as daunting box-ticking exercises. We need to be careful that we do not remove the heart from the gifted and talented agenda by allowing it to become mechanistic.

In 2005, the *Times Educational Supplement* ran a series entitled, 'What Is Education For?' This is a good question, and Montgomery (1990) suggested a need to redefine the central objectives in teaching as (a) enabling pupils to think efficiently and (b) communicating those thoughts succinctly.

Teaching pupils to think has been an important focus within gifted and talented provision, and it is a necessity for all students in our technological age. I often tell teachers that they can ask me any question, and I will be able to give them an answer, as long as I have access to a Google search engine. I have instant access to a wealth of information, but what I need to be able to do then is analyse it, criticise it, and make links to what I already know and understand. Lewis and Smith (1993) defined higher order thinking as follows: 'Higher order thinking occurs when a person takes new information and information stored in memory and interrelates and/or rearranges and extends this information to achieve a purpose or find possible answers in perplexing situations' (p. 136).

I would argue that higher order thinking is a life skill and that it is our duty to equip today's pupils to engage in such thinking. One of the slides shown on the G&T co-ordinators' course has the text, 'Are pupils too busy working to have time to think?' Our challenge is to ensure that pupils are not so busy drilling factual content that they have no time and space to reflect on it. Much more than the facts, the thinking about the content is the life skill that lasts; teaching for thinking is creative, exciting teaching. It is my belief that if pupils have learned to think critically (which is after all, the evaluative, verificative part of the creative process) they will also do better in external one-time tests than if they have merely crammed in course-specific content in order to gain good marks. In my opinion, these are key messages from the gifted and talented field that have important implications for the whole education system.

Contact address: h.wilson@brookes.ac.uk

Future Perspectives

Suggested priorities for gifted education over the next decade

There are currently major challenges facing an English education system that is so content laden and assessment driven. Teaching to the test and to short term targets has threatened the creativity and excitement that surely should be central to our lessons, so that pupils come to love learning and develop into the creative thinkers that our society needs. Thinking about the content is the life skill that lasts; teaching for thinking is creative, exciting teaching. When pupils have learnt to think critically, they will do better in the external tests than if they have merely crammed content. Our teachers need to be released, so that they cease to be slaves to content but instead are actively encouraged to exploit the curriculum to encourage deep thinking. In my opinion, this is a key message from the gifted and talented field: teach for challenge on an inclusive basis and see standards for all rise.

Helen Wilson

31

Educating for enquiry: personalising learning through dialogic teaching

Robert Fisher

Brunel University, UK

The personalising of learning, which means putting the student or learner at the heart of the educative process, has always been the essence of effective teaching and of lifelong learning (Fisher 2005). It has a moral basis in the fact that education is about persons in all aspects of their humanity, not just bundles of specific gifts and talents, but people in their wholeness, including the physical, emotional, intellectual, social and economic aspects of their being. Students need to be inducted into knowledge about the world but also into an understanding of themselves as persons of particular gifts and talents. To be fully educated, students need more than individual learning. They need what will be defined here as 'personalised learning'.

Personalised learning

The personalisation of education in this country is often treated as a version of what is called customisation in the business world. It represents a consumer-led approach to education, where what matters is the collection of, and response to, personal data about particular educational achievements. However, personalisation means more than that. It is about persons, not people just as functions, or what they can do within a society, but as individuals with their own unique purposes within that society.

'What is a person?' is a fundamental question for educators and for learners. One way to engage students in responding to this question is to ask them in what ways they think they are similar to, and different from, a cabbage (or a computer or any other physical object). In discussions with students of any age, the factors that are often identified as making them different from a cabbage include the fact that they are active, emotional, rational, imaginative and social in ways cabbages (or computers) are not. If there are indeed such differences, then they will need to be educated as persons, with these qualities (and not as cabbages or computers).

Persons are not merely the functions they fulfil and the skills and standards they can achieve, but are, more fundamentally, the inner purposes of their lives as human beings living among others. These purposes include self-expression, a sense of self worth and self-knowledge, as well as social relationships with, and knowledge of others. We find out what makes us individual by being in communion with ourselves and with others. As Maria, aged nine put it, 'It is not enough to just go round and round in your own thoughts, you need to get others to tell you what they think or how else are you going to get more thoughts?' Dialogue enables us to fulfil human needs and purposes through the capacities we possess, in order to express ourselves as individuals and through our ability to benefit from the thinking of others. Personalising learning through dialogue is about making all students special. It recognises that as humans, they need practice in communicating what they think, and in responding to the thinking of others. In short they learn best to become themselves through dialogue with others.

At the heart of personalised education is self-expression through talk. As Peter, aged eight, put it: 'A good teacher is interested in what you are thinking'. Talk is the most effective means of finding out what children are thinking, feeling or learning. However research shows that the quality of classroom talk has the power both to enable and to inhibit cognition and learning (Alexander 2006). In recent years there has been a growing realisation of the central importance of dialogue in stimulating thinking and learning (Fisher 2003; Mercer 2000). Most teacher-talk has traditionally been not dialogic, but rather monologic, where a teacher informs the student of certain prescribed forms of knowledge. Learning by rote, recitation or instruction is characterised by the superiority of the first voice (the teacher) over the second voice (the student). The theorist Bakhtin describes this form of dialogue as 'official monologism'. It depends upon an asymmetry of power between two voices within a dialogue. This asymmetry arises from a third voice implicit in the dialogue (Bakhtin 1986).

This 'third person', or 'third voice', stands outside the dialogue and acts as a point of reference or authority. This third voice may be a set of rules, sacred text, received view, school curriculum or other source of authority. This authority constrains the openness or creativity of the discussion. It sets the educational goal and directs the discussion. One question Bakhtin poses for any dialogue is: 'Where is the reference point of authority?' In essence, this asks us to consider who is asking the questions.

Teacher talk often centres on a deficit or ignorance on the part of the second voice (child), which is responded to by the first voice (teacher), who interprets the third voice in the given situation. This strategy is useful for teaching through instruction or demonstration, but it does not necessarily involve children in self-expression, thinking or dialogue. There are dialogic strategies that do put the personal voice of the student at the heart of the learning process. One such strategy, being researched in more than 30 countries around the world, is the community of enquiry. This approach argues that all children, whatever their gifts and talents, need to be educated in inclusive communities of philosophic enquiry. It provides the opportunity for students to practise the skills of shared enquiry by engaging in discussion about philosophical or conceptual questions of their own choosing, as well as issues of personal concern.

Philosophical dialogue

'I think philosophy makes you think more because it gives you time to think' (Paul, aged eight).

Teacher talk is transformed into dialogue when pupils take a more active role in discussion, prompted by open, structured, and cumulative questions (Fisher 2003). This is sometimes called the Socratic method, which is essentially the process of asking questions in ways that help students learn to question their beliefs and the beliefs of others. It is about enquiring with an open mind, a process of unlearning, where presuppositions and assumptions are exposed and interrogated.

Socrates was famous for his pose of 'scholarly ignorance', saying he was the wisest of men because he knew the limitations of his knowledge. Socratic dialogue invites a range of opinions and creative ideas. The aim of Socratic dialogue is to let the child's mind become a moving prism catching light from as many different angles as possible. Some forms of Socratic dialogue, however, are merely concealed forms of teacher talk, where the questioning leads only to a closed conclusion. This kind of dialogue is often used by teachers to scaffold instruction, as in, 'Who can tell me the answer to this?' rather than, 'Who can give me an (or another) answer?' Genuine Socratic dialogue is a creative process when it invites the free expression of ideas and is not limited by prescribed ends. The role of the dialogic teacher is that of questioner, and the child's voice can assert itself in unpredicted and challenging ways. As Terri, aged ten, describes, 'It's like an adventure – you never know where a discussion is going . . . and it always seems to end up with another question!'

Dialogic teaching

According to Alexander (2006), dialogic teaching is (a) collective – teachers and children address learning tasks together, whether as a group or as a class; (b) reciprocal – teachers and children listen to each other, share ideas and consider alternative viewpoints; (c) cumulative – teachers and children build on their own and others' ideas, and chain them into coherent lines of thinking and enquiry; (d) supportive – children articulate their ideas freely, without fear of embarrassment over 'wrong' answers, and they help each other to reach common understandings; and (e) purposeful – teachers plan and steer classroom talk with specific educational goals in view.

This list omits a key principle of dialogic teaching and that is cognitive challenge. It is this that turns teaching into learning. Dialogic teaching is not just getting children to say what they think, but also involves challenging them to think in new ways. The importance of open (or Socratic) questions, in teaching and in learning, is that they offer cognitive challenge. An open-ended question allows for a possible range of answers, hence it encourages more flexible thinking, allows depth of discussion and encourages better assessment of children's beliefs. Furthermore, it tests the limits of knowledge rather than just one item of knowledge, offers the possibility to clear up misunderstandings, and can result in unanticipated and unexpected answers, new hypotheses, and connections to previous knowledge. When asked, 'Is there a difference between knowing something and believing something?' a child replied, 'Yes there is because, for example, I believe in Father Christmas, but I know he doesn't exist!' Another child said, 'I don't want to know if Father Christmas exists or not. I enjoy wondering whether he does and the magic'.

The community approach to enquiry in the classroom involves not one or two voices creating single viewpoints but many voices creating multiple viewpoints. It is sustained by the use of complex, open-ended questions and elaborate explanatory responses – from teachers as well as from children. Children's own questions form the starting-point for an enquiry or discussion, which can be termed 'philosophical'. Here is an example of the questions raised after reading a 'poem for thinking', 'The Magic Box', by Kit Wright (Fisher 1997), with a mixed group of seven to ten year olds at Burunda State School in Brisbane:

- Can your imagination change who you are?
- If a picture paints a thousand words, can a word paint a thousand pictures?
- Does imagination only affect your mind?
- Can a poem affect your imagination?
- Can our imagination influence the way we live?

- Is our imagination a door into another world?
- Are there any limits to our imagination?
- Can a poem change your life/ the world/ the universe?
- Can a poem lead to another poem?
- What gives us the will to live?

It is not enough for the teacher to be the facilitator of questions and generalised discussion. Philosophical dialogue differs from mere conversation by the presence of cognitive challenge. The philosophically intelligent teacher digs for depth by challenging the thinking of individuals and the group. The questions that children raise need to be connected, extended, and further refined through discussion. For example, when one class chose as the question for discussion, 'What does it mean to be beautiful?' The teacher asked them what kind of question this was, and got responses that included, 'an open-ended question' and 'a philosophical question'. She then asked, 'What is a philosophical question?' She was answered, 'A question that has no one right answer but many possible answers that might be right or wrong or partially right and partially wrong'. She delved deeper by asking probing questions such as, 'What do you mean by beautiful?' 'Can you be beautiful and ugly?' 'Is beauty on the inside and outside?'

An example of an enquiry being sustained by the use of complex open-ended questions and elaborate explanatory responses: a teacher using a story that includes the theme of truth, such as Aesop's fable, 'Mercury and the Axe', might prepare a number of open-ended prompt questions to encourage children to discuss the nature of truth. Here is an excerpt from one such classroom discussion with six year olds:

> *Teacher:* What do we mean when we say something is true?
> *Child:* It means it really happened, it's not pretend . . . it's real. That's true.
> *Teacher:* Can you think something is true when it is not true?
> *Child:* Sometimes you say something you think is true. It's not a lie if you think it is true.
> *Child:* I disagree with that because you could think something was true and say it was true when it was not true.
> *Teacher:* Can you give an example?
> *Child:* Well, you could say it is raining because you thought it was raining and it was only birds on the roof. You can say something you think is true although in fact it is not true.
> *Child:* You can only tell if something is true if you or somebody sees it with their own eyes and ears. That is why there are many people [who] think things are true, like ghosts or witches, that sort of thing. But you might be wrong, so you have to check it first before you say it's true.
> *Child:* It's not true because you say it is, but it might be.

This philosophical dialogue was framed by a teaching method called 'community of enquiry', which is derived from the tradition of 'Philosophy for Children' (commonly abbreviated to P4C). It is a special form of collaborative enquiry where the agenda of research questions and the rules of discussion are defined by the students themselves.

Community of enquiry

'It helps you ask questions. It shows you there can be many answers to one question (and) it makes you think that everything must have a reason' (John, aged ten).

A community of enquiry is a form of dialogic teaching that emphasises the development of critical and creative thinking through questioning, and dialogue between children and teachers and between children and children. Researchers have reported striking cognitive gains through this approach in the classroom, including enhancing cognitive and communicative skills (Topping and Trickey 2006). The practice of being in a community of enquiry also helps develop habits of intelligent behaviour. These habits of intelligent behaviour include being (a) curious, through asking open and interesting questions; (b) collaborative, through engaging in thoughtful dialogue; (c) critical, through giving reasons and evidence; (d) creative, through generating and building on ideas; and (d) caring, through developing awareness of the needs of self and others.

Philosophical dialogue develops the kinds of thinking, as Karl says, that children may not use in other lessons, including philosophical intelligence, the capacity to ask and seek answers to existential questions. Secondly, philosophical enquiry provides a means for children to develop discussion skills, the capacity to engage in thoughtful conversations with others. Thirdly, philosophical discussion of complex objects of intellectual enquiry such as stories enhances critical thinking and verbal reasoning, the capacity to draw inferences and deductions from all kinds of texts. Fourthly, philosophical enquiry helps develop creative thinking, the capacity to generate hypotheses and build on the ideas of others. Fifthly, doing philosophy with children helps develop emotional intelligence, the capacity to be self-aware and caring towards others, providing essential practice in active citizenship and participative democracy. In Philosophy for Children, dialogue takes place in a community of enquiry. See Table 8 below for a format of activities for developing a community of enquiry.

During a dialogue, philosophical intelligence is stimulated by two kinds of challenge, both internal and external activity of mind. To encourage intellectual activity, time for individual opportunities for thinking should be built into any dialogue or philosophical research. That might include time for thinking before we start, e.g. focusing exercises, meditation; building in thinking time during a discussion, e.g. a mini-plenary; and thinking at the end, or plenary review.

Table 8 Stories for thinking: a format of activities for developing a community of enquiry

1. Focusing exercise – e.g. discussing learning objectives, agreeing on rules for discussion, using a thinking game or relaxation exercise to ensure alert, yet relaxed, attention

2. Sharing a stimulus – a story, poem, picture or other stimulus for creative thinking is presented

3. Thinking time – children think of what is strange, interesting or unusual about the stimulus, and share their thoughts and questions with a partner

4. Questioning – children ask their own (or shared) questions which are written on a board, these are discussed, related, and one chosen (or voted for) by the children to start the enquiry

5. Discussion – children are asked to respond, building on each other's ideas through dialogue, with the teacher probing for reasons, examples and alternative viewpoints

6. Plenary review – the discussion is reviewed (e.g. using a graphic map) and children reflect on the discussion and what they have learnt from it

7. Further activities – children engage in follow-up activities to further explore the stimulus in creative ways in class or at home

A useful teaching strategy is 'think–pair–share', where there is time for individual reflection, then trying out ideas with a partner, before sharing ideas with the whole group.

Focusing the discussion

There will be no philosophical interest in the topic or story unless there is something interesting or puzzling in it, for example by asking, 'What is strange about (what you have, heard, read, seen)?' 'What is it that puzzles you?', or 'What did you find interesting?'

Asking for reasons

We need to give a reason or reasons for our puzzlement and explain what we think and why it seems strange or interesting, for example by asking, 'What makes you say that?', 'What reasons do you have?' or 'Why do you agree or disagree with X?'

Probing assumptions

Our reasons will be based on other assumptions. We can probe these, for example by asking, 'How do you know?', 'Why do you think that?' or 'What have you based that on?'

Comparing and contrasting

During a dialogue the children will often come up with several different ideas, some related, and others not. We need to help them see connections, make distinctions, and to clarify their thinking by asking them to compare and contrast different ideas and assumptions; for example, by asking, 'How is X similar to Y?', 'Is X the same as Y?' or 'How is X different from Y?'

Making judgements and exploring implications

We can help children suggest solutions to what is puzzling, and to formulate and explore the judgements they make and the implications of what they have said; for example, by asking, 'What do you conclude from that?', 'What does that tell us?' or 'What follows from that?'

Further creative activities can follow the philosophical dialogue to help children explore the ideas and concepts further; for example, by expressing them visually, verbally, physically or by other forms of creative expression. The following is part of a discussion with a group of six-year-old children after they had read 'The Cats and the Chapatti' (Fisher 1999). They had chosen to answer Anna's question about the story, 'Why did they quarrel?'

> *Child*: There were some animals quarrelling.
> *Teacher*: What were they saying?
> *Child*: 'No, you can't', 'Yes you can' . . . that sort of thing.
> *Child*: They were contradicting each other.
> *Teacher*: So a quarrel is like a contradiction?

Child: (after a pause for thought) Yes.

Child: They were quarrelling with each other.

Teacher: Can you quarrel with yourself?

Child: You can't quarrel with yourself. You need to have more than one person.

Child: You can quarrel with yourself. You could punch yourself. Your brain quarrels with you . . . if you want to test yourself.

Child: I disagree with Sarah. You can't quarrel with yourself. You haven't done anything to yourself.

Child: If you punch your leg, it can't say no. Your brain says no.

Teacher: Can animals say 'Yes' and 'No'?

Child: No, only people can say 'Yes' and 'No'. That's how we are different from animals.

The community of enquiry is an effective strategy for finding questions that genuinely perplex and puzzle pupils. What is special about the community of enquiry is that the children them-selves pose the agenda of questions for discussion. Finding the best research question for critical enquiry is a challenge to any gifted mind, as many doctoral-level researchers have found. As one child put it, it gets your mind 'dancing' with possibilities. Philosophical inquiry puts personalised learning into practice, allowing individual children to share what is uncertain in experience, the nature of the puzzlement, and to generate hypotheses towards a solution to possible puzzles. Communal inquiry not only aims to solve common problems, but the process itself is one that cultivates philosophical and democratic dispositions and habits. Unlike other kinds of inquiry, philosophical inquiry deals with uncertainties found in widespread social conditions and aims, translating these into conflicts of organised interests and institutional claims. As Dewey argued, philosophical thinking encourages individuals to criticise existing aims, practices, and institutions, to challenge prevailing values, and to create their own models of values and relationships (Burgh et al. 2006; Dewey 1916).

Once started, a dialogue can be developed in countless creative ways. As Paul, aged eight, put it: 'There is never a last word because there can always be another word!' Philosophical dialogue is a kind of discursive game that uses questions to probe children's thinking, but also allows for playful exploration and evaluation of ideas. It allows what Bakhtin (1986) called a 'carnival' of ideas, where all potential authorities may be questioned. This may distract from what Lipman (2003) calls the 'forward' movement of Socratic dialogue, for it allows for byways to be explored and for the playful exploration of alternative ideas. Fully to engage the philo-sophic mind, we need to allow for playfulness, for experiments with ideas that may fail, and for openness in the exploration of ideas. More than that, we need to relish playful humour and 'honest nonsense' within dialogue. It does not always succeed in communicating good ideas, but it allows students undirected ownership and free expression of their thoughts. In this sense creative dialogue can be liberating, the focus of authority now being fully on the student. It frees them to explore ideas that are 'out of the box', outside the agenda of questions and beyond the given objectives.

Philosophical discussion is a kind of personalised learning that allows the playfulness of possibility thinking, by inviting the creation of possible worlds. This kind of playful dialogue, which can be described as Menippean, is about having permission to exercise philosophical intelligence to enter possible worlds and think 'impossible things'.

In a discussion of the brain, Leigh, aged ten, said, 'My brain is like an anthill, with millions of tiny passageways. There is always something going on in my head. The ants in my mind never seem to rest. I just hope there are not any anteaters!' (Fisher 2003). The use of metaphor shows the playfulness characteristic of a creative dialogue, as does the use of humour. In a discussion about wanting things, Danielle, aged ten, plays with the image of a ladder. What she says might also apply to the personalising of learning, the open-ended nature of dialogic enquiry and the inner purposes of education, which we need to focus on and constantly to redefine:

> If you want something very much you have to think how to get it. It's like you're on a ladder. The ladder is a way of getting to it just a little bit at first and then another little bit. I want lots of things but I don't know what I want at the end of the ladder. Maybe it keeps getter longer and you never get to the end. You can give up or you can keep climbing and see.

Contact address: rfcreative@btconnect.com

Future Perspectives

Suggested priorities for gifted education over the next decade

Gifted education will become inclusive. A child (any child) will be seen to have a gift in a domain, if it emerges as a relative strength or focus of interest. The provision for gifted children will be available for all children in terms of both personalised and pluralised learning. Personalised learning will focus on developing their strengths and research interests but also the inner purposes of their lives as human beings living among others, including self-expression, self-knowledge and metacognitive awareness. Learning will come to be seen not as about 'acceleration', but as about a full, rich and pluralised education – 'slow learning' in its best sense, not dull or routinised but as engagement in rich tasks and personal research projects undertaken over time. Education will be about depth but equally about breadth, focusing on projects that are diversified, pluralised and require working in different communities of enquiry with creative partners and critical friends.
Robert Fisher

Part 5

Expanding horizons: supporting gifted development more broadly

Many chapters in this volume endorse expanding the scope of gifted education in one way or another, increasing the diversity of learners who are included in gifted programming, and supporting gifted development more broadly across the population. None goes so far as to write, 'Every child is a gifted child', but many would agree that we must do a better job collectively of looking for gifted possibilities more inclusively. Across this book, authors are arguing that we need simultaneously to meet the learning needs of students who are significantly advanced relative to their age peers in one school subject or another without pigeon-holing them, and also to foster gifted-level learning much more broadly in more diverse kinds of learners. In this section, we have grouped those chapters that make these concepts their major focus of attention.

In the section's opening chapter, Bob Sternberg describes the WICS model, discussing how the underlying principles – wisdom, intelligence, creativity, synthesised – come together in gifted development. In harmony with many of the other chapters in this volume, but challenging much of the current practice in gifted education, he argues that wisdom, intelligence, creativity are all fluid and modifiable, and can be learned. Gifted education has historically been vulnerable to charges of elitism and exclusivity, and Joyce VanTassel-Baska's chapter also focuses on addressing these concerns, focusing specifically on issues of cultural diversity. She describes progress in the field, providing recommendations concerning teacher preparation, curriculum design, instructional tools, and assessment techniques.

Ian Warwick has been working with inner city students and educators for many years now to develop a broad-based approach to gifted education that can be available to every student and teacher. He has written a chapter with Dona Matthews on an initiative currently in place in London. They observe that there are enormous benefits not only for families and students, but also for schools and for society as a whole when educators see cultural diversity as a strength to be capitalised on, rather than a problem to be solved.

Belle Wallace makes the case that giftedness develops, and that all children's learning capacities can be improved. She has developed a practical tool for teachers, an inclusive, cross-curricular model called *Thinking Actively in a Social Context* (TASC), and describes how TASC can be used to improve children's learning capacities by teaching the processes underpinning problem-solving and thinking. In her chapter, Marie Huxtable describes how she uses TASC, among other tools, in her work to support children in developing their own giftedness, and schools in providing inclusive and inclusional gifted education provisions.

Barry Hymer has written his chapter from the stance of a practitioner researching his own practice as an educator in the field of giftedness. He describes the colourfully inclusional process of developing his G-T CReATe model, emphasising the benefits of educational policies that eschew gifted identification for a clearer focus on gift-creation. As do many of the authors of chapters in this volume, Hymer cites Carol Dweck's work as seminal to and supportive of his own. In her chapter, Dweck has adapted an interview that was published in *Gifted Education International* where she describes her fascinating research on the malleability of intelligence, and the important effect that mindsets can have on intellectual and academic functioning and success, demonstrating that intelligence, creativity, and giftedness are not the fixed traits that much historical work in the field assumes.

In the final chapter of the section and the volume, Sally Reis addresses the turning points she sees occurring in gifted education at the end of the first decade of the twenty-first century. These include expanding conceptions of the multidimensionality of giftedness and talent development, ensuring challenge for gifted and talented students, making a difference for underserved populations, changing our focus from ways to identify gifted students to the ways we develop gifts and talents, and applying 'gifted' education pedagogy to talent development, with a focus on strengths, not deficits. Without having read this book, she presciently identified the major themes that run through its chapters. We endorse her position, and hope that her prescience is as spot-on a description of gifted educational policies and practices around the world as it is of the themes that run through the chapters in this volume.

32

Wisdom, intelligence, creativity, synthesised: a model of giftedness

Robert J. Sternberg
Tufts University, US

Giftedness is, in large part, a function of creativity in generating ideas, analytical intelligence in evaluating the quality of these ideas, practical intelligence in implementing the ideas and convincing others to value and follow the ideas, and wisdom to ensure that the decisions and their implementation is for the common good of all stakeholders. The model is referred to as WICS – wisdom, intelligence, creativity, synthesised – although the order of elements in the acronym is intended only to make it pronounceable (Sternberg 2003d, 2003f, 2005a, 2005).

Creativity, intelligence, and wisdom are all modifiable (Sternberg and Grigorenko 1999). People can develop their creativity, intelligence and wisdom. Thus, one is not 'born' gifted. Rather, giftedness in wisdom, intelligence, and creativity is, to some extent, a form of developing competency and expertise (Sternberg 1998a, 1999b, 2003a, 2005a, 2005b, 2006) whereby genes interact with environment. The environment strongly influences the extent to which we are able to utilise and develop whatever genetic potentials we have (Grigorenko and Sternberg 2001; Sternberg and Arroyo 2006; Sternberg and Grigorenko 1997, 2001).

Giftedness involves both skills and attitudes. The skills are developing competencies and expertise. The attitudes concern how one employs the skills one has developed. Someone who has the skills but not the attitudes will fail to deploy the skills. Someone who has the attitudes but not the skills will fail to deploy the skills successfully.

Some traditional models of giftedness stress identification of fixed traits or behaviours that make people gifted; other models instead emphasise the interaction between internal attributes and situations (Sternberg and Davidson 1986, 2005). In general, one might say that there are three received views of the nature of giftedness. The first is that giftedness is a superfluous or outdated concept (Borland 2003b, 2005). According to this view, giftedness is a social invention that serves to create divisions in society that have no constructive purpose. Indeed, it creates divisions where they should not be. The techniques that have been developed for gifted education can and should be used for all education, and then would be advantageous for all children.

A second view is that giftedness is measured well by traditional assessments, whether intelligence test scores (IQ), SAT reasoning tests, or other conventional measures of *g*-based abilities. For example, Julian Stanley and his collaborators (Benbow et al. 1996; Brody and Stanley 2005; Stanley and Brody 2001) have made extensive use of the SAT and related tests in their talent searches, identifying children as gifted based on their SAT scores. Robinson (2005) and

Gallagher (2000) have been major supporters as well of traditional psychometric approaches to the assessment of giftedness. The basic idea in their view is that traditional tests tell us most of what we need to know for assessing who is gifted. A third view is that conventional tests are largely incomplete – that they measure some of what is relevant to giftedness, but not all of it and, in most cases, not even most of it (Feldhusen 2005; Freeman 2005; Gardner 1983; Gordon and Bridglall 2005; Mönks and Katzko 2005; Reis 2005; Renzulli 1977b, 1986, 2005; Runco 2005).

These models differ in their details. For example, Renzulli emphasises the importance of above-average ability, creativity and task commitment in his model. Gardner (1983, 1999) emphasises the importance of eight multiple intelligences. The model presented in this chapter is of this third kind, emphasising skills including but also going beyond intelligence as measured by conventional tests.

This chapter considers the elements of creativity, intelligence and wisdom, in that order, because it represents the order in which the elements often are initially used. As gifted perform-ance evolves, however, the elements become interactive and so order becomes less relevant. The chapter then considers how the concepts can be employed in teaching and assessment, and finally, how they can be employed in identifying the gifted.

Creativity

Creativity refers to the skills and attitudes needed for generating ideas and products that are (a) relatively novel, (b) high in quality, and (c) appropriate to the task at hand. Creativity is important for giftedness because it is the component whereby one generates the ideas that will influence others.

Creative giftedness as a confluence of skills and attitudes

A confluence model of creativity (Sternberg and Lubart 1995, 1996) suggests that creative people show a variety of characteristics. These characteristics represent not innate abilities, but rather, largely, decisions (Sternberg 2000c). In other words, to a large extent, people decide to be creative. Creativity is in large part attitudinal. What are the elements of the creative attitude (Kaufman and Sternberg 2006; Sternberg 1999)?

Problem redefinition

Creative individuals do not define a problem the way everyone else does. They decide on the exact nature of the problem using their own judgement. Most importantly, they are willing to defy the crowd in defining a problem differently from the way others do (Sternberg 2002a; Sternberg and Lubart 1995). Gifted individuals are more willing to redefine problems and better able to do so.

Problem analysis

Creative individuals are willing to analyse whether their solution to the problem is the best one possible. Gifted individuals are more willing to analyse their own decisions, and better see their strengths and weaknesses. They recognise that they are not always right and that not all their work is their best work, and they are self-critical in analysing the quality of their own work.

Selling a solution

Creative individuals come to realise that creative ideas do not sell themselves; rather, creators have to decide to sell their ideas, and then decide to put in the effort to do so. Gifted individuals are better salespeople. They persuade others of the value of their ideas and to follow those ideas. They thus need to be able to articulate the value of their idea in a clear and persuasive way – a skill very different from that which is required to do well on an IQ test.

Recognising how knowledge can both help and hinder creative thinking

Creative people realise that knowledge can hinder as well as facilitate creative thinking (Frensch and Sternberg 1989; Sternberg 1985). Sometimes people become entrenched and susceptible to tunnel vision, letting their expertise hinder rather than facilitate the exercising of their gifted-ness. Gifted people are more likely to recognise their own susceptibility to entrenchment and take steps to battle against it, such as seeking able advisors, new ideas from novices, and so forth.

Willingness to take sensible risks

Creative people recognise that they must decide to take sensible risks, which can lead them to success but also can lead them, from time to time, to fail (Lubart and Sternberg 1995). Gifted people are more willing to take large risks and to fail as often as they need in order to accomplish their long-term goals.

Willingness to surmount obstacles

Creative people are willing to surmount the obstacles that confront anyone who decides to defy the crowd. Such obstacles result when those who challenge paradigms confront those who accept them as assumptions (Kuhn 1970; Sternberg and Lubart 1995). All gifted people encounter obstacles. Curiously, gifted people are particularly susceptible to obstacles, because they often want to move followers more quickly and further than the followers might be ready for. So the gifted person needs great resilience in order to accomplish his or her goals.

Belief in one's ability to accomplish the task at hand

Creative people believe in their ability to get the job done. This belief is sometimes referred to as self-efficacy (Bandura 1996). Gifted people believe in themselves and their ideas – not necessarily in the value of every single idea, but in the value of their overall strategy for their contributions.

Willingness to tolerate ambiguity

Creative people recognise that there may be long periods of uncertainty during which they cannot be certain they are doing the right thing or that what they are doing will have the outcome they hope for. The more gifted the people, the greater the ambiguity, because they try to make large changes that can create transformational change for others as well as themselves.

Willingness to find extrinsic rewards for the things one is intrinsically motivated to do

Creative people almost always are intrinsically motivated for the work they do (Amabile 1983, 1996). Creative people find environments in which they receive extrinsic rewards for the things they like to do anyway. Gifted children remain gifted as adults if they love what they do.

Continuing to grow intellectually rather than to stagnate

Creative people avoid, as far as possible, getting stuck in their patterns of thought. Their thinking evolves as they accumulate experience and expertise. They learn from experience rather than simply letting its lessons pass them by. Lifelong gifted people do not flame out as time passes them by. Rather, they adapt to changing circumstances.

Our research on creativity (Lubart and Sternberg 1995; Sternberg and Lubart 1995) has yielded several conclusions. First, creativity often involves defying the crowd, or as we have put it, buying low and selling high in the world of ideas. Creative people are good investors: they do what needs to be done, rather than just what other people or polls tell them to do (Lubart, this volume). Second, creativity is relatively domain specific. Third, creativity is weakly related to traditional intelligence, but certainly is not the same thing as academic intelligence. In general, it appears that there is a threshold of IQ for creativity, but it is probably about 120 or even lower (see review in Sternberg and O'Hara 2000). So let us next consider the role of intelligence in giftedness.

Intelligence

Intelligence would seem to be important to giftedness, but how important? Intelligence, as conceived of here, is not just intelligence in its conventional narrow sense – some kind of general factor (g) (Demetriou 2002; Jensen 1998, 2002; Spearman 1927; see essays in Sternberg 2000e; Sternberg and Grigorenko 2002) or as IQ (Binet and Simon 1905; Kaufman 2000; Wechsler 1939), but rather, in terms of the theory of successful intelligence (Sternberg 1997a, 1999d, 2002b). Successful intelligence is defined as the skills and attitudes needed to succeed in life, given one's own conception of success, within one's sociocultural environment. Successfully intelligent people balance adaptation to, shaping of, and selection of environments by capitalising on their strengths and compensating for or correcting their weaknesses. Gifted individuals, from this viewpoint, are not necessarily good at everything. Two particular aspects of the theory of successful intelligence are especially relevant. These are academic and practical intelligence (see also Neisser 1979).

Academic intelligence

Academic intelligence refers to the memory and analytical skills and attitudes that in combination largely constitute the conventional notion of intelligence – the skills and attitudes needed to recall and recognise but also to analyse, evaluate and judge information. The literature on giftedness is in large part a literature on academic intelligence (see, e.g. essays in Sternberg and Davidson 1986, 2005). Certainly academic intelligence is important to giftedness and to gifted leadership. But there are many people who have been gifted intellectually who have not become gifted leaders. They lacked the other qualities of WICS.

258

The academic skills and attitudes matter for giftedness, because gifted individuals need to be able to retrieve information that is relevant to leadership decisions (memory) and to analyse and evaluate different courses of action, whether proposed by themselves or by others (analysis). The long-time primary emphasis on academic intelligence (IQ) in the literature relating intelligence to giftedness perhaps has been unfortunate. Indeed, recent theorists have been emphasising other aspects of intelligence, such as emotional intelligence (e.g. Caruso et al. 2002; Goleman 1998a, 1998b) or multiple intelligences (Gardner 1995). Here the emphasis is on practical intelligence (Hedlund et al. 2003, 2006; Sternberg et al. 2000; Sternberg and Hedlund 2002), which has a somewhat different focus from emotional intelligence. Practical intelligence is a part of successful intelligence. Practical intelligence is a core component of giftedness, and will therefore receive special attention here.

Practical intelligence

Practical intelligence is the set of skills and attitudes used to solve everyday problems by utilising knowledge gained from experience in order purposefully to adapt to, shape and select environments. It thus involves changing oneself to suit the environment (adaptation), changing the environment to suit oneself (shaping), or finding a new environment within which to work (selection). One uses these skills to (a) manage oneself, (b) manage others and (c) manage tasks.

Different combinations of intellectual skills engender different types of giftedness. Gifted people vary in their memory skills, analytical skills and practical skills. A gifted individual who is particularly strong in memory skills but not in the other kinds of skills may have vast amounts of knowledge at his or her disposal, but be unable to use it effectively. A gifted individual who is particularly strong in analytical skills as well as memory skills may be able to retrieve information and analyse it effectively, but may be unable to convince others that his or her analysis is correct. A gifted individual who is strong in memory, analytical, and practical skills is most likely to be effective in influencing others. But, of course, there exist gifted people who are strong in practical skills but not in memory and analytical skills (Sternberg 1997b; Sternberg et al. 2000). In conventional terms, they are 'shrewd' but not 'smart'. They may be effective or even gifted in getting others to go along with them, but they may end up leading these others down garden paths.

Gifted individuals need to be high in practical intelligence. Their creativity may help them generate wonderful ideas, but it will not ensure that they can implement the ideas or convince others to follow the ideas. Many creative individuals have ended up frustrated because they have been unable to convince others to follow up on their ideas. Many analytically intelligent individuals have been frustrated because they could analyse ideas well, but not persuade others of the value of their ideas.

My colleagues and I (Hedlund et al. 2003; Sternberg et al. 1995; Sternberg et al. 2000; Sternberg and Wagner 1993; Sternberg et al. 1993; Wagner and Sternberg 1985; Wagner 1987, 2000) have taken a knowledge-based approach to understanding practical intelligence. Individuals draw on a broad base of knowledge in solving practical problems, some of which is acquired through formal training and some of which is derived from personal experience. Much of the knowledge associated with successful problem solving can be characterised as tacit. It is knowledge that may not be openly expressed or stated; thus individuals must acquire such knowledge through their own experiences. Furthermore, although people's actions may reflect their knowledge, they may find it difficult to articulate what they know. For their own contributions, what matters is not so much what tacit knowledge they can articulate, but rather, how much of this knowledge they can apply. However, to serve as effective mentors, it helps greatly if they can articulate as well as act on this knowledge.

The main findings (reviewed in Sternberg et al. 2000) from tacit-knowledge research are that (a) tacit knowledge tends to increase with experience; (b) it correlates minimally and sometimes not at all with scores on tests of academic intelligence; (c) it does not correlate with personality; (d) it predicts job performance significantly; and (e) it provides significant incremental prediction over conventional academic-intelligence measures.

Wisdom

An individual can have all of the skills and attitudes described above and still lack an additional quality that, arguably, is the most important yet rarest quality a gifted person can have: wisdom (see also Baltes and Staudinger 1993, 2000). Wisdom is viewed here in terms of a proposed balance theory of wisdom (Sternberg 1998b), according to which an individual is wise to the extent he or she uses successful intelligence, creativity, and knowledge as moderated by values (a) to seek to reach a common good, (b) by balancing intrapersonal (one's own), interpersonal (others') and extrapersonal (organisational/institutional/spiritual) interests, (c) over the short and long term, to (d) adapt to, shape, and select environments. Wisdom is in large part a decision to use one's intelligence, creativity, and experience for a common good.

Wise people do not look out just for their own interests, nor do they ignore these interests. Rather, they skilfully balance interests of varying kinds, including their own, those of their stakeholders, and those of the organisation for which they are responsible. They also recognise that they need to align the interests of their group or organisation with those of other groups or organisations because no group operates within a vacuum. Wise individuals realise that what may appear to be a prudent course of action over the short term does not necessarily appear so over the long term. Giftedness in wisdom is a matter of balance – skilful balance of the various interests and of the short and long terms in making decisions.

Gifted leaders who have been less than fully successful often have been so because they have ignored one or another set of interests. For example, Richard Nixon and Bill Clinton, in their respective cover-ups, not only failed to fulfil the interests of the country they led, but also failed to fulfil their own interests. Their cover-ups ended up bogging down their administrations in scandals rather than allowing them to make the positive accomplishments they had hoped to make. Freud was a great leader in the fields of psychiatry and psychology, but his insistence that his followers (disciples) conform to his own system of psychoanalysis led him to lose those disciples and the support they might have continued to lend to his efforts. He was an expert in interpersonal interests, but not as applied to his own life. Napoleon lost sight of the extrapersonal interests that would have been best for his own country. His disastrous invasion of Russia, which appears to have been motivated more by hubris than by France's need to have Russia in its empire, partially destroyed his reputation as a successful military leader and paved the way for his later downfall.

Gifted individuals can be intelligent in various ways and creative in various ways; but intelligence and creativity do not guarantee wisdom. Indeed, probably relatively few gifted individuals at any level are particularly wise. Yet the few individuals who are wise to the point of being gifted – perhaps Nelson Mandela, Martin Luther King, Mahatma Gandhi, Winston Churchill, Mother Teresa – leave an indelible mark on the people they lead and, potentially, on history. It is important to note that wise people and especially leaders are probably usually charismatic, but that charismatic leaders are not necessarily wise, as Hitler, Stalin and many other charismatic leaders have demonstrated over the course of time.

Much of the empirical data on wisdom has been collected by the late Paul Baltes and his colleagues. Over time, they (e.g. Baltes et al. 1992; Baltes and Staudinger 1993) have collected a wide range of data showing the relevance of wisdom for gifted performance. For example, Staudinger et al. (1997) found that measures of intelligence and personality (as well as their interface) overlap with but are non-identical to measures of wisdom in terms of constructs measured. And Staudinger et al. (1992) showed that leading human-services professionals out-performed a control group on wisdom-related tasks. The professionals thought more con-textually in terms of life pragmatics than did the control participants. Staudinger and her colleagues also showed that older adults performed as well on such tasks as did younger adults, and that older adults did better on such tasks if there was a match between their age and the age of the fictitious characters about whom they made judgements. Baltes et al. (1995) found that older individuals in leadership positions who were nominated for their wisdom performed as well as did clinical psychologists on wisdom-related tasks. They also showed that up to the age of 80, older adults performed as well on such tasks as did younger adults. In a further set of studies, Staudinger and Baltes (1996) found that performance settings that were ecologically relevant to the lives of their participants and that provided for actual or 'virtual' interaction of minds increased wisdom-related performance substantially. These results suggest that part of wise leadership is achieving a meeting of minds, rather than merely imposing the view of the leader's mind on the minds of the followers.

Synthesis

Gifted leadership requires each of the elements of WICS. Without creativity, one cannot truly be a gifted leader, as leaders constantly confront novel tasks and situations. Without creativity to deal effectively with such situations, leaders fail. Similarly, without the application of a high level of intelligence, one cannot be a gifted leader. A leader may have creative ideas, but ones that are either flawed from the outset or that fail in implementation. The leader needs the intelligence to distinguish good from bad ideas, and to ensure that followers follow rather than ignore or rebel against the leader. And without wisdom, a leader may choose a path that benefits his or her cronies, but few others, as in the case of Mugabe or Saddam Hussein. Gifted leadership requires WICS.

Teaching for WICS

Teaching for WICS involves several different principles (Sternberg 1998c, 2004b; Sternberg and Grigorenko 2000; Sternberg, Torff and Grigorenko 1998a, 1998b). Because students have different life goals and hence different outcomes that, for them, are successful, success needs to be defined in terms that are meaningful to students as well as to the institution. Students take courses for many reasons. How can teachers translate a wide range of students' needs into effective teaching and assessment strategies? They can (1) provide numerous examples of con-cepts that cover a wide range of applications; (2) give students multiple and diverse options in assessment; and (3) grade student work in a way that preserves the integrity of the course as well as the integrity of the students' varied life goals.

Students need support to capitalise on their strengths and at the same time help them correct or compensate for weaknesses. Think back to your three or four best teachers. Were they identical in their methods of instruction and assessment? Did they all achieve their success in the same way? Almost certainly they did not. People succeed (and fail) for different reasons.

261

One teacher might stand out for the lectures she gave, another for her facilitation of group discussions, a third for his serving as a role model to emulate. Just as professionals (in all fields) succeed (and fail) in different ways, so do students. In order to maximise students' opportunities for success, it is important to enable them to capitalise on their strengths and to correct or compensate for weaknesses. Teaching in this way maximises students' achievement (Sternberg et al. 1999).

These facts have several implications. First, there is no one right way of teaching and learning. Different students learn and think in different ways. Second, there is no one right way of assessing students' achievement. Experience suggests that some students excel in multiple-choice tests, others in essays. Some students do well so long as the questions are limited to factual recall, whereas others do better if they are allowed to show their deeper understanding, perhaps of fewer facts. Unidimensional assessments (e.g. tests that are all multiple-choice, all short-answer, or all essay) often fail to enable students to capitalise on strengths. Third, we should teach and assess to weaknesses as well as to strengths. Some teachers might misunderstand the message here as a plea for extreme individualisation – an individualised programme for each student. Such a programme is usually impractical, especially at the introductory level, and often is counterproductive. Students need to learn to correct or compensate for their weaknesses as well as to capitalise on strengths. Thus it is important that students be intellectually uncomfortable some of the time, just as it is important for them to be intellectually comfortable and secure some of the time.

Students need to learn to balance adaptation to, shaping of, and selection of environments. The balance of these three responses to the environment has certain implications for teaching. First, students, like teachers, need to develop flexibility. A rigid classroom or institutional environment is likely to foster rigidity in the thinking of the students in it. Second, students need to be allowed and even encouraged to take risks and to make mistakes. People often learn more from their mistakes and failures than from their successes. An environment that does not allow students to make mistakes or ever to fail in their endeavours deprives the students of important learning opportunities. Third, students need to learn how to overcome obstacles when they seek to shape the environment in ways others may not like or appreciate. Fourth, teaching and assessment should balance use of analytical, creative, practical and wisdom-related thinking. Thinking always requires memory and the knowledge base that is accessed through the use of our memories. One cannot analyse what one knows if one knows nothing. One cannot creatively go beyond the existing boundaries of knowledge if one does not know what those boundaries are. And one cannot apply what one knows in a practical manner if one does not know anything to apply. At the same time, memory for facts without the ability to use those facts is useless.

It is for this reason that we encourage teachers to teach and assess achievement in ways that enable students to analyse, create with, and apply their knowledge. When students think to learn, they also learn to think. And there is an added benefit: students who are taught analytically, creatively, and practically perform better on assessments, apparently without regard to the form the assessments take. That is, they outperform students instructed in conventional ways, even if the assessments are for straight factual memory (Sternberg, Torff and Grigorenko 1998a, 1998b). Moreover, our research shows that these techniques succeed, regardless of subject-matter area. But what exactly are the techniques used to teach analytically, creatively and practically?

Teaching analytically means encouraging students to (a) analyse, (b) critique, (c) judge, (d) compare and contrast, (e) evaluate, and (f) assess. When teachers refer to teaching for critical thinking, they typically mean teaching for analytical thinking. Teaching creatively means encouraging students to (a) create, (b) invent, (c) discover, (d) imagine if . . ., (e) suppose that . . ., (f) predict. Teaching for creativity requires teachers not only to support and encourage creativity, but also to role-model it and to reward it when it is displayed (Sternberg and Lubart 1995; Sternberg and Williams 1996). In other words, teachers need not only to talk the talk, but also to walk the walk. And teaching practically means encouraging students to (a) apply, (b) use, (c) put into practice, (d) implement, (e) employ, (f) render practical what they know. Such teaching must relate to the real practical needs of the students, not just to what would be practical for individuals other than the students (Sternberg et al. 2001).

Teaching for wisdom means encouraging students to (a) think dialogically (i.e. see alternative points of view); (b) think dialectically (i.e. understand that what is true in a social context can change over time); (c) think for the long term as well as the short term; (d) think about how actions can be directed toward a common good; (e) think about how actions can balance one's own, others' and institutional interests.

Clearly, it is possible to implement teaching for WICS in a wide variety of academic contexts.

We know that the theory works through evaluation of its application in the identification of giftedness – see for instance The Rainbow Project (Sternberg and the Rainbow Project Collaborators 2005, 2006) and early findings from the Aurora Project (Chart et al. 2008) – and in the improved prediction of success in higher education (e.g. Hedlund et al. 2006; Stemler et al. 2006).

Conclusion

There probably is no model of giftedness that will totally capture all of the many facets – both internal and external to the individual – that make for giftedness. The WICS model may come closer than some models, however, in capturing dimensions that are important. It is based upon the notion that a gifted individual, in the ideal, decides to synthesise wisdom, intelligence and creativity. Gifted leadership requires such a synthesis.

A gifted leader needs exceptional creative skills and attitudes, firstly to come up with ideas, academic skills and attitudes to decide whether they *are* good ideas; secondly practical skills and attitudes to make the ideas work and convince others of the value of the ideas; and thirdly wisdom-based skills and attitudes to ensure that the ideas are in the service of the common good rather than just the good of the leader or perhaps some clique of family members or followers. A leader lacking in creativity will be unable to deal with novel and difficult situations, such as a new and unexpected source of hostility. A leader lacking in academic intelligence will not be able to decide whether his or her ideas are viable and a leader lacking in practical intelligence will be unable to implement his or her ideas effectively. An unwise leader may succeed in implementing ideas, but may end up implementing ideas that are contrary to the best interests of the people he or she leads.

The WICS model suggests that we need to broaden the way we conceive of giftedness in childhood as well as in adulthood. Giftedness is not just a matter of ability-test scores or of grades. The state of the world makes clear that what the nations of the world need most is gifted leaders, not just individuals who get good grades, or good test scores, or who have the skills that will get them into elite colleges, which in turn will prepare them to make a lot of money. Each nation needs to identify and develop giftedness in terms of a model broader than the traditional model of general ability. WICS is one such model.

Author notes

Preparation of this chapter was supported by Contract MDA 903-92-K-0125 from the U.S. Army Research Institute, by Grant Award # 31-1992-701 from the United States Department of Education, Institute for Educational Sciences, as administered by the Temple University Laboratory for Student Success and by Grant R206R00001 from the same organisation. Grantees undertaking such projects are encouraged to express freely their professional judgement. This chapter, therefore, does not necessarily represent the position or policies of the U.S. Army Research Institute or the U.S. Department of Education and no official endorsement should be inferred.

Contact address: robert.sternberg@tufts.edu

Future Perspectives

Suggested priorities for gifted education over the next decade

My hope is that the future of gifted education will be constructed on a broader theoretical basis than that which has led to identification relying so heavily on traditional measures of intelligence, or g (the general factor of intelligence). We have constructed a battery, Aurora, that measures the creative and practical aspects as well as the analytical aspect, and we have devised curricula for gifted students that allow all students both to capitalise on their strengths and to compensate for or correct their weaknesses. The students who score the highest on conventional tests are not necessarily those who will be creative musicians, scientists, writers, entrepreneurs, or whatever. Indeed, there is, for better or worse, some validity to the dictum that it is the fate of A students to be managed by B and C students. We need to develop in all students, including our gifted ones, the creative, practical, and wisdom-based skills they will need to cope in the world of the future and to excel.

Robert J. Sternberg

33

Fostering giftedness in urban and diverse communities: context-sensitive solutions

Ian Warwick
London Gifted and Talented, UK

Dona J. Matthews
Ontario Institute for Studies in Education of the University of Toronto, Canada

The problem: gifted education and social equity

What we understand as giftedness and what we define as success are inherently connected to our cultural values. Because giftedness is context-specific and socially constructed, gifted education can become one of the means whereby schools unwittingly perpetuate social inequities, including racism and economic disadvantage (Borland 2005; Gillborn 2005b). We know that across settings and nations, minority students are under-represented in gifted programming (Butler-Por 1993; Callahan 2005; Ford and Thomas 1997; Graham in press; van der Westhuizen 2007). While this is allowed to continue, the credibility of the field is undermined in ways that jeopardise not only social equity, but also funding and public support.

The concept of 'institutional racism' was defined by the Stephen Lawrence Inquiry (Macpherson 1999) as 'processes, attitudes and behaviour which amount to discrimination through unwitting prejudice, ignorance, thoughtlessness and racist stereotyping which disadvantage minority ethnic people'. Some critics argue that such inequities, whether intended or not, are a predictable result of any kind of gifted education. For example, 'Whether or not the intention of gifted programs is to reproduce existing economic and racial hierarchies or to produce cultural capital held by an elite group of students, these are in fact the consequences of such a system' (Sapon-Shevin 1994, p. 192). It has too often been true that, 'Gifted programmes are serving to widen the gap between society's 'haves' and 'have-nots' and between white and minority families by disproportionately serving the children of the former and neglecting the children of the latter' (Borland 2004, p. 6)

However, some critics point out that where gifted and talented (G&T) education is not specifically addressed, educational progress is 'not so much a question of intellectual merit but rather a question of affluence, with the most affluent receiving the best education and therefore achieving most highly. This suggests significant intellectual ability being untapped and unnoticed' (Campbell et al. 2004, p. 4). The creation of better opportunities is not enough, however, because even in a well-designed system, selectively low aspiration levels, combined with limited access to opportunities, means that 'those reaping the most benefit will be largely from affluent groups' (Campbell et al. 2004, p. 4). There are dangers, then, both in providing gifted education, and also in not doing so.

The situation in the United Kingdom

The under-representation in gifted programming of culturally and linguistically diverse students – most of whom are found in the larger urban centres – has concerned many researchers and educators worldwide. In the UK, Gillborn (2005b) has drawn attention to the fact that, according to Department for Children, Schools and Families statistics, white pupils are, proportionately, at least twice as likely to be identified as gifted, as are pupils from minority ethnic backgrounds. Although there are hopeful signs – in response to earlier reports, the situation has become significantly better for many of the under-represented groups – there is still work to be done. For example, only about 7 per cent of students from the Pakistani community are identified as gifted, as compared with a population average of 10.3 per cent. On the basis of these observations, Gillborn argues against gifted programming altogether, noting that plans to 'enhance G&T provision threaten further to institutionalise the race inequalities that have scarred the system for decades' (p. 1).

This is the conundrum then: gifted programming leads to social inequity, but we incur other social inequities when we do nothing to support gifted development, to say nothing about the loss to society of abilities that are left under-challenged and undeveloped. One solution is to identify two different and equally important objectives for gifted education: (a) to meet the learning needs of exceptionally advanced students, ensuring that giftedness and talent *are* developed; and (b) to use what we learn about giftedness to foster high-level ability more broadly across the population, paying particular attention to those groups that are under-represented in gifted programming, including children from families that are socio-economically disadvantaged, or linguistically, racially, or culturally different than the mainstream (Renzulli 2002).

A system-wide solution: a public health model of talent development

Beginning with the second objective, we can break down the historic link between disadvantage and educational underachievement most effectively in a system that seeks excellence for all its students, and secures access for all to as full a range of learning opportunities as possible. The public health approach to schooling means intentionally moving toward a population where the pool of highly competent people is as large and diverse as possible (Matthews et al. in press; Worrell in press).

In thinking about issues of inclusion and equity as they apply to the first objective for gifted education – addressing the learning needs of those students who are so exceptionally advanced that they require differentiated programming – there are two critical questions, one involving the identification of giftedness and talent, and the other involving programming. In the London context, these two questions have been framed as follows:

1 How can local authorities and schools do a better job of identifying linguistically, racially, and culturally diverse students as members of the G&T population?
2 What are the general and specific issues relating to the provision of G&T programming for linguistically and culturally diverse groups?

While there are good examples of effective and interesting practice, there has not been systematic national consideration of how to provide appropriate and meaningful teaching and learning for these groups.

Realising Equality and Achievement for Learners (REAL)

The Realising Equality and Achievement for Learners (REAL) project is a network comprising several clusters of primary and secondary schools that work together to examine their schools' current provisions for the distinct needs of Black/Minority/Ethnic (BME) and English as an Additional Language (EAL) students. The project contributes to the understanding of the general and specific issues relating to gifted and talented students from these groups, and is working to develop a long term sustainable action plan for improvement. By choosing to address educational disadvantage, the project targets the problem of under-representation of minority ethnic groups in the G&T programme.

The project was initially set up in 2006 between London Gifted & Talented, the Department for Children, Schools and Families (DCSF, but at that time known as the DfES), and three London local authorities. Three local authorities outside of London are also taking on the full programme. There are currently 28 local authorities and 87 schools involved in the second year of the REAL project. The project team works with schools and teachers to discover what gaps they themselves are working to close, adding the leverage and expertise of the team, and documenting the efforts in ways that can be understood by fellow professionals in the context of their own diverse experiences. The collaborative documentation process is a key to effective sharing of good ideas for practice. The project is part of the move toward raising the standards of education for all ethnic and linguistic minority pupils, but it plays a distinctive and complementary role. REAL projects are locally developed by schools and local authorities, and the ideas and practices involved are being made available for others to adopt and adapt. These projects provide schools and teachers with additional resources, and with opportunities to develop and fine tune their innovative ideas and practices in local contexts. They also work toward ensuring a degree of transferability.

The REAL project aims to

- improve the quality of identification, provision, and support for gifted and talented learners from the Black/Minority/Ethnic (BME) and English as an Additional Language (EAL) populations, especially underachievers;
- improve access to G&T opportunities for underachieving BME/EAL learners from disadvantaged backgrounds locally, regionally and nationally;
- improve support to schools and school leaders for this cohort of students;
- raise expectations of students, parents, staff and the wider community for this group; and
- improve knowledge and understanding of BME, EAL and G&T issues in a range of schools.

Based on their work with schools and local authorities, REAL is developing a set of tools and resources which can be adapted to the needs of other schools and local authorities nationally and internationally. The advantage of this model is that once innovative practice, ideas, and resources are located they will be trialled across other 'shadow' local authorities in London and nationally. When these are found to be both scaleable and transferable, they can then be shared with many other locations around the country, and around the world.

The core objectives are simple, although not simple to achieve. Success requires that families from diverse groups increase their awareness and capacity to support their gifted and talented young people. Schools also need to increase their awareness of this cohort, accompanied by increased knowledge, skills, and understanding. And finally, in addition to specific data from schools and local authorities, policy makers need a raised awareness level, as well as increased knowledge and understanding.

The national strategy for gifted and talented education is driven by a commitment to provide a stretching and challenging environment for those who are disadvantaged or might otherwise be excluded from opportunities to realise their potential. While this goal is very much in line with those of the REAL project, there are some serious barriers to equity faced by educators wishing to implement this strategy. The most serious, perhaps, results from the fact that where standardised test scores drive gifted identification, G&T cohorts tend to be less inclusive of those

- who have an incomplete prior attainment history;
- who achieve relatively less well in written work;
- whose achievements are outside the prescribed school curriculum (for instance, culturally specific gifts and talents), in areas that are unknown to, or unrecognised by, the school;
- for whom there may be cultural or other barriers to participation;
- who are not given the opportunity to demonstrate new or hidden gifts and talents through provision; and/or
- who are currently underachieving.

Another concern, observed on a whole school level, is the over-representation of some ethnic and gender groups within the population identified as talented, particularly in relation to sporting ability, which may mask their under-representation on gifted lists.

The REAL network is a professional space – both virtual and real – where colleagues can exchange dialogue, share ideas and increase their own expertise. Network members are expected to bring assets to the network, but equally to leave it enriched by their collaboration with others, and also ready to feed their learning on into new networks. Through these activities, colleagues interrogate their own beliefs, practices and experiences with a view to enhancing them. The issues they face are illustrated in Figure 18.

Strategies that effectively identify and address the needs of G&T BME/EAL learners focus on the centre of these three rings. In each other case, there is a risk that needs will not be identified, that the necessary supports will not be put in place, and that underachievement will result.

The REAL project provides an interactive vehicle for teachers and schools to develop a meaningful set of core practice-based ideas, suggestions, and interpretations, such as carefully structured motivational teaching, and properly structured language teaching. The project also provides information on related issues such as management support; staff time and effort; staff development; pupil population characteristics; and pupil responses. Furthermore, where appropriate, the project provides samples of curriculum material and other documents used by participating schools. In these ways, the REAL project aims to encourage the growth of local professional expertise, and to help make general principles locally relevant.

The primary task of the REAL project team is to ensure that the tools and approaches that are collegially developed are not locked to a particular context but are flexible enough to be transferred and taken up in a variety of educational contexts, while maintaining coherence and integrity. Rigorous and monitored quality assurance has had a formative impact within the project and ensures that output and assets can be used in the wider national and international context without the need for further modification and trialling.

One of the ways in which REAL is trying to tackle the challenge of representation is

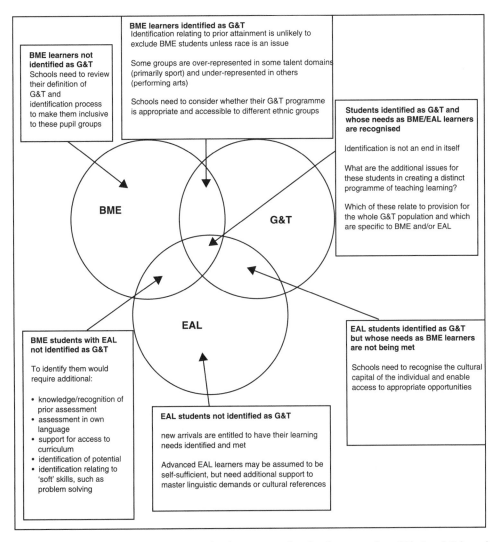

Figure 18 Identifying and addressing complex learning needs: what happens when Gifted and Talented education intersects with Black/Minority/Ethnic and English as an Additional Language

through examining how educators respond to new arrivals in their schools. Many of the assessment tools used to identify giftedness rely on past performance data, so how is it possible to assess the potential for excellence in a child who has recently arrived from Poland, for example, without a word of English, and no accompanying information from former teachers? Hounslow — one of the REAL local authorities — is situated close to Heathrow airport where many new arrivals to Britain land. Hounslow schools receive a high percentage of students from around the world, and have started to develop innovative ways of giving all their students equal opportunities to have their giftedness recognised. One of these is the *new arrivals assessment procedure*, based on the underlying assumption that all new arrivals could potentially require gifted services, and that it is incumbent on educational professionals to find this out.

The Initial Assessment pack has been created to help teachers assess and respond to the various needs of EAL new arrivals. According to most secondary school handbooks, high scores on standardised tests are required for gifted identification. Individual subject department nominations may also be taken into consideration. Somewhat predictably, new arrivals with English as an additional language and gifted learning needs are often not spotted, at least in the short term, due to their lack of ability in English, and the time it takes for them to settle and express themselves through their skills and talents in an academic setting.

The aim of the initial assessment activity was to shorten dramatically the G&T identification period for new arrivals. The guidelines for conducting oral interviews with students in their mother tongue were developed in order to gauge verbal fluency and previous educational experiences. These interviews help teachers set reading, writing, and mathematics tests at appropriate levels, and better comprehend new arrivals' abilities in less anglocentric ways.

The initial assessment process takes place over the course of six to eight weeks. Within the assessment pack reading and writing tasks, for example, are administered as soon as possible. Within two to three weeks, the English department follows up on how the student performs in lessons, and how he or she responds to ongoing academic tasks, which adds to the quality and depth of the assessment. Baseline measures – for example the 1000-word level test – are re-tested within six weeks to provide a sense of learning progression.

Another challenge for some BME and EAL students concerns their academic vocabulary. Students who have lived in Britain all their lives and are considered fluent in English may still, for example, speak only Punjabi at home. This can create problems with the more advanced English required at higher academic levels; if you have only heard the word for 'ignite' in Punjabi at home, for example, it can be more difficult to recognise and use it appropriately in advanced science lessons. This can lead to achievement barriers for G&T students, as precise English words, metaphors, figurative language and socially referenced phrases are often needed to attain the highest grades in examinations.

Currently, the work being undertaken by REAL for advanced learners of English addresses two core subjects, science and English. One focus is on developing and supporting acquisition of an Academic Word List, and a second addresses difficulties in the use of figurative and literal language. Strategies that have been identified by REAL participants as useful, and highlighted as transferable, include

- focusing on idioms and how they are used for effect;
- teaching the uses of literal and figurative language and illustrating the effects of these in texts;
- providing language enrichment and experimentation activities;
- promoting examples of language in context; and
- broadening students' language experiences.

When parents or caregivers of potentially gifted and talented students lack social capital, English language proficiency, or understanding of the British education system, they are often reluctant to become as fully involved in their child's education or to help them with their homework. We know that children's progress is greatly supported by help with further reading at home and academic conversations at home (Matthews et al. in press; Worrell in press), and educators who are committed to social equity understand that their responsibilities include helping parents and caregivers to help their children.

Several areas where parents want guidance and information have become clearer from sustained conversations with parents involved in the REAL project. These include

- detailed overviews of the English education system, including the expected National Curriculum levels for each key stage;
- explanations of the concepts of G&T, with specific reference to their children's education;
- ways that everyday practices such as shopping and cooking can be opportunities to develop language and maths skills;
- the importance of mastery and use of the home language in the development of higher order thinking;
- social and emotional aspects of learning, including the roles of praise and encouragement;
- strategies for increasing communication between home and school; and
- signposting G&T bilingual resources and services for further help and assistance.

In the course of implementing the REAL project, it became clear that many disadvantaged, immigrant, and minority students had unrecognised G&T abilities. Islington, for example, is an extremely diverse London borough with a particularly high Turkish and Bangladeshi population. Through contacting parents and inviting them to language support classes, Bilingual Community Officers in Islington began conversations with parents about their children's G&T learning needs. Discovering that a number of potentially high achievers in mathematics had not been recognised by their schools or parents, a REAL project activity was undertaken in four schools. A Turkish or Bengali/Sylheti speaking teacher taught a group of parents once a week for approximately three hours about the mathematics that their children were learning in school. Turkish and Bengali-speaking teaching assistants were employed to give additional support in class to the targeted pupils, and to link the work in class to homework and to the work with parents. A greater understanding of how mathematics is taught, and additional help in their own English, helps parents relate to their children's abilities, and feel more confident in working with them at home.

The concept of G&T can be difficult to translate into different languages and cultures. Working with Somali families, for example, community officers encountered comprehensive support for the academic emphasis inherent in the notion of giftedness, but less support for talent development. Traditional academic and scientific qualifications are usually valued as a route to financial success, whereas certain kinds of talent can be seen as incompatible with some communities' religious and moral values.

Where talents are regarded with concern, educators must find sensitive ways to communicate with families. One emphasis of the REAL project has been highlighting the ways that celebrating musical and artistic talents, for example, can lead to students' increased motivation in other areas of learning, greater educational achievement, and transferable skills. A further task involves working with community groups and their local schools to identify and celebrate culturally relevant and valued talents, which can then be incorporated into the identification processes used within those schools.

An online resource bank, toolkit and DVD are in production and will further support a much wider range of school leaders, G&T co-ordinators, and other teachers, in identifying and supporting BME and EAL learners. Early versions of these resources are already helping to ensure that school leaders and local authorities better understand the disadvantaged G&T agenda, and are aware that race equality is an essential requirement of effective G&T provision.

Moving on from here

In the increasingly diverse urban settings of the global village that we inhabit at the beginning of the twenty-first century, we have seen that schools, children, and communities benefit when educators and policymakers revisit their definitions and practices for supporting giftedness and talent development, and when they work to ensure that identification and programming methods intentionally and proactively target students from diverse populations. 'Realising Equality and Achievement for Learners' is a project that yields practical examples of collegial, interactive, context-sensitive strategies that are enabling schools and local authorities to address some thorny and complex issues as they move toward the kind of social equity and inclusion that enriches us all.

If we are to avoid the unintended consequences of social inequity that have plagued gifted education, our goals and expectations need to be clear, transparent and transferable. Educators need to hold high expectations of their culturally diverse and often multilingual students. We must learn how to celebrate cultural diversity most effectively, to see it as a strength to be capitalised on, rather than a problem to be solved. This means finding ways to increase the motivation and self esteem of all students. It also means becoming fully aware and respectful of diverse family and community cultures, which can differ substantially from dominant educational cultures.

For everyone's sake, the cohort of gifted and talented students must be drawn from all communities. This is achieved in part through the kinds of considerations, understandings, emphases, and strategies being discovered in work on the REAL project. The other part in the two-part solution discussed here is the implementation of a public health approach to education generally, whereby we support a larger and more diverse pool of people in mastering the basic skills that go into higher-level achievement, skills such as literacy, numeracy, spatial skills, and technological skills. When we foster as high a level of skills mastery as possible across the population – paying particular attention to those populations that tend to be under-represented in gifted and talented programming – we reap rich rewards over time in diverse kinds of scientific, artistic, intellectual, technological, physical, and social discoveries and achievements.

Contact address: ian.warwick@londongt.org

Future Perspectives

Suggested priorities for gifted education over the next decade

Within the UK, the future of gifted education must be based on social justice. All students are entitled to be stretched and challenged, and the most effective gifted and talented provision is rooted in good teaching and learning within the daily classroom. The educational system must seek excellence for all its students and ensure that race equality is seen as an essential requirement. It needs to be completely committed to breaking down the barriers that prevent individuals from realising their potential and to look outwards to raise the aspirations of students, families and their wider community. Gifted students represent a widely heterogeneous group. Our job must be to ensure that schools are in a position to be able to identify the potential of all children and give them the means to achieve it.   Ian Warwick and Dona J. Matthews

34

The role of gifted education in promoting cultural diversity

Joyce VanTassel-Baska

College of William and Mary, US

The field of gifted education has frequently been perceived as elitist and a burr in the side of educators who promote egalitarian practices, such as inclusion and a common curriculum for all. Yet the field has made many advances in promoting cultural diversity and identifying students from culturally diverse backgrounds, and these should be viewed as positive signs. Gifted children should be found and nurtured in every cultural group in the world today. Thoughtful educators must be vigilant and sensitive to the processes that can be employed to make that happen and have the will to carry it out.

Research on the efficacy of finding under-represented populations, including the culturally diverse, has become a cottage industry, with new tools and approaches emerging over the last ten years (Bracken and McCallum 1998; Lohman 2005; Naglieri and Ford 2003; VanTassel-Baska et al. 2002). Moreover, strategies and techniques for working effectively for diverse learners have been advocated in the context of multicultural curriculum for the gifted (Ford and Harris 2000; VanTassel-Baska 2004). The field of gifted education has also developed targeted programmes for culturally diverse learners and their families to promote positive transition to college (Olszewski-Kubilius and Scott 1992), to enhance academic development over time (Johnsen et al. 2007), and to promote advanced learning in schools (Bracken et al. 2007; Coleman et al. 2007).

In addition to these approaches in the elementary and secondary school levels, there has been a movement in America to develop national standards for the preparation of teachers of the gifted, which emphasise working with culturally diverse learners as a prominent part of the overall process (VanTassel-Baska and Johnsen 2007). Finally, our funding stream as a field at the federal level for the past 20 years, the Jacob Javits Act, has also targeted funds for research and development efforts to be directed to emphasising the needs of low-income and other under-represented groups. Thus, it may be fair to suggest that gifted education has contributed substantively to understanding how to address cultural diversity and enhancing learning for all.

This chapter will enumerate two of the emphases mentioned above as illustrations of how the field of gifted education in the US has focused on the cultural diversity agenda. The chapter concludes with a set of recommendations for schools to consider in implementing gifted programmes sensitive to cultural diversity.

Case illustration #1: The role of alternative assessment

Based on our current understanding of the problem of under-representation of low-income and minority students in gifted programmes and preliminary studies, the use of performance-based assessment as a non-traditional tool for enhancing the possibility of greater representation of such students in these programmes appears to be a promising development (VanTassel-Baska et al. 2002). Research literature on non-traditional assessment suggests that alternative assessment has its theoretical assumptions in the belief that abilities are malleable and developmental, in contrast to the conservative assumptions that view abilities as relatively stable. Critics of traditional assessment tools suggest that ability measures are often embedded in a cultural context where non-mainstream students (e.g. students from poverty, minority students) are often placed in a disadvantaged position. Dynamic or alternative assessment is non-traditional in that it focuses on tapping fluid rather than crystallised abilities. Such an approach is used to assess cognitive abilities that are frequently not apparent when most forms of traditional standardised tests are used. This type of assessment usually consists of a test-intervention-retest format, with the focus on the improvement students make after an intervention, specifically based on their learning cognitive strategies related to mastery of the testing task (Feuerstein 1986; Kirschenbaum 1998).

Performance task assessment is one type of dynamic assessment (VanTassel-Baska et al. 2002). Performance assessments focus on challenging, open-ended problems that require high level thinking and problem-solving, and put an emphasis on the process the student uses to come to an answer rather than on whether or not the student can quickly find the right answer. In 1998, the State Department of Education in South Carolina contracted with The Center for Gifted Education at The College of William and Mary to develop performance task protocols as a pilot project to assess their efficacy in identifying low socio-economic status (SES) and African American students within the state. Based on pilot, field test and statewide implementation data from the project, the performance tasks proved to be useful tools toward this end, finding in the range of 12–18 per cent more under-represented students (VanTassel-Baska et al. 2002).

Based on the success of these performance tasks in locating more under-represented students for gifted programmes, they were officially adopted as a third dimension of the state identification system (Dimension C) in 1999. Therefore, a statewide implementation of performance task assessment in addition to traditional ability and achievement identification method was institutionalised in the state of South Carolina.

Now students in South Carolina may be admitted to gifted programmes through meeting specified criteria on a group or an individual ability measure (Dimension A), a group achievement measure in the verbal or mathematical domain (Dimension B), and/or verbal or nonverbal performance tasks (Dimension C). Verbal performance-based assessments refer to verbal reasoning tasks that require written responses or correct manipulation of words. Nonverbal performance-based assessments refer to mathematical and spatial tasks. All of the performance-based assessment tasks are verbally mediated and assisted through a pre-teaching process on the test item prototype.

'Traditionally-identified gifted students' refers to students who qualified either (1) through reaching the 96th percentile or above on an ability test or (2) through meeting the criteria of a combination of 90th percentile or higher on ability test and 94th percentile or higher on an achievement measure. 'Performance task-identified students' were defined as gifted students who qualified (1) through meeting the criteria of 80 per cent correct rate on verbal or nonverbal performance tasks and (2) through meeting the standard of the 90th percentile on an ability test or the 94th percentile on an achievement test.

Since the inception of statewide use of performance assessments for the identification of gifted students in the 1999–2000 school year, all school districts in South Carolina have participated in the testing. In a follow-up study of statewide gifted student identification profiles over six years (2000–2005), VanTassel-Baska et al. (2007, in press) found that performance tasks protocols consistently identified higher percentages of low income (23 per cent) and African American students (14 per cent) than traditional identification tools (18 per cent and 11 per cent, respectively). Despite the fact that a great majority of gifted students came from middle-class or above family background regardless of the identification method employed (81.4 per cent traditional method versus 77 per cent performance tasks), performance task protocols demonstrated important advantages in identifying more under-represented populations.

Except for students who qualified for gifted services through a 96th percentile or above on an ability measure, the current gifted regulations allowed students to be identified through the combination of either a verbal or a non-verbal score (i.e. mathematical, quantitative or spatial) from any two types of assessment, namely, ability (A), achievement (B) or performance tasks (C).

The six year trend analysis findings suggested that a higher percentage of performance task-identified students (40.5 per cent) than traditionally identified students (20.8 per cent) fell into the category of being identified in one content domain only by meeting the criteria for achievement and performance-based assessment. This suggests a higher proportion of unbalanced identification profiles (verbal or nonverbal only) among performance task-identified students, and doubles what was found among traditionally identified students. Moreover, a large majority of both groups of gifted students, regardless of identification approaches, qualified for the programme through the non-verbal area (quantitative, mathematical, or spatial).

How well did performance task-identified students fare in gifted programmes in terms of academic outcomes? Their performance on the English and Mathematics portion of the state standardised test (PACT) were examined in comparison to those of traditionally identified students over four years (2001–2004).

The multivariate tests showed that there were overall performance differences on the English language arts and math component of PACT 2001 to PACT 2004 between students who were identified through alternative methods ($F = 3.32$, $p = 0.000$, $\eta^2 = 0.008$), favoring students identified traditionally. The performance mean differences among students identified through different dimensional combinations ranged from 3 to 9 points in English language arts and 3 to 11 points in mathematics across four years (2001–2004), translating into a 0.2 to 0.6 difference on Cohen's d effect size index.

Although the academic outcomes for the alternatively-identified gifted student population were not as strong as those attained by students identified more traditionally, the in-depth qualitative study on these learners revealed a positive picture of adjustment. Programme participation brought more opportunities, stimulation, and inspiration into the young lives of many students from disadvantaged families, and hope to their parents as well. The level of appreciation among both students and parents was overwhelming. The elevated self-esteem and motivation to learn among students, who would otherwise be bored and daydreaming in a regular class, was powerful.

Importantly, the many perspectives shared among teachers, parents, and students themselves suggested the beneficial nature of gifted identification and programming for these students. Many common yet diverse characteristics were cited for these students, ranging from being strong learners in several ways, to being limited in motivation, organisation, and the ability to work with peers. It is fair to conclude, however, after three to four years in the gifted programme, these students in general had gained important new skills, enhanced their academic performances (i.e. grade point averages) and felt renewed confidence in their own abilities.

275

The studies in South Carolina over a six year period suggest that, in general, performance-based assessment on a statewide basis has steadily contributed to greater numbers of both low income and minority students being identified for gifted programmes than would have been found through existing protocols, although the majority of students identified are higher socio-economic status and Caucasian. Moreover, the profiles of students identified through non-traditional means are more heavily weighted toward non-verbal abilities, are slightly more likely to be female, and present an uneven profile of ability between verbal and nonverbal aptitudes. Performance on high stakes state testing (PACT) suggests that these gifted students are less proficient and advanced than their traditionally identified counterparts across four years, although the differences between the two groups were educationally insignificant compared to the self-reported long term positive programme impact (VanTassel-Baska et al. 2005).

At a practical level, these studies continue to demonstrate the importance of using non-traditional assessments in tandem with traditional ones to find and serve under-represented gifted students. The results also challenge practitioners to match programme intervention to ability and aptitude information in order to achieve an optimal match for students in programmes.

Case illustration #2: The role of national teacher education standards

Coherent standards in education offer a variety of benefits. The content of standards from early elementary school through to the end of secondary education helps to ensure that students learn what they need to know for high level functioning in the twenty-first century. National groups that were broadly representative of the professions and the educational community have put more than ten years of work into the development of various sets of content standards. The input of these groups was further shaped by public comments on multiple drafts of their work. Such thoughtful consideration of what America's students and teachers should be learning has not occurred since the 1960s (Vinovskis 1996). These standards also help to ensure educational quality across school districts and educational institutions. Every student has the right to a challenging curriculum and to the pedagogical support needed to master it effectively. The standards call for systemic implementation that should leave no child behind (Wang et al. 1993).

The National Council for Accreditation of Teacher Education (NCATE) standards for teacher preparation also emphasise this cohesive implementation strategy. The standards provide educators with guide-posts to mark the way to providing students and candidates in higher education with meaningful outcomes to work toward. Because the standards are designed on a model of professional competencies, educators work on optimising knowledge, skills and dispositions through a focus on behaving like the professionals they will become.

Analysis of differences from earlier teacher education standards

The field of gifted education has been working from a set of standards, initially developed by the Council for Exceptional Children (CEC) and the Talented And Gifted Association (TAG) in 1985, that provided over 100 standards for programmes to fulfil, many of which were more focused on special education issues and language. The major differences between this older set of standards and the revised standards centre on the following areas:

1   The new standards emphasise state of the art research-based best practice in the field of gifted education. While the older set of standards was developed to reflect the best indicators for practice at the time, the field has evolved more fully since the initial adoption of the original NCATE standards in gifted education. The current set of standards has a fully developed set of research, literature, and practice-based studies that support each of the indicators and provide the field an appropriate base on which to develop teacher leaders for the future.

2   The new standards were carefully developed through consensus and over time. The older set of standards was developed primarily through the efforts of only one of the national organisations and adhered very closely to special education language and even spirit in the instructional and assessment standards areas. Consequently, the standards were criticised by many university educators as not being truly reflective of the thinking in the field of gifted education. The joint task force approach employed in the development of these standards over the past three years speaks strongly to the cohesion within the field on the content emphases of the standards being well aligned with desired practice.

3   The new standards reflect a much stronger integrated emphasis on diversity. They ensure that all types of diversity – cultural, linguistic, intellectual, sexual orientation and disabilities – are referenced in the indicators and integrated into each of the standards so that issues of cultural stereotyping, tolerance for differentness and celebration of multiculturalism, for example, can be found to be important parts of the new standards.

4   The new standards reflect a stronger emphasis on appropriate differentiated practice. They reflect added depth and breadth to the indicators related to both instructional planning and strategies with more tailored emphases, essential to building strong programmes of study for teachers in this area. The emphasis in assessment on both identification and learning has enhanced and sharpened the focus for measurement tools to be taught and used in programmes.

5   The new standards emphasise cognitive science research and findings from other related domains of learning beyond the gifted community. They are grounded in the most recent research on learning strategies that emphasise higher level thinking, use of concept mapping, an emphasis on meta-cognition, and problem-solving as central to the preparation of teachers to work with our best learners. These emphases were not included to the same degree in the older standards.

6   The new standards reflect an evolving field that shows deep connections to issues in general and special education. They reflect an awareness of the connections among gifted, special, and general education in respect to linkages to content expertise in instructional strategies, consonant with the educational reform agenda and to the use of technology. Moreover, the central role of diversity and collaboration echoes the major themes of both general and special education. Study of trends and issues in the field of gifted education by necessity traverses this broader landscape.

These new standards are important to the field of gifted education because they define the essential knowledge and skills that teachers need to acquire to be effective in teaching gifted and talented students in the classroom. Moreover, they help in gaining consensus among professionals who prepare future teachers, thus achieving consistency across teacher preparation programmes. They identify for others the legitimacy of gifted education not only in the area of teacher preparation but also as a separate field of study at the higher education level that is based on a strong foundation of research (Darling-Hammond et al. 1999; VanTassel-Baska 2004; Yinger 1999).

The process used in developing this set of standards for teachers of students with gifts and talents included a variety of stakeholders and followed validation procedures outlined by the CEC and approved by NCATE in 2001 (CEC 2003, p. 146). These procedures included the appointment of a small work group that guided the development of an underlying professional literature base for each standard set of indicators, the approval of this work by the Knowledge and Skills Committee of CEC, based on a survey of 200 educators in the field of gifted education, the application for approval to the NCATE Policy Board, and the final approval by that Board of the new standards complete with the research evidence supporting them. A National Association for Gifted Children (NAGC) task force was created four years ago to shepherd this process and to ensure tight collaboration among the organisations of CEC, CEC-TAG and NAGC as well as the larger field of university personnel and educators at all stages of the work.

Throughout the process, the task force was careful to ensure that the new initial standards emphasised diversity. Given the continuing and significant under representation of specific groups receiving educational services for the gifted and talented, it was critical that the standards stress the preparation of teachers who support the learning of all gifted students and not privilege some groups over others (TAG 2001). Of the 32 knowledge and 38 skill standards, 27 (38.5 per cent) explicitly address diversity.

Introduction to the Standards

All of the 70 initial indicators are organised into ten CEC content standards: Standard 1, Foundations; Standard 2, Development and Characteristics of Learners; Standard 3, Individual Learning Differences; Standard 4, Instructional Strategies; Standard 5, Learning Environments and Social Interactions; Standard 6, Language and Communication; Standard 7, Instructional Planning; Standard 8; Assessment; Standard 9, Professional and Ethical Practice; and Standard 10, Collaboration. Each set of underlying emphases is divided into knowledge and skills essential to the work of personnel preparation.

Standard 1 emphasises the knowledge-based foundation of the gifted education field that traces the theoretical, historical, and research-based constructs central to understanding this specialised area of individual differences and the manifestation of them in policies at all levels of the educational enterprise. This component also emphasises key issues and societal and economic factors that impact the development of intellectual talent more broadly. Standards 2 and 3 emphasise how gifted learners are different from other learners in respect to characteristics, developmental trajectories, and idiosyncratic ways of learning. Attention is given to the added differences that accrue due to cultural background, poverty and learning problems that sometimes accompany giftedness.

Standards 4 and 7 focus on instructional strategies and instructional planning respectively. Standard 4 emphasises the pedagogical approaches that have been found effective in working with gifted learners, including those from diverse backgrounds. It also stresses the importance of using management strategies, including assistive technology, that respond to exceptional student learning needs. Standard 7 focuses on the products necessary to differentiate curriculum for gifted learners including learning plans, units, and scope and sequence documents. Emphasis is also placed on differentiation features that can be matched to different domains and student differences.

Standards 5, 6 and 10 emphasise the nature of learning environments for the gifted that provide optimal contexts for learning personal, social and intellectual skills, the development of oral and written language and communication skills at appropriate levels of advancement, using appropriate technologies. Moreover, the collaboration standard focuses on the multiple types of collaboration necessary to be effective in developing programmes for these learners from families, to school personnel, to various community groups. Standard 8 explicates the knowledge and skills essential for identification of gifted learners, including the use of multiple methods for finding underrepresented populations, as well as the knowledge and skills needed to assess learning in programmes. Finally, Standard 9 focuses on professional and ethical practice in relating to students and other individual stakeholders in the gifted education enterprise and challenges teachers to strive for continuous improvement through professional development and reflection on practice. The full set of standards and their descriptions may be found at both the NAGC website (http://www.nagc.org) and the CEC website (http://www.cec.sped.org).

Implications of the new standards

What do the new standards mean for the field of gifted education? They represent a new era in consensus on what teachers of the gifted must know, understand and be able to demonstrate competency in. Recognised by over 500 American universities as the referent organisation for standards in teacher education programmes, NCATE standards in gifted education are now being used for institutional and programme reviews. Thus, first and foremost, the passage of the new standards should bring coherence to teacher education programmes nationwide at the initial level of certification or endorsement as well as master's level coursework in gifted education. For universities not NCATE-accredited, it offers a research-based set of standards officially sanctioned by the two national organisations and the field as a whole.

Secondly, the standards may influence more colleges of education to offer an endorsement strand of gifted courses under an existing master's programme and to ensure that pre-service candidates have at least one course in gifted education before they graduate.

Finally, the passage of the standards also signals a new era for the professional development of teachers who are not candidates for endorsement, certification, or a master's degree in gifted education. It provides a research-based agenda for professional development workshops, allowing choice and flexibility in the emphases but providing the overall blueprint for activity on all relevant topics deemed essential by the field in the equipping of teachers to work successfully with these learners. Thus local gifted programme coordinators working in concert with staff development departments can articulate the content demands for working with regular classroom teachers in gifted education and push for more systematic opportunities on an annual basis.

Conclusions

Based on the case illustration of performance-based assessment as an important tool in identifying culturally diverse gifted learners, and the case illustration of teacher education standards that emphasise diversity, one can see examples of how the field of gifted education has made progress in its cultural diversity agenda. However, much remains to be done, especially in the area of implementation of alternative assessment, specialised curricula and programmes, and the preparation of personnel.

Thus a set of recommendations for implementation of these initiatives should be part of all teacher education institutions and school settings. These recommendations should be focused on the preparation of teachers of the gifted in cultural competencies, the use of multi-cultural curriculum and instructional tools, and the use of traditional and alternative assessments to find giftedness in under-represented groups. The development of early childhood programmes and transition services should target these students early, and provide necessary follow-up at key stages of learning. Value-added instruction in core academic areas should be routinely provided to bolster the skills and concepts being taught. Social-emotional support structures are necessary at all levels, which would include counselling, mentoring and tutorials. Finally, there is a critical need to honour the contributions of all cultures to history, to the arts and to the framing of national culture as well as world culture.

Contact address: jlvant@wm.edu

Future Perspectives

Suggested priorities for gifted education over the next decade

The US context for operating gifted programmes in elementary and secondary schools may be seen as a patchwork quilt of options, available in some locales but not others. Only 11 states mandate funding to support programmes and services to this population, for example. University level preparation programmes for educators of the gifted are also sporadic. Only 77 institutions offer masters level coursework or doctoral study in this field. Currently there is an overemphasis on accountability testing that focuses energy and resources on students below proficiency, thereby ignoring the gifted learner in schools and classrooms. There is also a widespread belief that gifted students will succeed by themselves. A proactive response to such issues is required. We must set goals for a systematic approach to K-12 programme development in all our states, a required teacher preparation programme of at least 12 graduate hours linked to university coursework available in every state, and we must create systems of opportunity for promising children from poverty and diversity.

Joyce VanTassel-Baska

35

Developing pupils' problem-solving and thinking skills

Belle Wallace

Director of TASC International
Editor of Gifted Education International

In this chapter, I make the case that all children's learning capacities can be improved through the systematic and coherent teaching of the processes underpinning problem solving and thinking. I argue that this can be achieved via the implementation of an inclusive, cross-curricular model called Thinking Actively in a Social Context (TASC).[1] This model was initially derived from a longitudinal action research project carried out with multi-cultural learners in some of the most disadvantaged areas of South Africa, and has subsequently been used as the base for the development of problem-solving curricula in various countries.

There is widespread agreement that the teaching of thinking and problem-solving skills is a key factor in the development of pupils' autonomy, self-confidence, and 'learning how to learn' skills; and that all these attributes should be priority targets in schools (cf. Costa [ed.] 2001). However, many national curricular developments have tended to promote the memorisation of content for its own sake, rather than emphasising the opportunities for thinking and problem solving that could arise from the content. In this chapter, I suggest coherent and universal framework whereby the content of a prescribed curriculum can be used as the basis for the development of a problem-solving and thinking skills pedagogy. The acronym TASC was developed with four main ideas in mind:

Thinking

The essential message of TASC is that whilst all children are capable of thinking and improving their performance, they need to believe and know through experience that they can think, and are making positive progress in their thinking and problem-solving capacity.

Actively

To maintain their motivation to learn, children need to have ownership of their learning and participate actively in decision-making. They need to understand not just the 'what', but also

---

[1] The principles of TASC were subsequently embedded in a whole school, multi-cultural series of Language and Thinking texts entitled: 'Language in My World', and 'Reading in My World': Publisher: Nasou Via Africa, Cape Town, South Africa.

the 'why' and 'how' of their learning. This understanding through real-life, hands-on learning generates motivation, high self-esteem and confidence (Watkins et al. 2007).

Social

The hope for the future lies in the global recognition that as individuals we are not just developing from dependence to independence – we are also growing to appreciate that we are interdependent in a global community, with responsibilities to the community, and, consequently, rights earned within the community. Hence, children need to work collaboratively and cooperatively, to practise their thinking and to share ideas with others, taking responsibility for their decisions and actions.

Context

Children's learning needs to be relevant to their lives, extending from their immediate context, and becoming wider and deeper from there. Importantly, they need to understand both the links to, and the gaps between, their home culture, the school culture, and ever-wider into the global culture, learning over time to bridge the contextual gaps with understanding and confidence.

Early seeds from which TASC emerged and evolved

Robert Sternberg (1983, 1985, 1986, this volume) has led the way in making the case that intelligence can be developed, and argues that thinking and problem-solving skills are used in all aspects of life. Importantly, he observes, all pupils can be taught to improve and extend their working repertoires of skills for planning, carrying out tasks, monitoring, reflecting on their progress, and transferring these skills into other domains. He suggests that intelligent behaviour involves the processes of adapting, shaping and selecting real-world environments using analytical, creative and practical skills; and that the levels of all pupils' intellectual functioning can be raised through a problem-solving and thinking skills-based curriculum. Carol Dweck is making a similar argument about intelligence as an ability that develops, from the standpoint of her research in developmental psychology (see Dweck this volume).

There exists evidence (Brown 1987; Brown and Campione 1994) that learners need to use a wide range of thinking tools, both consciously and consistently across the curriculum, if such skills are to be transferred into a working repertoire of learning tools. An ad hoc scattering of thinking skills across lessons does not provide the learner with a comprehensive set of problem-solving and thinking tools that are autonomised and transferred into life. It makes educational sense then to have a coherent, whole-school policy for developing, implementing and monitoring a curriculum that systematically integrates a range of problem-solving and thinking skills within real-life situations, across the curriculum and within subject areas. Moreover, the ethos of the school needs to be a celebration of individual qualities with understanding and acceptance of difference.

Another leading thinker who has contributed greatly to the development of TASC, through an understanding of how children best learn, is Lev Vygotsky (Cole 1985; Vygotsky 1978). Vygotsky demonstrated that the development of language, through guided classroom dialogue, pupil interaction and the democratic sharing of ideas, is essential for successful learning. He stressed that when a teacher-mentor leads learners to negotiate their own meanings from the

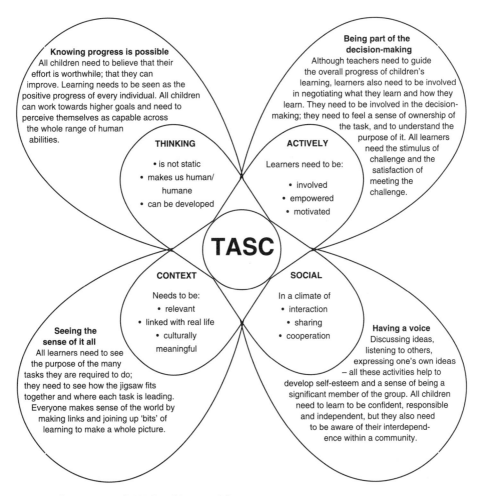

Figure 19 The meaning of TASC and its essential tenets

bases of their own experiential knowledge, then learners are motivated and empowered to learn. Vygotsky also stressed that the most effective route to independent competence is through the initial and sensitive teacher-mentor's scaffolding of the support necessary for the apprentice learner gradually to become autonomous.

More recently, neuropsychologists (see for example Geake this volume) have demonstrated that pupils need to link new learning with previous learning, seeing the relevance and the application of their current learning and also where the current learning is leading. The brain needs actively to construct mental maps of linked ideas and understanding, thus extending and constructing neural pathways. Moreover, unless children's learning is firmly embedded in an active problem-solving process, then much of the factual content is lost, and enormous time is wasted both for teaching and learning.

All learners need a rich language base since language is the major medium of communication in most teaching-learning processes. Learners need to talk and discuss in order to practise and straighten out their thinking, and the talk needs to begin with their home language, before it can be extended to accommodate the language of school learning.

Bandura (1971, 1982) discussed the vital role played by senior learners and adults when they model a desired behaviour for the young learner. Patterns of behaviour are 'caught rather than taught'. Therefore, it is essential for teachers to model and to verbalise their thinking behaviour: how else can learners reflect back the behaviour through practice and then make it their own? Moreover, Bandura has also drawn attention to the direct link between positive self-concept and self-esteem, and the motivation needed to persevere with a learning task. Recently Damasio (1999) has confirmed, through neurobiological research, the close interplay between cognition and emotion, and has underlined the essential role of positive self-concept in success-ful learning. All learners learn when they can build on success; and that raises the question of how teachers assess learners' work and how they provide feedback that supports, and yet gives guidance for improvement.

Using a broad base of understanding derived mainly from the work of Sternberg, Vygotsky, and Bandura, from 1984 to 1993, Belle Wallace and Harvey Adams surveyed the major world-wide problem-solving and thinking skills initiatives, and visited the key projects then currently operating. Adopting an eclectic approach, we simultaneously conducted an intensive action research project with diverse groups of multi-cultural learners and their teachers. Problem-solving and thinking skills strategies and methodologies were trialled, evaluated, and reflected upon by the researchers, a team of educational psychologists, the participating teachers, and, importantly, the pupils. Gradually a pragmatic working model emerged for the teaching and learning of thinking and problem-solving skills, and the seeds of TASC grew (Wallace and Adams 1993a, 1993b).

TASC is an inclusive framework designed to be embedded across the curriculum, developing the collective and interactive human abilities of social, emotional, spiritual, linguistic, mathemat-ical, scientific, mechanical/technical, visual/spatial, auditory/musical and movement/physical domains. When a school is actively celebrating the wide spectrum of human potential and all pupils feel valued, then it is easier to differentiate activities according to their learning needs without giving high status to some subjects or to 'able' pupils over others. Thus the policy of inclusion embraces and accommodates differentiation.

We need to ask ourselves what competencies and understandings children will need to enable them to function effectively in their world of tomorrow. The future scenario of possible world problems often looks bleak, and curricula are often locked into the scenarios of the past. However, curricula need to be oriented towards the future; the competencies children will need lie, for example, in their potential to understand and reconcile cultural differences on a worldwide scale; to cope with fast-moving change; effectively to use new inventions to improve life for all; to foster changes in the environment that will ensure its safe survival; and to nurture and preserve all that is beautiful and enriching within human cultures. All these competencies are developed through active and real problem solving. It is through the processes of thinking and reflecting, using all their human abilities, the children will acquire the self-confidence and the resilience to function effectively in their world.

Involving TASC

Adopting the TASC approach does not mean a major overhaul of teachers' pedagogy since the skills can be developed incrementally, consolidated, and then extended. However, when adopt-ing the TASC approach, it is more productive to develop a school-wide approach so that pupils receive a coherent message across the curriculum. (See the TASC Problem-Solving Wheel, Figure 20.)

Figure 20 TASC: Thinking Actively in a Social Context. The TASC Problem-Solving Wheel

There are certain essential teaching and learning processes that underlie the whole classroom methodology, as outlined below. Essentially, the role of the teacher changes from 'the information giver' to the 'constructor of knowledge with the learner'. TASC concerns the training of the brain. Learners need to understand that they can exercise and train the brain like an athlete trains his or her muscles. Moreover, learners need to realise that they are not stuck at any set level of performance, and talking about their thinking processes and ways of improving them can lead to positive growth (see Dweck, this volume for evidence of this). TASC aids understanding of the problem-solving process, because the two-dimensional TASC wheel replicates the complex, interactive, and recursively spiral mental processes of the creative process. Referring back to any previous stage can clarify the initial thinking as necessary, and referring forward can clarify purpose and direction.

Group work should be used as often as possible so that learners can negotiate meaning and understanding amongst themselves. However, group work skills need to be carefully trained and the purpose of the debate and discussion rigorously established and timed. Training in listening skills and taking turns is also important. When reflecting on the thinking process, learners also need to reflect on how well they worked as a team. Furthermore, when teachers are leading the learning interaction they need to verbalise the thinking processes, the thinking language, and the stages of the problem-solving wheel that are being used. This is essentially the modelling of thinking processes. Pupils acquire thinking strategies when the teacher first scaffolds the thinking behaviour by giving examples, then gives learners relevant guided practice, and gradually withdraws the scaffolding as the learner gains competence.

Working through the stages of the TASC Problem-Solving Wheel

Gather and organise

This concerns the learner asking 'What do I know about this?' Using and improving the memory is an important part of the problem-solving process, and the memory improves and works more efficiently when the brain can make links between 'bits' of information (Geake, this volume). Rather than assuming that learners know nothing about a proposed curriculum topic, the teacher first needs to gather from the learners what they already know about the topic. All learners need to bring into their working memory the network of knowledge and ideas they already have. Often, the 'able' learners may lead the others, but equally often, a teacher can be surprised by an unexpected contribution from a supposedly 'less able' pupil. All the learners' contributions can be recorded quickly in key words or phrases on to a large sheet of paper or interactive white board, which the teacher can use as a way to encourage the class (or group) to organise the knowledge – making links and grouping ideas. This collective mind map helps learners to organise ideas in a coherent way, allowing the teacher to see the wholeness or fragmentation of the learners' knowledge framework, then to help them refine and extend it. The collective mind map can be followed by asking the pupils to identify, and then work on, key aspects or issues to extend the initial collection of ideas, identifying any 'missing' knowledge, discussing ways to research, and identifying the relevant skills that are needed.

It is also important, at this stage, to discuss the themes, purposes, and concepts underlying the range of tasks. Groups can then be allocated (or can choose) from a range of tasks that they research, develop, and present to the rest of the class. Obviously, this means that learners need to develop a repertoire of research skills and to be clear about the questions they are researching. Auditing what children already know before completing the fine planning of a topic is a major key to effective differentiation of learning tasks, as well as an essential stage in assessment for learning.

Identify: what is the task?

Clarifying the task involves both analytical and creative thinking. Identifying key questions for further research encourages ownership of the learning journey. Many learners lose sight of the task they are undertaking, get lost in detail, or become distracted by irrelevant issues, and so it is important for them to identify and keep the purpose of the learning task clearly in mind. Also, many pupils get sidetracked by the rush to produce a quickly finished and decorated product as an end in itself, rather than thinking about the purposes and strategies for clarifying, presenting, and vividly communicating their ideas. In addition, learners must understand the criteria that will make the task successful or excellent.

Generate: how many ideas can I think of?

Generating ideas is another component of creative thinking. Frequently, learners fasten their efforts on the first idea they think of. 'Able' learners might anticipate the fast and easy completion of a task, while 'less able' learners might cling to the security of the one right answer. So it is important to encourage all learners to stop and think again, to take thinking risks and to consider several ideas before deciding on the best idea or course of action.

Decide: which is the best idea?

The dominant thinking tools that come into play at this stage are critical, analytical and evaluative thinking. When making decisions, learners need to prioritise and to give reasons for their choices, rather than deciding impulsively on a course of action or a solution. Then the course of action needs to be planned, and the possible solution trialled.

Implement: let's do it!

We live in a literate, numerate, technical world, and these skills are important. However, children also need to express their ideas across a fuller range of abilities as often as possible. To do this, they need to acquire skills in the creative and performing arts, within diverse subject domains, and in the world of information technology. They also need to acquire a wide range of recording skills that encourage maximum thinking and minimum recording, such as mind maps, flow charts, diagram formats and other such visual depictions.

Evaluate: how well did I do?

The skill of self-evaluation needs to be trained. Firstly, the teacher helps the learners to talk about the purpose of the task, and demonstrates or displays examples of 'good work', across a range of human abilities, eliciting reasons why the work is good. Gradually, learners themselves need to establish the criteria that they will use to evaluate their product; otherwise, they perpetuate the common practice of simply providing what they think the teacher wants. The process of evaluation needs to be both formative and summative, with learners feeling that every task can be improved because they are learning how to learn.

Communicate: let's tell someone!

When we communicate and disseminate, we straighten out our ideas and get them to cohere. In many primary schools, children give talks or performances to other classes. Good though this practice is, it can be extended: for example, when older children write poems, story-books and reference books which they or younger children really use, or when learners give demonstrations or performances to teach and communicate to other learners. Pupils need a real audience in order to feel the thrill of communicating and sharing their ideas and the results of their efforts. Also, any display of children's work needs to celebrate the stages of thinking and preparation by displaying the evidence of it. Using the TASC wheel as the centre for the display prompts children to analyse each stage of their thinking and to share that thinking with others.

Learn from experience: what have I learned?

The final stage of reflecting is both a formative and summative process that aims at consolidating and transferring what has been learned. This includes reflecting on the major competencies being developed, the learning processes that were used, and the efficiency of the whole problem-solving process. It is also important to reflect on which general and subject-specific skills have been practised, and what important content has been covered. This 'thinking about

287

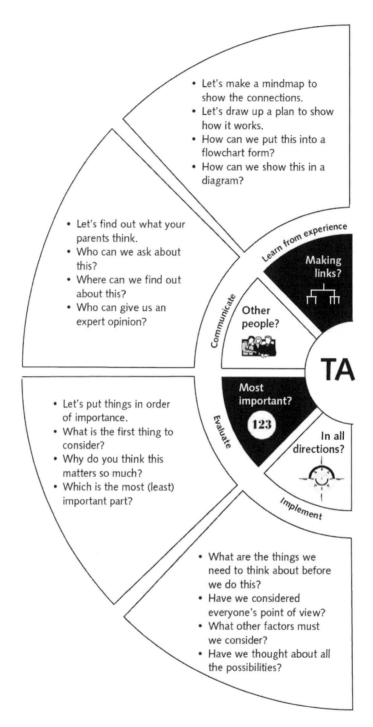

Figure 21 The Core Tools for Effective Thinking

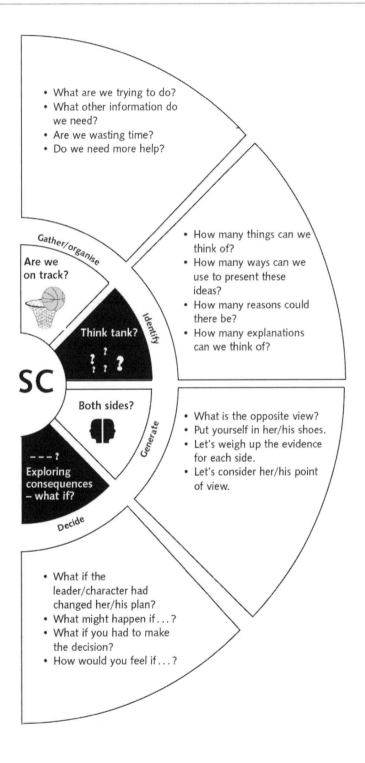

thinking' or metacognitive stage is vital if learners are to consolidate and transfer skills across the curriculum. An essential question for learners to ask is, 'How can we use what we have learned both in other subjects and in our everyday lives?' Users of the model find that it is a good idea to refer back to the original mind map constructed in the 'Gather and Organise' stage, and to extend it with new knowledge. Doing this enables the pupils to analyse the extension of their knowledge, and enables the brain to crystallise what has been learned.

The reader may well comment that the demand of any centralised curriculum does not allow time for a problem-solving, thinking skills approach to learning. And, indeed, a centralised curriculum is usually overcrowded with content that has to be covered in a specified time. However, teachers commonly complain that most learners do not remember what they have been taught, so work has to be repeated – and this, incidentally, is a source of great frustration to those pupils who do retain and remember. If learners were taught within a problem-solving, thinking skills paradigm, then they would consolidate and remember far more first time round, and the time that is spent on repetition would be considerably reduced. Also, a problem-solving, thinking skills approach develops learners' abilities to learn more efficiently as they acquire and automatise a wide range of learning tools. The TASC approach incorporates a wide range of tools for effective thinking that feed additional skills into the problem-solving wheel. While there are many tools for effective thinking, Figure 21 shows the essential core of these.

Assessment of the TASC problem-solving process

Teachers need to use their professional judgement to make qualitative assessment of children's progress, and this is not difficult with regard to the TASC process. Equally important is the need to help learners develop the skills for self-assessment and self-evaluation. Figure 21, above, gives a range of criteria that can be used in assessing pupils' work. These criteria need to be discussed and shared with the children when they are using the processes of the TASC wheel, so that they may gain an understanding of the evaluative process, and learn useful skills for self-monitoring and review.

Conclusion

The original purpose of our longitudinal action research was to develop a universal framework for developing problem-solving and thinking skills that can be applied in any multi-cultural, mixed-ability classroom. The underlying conceptual foundation is that all learners can improve their thinking skills, and hence their intelligence for living, and using effective tools for life-long learning. In a school culture where 'every child matters' and learning is personalised, not only are learners actively engaged in constructing knowledge, they are actively engaged in constructing themselves as independent, confident and successful learners.

We are living in a time of rapid change and renaissance with the proliferation of new knowledge, new values and new technologies. What skills will a child who is currently five years old need, in order to function effectively and with joy when that child is twenty-five years old? There will surely be technologies available and work to do that we do not yet know about, and have not even imagined. One thing we do know, however, is that hunger, poverty, global warming, religious hatreds and civil disagreements are problems that will need to be solved if we are to sustain life on earth. In order to help children grow into creatively productive adults, and to increase the likelihood of their inheriting and passing on a world rich with sustainable potential, we can start by developing and sharing tools that help them learn to think actively in social contexts. I recommend TASC to your consideration, as a model that can be used effectively to these ends.

Contact address: belle.wallace@btinternet.com

Future Perspectives

Suggested priorities for gifted education over the next decade

It has been frequently said that, as educators, our greatest challenge is to teach the children and young people in our care not *what* to learn but *how* to learn and *how* to think and solve problems. Current government initiatives in the UK say that the curriculum needs to be skills-based rather than content-driven, learning needs to be relevant to life and that pupils need to play a real part in decision-making and maintain ownership of their learning pathways. These are, indeed, very desirable learning outcomes. However, the greatest challenge still remains. In order to achieve this curriculum transformation, teachers will need to change their role from one of dispensing information to one of facilitating enquiry and problem-solving. This is the real challenge to educators if our young people are to build a different future for themselves.

Belle Wallace

36

Creating inclusive and inclusional understandings of gifts and talents through living educational theory research

Marie Huxtable

Bath and North East Somerset Local Authority's Children's Services, UK

You know the scenario: brisk introductions and the simple question, 'What do you do?' I am struck speechless. I can give you my job title or tell you at length the activities that make up my day, but that doesn't seem really to answer the question in any meaningful way; neither title nor diary communicates what it is that I am so passionately wanting to contribute through my paid employment coordinating and developing gifted and talented education in an English local authority. Let me pose a problem. Try to answer this question, without using your job title: 'What do you do?' For instance, if you work as a teacher you cannot just answer, 'I teach'; so what do you say?

Perhaps it is easier if people ask, 'What are you trying to do?' I can then explain how I am trying to contribute to the implementation of my employer's vision statement: 'We want all children and young people to do better in life than they ever thought they could. We will give children and young people the help that they need to do this' (Bath and North East Somerset School Improvement and Achievement Policy 2007, p. 4, downloaded from www.bathnes.gov.uk June 2007).

This at least carries some indication of the values that drive me. I could add that the purpose of my work is to enable children and young people to know themselves, growing as thoughtful, thought-full learners, developing aspirations and the confidence and competence to pursue them to the benefit of themselves and others. Moreover, I wish for them to be able to contribute to, and benefit from, their own learning and that of others. Does this give you a feel for what I value, or a clue as to the educational theories that attract me and that I seek to embody in my practice?

Now if I also tell you, in response to your question about what I do, that I run workshops for children, encourage educators to construct and make public accounts of their own 'living theory' research (Whitehead 1993; Whitehead and McNiff 2006), and talk with people, would you have more of a picture of what I do? If so, I think it is because you are beginning to have some insight into the values which form the bedrock of my practice and against which I test my productivity and success. To enable you to get beyond a list of activities, I need to communicate more clearly what my educational values are. Without that, there is no shared space for real conversation, the kind of discourse that can be useful in our quests to improve our educational experiences and contributions.

It is these values, which have drawn me to living theory research (Whitehead 1993), a methodology in which researchers' descriptions and explanations of their values, theories, learning, and educational development are recognised as shaping the meaning and significance of their practice. I like the way theory and practice are recognised in this approach to research as being dynamically interrelated and living, as evolving in response to interpersonal and intra-personal actions and reactions in a living world of which I am inextricably a part. I can see this research methodology being relevant to all, including children, as we seek to live fulfilling, worthwhile lives.

I do not believe that the efficacy of what I do can be determined by 'value added' indicators such as how many young people gain top examination grades 'early', or how many go to prestigious universities. Inevitably there are some givens but they are only a small part of the story. Educational practice is values-laden so I believe it is very important for me continu-ally to check whether in practice I am still being true to myself, to clarify and test myself against my evolving standards of judgements which arise through the process of researching my practice: 'These theories are living in the sense that they are our theories of practice, generated from within our living practices, our present best thinking that incorporates yester-day into today, and which holds tomorrow already within itself' (Whitehead and McNiff 2006, p. 3).

I am committed to improving the educational experience of all children and young people – with the intention of contributing to the opportunity for us all to live satisfying and productive lives in a humane world. This is what I understand to be inclusive education, alongside the more common understanding of all learners being included in the learning of the mainstream class-room. However, I draw a distinction between 'inclusive' and 'inclusional': 'inclusional' theory and practice is inclusive but not all theories that underpin inclusive practice are inclusional. When I use the word 'inclusional' I am working with an idea of Rayner's (2004), described by Whitehead and McNiff (2006, p. 40) as a dynamic awareness of space and boundaries that is connective, reflective and co-creative. Alder-Collins (2007) describes an inclusional pedagogy as creating a space for informed listening which acknowledges the differences of the other as a celebration of diversity and the boundaries that are permeable and dynamic. 'My space, as a space, needs to be both bounded and open, bounded in the sense that it can take on the charge/ energy/association of being associated with study as opposed to being unbounded as in social activities, and open in the sense that students can develop a feeling of ownership and of belonging in the space' (p. 293).

As with 'inclusive' and 'inclusional', so with other key terms: in my work I also make a distinction between 'gifts' and 'talents'. If 'gift' is used relationally in this way, 'talents' might be used to describe the skills, dispositions and understandings that are developed and deployed in an educational process that leads to creating and offering valued and valuable gifts.

I don't believe I can, or should, try to tell people how to live their lives. I do want to contribute to the possibility of their acquiring and creating insights, understandings, skills, attitudes and knowledge about themselves and the world, which will help them. I do not believe it is possible to predict what contributions a person will make to the world during their lifetime but I do believe that they can be influenced for better or worse. I am seeking ways of improving the contribution I make through the lens of gifted and talented education by developing inclusive (integrating all pupils in the mainstream) and inclusional (a dynamic relational awareness of space and boundaries where all can be held) living educational theory and practice, focusing on gifts and talents as dynamic, living educational concepts. Although the differences in the language used, such as 'gifts and talents', 'gifted and talented people', or 'gifted and talented education' might appear trivial, the consequences are not. How can one recognise the gift of 'inspirational light', an 'attentive ear', a 'creative space' when you seek to 'define and categorise' people or even singular skills or events?

And language reflects cultures. I did not realise how culturally determined a great deal of the education policy I am familiar with is until I read Joan Freeman's observations on cultural differences: 'The major cultural dichotomy affecting educational provision for the gifted and talented is between the largely Eastern perception – "all children have gifted potential" – and the largely Western one – "only some children have gifted potential" ' (Freeman 2002, p. 9). Freeman demonstrates that 'gifted and talented' is not a universal truth, and White (2006) offers further compelling insights as to the shared roots of western notions of intelligence and curriculum. I am encouraged by Freeman's reflection: 'The human spirit survives most attempts to be categorised, selected and treated in accord – for good or ill' (p. 188).

Whitehead (2007) distinguishes 'living logics' from the propositional and dialectical logics used in the majority of research accounts, as a logic that emerges in the course of the evolution of one's own form of life, with responses to the possibilities that life itself permits. He advocates the use of a living logic in the generation of explanations of educational influence in one's own learning, in the learning of others and in the learning of social formations. Through working with living logics and epistemologies I believe I can contribute to evolving, rather than revolving, educational theory and practice. I was just becoming acquainted with living theory when I wrote to Jack Whitehead:

> Why do I do what I do? I want children to grow as people who are comfortable in their own skin, knowing themselves, liking themselves, at peace with themselves, knowing what they want to work on, to improve, and to have the courage to change and accept their own stumbling and that of other people as part of the journey. I believe that an individual learns what they see themselves capable of learning and what is of value to them. The striving for excellence seems to carry with it a hope of personal fulfilment and when that personal ambition coincides with the needs of others, carries with it a hope for the progression of all of us and 'twice affirmation' for the individual.
>
> (Personal correspondence, October 2005)

What these words do not communicate is the inner pleasure, the feelings of camaraderie, laughter, love, the joy of being alive, the delight in recognition, affirmation and creativity – the very essence of educational values that I do not want to lose from sight. As Eisner (1997) and Whitehead (2005) have said, other forms of representation are needed which is why I now use video-narratives in my research which I believe communicates better the dynamic and relational qualities of the living values that give meaning and purpose to practice. I am not suggesting that life is or could be one big smile, but I choose to focus on the pleasure as I tend to get what I look for, and whilst I appreciate the inevitability of struggle, frustration, angst and toil, they serve a purpose which for me is in part communicated in these photographs (see Figure 22): the pleasure of living a fulfilling, worthwhile, socially connected life.

I ask you to look at the images and experience the pleasure that I feel in my work, and understand that I am trying to show you something of myself and not to comment on the individuals in the pictures. I have selected these images with considerable care as I believe they communicate something of my educational values. Look beyond what for me are delightful images. I did not take these photographs; it took a focused intention on the behalf of others to create, value and offer them. I believe they say as much about my educational values and standards of judgement in selecting them as of the educators who took them. These are brief

Figure 22 The pleasure in learning

moments, caught and transfixed as images which can be lost at the bottom of some dusty drawer, but the feelings and understandings communicated have become part of a living memory with the power to influence those you see and others, yourself included, who are beyond the lens. How might it transform practice if we sought data in the form of photographs or video to enable us to research and hold ourselves accountable?

Now, humour me and look again at the little girl, the top right-hand side photo in Figure 22. Try to see this child's gifts and talents not as abstractions, but rather happening in the crafting of the artefact, her intention, the connection between herself and the photographer, Belle Wallace (this volume). Try to see in the child's eyes, her smile, the way she is, and in the pleasure that can be felt flowing between the child and Belle at that 'in the moment' moment, co-created in the receptive, responsive flow within and between them. The pleasure in the flow of connection in the mutual valuing of the gifts created is something that can be felt also in the bottom right-hand side photo in Figure 1, taken by Joy Mounter. It is not just in the obvious connection being expressed in the foreground but within the educational context that Joy created and is part of in taking this photograph. She wrote:

> This picture for me holds so much emotion and joy. It describes the journey to emotional learning and celebration in my classroom. The moment when two children shared their joy of learning and success at solving a problem with each other spontaneously.
>
> (Mounter 2006)

I myself have no account to offer of how these children explain what they are feeling and the understandings they are evolving of themselves, their own values, and educational theories. This is their job, and theirs alone. Any temptation I might have to account for their own practice is,

295

I believe, an example of the way that 'good' practice is currently understood and colonised by a dominant paradigm: for me, it is only through working with educators and 'learners' to create their own living educational theory research accounts of their learning that we can begin really to understand how we are improving gifted and talented educational practice.

Dweck (1999) gives a very plausible theoretical explanation for the veracity of the well known saying, commonly attributed to Henry Ford, 'If you think you can or you think you can't, you are probably right', or in the words of one of Joy Mounter's pupils, 'I have learnt to never underestimate my skills of craft and learning, because nothing is impossible to a child with imagination' (learning evaluation by R., aged 10). Learning is in the province of the learner, not in the bestower of extrinsic rewards (product praise, grades scores, trophies).

While I have not budged from a lifetime's assertion that most people can accomplish most things, given sufficient time and a supportive social and educational context, I do recognise that the realisation of an ambition requires more than just a dream. Saying, 'This is how I want things to be' does not make them so. What is needed to move from dreaming to the possibility of a living reality? I believe the question is one that has many possible answers; the 'right ones' are those that carry hope for a person to live a satisfying and productive life contributing to a humane society. I believe that I neither have the right nor the ability to answer the question for another, but as an educator I am continually asking, 'How do I contribute to the possibility of a person creating "right answers" for themselves'? a question which leads to my understanding my responsibilities in this way:

> My challenge is how to enable a youngster to build an understanding of what they want to commit time and effort to that will enable them to live satisfying and productive lives without imposing my own values and needs. This moves me from an impositional peda-gogy to an inclusional one where there is a co-creative space between people; where there is a mutuality as each contributes and benefits from their own and the other's learning, skills, understandings, values.
>
> (Huxtable 2006, p. 14)

Referring to a mutual colleague, Moria Laidlaw expressed something similar in an email to me in April 2007:

> Maturity, I believe, is taking responsibility for one's self in the world. He does that all the time. He doesn't project. He doesn't take on stuff he can't follow through. He speaks the truth, whether it's easy or not. He commits to things he's chosen to commit to. He reasons rather than emotes. And so on. He knows what he is and what he's doing and he takes account of the effects he has in the world and on others as well as on himself.

I would feel I had contributed something really useful if there were an explicit appreciation that one of the most important gifts educators can create, value, and offer their students is an educational space in which to mature. It is not a passive space. Wine maturing is not liquid doing nothing in vast vats in dark cellars for decades. There are active transformational processes at work. How can one therefore recognise this 'creative space', the gift of 'inspirational light' and an 'attentive ear', when one seeks to define and categorise people, or even singular skills or events? In thinking about this question, consider the following excerpt from Barry Hymer's reflection (2002, pp. 1–2) on a moment in a classroom:

> By the time I got around to Robert's desk, he'd managed an illegible sentence, in his

typically tight, misspelled and dysfluent script. I asked him what he'd written and there was a long pause as he tried to make sense of his work. Then he replied, in a voice so slow and soft I hardly heard him, 'Even the winter leaves have their own secret colours'.

That was it. One line. But what a line! It was mid-summer, and Robert had found and studied a solitary, decaying winter-leaf. And in his observations and his slow reflections Robert captured an image that contained a most deliberate metaphor. He was saying, I'm convinced, 'Mr Hymer, notice me. I know I've not got a great deal going for me in school, but just sometimes, in some situations, I can do things that will amaze you'.

How would you understand the shared gift creation involved? I understand them as dynamic, living, and relational, each gift discernible but not separable; a relational dynamic, understood in the crafting over time, in the moment of the offering, and in the valuing through use in the tomorrow. Shekerjian (1991, p. 1) stated 'Everyone has an aptitude for something. The trick is to recognise it, to honour it, to work with it'. So, we can see in this exchange a recognition of value toward the other from both teacher and student. This communicates to me an active and creative appreciation of the unique qualities of self, and suggests that, by devoting effort, a person can create that which is valued and valuable. I contend that aptitude will go nowhere without passionate energy, the sources of which are unique to the individual: interest, curiosity, dedication to an ideal, family, love, public applause, a thirst for knowledge creation. Without focused energy nothing happens.

I am trying to describe a world that provides an energised space for maturation, one which opens minds to possibilities of growing as the person one chooses to be. In my work I am particularly focused on children and young people but I recognise it is not possible to contribute to a world of educational quality in which they can grow affectively, cognitively and physically unless the adults also value themselves and are growing. So a question that I must be mindful of is, 'How do I recognise, generate, develop, and share my own gifts and talents?' Similarly, you might ask yourself how, as an adult engaged in gifted and talented education, you are asking and researching such questions.

A dominant educational practice is rooted in fixed logics and epistemologies where a hypothesis is offered in terms of an answer, and the only acceptable test is whether the answer is 'proved' at the end of the period to be right or not right. A shift in thinking and methodologies is needed to enable educators and students to question the 'rightness' of a question, and to evolve their own diverse answers within which they can experiment, create, value, and offer various gifts, thereby coming to know the person they want to be and creating the future they want to live. How much time and effort is devoted by educators to listening to their pupils, helping them formulate their own questions that are interesting to them, helping them reflect on what really matters to them, their values, and self theories, helping them to recognise their aptitudes and to create gifts, articulating the judgements they are making, and engaging them in profound learning?

In living educational theory, research questions and answers do not stand apart but are recognised to be in dynamic, organic, receptive-responsive relationships, and it is the individual's values, theories, and practice, as well as their activities, which are researched. The Thinking Actively in a Social Context (TASC) wheel (Wallace et al. 2004) is an excellent vehicle with which to include gifted children in research. Pupils and teacher co-create a multi dimensional explanation of their own learning with TASC (see Wallace this volume).

Children and educators are continually developing their talents for gift creation. I have found these gifts valuable as they contribute to my thinking, my practice, and my life. According to my values, whether or not any of the people I seek to help, become noticeable on national or world stages now, or some time in the future, is not the final validation of what I am advocating. What ultimately matters to me, and is the reason why I have sought to share these stories and images, is whether the people involved, teachers and students (learners, all) continue to contribute the gifts they create, value, and offer to the evolution of a world worth living in.

(The views expressed here not necessarily those of Bath and North East Somerset Council.)

Contact address: marie_huxtable@yahoo.co.uk

Future Perspectives

Suggested priorities for gifted education over the next decade

To progress, 'gifted education' has to look to a different logic and values base than has dominated our education system in England since Galton and the beginning of mandatory schooling in the nineteenth century. Teachers are still torn between having to respond to the traditional demands of the establishment to define and categorise children, and their desires as educators to improve educational practice, which has a democratising and emancipating intent. In this chapter I have offered one possibility for evolving inclusive and inclusional gifted and talented educational theory and practice. How fast we will progress I think will depend on the willingness of educators to face themselves and others; their courage to recognise their own embodied values and theories that are communicated through their practice, their energy and willingness to research themselves and contribute to their own learning and that of us all, and their focused intention to influence national policy.

Marie Huxtable

37

Beyond compare? Thoughts towards an inclusional, fluid and non-normative understanding of giftedness

Barry J. Hymer

Centre for Learning and Teaching, Newcastle University, UK

This chapter is written from the stance of a practitioner researching his own practice as an educator in the field of giftedness. I describe how a model of gift-creation has emerged through critical responsiveness to my own practice, and I offer a parallel description of the conditions under which gifts can be grown – rather than identified. These descriptions underlie an argument for shifting professional focus from dominant twentieth-century western rationalist approaches to the field of gifted and talented education, with their deterministic, dualistic, individualistic, pragmatic, tool-for-result (cf. Vygotsky 1978), and knowing-centred associations, towards a concept of giftedness which is co-constructed (not identified) in a social, relationally respectful, activity-oriented, dialectical, tool-and-result (Newman and Holzman 1993; Vygotsky 1978) manner and context.

At the heart of my own research journey has been a growing dissatisfaction with elements of my practice as a consultant and trainer in gifted and talented education within the United Kingdom, and profound concerns with the implications for learners of dominant 'mystery' models of gifted education (Matthews and Foster 2006). My sense of being a 'living contradiction' (Whitehead 1989, 1993) has been nurtured by this dominant discourse at three levels: (a) at the level of content, a perceived emphasis on traditional test-and-place mantras and an implied belief in the existence of the 'naturally gifted' student, in the face of overwhelming evidence of the fluidity of such abstract and socially-constructed concepts as 'intelligence' or 'ability' (e.g. Adey et al. 2007; Dweck 1999, 2006; Hart et al. 2004; Sternberg 2004a, 2004c; Sternberg and Davidson 1986); (b) at the level of process, my adoption of a declarative, superficially authoritative 'expert-speak' delivery style at conferences, workshops, and training days, despite a personal commitment to the power and value of dialogical, co-constructivist practices; and (c) at the level of product, an implied faith in the viability of transferred (i.e. efficiently transmitted) 'objective' knowledge, understandings and practices, despite a recognition of the salience of contextual factors in knowledge-creation and a rejection of the 'banking' concept of education (Freire 1993).

As a psychologist and educator trained within the standard social sciences tradition of the neutral, disinterested outsider, I had been conditioned to believe that as a teacher I could ensure 'successful learning' principally through focusing my energies on the quality and rigour of my arguments and evidence-base (an empirical foundation), and the technical 'efficiency' and persuasiveness of my presentations (the dark arts and tools of sophistry). However, the evaluative feedback I have received in the course of recent research (Hymer 2007) has suggested, on the contrary, that beyond certain baseline presentational skills (e.g. of timekeeping, voice-projection, pace, use of audio-visual aids, content-audience match, etc.) only a relatively small part of the significant meanings (deep learning) gained by participants can be attributable to the course content ('knowledge') and presentational technique. What has struck me over the course of my research is how seldom people comment on being convinced, impressed, or transformed by the 'research evidence' underpinning an approach – even though 'evidence-base' (and I mean by this empirical evidence from within the hypothetico-deductive method) was, and to some extent remains, one of my most frequently invoked claims to credibility and legitimacy. What they do (and frequently) comment on is the personal knowledge, by which I include insights, principles, values, beliefs, practices, etc. that they have constructed through dialogue with me and with others. This is for me where learning becomes most real, meaning-ful, and 'inclusional' as described by Rayner (2004, p. 51): '. . . the idea that *space*, far from passively surrounding and isolating discrete, massy objects, is a vital, dynamic inclusion within, around and permeating natural form across all scales of organisation, allowing diverse possi-bilities for movement and communication'. It is where knowledge transcends any single 'knower,' and in the spirit of the African tribal concept of *ubuntu*, the dialectical unity of knowledge reflects the strength of its community of learners – being simultaneously distributed and personalised, dispersed but not attenuated, directed but also reciprocal:

A culture in its very nature is a set of values, skills and ways of life that no one member of the society masters. Knowledge in this sense is like a rope, each strand of which extends no more than a few inches along its length, all being intertwined to give a solidity to the whole. The conduct of our educational system has been curiously blind to this interdependent nature of knowledge. We have 'teachers' and 'pupils', 'experts' and 'laymen'. But the community of learning is somehow overlooked. (Bruner 1966, p. 126)

I sent this passage to my friend and colleague Marie Huxtable, inviting her thoughts, and received this response (e-mail dated 30 July 2006):

I like the analogy. . . . When I first started struggling with high ability ideas I did a talk where I used the image of a plait – with means, motives and opportunities as the strands. I think a 'challah' is better – that is a plaited bread – each strand is still distinct but impossible to separate from the other – each is the whole so to speak – and bread with its link with life I quite like as well.

Marie's image resonated with me. Perhaps significant in her development of the analogy from rope to challah is the possible further progression of the metaphor: the implication that the indivisibility of the breaded strands is most apparent when these are baked. Is the presentational or workshop content nothing but the raw materials, the doughy mix? Its planning and 'delivery' the plaiting? But does dialogue do the baking? Certainly the dialogical methods of Socrates, Wittgenstein, Bakhtin, Lipman, Vygotsky and others see little merit in the instrumental con-structions rejected by Bruner (above), preferring the dialectical unity of reciprocal meanings, co-constructed. Where once I believed I had a choice to make between (a) a rationalist, deductive route to the teaching and learning dialectic, and (b) a romantic, purely inductive alternative – or maybe (c) a hybrid of the two – I now acknowledge the generative-transformational power of the relational, social element. It is an avenue well-advanced by Friedman:

The true teacher is not the one who pours information into the student's head as through a funnel – the old-fashioned 'disciplined' approach – or the one who regards all potentialities as already existing within the student and needing only to be pumped up – the newer 'progressive' approach. It is the one who fosters genuine mutual contact and mutual trust, who experiences the other side of the relationship, and who helps his pupils realise, through the selection of the effective world, what it can mean to be a man.

(Cited in Buber 2002, pp. xvii–xviii)

I have over time and in response to feedback become emboldened by the realisation that on occasion to replace the propositional, declarative, expert-speak mode of presentational style with one more dialogical, fallible, and open to correction and provocation has carried fewer dangers than I'd feared, and provided more space for the living of such values as individual intellectual respect and the conditions conducive to generative-transformational giftedness. I use the term 'generative-transformational giftedness' tentatively because I see it as embodying not so much a reified 'thing,' as we have objectified 'intelligence' or 'giftedness' in the twentieth century, but rather a limpid process-state, fluid and changeable, and simultaneously both a value in and of itself, and a relational outcome. What I describe as generative-transformational giftedness, and the conditions under which I suggest it arises, is proposed as a theoretical scientific model – not a literal picture of 'reality' – but a personally meaningful, partial and provisional way of imagining the unobservable.

The model is influenced by the Deweyan (and proto-Vygotskyan) emphasis on the significance of the future in the present: 'Everything we see in children is transitional, promises and signs of the future . . . not to be treated as achievements, cut off and fixed; they are prophetic, signs of an accumulating power and interest' (Dewey 1902, p. 14). This in turn anticipates the malleable or incremental self-theory of intelligence described by Dweck: 'For (people holding an incremental view of intelligence) intelligence is not a fixed trait that they simply possess, but something they can cultivate through learning' (1999, p. 3).

There is also a clear connection to the Marxian-Vygotskyan concept of development as continuously emergent, relational human activity – with the search for method as being necessarily 'tool-and-result' (Vygotsky 1978) rather than 'tool-for-result'. Neither the tool (e.g. my presentation of 'good knowledge') nor the result (e.g. the insights and learning demonstrated by the audience-responders) is, except in a shallow transmission-of-knowledge sense, independently meaningful – they exist synergistically, reciprocally, germinating together, '. . . influencing each other in complex and changing ways as the totality tool-and-result develops' (Holzman 1997, p. 58). This is for me most in evidence not in the full flow of presentation-mode, but in the gaps, the hiatuses, the moments of reflection, challenge, and dialogue with the community, where I can jettison the declarative 'expert-speak' power-over position in favour of something much more social, relational, activity-oriented, and dialectical in its nature. In the words of one participant at a whole-school training event (23 September 2005): 'I have learned a lot in this session – but I don't think he 'taught' me anything. How has this happened?'

It is at these moments that I can inform and develop my own grasp of the subject matter, refining, cultivating, pruning – growing it, and an 'audience' can do the same. In short, I have come to see myself as performing when delivering a well-rehearsed 'script' (past learning), but as performing above myself when in true dialogue with others (new, two-way learning). In the Vygotskyan sense, this performatory function is associated with learning, not ego, and betrays no sense of inauthenticity or deception. We wear a mask without inhibition or guilt – to 'act up,' to play the 'role' of learner, and through this play to habituate to and advance within the learning role. In the words of Keleman (2001, p. 95), 'In the facades we put on for others we demonstrate our potential'.

The gaps are significant. It may be no accident that teachers who hold as inviolable their pupils' capacities to think for themselves and to remember that 'a body of knowledge is given life and direction by the conjectures and dilemmas that brought it into being and sustained its growth' (Bruner 1966, p. 159) often eschew the hegemonic concept of teaching to ability (and for which mixed-ability classes are by definition no antidote) in favour of inclusivity of opportunity, open-ended learning outcomes, creativity, challenge and personalised enquiry (Hannaford 2005; Hart et al. 2004; Jeffrey and Woods 2003; Mant et al. 2007; Wilson et al. 2005). A vivid example from Hart et al.'s seminal study is Anne, a Year 1 teacher who talks about children's 'spontaneous, unpredictable acts of meaning-making' (p. 63) happening in the gaps:

> There has to be a structure, with gaps in. . . . Is this an adequate or a satisfactory definition of a learning without limits school or classroom? Only if there is an accompanying account of what might fill those gaps. She is abundantly clear: with the children's acts of meaning-making, problem-solving, invention, imagination and discovery. Anne and her colleagues, the constraints of [official requirements] and so on, may set the structures, but in the gaps, the children take the lead.
>
> (pp. 64–65)

It is in these social, relational, activity-oriented, generative-transformational, dialectical moments that I personally have sensed a vitality and engagement amongst the communities with which I work, moments where they and I can discard our received roles as teacher/ student, expert/novice, actor/spectator, full jug/empty glass, and take on a different stance, showing the value of individual intellectual respect for our uniquely constructed meanings, and permitting the creation of generative-transformational giftedness – embracing those fluid, inclusional conditions which nurture thinking with clarity, insight, and creativity, to produce new meanings and create new products and achievements.

As part of my research into my own practice as an educator in the field of giftedness, I have invited participants to comment directly on their experiences of me, and the 'degree of fit' they perceive between my message and my practice. I have also invited them to reflect more intro-spectively on their own values, practices, and educational intentions and ambitions. In review-ing post-event evaluation returns, I am encouraged if individuals feel they have had the opportunity to be part of the experience, not just the recipient of it, to have been challenged to think critically for themselves – even (especially?) to the point of rejecting aspects of my own 'truth,' to ask their own questions not just to respond to mine, and to sense a congruence between my implicit values and my explicit practice: 'Our values need to be seen in lived relation with others. For them to make sense, the values themselves need to be understood as real-life practices, not as abstract concepts' (Whitehead and McNiff 2006, p. 58).

I am encouraged, because it is at these times that I see generative-transformational giftedness in gestation and emergence, evidence of my living my core personal and educational values and realising the relationally dynamic epistemological standards of judgement which are both consisting in and attendant on these values. I have come to use the notion of generative-transformational giftedness in pursuit of conceptual clarity, yet recognising its complexity and its association with established meanings. This brings with it both possibilities and hazards. As intimated earlier, what I mean by invoking the term 'giftedness' is giftedness in a non-psychometric sense of 'gifted disposition' – a tendency to think with clarity, creativity, original-ity, and insight in a certain way under certain conditions. This draws on but also extends the term as used by Perkins et al. (1993), who define a disposition as a 'tendency to think or behave in certain ways under certain conditions'. What are the 'ways' and the 'conditions' specifically in relation to generative-transformational giftedness? I suggest that these are categorisable under the following five emergent criteria for gift-creation, captured in the acronym, G-T CReATe[1]:

Generative-Transformational

Poor is the pupil who does not surpass his master.

(Leonardo da Vinci, 1452–1519)

This super-ordinate term is borrowed from McNiff et al., who note, 'This idea of generative power acts as the basic unit of energy whereby each thing may transform itself endlessly in the process of its own realisation of potential' (McNiff et al. 1992, p. 35). It draws also on the notion of praxis as used by Freire (1993), as the generative combination of reflection and action which exist '. . . in such radical interaction that if one is sacrificed – even in part – the other immediately suffers. There is no true word that is not at the same time a praxis. Thus, to speak a true word is to transform the world' (p. 68).

Within the field of giftedness, the generative-transformational element is realised when the conditions are created for the learner's transcendence from the particular known to the indeterminate unknown, and the resultant creation of a new insight, meaning, service or product which fell outside the predicted range of expectations for that learning episode. There is a clear implication here, that the generative transformational (G-T) criterion is unlikely to be met in the traditional objectivist classroom, with its linear progression from assumed ignorance to received enlightenment, and in which all educational tools are bent to the will of (existing) knowledge transmission. Rather, the generative transformational criterion is more easily met in the co-constructivist classroom of active, collaborative, learner-driven, and metacognitive learning (Watkins et al. 2007), where existing meanings can be worked on, challenged and transformed, generating new connections and new meanings.

Contradictory/Dialectical

Without contraries, there is no progression.

(William Blake, 1757–1827)

We learn most from the moments that jar, not from the moments that gel. In the words of a teacher at a recent (18 October 2007) school training day, 'I learn best when I'm intellectually uncomfortable – that's what really stretches me'. The contradictory-dialectical (C) criterion for gift-creation comprises the catalytic reaction that comes about in response to the juxtaposition of ideas, thoughts, beliefs and experiences, which have an analytical tension at the surfaces, but synthetic power in the depths. In this instance, I argue that the meanings generated by the speakers consist of a dialectical unity, not a relationship of cause or tool (e.g. the teacher's presentation of content to her class) and effect or result (e.g. a consequent 'comprehension'

---

[1] This model, and its theoretical underpinnings, are described in more detail than can be accommodated in this chapter in a forthcoming book, *Gifts, Talents and Education: A Living Theory Approach* by M. Huxtable, B. Hymer, and J. Whitehead (London: John Wiley, in press)

transmitted to the listeners), but rather a Platonic understanding that permits multiple, contradictory ways of thinking, and a simultaneous holding of the one and the many. '[T]he dialectical unity rather than metaphysical duality was central [to the totality of Vygotsky's enterprise]' (Holzman 1997, p. 59). Whilst this might ultimately resolve itself as a preference for one thought or solution over another, this is not required, and it may not even be desirable: 'The beginning of wisdom is the discovery that there exist contradictions of permanent tension with which it is necessary to live and that it is above all not necessary to seek to resolve' (Gorz, quoted in Ball 1998, p. 81).

Relational

> In all things we learn only from those we love.
>
> (Johann Wolfgang von Goethe, 1749–1832)

The relational (R) criterion is characterised by a power-with or power-through rather than power-over relationship between teacher and student – a relationship which is respectful of the different-ness of the other, yet also secure in one's own integrity and open to the creation of something new – 'All real living is meeting' (Buber 2002, p. xiv).

The relational element is germane to the field of gifted education, as it is to all true education, and it is this element that prevents the field from being reduced to arguments over the merits or otherwise of such 'technical fixes' as acceleration, or to a reliance on the direct instruction of the keyboard age. We respond best to those who convey the immeasurable virtues of empathy, trust, congruence, and recognition, and this has implications for us as educators: we see the power of the relational especially when this is harnessed with the (intellectually) activity-oriented dimension (below), as in this mother's reflections on the re-creation of her son's 'giftedness':

> This academic year our very bright six-year-old son is absolutely loving school. Why, after two years of absolute trauma, boredom and deliberate misbehaviour, has our son become a motivated, excited, learning-driven child? I put it down to one thing: the teacher. She likes him, she knows how to challenge him mentally, and to make work fun. She pitches work at the right level for him, and is firm when she needs to be. So here's three very heartfelt cheers to all those teachers out there, who are challenged by these kids, rather than see them as a problem.
>
> (Mother on a high-ability weblist posting, December 2004)

The response to this posting, from a Dutch educator, captures beautifully the respectful, relational 'we' in this gift-creating dynamic:

> The enrichment tasks teachers write can be very challenging and inspiring, but if they fail to motivate, give just and fair feedback, approach the kids as seriously as they do their friends and colleagues, then the whole project very often fails.
>
> (Heleen Wientjes, Utrecht University, high-ability weblist posting,
> December 2004)

Wientjes' comment echoes Hargreaves' study of interpersonal relations in education (1975), as much as it does Freire's belief that '[The teacher's] efforts must be imbued with a profound trust in people and their creative power. To achieve this, they must be partners of the students in their relations with them' (Freire 1993, p. 56).

Activity-oriented

I'm a playing boy, not a working boy.

(Tom, aged 5)

The activity-oriented (A) criterion is evident in the context of active participation in a learning experience: that intellectual activity generated in a learning episode that leads to the creation of meaning in the minds of the community. It arises from dialogical activity that is generated between the various members of the learning community, and is a function of the quality of that external and internal (reflective and metacognitive) dialogue. Bruner (1966, p. 117) speaks of 'the energising lure of uncertainty made personal by one's effort to control it', and proceeds to argue that, 'To channel curiosity into more powerful intellectual pursuits requires precisely that there be (a) transition from the passive, receptive, episodic form of curiosity to the sustained and active form' (p. 117).

Watkins et al. (2007) regard active learning as being one of five core classroom processes for promoting effective learning, and understand the term to go way beyond 'learning by doing', to involve elements which are variously behavioural (the use and creation of materials), cognitive (the construction of new meaning), and social (the engagement with others as collaborators and resources). It is this integrated sense of 'active' that is embraced in the G–T CReATe model, a Vygotskyan method which '. . . is activity-based rather than knowledge/epistemology-based . . . Knowledge is not separate from the activity of practising method; it is not "out there" waiting to be discovered through the use of an already-made tool' (Holzman 1997, p. 52).

Temporal/Social

Whilst a child can think *for* herself, she can't think *by* herself.

(Lawrence Stenhouse, 1926–1982)

Traditional western conceptualisations of giftedness have tended to emphasise the majesty of the individual mind over the humility of the social mind – what might be termed the 'exo-mind'. The wisdom of this emphasis can be questioned in the light of what we know about how, in reality, knowledge tends to be generated – rarely through some lonely spasm of intellectual brilliance, but more frequently through a hard and social passage in which know-ledge is shared, challenged, modified, and built upon. John Waller (2004) concludes his careful exploration of scientific breakthroughs with the reflection that no achievement in science is exclusively the product of one brain. And the eminent twenty-first-century scientist, Gill Samuels (inventor of Viagra, amongst other pharmaceutical breakthroughs) observed in an interview that she '. . . was one of a team of a thousand, it took us thirteen years, and we didn't set out to invent Viagra' (*The Independent*, 9 June 2005) – at a stroke capturing the essence of the Temporal-Social (Te) element in the G–T CReATe model: the creative harnessing of the exo-brain, dogged persistence over time, and the flexibility to connect unexpected findings with alternative objectives. Within this model, the social element is social in the Vygotskyan sense that 'what I can do with your help today, I can do alone tomorrow', in Rayner's (2004) sense of inclusionality, or in the African cultural notion introduced earlier, of *ubuntu* – 'I am who I am because of who we all are'.

The Temporal-Social element of this model leads one to expect divergences from linear-sequential expectations in gifted performance (e.g. David Jesson's research at York University (Jesson 2005), which found that only 28 per cent of pupils identified as gifted or talented in primary school went on to achieve their expected three A-grades at A-level, whilst many teenagers not previously highlighted as very able did achieve top grades), whereas traditional models are puzzled by such divergences, or seek to 'fix' these through ever more rigorous tracking and monitoring procedures, and ever-younger identification – within the United Kingdom, as early as four.

Having discussed the components of the G-T CReATe model, it is now possible to offer a compare-and-contrast representation of the values underpinning the traditional conceptualisation of giftedness, and those of the proposed model, as well as a brief summary of their contrasting emphases within the school and classroom:

Table 9   Two models of giftedness, reflecting contrasting ontological and epistemological stances

Domain	Traditional Conceptualisation	G-T CReATe Conceptualisation
Gift-identification?	Yes; test & classify; the earlier the better	No; focus instead on gift-creation; happens at moments of coincidence between opportunity and need
Educators' emphasis	'objective' data from past performances	creating opportunities for present and future learning
G&T cohorts and labels?	Yes; distinct teaching and learning provision (often acceleration) on the grounds of ability and identification	No; inclusive initial provision, but extension opportunities on the grounds of interest and application
Nature or nurture?	Emphasis on individual intelligence and the provenance of nature, genetics, background influences	Emphasis on the impact of social factors in learning, on motivation and distributed intelligence
Teacher's role?	Teacher as neutral, impartial arbiter, separate from and independent of individual students	Teacher as involved co-participant in the construction of gifts and talents
Co-ordinator's role?	Co-ordinator role: administrator of systems for identification, tracking and monitoring	Co-ordinator role: peer-coach and co-learner, alert to new learning and teaching methodologies for dissemination and championing
Expectations for performance over time?	Assumptions of linear progression in performance based on fixed ability	Assumptions of variable performance based on (e.g.) temporal-social, relational factors
Integration of affective factors?	Cognitive-emotional duality	Cognitive-emotional dialectical unity
Self theory? (Dweck 1999)	Feeds fixed, entity-approach to intelligence and performance-led orientation	Feeds growth-focused, incremental-approach to intelligence and learning or mastery-led orientation

Evidence of accountability?	Accountability through evidence of student performances and tracking and monitoring systems	Accountability through evidence of student learning, including 'soft data' (e.g. commitment, interest)

It remains to be seen whether, in the twenty-first century, educational policy will remain committed to the identification of the individually gifted child, and consequent provision for her needs, or instead will embrace the practical implications of 'mastery' models (Matthews and Foster 2006) such as G-T CReATe, which eschew gifted identification for a clearer focus on gift-creation. While the latter ambition is the more demanding, it is my belief that it is educationally more authentic.

Contact address: Stillthinkinguk@aol.com

Future Perspectives

Suggested priorities for gifted education over the next decade

The challenges of the twenty-first century are in many ways very different from those of yesteryear: in an age of automation and near-instantaneous cross-global communication very few individuals will have jobs for life; skills of knowledge-access and knowledge-generation trump skills of data-accumulation and knowledge-retention; creativity and design skills (calling upon reflection and meta-cognition) reign over easily-outsource-able skills of application, implementation and production (processing speed efficiencies); and, in an age of ecological imbalances and uneven distribution of resources, interpersonal and intrapersonal skills, values and mindsets take precedence over skills honed for the efficient exploitation of diminishing natural resources. Implications for the field of giftedness arise implicitly from all of these shifts: we need to embrace the dynamic processes of learning rather than its crystallised products and see an obsession with identification and labelling strategies for the few (visible performance), give way to a serious consideration of the factors underpinning gift-creation (leading to long-term learning) for all.   Barry J. Hymer

38

Self-theories and lessons for giftedness: a reflective conversation

Carol S. Dweck
Stanford University, US

Editorial Note: This chapter takes the form of an interview with Carol Dweck about her and her graduate and post-doctoral students' current work, especially as this relates to the field of giftedness. Conducted by Susan Veronikas and Michael F. Shaughnessy, the interview was first published in *Gifted Education International 19*, 2004, 27–33 and has been updated by Carol Dweck for this volume.

Could you give us a general overview of your current work?

My graduate and post-doctoral students and I are working on a number of projects that I am very excited about. We are exploring different ways in which thinking of intelligence as a fixed trait (a 'fixed' mindset) versus a malleable quality that can be developed (a 'growth mindset') influences students' motivation and achievement. In past work we have found that holding a fixed mindset makes students overly concerned with how smart they are, and leads them to avoid challenges, devalue effort and under-perform in the face of difficulty. In contrast, holding a growth mindset makes students more concerned with learning (rather than looking smart) and leads them to seek challenges, value effort, and shine in the face of difficulty. Here are examples of a few projects.

Mindset intervention

We (myself, Lisa Blackwell and Kali Trzesniewski) have completed a very successful intervention in which we taught at-risk junior high school students (aged 12–14) to think of their intelligence in a more growth-oriented way. By showing them that the brain forms new connections every time they learn, we gave them the message that intellectual skills can be expanded, and we explained how to apply this to their schoolwork. These students (compared to a control group that only received training in study skills) showed significant increases in their motivation, which had been poor, and their grades, which had been declining. The results of this intervention were published in the journal *Child Development* in February, 2007.

Buoyed by these results, we have now designed a series of colourful and engaging computer modules that deliver the intervention and, with a large sample of students, we are testing the impact on students' motivation and achievement. This intervention (called 'Brainology') teaches students about the brain, how it works, how it changes with learning, and what students can do to make it work better and grow smarter over time. The first group of students who went through the programme unanimously reported that they had changed their ideas about how learning occurs and how they now go about it. Here are some samples of their responses:

My favorite thing from Brainology is the neurons part where when u learn something there are connections and they keep growing. I always picture them when I'm in school.

I did change my mind about how the brain works . . . I will try harder because I know that the more you try the more your brain works.

The Brainology programme kind of made me change the way i work and study and practice for school work now that i know how my brain works and what happens when i learn.

Thank you for making us study more and helping us build up our brain! I actually picture my neurons growing bigger as they make more connections.

I imagine the neurons making connections in my brain and I feel like I am learning something.

I will try harder because I know that the more you try the more your brain works.

Women and mathematics

We (myself, Catherine Good and Aneeta Rattan) carried out a large study at Columbia University concerning talented females and mathematics, and exploring the effects of believing that mathematical intelligence is a fixed trait versus an ability that can be developed. We wondered whether females who believe their mathematical ability is a fixed trait are more susceptible to 'stereotype threat' – that is, whether their mathematical motivation and perform- ance would suffer in environments that evoke the stereotype of low mathematical ability on the part of females.

We have several fascinating findings. First, females in calculus who held a fixed view of mathematical ability showed a sharp decline in their confidence and sense of belonging in mathematics over the course of the semester, and this decline was especially pronounced for those who encountered stereotyping in their mathematics class. This decreased sense of belong- ing was accompanied by a drop in their grades and by a drop in their intention to pursue mathematics in the future. These were talented females; yet their belief in fixed mathematical ability made them vulnerable.

Women who had a growth mindset were not adversely affected by encountering stereotypes. They were able to maintain their confidence, sense of belonging, and grades. The stereotype tells women: 'We think your group has less mathematical ability'. A growth mindset tells women that even if this has been true, their group can acquire those skills. It would be wonder- ful to eradicate the stereotype. Until then, a growth mindset seems to allow women to cope with it better.

Second, we have shown in a simulation experiment with college students that giving 'teachers' a fixed versus growth mindset about mathematical ability creates striking differences in how much they use stereotypes in dealing with their male and female students. Giving them a growth mindset essentially wiped out stereotyping on many measures, whereas giving them a fixed mindset led them to show an alarming degree of differential treatment of males and females.

Third, in studies with middle school students (aged 11–14), we taught a mathematics lesson in a fixed-mindset way (referring to great mathematicians as born geniuses) or a growth-mindset way (referring to people who were passionate about mathematics and became great mathematicians). Females taught in the fixed way were later susceptible to stereotype threat, falling into poor performance when they worked on difficult problems. Those taught in the growth-mindset way were not. They were able to withstand challenges and maintain their motivation and performance. Thus these mindsets about mathematical ability seem to have important implications for how susceptible students *and* teachers are to stereotypes.

Attention and learning

We (myself, Jennifer Mangels, Catherine Good, Brady Butterfield and Justin Lamb) are also looking at psycho-physiological measures (brain waves) to measure students' attention and to see how students with the different mindsets go about learning. We have found that students with the fixed mindset are so concerned about how smart they are that they direct all their attention on a learning task to whether their answers are right or wrong, and pay little attention to information that will help them learn. In contrast, those with the growth mindset pay attention to both: information about how they have done and about how they can improve. As a result, they do better on a re-test of the answers they got wrong. This means that many very bright students with a fixed mindset may go around their worlds with little desire to learn, robbing themselves of countless opportunities to expand their skills and knowledge. This work was published in the journal *Social Cognitive Affective Neuroscience*, October 2006.

The roots of mindsets

We (myself, Melissa Kamins and Allison Master) are examining the roots of mindsets in early childhood and looking at how they contribute to a hardy versus vulnerable sense of self-worth. We are finding that an early fixed mindset is associated with a strong sense of 'contingent self-worth', the feeling that bad behaviour or bad outcomes mean you are a globally bad, unworthy person. We are also looking at parental practices that foster the different mindsets in children.

Other projects include (a) how mild depression impairs versus motivates students with different mindsets; (b) how students' mindsets affect the accuracy of their self-knowledge about their abilities; (c) how students with different mindsets repair their self-esteem; and (d) how educational environments communicate mindsets to students.

How do you teach students to value hard work, learning and challenges?

In the framework of fixed intelligence, hard work and challenges are bad things. When students believe in fixed intelligence, their primary goal is to look and feel smart. Since it is a framework in which 'you have it or you don't', they want to look and feel as though they have it. Instead of challenging themselves and learning, they put the premium on tasks that are more certain to validate their intelligence. Students working in this framework also tell us that hard work makes them feel dumb – if you really have ability, you should not have to work. So, this framework is really detrimental to valuing challenges, learning and hard work.

In the framework of malleable intelligence, hard work and challenges are good things. Students who believe in malleable intelligence put a much higher value on learning and challenging themselves. They also highly value effort, realising that even geniuses need to work hard to reach their potential. Therefore, orienting students toward increasing their abilities through effort is an extremely important part of education. It is also important not to praise students for doing things quickly and easily, since this means they were not challenged, did not work hard, and learned little. Too often adults use this as an opportunity to tell kids how smart they are, but then 'smart' comes to mean doing everything quickly and easily, rather than taking on challenges. Instead, we should apologise to them for wasting their time with a task they could not profit from, and praise them when they stick to something, try different strategies, and generally apply themselves to something difficult.

We should also model enjoying challenges ('This one is hard, so it should be fun!') and being intrigued and informed by mistakes ('Well, that didn't work. How interesting! What does that tell us? What should we try next?'). Finally, we should be sure to show our pleasure when children make progress – to point out how they challenged themselves, worked hard, and improved. Pleasure in hard work, learning, and challenges can be communicated to students in all of these ways. In my book, *Mindset*, I give many more examples.

Is motivation more important than intelligence?

This is like asking if nurture is more important than nature. They are inseparable. Motivation is the motor for intelligence: it is what allows students to use their intellectual ability to full advantage and to increase their intellectual skills over time. There is a common but erroneous belief among many students (and teachers) that intelligence is all you need. Yet there are many examples of brilliant young people who end up accomplishing very little. There are also many examples of people who made huge contributions to arts, humanities and science who did not seem all that promising early on, but became passionate about an area and became brilliant at it.

Interestingly, more and more research (for example, by Anders Ericsson and his colleagues) is showing that what distinguishes people who achieve great things from their equally talented peers is how much effort they put in. Plain old dedication seems to be the foundation of important and creative contributions. Thomas Edison's biographer tells us that by all standards Edison was an ordinary boy who then began a lifelong love affair with technology. Over time, he came to embody what we call a 'genius'.

I have to confess that I do sometimes wonder whether what children come with is not talent or ability – but fascination with something. Prodigies, for example, are not just little founts of knowledge and skills, but are riveted by numbers, words, or music. Wouldn't it be interesting if the fascination comes first and the ability comes second?

Labelling children as gifted: What are the pros, cons and concerns?

My concern about giving children the label 'gifted' is that when we do so, we are in danger of conveying a fixed mindset. We are, in essence, telling them that they have been given a 'gift', a fixed ability that sets them apart from others and makes them more special than others. I worry that some children will become so focused on showing they deserve the label that they will stop challenging themselves, avoiding any situation that might reveal any inadequacy and show that they do not have the gift.

I also worry that the word 'gift' itself implies that no effort is involved in the attainment of intellectual excellence. It is just something that is bestowed upon the lucky few, who because of it are destined to be successful. Indeed, if children believe that they simply have to sit there with their gift and success will come, this is a recipe for disappointment. I have received many letters from gifted children who are now disappointed adults. They waited and success did not arrive. They never learned how to work hard and persevere toward their goals because nobody told them they would have to.

I have no problem with gifted programmes that provide enrichment and that allow high achieving students to be challenged. Such programmes should convey loudly and clearly that students' current ability is just the starting point and that challenge, effort, and learning are the only way to fulfil their potential. These programmes should give numerous examples of highly accomplished people and the devotion that it took for them to make their contributions. In short, gifted students need the same motivational lessons that all children need, but maybe more so, since many of them may have been coasting along and receiving accolades.

Tell us about children's approaches to schoolwork . . . are there male-female differences, racial-ethnic differences or socio-economic differences?

We have shown that the same motivational principles hold across males and females, and across racial, ethnic, and socio-economic groups. Some groups may be more vulnerable because of stereotypes, and actually, research is showing that these more vulnerable groups are the ones that are being helped the most by growth-mindset interventions. Stereotypes, it seems, have less force when you believe the skills in question can be acquired.

What do you mean by 'contingent worth'? Why is it important?

By 'contingent worth', I mean the idea that you are worthy when you are succeeding and unworthy when you are not. Everyone is disappointed when they don't do well, but only some children lose their self-respect and their sense of being a deserving individual. This is important because when it happens, they become unable to function adaptively. We have studied this mostly in young children, and found that a fixed mindset can contribute to contingent self-worth. These children conclude they are bad people when they fail or are criticised, and become too paralysed to fix the problem.

How do the types of praise children receive affect them? Can praising intelligence be a negative thing?

People in our society want their children to feel good about themselves and they think the way to accomplish this is to praise their children's intelligence. Is this correct? Does it work?

In a series of studies, we gave students praise for their intelligence or praise for their effort after they succeeded on a challenging task. Compared to those who were praised for effort, those praised for intelligence fell into a fixed mindset; wanting to avoid a challenging learning task in favour of one that could make them look smart over and over again. Then, following some difficult problems, those praised for intelligence concluded that they were not smart after all – since success meant they were smart, failure meant they were not. What is more, they now lost their enjoyment of the task, and their performance fell off dramatically.

Those who were praised for effort remained learning-oriented and, even in the face of difficulty, maintained their enjoyment and high level of performance. Effort praise, by the way, is just one type of 'process' praise – praising the process children are engaged in. It could have been praise for their strategies, their careful thinking, or the like. It is praise that keeps them focused on their engagement with the task, and allows them to maintain (or even intensify) that focus when the task gets harder. Intelligence praise, by contrast, puts the focus on the child and the evaluation of his or her abilities. Interestingly, children loved the intelligence praise. They got self-satisfied smiles on their faces that we never saw in the effort-praised children. But their self-satisfaction was short-lived. One bout of difficult problems was enough to blow it away. We have demonstrated these effects in children as young as four and a half years of age. Even telling a child he or she is a good 'draw-er' made them lose their confidence and zest when they later made mistakes.

Gifted and talented children are easy targets for 'intelligence praise'. Parents and educators are delighted with what these children can do, and eager to heap praise on them for their unusual performance. This temptation should be resisted. Early promise so often remains unfulfilled, and I wonder how much of this is because of our well-meant, but misguided praise.

What exactly are self-theories? How do they affect development?

Self-theories (or mindsets) are the beliefs that children form about their personal qualities; for example, about their intelligence. As I have been discussing, believing that intelligence is a fixed trait that cannot be changed, has different effects from believing that it is a malleable quality that can be developed. We are finding that children with the growth mindset fare better across challenging developmental transitions, than do those with the fixed mindset. Believing that their qualities can be cultivated allows children to falter and recover, and to explore new subjects and interests in a curious, learning mode.

Believing that their traits are carved in stone makes mistakes and challenges – so common during times of transition – threatening to these students. They fear they will find out they are dumb rather than smart, and that everyone else will find this out about them too. These challenges may cause children to slacken their effort (just when more effort is needed) so as not to seem to care and so as not to try and still fail. It is hard for students to confront a challenging developmental transition successfully when they are running the other way to save their egos. In short, a mindset in which challenge, effort, growth and learning are sought is one that serves children well across development.

Why are confidence and success not enough?

Society tends to think they are. I've seen in my work that they're not. Many of the most confident students, who have had lots of success, still avoid challenges and falter in the face of difficulty. For example, many students with the fixed view of intelligence have high levels of confidence as they confront a task, but if things go wrong, they lose interest in it and they lose the desire and ability to work toward mastery. What we should be working toward is not puffing up students' intellectual self-confidence but building a learning-oriented confidence that withstands setbacks and keeps students on track, expending effort when they need it most.

We have shown that this is best promoted by focusing students on the goal of learning (expanding their abilities) and teaching them the efficacy of effort and strategy use in the face of obstacles.

How do we convince all students that although grades are important, learning is more important?

We recently completed a study of students in a chemistry course leading to medical school, the entry course to the curriculum required for medical school application. All students thought that grades were critically important, but those who said that learning was most important were the ones who used the best study strategies, bounced back from initially disappointing grades, and did best in the course. I think the finding that focusing on learning can help you get better grades in challenging courses makes a convincing argument!

What should parents do for students who are not motivated to succeed in academic pursuits?

Often students who are not motivated are hung up on their abilities. They fear they will expose themselves and that their parents will be ashamed to have a child who is not smart. If they do not try hard, they can preserve a sense of themselves as smart (but unmotivated): 'If I really cared, I *could* do well'. Often parents and teachers respond to this with intelligence praise. They think that if they tell these students they are smart, it will give them confidence and re-motivate them. But that just compounds the problem. It keeps the students in their fixed-intelligence framework, still worrying whether they are smart or not and still unwilling to take the risk of trying hard. Instead, parents and teachers would do better to follow the suggestions I outlined above: teach and praise effort, strategies, learning and improvement.

How can intelligence tests and their results be more properly used? Or, how can we use intelligence tests and their results more intelligently?

Intelligence tests were invented by Alfred Binet, who had a radical growth-mindset. He believed that the most basic capacity to learn could be transformed through education. He invented the IQ test simply as a diagnostic tool, to identify children who were not profiting from their current school instruction, so he could devise educational techniques that would suit their learning styles better. This was a great idea. Tests used as diagnostic tools, to identify a student's strengths and weaknesses in order to best teach that student, are still a good idea. However, if an IQ test is used for this purpose, perhaps it should be given another name!

The real danger of these tests is that many educators come to believe (erroneously) that they are a good index of how intelligent children are and what their intellectual potential is. The public needs to be educated: the fact is that nothing can measure intellectual potential. It is something that unfolds as children work hard and learn. Moreover, scientific research is showing that many of the most basic parts of intelligence can be changed with training.

The bottom line is: By all means, use tests to diagnose what a children need to learn, but not simply to label them or to place them into fixed categories.

In our high stakes testing society, with such an emphasis on grades and student achievement on standardised tests, what kind of message are we sending our students and children?

It is not a good message and we have to be careful not to make it even worse. In the high stakes testing atmosphere we must be careful not to let students think that these tests measure their underlying capacity or intelligence. In one study, we showed fixed- and growth-minded school children a test of ability, and later asked them what they thought it measured – their ability in that area? Their intelligence? Their intelligence when they grew up? Students with a growth mindset said 'yes' to the first (after all that is what we told them), but 'no' to the next two. No current test could tell them how smart they would be when they were grown up. However, students with a fixed mindset said 'yes' to all three – they thought a single test could tell them how smart they would be for the rest of their lives. Students must learn that tests can measure what they know now, but tests cannot tell them about their potential for learning in the future.

Many students 'fall apart' when they get to junior high or middle school (age 11–14). Have they been 'spoon fed' for too long, and are then unable to function autonomously? Or have other things happened?

In our studies, we have watched students fall apart at this time. Many of them have not confronted this kind of challenge before, and those with the fixed mindset are petrified that they will be found to be unintelligent. An emphasis on a growth-mindset orientation and on challenge, learning, and effort before then would have helped students cope when the going got rough. In fact, our intervention has shown that teaching students a growth mindset allowed them to fare better both in terms of their motivation and their grades at this very time.

Who has most influenced you and why?

The people who have influenced me most over the years are my graduate students, who are the most extraordinary group of people. They have not only been my collaborators on this rewarding, adventurous journey of research, but they are the ones who have taught me how to be a mentor. Two other people influenced me greatly – two little boys in one of my first studies. As they confronted highly difficult problems, they welcomed the challenge with glee. I was astounded that they could happily greet what I considered to be a highly threatening situation. They became my role models and as, through my research, I've discovered their secrets, I have tried to emulate them.

Of what professional and personal accomplishment are you most proud?

I am extremely proud of my past and current students and the wonderful contributions they are making. I am very proud that our work is benefiting teachers and students. More personally, I am proud that I have become more like the two little boys in my early study.

Contact address: dweck@psych.stanford.edu

Future Perspectives

Suggested priorities for gifted education over the next decade

It is critical for gifted education to take a modern view of giftedness and talent, one that fits with solid research findings. Past perspectives simply categorised people as gifted or not gifted, erroneously portrayed giftedness as a stable thing, and sought more to measure and reward giftedness and talent than to develop it. We now recognise that talent is often very specific, that it can wax and wane over time, and that it can be stifled by the wrong kind of praise or well-meant encouragement. Many of our gifted young people today need constant praise, become afraid of challenges, and fall apart when things do not come easily to them. As a result, they lose their ability to grow. The most important task facing us today is how to develop and sustain talent by fostering a love of learning, a zest for challenge, and resilience in the face of setbacks.

Carol S. Dweck

39

Turning points and future directions in gifted education and talent development

Sally M. Reis

Neag Center for Gifted Education and Talent Development
The University of Connecticut, US

What will be the turning points in the education of gifted and talented students in the next several decades? As we complete the first decade of the new century, it is appropriate to reflect on the extraordinary changes and advances that have occurred in the last several decades in our field. Consensus on the turning points of the past century may be difficult to reach and admittedly, this perspective is filtered through the lens of one American woman who has spent the majority of her professional life in this area. The turning points suggested as a focus for the next several decades include the following: (1) expanding conceptions of the multidimensionality of giftedness and talent development, (2) eradicating the continued absence of challenge for gifted and talented students, (3) making a difference for underserved populations, (4) changing our focus from ways to identify gifted students to the ways we develop gifts and talents, and finally, (5) applying 'gifted' education pedagogy to talent development, with a focus on strengths, not deficits.

Expanding conceptions of giftedness and talent

In the past century, we have come to understand that gifted learners are not a homogeneous group; rather, they are diverse, varied, and unique. A thorough review of the research on gifted and talented learners indicates the many different characteristics among this diverse group of young people and adults. Research conducted in the 1980s and 1990s has provided data that support notions of multiple components in intelligence. This is particularly evident in the reexamination of 'giftedness' by Sternberg and Davidson (1986) in their publication of two books published twenty years apart on *Conceptions of Giftedness*. The different conceptions of giftedness presented, although distinct, are interrelated in several ways. Most theorists and researchers define giftedness in terms of multiple qualities, not all of which are intellectual. Motivation, high self-concept, and creativity are key qualities in many of these broadened conceptions of giftedness (Renzulli 1986, 2006).

The most recent American definition, which was cited in the most recent national report on the state of gifted and talented education, states that children and youth with outstanding talent perform or show the potential for performing at remarkably high levels of accomplishment when compared with others of their age, experience, or environment. They require services or activities not ordinarily provided by the schools. Outstanding talents are present in children and youth from all cultural groups, across all economic strata, and in all areas of human endeavour (U.S. Department of Education 1993, p. 26).

Though many school districts adopt this or other broadened conceptions and definitions as their philosophy, others still only pay attention to 'intellectual' ability when both identifying and serving students. And, even though many psychologists and educators recognise broadened definitions of giftedness and intelligence, many students with gifts and talents continue to be unrecognised and underserved. This oversight should be recognised and overcome in the future.

Conceptions of high achievement as opposed to creative productive giftedness

A discussion of high intellectual ability or potential, and high creative ability or potential, is presented in two separate sections because existing research and discussion often identify two broad categories, which Renzulli (1986, 2006) appropriately referred to as either 'high achievement/schoolhouse giftedness' and/or 'creative/productive giftedness'. Schoolhouse giftedness refers to test-taking, lesson-learning, or academic giftedness, and individuals who fall into this category generally score well on more traditional intellectual or cognitive assessments and perform well in school. Creative/productive giftedness, on the other hand, is reflected in individuals who tend to be producers (rather than consumers) of original knowledge, materials, or products and who employ thought processes that tend to be inductive, integrated, and problem oriented. It is important that we recognise and encourage both types of giftedness in this current century.

A continued lack of challenge for gifted and talented students

The belief espoused in school reform that children from all economic and cultural backgrounds must reach their full potential has not been extended to America's most talented students: 'They are under-challenged and therefore underachieve' (U.S. Department of Education 1993, p. 5). The report further indicates that our nation's talented students are offered a less rigorous curriculum, read fewer demanding books and are less prepared for work or postsecondary education than top students in many other industrialised countries. Talented children from economically disadvantaged homes or from culturally or linguistically diverse groups are especially neglected, the report also indicates, and many of them will not realise their potential without some type of intervention.

Boredom and repetition in school for academically talented students

For too long, American students have failed to be stimulated in school, especially in elementary and middle school. Research conducted by the National Research Center on the Gifted and Talented has analysed what occurs in American classrooms for high ability students. The results portray a disturbing pattern. The Classroom Practices Survey (Archambault et al. 1993) was conducted to determine the extent to which gifted and talented students receive differentiated education in regular classrooms. Sixty-one per cent of approximately 7300 randomly selected third and fourth grade teachers in public and private schools in the United States reported that they had *never* had any training in teaching gifted students. This result was consistent for all types of schools sampled and for classrooms in various parts of the country and for various types of communities.

The Classroom Practices Observational Study (Westberg et al. 1993) examined the instructional and curricular practices used with gifted and talented students in regular elementary classrooms throughout the United States. Systematic observations were conducted in 46 third and fourth grade classrooms to identify how classroom teachers meet the needs of gifted students in the regular classroom. The results indicated little differentiation in the instructional and curricular practices, including grouping arrangements and verbal interactions, for gifted students in the regular classroom. In all content areas in 92 observation days, gifted students rarely received instruction in homogeneous groups (21 per cent of the time), and more alarmingly, the target gifted students experienced no instructional or curricular differentiation in 84 per cent of the instructional activities in which they participated.

In a study on curriculum compacting (Reis et al. 1993), the effects of using a plan called curriculum compacting (Reis et al. 1992) was examined to modify the curriculum and eliminate previously mastered work for high ability students. The work that is eliminated is content that is repeated from previous textbooks or content that may be new in the curriculum but that some students already know. When classroom teachers eliminated between 40–50 per cent of the previously mastered regular curriculum for high ability students, no differences were found between students whose work was compacted and students who did all the work in reading, math computation, social studies and spelling. And in some content areas, scores were actually higher when this elimination of previous mastered content took place. Several other recent studies in reading and in middle school differentiation (Reis et al. 2003; Tomlinson 1995) suggest that advanced students continue to remain under-challenged in many classrooms in the United States.

The ramifications of the lack of challenge for gifted students

Three ramifications clearly exist for gifted and high-potential students in our schools. First, they remain unchallenged; their development may be delayed or even halted. If instructional materials are not above the students' current level of knowledge or understanding, learning is less efficient and intellectual growth may stop. It is, for example, not surprising to find very talented first graders in an urban school who read on a fifth grade level, but who are reading only slightly above grade level when they enter fifth grade. Second, too many of our brightest students never learn to work, and consequently they acquire poor work habits. In a study (Reis et al. 1995) conducted on high ability urban high school students, half of the previously identified gifted students we studied were underachieving in school. When these students provided insights about why they were doing poorly in high school, they blamed elementary school programmes that were too easy. One student's representative comment summarised the attitude of the majority of students involved in the study: 'Elementary school was fun. I always received top grades on my report card. I never studied when we were in class and I never had to study at home'. The problem of systematically learning *not* to work exists in all types of schools in rural, suburban and urban areas, undoubtedly in many countries in addition to America, and seems to be an area of increasing importance in educating gifted and talented students.

Underserved diverse populations in gifted education

Unfortunately, the majority of young people participating in gifted and talented programmes across the country continue to represent the majority culture. Few doubts exist regarding the reasons that economically disadvantaged and other minority group students are under-represented in gifted programmes. Test bias and inappropriateness have been mentioned as one reason, given the continued reliance on traditional identification approaches. Groups that have been traditionally underrepresented in gifted programmes could be better served, according to Frasier and Passow (1994), if the following elements were considered: new constructs of gifted-ness; attention to cultural and contextual variability; the use of more varied and authentic assessment; performance identification; identification through learning opportunities; and attention to both absolute attributes of giftedness – the traits, aptitudes, and behaviours uni-versally associated with talent – as well as the specific behaviours that represent different manifestations of gifted potential and performance as a consequence of the social and cultural contexts in which they occur.

In a three-year study of 35 economically disadvantaged, ethnically diverse, talented high school students who either achieved or underachieved in their urban high school, specific reasons were found that contributed to either excellent or poor achievement (Reis et al. 1995). Qualitative methods were used to identify a number of common personal characteristics exhib-ited by the high achieving participants in this study, including motivation and inner will, positive use of problem solving, independence, realistic aspirations, heightened sensitivity to each other and the world around them, and appreciation of cultural diversity. A determination to succeed was consistently echoed by most of the participants in this study, despite what could be considered prejudice levelled against them. Rosa, one of the participants in the study, said that she had experienced various types of prejudice in her community, and occasionally in academic experiences. She believed that she experienced prejudice because she is both intelli-gent and Hispanic. This prejudice occurred in school, coming from teachers as well as students, and in the summer programmes she participated in for high achieving students – which were held at some of the most prestigious private schools in the state. She explained, 'I know that people will occasionally look at me and say, when they find out that I'm smart, "How can that be? She's Puerto Rican" ' (p. 102).

Each of the high achieving participants in this study referred to an internal motivation that kept them driven to succeed in their urban environment. One participant referred to this drive as an 'inner will' which contributed to the strong belief self-observed in the participants. Resilience was also exhibited by many of the participants in this study, as the majority came from homes that had been affected by periodic or regular unemployment of one or more parents, poverty, family turmoil caused by issues such as alcohol, drugs, and mental illness, and other problems. All participants also lived in a city in which violence, drugs, poverty, and crime were factors. Despite these challenges, the majority of the high achieving participants in this study developed the resilience necessary to overcome problems associated with their families, their school and their environment. The courage and resilience they displayed seem remarkable, and yet they simply accepted their circumstances and took advantage of the opportunities given to them.

Culturally diverse gifted students and those who are acquiring English represent a hetero-geneous group. According to Kitano and Espinosa (1995), 'Their diversity suggests a need for a broad range of programmes that provide options for different levels of primary and English language proficiency, different subject–matter interests, and talent areas' (p. 237). New strategies are necessary to identify diverse gifted students and provide them with both developmentally appropriate curricula and enriched programmes that evoke a gifted student's potential, broader conceptions of intelligence, alternative definitions of giftedness, and assessment models developed for specific populations.

Gifted girls and women

What factors cause some smart, young girls with hopes and dreams to become self-fulfilled, talented women in their later lives? While some research has addressed the issue, much more is needed. Some research (Arnold 1995; Bell 1989; Cramer 1989; Hany 1994; Kline and Short 1991; Kramer 1991; Leroux 1988; Perleth and Heller 1994; Reis 1987, 1998; Reis and Callahan 1989; Subotnik 1988) has indicated that gifted females begin to lose self-confidence in elementary school, which continues through college and graduate school. These young women may increasingly doubt their intellectual competence; perceive themselves as less capable than they actually are; and believe that boys can rely on innate ability while they themselves must work hard. Talented girls, it is also said, choose more often to work in groups, and are more concerned about teacher reactions, more likely to adapt to adult expectations, and less likely than boys to describe themselves or to be described as autonomous and independent. But some bright girls also use affiliations and their relationships to assess their level of ability, and to achieve at higher levels, and often believe that their grades will be higher if their teachers like them.

A comprehensive analysis of gifted females (Reis 1998) offered numerous suggestions on how their needs can be better met across the lifespan, including research on talented girls' social and emotional development through elementary and secondary school. Conclusions from this research suggest that girls achieve well in school, but less well in life, when their self-confidence and self-perceived abilities decrease. Simply put, the adult level professional achievement of women is lower than that of males of comparable ability. Some gifted females value their own personal achievements less as they get older, which may indicate that the ageing process has a negative impact on both the achievement and the self-confidence of gifted females. Reis (1998) also found however, that as gifted females approach middle to later age, many of the conflicts they faced as young women decrease and they are able to excel. However, any examination of the highest levels of adult creative productivity from Nobel prizes to other prizes in literature, science or the arts reflects higher levels of male professional productivity. Continued interest in this topic should result in future research.

Underachieving gifted learners

Student performance that falls noticeably short of potential, especially for young people with high ability, is bewildering and perhaps the most frustrating of all challenges both teachers and parents face. Some students underachieve or fail in school for obvious reasons: excessive absences from school, poor performance, disruptive behaviour, low self-esteem, family problems, and poverty. In addition to the risk factors that predict the reasons most students fail, another long-standing problem which causes underachievement in gifted or high potential students is the inappropriate curriculum and content which some of them encounter on a daily basis. The hundreds of hours spent each month in classrooms in which students rarely encounter new or challenging curriculum, the boredom of being assigned routine tasks mastered long ago, the low levels of discussion, and the mismatch of content to students' ability lead to frustration on the parts of many of our brightest students. In fact, dropping out of school is the only way that some students believe they can address these issues effectively.

Reis and McCoach (2000) identified specific characteristics of gifted underachievers, which may provide helpful insights for educators regarding the performance of some of their students. These characteristics include high or variable abilities, especially verbal and/or visual/motor; good knowledge, memory and motivation in areas of strength and interest; possible creative talents; low course grades relative to ability; variable scores on standardised achievement tests; preference for non-traditional rewards; poor organisation and time management; lack of homework production; and unrealistically low or high self-concept. Reis and McCoach (2000) also provided a comprehensive summary of research on gifted students who underachieve, and summarised the limited interventions studied to address this area.

A change in direction: focusing on developing gifts and talents in children

In the past, the general approach to the study of gifted persons could easily lead the casual reader to believe that giftedness is an absolute condition that is magically bestowed upon a person in much the same way that nature endows us with blue eyes, red hair, or a dark complexion (Renzulli 1980). This position is not supported by the current research cited in this article. The multiple lists of traits and characteristics – some for girls and some for boys; some for students from the majority culture, others for students from diverse cultural backgrounds indicate the diversity of talents in different populations. For too many years educators have pretended that we can identify one set of specific traits of gifted children in an unequivocal fashion. Many people have been led to believe that certain individuals have been endowed with a golden chromosome that makes him or her 'a gifted person'. This belief has led further to the mistaken idea that all we need to do is find the right combination of traits that prove the existence of this 'gift'. The use of terms such as 'the truly gifted' and 'the highly gifted', only serve to confuse the issue. The misuse of the concept of giftedness has given rise to both criticism and confusion about both identification and programming, and the result has been many mixed messages sent to educators and the public at large resulting in a justifiable scepticism about the credibility of the gifted education movement and our ability both to define and to offer services that are qualitatively different from general education.

Joseph Renzulli and I advocate a fundamental change in the ways the characteristics and traits of giftedness should be viewed in the future (Renzulli and Reis 1987). The characteristics of advanced learners must be identified within various population groups. That is, we should attempt to identify the characteristics of talented students within each educational context and population. This information should be used to help us differentiate between all students and those who need different levels of service, or a continuum of services (Renzulli 1994; Renzulli and Reis 1997) in school to realise their potential. This shift might appear insignificant, but we believe that it has implications for the way that we think about the characteristics of giftedness and the ways in which we should structure our identification and programming endeavours. This change may also provide the flexibility in both identification and programming endeavours that will encourage the inclusion of diverse students in our programmes.

Defining our populations, then deciding which services are offered to all students and what is qualitatively necessary for gifted students based on the traits of the population, will help us to develop programmes that are internally consistent. At a very minimum, educators must acknowledge that giftedness is manifested by different traits in different populations, and we must develop programmes that reflect the diversity of talent in our culture.

A continuum of services

We recommend that a broad range of special services (Renzulli 1994; Renzulli and Reis 1997) be implemented at the national and local level to develop a comprehensive programme for total talent development, which challenges all students who are capable of working at the highest levels of their abilities and special interest areas. These services may include: individual or small group counselling, direct assistance in facilitating advanced level and accelerated work, arranging mentorships with faculty members or community persons, and making other types of connections between students, their families, and out-of-school persons. Direct assistance also involves setting up and promoting student, faculty and parental involvement in special programmes such as those that develop creativity, provide acceleration, and give opportunities for state and national essay, mathematics, and history contests. Another type of direct assistance includes arranging out-of-school involvement for individual students in summer programmes, accelerated learning opportunities, on-campus courses, special schools, theatrical groups, scientific expeditions and apprenticeships at places where advanced level learning opportunities are available. Provision of these services to students whose learning needs match the services is one of the responsibilities of the gifted programme teacher or an enrichment team of teachers and parents who work together to provide options for advanced learning.

Applying 'gifted' education pedagogy to develop talents in students: focusing on strengths, not deficits

Much that has been learned and developed in gifted programmes can be adapted to offer exciting, creative alternatives in instruction and curriculum for all students, understanding that if this were to occur, truly advanced services could be targeted for those who really need them. A rather impressive menu of exciting curricular adaptations, independent study and thinking skill strategies, grouping options, and enrichment strategies have been developed in gifted programmes which could be used to improve schools. Our work in the Schoolwide Enrichment Model (Renzulli and Reis 1985, 1997) has been field tested and implemented by hundreds of school districts across the country and around the world for the last twenty years. Experiences with Schoolwide Enrichment have led us to realise that when an effective approach to enrichment is implemented, all students in the school benefit and the entire school begins to improve. This approach seeks to apply strategies used in gifted programmes to the entire school population, emphasising talent development in *all* students through a variety of acceleration and enrichment strategies that have been discussed earlier. Not all students can, of course, participate in all advanced opportunities but many can work far beyond what they are currently asked to do. It is clear that our most advanced students need different types of educational experiences than they are currently receiving and that without these services, talents may not be nurtured in many students. Gifted and talented students flourish in an environment that nurtures and tries to develop the talents of all children, and the unique needs of gifted students are better served in an environment that seeks to maximise the potential of all students.

We seldom study how gifted programme participants benefit from their experiences, and we rarely ask what else we should have been doing for gifted students who had some programme involvement. It is clear that a continuum of services should be made available representing a variety of different approaches, including acceleration, counselling, regular curriculum modification and differentiation, separate classes, and a pull-out or resource room component. Longitudinal studies should also investigate the acquisition of self-regulated, self-directed learning, given the current explosion of knowledge available on the web. Studies should investigate how gifted students can gain access to this information while also learning the skills of synthesis, analysis, and evaluation necessary to understand how to interpret the large body of information they encounter. New opportunities for gifted students must include opportunities for advancement through the regular curriculum at an appropriately challenging rate and pace; depth and advanced content; independent, self-directed learning challenges; acceleration, independent study; and varied learning opportunities based on interest, learning styles, product preferences and modality preferences.

Contact address: sally.reis@uconn.edu

Future Perspectives

Suggested priorities for gifted education over the next decade

In the next ten years, we must work to ensure that teachers and gifted programme coordinators focus on opportunities for creative productivity in high potential and gifted children. With a current national and international focus on testing and assessment and standardisation of curriculum, we can kill the joy that our most able students have both in school and in creative endeavours. We must refocus our efforts and ensure that our schools and programmes help to create a new generation of artists, scholars, researchers, and producers in every field that will use their talents to preserve our earth and grow as individuals. We should create opportunities that will enable them to lead satisfying lives that will ultimately enable them to develop their gifts, pursue their passions, and find meaningful and challenging work that will make our world a healthier, more beautiful and peaceful place.

Sally M. Reis

References

Abroms, K. I. (1985) Social giftedness and its relationship with intellectual giftedness, in J. Freeman, (ed.), *The psychology of gifted children: Perspectives on development and education*. Chichester: Wiley. (pp. 201–218)

Adey, P. and Shayer, M. (1994) *Really raising standards: Cognitive intervention and academic achievement*. London: Routledge.

Adey, P., Csapo, B., Demetriou, A., Hautmaki. J. and Shayer, M. (2007) Can we be intelligent about intelligence? Why education needs the concept of plastic general ability. *Educational Research Review*, 2:2, 75–97.

Ainley, M. D. (1993) Styles of engagement with learning: Multidimensional assessment of their relationship with strategy use and school achievement. *Journal of Educational Psychology*, 85(3), 395–405.

Albert, R. S. (1975) Toward a behavioral definition of genius. *American Psychologist*, 30, 140–151.

Albrecht, K. (2006) *Social intelligence. The new science of success*. San Francisco, CA: Jossey-Bass.

Alder-Colins, J. (2007) Developing an inclusional pedagogy of the unique: How do I clarify, live and explain my educational influences in my learning as I pedagogise my healing nurse curriculum in a Japanese University? Unpublished doctoral dissertation. University of Bath.

Alexander, P. A. and Muia, J. (1982) *Gifted education: A comprehensive roadmap*. Rockville, MD: Aspen.

Alexander, P. A., Parsons, J. L. and Nash, W. R. (1996) *Towards a theory of creativity*. Paper produced for the National Association of Gifted Children. Washington D.C.: NAGC Press.

Alexander R. (2006) (3rd ed.) *Towards dialogic teaching: Rethinking classroom talk*. Cambridge: Dialogos.

Allard, B. and Sundblad, B. (1991) Skrivandets genes. [*The genesis of school writing – focusing on spelling and related conventions*]. Stockholm University: Department of Education.

Amabile, T. M. (1982) Social psychology of creativity: A consensual assessment technique. *Journal of Personality and Social Psychology*, 43, 997–1013.

Amabile, T. M. (1983) *The social psychology of creativity*. New York: Springer-Verlag.

Amabile, T. M. (1996) *Creativity in context*. Boulder, CO: Westview.

Amabile, T. M., Conti, R., Coon, H., Lazenby, J. and Herron, M. (1997) Assessing the work environment for creativity. *Academy of Management Journal*, 39(5), 1154–1184.

American heritage electronic dictionary (3rd ed.). (1992). Boston: Houghton Mifflin.

American Psychiatric Association (1994) *Diagnostic and statistical manual of mental disorders*. (4th ed.) Washington, D.C.: Author.

Andreani, O. and Pagnin, A. (1993) Nurturing the moral development of the gifted. In K. Heller, F. Mönks, and H. Passow (eds.), *International handbook of research and development of giftedness and talent*. Oxford: Pergamon Press. (pp. 539–553)

Angoff, W. H. (1988) The nature–nurture debate, aptitudes, and group differences. *American Psychologist*, 41, 713–720.

APA Work Group of the Board of Educational Affairs (1997) *Learner-centered psychological principles: A framework for school reform and redesign.* Washington, D.C.: American Psychological Association.

Apple, M. W. (1982) Education and cultural reproduction: A critical reassessment of programs for choice, in R. Everhart (ed.), *The public school monopoly: A critical analysis of education and the state in American society.* Cambridge, MA: Ballinger. (pp. 503–541)

Archambault Jr., F. X., Westberg, K. L., Brown, S. W., Hallmark, B. W., Emmons, C. L. and Zhang, W. (1993) *Regular classroom practices with gifted students: Results of a national survey of classroom teachers.* Storrs: The National Research Center on the Gifted and Talented, University of Connecticut. (Research Monograph #93102).

Archambault, R. D. (ed.) (1964) *John Dewey on education: Selected writings.* Chicago: University of Chicago Press.

Arnold, K. D. (1995) *Lives of promise: What becomes of high school valedictorians?* San Francisco: Jossey-Bass.

ASPEN Asperger Syndrome Educational Network. http//www.asperger.org

Asperger, H. (1944/1991) Autistic psychopathy in childhood. (pp. 37–92). In U. Frith, (ed.), *Autism and Asperger syndrome.* Cambridge: Cambridge University Press.

Assouline, S. G., Colangelo, N., Lupkowski-Shoplik, A. E., Lipscomb, J. and Forstadt, L. (2003) *The Iowa Acceleration Scale – 2nd Edition.* Scottsdale AZ: Great Potential Press.

Attwood, T. (1998). *Asperger's Syndrome: A guide for parents and professionals.* Philadelphia: Taylor and Francis.

Attwood, T. (2000) *Asperger Syndrome: A guide for parents and professionals.* London: Jessica Kingsley.

Baer, J. (1991) Depression, general anxiety, test anxiety, and rigidity of gifted junior high and high school children. *Psychological Reports*, 69, 1128–1130.

Bakhtin, M. M. (1986) *Speech genres and other late essays.* C. Emerson and M. Holquist (eds.), Trans. V. W. McGee. Austin, TX: University of Texas Press.

Balchin, T. (2002) Male teachers in primary education. *Forum, the Journal for Promoting 3–19 Comprehensive Education*, 44(1), pp. 28–34.

Balchin. T. (2005a) Identifying gifted and talented students through creative behaviour. *The Journal of the National Association for Gifted Children*, 10(1), 20–26.

Balchin, T. (2005b) A creativity feedback package for teachers and students of design and technology in the UK. *International Journal of Design and Technology Association*, 10(2), 31–43.

Balchin, T. (2006) Assessing creativity through consensual assessment, in N. Jackson and J. Cowan, (eds.), *The challenge of creativity assessment in higher education*, Routledge: Oxon, (pp. 173–182).

Balchin, T. (2007a) Identifications of the gifted: the efficacy of teacher nominations in English schools. *Journal of the National Association for Gifted Children*, 11(1), 5–17.

Balchin, T. (2007b) Assessing Creative Outcomes in British Schools. *Creative Learning Today*, 15(2), April 2007, 1–2, 7.

Balchin, T. (2008a) Improving the quality of G&T nominations: Tackling creativity. *Gifted Education International.*

Balchin, T. (2008b) Balancing identifications: Encouraging parental feedback and recanting the National Register. *Journal of the National Association for Gifted Children*, 12(1), 6–14.

Balchin, T. (in press) Teacher nominations of giftedness: Investigating the beliefs of English G&T co-ordinators. *Journal for the Education of the Gifted*, 31(4).

Baldwin, A. Y. (2002) Discovering the different faces of giftedness: A challenge for the new millennium. Proceedings of the 13th Biennial World Conference in Istanbul August 1999. In B. Clark (ed.), *Gifted and talented: A challenge for the new millennium.* Northridge CA: WCGTC. (pp. 28–33)

Ball, S. J. (1998) Educational studies, policy entrepreneurship and social theory. In R. Slee, G. Weiner and S. Tomlinson (eds.), *School effectiveness for whom? Challenges to the school effectiveness and school improvement movements.* London: Falmer Press.

Baltes, P. B. and Staudinger, U. M. (1993) The search for a psychology of wisdom. *Current Directions in Psychological Science*, 2, 75–80.

Baltes, P. B. and Staudinger, U. M (2000) Wisdom: A metaheuristic (pragmatic) to orchestrate mind and virtue toward excellence. *American Psychologist*, 55, 122–135.

Baltes, P. B., Smith, J. and Staudinger, U. M. (1992) Wisdom and successful aging. In T. Sonderegger (ed.), *Nebraska Symposium on Motivation* (Vol. 39). Lincoln, NE: University of Nebraska Press. (pp. 123–167)

Baltes, P. B., Staudinger, U. M., Maercker, A. and Smith, J. (1995) People nominated as wise: A comparative study of wisdom-related knowledge. *Psychology and Aging*, 10, 155–166.

Bandura, A. (1971) *Social Learning Theory*. Englewood Cliffs, NJ: Prentice Hall.

Bandura, A. (1982) Self-efficacy mechanism in human agency. *American Psychologist*, 37, 122–147.

Bandura, A. (1986) *Social foundation of thought and action: A social cognitive theory*. Englewood Cliffs, NJ: Prentice Hall.

Bandura, A. (1996) *Self-efficacy: The exercise of control*. New York: W. H. Freeman.

Bandura, A. (2003) *Self-efficacy. The exercise of control*. New York: W. H. Freeman.

Bar-On, R. and Parker J. D. (2000) EQ-i:YV. BarOn Emotional Quotient Inventory: Youth Version. *Technical Manual*. New York: MHS.

Baron-Cohen, S. (2002) The extreme male brain theory of autism. *Trends in Cognitive Sciences*, 6(6), 248–254.

Baum, S. (1984) Meeting the needs of the learning disabled gifted student. *Roeper Review*, 7, 16–19.

Baum, S. (1988) An enrichment program for gifted learning disabled students. *Gifted Child Quarterly*, 32(10), 226–230.

Baum, S., Owen, S. V. and Dixon, J. (1991) *To be gifted and learning disabled: From identification to practical intervention strategies*. Masfield, CT: Creative Learning Press.

Baum, S., Olenchak, F. R. and Owen, S. V. (1998) Gifted students with attention deficits: Fact and/or fiction? Or, can we see the forest fort he tree? *Gifted Child Quarterly*, 42(2), 96–104.

Baumert, J. and Lehmann, R. et al. (1997) *TIMSS – Mathematisch-naturwissenschaftlicher Unterricht im internationalen Vergleich* [Instruction in Mathematics and the Sciences]. Opladen: Leske + Budrich.

Beauchamp, T. and Childress, J. (2001) *Principles of biomedical ethics* (5th edn.). Oxford: Oxford University Press.

Bebeau, M., Rest, J. and Yamoor, C. (1985) Measuring dental students' ethical sensitivity. *Journal of Dental Education*, 49(4), 225–235.

Bebeau, M., Rest, J. and Narvaez, D. (1999) Beyond the promise: a perspective on research in moral education. *Educational Researcher*, 28(4), 18–26.

Belanger, J. and Gagné, F. (2006) Examining the size of the gifted/talented population from multiple identification criteria. *Journal for the Education of the Gifted*, 30(2), 131–163.

Bell, L. A. (1989) Something's wrong here and it's not me: Challenging the dilemmas that block girls' success. *Journal for the Education of the Gifted*, 12(2), 118–130.

Benbow, C. P., Lubinski, D. and Suchy, B. (1996) Impact of the SMPY model and programs from the perspective of the participant. In C. P. Benbow and D. Lubinski (eds.), *Intellectual talent: Psychometric and social issues*. Baltimore, MD: Johns Hopkins University Press. (pp. 206–300)

Berninger, V. W. (2004) 'The role of mechanics in composing of elementary students. A review of research and intervention', Keynote: Annual DCD Conference, Oxford, April.

Besançon, M. and Lubart, T. I. (in press) Differences in the development of creative competencies in children schooled in diverse learning environments. *Learning and Individual Differences*.

Besançon, M., Guignard, J-H. and Lubart, T.I. (2006) Haut potentiel, créativité chez l'enfant et éducation. *Bulletin de Psychologie*, 59(5), 491–504.

Besemer, S. P. (1998) Creative Product Analysis Matrix: Testing the model structure and a comparison among products – three novel chairs. *Creativity Research Journal* 11(4), 333–346.

Besemer, S. P. and Treffinger, D. H. (1981) Analysis of creative products: review and synthesis. *Journal of Creative Behavior* 15(3), 158–178.

Billig, M. (1999) *Freudian repression: Conversations creating the unconscious*. Cambridge University Press: Cambridge.

Binet, A. (1911) *Idées modernes sur les enfants*. [Modern ideas about children]. Paris: Flammarion.

Binet, A. and Simon, T. (1905) Méthodes nouvelles pour le diagnostic du niveau intellectuel des anormaux. *L'Année Psychologique*, 11, 191–336.

Binfet, J. (1995) Identifying the themes in student-generated moral dilemmas. A paper presented at the annual meeting of the American Educational Research Association, April 18th, 1995, San Francisco, CA.

Black, P. and Harrison, C. (2004) *Science Inside the Black Box*. London: nferNelson.

Black, P. and Wiliam, D. (1998) *Inside the Black Box*. London: nferNelson.

Blackwell, L., Trzesniewski, K. and Dweck, C. S. (2007) Implicit theories of intelligence predict achievement across an adolescent transition: A longitudinal study and an intervention. *Child Development*, 78. 246–263.

Bleuler, E. (1951) *Textbook of psychiatry*. A.A. Brill (ed.). New York: Dover.

Bloom, B. S. (ed.) (1985) *Developing talent in young children*. New York: Ballentine Books.

Borland, J. H. (2003) The death of giftedness. In J. H. Borland (ed.), *Rethinking gifted education*. New York : Teachers College Press. (pp. 105–124)

Borland, J. H. (2004) *Issues and practices in the identification and education of gifted students from underrepresented groups*. Storrs, CT: The National Research Center on the Gifted and Talented. (pp. 1–35)

Borland, J. H. (2005) 'Gifted education without gifted children: The case for no conception of giftedness'. In R. J. Sternberg and J. E. Davidson (eds.), *Conceptions of giftedness*. Cambridge: Cambridge University Press. (pp. 1–19)

Borland, J. H. et al. (Guest eds.) (2002) A quarter century of ideas on ability grouping and accelerations. Special Issue. *Roeper Review*, 24, 100–177.

Bouchard, T. J. (1997) IQ similarity in twins reared apart: Findings and responses to critics. In R. J. Sternberg and E. Grigorenko (eds.), *Intelligence, heredity, and environment*. New York: Cambridge University Press. (pp. 126–160)

Boultinghouse, A. (1984) What is your style? A learning styles inventory for lower elementary students. *Roeper Review*, 6, 208–210.

Brabeck, M., Rogers, L., Sirin, S., Handerson, J., Ting, K. and Benvenuto, M. (2000) Increasing ethical sensitivity to racial and gender intolerance in schools: Development of the racial ethical sensitivity test (REST). *Ethics and Behavior*, 10(2), 119–137.

Bracken, B. A. and McCallum, R. S. (1998). *Universal Nonverbal Intelligence Test*. Itasca, IL: Riverside Publishing.

Bracken, B. A., VanTassel-Baska, J., Brown, E. F. and Feng, A. (2007) Project Athena: A tale of two studies. In J. VanTassel-Baska and T. Stambaugh (eds.), *Overlooked gems: A national perspective on low-income promising learners*. Washington, DC: National Association for Gifted Children. (pp. 63–67)

Braggett, E. J. (1985) Education of gifted and talented children: Australian provision. Canberra: Commonwealth Schools Commission.

Bransford, J. D., Brown, A. L. and Cocking, R. R. (2000) *How people learn: Brain, mind, experience, and school*. Washington D.C.: National Academy Press.

Brody, L. E. (2004) Grouping and acceleration practices in gifted education. In S. M. Reis (ed.), *Essential readings in gifted education*, (vol.III). Thousand Oaks, CA: Corwin Press.

Brody, L. E. and Stanley, J. C. (2005) Youths who reason exceptionally well mathematically and/or verbally. In R. J. Sternberg and J. E. Davidson (eds.), *Conceptions of giftedness* (2nd edn). New York: Cambridge University Press. (pp. 20–37)

Brody, L. E., Muratori, M. C. and Stanley, J. C. (2004) Early entrance to college: Academic, social, and emotional considerations. In N. Colangelo, S. G. Assouline and M. U. M. Gross (eds.), *A nation deceived: How schools hold back America's brightest students (Volume II)*. Iowa City, IA.: Belin and Blank International Center for Gifted Education and Talent Development, University of Iowa. (pp. 97–108)

Brooks, R. (1985) Delinquency among gifted children. In J. Freeman (ed.), *The psychology of gifted children*. London: Wiley. (pp. 297–308)

Broussard, S. C. and Garrison, M. E. B. (2004) The relationship between classroom motivation and academic achievement in elementary-school-aged children, *Family and Consumer Sciences Research Journal*, 33(2), 106–120.

Brown, A. L. (1987) Metacognition, executive control, self-regulation and other mysterious mechanism. In

F. E. Weinert and R. H. Kluwe (eds.), *Metacognition, motivation, and understanding*. Hillsdale, NJ: Lawrence Erlbaum Associates, Inc. (pp. 655–116)

Brown, A. L., Campione, J. C. (1994) Guided discovery in a community of learners. In K. McGilly (ed.), *Classroom lessons: Integrating cognitive theory and classroom ractice*. Cambridge, Mass, MIT Press.

Bruner, J. S. (1966) *Toward a theory of instruction*. Cambridge, MA: Harvard University Press.

Bruner, J. S. (1996) *The culture of education*. Cambridge, MA: Harvard University Press.

Bu, Y. M., Chen, K. W., Chen, H. S. and Tse, S. K. (1999a) *Readings in Chinese language*, vol. 3, 3rd edn. Hong Kong: Oxford University Press. [in Chinese]

Bu, Y. M., Chen, K. W., Chen, H. S. and Tse, S. K. (1999b) *Readings in Chinese language*, vol. 4, 3rd edn. Hong Kong: Oxford University Press. [in Chinese]

Buber, M. (2002) *Between man and man*. London: Routledge.

Buescher, T. M., Olszewski, P. and Higham, S. J. (1987, April) *Influences on strategies adolescents use to cope with their own recognized talents*. Paper presented at the biennial meeting of the Society for Research in Child Development, Baltimore, MD.

Burgh G., Field T. and Freakley M. (2006) *Ethics and the community of enquiry*. Melbourne: Thompson.

Burns, D., Johnson, S. and Gable, R. (1998) Can we generalize about the learning style characteristics of high academic achievers? *Roeper Review*, 20, 276–281.

Burton-Szabo, S. (1996, January/February) Special classes for gifted students? Absolutely! *Gifted Child Today*, 19(1), 12–15.

Butler-Por, N. (1993) Underachieving gifted students. In K. A. Heller, F. J. Mönks, and A. H. Passow (eds.), *International handbook of research and development of giftedness and talent*, Oxford: Pergamon. (pp. 649–668)

Cabeza, R. and Nyberg, L. (2000) Imaging cognition II: An empirical review of 275 PET and fMRI studies. *Journal of Cognitive Neuroscience* 12(1), 1–47.

Callahan, C. M. (1993) Evaluation programs and procedures for gifted education: International problems and solutions. In K. A. Heller, F. J. Mönks and A. H. Passow (eds.), *International handbook of research and development of Giftedness and Talent*. Oxford: Pergamon. (pp. 605–618)

Callahan, C. M. (1996) A critical self-study of gifted education: Healthy practice, necessary evil, or sedition? *Journal for the Education of the Gifted*, 19, 148–163.

Callahan, C. M. (2000) Evaluation as a critical component of program development and implementa-tion. In K. A. Heller, F. J. Mönks, R. J. Sternberg and R. F. Subotnik (eds.), *International handbook of giftedness and talent* (2nd edn). Oxford: Pergamon/Amsterdam: Elsevier. (pp. 537–547)

Callahan, C. M. (2005) Identifying gifted students from underrepresented populations, *Theory into Practice*, Spring 44, 98–104.

Calvert, G. A., Campbell, R. and Brammer, M. J. (2000) Evidence from functional magnetic resonance imaging of crossmodal binding in human heteromodal cortex. *Current Biology*, 10(11), 649–657.

Campbell, A. V. (2003) The virtues (and vices) of the four principles. *Journal of Medical Ethics*, 29: 292–296.

Campbell, J. R., Hombo, C. M. and Mazzeo, J. (2000) NAEP 1999 trends in academic progress: Three decades of student performance. *Education Statistics Quarterly*, 2 (4). NCES 2000469. Washington D.C.: U.S. Department of Education.

Campbell, J. R., Wagner, H. and Walberg, H. J. (2000) Academic competitions and programs designed to challenge the exceptionally talented. In K. A. Heller, F. J. Mönks, R. J. Sternberg and R. F. Subotnik (eds.), *International handbook of giftedness and talent* (2nd edn). Oxford: Pergamon/Amsterdam: Elsevier. (pp. 523–535)

Campbell, R. J., Eyre, D., Muijs, R.D., Neelands, J. G. A. and Robinson, W. (2004) *The English model: Context, policy and challenge*. Warwick: National Academy for Gifted and Talented Youth.

Candolle, A. de (1873) *Histoire des sciences et des savants depuis deux siècles*. Geneve: Georg.

Carlsson, I., Wendt, P. E. and Risberg, J. (2000) On the neurobiology of creativity. Differences in frontal activity between high and low creative subjects. *Neuropsychologia*, 38, 873–885.

Caruso, D. R., Mayer, J. D. and Salovey, P. (2002) Emotional intelligence and emotional leadership. In R. E. Riggio, S. E. Murphy and F. J. Pirozzolo, *Multiple intelligences and leadership*. Mahwah, NJ: Lawrence Erlbaum Associates, Inc. (pp. 55–74)

Cash, A. (1999a) Autism: The silent mask. In A. Y. Baldwin and W. Vialle (eds.), *The Many Faces of Giftedness*. Albany NY: Wadsworth Publishing. (pp. 209–236)

Cash, A. (1999b) A profile of gifted individuals with autism: The twice-exceptional learner. *Roeper Review*, 22, 22–27.

Cassandro, V. J. (1998) Explaining premature mortality across fields of creative endeavor. *Journal of Personality*, 66, 805–833.

Cattell, R. B. (1971) *Abilities: Their structure, growth, and action*. Boston: Houghton Mifflin.

Chaffey, G. W. (2002) 'Identifying Australian Aboriginal children with high academic potential using dynamic testing'. Unpublished Ph.D. Thesis, University of New England, Australia.

Chaffey, G. W., Bailey, S. B. and Vine, K. W. (2003). Identifying high academic potential in Australian Aboriginal children using dynamic testing. *The Australasian Journal of Gifted Education*, 12 (1), 42–55.

Chaffey, G. W., McCluskey, K. and Halliwell, G. (2005) Using Coolabah dynamic assessment to identify Canadian Aboriginal children with high academic potential: A cross-cultural study. *Gifted and Talented International*, 20 (2), 50–59.

Chaffey, G. W. and Bailey, S. (2006) Coolabah dynamic assessment: Identifying high academic potential in at risk populations. In B. Wallace and G. Eriksson (eds.), *Diversity in Gifted Education. International Perspectives on Global Issues*. London: Routledge. (pp. 101–142)

Chan, D. W. (1998) The development of gifted education in Hong Kong, *Gifted Education International*, 13, 150–158.

Chan, D. W. (2003) Dimensions of emotional intelligence and their relationships with social coping among gifted adolescents in Hong Kong. *Journal of Youth and Adolescence*, 32 (6), 409–418.

Chart, H., Grigorenko, E. L. and Sternberg, R. J. (2008) The Aurora Battery: Toward better identification of giftedness. In Plucker, J. A. and Callahan, C. (eds.), *Critical issues and practices in gifted education*. Waco, TX: Prufrock Press. (pp. 281–301)

Chesson, R., McKay, C. and Stephenson, E. (1991) The consequences of motor/learning difficulties in school age children and their teachers: Some parental views. *Support for Learning* 6(4), 172–77.

Cimpian, A., Arce, H., Markman, E. M. and Dweck, C. S. (2007) Subtle linguistic cues impact children's motivation. *Psychological Science*, 18, 314–316.

Clark, B. (1992) *Growing up gifted*. New York: Merrill.

Clark, B. (1997) *Growing up gifted: Developing the potential of children at home and at school* (5th edn.). Upper Saddle River, NJ: Prentice-Hall.

Clark, C. and Shore, B. (1998) *Educating students with high ability*. Paris: UNESCO.

Claxton, G. L. (1997) *Hare brain, tortoise mind: Why intelligence increases when you think less*, Fourth Estate: London: HarperSanFrancisco.

Claxton, G. L (1998) *Hare brain, tortoise mind*. London: Fourth Estate Ltd.

Claxton, G. L (1999a) *Wise up: The challenge of lifelong learning*. London and New York: Bloomsbury.

Claxton, G. L (1999b) *Wise up: Learning to live the learning life*. Stafford: Network Educational Press.

Claxton, G. L. (2002) *Building learning power: helping young people become better learners*. Bristol: TLO Ltd.

Clements, S. D. (1966) *National project on minimal brain dysfunction in children – terminology and identification*. Monograph No 3, Public Health Service Publication 1415. Washington, D.C.: Government Printing Office.

Coffield, F., Moseley, D., Hall, E. and Ecclestone, K. (2004) *Learning styles and pedagogy in post-16 learning: A systematic and critical review* (Report No. 041543). London: Learning and Skills Research Centre.

Colangelo, N. (1982) Characteristics of moral problems as formulated by gifted adolescents. *Journal of Moral Education*, 11(4), 219–232.

Colangelo, N. (2002) Counseling gifted and talented students. *The National Research Center on the Gifted and Talented Newsletter*. Fall, 5–9.

Colangelo, N., Assouline, S. G. and Gross, M. U. M. (eds.). (2004) *A nation deceived: How schools hold back America's brightest students. The Templeton National Report on Acceleration, Vols. I and II*. Iowa City, IA: Belin and Blank International Center for Gifted Education and Talent Development, University of Iowa.

Colangelo, N., Assouline, S. G. and Lupkowski-Shoplik, A. E. (2004) Whole-grade acceleration.

In N. Colangelo, S. G. Assouline, and M. U. M. Gross (eds.), *A nation deceived: How schools hold back America's brightest students (Volume II)*. Iowa City, IA: Belin and Blank International Center for Gifted Education and Talent Development, University of Iowa. (pp. 77–86)

Cole, M. (1985) The zone of proximal development: Where culture and cognition create each other. In J.V. Wertsch (ed.), *Culture, Communication and Cognition: Vygotskian Perspectives*. New York: Cambridge University Press.

Coleman, L.J. (2004) Is consensus on a definition in the field possible, desirable, necessary? *Roeper Review*, 27, 10–11.

Coleman, M. R. and Gallagher, J. J. (1995) The successful blending of gifted education with middle schools and cooperative learning: Two studies. *The Journal for the Education of the Gifted*, 18, 362–384.

Coleman, M. R., Coltrane, S. S., Harradine, C. and Timmons, L.A. (2007) Impact of poverty on promising learners, their teachers, and their schools. In J. VanTassel-Baska and T. Stambaugh (eds.), *Overlooked gems: A National perspective on low-income promising learners*. Washington, D.C.: National Association for Gifted Children. (pp. 59–61)

College Board (2001) *Advanced placement program*. http://www.collegeboard.org

Colon, P. T. and Treffinger, D.J. (1980) Providing for the gifted in the regular classroom: Am I really MAD? *Roeper Review*, 3, 18–21.

Connelly, V. and Hurst, G. (2001) The influence of handwriting fluency on writing quality in later primary and early secondary education *Handwriting Today* 2, 50–57.

Connelly, V. Dockrell, J. and Barnett, A. (2005) The slow handwriting of undergraduate students constrains the overall performance in exam essays. *Educational Psychology* 25 (1), 99–109.

Conti, R., Amabile, T. M. and Pollak, S. (1995) The positive impact of creative activity: Effects of creative task engagement and motivational focus on college students' learning. *Personality and Social Psychology Bulletin*, 21, 1107–1116.

Conti, R., Coon, H. and Amabile, T. M (1996) Evidence to support the componential model of creativity: Secondary analyses of three studies. *Creativity Research Journal*, 9(4), 385–389.

Cooper, P. and Ideus, K. (1995) 'Is attention deficit hyperactivity disorder a Trojan horse?' *Support for Learning*, 10(1), 29–34.

Corn, A. (1986) 'Gifted students who have a visual difficulty. Can we meet their educational needs?' *Education of the Visually Handicapped*, 18(2), 71–84.

Corno, L. (1993) The best-laid plans: Modern conceptions of volition and educational research. *Educational Researcher*, 22, 14–22.

Corno, L. and Mandinach, E. (1983) The role of cognitive engagement in classroom learning and motivation. *Educational Psychologist*. 18, 88–109.

Corno, L. and Snow, R. E. (1986) Adapting teaching to individual differences among learners. In M. C. Wittrock (ed.), *Handbook of research on teaching* (3rd edn) New York: Macmillan. (pp. 605–629)

Costa, A. L. (ed.) (2001) *Developing minds – A resource book for teaching thinking*, 3rd edn. Alexandria, VA: ASCD.

Council for Exceptional Children (2003) *What every special educator must know: Ethics, standards, and guidelines for special educators* (5th edn). Washington, D.C.: Author.

Cox, C. (1926) *The early mental traits of three hundred geniuses*. Stanford, CA: Stanford University Press.

Craft, A. (2000) *Creativity across the primary curriculum*. London: Routledge.

Cramer, R. H. (1989) Attitudes of gifted boys and girls towards math: A qualitative study. *Roeper Review*, 11, 128–133.

Cramond, B. (2004) Can we, should we, need we agree on a definition of giftedness? *Roeper Review*, 21(1), 15.

Creţu, C. (1993) Global success in learning. How to improve it?, work presented at The Third European Conference of ECHA in Munich, abstract. In Hany, E. A. and Heller, K. A. (eds.), *Competence and responsibility, vol. I*. Göttingen: Hogrefe.

Creţu, C. (1996) The Global Success model. In *International Conference on Giftedness, Social Educational Problems*, ACTAS, ISMAI, Porto, Portugal. (pp. 238–258) [available in English and Spanish]

Creţu, C. (1997) *The Success psychology and education*. ed. Polirom, Iasi-RO [available in Romanian].

Creţu, C. (1998) *The Global Success Model*, work presented at The European Conference of ECHA in Oxford, UK.

Cronbach, L. J. and Snow, R. W. (1977) *Aptitudes and instructional methods: A handbook for research on interactions*. New York: Irvington.

Cropley, A. J. (1997) Fostering creativity in the classroom: General principles. In M. Q. Runco (ed.), *The creativity research handbook*, 1, Cresskill, NJ: Hampton Press. (pp. 83–114)

Cropley, A. J. (2006) In praise of convergent thinking. *Creativity Research Journal*, 18(3), 391–404.

Cross, T. L., Coleman, L. J. and Stewart, R. A. (1995) Psychosocial diversity among gifted adolescents: An exploratory study of two groups. *Roeper Review*, 17(3), 181–185.

Csikszentmihalyi, M. (1982) Learning, 'flow', and happiness. In R. Gross (ed.), *Invitation to lifelong learning*. Chigargo: Follett. (pp. 167–187)

Csikszentmihalyi, M. (1990) *Flow: the psychology of optimal experience*. New York: Harper Perennial.

Csikszentmihalyi, M. (1996) *Creativity: Flow and the psychology of discovery and invention*. New York: Harper Perennial.

Csikszentmihalyi, M. (1999) Implication of a system perspective for the study of creativity. In Sternberg, R. J. (ed.), *Handbook of creativity*. New York: Cambridge University Press. (pp. 313–335)

Csikszentmihalyi, M., Rathunde, K. and Whalen, S. (1993) *Talented teenagers: The roots of success and failure*. Cambridge: Cambridge University Press.

Dabrowski K. (1979) *Dezintegracja pozytywna*, Warszawa: Państwowy Instytut Wydawniczy.

Dabrowski, K. (1964) *Positive desintegration*. London: Little Brown.

Dabrowski, K. and Piechowski, M. M. (1977) Theory of levels of emotional development (vol.1, *Multilevelness and positive disintegration*). Oceanside, NY: Dabor

Dahlgren, G. and Olsson, L-E. (1985). *Läsning i barnperspektiv* [Reading in children's perspective]. Göteborg Studies in Educational Sciences 51. Acta Universitatis Gothoburgensis.

Dai, D. Y. and Renzulli, J.S., in press, 'Snowflakes, living systems, and the mystery of giftedness', *Gifted Child Quarterly*.

Dai, D. Y., Moon, S. and Feldhusen, J. (1998) Achievement motivation of gifted students: A social cognitive perspective. *Educational Psychologist*, 33(2), 45–63.

Damasio, A. R. (1999) *The feeling of what happens: Body, emotion and the making of consciousness*. London: William Heinemann

Damasio, A. R. (2001) Some notes on brain, imagination and creativity. In K. H. Pfenninger and V. R. Shubik (eds.), *The origins of creativity*. Oxford: Oxford University Press. (pp. 59–68)

Darling-Hammond, L., Wise, A. and Klein, S. (1999) *A license to teach, raising standards for teaching*. San Francisco: Jossey-Bass.

Darling-Hammond, L., Chung, R. and Frelow, F. (2002) Variation in teacher preparation: How well do different pathways prepare teachers to teach? *Journal of Teacher Education*, 53, 286–302.

Dauber, S. L. and Benbow, C. P. (1990) Aspects of personality and peer relations of extremely talented adolescents. *Gifted Child Quarterly*, 34(1), 10–14.

Davies, T. (2000) Confidence! Its role in the creative teaching and learning of Design and Technology. *Journal of Technology Education*, 12(1), 18–31.

Davis, G. A. and Rimm, S. B. (1998) *Education of the gifted and talented*. (4th edn). Needham Heights: Allyn and Bacon.

Davis, G. A., and Rimm, S. B. (2004) *Education of the gifted and talented* (5th edn). Boston: Allyn and Bacon.

De Souza Fleith, D. (2000) Teacher and student perceptions of creativity in the classroom environment. *Roeper Review*, 22(2), 148–158.

De Waele, M., Morval, J. and Sheitoyan, R. (1993) *Self-management in organizations: The dynamics of interaction*. Seattle, WA: Hogrefe and Huber.

Dehaene, S. (1997) *The number sense: How the mind creates mathematics*. Oxford: Oxford University Press.

Dehaene, S., Kerszberg, M. and Changeux, J-P. (1998) A neuronal model of a global workspace in effortful cognitive tasks. *Proceedings of the National Academy of Sciences USA*, 95, 14529–14534.

DeHann, R. F. and Havighurst, R. J. (1961) *Educating gifted children* (rev. edn). Chicago: University of Chicago Press.

Delaubier, J.-P. (2002) *La scolarisation des élèves « intellectuellement précoces ». Rapport à Monsieur le Ministre de l'Education Nationale.* [Intellectually precocious children's schooling. Report to the Education Minister]. Paris: Ministère de l'Education Nationale. [Can be downloaded from http://www.education.gouv.fr].

Delbridge-Parker, L. and Robinson, D. C. (1988) Type and academically gifted adolescents. *Journal of Psychological Type,* 17, 66–72.

Demetriou, A. (2002) Tracing psychology's invisible giant and its visible guards. In R. J. Sternberg and E. L. Grigorenko (eds.), *The general factor of intelligence: How general is it?* Mahwah, NJ: Lawrence Erlbaum Associates, Inc. (pp. 3–18)

Dennis, W. (1966) Creative productivity between the ages of 20 and 80 years. *Journal of Gerontology,* 21, 1–8.

Deutsches PISA-Konsortium (ed.) (2001) *PISA 2000 – Basiskompetenzen von Schülerinnen und Schülern im internationalen Vergleich* [Basic competencies of students in the international perspective]. Opladen: Leske + Budrich.

Deutsches PISA-Konsortium (ed.) (2002) *PISA 2000 – Die Länder der Bundesrepublik Deutschland im Vergleich* [The Länder of the Federal Republic of Germany compared]. Opladen: Leske + Budrich.

Dewey, J. (1902) *The child and the curriculum.* Chicago: University of Chicago Press.

Dewey, J. (1916) *Democracy and education.* New York: The Free Press (Macmillan).

DfEE (1999) *Excellence in cities.* London: London: The Stationery Office.

DfEE /QCA (1999) *The National Curriculum for England (Design and Technology).* London : DfEE/QCA.

DfES (2003) *Excellence and enjoyment: a strategy for primary schools.* London: Department for Education and Skills.

DfES (2004–2009) *Personalised learning.* London: DfES.

DfES (2005) *Ethnicity and education: The evidence on minority ethnic pupils.* London: DfES.

DfES (2006a) *Identifying Gifted and Talented Pupils.* Nottingham: DfES Publications.

DfES (2006b) *National Quality Standards in Gifted and Talented Education.* London: DfES.

DfES/QCA (2000) *Curriculum guidance for the foundation stage.* London: Department of Education and Skills / Qualifications and Curriculum Authority.

Dietrich, A. (2004) Cognitive neuroscience of creativity. *Psychonomic Bulletin & Review,* 11(6), 1011–1026.

Diezmann, C. M. and Watters, J. J. (2001) The collaboration of mathematically gifted students on challenging tasks. *Journal for the Education of the Gifted,* 25, 7–31.

Digman, J. M. (1990) Personality structure: Emergence of the five-factor model. In M. R. Rosenzweig and L. W. Porter (eds.), *Annual Review of Psychology* 41, Palo Alto, CA: Annual Reviews, 417–440.

Dollinger, S. and Shafran, M. (2005) Note on the consensual assessment technique in creativity research. *Perceptual and Motor Skills,* 100(31), 592–598.

Donoghue, E. F., Karp, A. and Vogeli, B. R. (2000) Russian schools for the mathematically and scientifically talented: Can the vision survive unchanged? *Roeper Review,* 22, 121–122.

Dorfman, L. (2000) Research on gifted children and adolescents in Russia: A chronicle of theoretical and empirical development. *Roeper Review,* 22, 123–131.

Drubach, D. (2000) *The brain explained.* Upper Saddle River, NJ: Prentice-Hall, Inc.

Duncan, J. (2001) An adaptive coding model of neural function in prefrontal cortex. *Nature Reviews Neuroscience,* 2(11), 820–829.

Dunn, L M. and Dunn, L. M. (1981) *PPVT-R: Peabody Picture Vocabulary Test Revised.* Circles Pines, MN: American Guidance Service (AGS) Publishing.

Dunn, R. (1993) The learning styles of gifted adolescents in nine culturally diverse nations. *InterEd,* 20(64), 4–6.

Dunn, R. (1998) Learning styles, creativity, and talent development. In D. J. Treffinger and K. W. McCluskey (eds.), *Teaching for talent development.* Sarasota, FL: Center for Creative Learning. (pp. 45–52)

Dunn, R. and Price, G. E. (1980) The learning style characteristics of gifted students. *Gifted Child Quarterly,* 24, 33–36.

Dunn, R., Dunn, K. and Price, G. E. (1975) *Learning style inventory.* Lawrence, KS: Price Systems.

Dunn, R., Dunn, K. and Treffinger, D. J. (1992) *Bringing out the giftedness in your child.* New York: John Wiley.

Dweck, C.S. (1999) *Self-Theories: Their role in motivation, personality and development.* Philadelphia: Taylor and Francis/Psychology Press.

Dweck, C. S. (2000) *Self-Theories: Their role in motivation, personality and development.* Philadelphia: Psychology Press

Dweck, C. S (2006) *Mindset: The new psychology of success.* New York: Random House.

Dweck, C. S. and Leggett, E. L. (1988) A social-cognitive approach to motivation and personality. *Psychological Review*, 95, 256–273.

Dweck, C. S., Chiu, C. and Hong, Y. (1995) Implicit theories and their role in judgments and reactions: A world from two perspectives, *Psychological Inquiry*, 6, 267–285.

Dworkin, R. (1977) *Taking rights seriously.* Boston: Harvard University Press.

Eder, D. (1985) The cycle of popularity: Interpersonal relations among female adolescents. *Sociology of Education*, 58, 154–165.

Edfeldt, Å. W. (1962) *Concerning freshmen's reading ability.* Research Reports, Vol. 3, May 1962. Stockholm University: Department of Education.

Edfeldt, Å. W. (1990a) The Huey legacy: A cognitive evaluation. *Early Child Development and Care*, 59, 53–72.

Edfeldt, Å. W. (1990b) *Teaching analytical reading with newspapers as sole reading text.* Stockholm University: Department of Education Research Bulletins, XIV:2.

Edwards, J. (1994) *The Scars of Dyslexia* London: Cassell

Einstein, A. (1946). Autobiographical notes. (2–94) In P. A. Schilpp (ed.), *Albert Einstein: Philosopher – scientist.* Evanston, IL: Library of Living.

Eisner, E. (1997) The Promise and Perils of Alternative Forms of Data Representation. *Educational Researcher*, 26(6), 4–10.

Enersen, D. L. (1993) Summer residential programs: Academics and beyond. *Gifted Child Quarterly*, 37, 169–176.

Entine, J. (2000) *Taboo: Why Black athletes dominate sports and why we are afraid to talk about it.* New York: Public Affairs.

Ericsson, K. A. (1996a) The acquisition of expert performance: An introduction to some of the issues. In K. A. Ericsson (ed.), *The road to expert performance: Empirical evidence from the arts and sciences, sports, and games.* Mahwah, NJ: Lawrence Erlbaum Associates, Inc. (pp. 1–50)

Ericsson, K. A. (ed.) (1996b) *The road to excellence: The acquisition of expert performance in the arts and sciences, sports, and games.* Mahwah, NJ: Lawrence Erlbaum Associates, Inc.

Ericsson, K. A. and Charness, N. (1994) Expert performance: its structure and acquisition, *American Psychologist*, 49, 725–47.

Ericsson, K. A., Krampe, R. T. and Tesch-Römer, C. (1993) The role of deliberate practice in the acquisition of expert performance. *Psychological Review*, 100, 363–406.

Ericsson, K. A., Charness, N., Feltovich, P. J. and Hoffman, R. R. (eds.) (2006) *The Cambridge handbook of expertise and expert performance.* New York: Cambridge University Press.

European Agency for Development in Special Needs Education (2003) *Special needs education in Europe: thematic publication.* Middelfart: European Agency for Development in Special Needs Education.

European Council (1994) *Recommendation 1248, relating to the education of the exceptionally gifted children.* Retrieved 14/01/2008 from http://assembly.coe.int/main.asp?Link=/documents/adoptedtext/ta94/erec1248.htm.

Evered, L. and Nayer, S. (2000) Novosibirsk's School for the Gifted – changing emphases in the New Russia. *Roeper Review*, 23, 22–24.

Ewing, N. J. and Yong, F. L. (1992) A comparative study of the learning style preferences among gifted African-American, Mexican-American, and American-born Chinese middle grade students. *Roeper Review*, 14, 120–123.

Eysenck, H. J. (1993) Creativity and personality: Suggestions for a theory. *Psychological Inquiry*, 4, 147–178.

Eysenck, H. J. (1995) *Genius: the Natural History of Creativity.* Cambridge: Cambridge University Press.

Feather, N. T. (1991) Human values in global self-esteem, and belief in a just world, in *Journal of Personality*, 59.

334

Feldhusen, J. F. (1986) A conception of giftedness. In R. J. Sternberg and J. E. Davidson (eds.), *Conceptions of giftedness*. New York: Cambridge University Press. (pp. 112–127)

Feldhusen, J. F. (2003a) Beyond general giftedness: New ways to identify and educate gifted, talented, and precocious youth. In J. H. Borland (ed.), *Rethinking gifted education*. New York: Teachers College Press. (pp. 34–45)

Feldhusen, J. F. (2003b) The nature of giftedness and talent and the pursuit of creative achievement and expertise, *Gifted and Talented*, 7, 3–5.

Feldhusen, J. F. (2005) Giftedness, talent, expertise, and creative achievement. In R. J. Sternberg and J. E. Davidson (eds.), *Conceptions of giftedness* (2nd edn). New York: Cambridge University Press. (pp. 64–79)

Feldman, D. H. with Goldsmith, L. T. (1986) *Nature's gambit: Child prodigies and the development of human potential*. New York: Basic Books.

Ferrando, M. (2006) Creatividad e Inteligencia Emocional: Un estudio empírico en alumnos con altas habilidades. Published Ph.D. thesis. Universidad de Murcia.

Ferrando, M. and Bailey R. (2006) 'Emotional Intelligence in G&T: a Pilot Study'. Paper presented to the British Educational Research Association (BERA). September Warwick University (UK).

Ferrando, M., Ferrandiz, C., Prieto, M. D., Sanchez, C., Hernandez, D., Serna, B. and Lopez, J. (2007) *Socio-Emotional Intelligence in G&T and Non-G&T Pupils*. Paper presented in the World Council for Gifted and Talented Children, 17th Biennial World Conference. University of Warwick (UK).

Feuerstein, R. (1986) Learning to learn: Mediated learning experiences and instrumental enrichment. *Special Services in the Schools*, 3, 49–82.

Feynman, R., Leighton, R. and Hutchings, E. (ed.) (1997). *'Surely You're Joking, Mr. Feynman!': Adventures of a Curious Character*. New York: W. W. Norton

Field, G. (2007) 'The effect of using Renzulli Learning on student achievement: An investigation of Internet technology on reading fluency, comprehension, and social studies'. The University of Connecticut: Unpublished doctoral dissertation.

Fisher, R. (1997) *Games for thinking*. Oxford: Nash Pollock.

Fisher, R. (1999) *First stories for thinking*. Oxford: Nash Pollock.

Fisher, R. (2001) *Values for thinking*, Oxford: Nash Pollock.

Fisher, R. (2003) (2nd edn) *Teaching thinking: Philosophical enquiry in the classroom*. London: Continuum.

Fisher, R. (2005) (2nd edn) *Teaching children to learn*. Cheltenham: Stanley Thornes.

Flack, J. (2000) The definition of giftedness: How can we help promote the work ethic in gifted students? *Understanding Our Gifted*, 13(1), 9–10.

Flavell, J. H. (1985) *Cognitive development*. Englewood Cliffs, NJ: Prentice Hall.

Flutter, J. and Rudduck, J. (2004) *Consulting pupils: What's in it for schools?* London: RoutledgeFalmer.

Folsom, C. (2004) Complex teaching and learning: Connecting teacher education to student performance. In E. Guyton (ed.), *Association of Teacher Educators Yearbook*. Reston, VA. Association of Teacher Educators. (pp. 205–231)

Folsom, C. (2006) Making conceptual connections between gifted and general education: Teaching for intellectual and emotional learning (TIEL), *Roeper Review*, 28, 2, 79–87.

Ford, D. Y. (1996) *Reversing underachievement among gifted black students: Promising programs and practices*. New York: Teachers College Press.

Ford, D.Y. and Thomas A. (1997) Underachievement among gifted minority students: Problems and promises in recruitment and retention, *Journal of Special Education*, 32, 4–14.

Ford, D.Y. and Harris III, J.J. (2000) A framework for infusing multicultural curriculum into gifted education. *Roeper Review*, 23(1), 4–10.

Frangou, S., Chitins, X. and Williams, S. C. (2004) Mapping IQ and gray matter density in healthy young people. *NeuroImage*, 23(3), 800–805.

Frankl, V. E. (1967) *Psychotherapy and existentialism: Selected papers on logotherapy*. New York: Simon and Schuster.

Frasier, M. M., and Passow, A. H. (1994) *Towards a new paradigm for identifying talent potential*. Storrs, CT: University of Connecticut, The National Research Center on the Gifted and Talented.

Frasier, M. M., García, J. H. and Passow, A. H. (1995) *A review of assessment issues in gifted education and their implications for identifying gifted minority students.* Storrs, CT: University of Connecticut, The National Research Center on the Gifted and Talented.

Freeman, J. (1979) *Gifted children.* Lancaster, UK: MTP Press.

Freeman, J. (1983) Emotional problems of the gifted child. *Journal of Child Psychology and Psychiatry,* 24 (3), 481–485.

Freeman, J. (1985) *The psychology of gifted children.* London: John Wiley & Sons.

Freeman, J. (1998) *Educating the very able: current international research.* London: Ofsted.

Freeman, J. (2000) Families: The essential context for gifts and talents. In K. A. Heller, F. J. Mönks, R. J. Sternberg and R. F. Subotnik (eds.), *International handbook of giftedness and talent* (2nd edn). Oxford: Pergamon/Amsterdam: Elsevier. (pp. 573–585)

Freeman, J. (2001) *Gifted children grown up.* London: David Fulton Publishers.

Freeman, J. (2002) Out-of-school educational provision for the gifted and talented around the world. A report to the DfES. Retrieved 22/4/2007 from http://www.joanfreeman.com/mainpages/freepapers.htm.

Freeman, J. (2003) Gender differences in gifted achievement in Britain and the USA. *Gifted Child Quarterly,* 47, 202–211.

Freeman, J. (2005) Permission to be gifted: How conceptions of giftedness can change lives. In R. J. Sternberg and J. E. Davidson (eds.), *Conceptions of giftedness* (2nd edn). New York: Cambridge University Press. (pp. 80–97)

Freeman, J. (2006) Giftedness in the long term, *Journal for the Education of the Gifted,* 29(4), 384–403.

Freinet, C. (1994) *Oeuvres pédagogiques. Tome 1.* Lonrai, France: Seuil.

Freire, P. (1993) *Pedagogy of the oppressed.* London: Penguin Books.

Frensch, P. A. and Sternberg, R. J. (1989) Expertise and intelligent thinking: when is it worse to know better? In R. J. Sternberg (ed.), *Advances in the psychology of human intelligence.* Volume 5 Hillsdale, NJ: Lawrence Erlbaum Associates, Inc. (pp. 157–188)

Frith, U. (ed.) (1991) *Autism and Asperger syndrome.* Cambridge: Cambridge University Press.

Fryer, M. (1996) *Creative teaching and learning.* London: Paul Chapman Publishing.

Furlong, J. (2004) BERA at 30. Have we come of age? *British Educational Research Journal,* 30(3).

Gagné, F. (1985) Giftedness and talent: Reexamining a reexamination of the definitions. *Gifted Child Quarterly,* 29, 103–112.

Gagné, F. (1991) Toward a differentiated model of giftedness and talent. In N. Colangelo and G. A. Davis (eds.), *Handbook of gifted education.* Boston: Allyn and Bacon. (pp. 65–80)

Gagné, F. (1993) Constructs and models pertaining to exceptional human abilities. In K. A. Heller, F. J. Mönks and A. H. Passow (eds.), *International handbook of research and development of giftedness and talent.* Oxford: Pergamon Press. (pp. 63–85).

Gagné, F. (1995) From giftedness to talent: A developmental model and its impact on language of the field, in *Roeper Review,* 18(2).

Gagné, F. (1997) Critique of Morelock's (1996) definitions of giftedness and talent. *Roeper Review,* 20(2), 76.

Gagné, F. (1998) A proposal for subcategories within the gifted or talented populations. *Gifted Child Quarterly,* 42, 87–95.

Gagné, F. (2000) Understanding the complex choreography of talent development through DMGT-based analysis. In K. A. Heller, F. J. Mönks, R. J. Sternberg and R. Subotnik (eds.), *International handbook for research on giftedness and talent* (2nd edn). Oxford: Pergamon Press. (pp. 67–79)

Gagné, F. (2003) Transforming gifts into talents: The DMGT as a developmental theory. In N. Colangelo and G. A. Davis (eds.), *Handbook of gifted education* (3rd edn). Boston: Allyn and Bacon. (pp. 60–74)

Gagné, F. (2004) Transforming gifts into talents: The DMGT as a developmental theory. *High Ability Studies,* 15, 119–147.

Gagné, F. (2005) From gifts to talents: The DMGT as a developmental model. In R. J. Sternberg and J. E. Davidson (eds.), *Conceptions of giftedness* (2nd edn). Cambridge: Cambridge University Press. (pp. 98–119)

Gagné, F. and Gagnier, N. (2004) The socioaffective and academic impact of early entrance to school. *Roeper Review*, 26(3), 128–139.

Gallagher, J. J. (1985) *Teaching the gifted child* (3rd edn). Boston: Allyn and Bacon.

Gallagher, J. J. (2000) Changing paradigms for gifted education in the United States. In K. A. Heller, F. J. Mönks, R. J. Sternberg and R.F. Subotnik (eds.), *International handbook of giftedness and talent* (2nd edn). Oxford: Pergamon/Amsterdam: Elsevier. (pp. 681–693)

Gallagher, J. J., Coleman, M. R. and Nelson, S. (1993) *Cooperative learning as perceived by educators of gifted students and proponents of cooperative education*. University of North Carolina at Chapel Hill, Gifted Education Policy Studies Program.

Gallagher, J. J, Harradine, C. C. and Coleman, M. R. (1997) Challenge or boredom? Gifted students' views on their schooling. *Roeper Review*, 19(3), 132–136.

Gallagher, S. A. (1990) Personality patterns of the gifted. *Understanding our Gifted*, 3, 11–3.

Galton, F. (1869) *Hereditary genius: An inquiry into its laws and consequences*. London: Macmillan.

Galton, F. (1874) *English men of science: Their nature and nurture*. London: Macmillan.

Galton, F. (1892/1962) *Hereditary genius: An inquiry into its laws and consequences*. New York: Meridian Books.

Galton, M. and MacBeath, J. with Page, C. and Steward, S. (2002) *A Life in teaching? The impact of change on primary teachers' working lives*. Survey for NUT.

Gardner, H. (1983) *Frames of mind: The theory of multiple intelligences*, Basic Books, New York.

Gardner, H. (1993a) *Creating Minds: An anatomy of creativity seen through the lives of Freud, Einstein, Picasso, Stravinsky, Eliot, Graham, and Gandhi*. New York: Basic Books.

Gardner, H. (1993b) *Multiple intelligences: The theory in practice*. New York: Basic Books

Gardner, H. (1995) *Leading minds*. New York: Basic Books.

Gardner, H. (1999) *Intelligence reframed: multiple intelligence for the 21st century*. New York: Basic Books.

Gardner, H. (2000) The giftedness matrix: A developmental perspective. In R.C. Freidman, and B.M. Shore (eds.), *Talents unfolding: Cognition and development* Washington, DC: American Psychological Association. (pp. 77–88)

Garland, A. F. and Ziegler, E. (1999) Emotional and behavioural problems among highly intellectually gifted youth. *Roeper Review*, 22(1), 41–44.

Gath, D., Tennent, G. and Pidduck, R. (1970) Psychiatric and social characteristics of bright delinquents. *British Journal of Psychology*, 116, 515–516.

Geake, J. G. (2004) How children's brains think: Not left or right but both together. *Education 3–13*, 32(3), 65–72.

Geake, J. G. (2006) Mathematical brains. *Gifted and Talented*, 10(1), 2–7.

Geake, J. G. (2007a) The neuropsychology of giftedness. In L. Shavinina (ed.), *International handbook of giftedness*, Springer Science (in press).

Geake, J. G. (2007b) Fluid analogising: A cognitive neuroscience construct of giftedness. *Roeper Review*, (in press).

Geake, J. G. and Cooper, P.W. (2003) Implications of cognitive neuroscience for education. *Westminster Studies in Education*, 26(10), 7–20.

Geake, J. G. and Dodson, C. S. (2005) A neuro-psychological model of the creative intelligence of gifted children. *Gifted & Talented International*, 20(1), 4–16.

Geake, J. G., and Hansen, P. (2005) Neural correlates of intelligence as revealed by fMRI of fluid analogies, *NeuroImage*, 26(2), 555–564.

Geake, J. G. and Hansen, P. (in press) Neural correlates of creative intelligence as determined by abilities at fluid analogising: An fMRI study.

George, D. (1992) *The challenge of the able child*. London: David Fulton.

Georgsdottir, A. S. and Lubart, T. I. (2003) La flexibilité cognitive et la créativité. [Cognitive flexibility and creativity] *Psychologie Française*, 48(3), 29–40.

Georgsdottir, A. S., Jacquet, A. Y., Pacteau, C. and Lubart, T. (2000) La flexibilité cognitive: une exemple de variabilité intra-individuelle liée à la créativité [Cognitive flexibility: an example of intra-individual variability linked to creativity]. Colloque 'invariants & variabilité dans les sciences cognitives' ['Invariants and variability in cognitive science' conference]. Paris, France.

337

Georgsdottir, A. S., Ameel, E. and Lubart, T. I. (2002) Cognitive flexibility and logical reasoning in school aged children. XVIIth Biennial Meeting of the International Society for the Study of Behavioural Development (ISSBD). Ottawa, Canada.

Geschwind, N. and Galaburda, A. (1987) *Cerebral lateralization: Biological mechanisms, associations, and pathology.* Cambridge, MA: MIT Press.

Getzels, J. W. and Csikszentmihalyi, M. (1976). *The creative vision: A longitudinal study of problem finding in art.* New York: Wiley.

Ghiselin B. (1952) *The creative process.* Los Angeles: University of California Press.

Gibbons, M., Nowotny, H., Limoges, C., Trow, M., Schwartzman, S. and Scott, P. (1994) *The new production of knowledge; the dynamics of science and research in contemporary societies.* London: Sage

Gillborn, D. (2005) Memorandum submitted by Professor David Gillborn (University of London) on the Education White Paper (2005): *Race inequality, 'gifted & talented' students and the increased use of 'setting by ability'.* House of Commons Select Committee on Education and Skills. London: United Kingdom Parliament.

Gilligan, C. (1982) *In a different voice.* Cambridge, MA: Harvard University Press.

Gillon, R. (1985) *Philosophical medical ethics* Chichester: John Wiley & Sons.

Gilmore, C. K., McCarthy, S. E. and Spike, E. (2007) Symbolic arithmetic knowledge without instruction. *Nature,* 447, 589–591.

Gold, M. J. (1965) *Education of the intellectually gifted.* Columbus, Oh: Charles E. Merrill.

Goleman, D. (1995) *Emotional intelligence,* Bantam Books, NY.

Goleman, D. (1998a) *Working with emotional intelligence.* New York: Bantam.

Goleman, D. (1998b) What makes a good leader? *Harvard Business Review, November–December,* 93–102.

Goleman, D. (2006) *Social intelligence.* New York: Bantam Books.

Gordon, E. W. and Bridglall, B. L. (2005) Nurturing talent in gifted students of color. In R. J. Sternberg and J. E. Davidson (eds.), *Conceptions of giftedness* (2nd edn). New York: Cambridge University Press. (pp. 120–146)

Gottfried, A. E. (1990) Academic intrinsic motivation in young elementary school children. *Journal of Education Psychology* 82(3), 525–538.

Gottfried, A. W., Cook, C. R., Gottfried, A. E. and Morris, P. E. (2005) Educational characteristics of adolescents with gifted academic intrinsic motivation: A longitudinal investigation from school entry through early adulthood. *Gifted Child Quarterly,* 49(2), 172.

Gottfried, A. W., Gottfried, A. E. and Guerin, D. W. (in press) Issues in early prediction and identification of intellectual giftedness. In F. D. Horowitz, R. F. Subotnik and D. J. Matthews (eds.), *The development of giftedness and talent across the lifespan.* Washington, D.C.: American Psychological Association.

Gowan, J. C. and Bruch, C. B. (1971) *The academically talented student and guidance.* Boston: Houghton Mifflin.

Graham, S. (in press) Giftedness in adolescence: African American gifted youth and their challenges from a motivational perspective. In F. D. Horowitz, R. F. Subotnik and D. J. Matthews (eds.), *The development of giftedness and talent across the lifespan,* Washington, D.C.: American Psychological Association.

Grandin, T. (1992) An inside view of autism. In E. Schopler and G. B. Mesibov (eds.), *High functioning individuals with autism.* New York: Plenum Press. (pp. 105–128)

Grandin, T. (2006) *Thinking in pictures, expanded edition: My Life with Autism.* New York: Vintage Books.

Grant, H. and Dweck, C. S. (2003) Clarifying achievement goals and their impact. *Journal of Personality and Social Psychology,* 85, 541–553.

Gray, J. R., Chabris, C. F. and Braver, T. S. (2003) Neural mechanisms of general fluid intelligence. *Nature Neuroscience,* 6(3), 316–322.

Greenwood, C. R. (1991) Longitudinal analysis of time, engagement, and achievement in at-risk versus non-risk students. *Exceptional Children,* 57(6), 521–536.

Griggs, S. A. and Dunn, R. (1984) Selected case studies of the learning style preferences of gifted students. *Gifted Child Quarterly,* 28, 115–119.

Griggs, S. A. and Price, G. E. (1980a) Learning styles of gifted versus average junior high school students. *Phi Delta Kappan,* 61, 361.

Griggs, S. A. and Price, G. E. (1980b) A comparison between the learning styles of gifted versus average suburban junior high school students. *Roeper Review*, 3, 7–9.

Grigorenko, E. L. (2000) Russian gifted education in math and science: Tradition and transformation. In K. A. Heller, F. J. Mönks, R. J. Sternberg and R. F. Subotnik (eds.), *International handbook of research and development of giftedness and talent*. Amsterdam, Holland: Elsevier.

Grigorenko, E. L. and Clinkenbeard, P. R. (1994) An inside view of gifted education in Russia. *Roeper Review*, 16, 167–171.

Grigorenko, E. L. and Sternberg, R. J. (1998) Dynamic testing. *Psychological Bulletin*, 124(1), 75–111.

Grigorenko, E. L. and Sternberg, R. J. (eds.) (2001) *Family environment and intellectual functioning: A life-span perspective*. Mahwah, NJ: Lawrence Erlbaum Associates, Inc.

Gross, M. U. M. (1989) The pursuit of excellence or the search for intimacy? The forced-choice dilemma of gifted youth. *Roeper Review*, 11 (4), 189–194.

Gross, M. U. M. (1993) *Exceptionally gifted children*. New York: Routledge.

Gross, M.U.M. (1998) Fishing for the facts: A response to Marsh and Craven, 1997. *Australian Journal of Gifted Education*, 7(1), 10–23.

Gross, M. U. M. (2004) *Exceptionally gifted children*. London: Routledge.

Grossberg, L. N. and Cornell, D. G. (1988) Relationship between personality adjustment and high intelligence: Terman versus Hollingworth. *Exceptional Children*, 55, 266–272.

Grotz, P. (1990). Arbeitsgemeinschaften für besonders befähigte Sekundarstufenschüler. Erfahrungen mit einem Förderprogramm an Schulen in Baden-Württemberg [Enrichment programs at the secondary schools of Baden-Württemberg]. In H. Wagner (ed.), *Begabungsförderung in der Schule* [Nurturing gifted students at school] Bad Honnef: Bock. (pp. 13–28)

Gubbay, S. S. (1976) *The clumsy child*. London: W.B. Saunders.

Guignard, J-H. and Lubart, T. I. (2006) A comparative study of convergent and divergent thinking in intellectually gifted children. *Gifted and Talented International*, 22(1).

Guilford, J. P. (1950) Creativity. *American Psychologist*, 5, 444–454.

Guilford, J. P. (1959) Three faces of intellect. *American Psychologist*, 14, 469–479.

Guilford, J. P. (1967) *The nature of human intelligence*. New York: McGraw-Hill.

Guilford, J. P. (1977) *Way beyond the IQ*. Buffalo, NY: Creative Education Foundation.

Guillberg, C. (1991) Asperger's Syndrome in 23 Swedish Children. *Developmental Medicine and Child Neurology*, 31, 520–31.

Hacker, D. J., Dunlosy, J. and Grassner, A. E. (eds.) (1998) *Metacognition in educational theory and practice*. Mahwah, NJ: Lawrence Erlbaum Associates.

Hadamard, J. (1945) *The psychology of invention in the mathematical field*. Princeton, NJ: Princeton University Press.

Haier, R. J. and Denham, S. A. (1976) A summary profile of the nonintellectual correlates of mathematical precocity in boys and girls. In D. P. Keating (ed.), *Intellectual talent research and development*. Baltimore, MD: Johns Hopkins University Press. (pp. 225–241)

Haier, R. J., Jung, R. E., Yeo, R. A., Head, K. and Alkire, M. T. (2004) Structural brain variation and general intelligence. *NeuroImage*, 23(1), 425–433.

Hall, C. and Shulz, R. (2003) Tensions in teaching and teacher education: professionalism and professionalisation in England and Canada. *Compare* 33(3), 369–383.

Hallam, S. and Ireson, J. (2006) Secondary school pupils' preferences for different types of structured grouping practices, *British Educational Research Journal* 32(4): 583–599.

Hannaford, C. (2005) *Fairer schools: Fairer society*. Utbildning & Demokrati; Sweden: Örebro University.

Hany, E.A. (1993) Methodological problems and issues concerning identification. In K. A. Heller, F. J. Mönks and A. H. Passow (eds.), *International handbook of research and development of giftedness and talent*. Oxford: Pergamon. (pp. 209–232)

Hany, E. A. (1994) The development of basic cognitive components of technical creativity: A longitudinal comparison of children and youth with high and average intelligence. In R. F. Subotnik and K. D. Arnold (eds.), *Beyond Terman: Contemporary longitudinal studies of giftedness and talent*. Norwood, NJ: Ablex. (pp. 115–154)

Hany, E. A. (1997) Modeling teachers' judgment of giftedness: A methodological inquiry of biased judgment. *High Ability Studies*, 8, 159–178.

Hany, E. A. (2000) Begabtenförderung in Deutschland als Scheinbehandlung? – Ein freundschaftlicher Frontalangriff [Nurturing the gifted in Germany as a dummy treatment? – A friendly frontal attack]. In H. Joswig (ed.), *Begabungen erkennen – Begabte fördern* [Identifying and nurturing the gifted] Rostock: Univ. Rostock, Phil. Fak. (pp. 133–143)

Hany, E. A. (2001) Identifikation von Hochbegabten im Schulalter. In K. A. Heller (ed.), *Hochbegabung im Kindes- und Jugendalter* [High ability in childhood and adolescence] (2nd edn). Göttingen: Hogrefe. (pp. 41–169)

Hany, E. A. (2004) Determinanten besonderer Leistungen im Kontext von Spezialschulen: Konsequenzen für die Schülerauswahl [Determinants of excellence in the context of gifted schools: consequences for the talent search]. *Psychologie in Erziehung und Unterricht*, 51, 40–51.

Hany, E. A. and Heller, K. A. (1992). *Förderung besonders befähigter Schüler in Baden-Württemberg: Ergebnisse der Wissenschaftlichen Begleitforschung* [Nurturing gifted students in Baden-Württemberg: Results of program evaluation]. In Ministerium für Kultus und Sport (MKS) (ed.), Heft 15 der Reihe 'Förderung besonders befähigter Schüler', Baden-Württemberg. Stuttgart: MKS.

Hargreaves, D. H. (1975) *Interpersonal Relations and Education*. London: Routledge & Kegan Paul.

Hargreaves, D. H. (1996) 'Teaching as a research-based profession: Possibilities and prospects', the Teacher Training Agency Annual Lecture, London: TTA.

Harker, E. (2006) How can I carry out Masters level educational research without abandoning my own educational values? Masters Educational Enquiry: University of Bath. Retrieved 22/4/2007 from http://www.jackwhitehead.com/tuesdayma/ehee06.htm.

Harrington, D. M., Block, J. H. and Block, J. (1987) Testing aspects of Carl Rogers's theory of creative environments: Child rearing antecedents of creative potential in young adolescents. *Journal of Personality and Social Psychology*, 4, 851–856.

Harrison, J. (1998) Improving learning opportunities in mainstream secondary schools and colleges for students on the autistic spectrum. *British Journal of Special Education* 23, 4, pp. 179–83

Hart, B. & Risley, T. (1995) Meaningful differences in everyday experience of young American children. Baltimore: Paul Brookes Publishing Co.

Hart, S., Dixon, A., Drummond, M.J. and McIntyre, D. (2004) *Learning without limits*. Maidenhead: Open University Press.

Harter, S. (1986) *Manual for self-perception profile for adolescents*. Denver, CO: University of Denver Press.

Hayes, J. R. (1989) *The complete problem solver* (2nd edn). Hillsdale, NJ: Lawrence Erlbaum Associates, Inc.

Hedlund, J., Forsythe, G. B., Horvath, J. A., Williams, W. M., Snook, S. and Sternberg, R. J. (2003) Identifying and assessing tacit knowledge: Understanding the practical intelligence of military leaders. *Leadership Quarterly*, 14, 117–140.

Hedlund, J., Wilt, J. M., Nebel, K. R., Ashford, S. J. and Sternberg, R. J. (2006) Assessing practical intelligence in business school admissions: A supplement to the graduate management admissions test. *Learning and Individual Differences*, 16, 101–127.

Heilman, K. M., Nadeau, S. E. and Beversdorf, D. O. (2003) Creative innovation: possible brain mechanisms. *Neurocase*, 9, 369–379.

Heller, K. A. (1995) Evaluation of programs for the gifted. In M. Katzko and F. J. Mönks (eds.), *Nurturing talent: Individual needs and social ability*. Assen/Maastricht: Van Gorcum. (pp. 264–268)

Heller, K. A. (1999) Individual (learning and motivational) needs versus instructional conditions of gifted education. *High Ability Studies*, 9, 9–21.

Heller, K. A. (ed.). (2001) *Hochbegabung im Kindes- und Jugendalter* (2nd edn) [High ability in childhood and adolescence]. Göttingen: Hogrefe.

Heller, K. A. (2002a) Identifying and nurturing the gifted in math, science, and technology. In Korean Educational Development Institute (ed.), *International Conference on Education for the Gifted in Science* Seoul: KEDI. (pp. 49–90)

Heller, K. A. (Guest Editor). (2002b) Program evaluation. *European Journal of Psychological Assessment*, 18, Issue 3 (Special Section), 187–241.

Heller, K. A. (2003) Das Gymnasium zwischen Tradition und modernen Bildungsansprüchen [The German Gymnasium between tradition and modern requirements]. *Zeitschrift für Pädagogik*, 49, 213–234.

Heller, K. A. (2004) Identification of gifted and talented students. *Psychology Science*, 46, 302–323.

Heller, K. A. (2005a) Education and counseling of the gifted and talented in Germany. *International Journal for the Advancement of Counselling*, 27, 191–210.

Heller, K. A. (2005b) The Munich Model of Giftedness and its impact on identification and programming. *Gifted and Talented International*, 20, 30–36.

Heller, K. A. and Hany, E.A. (1996) Psychologische Modelle der Hochbegabtenförderung [Psychological models of gifted education]. In F.E. Weinert (ed.), *Psychologie des Lernens und der Instruktion, Vol. 2 der Pädagogischen Psychologie (Enzyklopädie der Psychologie)* Göttingen: Hogrefe. (pp. 477–513)

Heller, K. A. and Lengfelder, A. (2000) *German Olympiad Study on Math, Physics and Chemistry*. Invited Paper for the AERA Annual Meeting 2000 in New Orleans (USA).

Heller, K. A. and Lengfelder, A. (2006) Evaluation study of the International Academic Olympiads. Three decades of cross-cultural and gender findings from North-American, European and East-Asian Olympians. In H. Helfrich, M. Zillekens and E. Hölter (eds.), *Culture and development in Japan and Germany*. Münster: Daedalus. (pp. 155–170)

Heller, K. A. and Perleth, Ch. (2004) Adapting conceptual models for cross-cultural applications. In J. R. Campbell, K. Tirri, P. Ruohotie and H. Walberg (eds.), *Cross-cultural research: Basic issues, dilemmas, and strategies*. Hämeenlinna, Finland: Research Centre for Vocational Education / University of Tampere, Finland. (pp. 81–101)

Heller, K. A. and Perleth, Ch. (2007) *Münchner Hochbegabungs-Testbatterie (MHBT)* [Munich High Ability Test Battery]. Göttingen: Hogrefe.

Heller, K. A. and Reimann, R. (2002) Theoretical and methodological problems of a 10-year-follow-up program evaluation study. *European Journal of Psychological Assessment*, 18, 229–241.

Heller, K. A. and Viek, P. (2000) Support for university students: Individual and social factors. In C. F. M. van Lieshout and P. G. Heymans (eds.), *Developing talent across the life span*. Hove: Psychology Press/ Philadelphia: Taylor and Francis. (pp. 299–321)

Heller, K. A., Mönks, F. J. and Passow, A. H. (eds.). (1993) *International handbook of research and development of giftedness and talent*. Oxford: Pergamon.

Heller, K. A., Mönks, F. J., Sternberg, R. J. and Subotnik, R. F. (eds.) (2000) *International handbook of giftedness and talent* (2nd edn, revised reprint 2002). Oxford/Amsterdam: Pergamon/Elsevier.

Heller, K. A., Perleth, C. and Lim, T. K. (2005) The Munich Model of Giftedness designed to identify and promote gifted students. In R. J. Sternberg and J. E. Davidson (eds.), *Conceptions of giftedness* (2nd edn). New York: Cambridge University Press. (pp. 147–170)

Hemery, D. (1986) *The pursuit of sporting excellence: A study of sport's highest achievers*. London: Willow Books.

Henderson, S. E. and Green, D. (2001) Handwriting problems in children with Asperger Syndrome *Handwriting Today*, 2, 65–71

Henderson, S. E., Stainthorp, R., Barnett, A. and Scheib, B. (2001) Handwriting policy and practice in primary schools. Paper presented at the British Psychological Society Education and Developmental Sections Joint Annual Conference September, England: Worcester University.

Henderson, V. and Dweck, C. S. (1990) Adolescence and achievement. In S. Feldman and G. Elliott (eds.), *At the threshold: Adolescent development*. Cambridge, MA: Harvard University Press. (pp. 308–329)

Hermelin, B. (2001) *Bright spiders of the mind: A personal story of research with autistic savants*. London: Jessica Kingsley.

Herrnstein, R. J. and Murray, C. (1994) *The bell curve: Intelligence and class structure in American Life*. New York: Free Press.

Hewston, R. (2006) *The First Annual Survey of the Workloads and Support Needs of Gifted and Talented Co-ordinators in Secondary Schools in England. An Occasional Paper for the National Academy for Gifted and Talented Youth* (NAGTY): University of Warwick Press.

Hickey, M. (2001) An application of Amabile's Consensual Assessment Technique for rating the creativity of children's musical compositions. *Journal of Research in Music Education*, 49(3), 234–244.

Hiebert, E. F. and Raphael, T. E. (1996). *Psychological perspectives on literacy and extensions to educational practice.* In D. C. Berliner & R. C. Calfee (eds.), *Handbook on educational psychology.* New York: Macmillan. (pp. 550–602)

Hobson, J. R. (1963) High school performance of underage pupils initially admitted to kindergarten on the basis of physical and psychological examinations. *Educational and Psychological Measurement,* 23, 159–170.

Hoehn, L. and Birely, M. K. (1988) Mental processing preferences of gifted children. *Illinois Council for the Gifted Journal,* 7, 28–31.

Holahan, C. K. and Sears, R. R. (1995) *The gifted group in later maturity.* Stanford, CA: Stanford University Press.

Holling, H. and Kanning, U. P. (1999) *Hochbegabung* [High ability]. Göttingen: Hogrefe.

Hollingworth, L. S. (1942) *Children above 180 IQ Stanford-Binet: Origin and development.* Yonkers-on-Hudson, NY: World.

Holton Gerald (1972) On trying to understand scientific genius. *American Scholar,* 41, 95–110.

Holzman, L. (1997) *Schools for growth – radical alternatives to current educational models.* Mahwah, NJ: Lawrence Erlbaum Associates, Inc.

Hong, E. and Milgram, R. M. (1996) The structure of giftedness: The domain of literature as an example. *Gifted Child Quarterly,* 40, 31–40.

Horowitz, F. D. (1987) A developmental view of giftedness. *Gifted Child Quarterly,* 31, 4, 165–168.

Horwitz, R. A. (1979). Psychological effects of the open classroom. *Review of Educational Research,* 49(1), 71–85.

Howe, A. (2004) Science is creative. *Primary Science Review,* 81 Jan/Feb 2004, 14–16; Association for Science Education.

Howe, M. J. A. (1990) *The origins of exceptional abilities.* Oxford: Basil Blackwell.

Howe, M. J. A. (1999) *Genius explained.* Cambridge: Cambridge University Press.

Huey, E. B. (1908) *The Psychology and pedagogy of reading.* New York: Macmillan.

Hunsaker, S. L. and Callahan, C. M. (1995) Creativity and giftedness : Published instruments uses and abuses. *Gifted Child Quarterly,* 39, 110–114.

Husén, T. and Postlethwaithe, T. N. (eds.) (1985) *The international encyclopedia of education, I–X.* Oxford: Pergamon.

Huxtable, M. (2006) Making public my embodied knowledge as an educational psychologist in the enquiry, How can (do) I improve my practice as a Senior Educational Psychologist? A paper presented at British Educational Research Association Conference, 2006.

Hyde, J. S., Fennema, E. and Lamon, S. J. (1990) Gender differences in mathematics performance: A meta-analysis. *Psychological Bulletin,* 107 (2), 139–155.

Hymer, B. J. (2007) How do I understand and communicate my values and beliefs in my work as an educator in the field of giftedness? Doctoral dissertation, University of Newcastle Upon Tyne.

Hymer, B. J. with Michel, D. (2002) *Gifted and talented learners: Creating a policy for inclusion.* London: David Fulton

Ikonen-Varila, M. (2000) Moraalipäättelyn kehittyneisyys, normisosialisaatio ja toimintastrategiat [Development of ethics, norm-sosialization and strategic plans]. In J. Hautamäki, P. Arinen, A. Hautamäki, M. Ikonen-Varila, S. Kupiainen, B. Lindholm, M. Niemenvirta, P. Rantanen, M. Ruuth and P. Scheinin (eds.), *Oppimaan oppiminen yläasteella. Oppimistulosten arviointi 7/2000.* Helsinki: Opetushallitus. (pp. 215–238)

Isaksen, S. G. and Treffinger, D. J. (2004) Celebrating 50 years of reflective practice: Versions of creative problem solving. *Journal of Creative Behavior.* 38 (2), 75–101.

Isaksen, S. G., Dorval, K. B. and Treffinger, D. J. (2000) *Creative approaches to problem solving.* (2nd edn.) Dubuque, IA: Kendall-Hunt.

Jaksa, P. (1999) The flowers and the thorns. *FOCUS Reprint Newsletter of the National ADDA* pp. 1–4. http://www.add.org.com.

Janis, I. L. (1972) *Victims of groupthink.* Boston: Houghton Mifflin.

Janos, P. and Robinson, N. (1985) Psychosocial development in intellectually gifted children. In

F. Horowitz and M. O'Brien (eds.), *The gifted and talented: Developmental perspectives*. Washington, D.C.: American Psychological Association. (pp. 149–195)

Jeffrey, B. and Woods, P. (2003) *The creative school – a framework for success, quality and effectiveness*. London: Routledge Falmer.

Jeltova, I. and Grigorenko, E. L. (2005) Systemic approaches to giftedness: Contributions of Russian psychology. In Sternberg, R. J. and Davidson, J. E. (eds.), *Conceptions of giftedness*. New York: Cambridge University Press.

Jenkins, J., Jewell, M., Leicester, N., O'Connor, R., Jenkins, L. and Troutner, N. (1994) Accommodations for individual differences without classroom ability groups: An experiment in school restructuring. *Exceptional Children*, 60, 344–358.

Jensen, A. R. (1969) How much can we boost IQ and scholastic attainment? In *Environment, Heredity and Intelligence*. Cambridge, MA: Harvard Educational Review.

Jensen, A. R. (1998) *The g factor*. Westport, CT: Greenwood/Praeger.

Jensen, A. R. (2002) Psychometric *g*: Definition and substantiation. In R. J. Sternberg and E. L. Grigorenko (eds.), *The general factor of intelligence: How general is it?* Mahwah, NJ: Lawrence Erlbaum Associates, Inc. (pp. 39–53)

Jesson, D. (2005) The Comparative Evaluation of GCSE Value-Added Performance by Type of School and LEA; Discussion Papers 00/52, Department of Economics, University of York.

Johnsen, S. K. (2004) Performance assessment plan for gifted and talented education program. Program for preparing school professionals submitted and approved by the Council for Exceptional Children and nationally recognized by NCATE. Unpublished manuscript, Waco, TX: Department of Educational Psychology, Baylor University.

Johnsen, S. K., Feuerbacher, S. and Witte, M. M. (2007) Increasing the retention of gifted students from low-income backgrounds in university programs for the gifted: The UYP Project. In J. VanTassel-Baska (ed.), *Serving gifted learners beyond the traditional classroom*. Waco, TX:Prufrock Press. (pp. 55–79)

Joint Committee on Standards for Educational Evaluation/Sanders, J.R. (1994) *The program evaluation standards: How to assess evaluations of educational programs?* Thousand Oaks, CA: Sage.

Jordan, R. and Jones, G. (2001) *Meeting the Needs of Children with Autistic Spectrum Disorders*. London: David Fulton

Kaiser, C. (2007) Listening with your eyes. *Scientific American Mind*, 18(2), 24–29.

Kamin, L. J. (1974) *The science and politics of IQ*. Maryland: Erlbaum.

Kamins, M. and Dweck, C. S. (1999) Person vs. process praise and criticism: Implications for contingent self-worth and coping. *Developmental Psychology*, 35, 835–847.

Kanevsky, L. (1992) The learning game. In P. Klein and A. J. Tannenbaum (eds.), *To be young and gifted* Norwood, NJ: Ablex. (pp. 204–241)

Kanevsky, L. and Keighley, T. (2003) To produce or not to produce? Understanding boredom and the honor in underachievement *Roeper Review*, 26, 20–28.

Kanner, L. (1943) Autistic disturbances of affective contact. *Nervous Child*, 2, 217–50.

Karnes, F. and Brown, K. (1981) Moral development and the gifted: An initial investigation. *Roper Review*, 3, 8–10.

Karp, A. (2003) Thirty years after: The lives of former winners of Mathematical Olympiads. *Roeper Review*, 25, 83–92.

Katz, M. B. (1975) *Class, bureaucracy, and schools*. Praeger, New York.

Kaufman, A. S. (2000) Tests of intelligence. In R. J. Sternberg (ed.), *Handbook of intelligence*. New York: Cambridge University Press. (pp. 445–476)

Kaufman, J. C. (2003) The cost of the muse; poets die young. *Death Studies*, 27, 813–821.

Kaufman, J. C. and Sternberg, R. J. (eds.) (2006) *The international handbook of creativity*. New York: Cambridge University Press.

Keating, D. P. (in press). Developmental science and giftedness: An integrated life-span perspective. In F. D. Horowitz, R. F. Subotnik and D. J. Matthews (eds.), *The development of giftedness and talent across the lifespan*. Washington, D.C.: American Psychological Association.

Kelemen, L. (2001) *To kindle a soul*. Southfield, Michigan: Targum Press.

343

Kellmer-Pringle, M. (1970) *Able misfits*. London: Longman.

Kerry, T. (1983) *Finding and helping the able child*. London: Croom Helm

Kimbell, R., Stables, K., Miller, S., Wheeler, T., Wright, R. and Balchin, T. (2004). Assessing design innovation: a research and development project for the Department for Education and Skills (DfES) and the Qualifications and Curriculum Authority (QCA). Goldsmiths College, University of London.

King, A. (1993) From sage on the stage to guide on the side. *College Teaching*, Vol. 41, 1993, 30–35.

Kirschenbaum, R. J. (1998) Dynamic assessment and its use with underserved gifted and talented populations. *Gifted Child Quarterly*, 42, 140–147.

Kitano, M. K. and Espinosa, R. (1995) Language diversity and giftedness: Working with gifted English language learners. *Journal for the Education of the Gifted*, 18, 234–54.

Kline, B. E. and Short, E. B. (1991) Changes in emotional resilience: Gifted adolescent females. *Roeper Review*, 13, 118–121.

Koestler, A. (1964) *The act of creation*. New York: Macmillan

Kohlberg, L. (1969) Stage and sequence: The cognitive-developmental approach to socialization. In D. A. Goslin (ed.), *Handbook of socialization theory and research*. Chicago: Rand McNally. (pp. 347–480)

Kohlberg, L. (1984) *The psychology of moral development. Vol 2. Essays on moral development*. San Francisco: Harper and Row.

Konrad, M. and Trela, K. (2007) Go 4 It . . . Now! Extending writing strategies to support all students, *Teaching Exceptional Children*, vol. 39, no. 4, pp. 42–51.

Koshy, V. (2002) *Teaching gifted children 4–7: A Guide for Teachers*. London: David Fulton.

Koshy, V. (2005) *Action research for improving practice*. London: Sage/Paul Chapman.

Koshy, V. and Robinson. N. (2006) Too long neglected: Gifted young children. European early childhood. *Education Research Journal*, 14, 2, 113–126.

Koshy, V., Mitchell, C. and Williams, M. (2006) *Nurturing Gifted and Talented Children at Key Stage 1. A Report of Action research Projects*. DfES.

Kosslyn S. M. (1983) *Ghosts in the mind's machine. Creating and using images in the brain*. New York: W.W. Norton and Company.

Kramer, L. R. (1991) The social construction of ability perceptions: An ethnographic study of gifted adolescent girls. *Journal of Early Adolescence*, 11(3), 340–362.

Kratzig, G. P. and Arbuthnott, K. D. (2006) Perceptual learning style and learning proficiency: A test of the hypothesis. *Journal of Educational Psychology*, 98(1), 238–246.

Kriegseis, A., Hennighausen, E., Rösler, F. and Röder, B. (2006) Reduced EEG alpha activity over parieto-occipital brain areas in congenitally blind adults. *Clinical Neurophysiology*, (in press).

Kristensen, P. and Bjerkedal, T. (2007, June 22) Explaining the relation between birth order and intelligence. *Science*, 316, 1717.

Kuhn T. S. (1970) *The structure of scientific revolutions*. Chicago: Chicago University Press.

Kulik, J. A. (1997) Ability grouping. In N. Colangelo and G. A. Davis (eds.), *Handbook of gifted education (V. II)*. Needham Heights, MA: Allyn & Bacon. (pp. 230–242)

Kulik, J. A. (2004) Meta-analytic studies of acceleration. In N. Colangelo, S. G. Assouline and M. U. M. Gross (eds.), *A nation deceived: How schools hold back America's brightest students (Volumes II)*. Iowa City, IA.: Belin and Blank International Center for Gifted Education and Talent Development, University of Iowa. (pp. 13–22)

Kushman, J. W., Sieber, C. and Harold, K. P. (2000) *This isn't the place for me: School dropout*. American Counseling Association. (pp. 471–507).

Laidlaw, M. (2006) How might we enhance the educational value of our research-base at the New University in Guyuan? Researching stories for the social good. Inaugural Professorial Lecture by Moira Laidlaw, Ningxia Teachers University 13/6/2006. Retrieved 6/5/2007 from http://www.jackwhitehead.com/china/mlinaugural.htm.

Lakoff, G. and Johnson, M. (1980) *Metaphors we live by*. Chicago: Chicago University Press.

Lakoff, G. and Johnson, M. (1999) *Philosophy in the flesh. The embodied mind and its challenge to western thought*. New York: Basic Books.

Landau, E. (1991) *The courage to be gifted*. Melbourne: Hawker Brownlow Education.

Lao, S. (2000) *An annotation to Daxue and Zhongyong*. Hong Kong: The Chinese University Press. [In Chinese]

Lautrey, J. (Ed). (2002) *L'état de la recherche sur les enfants dits surdoués. Rapport à la Fondation de France*. [*the Current State of Research Concerning Children Known as Gifted. Report to the Fondation de France*]. Paris: Université Paris 5, Laboratoire Cognition et Développement.

Lautrey, J. (2004) Les modes de scolarisation des enfants à haut potentiel et leurs effets. *Psychologie Française*, 49, 337–352.

Lee, K. H., Choi, Y. Y., Gray, J. R., Cho, S. H., Chae, J.-H., Lee, S. and Kim, K. (2006) Neural correlates of superior intelligence: Stronger recruitment of posterior parietal cortex. *NeuroImage* 29(2), 578–86.

Lee, W. O. (1996) The cultural context for Chinese learners: Conceptions of learning in the Confucian tradition. In D. A. Watkins and J. B. Biggs (eds.), *The Chinese learner: Cultural, psychological, and contextual influences*. Hong Kong: Comparative Education Research Centre. (pp. 25–42)

Lehman, H. C. (1953) *Age and achievement*. Princeton, NJ: Princeton University Press.

Lengfelder, A. and Heller, K. A. (2002) German Olympiad studies: Findings from a retrospective evaluation and from in-depth interviews. Where have all the gifted females gone? *Journal of Research in Education*, 12, 86–92.

Leroux, J. A. (1986) The gifted in middle school. *Roeper Review*, 9, 72–77.

Leroux, J. A. (1988) Voices from the classroom: Academic and social self-concepts of gifted adolescents. *Journal for the Education of the Gifted*, 11(3), 3–18.

Lessinger, L. M. and Martinson, R. A. (1961) The use of the California Psychological Inventory with gifted pupils. *Personnel and Guidance Journal*, 39, 572–575.

Leu Jr., D. J., Leu, D. D. and Coiro, J. (2004 *Teaching with the Internet: New literacies for new times* (4th edn). Norwood, MA: Christopher-Gordon.

Leu, D. J., Zawilinski, L., Castek, J., Banerjee, M., Housand, B., Liu, Y. and O'Neil. M (2005) What is new about the new literacies of online reading comprehension? In A. Berger, L. Rush and J. Eakle (eds.), *Secondary school reading and writing: What research reveals for classroom practices*. Chicago: National Council of Teachers of English/National Conference of Research on Language and Literacy.

Lewis, A. and Smith, D. (1993) Defining higher order thinking, *Theory into Practice* 32(3).

Li, A. K. F. and Adamson, G. (1995) Siblings of gifted secondary school students: Self-perceptions and learning style preference. *Roeper Review*, 18, 152–153.

Lidz, C. S. (1997) Dynamic assessment approaches. In D. S. Flanagan, J. L. Genshaft and P. L. Harrison (eds.), *Contemporary intellectual assessment*. New York: The Guilford Press. (pp. 281–296)

Limont, W. (1996) *Analiza wybranych mechanizmów wyobraźni twórczej*. Toruń: Wydawnictwo Uniwersytetu Mikołaja Kopernika.

Limont, W. (2004) Poznawcze i twórcze funkcje metafory wizualne. In S. Popek, R. E. Bernacka, C. W. Domański, B. Gawda, D. Turska (eds.), *Twórczość w teorii i praktyce*. Lublin: UMCS. (103–112)

Lindauer, M. S. (2003) *Aging, creativity, and art: A positive perspective on late-life development*. New York: Kluwer Academic/Plenum Publishers.

Lipman, M. (2003) (2nd edn) *Thinking in education*, Cambridge: Cambridge University Press.

Lohman, D. F. (2005) An aptitude perspective on talent: Implications for identification of academically gifted minority students. *Journal for the Education of the Gifted*, 28, 333–360.

Lovaglia, M. J., Lucas, J. W., Houser, J. A., Thye, S. R. and Markovsky, B. (1998) Status processes and mental ability test scores. *American Journal of Sociology*, 104(1), 195–228.

Lovaglia, M. J., Thompkins, D., Lucas, J. and Thye, S. (2000) 'The shadow of the future: How negative expectations cloud test performance'. Paper presented at the Fifth Biennial Wallace National Research Symposium on Talent Development, The University of Iowa, Iowa City, USA.

Lubart, T. I. (1994) Creativity. In R. J. Sternberg (ed.), *Thinking and problem solving*. New York: Academic Press. (pp. 289–332)

Lubart, T. I. (1999) Componential models of creativity. In M. A. Runco and S. Pritzer (eds.), *Encyclopedia of creativity*. New York: Academic Press. (pp. 295–300)

Lubart, T. (Éd). (2006). *Enfants exceptionnels. Précocité intellectuelle, haut potentiel et talent* [Exceptionnal children. Intellectual precocity, high potential and talent.]. Rosny sous Bois 93: Bréal.

Lubart, T. I. and Lautrey, J. (1995) Relationships between creative development and cognitive development. Seventh European Conference on Developmental Psychology, Krakow, Poland.

Lubart, T. I. and Lautrey, J. (1998) Family environment and creativity. XVth Biennial Meeting of the International Society for the Study of Behavioral Development (ISSBD). Bern, Switzerland.

Lubart, T. I. and Sternberg, R. J. (1995) An investment approach to creativity: Theory and data. In S. M. Smith, T. B. Ward and R. A Finke (eds.), *The creative cognition approach*. Cambridge, MA: MIT Press. (pp. 271–302)

Lubart, T. I., Jacquet, A-Y., Pacteau, C. and Zenasni, F. (2000) 'Creativity in children's drawings and links with flexible thinking'. XXVII International Congress of Psychology, Stockholm, Sweden.

Lubinski, D. (2004) Long-term effects of educational acceleration. In N. Colangelo, S. G. Assouline and M. U. M. Gross (eds.), *A nation deceived: How schools hold back America's brightest students (Volumes II)*. Iowa City, IA: Belin and Blank International Center for Gifted Education and Talent Development, University of Iowa. (pp. 23–38)

Lubinski, D. and Benbow, C. (2000) States of excellence. *American Psychologist*, 55, 137–150.

Luria, A. R. (1968) *The Mind of a mnemonist: A little book about a vast memory*. Cambridge, MA: Harvard University Press.

Lykken, D. T. (1982) Research with twins: The concept of emergenesis. *Psychophysiology*, 19, 361–373.

Lykken, D. T. (1998) The genetics of genius. In A. Steptoe (ed.), *Genius and the mind: Studies of creativity and temperament in the historical record*. New York: Oxford University Press. (pp. 15–37)

Lykken, D. T., McGue, M., Tellegen, A. and Bouchard Jr., T. J. (1992). Emergenesis: Genetic traits that may not run in families. *American Psychologist*, 47, 1565–1577.

MacArthur, D. G. and North, K. N. (2005) Genes and human elite athletic performance. *Human Genetics*, 116, 331–339.

McCallister, C., Nash, W. R. and Meckstroth, E. (1996) The social competence of gifted children: Experiments and experience. *Roeper Review*, 18(4), 273–276.

McCann, S. J. H. (2001) The precocity-longevity hypothesis: Earlier peaks in career achievement predict shorter lives. *Personality and Social Psychology Bulletin*, 27, 1429–1439.

McCluskey, K. W., Baker, P. A., Bergsgaard, M. and McCluskey, A. L. A. (2003) Interventions with talented at-risk populations with emotional and behavioural difficulties. In D. Montgomery (ed.), *Gifted and talented with SEN: Double exceptionality*. London: David Fulton. (pp. 168–185)

McCoach, B. D. and Siegle, D. (2003) Factors that differentiate underachieving gifted students from high-achieving gifted students, *Gifted Child Quarterly*, 47, 2, 144–154.

McCrae, R. R., Costa Jr., P. T., Ostendorf, F., Angleitner, A., Hrebickova, M., Avia, M. D., Sanz, J., Sanchez-Bernardos, M. L., Kusdil, M. E., Woodfield, R., Saunders, P. R. and Smith, P. B. (2000) Nature over nurture: Temperament, personality, and life span development. *Journal of Personality and Social Psychology*, 78, 173–186.

McManus, I. C. and Bryden, M. P. (1991). Geschwind's theory of cerebral lateralization: Developing a formal, causal model. *Psychological Bulletin*, 110, 237–253.

McNiff, J., Whitehead, J. and Laidlaw, M. (1992) *Creating a good social order through action research*. Bournemouth: Hyde.

Macpherson, W. (1999) *The Stephen Lawrence Inquiry: Report of an inquiry*. Retrieved 17/9/2007 from http://www.archive.official-documents.co.uk/document/cm42/4262/sli-00.htm.

Maddux, C. D. (1983) Early school entry for the gifted: New evidence and concerns. *Roeper Review*, 5 (4), 15–17.

Maker, J. C. (1993) Creativity, intelligence, and problem solving: A definition and design for cross-cultural research and measurement related to giftedness. *Gifted Education International*, 9, 68–77.

Maker, J. C. (1996) Identification of gifted minority students: A national problem, needed changes and a promising solution. *Gifted Child Quarterly*, 40, 41–50.

Maker, J. C. and Nielson, A. B. (1995) *Teaching/learning models in education of the gifted* (2nd edn). Austin, TX: Pro-Ed.

Mandler, G. (1995) Origins and consequences of novelty. In S. M. Smith, T. B. Ward and R. A. Finke (eds.), *The creative cognition approach*. Cambridge, MA: MIT Press. (pp. 9–25)

Mangels, J. A., Butterfield, B., Lamb, J., Good, C. D. and Dweck, C. S. (2006) Why do beliefs about intelligence influence learning success? A social-cognitive-neuroscience model. *Social, Cognitive, and Affective Neuroscience*, 1, 75–86.

Mansell, W. (2007) *Education by numbers: The tyranny of testing.* London: Politico's Publishing Ltd.

Mant, J., Wilson, H. and Coates, D. (2007) The effect of increasing conceptual challenge in primary science lessons on pupils' achievement and engagement. *The International Journal of Science Education*, 29 (14), 5 November, 2007, pp. 1707–1719

Mares, L. and Byles, J. (1994) *One step ahead.* Melbourne: Hawker Browntow Education.

Marland, S. P. (1972) *Education of the gifted and talented: Report to the Congress of the United States by the U. S. Commissioner of Education.* Washington, D.C.: U.S. Government Printing Office.

Marsh, H. S. and Parker, J. W. (1984) Determinants of student self-concept. Is it better to be a relatively large fish in a small pond even if you don't learn to swim as well? *Personality and Social Psychology*, 47 (1), 213–231.

Marsh, H.S., Chesser, D., Craven, R. and Roche, L. (1995) The effects of gifted and talented programs on academic self-concept: The big fish strikes again. *American Educational Research Journal*, 32(2), 285–319.

Martinková, M. (1995) *Matej. O chlapcovi, ktorý rozpráva kreslením.* Bratyslava: Škola pre mimoriadne nadané deti a Gymnázium.

Martinková, M. (2006) *Chlapec, ktorý myslí v obrazoch a vyjadruje sa kresbou Sprievodca malého, nadaného autistu.* Bratislava: Vydavateľstvo Európa.

Marton, F. (1981) Phenomenography: describing conceptions of the world around us. *Instructional Science*, 10, 177–200.

Marton, F. and Säljö, R. (1976) Qualitative differences in learning. *British Journal of Educational Psychology*, 46, 115–127.

Marton, F. and Säljö, R. (1984) Approaches to learning. In F. Marton, D. Hounsell and N. Enthwistle (eds.), *The experience of learning.* Edinburgh: Scottish Academic Press. (pp. 39–58)

Matsagouras, E. (2000) *School classroom* [in Greek]. Athens: Gregory publ.

Matsagouras, E. (2004) *Cross-curricularity in school knowledge* [in Greek]. Athens: Gregory publ.

Matthews, D. J. and Foster, J. F. (2005) *Being smart about gifted children: A guidebook for parents and educator.* Scottsdale, AZ: Great Potential Press.

Matthews, D. J. and Foster, J. F. (2006) Mystery to mastery: Shifting paradigms in gifted education, *Roeper Review*, 28, 2, 64–9.

Matthews, D. J. and Kitchen, J. (in press) Allowing idiosyncratic learners to thrive: Policy implications of a study of school-within-a-school gifted programs, *Journal of School Choice.*

Matthews, D. J., Foster, J. F., Gladstone, D., Schieck, J. and Meiners, J. (in press) Supporting professionalism, diversity, and context within a collaborative approach to gifted education, *Journal of Educational and Psychological Consultation.*

Matthews, D. J., Subotnik, R. F. and Horowitz, F. D. (in press) A developmental perspective on giftedness and talent: Implications for research, policy, and practice. In F. D. Horowitz, R. F. Subotnik and D. J. Matthews (eds.), *The development of giftedness and talent across the lifespan*, Washington D.C.: American Psychological Association.

Mayer, J. D., Perkins, D. M., Caruso, D. and Salovey, P. (2001) Emotional intelligence and giftedness. *Roeper Review*, 23, 131–137.

Mayer, J. D., Salovey, P., and Caruso, D. R. (2002) *Mayer–Salovey–Caruso Emotional Intelligence Test (MSCEIT) user's manual.* Toronto: Multi-Health Systems.

Meador, K. (1999) Creativity around the globe. *Childhood Education*, 75(6), 324–25.

Meadows, S. (2006) *The child as thinker.* Abingdon, Oxon: Routledge.

Mednick, S. A. (1962) The associative basis of the creative process. *Psychological Review*, 69, 220–232.

Mercer, N. (2000) *Words and minds: How we use language to think together.* London: Routledge

Milgram, R. M. and Hong, E. (1999) Creative out-of-school activities in intellectually gifted adolescents as predictors of their life accomplishment in young adults: a longitudinal study. *Creativity Research Journal*, 12, 77–87.

Miller, I. A. (1996) Metaphors in creative scientific thought. *Creativity Research Journal*, Vol. 9, Nos. 2–3, 113–130.

Ministère de l'Education Nationale. (2006) *Repères et références statistiques sur les enseignements, la formation et la recherche, édition 2006*. [*Benchmarks and statistical informations on education, training and research*]. Paris: Author.

Mönks, F. J. (1996) 'Differentiation and integration: A historical and international perspective'. In International Conference in Giftedness, Social Educational Problems, ACTAS, ISMAI, Porto, Portugal, pp. 23–34.

Mönks, F. J. and van Boxtel, H. W. (1985) Gifted adolescents: A developmental perspective. In Freeman, J. (ed.), *The psychology of gifted children*. New York: John Wiley & Sons Ltd.

Mönks, F. J. and Ferguson, T. J. (1983) Gifted adolescents: An analysis of their psychosocial development, *Journal of Youth and Adolescence*, 12.

Mönks, F. J., Heller, K. A. and Passow, A. H. (2000) The study of giftedness: Reflections on where we are and where we are going. In K. A. Heller, F. J. Mönks, R. J. Sternberg and R. F. Sobotnik (eds.), *International handbook of giftedness and talent, 2nd edition* Amsterdam: Elsevier. (pp. 839–864)

Mönks, F. J. and Katzko, M. W. (2005) Giftedness and gifted education. In R. J. Sternberg and J. E. Davidson (eds.), *Conceptions of giftedness* (2nd edn) New York: Cambridge University Press. (pp. 187–200)

Montessori, M. (1958/2004) *Pédagogie scientifique: tome 2, éducation élémentaire*. Genève: Desclée de Brouwer.

Montgomery, D. (1985) *The special needs of able pupils in ordinary classroom*. Kingston: Learning Difficulties Research Project.

Montgomery, D. (1990) *Children with learning difficulties*. London: Cassell.

Montgomery, D. (1992) *Managing behaviour problems*. Sevenoaks: Hodder and Stoughton.

Montgomery, D. (ed.) (2000) *Able underachievers*. London: Whurr.

Montgomery, D. (2002) *Helping teachers improve through classroom observation* (2nd edition). London: David Fulton.

Montgomery, D. (ed.) (2003) *Gifted and talented with special educational needs: Double exceptionality*. London: David Fulton.

Montgomery, D. (2007) *Spelling, handwriting and dyslexia*. Abingdon, Oxon: Routledge.

Montgomery, D. (2008) Cohort analysis of writing in Year 7 after 2, 4, and 7 years of the National Literacy Strategy, *Support for Learning*, 23, 1 (in press).

Montgomery, J. (1997) *Health care law*. Oxford: Oxford University Press.

Montour, K. M. (1977) William James Sidis, the broken twig. *American Psychologist*, 32(4), 2625–79.

Moon, S. M., (2003) Personal talent. *Journal of High Ability Studies*, 14 (1), 5–23.

Morelock, M. J. (1996) On the nature of giftedness and talent: imposing order on chaos. *Roeper Review*, 19(1), 4–12.

Morelock, M. J. and Morrison, K. (1999) Differentiating 'developmentally appropriate': The multidimensional curriculum model for young gifted children. *Roeper Review*, 21, 195–200.

Mounter, J. (2006) 'How can I live my personal theory of education in the classroom to promote self reflection as a learner?' Masters Educational Enquiry: University of Bath. Retrieved 22/4/2007 from http://www.jackwhitehead.com/tuesdayma/joymounteree.htm.

Mueller, C. M. and Dweck, C. S. (1998) Intelligence praise can undermine motivation and performance. *Journal of Personality and Social Psychology*, 75, 33–52.

Mullis, I. V. S., Martin, M. O., Gonzalez, E. J. and Chrostowski, S. J. (2004) IEA's TIMSS 2003. International report on achievement in the mathematics cognitive domains. Chestnut Hill, MA: TIMSS & PIRLS International Study Center, Boston College.

Muratori, M. C. (2007) *Early entrance to college*. Waco, TX: Prufrock Press.

Muratori, M. C., Colangelo, N. and Assouline, S. G. (2003) Early entrance students: Impressions of their first semester of college. *Gifted Child Quarterly*, 47, 219–248.

Murdock, M. C. and Puccio, G. J. (1993) A contextual organiser for conducting creativity research. In S. G. Isaksen, M. C. Murdock, R. L. Firestien and D. J. Treffinger (eds.), *Understanding and recognising creativity: The emergence of a discipline*. Norwood, NJ: Ablex. (pp. 249–280)

Myers, I. B. (1980) *Gifts differing.* Palo Alto, CA: Consulting Psychologists Press.

Naglieri, J. A. and Ford, D. Y. (2003) Addressing underrepresentation of gifted minority children using the Naglieri Nonverbal Ability Test (NNAT). *Gifted Child Quarterly,* 47(2), 155–160.

Naglieri, J. A. and Kaufman, J. C. (2001) Understanding intelligence, giftedness and creativity using PASS theory. *Roeper Review,* 23(3), 151–156.

Narvaez, D. (1993) High achieving students and moral judgment. *Journal for the Education of the Gifted,* 16(3), 268–279.

Narvaez, D. (2001) *Ethical sensitivity.* Activity Booklet 1. Retrieved 2/3/2007 from http://www.nd.edu/~dnarvaez/.

Narvaez, D., Endicott, L. and Bock, T. (2002) Who should I become? Citizenship, goodness, human flourishing, and ethical expertise. In W. Veugelers and F. K. Oser (eds.), *Teaching in moral and democratic education.* Bern: Peter Lang.

Nathansen, J. (2001) An investigation of the curriculum provision for students diagnosed with Asperger Syndrome at a Further Education College. Unpublished MA SpLD dissertation London: Middlesex University.

National Association for Gifted Children and the Council of State Directors of Programs for of the Gifted (2005) *2004–2005 State of the states: A report by the National Association for Gifted Children and the Council of State Directors of Programs.* Washington, D.C.: Author.

National Autistic Society (1997) *Approaches to autism 3rd edition.* London: NAS.

Neber, H. (2004) Lehrernominierungen für ein Enrichment-Programm als Beispiel für die Talentsuche in der gymnasialen Oberstufe [Teacher Nomination for an Enrichment Program as an Example of Talent Search in Collage Prep Courses]. *Psychologie in Erziehung und Unterricht,* 51, 24–39.

Neber, H. (2006) Entdeckendes Lernen [Discovering learning]. In D. H. Rost (ed.), *Handwörterbuch Pädagogische Psychologie, 3. Aufl.* [Handbook of Educational Psychology, 3rd edn] Weinheim: Beltz/PVU. (pp. 115–120)

Neber, H. and Heller, K. A. (2002) Evaluation of a summer-school program for highly gifted secondary-school students: The German Pupils Academy. *European Journal of Psychological Assessment,* 18, 214–228.

Neihart, M. (1999) The impact of giftedness on psychological well-being: What does the empirical literature say? *Roeper Review,* 22(1), 10–17.

Neihart, M. (2000) Gifted children with Asperger's Syndrome. *Gifted Child Quarterly,* 44 (4), 222–230.

Neihart, M., Reis, S. M., Robinson, N. M. and Moon, S. M. (2002) *The social and emotional development of gifted students: What do we know?* Waco, TX: Prufrock Press.

Neisser, U. (1979) The concept of intelligence. In R. J. Sternberg and D. K. Detterman (eds.), *Human intelligence: Perspectives on its theory and measurement* Norwood, NJ: Ablex. (pp. 179–189)

Nelson, C.A. (1999) Neural plasticity and human development. *Current Directions in Psychological Science* vol. 8, pp. 42–45.

Nelson, K. C. (1989) Dabrowski's theory of positive disintegration. *Advanced Development,* 1, 1–14.

Nelson, S., Gallagher, J. J. and Coleman, M. R. (1993). Cooperative learning from two different perspectives. *Roeper Review,* 16, 117–121.

Newman, F. and Holzman, L. (1993) *Lev Vygotsky: Revolutionary scientist.* London: Routledge.

Nisbett, R. E., Peng, K., Choi, I. and Norenzayan, A. (2001) Culture and systems of thought: Holistic versus analytic cognition. *Psychological Review,* 108, 291–310.

Nussbaum, A.D. and Dweck, C.S. (2008) Defensiveness vs. remediation: Self-theories and modes of self-esteem maintenance. *Personality and Social Psychology Bulletin,* 34: 599–612.

Oakes, J. (1985) *Keeping track: How schools structure inequality.* New Haven, CT: Yale University Press.

O'Boyle, M. W., Benbow, C. P. and Alexander, J. E. (1995) Sex differences, hemispheric laterality, and associated brain activity in the intellectually gifted. *Developmental Neuropsychology,* 11, 415–443.

O'Boyle, M. W., Cunnington, R., Silk, T., Vaughan, D., Jackson, G., Syngeniotis, A. and Egan, G. (2005) Mathematically gifted male adolescents activate a unique brain network during mental rotation. *Cognitive Brain Research,* 25, 583–587.

OfSTED (2001). *Document No. HMI 334.* London: HMSO, OfSTED.

OfSTED (2005) *The Annual Report of Her Majesty's Chief Inspector for Schools 2004/5*. London: HMSO, OfSTED.

Ogbu, J. U. (1978) Minority education and caste: The American system in cross-cultural perspective, *American Educational Research Journal*, 15, 4, 570–72.

Ogbu, J. U. (1994) Understanding cultural diversity and learning. *Journal for the Education of the Gifted*, 17(4), 355–383.

Olszewski-Kubilius, P. M. and Scott, J. M. (1992) An investigation of the college and career counseling needs of economically disadvantaged minority gifted students. *Roeper Review*, 14(3), 141–148.

Owens, L. and Straton, R. G. (1980) The development of a cooperative, competitive and individualized learning preference scale for students. *British Journal of Educational Psychology*, 50, 147–161.

Pagnin, A. and Adreani, O. D. (2000) New trends in research on moral development in the gifted. In K. A. Heller, F. J. Mönks, R. Sternberg and R. Subotnik (eds.), *International handbook of giftedness and talent*. Oxford: Pergamon Press. (pp. 467–484)

Paris, S. G., Byrnes, J. P. and Paris, A. H. (2001) Constructing theories, identities, and actions of self-regulated learners. In B. Zimmerman and D. Schunk (eds.), *Self-regulated learning and academic achievement: Theoretical perspectives* Mahwah, NJ: Lawrence Erlbaum Associates, Inc. (pp. 253–288)

Parlett, M. and Hamilton, D. (1987) Evaluation as illumination: A new approach to the study of innovatory programmes. In R. Murphy and H. Torrance (eds.), *Evaluating education: Issues and methods*. London: PCP. (pp. 57–73)

Pereira, M. (ed.) (2006) Dossier: Les enfants à haut potentiel et l'école. [Exceptional children. Intellectual precocity, high potential and talent] *Bulletin de Psychologie*, 59 (5).

Perkins, D., Jay, E. and Tishman, S, (1993) Beyond abilities: a dispositional theory of thinking. *Merrill-Palmer Quarterly*, 39, 1, 1–21.

Perleth, C. and Heller, K. A. (1994) The Munich longitudinal study of giftedness. In R. F. Subotnik and K. K. Arnold (eds.), *Beyond Terman: Contemporary longitudinal studies of giftedness and talent*. Norwood, NJ: Ablex. (pp. 77–114)

Perrin, J. (1985) Preferred learning styles make a difference. *The School Administrator*, 42(7), 16.

Persson, R. S., Joswig, H. and Balogh, L. (2000) Gifted Education in Europe: Programs, Practices, and Current Research. In K. A. Heller, F. J. Mönks, R. J. Sternberg and R. F. Subotnik (eds.), *International handbook of giftedness and talent* (2nd edn) Oxford: Pergamon/Amsterdam: Elsevier. (pp. 703–734)

Pfeiffer, S. I. (2003) Challenges and opportunities for students who are gifted: What the experts say. *Gifted Child Quarterly*, 47, 161–169.

Piaget, J. (1969/2004) *Psychologie et pédagogie*. Paris: Folio Essai.

Piechowski M. M. (1979) *Developmental potential*. In N. Colangelo and R. T. Zaffran (eds.), *New Voices in Counseling the Gifted*. Dubuque, IA: Kendall/Hunt. (pp. 25–57)

Pierce, R. L. and Adams, C. M. (2004) One way to differentiate mathematics instruction. *Gifted Child Today*, 27(2), 58–66.

Pigiaki, P. (1995) Fundamental errors made in the design and introduction of career education into Greek schools. *International Journal of Vocational Education and Training*, 3 (1), 33–50.

Pintrich, P. R. (2000) The role of goal orientation is self-regulated learning. In M. Boekaerts, P. Pintrich and M. Zeidner (eds.), *Handbook of self-regulation*. New York: Academic. (pp. 452–502)

Plomin, R. (1995). Nature, nurture and intelligence (synopsis). In M. W. Katzko and F. J. Mönks (eds.), *Nurturing talent: Individual needs and social ability*. Assen, The Netherlands: Van Gorcum. (pp. 112–113)

Plomin, R. and Daniels, D. (1987) Why are children in the same family so different from one another? *Behavioral and Brain Sciences*, 10(1), 1–16.

Plomin, R., Owen, M. J. and McGuffin, P. (1994) The genetic basis of complex human behaviors. *Science*, 264.

Plucker, J. A. and McIntire, J. (1996) Academic survivability in high-potential, middle school students. *Gifted Child Quarterly*, 40(1): 7–14.

Polanyi, M. (1966) *The tacit dimensions*. Garden City, NY: Doubleday.

Pontecorvo, C. and Sterponi, L. (2002) Learning to argue and reason through discourse in educational settings. In G. Wells and G.L Claxton (eds.), *Learning for life in the 21st century: Sociocultural perspectives on the future of education*. Oxford: Blackwell.

Porath, M. (2006) The conceptual underpinnings of giftedness: developmental and educational implications. *Journal of High Ability Studies*, 17(2), 145–159.

Post, B. (2005) What we can learn from Russia's schools. *Phi Delta Kappan*, 86, 627–629.

Price, G. E., Dunn, K., Dunn, R. and Griggs, S. A. (1981) Studies in students' learning styles. *Roeper Review*, 4, 38–40.

Pring, L. and Hermelin, B. (1993) Bottle, tulip and wineglass: Semantic and structural picture processing by Savant Artists. *Journal of Child Psychology and Psychiatry*, 34(8), 1365–1385.

Quinn, S. (1995) *Marie Curie; a Life*. New York: Simon and Shuster.

Räsänen, A., Tirri, K. and Nokelainen, P. (2006) The moral and religious reasoning of gifted adolescence. In K. Tirri (ed.), *Nordic perspectives on religion, spirituality and identity*. Helsinki, Finland: University of Helsinki. (pp. 97–111)

Raskin, E. A. (1936) Comparison of scientific and literary ability: A biographical study of eminent scientists and men of letters of the nineteenth century. *Journal of Abnormal and Social Psychology*, 31, 20–35.

Raven, J. C. (2008) *Raven's Progressive Matrices*. London: Harcourt Assessment.

Rawls, J. (1976) *A theory of justice*. Oxford: Oxford University Press.

Rayner, A. D. M. (2004) Inclusionality and the Role of Place, Space and Dynamic Boundaries in Evolutionary Processes, *Philosophica*, 73, 51–70.

Reed, C. F. (2004) Mathematically gifted in the heterogeneously grouped mathematics classroom. *Journal of Secondary Gifted Education*, 15(3), 89–95.

Reeves, T. C., Herrington, J. and Oliver, R. (2002) Authentic activities and on-line learning. In A. Goody, J. Harrington and M. Northcote (eds.), *Quality conversations: Research and development in higher education, Vol. 25* Jamison. ACT: HERDSA. (pp. 562–567)

Reimann, R. (2002a) Differentielle Fördereffekte des achtjährigen Gymnasiums [Differential effects of the eight-year German gymnasium]. In K.A. Heller (ed.), *Begabtenförderung im Gymnasium* [Gifted education at the German gymnasium]. Opladen: Leske + Budrich. (pp. 167–178)

Reimann, R. (2002b). Persönlichkeits und Leistungsentwicklung im achtjährigen Gymnasium [Development of the personality and school achievement at the eight-year German gymnasium]. In K. A. Heller (ed.), *Begabtenförderung im Gymnasium* [Gifted education at the German gymnasium] Opladen: Leske + Budrich. (pp. 81–135)

Reis, S. M. (1987). We can't change what we don't recognize: Understanding the special needs of gifted females. *Gifted Child Quarterly*, 31(2), 83–88.

Reis, S. M. (1998) *Work left undone: Challenges and compromises of talented females*. Mansfield Center, CT: Creative Learning Press.

Reis, S. M. (2005) Feminist perspectives on talent development: A research-based conception of giftedness in women. In R. J. Sternberg and J. E. Davidson (eds.), *Conceptions of giftedness* (2nd edn). New York: Cambridge University Press. (pp. 217–245)

Reis, S. M. and Callahan, C. M. (1989) Gifted females: They've come a long way-or have they? *Journal for the Education of the Gifted*, 12(2), 99–117.

Reis, S. M. and McCoach, D. B. (2000) The underachievement of gifted students: what do we know and where do we go? *Gifted Child Quarterly*, 44 (3), 152–170.

Reis, S. M. and Renzulli, J. S. (1982) A case for the broadened conception of giftedness. *Phi Delta Kappan*, 63, 619–620.

Reis, S. M. and Renzulli, J. S. (1991) The assessment of creative products in programs for gifted and talented students. *Gifted Child Quarterly*, 35(3), 128–134.

Reis, S. M. and Renzulli, J. S. (1994) Research related to the Schoolwide Enrichment Triad Model. *Gifted Child Quarterly*, 38(1), 7–20.

Reis, S. M. and Westberg, K. L. (1994) An examination of current school district policies: Acceleration of secondary students. *Journal of Secondary Gifted Education*, 5(4), 7–17.

Reis, S. M., Burns, D. E. and Renzulli, J. S. (1992) *Curriculum compacting: The complete guide to modifying the regular curriculum for high ability students*. Mansfield Center, CT: Creative Learning Press.

Reis, S. M., Burns, D. E. and Renzulli, J. S. (1993) *Curriculum compacting: The complete guide to modifying the regular curriculum for high ability students*. Melbourne: Hawker Brownlow Education.

351

Reis, S. M., Hébert, T. P., Díaz, E. I., Maxfield, L. R. and Ratley, M. E. (1995) *Case studies of talented students who achieve and underachieve in an urban high school.* Storrs, CT: University of Connecticut, The National Research Center on the Gifted and Talented.

Reis, S. M., Gubbins, E. J., Briggs, C., Schreiber, F. J., Richards, S., Jacobs, J., Eckert, R. D., Renzulli, J. S. and Alexander, M. (2003) *Reading instruction for talented readers: Case studies documenting few opportunities for continuous progress (RM03184).* Storrs, CT: The National Research Center on the Gifted and Talented, University of Connecticut.

Renzulli, J. S. (1977a) The enrichment triad model: A guide for developing defensible programmes for the gifted and talented: Part II. *Gifted Child Quarterly,* 21, 237–243.

Renzulli, J. S. (1977b) *The enrichment triad model: A guide for developing defensible programs for the gifted and talented.* Mansfield Center, CT: Creative Learning Press.

Renzulli, J. S. (1978) What makes giftedness? Reexamining a definition. *Phi Delta Kappan,* 59, 180–184.

Renzulli, J. S. (1980) Will the gifted child movement be alive and well in 1990? *Gifted Child Quarterly,* 24, 3–9.

Renzulli, J. S. (1986) The three ring conception of giftedness: A developmental model for creative productivity. In R. J. Sternberg and J. E. Davidson (eds.), *Conception of giftedness.* New York: Cambridge University Press. (pp. 53–92)

Renzulli, J. S., (1987) What makes Giftedness? Re-examine a Definition. *Phi Delta Kappan,* 60, 3.

Renzulli, J. S. (1998) A rising tide lifts all ships: Developing the gifts and talents of all students. *Phi Delta Kappan,* 80(2), 105–111.

Renzulli, J. S., (1990) Torturing data until they confess: an analysis of the analysis of the three-ring conception of giftedness. *Journal for the Education of the gifted,* 13.

Renzulli, J. S. (2002) Expanding the conception of giftedness to include co-cognitive traits and to promote social capital. *Phi Delta Kappan,* 84, 1, 33–58.

Renzulli, J. S. (2003) Conception of giftedness and its relationship to the development of social capital. In N. Colangelo and G. A. Davis (eds.), *Handbook of gifted education,* 3rd edn. Boston: Allyn & Bacon. (pp. 75–87)

Renzulli, J. S. (2005) The three-ring conception of giftedness: A developmental model for promoting creative productivity. In R. J. Sternberg and J. E. Davidson (eds.), *Conceptions of giftedness,* 2nd edn. New York: Cambridge University Press. (pp. 246–279)

Renzulli, J. S. (2006) Dear Mr. and Mrs. Copernicus: We Regret to Inform You. . . . *SEM Articles.* University of Connecticut: National Research Centre on the Gifted and Talented. www.gifted.uconn.edu/sem/copernic.html.

Renzulli, J. S. and Reis, S. M. (1985) *The schoolwide enrichment model: A comprehensive plan for educational excellence.* Mansfield Center, CT: Creative Learning Press.

Renzulli, J. S., & Reis, S. M. (1997). *The schoolwide enrichment model: A how-to guide for educational excellence* (2nd ed.). Mansfield Center, CT: Creative Learning Press.

Renzulli, J. S. and Reis, S. M. (2003) The Schoolwide Enrichment Model: Developing creative and productive giftedness. In N. Colangelo and G. A. Davis (eds.), *Handbook of gifted education* (3rd edn). Boston: Allyn and Bacon. (pp. 184–203)

Resnick, L. (1999) Making America smarter. *Education Week Century Series,* 18(40), 38–40.

Rest, J. (1986) *Moral development: Advances in research and theory.* New York: Praeger.

Rhodes, M. (1961) An analysis of creativity. *Phi Delta Kappan,* 42, 305–310.

Richardson, T. M. and Benbow, C. P. (1990) Long-term effects of acceleration on the social-emotional adjustment of mathematically precocious youths. *Journal of Educational Psychology,* 82, 464–470.

Rieben, L. (1978) Intelligence et pensée créative [Intelligence and creative thinking]. Neuchâtel: Delachaux et Niestlé.

Rimland, B. (1978, August) Inside the mind of the autistic savant. *Psychology Today,* 68–80.

Rinaldi, C. (2006) *In dialogue with Reggio Emilia: Listening, researching and learning.* Abingdon, Oxon: Routledge.

Robinson, N. M. (2004) Effects of academic acceleration on the social-emotional status of gifted students.

In N. Colangelo, S. G. Assouline and M. U. M. Gross (eds.), *A nation deceived: How schools hold back America's brightest students (Volumes II)*. Iowa City, IA. (pp. 59–68)

Robinson, N. M. (2005) In defense of a psychometric approach to the definition of academic giftedness: A conservative view from a die-hard liberal. In R. J. Sternberg and J. E. Davidson (eds.), *Conceptions of giftedness (Vol. 2)*. New York: Cambridge University Press. (pp. 280–294)

Roe, A. (1953) *The making of a scientist*. New York: Dodd, Mead.

Roedell, W. C. (1986) Socioemotional vulnerabilities of young gifted children. *Journal of Children in Contemporary Society*, 18 (3–4), 17–29.

Rogers, C. R. (1949) Towards a theory of creativity. In Anderson, H. (ed.), *Creativity and its cultivation*. New York: Harper & Brothers Publishers.

Rogers, C. R. (1954) Toward a theory of creativity. *ETC: A Review of General Semantics*, 11, 249–260.

Rogers, K. B. (2002a) Grouping the gifted and talented. *Roeper Review*, 24(4), 103.

Rogers, K. B. (2002b) *Re-forming gifted education: How parents and teachers can match the program to the child.* Scottsdale, AZ: Great Potential Press.

Rogers, K. B. (2002c) Best Practice Research Summary Retrieved 1/7/2007 from http://www.isd194.k12.mn.us/g_BPrac.htm.

Rogers, K. B. (2004) The academic effects of acceleration. In N. Colangelo, S. G. Assouline and M. U. M. Gross (eds.), *A nation deceived: How schools hold back America's brightest students (Volumes II)*. Iowa City, IA. (pp. 47–58)

Rogers, W. (1996) High ability and underfunctioning in students with Asperger Syndrome. Geneva; Swiss International Schools Conference (October 1996).

Roid, G. H. (2003) *Stanford-Binet Intelligence Scales, Fifth Edition, Interpretive manual: Expanded guide to the interpretation of SB5 test results*. Itasca, IL: Riverside Publishing.

Rosenthal, R. and Jacobson, L. (1968) *Pygmalion in the classroom: Teacher expectation and pupils' intellectual development*. New York: Holt, Rinehart and Winston.

Rost, D. H. (ed.) (1993) *Lebensumweltanalyse hochbegabter Kinder* [Learning environment of gifted children]. Göttingen: Hogrefe.

Rost, D. H. (ed.) (2000) *Hochbegabte und hochleistende Jugendliche* [Highly gifted and productive adolescents]. Münster: Waxmann.

Rothman, G. R. (1992) Moral reasoning, moral behaviour, and moral giftedness: a developmental perspective. In P. S. Klein and A. J. Tannenbaum (eds.), *To be young and gifted*. New Jersey: Ablex. (p. 330)

Rowe, D. C. (1994) *The limits of family influence: genes, experience, and behavior*. New York: Guilford Press.

Rowe, D. C. (1997) Genetics, temperament, and personality. In R. Hogan, J. Johnson and S. Briggs (eds.), *Handbook of personality psychology*. San Diego, CA: Academic Press. (pp. 367–386)

Rudberg, S. (1956). Nobel Prize for Physics Presentation Speech to William Shockley. Speech notes from the archive website of the Nobel Foundation, http://www.nobel.se.

Ruf, D. (2002, November) Personality type and adjustment in highly gifted children. Paper presented at the annual meeting of the National Association for Gifted Children, Denver, CO.

Ruf, D. (2003) *Use of the SB5 in the assessment of high abilities. (Stanford-Binet Intelligence Scales, Fifth Edition Assessment Service Bulletin No. 3)*. Itasca, IL: Riverside.

Runco, M. A. (1992) The evaluative, valuative and divergent thinking of children. *Journal of Creative Behavior*, 25, 311–319.

Runco, M. A. (1993) Divergent thinking, creativity, and giftedness. *Gifted Child Quarterly*, vol. 37, 16–22.

Runco, M. A. (1999) Developmental trends in creative abilities and potential. In M. A. Runco and S. R. Pritzker (eds.), *Encyclopedia of creativity*. San Diego, CA: Academic Press. (pp. 537–540)

Runco, M. A. (2005) Creative giftedness. In R. J. Sternberg and J. E. Davidson (eds.), *Conceptions of giftedness* (2nd edn). New York: Cambridge University Press. (pp. 280–294)

Runco, M. A., and Albert, R. S. (1986) The threshold theory regarding creativity and intelligence: an empirical test with gifted and non-gifted children. *Creative Child and Adult Quarterly*, 11, 212–218.

Rypma, B., Prabhakaran, V., Desmond, J. E., Glover, G. H. and Gabrieli, J. D. (1999) Load-dependent roles of frontal brain regions in the maintenance of working memory. *NeuroImage*, 9, 216–226.

Sak, U. (2004). A synthesis of research on psychological types of gifted adolescents. *Journal of Secondary Gifted Education*, 15(2), 70–79.

Salili, F. (1996) Accepting personal responsibility for learning. In D. A. Watkins and J. B. Boggs (eds.), *The Chinese learner: Cultural, psychological, and contextual influences*. Hong Kong: Comparative Education Research Centre. (pp. 85–106)

Salili, F., Chiu, C. Y. and Lai, S. (2001) The influence of culture and context on students' achievement orientations. In F. Salili, C. Y. Chiu and Y. Y. Hong (eds.), *Student motivation: The culture and context of learning:* New York: Plenum. (pp. 221–247)

Sanders, D. (1994) Methodological considerations in comparative cross-national research. *International Social Science Journal* Vol. 46, No. 4, 513–521.

Sapon-Shevin, M. (1994) *Playing favourites: Gifted education and the disruption of community* Albany, NY: State University of New York Press.

Sassoon, R. (1990) *Handwriting: A New Perspective*. Cheltenham: Stanley Thornes.

Scarr, S. and McCartney, K. (1983) How people make their own environments: A theory of genotype-environment effect. *Child Development*, 54, 424–435.

Schank, R. C. and Cleary, C. (1995) Making machines creative. In S. M. Smith, T. B. Ward and R. A. Finke (eds.), *The creative cognition approach*. Cambridge, MA: MIT Press. (pp. 229–247)

Schewean, V.L., Saklofske, D. H., Widdifield-Konkin, L., Parker, J. and Kloosterman, P. (2006) Emotional Intelligence and Gifted Children. *E-Journal of Applied Psychology: Emotional Intelligence*, 2 (2), 30–37.

Schiever, S. W. and Maker, C. J. (1997) Enrichment and acceleration: An overview and new directions. In N. Colangelo and C. Davis (eds.), *Handbook of gifted education* (2nd edn). Boston: Allyn & Bacon. (pp. 113–125)

Schlicte-Hiersemenzel, B. (2000) The psychodynamics of psychological and behavioural difficulties of highly able children: Experiences from a psychotherapeutic practice. In D. Montgomery (ed.), *Able underachievers*. London: Whurr. (pp. 52–61)

Schoon, I. (2000) A life span approach to talent development. In K.A. Heller, F.J. Mönks, R.J. Stenberg and R.F. Subotnik (eds.), *International handbook of giftedness and talent*. Oxford: Elsevier. (pp. 213–225)

Schraw, G. and Graham, T. (1997) Helping gifted students develop metacognitive awareness, *Roeper Review*, 20, 4–8.

Schunk, D. (2001). Social cognitive theory of self-regulated learning. In B. Zimmerman and D. Schunk (eds.), *Self-regulated learning and academic achievement: Theoretical perspectives*. Mahwah, NJ: Lawrence Erlbaum Associates, Inc. (pp. 125–152)

Schutte, N. S., Malouff, J. M., Hall, L. E., Haggerty, D. J., Cooper, J. T., Golden, C. J. et al. (1998). Development and validation of a measure of emotional intelligence. *Personality and Individual Differences*, 25, 167–177.

Scriven, M. (1967) *The methodology of evaluation*. AERA Monograph Series on Curriculum Evaluation, No. 1. Chicago: Rand McNally.

Seagoe, M. (1974) Some learning characteristics of gifted children. In R. Martinson (ed.), *The identification of the gifted and talented*. Ventura, CA: Office of the Ventura County Superintendent of Schools.

Selby, E. C. and Treffinger, D. J. (2003) *Giftedness, creativity, and learning style*. In R. Dunn (ed.), Survey of research on the Dunn and Dunn learning styles model. Jamaica, NY: St. John's University.

Selby, E. C., Treffinger, D. J., Isaksen, S. G. and Lauer, K. J. (2004) The conceptual foundation of VIEW: A tool for assessing problem solving style. *Journal of Creative Behavior*, 38 (4), 221–243.

Selby, E. C., Shaw, E. J. and Houtz, J. C. (2005) The creative personality. *Gifted Child Quarterly*, 49 (4), 300–314.

Shagoury-Hubbard, R. (1996) *Workshop of the possible: Nurturing children's creative development*. York, MA: Stenhouse Publishers.

Sharan, S. (1980) Cooperative learning in small groups: Recent methods and effects on achievement, attitudes, and ethnic relations. *Review of Educational Research*, 50, 241–271.

Sharp, J. G., Byrne, J. and Bowker, R. (2007) VAK or VAK-uous? Lessons in the trivialisation of learning and the death of scholarship. *Research Papers in Education* (in press).

Shavinina, L. V. and Ferrari, M. (eds.) (2004) *Beyond knowledge: Extracognitive aspects of developing high ability*. Mahwah, NJ: Lawrence Erlbaum Associates, Inc.

Shaw, P., Greenstein, D., Lerch, J., Clasen, L., Lenroot, R., Gogtay, N., Evans, A., Rapoport, J. and Giedd, J. (2006) Intellectual ability and cortical development in children and adolescents. *Nature*, 440(7084), 676–679.

Shekerjian, D. (1991) *Uncommon Genius*. London: Penguin.

Shepard R. N. (1978) Externalization of mental images and the act of creation. In B. S. Randhawa and W. E. Coffman (eds.), *Visual learning, thinking, and communication*. New York: Academic Press, Inc. (pp. 133–191)

Sherrington, C. (1938) *Man on his nature*. Cambridge: Cambridge University Press.

Shi, J. (2004) Diligence makes people smart: Chinese perspective of intelligence. In R. J. Sternberg (ed.), *International handbook of intelligence*, Cambridge: Cambridge University Press. (pp. 325–343)

Shi, J. and Zha, Z. (2000) Psychological research on and education of gifted and talented children in China. In K. Heller, F. J. Mönks, R. Sternberg and R. Subotnik (eds.), *International handbook of research and development of giftedness and talent* (2nd edn). Oxford: Pergamon Press. (pp. 757–764)

Shonkoff, J. P. and Phillips, D. A. (2000) *From neurons to neighbourhoods: The science of early childhood development*. Washington, D.C.: National Academy Press.

Shore, B. M., Rejskind, G. and Kanevsky, L. S. (2003) Cognitive research on giftedness: a window on creativity and teaching for creativity. In D. Ambrose, L. M. Cohen and A. J. Tannenbaum (eds.), *Creative intelligence: toward theoretic integration*. Cresskill, NJ: Hampton Press. (pp. 181–210)

Silberman, S. (2001) The Geek Syndrome. *Wired Magazine Issue* 9, 12 Dec 2001. Retrieved 11/12/2007 from http://www.wired.com/wired/archive/9.12/

Silverman, L. K. (1989) Invisible gifts, invisible handicaps. *Roeper Review* 12, 1, 37–42.

Silverman, L. K. (1991) Family counseling. In N. Colangelo and G. A. Davis (eds.), *Handbook of gifted education*. Boston: Allyn and Bacon. (pp. 307–320)

Silverman, L. K. (1993) Counseling families. In L.K. Silverman (ed.). *Counseling the gifted and talented*. Denver, Colorado: Love Publishing Company.

Silverman, L. K. (1994) The moral sensitivity of gifted children and the evolution of society. *Roeper Review*, 17(2), 110–116.

Simonton, D. K. (1975a) Age and literary creativity: A cross-cultural and transhistorical survey. *Journal of Cross-Cultural Psychology*, 6, 259–277.

Simonton, D. K. (1975b) Sociocultural context of individual creativity: A transhistorical time series analysis. *Journal of Personality and Social Psychology*, 32, 1119–1133.

Simonton, D. K. (1984) *Genius, creativity, and leadership*. Cambridge, MA: Harvard University Press.

Simonton, D. K. (1987) Developmental antecedents of achieved eminence. *Annals of Child Development*, 5, 131–169.

Simonton, D. K. (1988a) Age and outstanding achievement: What do we know after a century of research? *Psychological Bulletin*, 104, 251–267.

Simonton, D. K., (1988b) Creativity, leadership and chance. In R. J. Stenberg (ed.), *The Nature of creativity: Contemporary psychological perspectives*. Cambridge University Press. Personality and Social Psychology Bulletin, 18.

Simonton, D. K. (1989) The swan-song phenomenon: Last-works effects for 172 classical composers. *Psychology and Aging*, 4, 42–47.

Simonton, D. K. (1991a) Career landmarks in science: Individual differences and interdisciplinary contrasts. *Developmental Psychology*, 27, 119–130.

Simonton, D. K. (1991b) Emergence and realization of genius: The lives and works of 120 classical composers. *Journal of Personality and Social Psychology*, 61, 829–840.

Simonton, D. K. (1992a) The social context of career success and course for 2,026 scientists and inventors. *Personality and Social Psychology Bulletin*, 18, 452–463.

Simonton, D. K. (1992b) Leaders of American psychology, 1879–1967: Career development, creative output, and professional achievement. *Journal of Personality and Social Psychology*, 62, 5–17.

Simonton, D. K. (1994) *Greatness: Who makes history and why*. New York: Guilford Press.

Simonton, D. K. (1996) Individual genius and cultural configurations : The case of Japanese civilisation. *Journal of Cross-Cultural Psychology*, 27, 354–375.

Simonton, D. K. (1997) Creative productivity: A predictive and explanatory model of career trajectories and landmarks. *Psychological Review*, 104, 66–89.

Simonton, D. K. (1999a) *Origins of genius: Darwinian perspectives on creativity.* New York: Oxford University Press.

Simonton, D. K. (1999b) Talent and its development: An emergenic and epigenetic model. *Psychological Review*, 106, 435–457.

Simonton, D. K. (2000a) Creative development as acquired expertise: Theoretical issues and an empirical test. *Developmental Review*, 20, 283–318.

Simonton, D. K. (2000b). Creativity: Cognitive, personal, developmental, and social aspects. *American Psychologist*, 55, 151–158.

Simonton, D. K. (2005) Giftedness and genetics: The emergenic-epigenetic model and its implications. *Journal for the Education of the Gifted*, 28, 270–286.

Simonton, D. K. (2007a) Creative life cycles in literature: Poets versus novelists or conceptualists versus experimentalists? *Psychology of Aesthetics, Creativity, and the Arts*, 1, 133–139.

Simonton, D. K. (2007b) Talent and expertise: The empirical evidence for genetic endowment. *High Ability Studies*, 18, 83–84.

Simonton, D. K. (2008) Scientific talent, training, and performance: Intellect, personality, and genetic endowment. *Review of General Psychology*, 12, 28–46.

Singh, H. and O'Boyle, M. W. (2004) Interhemispheric interaction during global-local processing in mathematically gifted adolescents, average-ability youth, and college students. *Neuropsychology*, 18(2), 671–677.

Sisk, D. A. (1982) Caring and sharing: Moral development of gifted students. *Elementary school journal*, 82, 221–229.

Sisk, D. A. (2000) Overcoming underachievement of gifted and talented students. In D. Montgomery (ed.), *Able Underachievers*. London: Whurr. (pp. 111–126)

Sisk, D. A. (2001) Creative leadership: a study of middle managers, senior level managers and CEOs. *Gifted Education International*, 15, 281–290.

Sisk, D. A. (2003) Gifted with behaviour disorders: Marching to a different drummer. In D. Montgomery (ed.), *Gifted and Talented Children with SEN* London: David Fulton. (pp. 131–154)

Slavin, R. E. (1991) Synthesis of research on cooperative learning. *Educational Leadership*, 48, 71–82.

Slavin, R. E. (2002) Evidence-based education policies: transforming educational practice and research. *Educational Researcher*, 31(7): 15–21.

Sloboda, J. A., Davidson, J. W., Howe, M. J. A. and Moore, D. G. (1996) The role of practice in the development of performing musicians. *British Journal of Psychology*, 87.

Smith, S. M., Ward, T. B. and Finke, R. A. (1995) Principles, paradoxes, and prospects for the future of creative cognition. In S. M. Smith, T. B. Ward and R. A. Finke, *The creative cognition approach*. Cambridge: MIT Press. (pp. 327–335)

Snow, R. E. and Swanson, J. (1992) Instructional psychology: Aptitude, adaptation, and assessment. *Annual Review of Psychology*, 43, 583–626.

Snyder, A. W. (2001) Paradox of the savant mind. *Nature*, 413, 251–252.

Snyder, A. W. and Bossomaier, T. (2004) Absolute pitch accessible to everyone by turning off part of the brain? *Organised Sound*, 9(2), 181–189.

Snyder, A. W., Bahramali, H., Hawker, H. T. and Mitchell, D. J. (2006) Savant-like numerosity skills revealed in normal people by magnetic pulses. *Perception*, 35(6), 837–845.

Snyder, A. W., Mulcahy, E., Taylor, J. L., Mitchell, D. J., Sachdev, P. and Gandevia, S. C. (2003) Savant-like skills exposed in normal people by suppressing the left fronto-temporal lobe. *Journal of Integrative Neuroscience*, 2(2), 149–158.

Snyder, C. R. and Lopez, S. J. (eds.) (2002) *Handbook of positive psychology*. Oxford: Oxford University Press.

Soloff, S. (1973) The effect of non content factors on the grading of essays. *Graduate Research in Education and Related Disciplines*, 6, 2, 44–54.

South Carolina State Department of Education: Technical Reports. http://www.myscschools.com/offices/assessment.

Southern, W. T. and Jones E. D. (2004) Types of acceleration: Dimensions and issues. In N. Colangelo, S. G. Assouline and M. U. M. Gross (eds.), *A nation deceived: How schools hold back America's brightest students. (Volume II.)* Iowa City, IA, University of Iowa. (pp. 5–12)

Spearman, C. (1927) *The abilities of man.* London: Macmillan.

Spence, J. T. and Helmreich, R. L. (1983) Achievement related motives and behavior. In J. T. Spence (ed.), *Achievement and achievement motives: Psychological and sociological approaches.* New York: Freeman. (pp. 7–68)

Spreacker, A. (2001) Educating for moral development. *Gifted Education International*, 15, 188–193. Bicester: A B Academic Publishers.

Stahl, S. A. (1988) Evidence to support matching reading styles and initial reading methods? A reply to Carbo. *Phi Delta Kappan*, 70, 317–322.

Stamm, M. (2003) Looking at long term effects of early reading and numeracy ability: A glance at the phenomenon of giftedness. *Gifted and Talented International*, 18, 1, 7–16.

Stanley, J. C. and Brody, L. E. (2001) History and philosophy of the talent search model. *Gifted and Talented International*, 16, 94–96.

Stapf, A. (2003) *Hochbegabte Kinder* [Highly gifted children]. München: C.H. Beck.

Starida, M. (1995) Issues of quality in Greek teacher education. *European Journal of Teacher Education*, 18 (1), 115–121.

Starr, R. (2003) 'Show me the light. I can't see how bright I am'. Gifted students with visual impairment. In D. Montgomery (ed.), *Gifted and Talented with Special Educational Needs; Double Exceptionality* London: David Fulton. (pp. 93–109)

Staudinger, U. M. and Baltes, P. M. (1996) Interactive minds: A facilitative setting for wisdom-related performance? *Journal of Personality and Social Psychology*, 71, 746–762.

Staudinger, U. M., Smith, J. and Baltes, P. B. (1992) Wisdom-related knowledge in life review task: Age differences and the role of professional specialization. *Psychology and Aging*, 7, 271–281.

Staudinger, U. M., Lopez, D. F. and Baltes, P. B. (1997) The psychometric location of wisdom-related performance: Intelligence, personality, and more? *Personality and Social Psychology Bulletin*, 23, 1200–1214.

Steele, C. M. and Aronson, J. (1995) Stereotype threat and the intellectual test performance of African Americans. *Journal of Personality and Social Psychology*, 69(5), 797–811.

Steineger, M. (1997) Clarion call to action. *Northwest Education* (Fall 1997). Portland, OR: Northwest Regional Educational Laboratory.

Stemler, S. E., Grigorenko, E. L., Jarvin, L. and Sternberg, R. J. (2006) Using the theory of successful intelligence as a basis for augmenting AP exams in psychology and statistics. *Contemporary Educational Psychology*, 31, 344–376.

Sternberg, R. J. (1983) Criteria for intelligence skills training. *Educational Researcher*, 12, 6.

Sternberg, R. J. (1985) *Beyond IQ: A triarchic theory of human intelligence.* New York: Cambridge University Press.

Sternberg, R. J. (1986) *Intelligence applied: Understanding and Increasing your intellectual skills.* San Diego, CA Harcourt Brace Jovanovich.

Sternberg, R. J. (1997a) The concept of intelligence and its role in lifelong learning and success. *American Psychologist*, 52, 1030–1037.

Sternberg, R. J. (1997b) *Successful intelligence.* New York: Plume.

Sternberg, R. J. (1997c) A triarchic view of giftedness: Theory and practice. In N. Colangelo and G. A. Davis (eds.), *Handbook of gifted education.* Boston, MA: Allyn and Bacon.

Sternberg, R. J. (1998a) Abilities are forms of developing expertise. *Educational Researcher*, 27, 11–20.

Sternberg, R. J. (1998b) A balance theory of wisdom. *Review of General Psychology*, 2(4), 347–365.

Sternberg, R. J. (1998c) Principles of teaching for successful intelligence. *Educational Psychologist*, 33, 65–72.

Sternberg, R. J. (ed.) (1999a) *Handbook of creativity.* Cambridge: Cambridge University Press.

Sternberg, R. J. (1999b) Intelligence as developing expertise. *Contemporary Educational Psychology*, 24, 259–375.

Sternberg, R. J. (1999c) A propulsion model of types of creative contributions. *Review of General Psychology*, 3, 83–100.

Sternberg, R. J. (1999d) The theory of successful intelligence. *Review of General Psychology*, 3, 292–316.

Sternberg, R. J. (2000a) Patterns of giftedness: A triarchic analysis. *Roeper Review*, 22, 231–235.

Sternberg, R. J. (2000b) Wisdom as a form of giftedness. *Gifted Child Quarterly*, 44, 252–260.

Sternberg, R. J. (2000c) Creativity is a decision. In B. Z. Presseisen (ed.), *Teaching for intelligence II: A collection of articles*. Arlington Heights, IL: Skylight Training and Publishing Inc. (pp. 83–103)

Sternberg, R. (2000d) Giftedness as developing expertise. In K. A. Heller, F. J. Mönks, R. Sternberg and R. Subotnik (eds.), *International handbook of giftedness and talent*. Oxford: Elsevier

Sternberg, R. J. (ed.) (2000e) *Handbook of intelligence*. New York: Cambridge University Press.

Sternberg, R. J. (2001) Giftedness as developing expertise: A theory of the interface between high abilities and achieved excellence. *High Ability Studies*, 12(2), 159–179.

Sternberg, R. J. (ed.) (2002a) *Psychologists defying the crowd*. Washington, D.C.: American Psychological Association.

Sternberg, R. J. (2002b) Successful intelligence: A new approach to leadership. In R. E. Riggio, S. E. Murphy and F. J. Pirozzolo (eds.), *Multiple intelligences and leadership*. Mahwah, NJ: Lawrence Erlbaum Associates, Inc. (pp. 9–28)

Sternberg, R. J. (2003a) What is an expert student? *Educational Researcher*, 32(8), 5–9.

Sternberg, R. J. (2003b) Giftedness according to the theory of successful intelligence. In N. Colangelo and GA Davis (eds.), *Handbook of gifted education*, 3rd edn. Boston: Allyn & Bacon. (pp. 75–87)

Sternberg, R. J. (2003c) WICS as a model of giftedness. *High Ability Studies*, 14, 109–137.

Sternberg, R. J. (2003d) WICS: A model of leadership in organizations. *Academy of Management Learning and Education*, 2, 4, 386–401.

Sternberg, R. (2003e) Wisdom and education. *Gifted Education International*, 17, 233–248.

Sternberg, R. J. (2003f) *Wisdom, intelligence, and creativity, synthesised*. New York: Cambridge University Press.

Sternberg, R. J. (2004a) Introduction to definitions and conceptions of giftedness. In *Essential readings in gifted education, Volume 1: Definitions and conceptions of giftedness*. London: Sage

Sternberg, R. J. (2004b) Teaching for wisdom: What matters is not what students know, but how they use it. In D. R. Walling (ed.), *Public education, democracy, and the common good*. Bloomington, IN: Phi Delta Kappan. (pp. 121–132)

Sternberg, R. J. (2004c) Lies we live by: misapplication of tests. In *Essential readings in gifted education, volume 2: Identification of students for gifted and talented programs*. London: Sage

Sternberg, R. J. (2005a) WICS: A model of giftedness in leadership. *Roeper Review*, 28(1), 37–44.

Sternberg, R. J. (2005b) The WICS model of giftedness. In R. J. Sternberg and J. E. Davidson (eds.), *Conceptions of giftedness* (2nd edn.). New York: Cambridge University Press. (pp. 327–342)

Sternberg, R. J. (2006) Reasoning, resilience, and responsibility from the standpoint of the WICS theory of higher mental processes. In R. J. Sternberg and R. F. Subotnik (eds.), *Optimizing student success in schools with the other three R's: Reasoning, resilience, and responsibility*. Greenwich, CT: Information Age Publishing. (pp. 17–37)

Sternberg, R. J. (2007) Cultural concepts of giftedness. *Roeper Review*, vol. 29, 160–165.

Sternberg, R. J. and Arroyo, C. G. (2006) Beyond expectations: A new view of the gifted disadvantaged. In B. Wallace and G. Eriksson (eds.), *Diversity in gifted education: International perspectives on global issue.s* London: Routledge. (pp. 110–124)

Sternberg, R. J. and Davidson, J. E. (eds.) (1986) *Conceptions of giftedness*. New York: Cambridge University Press.

Sternberg, R. J. and Davidson, J. E. (eds.) (2005) *Conceptions of giftedness* (2nd edn). New York: Cambridge University Press.

Sternberg, R. J. and Grigorenko, E. L. (eds.) (1997) *Intelligence, heredity, and environment*. New York: Cambridge University Press.

Sternberg, R. J. and Grigorenko, E. L. (1999) Myths in psychology and education regarding the gene environment debate. *Teachers College Record*, 100, 536–553.

Sternberg, R. J. and Grigorenko, E. L. (2000) *Teaching for successful intelligence.* Arlington Heights, IL: Skylight.

Sternberg, R. J. and Grigorenko, E. L. (eds.) (2001) *Environmental effects on cognitive abilities.* Mahwah, NJ: Lawrence Erlbaum Associates, Inc.

Sternberg, R. J. and Grigorenko, E. L. (eds.) (2002) *The general factor of intelligence: How general is it?* Mahwah, NJ: Lawrence Erlbaum Associates, Inc.

Sternberg, R. J. and Hedlund, J. (2002) Practical intelligence, *g*, and work psychology. *Human Performance,* 15, 143–160.

Sternberg, R. J. and Lubart, T. I. (1992) Creativity: Its nature and assessment. *School Psychology International,* 13(3), 243–253.

Sternberg, R. J. and Lubart, T. I. (1995) *Defying the crowd: Cultivating creativity in a culture of conformity.* New York: Free Press.

Sternberg, R. J. and Lubart, T. I. (1996) Investing in creativity. *American Psychologist,* 51(7), 677–688.

Sternberg, R. J. and Lubart, T. I. (1999) The concept of creativity: Prospects and paradigms. In R. J. Sternberg (ed.), *Handbook of creativity.* Cambridge: Cambridge University Press. (pp. 137–152)

Sternberg, R. J. and O'Hara, L. A. (2000) Intelligence and creativity. In R. J. Sternberg (ed.), *Handbook of intelligence.* New York: Cambridge University Press. (pp. 609–628)

Sternberg, R. J. and The Rainbow Project Collaborators (2005) Augmenting the SAT through assessments of analytical, practical, and creative skills. In W. Camara and E. Kimmel (eds.), *Choosing students: Higher education admission tools for the 21st century.* Mahwah, NJ: Lawrence Erlbaum Associates, Inc. (pp. 159–176)

Sternberg, R. J. and The Rainbow Project Collaborators (2006) The Rainbow Project: Enhancing the SAT through assessments of analytical, practical and creative skills. *Intelligence,* 34(4), 321–350.

Sternberg, R. J. and Wagner, R. K. (1993) The *g*–ocentric view of intelligence and job performance is wrong. *Current Directions in Psychological Science,* 2(1), 1–4.

Sternberg, R. J. and Williams, W. M. (1996) *How to develop student creativity.* Alexandria, VA: Association for Supervision and Curriculum Development.

Sternberg, R. J. and Zhang, L 1995 'What do we mean by giftedness? A pentagonal implicit theory', *Gifted Child Quarterly,* 39, 88–94.

Sternberg, R. J., Wagner, R. K. and Okagaki, L. (1993) Practical intelligence: The nature and role of tacit knowledge in work and at school. In H. Reese and J. Puckett (eds.), *Advances in lifespan development.* Hillsdale, NJ: Lawrence Erlbaum Associates, Inc. (pp. 205–227)

Sternberg, R. J., Wagner, R. K., Williams, W. M. and Horvath, J. A. (1995) Testing common sense. *American Psychologist,* 50(11), 912–927.

Sternberg, R. J., Torff, B. and Grigorenko, E. L. (1998a) Teaching for successful intelligence raises school achievement. *Phi Delta Kappan,* 79, 667–669.

Sternberg, R. J., Torff, B. and Grigorenko, E. L. (1998b) Teaching triarchically improves school achievement. *Journal of Educational Psychology,* 90, 374–384.

Sternberg, R. J., Grigorenko, E. L., Ferrari, M. and Clinkenbeard, P. (1999) A triarchic analysis of an aptitude–treatment interaction. *European Journal of Psychological Assessment,* 15(1), 1–11.

Sternberg, R. J., Forsythe, G. B., Hedlund, J., Horvath, J., Snook, S., Williams, W. M., Wagner, R. K. and Grigorenko, E. L. (2000) *Practical intelligence in everyday life.* New York: Cambridge University Press.

Sternberg, R.J., Castejón, J.L., Prieto, M.D., Hautamäki, J. and Grigorenko, E.L. (2001) Confirmatory factor analysis of the Sternberg triarchic abilities test in three international samples: An empirical test of the triarchic theory of intelligence. *European Journal of Psychological Assessment,* 17, 1–16.

Steven, M. S., Hansen, P. C. and Blakemore, C. (2006) Activation of colour-selective areas of the visual cortex in a blind synaesthete. *Cortex,* 42(2), 304–308.

Stevens, R. and Slavin, R. (1995) The cooperative elementary school: Effects of students' achievement, attitudes, and social relations. *American Educational Research Journal,* 32, 321–351.

Stevenson, H. (1998) Cultural interpretations of giftedness: The case of East Asia. In R. C. Friedman and K. B. Rogers (eds.), *Talent in context: Historical and social perspectives on giftedness.* Washington, D.C.: American Psychological Association. (pp. 61–77)

Stipek, D. J. and Ryan, R. H. (1997) Economically disadvantaged preschoolers: ready to learn but further to go. *Developmental Psychology*, 33(4), 711–723.

Storfer, M. D. (1990) *Intelligence and giftedness: The contributions of heredity and early environment*. San Francisco: Jossey-Bass.

Straughan, R. (1975) Hypothetical moral situations. *Journal of Moral Education*, 4(3), 183–189.

Strike, K. (1999) Justice, caring, and universality: In defence of moral pluralism. In M. Katz, N. Noddings and K. Strike (eds.), *Justice and caring. The search for common ground in education*. New York: Teachers College Press. (pp. 21–37)

Subotnik, R. (1988) The motivation to experiment: A study of gifted adolescents' attitudes toward scientific research. *Journal for the Education of the Gifted*, 11(3), 19–35.

Subotnik, R. F and Jarvin, L. (2005) Beyond expertise: Conceptions of giftedness as great performance. In R. J. Sternberg and J. E. Davidson (eds.), *Conceptions of giftedness*, 3rd edn. Cambridge: Cambridge University Press. (pp. 343–357)

Subotnik, R. F., Olszewski-Kubilius, P. and Arnold, K. D. (2003) Beyond Bloom: Revisiting environmental factors that enhance or impede talent development. In J. H. Borland (ed.), *Rethinking gifted education*. New York: Teachers College Press. (pp. 227–238)

Sue, S. and Okazaki, S. (1990) Asian-American educational achievements: A phenomenon in search of an explanation. *American Psychologist*, vol. 45, 913–920.

Sulloway, F. J. (1996) *Born to rebel: Birth order, family dynamics, and creative lives*. New York: Pantheon.

Swedish National Agency for Education (2004) *Pisa 2003 – svenska femtonåringars kunskaper och attityder i ett internationellt perspektiv* [Pisa 2003: Swedish fifteen-year olds' knowledge and attitudes in an international perspective] Report no. 254. Stockholm: Swedish National Agency for Education.

Swiatek, M. A. (1995) An Empirical Investigation Of The Social Coping Strategies Used By Gifted Adolescents. *Gifted Children Quarterly*, 39, 154–160.

Syer, C. A. and Shore, B. M. (2001, November) *NAGC members' understanding of inquiry-based learning*. Paper presented at the annual meeting of the National Association for Gifted Children, Cincinnati, OH.

Sylva, K. and Pugh, G. (2005) Transforming the early years in England. *Oxford Review of Education*. 31,1, pp. 11–27.

TAG (The Association for the Gifted). (April, 2001) *Diversity and developing gifts and talents: A national action plan*. Washington, D.C.: Author.

Tammet, D. (2006) *Born on a blue day*. London: Hodder & Stoughton.

Tanguay, F. B. (2002) *Nonverbal learning difficulties at school*. London: Jessica Kingsley.

Tannenbaum, A. J. (1983) *Gifted children: Psychological and educational perspectives*. New York: Macmillan.

Tannenbaum, A. J. (1986) *Giftedness: A psychological approach*. In R. J. Sternberg and J. E. Davidson (eds.), *Conceptions of giftedness*. New York: Cambridge University Press. (pp. 21–52)

Tannenbaum, A. J. (2000) A history of Giftedness in school and society. In K. A. Heller, F. J. Mönks, R. J. Stenberg and R. F. Subotnik (eds.) *International handbook of giftedness and talent*. Oxford: Elsevier.

Tannenbaum, A. J. (2003) Nature and nurture of giftedness. In N. Colangelo and G. A. Davis, *Handbook of gifted education*, 3rd edn. Boston: Allyn & Bacon. (pp. 45–59)

Tantam, D. (1988) Lifelong eccentricity and social isolation: II. Asperger's Syndrome or schizoid personality disorder? *British Journal of Psychiatry*, 153, 783–791.

Tan-Willman, C. and Gutteridge, D. (1981) Creative thinking and moral reasoning in academically gifted secondary school adolescents. *Gifted Child Quarterly*, 25(4), 149–153.

Taylor, C. W. (1968, December) Be talent developers as well as knowledge dispensers. *Today's Education*, 67–69.

Taylor, C. W. (1985) Cultivating multiple creative talents in students. *Journal for the Education of the Gifted*, 8 (3), 187–198.

Taylor, S. D. (1998) Minority students and gifted and talented programs: Perceptions, attitudes and awareness. Ph.D. Thesis, University of Sydney.

Teasdale, R. (2000) A case study in double exceptionality. *Educating Able Children*, 6 (2) 41–2.

Terman, L. M. (1925) *Mental and physical traits of a thousand gifted children*. Stanford, CA: Stanford University Press.

Terman, L. M. (1925–1929) *Genetic studies of genius*, Vols I–V. Stanford: Stanford University Press.

Terrassier, J-C. (1991/1999) *Les enfants surdoués, ou la précocité embarrassante* (4éme édition). [Gifted children or the awkward precocity]. Paris: ESF.

Tharp, R. and Gallimore, R. (1988) *Rousing minds to life*. Cambridge: Cambridge University Press.

Theories of learning: Social constructivism. Graduate Student Instructor: Teaching Resource Center, University of California, Berkeley. Retrieved 24/3/2007 from http://gsi.berkeley.edu/resources/learning/social.html

Thomas, G. (2004) Introduction: evidence and practice. In G. Thomas and R. Pring (eds.), *Evidence-based practice in education*. Maidenhead: Open University Press.

Thomas, N. G. and Berk, L. E. (1981) Effects of school environments on the development of young children's creativity. *Child-Development*, 52(4), 1153–1162.

Thompson, L. A. and Plomin, R. (1993) Genetic influence on cognitive ability. In K. A. Heller, F. J. Mönks and A. H. Passow (eds.), *International handbook of research and development of giftedness and talent* (pp. 103–113). Oxford: Pergamon.

Thorkildsen, T. (1994). Some ethical implications of communal and competitive approaches to gifted education. *Roeper Review*, 17, 54–57.

Tirri, K. (1996) *The themes of moral dilemmas formulated by preadolescents*. Resources in Education ED 399046.

Tirri, K. (2003) The moral concerns and orientations of sixth- and ninth-grade students. *Educational Research and Evaluation*, 9(1), 93–108.

Tirri, K. and Nokelainen, P. (2006) Gifted students and the future. *KEDI Journal of Educational Policy*, 3(2), 55–66.

Tirri, K. and Nokelainen, P. (2007) Comparison of Academically Average and Gifted Students' Self-rated Ethical Sensitivity. *Educational Research and Evaluation*, 13(6), 587–601.

Tirri, K. and Pehkonen, L. (2002) The moral reasoning and scientific argumentation of gifted adolescents. *The Journal of Secondary Gifted Education*, III, 3, 120–129.

Tjeldvoll, A. and Lingens, HG (eds.) (2000) *Torsten Husén: Conversations in comparative education*. Bloomington, IN: Phi Delta Kappa Educational Foundation.

Tomlinson, C. (1995) *How to differentiate instruction in mixed-ability classrooms*. Alexandria, VA: Association for Supervision and Curriculum Development ED 386301.

Tomlinson, C. A., Callaghan, C. M. and Lelli, K. M. (1997) Challenging expectation: Case studies of high potential, culturally diverse young children. *Gifted Child Quarterly*, vol. 41, no. 2, 5–17.

Topping K. J. and Trickey, S. (2006) Collaborative philosophical enquiry for school children. *School Psychology International*, 27, 599–614.

Torff, B. (ed.) (1997) *Multiple intelligences and assessment: A collection of articles*. Arlington Heights, IL: Skylight Training and Publishing.

Torrance, E. P. (1968) A longitudinal examination of the fourth grade slump in creativity. *Gifted Child Quarterly*, 12(4), 195–199.

Torrance, E. P. (1974a) *Torrance test of creative thinking*. Lexington, MA: Personal Press.

Torrance, E. P. (1974b) *Torrance tests of creative thinking: Norms-technical manual*. Lexington, MA: Ginn and Company.

Torrance, E. P. (1979) *The search for Satori and creativity*. Buffalo, NY: Bearly Limited.

Tortora, G. and Grabowski, S. (1996) *Principles of anatomy and physiology*. New York: Harper Collins College Publishers.

Toulmin, S. (1958) *The uses of argument*. New York: Cambridge University Press.

Treffert, D.A.(1989) *Extraordinary people: Understanding 'idiot savants'*. New York: Harper & Row.

Treffinger, D. J. (1980) The progress and peril of identifying creative talent among gifted and talented students. *Journal of Creative Behavior*, 14(1), 20–34.

Treffinger, D. J. (1981) *Blending gifted education with the total school program*. Buffalo, NY: DOK Publishers.

Treffinger, D. J. (1987) *Research on creativity assessment*. In S. G. Isaksen (ed.), *Frontiers of creativity research: Beyond the basics*. Buffalo, NY: Bearly Limited. (pp. 103–119)

Treffinger, D. J. (1995) School improvement, talent development and creativity. *Roeper Review*, 18(1) 93–97.

Treffinger, D. J. (1998) From gifted education to programming for talent development. *Phi Delta Kappan*, (79) 10, 752–755.

Treffinger, D. J. (2003) *Independent, self-directed learning: 2003 update*. Sarasota, FL: Center for Creative Learning.

Treffinger, D. J. (2005) Enabling differentiation through levels of service. *Creative Learning Today*, 14 (1), 1, 8–9.

Treffinger, D. J. and Barton, B. L. (1979, March–April) Fostering independent learning. *G/C/T Magazine*, 3–6.

Treffinger, D. J. and Isaksen, S. G. (2005) Creative problem solving: History, development, and implications for gifted education and talent development. *Gifted Child Quarterly*. 49 (4), 342–353.

Treffinger, D. J. and Nassab, C. A. (2000) *Thinking tools lessons*. Waco, TX: Prufrock Press.

Treffinger, D. J. and Nassab, C. A. (2005) *Thinking tool guides*. (Rev. edn). Sarasota, FL: Center for Creative Learning.

Treffinger, D. J. and Selby, E. C. (in press) Levels of Service (LoS): A contemporary approach to programming for talent development. In J. S. Renzulli (ed.), *Systems and models for developing programs for the gifted and talented*. (2nd edn). Mansfield Center, CT: Creative Learning Press.

Treffinger, D. J., Young, G. C., Selby, E. C. and Shepardson, C. A. (2002) *Assessing creativity: A guide for educators*. Storrs, CT: National Research Center on the Gifted and Talented, University of Connecticut.

Treffinger, D. J., Young, G. C., Nassab, C. A. and Wittig, C. V. (2004) *Enhancing and expanding gifted programs: The levels of service approach*. Waco, TX: Prufrock Press.

Treffinger, D. J., Young, G. C., and Nassab, C. A. (2005) *Giftedness and talent: Nature and definitions. A technical paper supporting the Levels of Service approach to talent development programming*. Sarasota, FL: Center for Creative Learning.

Treffinger, D. J., Nassab, C. A., Schoonover, P. F., Selby, E. C., Shepardson, C. A., Wittig, C. V. and Young, G. C. (2006) *The creative problem solving kit*. Waco, TX: Prufrock Press.

Treffinger, D. J., Isaksen, S. G. and Stead-Dorval, K. B. (2006) *Creative problem solving: An introduction*. (4th Edition). Waco, TX: Prufrock Press.

Treffinger, D. J., Selby, E. C., Isaksen, S. G. and Crumel, J. H. (2007) *Problem-solving style: An introduction*. Sarasota, FL: Center for Creative Learning.

Treffinger, D. J., Young, G. C., Nassab, C. A., Selby, E. C. and Wittig, C. V. (in press). *Talent development handbook for the levels of service approach*. Thousand Oaks, CA: Corwin Press.

Treffinger, D. J., Young, G. C., Nassab, C. A. and Wittig, C. V. (2004). *Enhancing and expanding gifted programs: The levels of service approach*. Waco, TX: Prufrock Press.

Trickey, S. and Topping, K. J. (2004) Philosophy for children: a systematic review. *Research Papers in Education*, 19(3), 365–380.

Trost, G. (1993) Prediction of excellence in school, university and work. In K. A. Heller, F. J. Monk and A. H. Passow (eds.), *International handbook of research and development of giftedness and talent*. Oxford: Pergamon Press.

Trost, G. (2000) Prediction of excellence in school, higher education, and work. In K. A. Heller, F. J. Mönks, R. J. Sternberg and R. F. Subotnik (eds.), *International handbook of giftedness and talent* (2nd edn). Oxford: Pergamon/Amsterdam: Elsevier. (pp. 317–327)

Tweed, R. G. and Lehman, D. R. (2002) Learning considered within a cultural context: Confucian and Socratic approaches. *American Psychologist*, vol. 57, 89–99.

Tzuriel, D. and Feuerstein, R. (1992) Dynamic group assessment for prescriptive teaching: Differential effect of treatment. In H. C. Haywood and D. Tzuriel (eds.), *Interactive Assessment*). New York: Springer-Verlag. (pp. 187–206)

Urban, K. K. and Sekowski, A. (1993) Programs and practices for identifying and nurturing giftedness and talent in Europe. In K. A. Heller, F. J. Mönks and A. H. Passow (eds.), *International handbook of research and development of giftedness and talent*. Oxford: Pergamon. (pp. 779–795)

U.S. Department of Education, Office of Educational Research and Improvement (1993). *National excellence: A case for developing America's talent*. Washington, D. C.: U.S. Government Printing Office.

Utay, C. and Utay, J. (1997) Peer-assisted learning: The effects of cooperative learning and cross-grade peer tutoring with word processing on writing skills of students with learning disabilities. *Journal of Computing in Childhood Education*, 8, 165–185.

van der Westhuizen, C. (2007) Undervalued and under-served: The gifted disadvantaged. *Gifted Education International*, vol. 23, 138–48.

Van Tassel-Baska, J. (1998) Appropriate curriculum for the talented learner. In J. Van Tassel Baska (ed.), *Excellence in educating gifted and talented learners*. Denver, CO: Love Publishing Company.

Van Tassel-Baska, J. (2004, May) The development of an NCATE conceptual framework, research base, and standards for gifted education. Presentation at the NAGC University Network Meeting, Crystal City, VA.

Van Tassel-Baska, J. and Feng, A. X. (2003) *Project STAR follow-up study*. Columbia, SC: South Carolina Department of Education.

Van Tassel-Baska, J. and Johnsen, S. K. (2007) Teacher education standards for the field of gifted education: A vision of coherence for personnel preparation in the 21st century. *Gifted Child Quarterly*, 51(2), 182–205.

Van Tassel-Baska, J. and Little, C. A. (eds.) (2003) *Content-based curriculum for high ability learners*. Waco, TX: Prufrock Press.

Van Tassel-Baska, J., Johnson, D. and Avery, L. D. (2002) Using performance tasks in the identification of economically disadvantaged and minority gifted learners: Findings from Project STAR. *Gifted Child Quarterly*, 46 (2), 110–123.

Van Tassel-Baska, J., Feng, A. X., Chandler, K., Quek, C. and Swanson, J. (2005) *Project STAR: A Two Year Research Study Report*. Williamsburg, VA: Center for Gifted Education, The College of William & Mary.

Van Tassel-Baska, J., Xuemei Feng, A., and De Brux, E. (2007) A Study of Identification and Achievement Profiles of Performance Task-Identified Gifted Students Over 6 Years, *Journal for the Education of the Gifted*, 31, 1, 7.

Van Tassel-Baska, J. Feng, A. X. and de Brux (in press). A study of performance task-identified gifted students' identification and achievement profiles over six years. *Roeper Review*.

Vasilyuk, F. (1991) *The psychology of experiencing: the resolution of life's critical situations*. Hemel Hempstead: Harvester Wheatsheaf.

Vinovskis, M. (1996) An analysis of the concept and uses of systemic educational reform. *American Educational Research Journal*, 33, 53–89.

von Karolyi, C. (2006) Grappling with complex global issues. Issue awareness in young highly gifted children: 'Do the claims hold up?' *Roeper Review*, 28, 3, 167–174.

Vrignaud, P. (2006) La scolarisation des enfants intellectuellement précoces en France: présentation des différentes mesures et de résultats de recherches [Intellectual precocious childrens' schooling in France: Description of the different measures and of the results of several researches]. *Bulletin de Psychologie*. Tome 59 (5), 485, 439–449.

Vrignaud, P. and Bonora, D. (2000) *Le traitement des surdoués dans les systèmes éducatifs. Rapport rédigé à la demande du Ministre de l'Education Nationale*. [Dealing With the Gifted in the Education Systems. Report on request of the Education Minister]. Paris: INETOP.

Vrignaud, P., Bonora, D. and Dreux, A. (2005) Counseling the gifted and talented in France: Minimising gift and maximising talent. *International Journal for the Advancement of Counseling*, 27, 211–228.

Vygotsky, L. S. (1978) *Mind in society. The development of higher psychological processes*. (Edited and translated by Cole, W. et al.) Cambridge MA: Harvard University Press.

Wagner, R. K. (1987) Tacit knowledge in everyday intelligent behavior. *Journal of Personality and Social Psychology*, 52(6), 1236–1247.

Wagner, R. K. (2000) Practical intelligence. In R. J. Sternberg (ed.), *Handbook of human intelligence*. New York: Cambridge University Press. (pp. 380–395)

Wagner, R. K. and Sternberg, R. J. (1985) Practical intelligence in real-world pursuits: The role of tacit knowledge. *Journal of Personality and Social Psychology*, 49, 436–458.

Wagner, R. K. and Sternberg, R. J. (1986) Tacit knowledge and intelligence in the everyday world. In R. J.

Sternberg and R. K. Wagner (eds.), *Practical intelligence: Nature and origins of competence in the everyday world*. Cambridge: Cambridge University Press. (pp. 51–83)

Walker, L., de Vries, B. and Trevethan, S. (1987) Moral stages and moral orientations in real-life and hypothetical dilemmas. *Child Development*, 58, 842–858.

Wallace, B. (2000a) *Teaching the very able child: Developing a policy and adopting strategies for provision*. London: David Fulton.

Wallace, B. (2000b) Walter. In A. Klin, F. R. Volkmar, and S. S. Sparrow (eds.), *Asperger Syndrome*. New York: Guilford. (pp. 434–442)

Wallace, B. and Adams, H. B. (eds.) (1993a) *Worldwide perspectives on the gifted disadvantaged*. Bicester, UK: AB Academic Publishers.

Wallace, B. and Adams, H. B. (1993b) *TASC Thinking actively in a social context*. Bicester, UK: AB Aacademic Publishers.

Wallace, B., Maker, J., Cave, D. and Chandler, S. (2004) *Thinking skills and problem-solving: An inclusive approach*. London: David Fulton.

Wallach, M. A. (1985) Creativity testing and giftedness. In F. D. Horwitz and M. O'Brien (eds.), *The gifted and talented: Developmental perspective*. Hyattsville, MD: American Psychological Association. (pp. 99–123)

Wallach, M. A. and Kogan, N. (1965) *Modes of thinking in young children*. New York: Holt, Rinehart & Winston.

Waller, J. (2004) *Leaps in the dark: The making of scientific reputations*. Oxford: Oxford University Press.

Waller, N. G., Bouchard Jr., T. J., Lykken, D. T., Tellegen, A. and Blacker, D. M. (1993) Creativity, heritability, familiality: Which word does not belong? *Psychological Inquiry*, 4, 235–237.

Wang, M., Haertel, G. and Walberg, H. (1993) Toward a knowledge base for school learning. *Review of Educational Research*, 63, 249–294.

Watkins, C., Carnell, E. and Lodge, C. (2007) *Effective learning in classrooms*. London: Paul Chapman Publishing.

Webb, R. M., Lubinski, D. and Benbow, C. P. (2007). Spatial ability: A neglected dimension in talent searches for intellectually precocious youth. *Journal of Educational Psychology*, 99, 2, 397–420.

Weber, M. (1930) *The Protestant ethic and the spirit of capitalism*. London: Allen and Unwin.

Wechsler, D. (1939) *The measurement of adult intelligence*. Baltimore: Williams & Wilkins.

Wechsler, D. (1950) Cognitive, conative, and nonintellective intelligence. *American Psychologist*, 5, 78–83.

Weinert, F. E. (1995) Learning from Wise Mother Nature or Big Brother Instructor: The Wrong Choice as Seen from an Educational Perspective. *Educational Psychologist*, 30(3), 135–142.

Weisberg, R. W. (1993) *Creativity: Beyond the myth of genius*. New York: Freeman.

Westberg, K. L., Archambault Jr., F. X., Dobyns, S. M. and Salvin, T. J. (1993) The classroom practices observation study. *Journal for the Education of the Gifted*, 16 (2), 120–146.

Whitmore, J. R. (1980) *Giftedness, conflict, and underachievement*. Boston: Allyn & Bacon.

Whitmore, J. R. (ed.) (1986). *Intellectual giftedness in young children: Recognition and development*. New York: Haworth.

White, J. (2006) *Intelligence, destiny and education: The ideological roots of intelligence testing*. Abingdon, Oxon: Routledge.

Whitehead, J. (1989) Creating a living educational theory from questions of the kind, 'How do I improve my practice?' *Cambridge Journal of Education*, 19, 1, 41–52

Whitehead, J. (1993) *The growth of educational knowledge: Creating your own living educational theories*. Bournemouth: Hyde Publications.

Whitehead, J. (2005) Living inclusional values in educational standards of practice and judgement. Keynote for the Act, Reflect, Revise III Conference, Brantford Ontario, 11/11/2005. Retrieved 9/5/2007 from http://www.jackwhitehead.com/monday/arrkey05dr1.htm.

Whitehead, J. (2007) Creating a world of educational quality through living educational theories. Paper presented at AERA 13/4/2007, Chicago. Retrieved 26/4/2007 from http://www.jackwhitehead.com/aera07/jwaera07.htm.

Whitehead, J. and McNiff, J. (2006) *Action research living theory*, London: Sage.

Whitmore, J. R. (1980) *Giftedness, conflict and underachievement*. Boston: Allyn and Bacon.

Whitmore, J. R. (ed.) (1986). *Intellectual giftedness in young children: Recognition and development*. New York: Haworth.

Whitmore, J. R. (1987) Conceptualizing the issues of underserved populations of gifted students. *Journal for the Education of the Gifted*, 10(3), 141–153.

Wickes, K. N. S. and Ward, T. B. (2006) Measuring gifted adolescents' implicit theories of creativity. *Roeper Review*, 28(3) 131–139.

Wilde, S., Wright, S., Hayward, G., Johnson. J. and Skerrett, R. (2006) Nuffield Review, Higher Education Focus Groups Preliminary Report, The Nuffield Review of 14–19 Education and Training. Retrieved 1/6/2007 from http://www.nuffield14–19review.org.uk/cgi/documents/documents.cgi?a=106&t=template.htm.

Wilson, H., Mant, J. and Coates, D. (2005) Creative science and conceptual challenge: Lessons from the AstraZeneca Science Teaching Trust Project. *G&T Update*, Issue 22, March 2005, pp. 5–7.

Winebrenner, S. and Delvin, B. (2001) *Cluster grouping of gifted students: How to provide full-time services on part-time budget*. ERIC document ED 397618.

Wing, L. (1981) Asperger's syndrome: A clinical account. Psychological Med 11(1) 115–29.

Wing, L. (1991) The relationship between Asperger's syndrome and Kanner's autism. In U. Frith, (ed.), *Autism and Asperger syndrome*. Cambridge: Cambridge University Press. (pp. 93–121)

Wing, L. (1996) *The autistic spectrum: A guide for parents and professionals*. London: Constable.

Winner, E. (1996) *Gifted children: Myths and realities*. New York: BasicBooks.

Winner, E. (2000a) Giftedness: Current theory and research, *Current Directions in Psychological Science*, 9, 153–156.

Winner, E. (2000b) The origins and ends of giftedness. *American Psychologist*, 55, 159–169.

Winstanley, C. (2004) *Too clever by half: A fair deal for gifted children*. Stoke on Trent: Trentham Books.

Wistedt, I. (2005) Gifted Education in Sweden. *ECHA News*, 19/2, 4.

Wong, W. (2006) Understanding dialectical thinking from a cultural-historical perspective. *Philosophical Psychology*, 19, 239–260.

Wood, K., Algozzine, B. and Avett, S. (1993) Promoting cooperative learning experiences for students with reading, writing, and learning disabilities. *Reading and Writing Quarterly: Overcoming Learning Difficulties*, 9, 369–376.

Worrell, F. C (in press), What does gifted mean? Personal and social identity perspectives on giftedness in adolescence. In F. D. Horowitz, R. F. Subotnik and D. J. Matthews (eds.), *The development of giftedness and talent across the lifespan*. Washington D.C.: American Psychological Association.

Wright, G. (2007) *The anatomy of metaphor*. Cambridge: Clare College.

Wu, E. H. (2005) Factors that contribute to talented performance: A theoretical model from a Chinese perspective. *Gifted Child Quarterly*, 49, 231–246.

Wu, E. H. (2006) Nurture over nature: A reflective review of Confucian philosophy on learning and talented performance. *Gifted Education International*, 21, 181–189.

Wu, X. (2003) *Analects made easy [Lun-yu-yi-du]*, Beijing: Chinese Social Sciences Publisher. [In Chinese].

Yapp, C. (2005) The renaissance of learning, educating able children. *The Journal of NACE* (National Association for Able Children in Education), Autumn, 8, 1: 131–35. London: David Fulton.

Yinger, R. (1999) The role of standards in teaching and teacher education. In G. Griffin (ed.), *The education of teachers: The 98th yearbook of the NSSE*. Chicago: University of Chicago Press. (pp. 85–113)

Young, R. (2000) *Uncommon genius* (video recording). Australian Broadcasting Commission.

Yussen, S. (1977) Characteristics of moral dilemmas written by adolescents. *Developmental Psychology*, 13(2), 162–163.

Zadeh, L. A. (1973) Outline of a new approach to the analysis of complex systems and decision processes. *IEEE Transactions on systems man and cybernetics*, vol. SMC-3.

Zadeh, L. A., Fu K. S., Tanaka, K. and Shimura, M. (coord.) (1975) *Fuzzy sets and their application to cognitive and decision processes*. New York: University of California, Berkeley, Academic Press.

Zajonc, R. B. (1976) Family configuration and intelligence. *Science*, 192, 227–235.

Zeichner, K. M. and Liston, D. P. (1996) *Reflective teaching: An introduction.* Hillsdale, NJ: Lawrence Erlbaum Associates, Inc.

Zeidner, M., Shani-Zinovich, I., Matthews, G. and Roberts, R. D. (2005) Assessing emotional intelligence in gifted and non-gifted school students: Outcomes depending on the measure. *Intelligence,* 33, 369–391.

Zenasni, F., Besançon, M. and Lubart, T. I. (in press). Creativity and tolerance of ambiguity: An empirical study. *Journal of Creative Behavior.*

Zhang, L. and Hui, S. K. (2001) From pentagon to triangle: A cross-cultural investigation of an implicit theory of giftedness. *Roeper Review,* vol. 25, 78–82.

Zhang, L. and Sternberg, R. J. (1998) The pentagonal implicit theory of giftedness revisited: a cross-validation in Hong Kong. *Roeper Review,* vol. 21.

Zhilin D. M. (2007) Work with gifted children in Russia. In The New Zealand Association for Gifted Children '*Tall Poppies*' online magazine (http://www.giftedchildren.org.nz/national/article9.php).

Ziegler, A. and Heller, K. A. (2000) Conceptions of Giftedness from a Meta-Theoretical Perspective. In K. A. Heller, F. J. Mönks, R. J. Sternberg and R. F. Subotnik (eds.), *International Handbook of Giftedness and Talent* (2nd edn). Oxford: Pergamon/Amsterdam: Elsevier. (pp. 3–21)

Zilmer, E. A., Harrower, M. Rizler, B. A. and Archer, R. P. (1995) *The quest for the Nazi personality: A psychological investigation of Nazi war criminals.* Hillsdale, NJ: Lawrence Erlbaum Associates, Inc.

Zimmerman, B. and Schunk, D. (eds.) (2001) *Self-regulated learning and academic achievement* (2nd edn). Mahwah, NJ: Lawrence Erlbaum Associates, Inc.

Index